Sandra

THE
EXPERIENCE OF LITERATURE

BRIEFER VERSION

THE EXPERIENCE OF LITERATURE

BRIEFER VERSION

LIONEL TRILLING
Columbia University

HOLT, RINEHART AND WINSTON

New York   Chicago   San Francisco   Atlanta
Dallas   Montreal   Toronto

COPYRIGHT ACKNOWLEDGMENTS

CITY LIGHTS BOOKS

for Allen Ginsberg, "A Supermarket in California" from HOWL and Other Poems, copyright 1956, 1959 by Allen Ginsberg; and "To Aunt Rose" from KADDISH and Other Poems, copyright 1961 by Allen Ginsberg. Reprinted by permission of City Lights Books.

COLLINS-KNOWLTON-WING, INC.

for Robert Graves, "The Climate of Thought," and "To Juan at the Winter Solstice" from Collected Poems of Robert Graves, Doubleday and Company. Reprinted by permission of Collins-Knowlton-Wing, Inc., copyright © 1955 by Robert Graves.

J. M. DENT & SONS LTD.

for Joseph Conrad, "The Secret Sharer," reprinted by permission of J. M. Dent & Sons Ltd. and the Trustees of the Joseph Conrad Estate.

for Dylan Thomas, "The Force that through the Green Fuse," "Do Not Go Gentle into that Good Night," "In My Craft or Sullen Art," and "Fern Hill" from Collected Poems of Dylan Thomas, copyright 1952 by Dylan Thomas, published by New Directions, reprinted in Canada by the permission of J. M. Dent & Sons Ltd. and the Trustees for the Copyrights of the late Dylan Thomas.

DOUBLEDAY & COMPANY, INC.

for Theodore Roethke, "Frau Bauman, Frau Schmidt, and Frau Schwartze," copyright 1952 by Theodore Roethke (Originally appeared in The New Yorker); and "Light Listened," copyright © 1964 by Beatrice Roethke as Executrix of the Estate of Theodore Roethke, from The Collected Poems of Theodore Roethke. Reprinted by permission of Doubleday & Company, Inc.

DUELL, SLOAN AND PEARCE

for E. E. Cummings, "anyone lived in a pretty how town," copyright 1939, 1940 by E. E. Cummings. From 50 Poems by E. E. Cummings, reprinted by permission of Duell, Sloan and Pearce, affiliate of Meredith Press.

E. P. DUTTON & CO., INC.

for Luigi Pirandello, Six Characters in Search of an Author, translated by Edward Storer, from the book Naked Masks: Five Plays by Luigi Pirandello. Edited by Eric Bentley. Dutton Paperback Edition. Copyright, 1922, by E. P. Dutton & Co., Inc. Renewal, 1950, in the names of Stefano, Fausto, and Lietta Pirandello. Reprinted by permission of the publishers.

FABER AND FABER, LTD.

for T. S. Eliot, "The Love Song of J. Alfred Prufrock," "The Hippopotamus," "The Hollow Men," "La Figlia Che Piange," "Sweeney among the Nightingales," "Journey of the Magi," and "Animula," from Collected Poems 1909–1962. Reprinted in Canada by permission of Faber and Faber Ltd.

for W. H. Auden, "In Memory of W. B. Yeats," "In Memory of Sigmund Freud," and "Musée des Beaux Arts" from Collected Shorter Poems 1927–1957. Reprinted in Canada by permission of Faber and Faber Ltd.

FARRAR, STRAUS & GIROUX, INC.

for Robert Lowell, "For the Union Dead." Reprinted with the permission of Farrar, Straus & Giroux, Inc. from For the Union Dead by Robert Lowell, copyright © 1960 by Robert Lowell.

for Bernard Malamud, "The Magic Barrel." Reprinted with the permission of Farrar,

PREFACE

This is an anthology designed to be used in college courses that undertake the study of literature in general, often with a view to "introducing" the student to an art that he perhaps thinks of as remote from his interest. Such courses have had an established place in the curriculum for a considerable time, and for almost as long their convenience has been served by books that bring together notable examples of the chief literary genres, usually, like this one, drama, fiction, and poetry. In its purpose, then, and in most of its elements, the present volume is of a familiar kind. What will not be familiar from similar anthologies is the commentaries, in the form of brief essays, that follow each of the plays and stories and certain of the poems. They have only one end in view —to make it more likely that the student's act of reading will be an experience, having in mind what that word implies of an activity of consciousness and response. Their intention, that is to say, is no other than that of every teacher of literature as he works with his students in the classroom.

That there are classrooms in which literature is the subject of instruction testifies to our recognition that the reading of literature is not always and necessarily an experience. As every teacher of literature knows, a student can proceed with diligence from the beginning of a work to its end and yet give but little response to what he reads. We count on what takes place in the classroom to initiate a more appropriate degree of activity. By means of the discussion he institutes, the teacher brings his students to understand that the work before them is an object that may be freely touched and handled, picked up, turned over, looked at from this angle or that, and, at least in some sense, possessed. The commentaries in this book have been supplied in the belief that something has been gained for the classroom situation if the student has previously been led to think about what he will be asked to talk about.

It will readily be seen that no special theory of literature or method of criticism informs what I have written. In some of the commentaries the emphasis falls on formal matters, such as imagery, diction, versification, tone, point of view, and so on. But I have not thought it necessary to limit myself to such considerations as being more truly, or more purely, literary than others. I have felt free to enter into the overt or implicit meanings of a work and to pursue (sometimes to question) its moral, or social, or religious ideas. I have not hesitated to refer to critical theories or canons of taste of the past. If a biographical or historical circumstance seems to be to the point, I have adduced it. In short, I have availed myself of any of the usual elements of literary discourse that I thought relevant to the work and useful to the student.

I can scarcely fail to be aware of the opinion of some teachers that students should not read anything *about* a work of literature. It is held that coherent discourse in print interferes with the student's perception and feeling, making his response to the work less immediate and sincere, less his own. This is a view that must be taken seriously, especially at the present time, when it may sometimes seem that literature exists chiefly to provide occasions for its being explicated, expounded, and judged, and that, as a consequence of so much public to-do, the individual reader's experience of literature has an ever-diminishing chance of being private and autonomous.

Yet a jealous concern for the privacy and autonomy of the experience of literature must not obscure the truth that the literary experience is, of its very nature, communal—it asks to be shared in discourse. It is certainly possible for literary discourse to become excessive and intrusive, yet in any developed culture the impulse to say things about literature and to take account of what others say about it is no less natural than the creation and the enjoyment of the art. We find a pleasure that seems instinctual not only in the emotions that are aroused by what we read in private but also in communicating them to each other, in trying to understand why we feel as we do, in testing our emotions by those that others tell us they have, in discovering what we might possibly feel beyond what we do feel. And discourse leads to dialectic: we disagree with others in observation and response and in the general principles that we and they have insensibly been led to form. This activity, in itself interesting and pleasant, has the effect of increasing the interest and the pleasure of the private experience. The belief that this is so makes the ground upon which all instruction in literature proceeds. There is, indeed, no other ground. The activity of discourse and dialectic takes various forms and among them there is really no difference in the way they relate to the individual's privacy and autonomy. The discourse of an essay and the dialectic it initiates between itself and the reader are not different in kind from the discourse and the dialectic that go on in the free but directed discussion of the classroom. Neither the discussion nor the essay can be supposed to violate the student's privacy or limit his autonomy— unless on this score the whole process of education is to be impugned!

Nothing could be further from the intention of the commentaries than to usurp or circumscribe the teacher's function. They could hardly say all that is to be said about the works to which they address themselves, and they have tried to say no more than will bring the student into a more intimate and more active connection with what he has read. They obviously do not seek to impose themselves as anything like doctrine and they will not have failed of their purpose if they arouse either the student or the teacher, or both together, to disagreement.

The serviceability of a teaching anthology of this kind is judged by criteria that are obvious enough. Its selection of examples of the various genres should be sufficiently large to permit catholicity and variety. The critical standards by which it makes its choice should be uncompromising, yet applied with the awareness that, among the innumerable works that command our admiration, some are more accessible to students than others and some are more teachable than others. It should assume that literature is a continuous enterprise and include on an equal footing both the traditional and the new. I have had these considerations in mind and a few others as well. In making choice of the works to be included I have preferred those that I thought would prove memorable to the student by reason of momentousness of theme and force of dramatic or intellectual energy. That a work had already proved memorable to many was a special recommendation: not all the works I have chosen are "great" but I have, I think, made preponderant those to which the adjective may be applied.

The plays and stories have been drawn from several literatures. The poems, for obvious reasons, are all English and American. Although the selection of poems for further reading is large, it does not pretend to be canonical, and this is especially to be said of the selection of contemporary poets. It is perhaps here that I should remark that I have thought it best that the poets of our own time who are included in this section of the anthology should be read without footnotes.

The examples of each genre are arranged chronologically, although there are a few violations of this order for particular reasons. Historical considerations in themselves are naturally not paramount in introductory courses in literature, yet literary study cannot proceed without awareness of the fact that from one age to another changes take place in the meanings of words, in aesthetic conventions, in intellectual and moral assumptions, and in modes of behavior. The order of chronology is a first means to this necessary awareness.

I was peculiarly fortunate in the help I was given with this book and I am deeply grateful to those who gave it. The work on the footnotes was begun by Kent Hieatt, continued by David Thompson, and completed by Terry Schutz. Bernard Lionel Einbond of Hunter College kindly took in charge the task of checking the textual accuracy of the poems. Seeing the book through the press with Brian Heald was to me a revelation of what editorial intelligence, precision, and efficiency can be and I shall always remember our collaboration with pleasure. To Stanley Burnshaw I owe an especial debt of gratitude not only for his many valuable suggestions but also for his unfailing sympathy and his supernal patience.

New York, N.Y.   L.T.
January 1967

This abridged edition of *The Experience of Literature* has been prepared in response to the needs of those teachers who wish to use the anthology together with other books or who give courses that are shorter than those for which the anthology in its original edition was designed.

I am very grateful to Professor Charles Kaplan for having undertaken to make the abridgment and for the judgment and experience he brought to the task.

L.T.

January 1969

CONTENTS

PART 3: POETRY

PART

1 DRAMA

OEDIPUS REX

SOPHOCLES

496–406 B.C.

SCENE

Before the palace of Oedipus, King of Thebes. A central door and two lateral doors open onto a platform which runs the length of the façade. On the platform, right and left, are altars; and three steps lead down into the "orchêstra," or chorus-ground. At the beginning of the action these steps are crowded by suppliants who have brought branches and chaplets of olive leaves and who sit in various attitudes of despair. OEDIPUS enters.

PROLOGUE

OEDIPUS.   My children, generations of the living
In the line of Kadmos,[1] nursed at his ancient hearth:
Why have you strewn yourselves before these altars
In supplication, with your boughs and garlands?
The breath of incense rises from the city
With a sound of prayer and lamentation.
                                        Children,
I would not have you speak through messengers,
And therefore I have come myself to hear you—
I, Oedipus, who bear the famous name.

[*To a* PRIEST.] You, there, since you are eldest in the company,
Speak for them all, tell me what preys upon you,
Whether you come in dread, or crave some blessing:
Tell me, and never doubt that I will help you
In every way I can; I should be heartless
Were I not moved to find you suppliant here.
        PRIEST.   Great Oedipus, O powerful king of Thebes!
You see how all the ages of our people
Cling to your altar steps: here are boys
Who can barely stand alone, and here are priests
By weight of age, as I am a priest of God,
And young men chosen from those yet unmarried;
As for the others, all that multitude,
They wait with olive chaplets[2] in the squares,
At the two shrines of Pallas,[3] and where Apollo[4]
Speaks in the glowing embers.
                                        Your own eyes
Must tell you: Thebes is tossed on a murdering sea
And can not lift her head from the death surge.
A rust consumes the buds and fruits of the earth;
The herds are sick; children die unborn,
And labor is vain. The god of plague and pyre
Raids like detestable lightning through the city,
And all the house of Kadmos is laid waste,

---

[1] Legendary founder of Thebes. This text of the play uses a transliteration of proper names that often differs from common usage. More frequently seen spellings are Cadmus, Creon, Tiresias, Jocasta (or Iocasta), Laius, Menoeceus, Phoebus, Athena, Bacchus, Dionysus, Polydorus, Cithaeron, Parnassus, Polybus, Phocis, Lycia, Cyllene, Polyneices, Eteocles.

[2] Wreaths of olive branches to be worn on the head; the olive symbolized peace.

[3] Pallas Athenê, goddess of war, handicraft, and wisdom and patron goddess of Athens.

[4] God of light and healing, among other things; one of the principal Greek gods. Apollo was thought to speak through the oracle at Delphi, where a priestess muttered incomprehensibly and was interpreted by priests or seers.

All emptied, and all darkened: Death alone
Battens upon the misery of Thebes.

You are not one of the immortal gods, we know;
Yet we have come to you to make our prayer
As to the man surest in mortal ways
And wisest in the ways of God. You saved us
From the Sphinx,[5] that flinty singer, and the tribute
We paid to her so long; yet you were never
Better informed than we, nor could we teach you:
A god's touch, it seems, enabled you to help us.

Therefore, O mighty power, we turn to you:
Find us our safety, find us a remedy,
Whether by counsel of the gods or of men.
A king of wisdom tested in the past
Can act in a time of troubles, and act well.
Noblest of men, restore
Life to your city! Think how all men call you
Liberator for your boldness long ago;
Ah, when your years of kingship are remembered,
Let them not say *We rose, but later fell*—
Keep the State from going down in the storm!
Once, years ago, with happy augury,
You brought us fortune; be the same again!
No man questions your power to rule the land:
But rule over men, not over a dead city!
Ships are only hulls, high walls are nothing,
When no life moves in the empty passageways.

     OEDIPUS.   Poor children! You may be sure I know
All that you longed for in your coming here.
I know that you are deathly sick; and yet,
Sick as you are, not one is as sick as I.
Each of you suffers in himself alone
His anguish, not another's; but my spirit
Groans for the city, for myself, for you.

I was not sleeping, you are not waking me.
No, I have been in tears for a long while
And in my restless thought walked many ways.
In all my search I found one remedy,
And I have adopted it: I have sent Kreon,

---

     [5] A monster that, according to legend, had plagued Thebes, singing the riddle, "What is it that walks on four legs in the morning, on two at midday, and on three in the evening?" Those who could not answer were devoured, but Oedipus, when asked, promptly replied, "Man, for he crawls in infancy, walks erect in maturity, and uses a staff in old age." This was the correct answer, and the Sphinx, on receiving it, destroyed herself. Kreon, who acted as regent of Thebes after the death of her king, Laïos, then offered Oedipus the throne and the hand of Iokaste, Laïos' widow and Kreon's sister.

Son of Menoikeus, brother of the Queen,
To Delphi, Apollo's place of revelation,
To learn there, if he can,
What act or pledge of mine may save the city.
I have counted the days, and now, this very day,
I am troubled, for he has overstayed his time.
What is he doing? He has been gone too long.
Yet whenever he comes back, I should do ill
Not to take any action the god orders.

PRIEST.   It is a timely promise. At this instant
They tell me Kreon is here.

OEDIPUS.   O Lord Apollo!
May his news be fair as his face is radiant!

PRIEST.   Good news, I gather: he is crowned with bay,[6]
The chaplet is thick with berries.

OEDIPUS.   We shall soon know;
He is near enough to hear us now. [*Enter* KREON]
                         O Prince:
Brother: son of Menoikeus:
What answer do you bring us from the God?

KREON.   A strong one. I can tell you, great afflictions
Will turn out well, if they are taken well.

OEDIPUS.   What was the oracle? These vague words
Leave me still hanging between hope and fear.

KREON.   Is it your pleasure to hear me with all these
Gathered around us? I am prepared to speak,
But should we not go in?

OEDIPUS.   Speak to them all.
It is for them I suffer, more than for myself.

KREON.   Then I will tell you what I heard at Delphi.
In plain words
The god commands us to expel from the land of Thebes
An old defilement we are sheltering.
It is a deathly thing, beyond cure;
We must not let it feed upon us longer

OEDIPUS.   What defilement? How shall we rid ourselves of it?

KREON.   By exile or death, blood for blood. It was
Murder that brought the plague-wind on the city.

OEDIPUS.   Murder of whom? Surely the god has named him?

KREON.   My lord: Laïos once ruled this land,
Before you came to govern us.

OEDIPUS.   I know;
I learned of him from others; I never saw him.

KREON.   He was murdered; and Apollo commands us now
To take revenge upon whoever killed him.

OEDIPUS.   Upon whom? Where are they? Where shall we find a clue
To solve that crime, after so many years?

[6] Laurel, an emblem of victory or excellence.

KREON. Here in this land, he said. Search reveals
Things that escape an inattentive man.

OEDIPUS. Tell me: Was Laïos murdered in his house,
Or in the fields, or in some foreign country?

KREON. He said he planned to make a pilgrimage.
He did not come home again.

OEDIPUS. And was there no one,
No witness, no companion, to tell what happened?

KREON. They were all killed but one, and he got away
So frightened that he could remember one thing only.

OEDIPUS. What was that one thing? One may be the key
To everything, if we resolve to use it.

KREON. He said that a band of highwaymen attacked them,
Outnumbered them, and overwhelmed the King.

OEDIPUS. Strange, that a highwayman should be so daring—
Unless some faction here bribed him to do it.

KREON. We thought of that. But after Laïos' death
New troubles arose and we had no avenger.

OEDIPUS. What troubles could prevent your hunting down the killers?

KREON. The riddling Sphinx's song
Made us deaf to all mysteries but her own.

OEDIPUS. Then once more I must bring what is dark to light.
It is most fitting that Apollo shows,
As you do, this compunction for the dead.
You shall see how I stand by you, as I should,
Avenging this country and the god as well,
And not as though it were for some distant friend,
But for my own sake, to be rid of evil.
Whoever killed King Laïos might—who knows?—
Lay violent hands even on me—and soon.
I act for the murdered king in my own interest.

Come, then, my children: leave the altar steps,
Lift up your olive boughs!
One of you go
And summon the people of Kadmos to gather here.
I will do all that I can; you may tell them that. [*Exit a* PAGE.]
So, with the help of God.
We shall be saved—or else indeed we are lost.

PRIEST. Let us rise, children. It was for this we came,
And now the King has promised it.
Phoibos[7] has sent us an oracle; may he descend
Himself to save us and drive out the plague.

[*Exeunt* OEDIPUS *and* KREON *into the palace by the central door. The* PRIEST
and the SUPPLIANTS *disperse right and left. After a short pause the* CHORUS
enters the orchêstra.]

7 Phoibus Apollo.

PÁRODOS[8]

CHORUS.　What is God[9] singing in his profound　　　　　　[STROPHE 1]
Delphi of gold and shadow?
What oracle for Thebes, the sunwhipped[10] city?

Fear unjoints me, the roots of my heart tremble.

Now I remember, O Healer, your power and wonder:
Will you send doom like a sudden cloud, or weave it
Like nightfall of the past?

Speak to me, tell me, O
Child of golden Hope, immortal Voice.

Let me pray to Athenê, the immortal daughter of Zeus,　　[ANTISTROPHE 1]
And to Artemis her sister
Who keeps her famous throne in the market ring,[11]

And to Apollo, archer from distant heaven—[12]

O gods, descend! Like three streams leap against
The fires of our grief, the fires of darkness;
Be swift to bring us rest!

As in the old time from the brilliant house
Of air you stepped to save us, come again!

Now our afflictions have no end,　　　　　　　　　　　[STROPHE 2]
Now all our stricken host lies down
And no man fights off death with his mind;

The noble plowland bears no grain,
And groaning mothers can not bear—

See, how our lives like birds take wing,
Like sparks that fly when a fire soars,
To the shore of the god of evening.[13]

The plague burns on, it is pitiless,　　　　　　　　　　[ANTISTROPHE 2]
Though pallid children laden with death
Lie unwept in the stony ways,

And old gray women by every path
Flock to the strand about the altars

---

[8] This is an ode chanted by the Chorus, who remain on stage hereafter and comment, always in chanted odes, on the action of the play. When the Chorus participates in the actual dialogue, only its leader (Choragos) speaks, but he speaks for the entire group.
[9] Apollo, worship of whom sometimes approached monotheism.
[10] Whipped by Apollo, who was sometimes identified with the Sun-god.
[11] Artemis was the goddess of hunting; she was usually associated with forests and hills, where wild animals predominate, but was sometimes thought of as a city goddess.
[12] Apollo was also the god of archery.
[13] Death.

There to strike their breasts and cry
Worship of Phoibos in wailing prayers:
Be kind, God's golden child!

There are no swords in this attack by fire,   [STROPHE 3]
No shields, but we are ringed with cries.

Send the besieger plunging from our homes
Into the vast sea-room of the Atlantic
Or into the waves that foam eastward of Thrace—[14]

For the day ravages what the night spares—

Destroy our enemy, lord of the thunder!
Let him be riven by lightning from heaven!

Phoibos Apollo, stretch the sun's bowstring,   [ANTISTROPHE 3]
That golden cord, until it sing for us,
Flashing arrows in heaven!
                    Artemis, Huntress,
Race with flaring lights upon our mountains!

O scarlet god, O golden-banded brow,
O Theban Bacchos[15] in a storm of Maenads,[16] [*Enter* OEDIPUS, *center.*]
Whirl upon Death, that all the Undying hate!
Come with blinding torches, come in joy!

SCENE I

OEDIPUS.   Is this your prayer? It may be answered. Come,
Listen to me, act as the crisis demands,
And you shall have relief from all these evils.

Until now I was a stranger to this tale,
As I had been a stranger to the crime.
Could I track down the murderer without a clue?
But now, friends,
As one who became a citizen after the murder,
I make this proclamation to all Thebans:

If any man knows by whose hand Laïos, son of Labdakos,
Met his death, I direct that man to tell me everything,
No matter what he fears for having so long withheld it.
Let it stand as promised that no further trouble
Will come to him, but he may leave the land in safety.

Moreover: If anyone knows the murderer to be foreign,
Let him not keep silent: he shall have his reward from me.

[14] The eastern half of the Balkan Peninsula.
[15] Dionysos; god of wine who is frequently represented with a scarlet face.
[16] Female attendants of Dionysos who were inspired to ecstatic frenzy by the god.

However, if he does conceal it; if any man
Fearing for his friend or for himself disobeys this edict,
Hear what I propose to do:

I solemnly forbid the people of this country,
Where power and throne are mine, ever to receive that man
Or speak to him, no matter who he is, or let him
Join in sacrifice, lustration, or in prayer.
I decree that he be driven from every house,
Being, as he is, corruption itself to us: the Delphic
Voice of Apollo has pronounced this revelation.
Thus I associate myself with the oracle
And take the side of the murdered king.

As for the criminal, I pray to God—
Whether it be a lurking thief, or one of a number—
I pray that that man's life be consumed in evil and wretchedness.
And as for me, this curse applies no less
If it should turn out that the culprit is my guest here,
Sharing my hearth.
                    You have heard the penalty.

I lay it on you now to attend to this
For my sake, for Apollo's, for the sick
Sterile city that heaven has abandoned.
Suppose the oracle had given you no command:
Should this defilement go uncleansed for ever?
You should have found the murderer: your king,
A noble king, had been destroyed!
                           Now I,
Having the power that he held before me,
Having his bed, begetting children there
Upon his wife, as he would have, had he lived—
Their son would have been my children's brother,
If Laïos had had luck in fatherhood!
(And now his bad fortune has struck him down)—
I say I take the son's part, just as though
I were his son, to press the fight for him
And see it won! I'll find the hand that brought
Death to Labdakos' and Polydoros' child,
Heir of Kadmos' and Agenor's line.
And as for those who fail me,
May the gods deny them the fruit of the earth,
Fruit of the womb, and may they rot utterly!
Let them be wretched as we are wretched, and worse!

For you, for loyal Thebans, and for all
Who finds my actions right, I pray the favor
Of justice, and of all the immortal gods.
    CHORAGOS.   Since I am under oath, my lord, I swear
I did not do the murder, I can not name

The murderer. Phoibos ordained the search;
Why did he not say who the culprit was?
    OEDIPUS.   An honest question. But no man in the world
Can make the gods do more than the gods will.
    CHORAGOS.   There is an alternative, I think—
    OEDIPUS.   Tell me.
Any or all, you must not fail to tell me.
    CHORAGOS.   A lord clairvoyant[17] to the lord Apollo,
As we all know, is the skilled Teiresias.
One might learn much about this from him, Oedipus.
    OEDIPUS.   I am not wasting time:
Kreon spoke of this, and I have sent for him—
Twice, in fact; it is strange that he is not here.
    CHORAGOS.   The other matter—that old report—seems useless.
    OEDIPUS.   What was that? I am interested in all reports.
    CHORAGOS.   The King was said to have been killed by highwaymen.
    OEDIPUS.   I know. But we have no witnesses to that.
    CHORAGOS.   If the killer can feel a particle of dread,
Your curse will bring him out of hiding!
    OEDIPUS.   No.
The man who dared that act will fear no curse.

               [*Enter the blind seer* TEIRESIAS, *led by a* PAGE.]
    CHORAGOS.   But there is one man who may detect the criminal.
This is Teirsias, this is the holy prophet
In whom, alone of all men, truth was born.
    OEDIPUS.   Teiresias: seer: student of mysteries,
Of all that's taught and all that no man tells,
Secrets of Heaven and secrets of the earth:
Blind though you are, you know the city lies
Sick with plague; and from this plague, my lord,
We find that you alone can guard or save us.

Possibly you did not hear the messengers?
Apollo, when we sent to him,
Sent us back word that this great pestilence
Would lift, but only if we established clearly
The identity of those who murdered Laïos.
They must be killed or exiled.
                 Can you use
Birdflight[18] or any art of divination
To purify yourself, and Thebes, and me
From this contagion? We are in your hands.
There is no fairer duty
Than that of helping others in distress.
    TEIRESIAS.   How dreadful knowledge of the truth can be
When there's no help in truth! I knew this well,
But did not act on it: else I should not have come.

---

17 Seer or priest.
18 Augurs observed the flight and behavior of birds, which supposedly revealed the future or the forgotten or unknown past.

OEDIPUS.   What is troubling you? Why are your eyes so cold?

TEIRESIAS.   Let me go home. Bear your own fate, and I'll
Bear mine. It is better so: trust what I say.

OEDIPUS.   What you say is ungracious and unhelpful
To your native country. Do not refuse to speak.

TEIRESIAS.   When it comes to speech, your own is neither temperate
Nor opportune. I wish to be more prudent.

OEDIPUS.   In God's name, we all beg you—

TEIRESIAS.   You are all ignorant.
No; I will never tell you what I know.
Now it is my misery; then, it would be yours.

OEDIPUS.   What! You do know something, and will not tell us?
You would betray us and wreck the State?

TEIRESIAS.   I do not intend to torture myself, or you.
Why persist in asking? You will not persuade me.

OEDIPUS.   What a wicked old man you are! You'd try a stone's
Patience! Out with it! Have you no feeling at all?

TEIRESIAS.   You call me unfeeling. If you could only see
The nature of your own feelings . . .

OEDIPUS.   Why,
Who would not feel as I do? Who could endure
Your arrogance toward the city?

TEIRESIAS.   What does it matter?
Whether I speak or not, it is bound to come.

OEDIPUS.   Then, if 'it' is bound to come, you are bound to tell me.

TEIRESIAS.   No, I will not go on. Rage as you please.

OEDIPUS.   Rage? Why not!

                              And I'll tell you what I think:
You planned it, you had it done, you all but
Killed him with your own hands: if you had eyes,
I'd say the crime was yours, and yours alone.

TEIRESIAS.   So? I charge you, then,
Abide by the proclamation you have made:
From this day forth
Never speak again to these men or to me;
You yourself are the pollution of this country.

OEDIPUS.   You dare say that! Can you possibly think you have
Some way of going free, after such insolence?

TEIRESIAS.   I have gone free. It is the truth sustains me.

OEDIPUS.   Who taught you shamelessness? It was not your craft.

TEIRESIAS.   You did. You made me speak. I did not want to.

OEDIPUS.   Speak what? Let me hear it again more clearly.

TEIRESIAS.   Was it not clear before? Are you tempting me?

OEDIPUS.   I did not understand. Say it again.

TEIRESIAS.   I say that you are the murderer whom you seek.

OEDIPUS.   Now twice you have spat out infamy. You'll pay for it!

TEIRESIAS.   Would you care for more? Do you wish to be really angry?

OEDIPUS.   Say what you will. Whatever you say is worthless.

TEIRESIAS.   I say you live in hideous shame with those
Most dear to you. You can not see the evil.
    OEDIPUS.   Can you go on babbling like this for ever?
    TEIRESIAS.   I can, if there is power in truth.
    OEDIPUS.   There is:
But not for you, not for you,
You sightless, witless, senseless, mad old man!
    TEIRESIAS.   You are the madman. There is no one here
Who will not curse you soon, as you curse me.
    OEDIPUS.   You child of total night! I would not touch you;
Neither would any man who sees the sun.
    TEIRESIAS.   True: it is not from you my fate will come.
That lies within Apollo's competence,
As it is his concern.
    OEDIPUS.   Tell me, who made
These fine discoveries? Kreon? or someone else?
    TEIRESIAS.   Kreon is no threat. You weave your own doom.
    OEDIPUS.   Wealth, power, craft of statesmanship!
Kingly position, everywhere admired!
What savage envy is stored up against these,
If Kreon, whom I trusted, Kreon my friend,
For this great office which the city once
Put in my hands unsought—if for this power
Kreon desires in secret to destroy me!

He has bought this decrepit fortune-teller, this
Collector of dirty pennies, this prophet fraud—
Why, he is no more clairvoyant than I am!
                                    Tell us:
Has your mystic mummery ever approached the truth?
When that hellcat the Sphinx was performing here,
What help were you to these people?
Her magic was not for the first man who came along:
It demanded a real exorcist. Your birds—
What good were they? or the gods, for the matter of that?
But I came by,
Oedipus, the simple man, who knows nothing—
I thought it out for myself, no birds helped me!
And this is the man you think you can destroy,
That you may be close to Kreon when he's king!
Well, you and your friend Kreon, it seems to me,
Will suffer most. If you were not an old man,
You would have paid already for your plot.
    CHORAGOS.   We can not see that his words or yours
Have been spoken except in anger, Oedipus,
And of anger we have no need. How to accomplish
The god's will best: that is what most concerns us.
    TEIRESIAS.   You are a king. But where argument's concerned
I am your man, as much a king as you.

I am not your servant, but Apollo's.
I have no need of Kreon's name.

Listen to me. You mock my blindness, do you?
But I say that you, with both your eyes, are blind:
You can not see the wretchedness of your life,
Nor in whose house you live, no, nor with whom.
Who are your father and mother? Can you tell me?
You do not even know the blind wrongs
That you have done them, on earth and in the world below.
But the double lash of your parents' curse will whip you
Out of this land some day, with only night
Upon your precious eyes.
Your cries then—where will they not be heard?
What fastness of Kithairon[19] will not echo them?
And that bridal-descant of yours—you'll know it then,
The song they sang when you came here to Thebes
And found your misguided berthing.
All this, and more, that you can not guess at now,
Will bring you to yourself among your children.

Be angry, then. Curse Kreon. Curse my words.
I tell you, no man that walks upon the earth
Shall be rooted out more horribly than you.

    OEDIPUS.   Am I to bear this from him?—Damnation
Take you! Out of this place! Out of my sight!
    TEIRESIAS.   I would not have come at all if you had not asked me.
    OEDIPUS.   Could I have told that you'd talk nonsense, that
You'd come here to make a fool of yourself, and of me?
    TEIRESIAS.   A fool? Your parents thought me sane enough.
    OEDIPUS.   My parents again!—Wait: who were my parents?
    TEIRESIAS.   This day will give you a father, and break your heart.
    OEDIPUS.   Your infantile riddles! Your damned abracadabra!
    TEIRESIAS.   You were a great man once at solving riddles.
    OEDIPUS.   Mock me with that if you like; you will find it true.
    TEIRESIAS.   It was true enough. It brought about your ruin.
    OEDIPUS.   But if it saved this town?
    TEIRESIAS [*To the* PAGE].   Boy, give me your hand.
    OEDIPUS.   Yes, boy; lead him away.

                           —While you are here
We can do nothing. Go; leave us in peace.
    TEIRESIAS.   I will go when I have said what I have to say.
How can you hurt me? And I tell you again:
The man you have been looking for all this time,
The damned man, the murderer of Laïos,
That man is in Thebes. To your mind he is foreign-born,
But it will soon be shown that he is a Theban,
A revelation that will fail to please.

    [19] A mountain near Thebes.

A blind man,
Who has his eyes now; a penniless man, who is rich now;
And he will go tapping the strange earth with his staff.
To the children with whom he lives now he will be
Brother and father—the very same; to her
Who bore him, son and husband—the very same
Who came to his father's bed, wet with his father's blood.

Enough. Go think that over.
If later you find error in what I have said,
You may say that I have no skill in prophecy.

[*Exit* TEIRESIAS, *led by his* PAGE. OEDIPUS *goes into the palace.*]

ODE I

CHORUS.   The Delphic stone of prophecies[20]   [STROPHE 1]
Remembers ancient regicide
And a still bloody hand.
That killer's hour of flight has come.
He must be stronger than riderless
Coursers of untiring wind,
For the son of Zeus[21] armed with his father's thunder
Leaps in lightning after him;
And the Furies[22] hold his track, the sad Furies.

Holy Parnassos' peak of snow[23]   [ANTISTROPHE 1]
Flashes and blinds that secret man,
That all shall hunt him down:
Though he may roam the forest shade
Like a bull gone wild from pasture
To rage through glooms of stone.
Doom comes down on him; flight will not avail him;
For the world's heart calls him desolate,
And the immortal voices follow, for ever follow.

But now a wilder thing is heard   [STROPHE 2]
From the old man skilled at hearing Fate in the wing-beat of a bird.
Bewildered as a blown bird, my soul hovers and can not find
Foothold in this debate, or any reason or rest of mind.
But no man ever brought—none can bring

20 The shrine at Delphi contained a large ceremonial stone that was called, because Delphi was thought to be at the center of the earth, Earth's Navel.
21 Apollo.
22 Hideous female deities who pursued and drove mad those who had committed such heinous crimes as patricide.
23 Parnassos was a mountain with two peaks, one of which was consecrated to Apollo and the Muses (goddesses of arts and sciences) and the other to Dionysos; the "peak of snow" would be the peak of Apollo and the Muses. Delphi was located on the southern slope of Parnassos.

Proof of strife between Thebes' royal house,
Labdakos' line,[24] and the son of Polybos;[25]
And never until now has any man brought word
Of Laïos' dark death staining Oedipus the King.

Divine Zeus and Apollo hold   [ANTISTROPHE 2]
Perfect intelligence alone of all tales ever told;
And well though this diviner[26] works, he works in his own night;
No man can judge that rough unknown or trust in second sight,
For wisdom changes hands among the wise.
Shall I believe my great lord criminal
At a raging word that a blind old man let fall?
I saw him, when the carrion woman[27] faced him of old,
Prove his heroic mind. These evil words are lies.

SCENE II

KREON.   Men of Thebes:
I am told that heavy accusations
Have been brought against me by King Oedipus.

I am not the kind of man to bear this tamely.

If in these present difficulties
He holds me accountable for any harm to him
Through anything I have said or done—why, then,
I do not value life in this dishonor.

It is not as though this rumor touched upon
Some private indiscretion. The matter is grave.
The fact is that I am being called disloyal
To the State, to my fellow citizens, to my friends.
    CHORAGOS.   He may have spoken in anger, not from his mind.
    KREON.   But did you not hear him say I was the one
Who seduced the old prophet into lying?
    CHORAGOS.   The thing was said; I do not know how seriously.
    KREON.   But you were watching him! Were his eyes steady?
Did he look like a man in his right mind?
    CHORAGOS.   I do not know.
I can not judge the behavior of great men.
But here is the King himself. [*Enter* OEDIPUS.]
    OEDIPUS.   So you dared come back.
Why? How brazen of you to come to my house,
You murderer!

[24] The family of Laïos.
[25] Polybos was thought to be Oedipus' father.
[26] Teiresias.
[27] The Sphinx.

Do you think I do not know
That you plotted to kill me, plotted to steal my throne?
Tell me, in God's name: am I coward, a fool,
That you should dream you could accomplish this?
A fool who could not see your slippery game?
A coward, not to fight back when I saw it?
You are the fool, Kreon, are you not? hoping
Without support or friends to get a throne?
Thrones may be won or bought: you could do neither.

    KREON.   Now listen to me. You have talked; let me talk, too.
You can not judge unless you know the facts.

    OEDIPUS.   You speak well: there is one fact; but I find it hard
To learn from the deadliest enemy I have.

    KREON.   That above all I must dispute with you.

    OEDIPUS.   That above all I will not hear you deny.

    KREON.   If you think there is anything good in being stubborn
Against all reason, then I say you are wrong.

    OEDIPUS.   If you think a man can sin against his own kind
And not be punished for it, I say you are mad.

    KREON.   I agree. But tell me: what have I done to you?

    OEDIPUS.   You advised me to send for that wizard, did you **not?**

    KREON.   I did. I should do it again.

    OEDIPUS.   Very well. Now tell me:
How long has it been since Laïos—

    KREON.   What of Laïos?

    OEDIPUS.   Since he vanished in that onset by the road?

    KREON.   It was long ago, a long time.

    OEDIPUS.   And this prophet,
Was he practicing here then?

    KREON.   He was; and with honor, as now.

    OEDIPUS.   Did he speak of me at that time?

    KREON.   He never did;
At least, not when I was present.

    OEDIPUS.   But . . . the enquiry?[28]
I suppose you held one?

    KREON.   We did, but we learned nothing.

    OEDIPUS.   Why did the prophet not speak against me then?

    KREON.   I do not know; and I am the kind of man
Who holds his tongue when he has no facts to go on.

    OEDIPUS.   There's one fact that you know, and you could tell it.

    KREON.   What fact is that? If I know it, you shall have it.

    OEDIPUS.   If he were not involved with you, he could not **say**
That it was I who murdered Laïos.

    KREON.   If he says that, you are the one that knows it!—
But now it is my turn to question you.

    OEDIPUS.   Put your questions. I am no murderer.

[28] Into Oedipus' background.

KREON.   First, then: you married my sister?
OEDIPUS.   I married your sister.
KREON.   And you rule the kingdom equally with her?
OEDIPUS.   Everything that she wants she has from me.
KREON.   And I am the third, equal to both of you?
OEDIPUS.   That is why I call you a bad friend.
KREON.   No. Reason it out, as I have done.
Think of this first: Would any sane man prefer
Power, with all a king's anxieties,
To that same power and the grace of sleep?
Certainly not I.
I have never longed for the king's power—only his rights.
Would any wise man differ from me in this?
As matters stand, I have my way in everything
With your consent, and no responsibilities.
If I were king, I should be a slave to policy.
How could I desire a sceptre more
Than what is now mine—untroubled influence?
No, I have not gone mad; I need no honors,
Except those with the perquisites I have now.
I am welcome everywhere; every man salutes me,
And those who want your favor seek my ear,
Since I know how to manage what they ask.
Should I exchange this ease for that anxiety?
Besides, no sober mind is treasonable.
I hate anarchy
And never would deal with any man who likes it.

Test what I have said. Go to the priestess
At Delphi, ask if I quoted her correctly.
And as for this other thing: if I am found
Guilty of treason with Teiresias,
Then sentence me to death. You have my word
It is a sentence I should cast my vote for—
But not without evidence!
                    You do wrong
When you take good men for bad, bad men for good.
A true friend thrown aside—why, life itself
Is not more precious!
                    In time you will know this well:
For time, and time alone, will show the just man,
Though scoundrels are discovered in a day.
CHORAGOS.   This is well said, and a prudent man would ponder it.
Judgments too quickly formed are dangerous.
OEDIPUS.   But is he not quick in his duplicity?
And shall I not be quick to parry him?
Would you have me stand still, hold my peace, and let
This man win everything, through my inaction?

KREON.   And you want—what is it, then? To banish me?

OEDIPUS.   No, not exile. It is your death I want,

So that all the world may see what treason means.

KREON.   You will persist, then? You will not believe me?

OEDIPUS.   How can I believe you?

KREON.   Then you are a fool.

OEDIPUS.   To save myself?

KREON.   In justice, think of me.

OEDIPUS.   You are evil incarnate.

KREON.   But suppose that you are wrong?

OEDIPUS.   Still I must rule.

KREON.   But not if you rule badly.

OEDIPUS.   O city, city!

KREON.   It is my city, too!

CHORAGOS.   Now, my lords, be still. I see the Queen,

Iokastè, coming from her palace chambers;

And it is time she came, for the sake of you both.

This dreadful quarrel can be resolved through her. [*Enter* IOKASTE.]

IOKASTE.   Poor foolish men, what wicked din is this?

With Thebes sick to death, is it not shameful

That you should rake some private quarrel up?

[*To* OEDIPUS.] Come into the house.

                              —And you, Kreon, go now:

Let us have no more of this tumult over nothing.

KREON.   Nothing? No, sister: what your husband plans for me

Is one of two great evils: exile or death.

OEDIPUS.   He is right.

                        Why, woman I have caught him squarely

Plotting against my life.

KREON.   No! Let me die

Accurst if ever I have wished you harm!

IOKASTE.   Ah, believe it, Oedipus!

In the name of the gods, respect this oath of his

For my sake, for the sake of these people here!

[STROPHE 1]

CHORAGOS.   Open your mind to her, my lord. Be ruled by her, I beg you!

OEDIPUS.   What would you have me do?

CHORAGOS.   Respect Kreon's word. He has never spoken like a fool,

And now he has sworn an oath.

OEDIPUS.   You know what you ask?

CHORAGOS.   I do.

OEDIPUS.   Speak on, then.

CHORAGOS.   A friend so sworn should not be baited so,

In blind malice, and without final proof.

OEDIPUS.   You are aware, I hope, that what you say

Means death for me, or exile at the least.

CHORAGOS.   No, I swear by Helios,[29] first in Heaven!   [STROPHE 2]
May I die friendless and accurst,
The worst of deaths, if ever I meant that!
    It is the withering fields
    That hurt my sick heart:
Must we bear all these ills,
    And now your bad blood as well?

OEDIPUS.   Then let him go. And let me die, if I must,
Or be driven by him in shame from the land of Thebes.
It is your unhappiness, and not his talk,
That touches me.
                    As for him—
Wherever he goes, hatred will follow him.
    KREON.   Ugly in yielding, as you were ugly in rage!
Natures like yours chiefly torment themselves.
OEDIPUS.   Can you not go? Can you not leave me?
    KREON.   I can.
You do not know me; but the city knows me,
And in its eyes I am just, if not in yours. [*Exit* KREON.]

                                                    [ANTISTROPHE 1]
    CHORAGOS.   Lady Iokastè, did you not ask the King to go to his chambers?
    IOKASTE.   First tell me what has happened.
    CHORAGOS.   There was suspicion without evidence; yet it rankled
As even false charges will.
    IOKASTE.   On both sides?
    CHORAGOS.   On both.
    IOKASTE.   But what was said?
    CHORAGOS.   Oh let it rest, let it be done with!
Have we not suffered enough?
    OEDIPUS.   You see to what your decency has brought you:
You have made difficulties where my heart saw none.

                                                    [ANTISTROPHE 2]
    CHORAGOS.   Oedipus, it is not once only I have told you—
    You must know I should count myself unwise
To the point of madness, should I now forsake you—
    You, under whose hand,
        In the storm of another time,
    Our dear land sailed out free.
        But now stand fast at the helm!

    IOKASTE.   In God's name, Oedipus, inform your wife as well:
Why are you so set in this hard anger?
    OEDIPUS.   I will tell you, for none of these men deserves

---

[29] The Sun-god.

My confidence as you do. It is Kreon's work,
His treachery, his plotting against me.

    IOKASTE.   Go on, if you can make this clear to me.

    OEDIPUS.   He charges me with the murder of Laïos.

    IOKASTE.   Has he some knowledge? Or does he speak from hearsay?

    OEDIPUS.   He would not commit himself to such a charge,
But he has brought in that damnable soothsayer
To tell his story.

    IOKASTE.   Set your mind at rest.
If it is a question of soothsayers, I tell you
That you will find no man whose craft gives knowledge
Of the unknowable.

            Here is my proof:
An oracle was reported to Laïos once
(I will not say from Phoibos himself, but from
His appointed ministers, at any rate)
That his doom would be death at the hands of his own son—
His son, born of his flesh and of mine!

Now, you remember the story: Laïos was killed
By marauding strangers where three highways meet;
But his child had not been three days in this world
Before the King had pierced the baby's ankles[30]
And left him to die on a lonely mountainside.

Thus, Apollo never caused that child
To kill his father, and it was not Laïos' fate
To die at the hands of his son, as he had feared.
This is what prophets and prophecies are worth!
Have no dread of them.

            It is God himself
Who can show us what he wills, in his own way.

    OEDIPUS.   How strange a shadowy memory crossed my mind,
Just now while you were speaking; it chilled my heart.

    IOKASTE.   What do you mean? What memory do you speak of?

    OEDIPUS.   If I understand you, Laïos was killed
At a place where three roads meet.

    IOKASTE.   So it was said;
We have no later story.

    OEDIPUS.   Where did it happen?

    IOKASTE.   Phokis, it is called: at a place where the Theban Way
Divides into the roads toward Delphi and Daulia.

    OEDIPUS.   When?

    IOKASTE.   We had the news not long before you came
And proved the right to your succession here.

    OEDIPUS.   Ah, what net has God been weaving for me?

    IOKASTE.   Oedipus! Why does this trouble you?

30 Perhaps to prevent his ghost from walking.

OEDIPUS.   Do not ask me yet.
First, tell me how Laïos looked, and tell me
How old he was.

    IOKASTE.   He was tall, his hair just touched
With white; his form was not unlike your own.

    OEDIPUS.   I think that I myself may be accurst
By my own ignorant edict.

    IOKASTE.   You speak strangely.
It makes me tremble to look at you, my King.

    OEDIPUS.   I am not sure that the blind man can not see.
But I should know better if you were to tell me—

    IOKASTE.   Anything—though I dread to hear you ask it.

    OEDIPUS.   Was the King lightly escorted, or did he ride
With a large company, as a ruler should?

    IOKASTE.   There were five men with him in all: one was a herald;
And a single chariot, which he was driving.

    OEDIPUS.   Alas, that makes it plain enough!

                         But who—
Who told you how it happened?

    IOKASTE.   A household servant,
The only one to escape.

    OEDIPUS.   And is he still
A servant of ours?

    IOKASTE.   No; for when he came back at last
And found you enthroned in the place of the dead king,
He came to me, touched my hand with his, and begged
That I would send him away to the frontier district
Where only the shepherds go—
As far away from the city as I could send him.
I granted his prayer; for although the man was a slave,
He had earned more than this favor at my hands.

    OEDIPUS.   Can he be called back quickly?

    IOKASTE.   Easily.
But why?

    OEDIPUS.   I have taken too much upon myself
Without enquiry; therefore I wish to consult him.

    IOKASTE.   Then he shall come.

                     <u>But am I not one also</u>
<u>To whom you might confide these fears of yours?</u>

    OEDIPUS.   That is your right; it will not be denied you,
Now least of all; for I have reached a pitch
Of wild foreboding. Is there anyone
To whom I should sooner speak?

Polybos of Corinth is my father.
My mother is a Dorian: Meropê.
I grew up chief among the men of Corinth
Until a strange thing happened—
Not worth my passion, it may be, but strange.

[handwritten margin note: lover Figure →]

At a feast, a drunken man maundering in his cups
Cries out that I am not my father's son!
I contained myself that night, though I felt anger
And a sinking heart. The next day I visited
My father and mother, and questioned them. They stormed,
Calling it all the slanderous rant of a fool;
And this relieved me. Yet the suspicion
Remained always aching in my mind;
I knew there was talk; I could not rest;
And finally, saying nothing to my parents,
I went to the shrine at Delphi.

The god dismissed my question without reply;
He spoke of other things.
     Some were clear,
Full of wretchedness, dreadful, unbearable:
As, that I should lie with my own mother, breed
Children from whom all men would turn their eyes;
And that I should be my father's murderer.

I heard all this, and fled. And from that day
Corinth to me was only in the stars
Descending in that quarter of the sky,
As I wandered farther and farther on my way
To a land where I should never see the evil
Sung by the oracle. And I came to this country
Where, so you say, King Laïos was killed.

I will tell you all that happened there, my lady.

There were three highways
Coming together at a place I passed;
And there a herald came towards me, and a chariot
Drawn by horses, with a man such as you describe
Seated in it. The groom leading the horses
Forced me off the road at his lord's command;
But as this charioteer lurched over towards me
I struck him in my rage. The old man saw me
And brought his double goad down upon my head
As I came abreast.
    He was paid back, and more!
Swinging my club in this right hand I knocked him
Out of his car, and he rolled on the ground.
       I killed him.

I killed them all.
Now if that stranger and Laïos were—kin,
Where is a man more miserable than I?
More hated by the gods? Citizen and alien alike
Must never shelter me or speak to me—
I must be shunned by all.

And I myself

Pronounced this malediction upon myself!

Think of it: I have touched you with these hands,
These hands that killed your husband. What defilement!

Am I all evil, then? It must be so,
Since I must flee from Thebes, yet never again
See my own countrymen, my own country,
For fear of joining my mother in marriage
And killing Polybos, my father.

Ah,

If I was created so, born to this fate,
Who could deny the savagery of God?

O holy majesty of heavenly powers!
May I never see that day! Never!
Rather let me vanish from the race of men
Than know the abomination destined me!

    CHORAGOS.   We too, my lord, have felt dismay at this.
But there is hope: you have yet to hear the shepherd.

        OEDIPUS.   Indeed, I fear no other hope is left me.

        IOKASTE.   What do you hope from him when he comes?

        OEDIPUS.   This much:
If his account of the murder tallies with yours,
Then I am cleared.

        IOKASTE.   What was it that I said
Of such importance?

        OEDIPUS.   Why, 'marauders', you said,
Killed the King, according to this man's story.
If he maintains that still, if there were several,
Clearly the guilt is not mine: I was alone.
But if he says one man, singlehanded, did it,
Then the evidence all points to me.

        IOKASTE.   You may be sure that he said there were several;
And can he call back that story now? He can not.
The whole city heard it as plainly as I.
But suppose he alters some detail of it:
He can not ever show that Laïos' death
Fulfilled the oracle: for Apollo said
My child was doomed to kill him; and my child—
Poor baby!—it was my child that died first.

No. From now on, where oracles are concerned,
I would not waste a second thought on any.

        OEDIPUS.   You may be right.

But come: let someone go

For the shepherd at once. This matter must be settled.

        IOKASTE.   I will send for him.
I would not wish to cross you in anything,
And surely not in this.—Let us go in. [*Exeunt into the palace.*]

ODE II

CHORUS. Let me be reverent in the ways of right, [STROPHE 1]
Lowly the paths I journey on;
Let all my words and actions keep
The laws of the pure universe
From highest Heaven handed down.
For Heaven is their bright nurse,
Those generations of the realms of light;
Ah, never of mortal kind were they begot,
Nor are they slaves of memory, lost in sleep:
Their Father is greater than Time, and ages not.

The tyrant is a child of Pride [ANTISTROPHE 1]
Who drinks from his great sickening cup
Recklessness and vanity,
Until from his high crest headlong
He plummets to the dust of hope.
That strong man is not strong.
But let no fair ambition be denied;
May God protect the wrestler for the State
In government, in comely policy,
Who will fear God, and on His ordinance wait.

Haughtiness and the high hand of disdain [STROPHE 2]
Tempt and outrage God's holy law;
And any mortal who dares hold
No immortal Power in awe
Will be caught up in a net of pain:
The price for which his levity is sold.
Let each man take due earnings, then,
And keep his hands from holy things,
And from blasphemy stand apart—
Else the crackling blast of heaven
Blows on his head, and on his desperate heart.
Though fools will honor impious men,
In their cities no tragic poet sings.

Shall we lose faith in Delphi's obscurities, [ANTISTROPHE 2]
We who have heard the world's core
Discredited, and the sacred wood
Of Zeus at Elis praised no more?
The deeds and the strange prophecies
Must make a pattern yet to be understood.
Zeus, if indeed you are lord of all,
Throned in light over night and day,
Mirror this in your endless mind:
Our masters call the oracle

Words on the wind, and the Delphic vision blind!
Their hearts no longer know Apollo,
And reverence for the gods has died away.

SCENE III

Enter IOKASTE
IOKASTE.   Princes of Thebes, it has occurred to me
To visit the altars of the gods, bearing
These branches as a suppliant, and this incense.
Our King is not himself: his noble soul
Is overwrought with fantasies of dread,
Else he would consider
The new prophecies in the light of the old.
He will listen to any voice that speaks disaster,
And my advice goes for nothing. [*She approaches the altar, right.*]
                                To you, then, Apollo,
Lycéan lord,[31] since you are nearest, I turn in prayer.

Receive these offerings, and grant us deliverance
From defilement. Our hearts are heavy with fear
When we see our leader distracted, as helpless sailors
Are terrified by the confusion of their helmsman.   [*Enter* MESSENGER.]
        MESSENGER.   Friends, no doubt you can direct me:
Where shall I find the house of Oedipus
Or, better still, where is the King himself?
        CHORAGOS.   It is this very place, stranger; he is inside.
This is his wife and mother of his children.
        MESSENGER.   I wish her happiness in a happy house,
Blest in all the fulfillment of her marriage.
        IOKASTE.   I wish as much for you: your courtesy
Deserves a like good fortune. But now, tell me:
Why have you come? What have you to say to us?
        MESSENGER.   Good news, my lady, for your house and your husband.
        IOKASTE.   What news? Who sent you here?
        MESSENGER.   I am from Corinth.
The news I bring ought to mean joy for you,
Though it may be you will find some grief in it.
        IOKASTE.   What is it? How can it touch us in both ways?
        MESSENGER.   The word is that the people of the Isthmus[32]
Intend to call Oedipus to be their king.
        IOKASTE.   But old King Polybos—is he not reigning still?
        MESSENGER.   No. Death holds him in his sepulchre.
        IOKASTE.   What are you saying? Polybos is dead?
        MESSENGER.   If I am not telling the truth, may I die myself.
        IOKASTE [*to a* MAIDSERVANT].   Go in, go quickly; tell this to your master.

31 Apollo was thought to have been born at Lycéa.
32 Corinth was an isthmus.

O riddlers of God's will, where are you now!
This was the man whom Oedipus, long ago,
Feared so, fled so, in dread of destroying him—
But it was another fate by which he died. [*Enter* OEDIPUS, *center*]

OEDIPUS.   Dearest Iokastê, why have you sent for me?

IOKASTE.   Listen to what this man says, and then tell me
What has become of the solemn prophecies.

OEDIPUS.   Who is this man? What is his news for me?

IOKASTE.   He has come from Corinth to announce your father's death!

OEDIPUS.   Is it true, stranger? Tell me in your own words.

MESSENGER.   I can not say it more clearly: the King is dead.

OEDIPUS.   Was it by treason? Or by an attack of illness?

MESSENGER.   A little thing brings old men to their rest.

OEDIPUS.   It was sickness, then?

MESSENGER.   Yes, and his many years.

OEDIPUS.   Ah!

Why should a man respect the Pythian hearth,[33] or
Give heed to the birds that jangle above his head?
They prophesied that I should kill Polybos,
Kill my own father; but he is dead and buried,
And I am here—I never touched him, never,
Unless he died of grief for my departure,
And thus, in a sense, through me. No. Polybos
Has packed the oracles off with him underground.
They are empty words.

IOKASTE.   Had I not told you so?

OEDIPUS.   You had; it was my faint heart that betrayed me.

IOKASTE.   From now on never think of those things again.

OEDIPUS.   And yet—must I not fear my mother's bed?

IOKASTE.   Why should anyone in this world be afraid,
Since Fate rules us and nothing can be foreseen?
A man should live only for the present day.

Have no more fear of sleeping with your mother:
How many men, in dreams, have lain with their mothers!
No reasonable man is troubled by such things.

OEDIPUS.   That is true; only—
If only my mother were not still alive!
But she is alive. I can not help my dread.

IOKASTE.   Yet this news of your father's death is wonderful.

OEDIPUS.   Wonderful. But I fear the living woman.

MESSENGER.   Tell me, who is this woman that you fear?

OEDIPUS.   It is Meropê, man; the wife of King Polybos.

MESSENGER.   Meropê? Why should you be afraid of her?

OEDIPUS.   An oracle of the gods, a dreadful saying.

MESSENGER.   Can you tell me about it or are you sworn to silence?

OEDIPUS.   I can tell you, and I will.
Apollo said through his prophet that I was the man

---

[33] Delphi, where Apollo's medium was the Pythia.

Who should marry his own mother, shed his father's blood
With his own hands. And so, for all these years
I have kept clear of Corinth, and no harm has come—
Though it would have been sweet to see my parents again.

MESSENGER.   And is this the fear that drove you out of Corinth?

OEDIPUS.   Would you have me kill my father?

MESSENGER.   As for that
You must be reassured by the news I gave you.

OEDIPUS.   If you could reassure me, I would reward you.

MESSENGER.   I had that in mind, I will confess: I thought
I could count on you when you returned to Corinth.

OEDIPUS.   No: I will never go near my parents again.

MESSENGER.   Ah, son, you still do not know what you are doing—

OEDIPUS.   What do you mean? In the name of God tell me!

MESSENGER.   —If these are your reasons for not going home.

OEDIPUS.   I tell you, I fear the oracle may come true.

MESSENGER.   And guilt may come upon you through your parents?

OEDIPUS.   That is the dread that is always in my heart.

MESSENGER.   Can you not see that all your fears are groundless?

OEDIPUS.   Groundless? Am I not my parents' son?

MESSENGER.   Polybos was not your father.

OEDIPUS.   Not my father?

MESSENGER.   No more your father than the man speaking to you.

OEDIPUS.   But you are nothing to me!

MESSENGER.   Neither was he.

OEDIPUS.   Then why did he call me son?

MESSENGER   I will tell you:
Long ago he had you from my hands, as a gift.

OEDIPUS.   Then how could he love me so, if I was not his?

MESSENGER.   He had no children, and his heart turned to you.

OEDIPUS.   What of you? Did you buy me? Did you find me by chance?

MESSENGER.   I came upon you in the woody vales of Kithairon.

OEDIPUS.   And what were you doing there?

MESSENGER.   Tending my flocks.

OEDIPUS.   A wandering shepherd?

MESSENGER.   But your savior, son, that day.

OEDIPUS.   From what did you save me?

MESSENGER.   Your ankles should tell you that.

OEDIPUS.   Ah, stranger, why do you speak of that childhood pain?

MESSENGER.   I pulled the skewer that pinned your feet together.

OEDIPUS.   I have had the mark as long as I can remember.

MESSENGER.   That was why you were given the name you bear.[34]

OEDIPUS.   God! Was it my father or my mother who did it?
Tell me!

MESSENGER.   I do not know. The man who gave you to me
Can tell you better than I.

OEDIPUS.   It was not you that found me, but another?

[34] *Oedipus* means "swell-foot."

MESSENGER.   It was another shepherd gave you to me.

OEDIPUS.   Who was he? Can you tell me who he was?

MESSENGER.   I think he was said to be one of Laïos' people.

OEDIPUS.   You mean the Laïos who was king here years ago?

MESSENGER.   Yes; King Laïos; and the man was one of his herdsmen.

OEDIPUS.   Is he still alive? Can I see him?

MESSENGER.   These men here
Know best about such things.

OEDIPUS.   Does anyone here
Know this shepherd that he is talking about?
Have you seen him in the fields, or in the town?
If you have, tell me. It is time things were made plain.

CHORAGOS.   I think the man he means is that same shepherd
You have already asked to see. Iokastè perhaps
Could tell you something.

OEDIPUS.   Do you know anything
About him, Lady? Is he the man we have summoned?
Is that the man this shepherd means?

IOKASTE.   Why think of him?
Forget this herdsman. Forget it all.
This talk is a waste of time.

OEDIPUS.   How can you say that,
When the clues to my true birth are in my hands?

IOKASTE.   For God's love, let us have no more questioning!
Is your life nothing to you?
My own is pain enough for me to bear.

OEDIPUS.   You need not worry. Suppose my mother a slave,
And born of slaves: no baseness can touch you.

IOKASTE.   Listen to me, I beg you: do not do this thing!

OEDIPUS.   I will not listen; the truth must be made known.

IOKASTE.   Everything that I say is for your own good!

OEDIPUS.   My own good
Snaps my patience, then; I want none of it.

IOKASTE.   You are fatally wrong! May you never learn who you are!

OEDIPUS.   Go, one of you, and bring the shepherd here.
Let us leave this woman to brag of her royal name.

IOKASTE.   Ah, miserable!
That is the only word I have for you now.
That is the only word I can ever have. [Exit into the palace.]

CHORAGOS.   Why has she left us, Oedipus? Why has she gone
In such a passion of sorrow? I fear this silence:
Something dreadful may come of it.

OEDIPUS.   Let it come!
However base my birth, I must know about it.
The Queen, like a woman, is perhaps ashamed
To think of my low origin. But I
Am a child of Luck; I can not be dishonored.
Luck is my mother; the passing months, my brothers,
Have seen me rich and poor.

                    If this is so,
How could I wish that I were someone else?
How could I not be glad to know my birth?

ODE III

    CHORUS. If ever the coming time were known   [STROPHE]
To my heart's pondering,
Kithairon, now by Heaven I see the torches
At the festival of the next full moon,[35]
And see the dance, and hear the choir sing
A grace to your gentle shade:
Mountain where Oedipus was found,
O mountain guard of a noble race!
May the god who heals us[36] lend his aid,
And let that glory come to pass
For our king's cradling-ground.

Of the nymphs that flower beyond the years,[37]   [ANTISTROPHE]
Who bore you, royal child,
To Pan of the hills[38] or the timberline Apollo,[39]
Cold in delight where the upland clears,
Or Hermês for whom Kyllenê's heights are piled?[40]
Or flushed as evening cloud,
Great Dionysos, roamer of mountains,[41]
He—was it he who found you there,
And caught you up in his own proud
Arms from the sweet god-ravisher[42]
Who laughed by the Muses' fountains?

SCENE IV

    OEDIPUS. Sirs: though I do not know the man,
I think I see him coming, this shepherd we want:
He is old, like our friend here, and the men

---

    [35] Almost every god who was at all important had a festival day, most of which were celebrated at the full moon.
    [36] Apollo.
    [37] Immortal nymphs; the Chorus is attempting to attribute immortality to Oedipus.
    [38] Pan was god of pastures, forests, flocks, and herds.
    [39] Apollo was also associated with the care of flocks and herds.
    [40] Hermês, the messenger of the gods and also a god of flocks, roads, trading, etc., was born on Mt. Kyllenê.
    [41] Dionysos, the god of wine (hence "flushed") and also of vegetation, was honored in ceremonies on Mt. Parnassos.
    [42] The nymph who is conjectured to have borne Oedipus.

Bringing him seem to be servants of my house.
But you can tell, if you have ever seen him.

[*Enter* SHEPHERD *escorted by servants.*]

CHORAGOS. I know him, he was Laïos' man. You can trust him.

OEDIPUS. Tell me first, you from Corinth: is this the shepherd
We were discussing?

MESSENGER. This is the very man.

OEDIPUS [*to* SHEPHERD]. Come here. No, look at me. You must answer
Everything I ask.—You belonged to Laïos?

SHEPHERD. Yes: born his slave, brought up in his house.

OEDIPUS. Tell me: what kind of work did you do for him?

SHEPHERD. I was a shepherd of his, most of my life.

OEDIPUS. Where mainly did you go for pasturage?

SHEPHERD. Sometimes Kithairon, sometimes the hills near-by.

OEDIPUS. Do you remember ever seeing this man out there?

SHEPHERD. What would he be doing there? This man?

OEDIPUS. This man standing here. Have you ever seen him before?

SHEPHERD. No. At least, not to my recollection.

MESSENGER. And that is not strange, my lord. But I'll refresh
His memory: he must remember when we two
Spent three whole seasons together, March to September,
On Kithairon or thereabouts. He had two flocks;
I had one. Each autumn I'd drive mine home
And he would go back with his to Laïos' sheepfold.—
Is this not true, just as I have described it?

SHEPHERD. True, yes; but it was all so long ago.

MESSENGER. Well, then: do you remember, back in those days,
That you gave me a baby boy to bring up as my own?

SHEPHERD. What if I did? What are you trying to say?

MESSENGER. King Oedipus was once that little child.

SHEPHERD. Damn you, hold your tongue!

OEDIPUS. No more of that!
It is your tongue needs watching, not this man's.

SHEPHERD. My King, my Master, what is it I have done wrong?

OEDIPUS. You have not answered his question about the boy.

SHEPHERD. He does not know . . . He is only making trouble . . .

OEDIPUS. Come, speak plainly, or it will go hard with you.

SHEPHERD. In God's name, do not torture an old man!

OEDIPUS. Come here, one of you; bind his arms behind him.

SHEPHERD. Unhappy king! What more do you wish to learn?

OEDIPUS. Did you give this man the child he speaks of?

SHEPHERD. I did.
And I would to God I had died that very day.

OEDIPUS. You will die now unless you speak the truth.

SHEPHERD. Yet if I speak the truth, I am worse than dead.

OEDIPUS [*to* ATTENDANT]. He intends to draw it out, apparently—

SHEPHERD. No! I have told you already that I gave him the boy.

OEDIPUS. Where did you get him? From your house? From somewhere
else?

SHEPHERD.   Not from mine, no. A man gave him to me.

OEDIPUS.   Is that man here? Whose house did he belong to?

SHEPHERD.   For God's love, my King, do not ask me any more!

OEDIPUS.   You are a dead man if I have to ask you again.

SHEPHERD.   Then . . . Then the child was from the palace of Laïos.

OEDIPUS.   A slave child? or a child of his own line?

SHEPHERD.   Ah, I am on the brink of dreadful speech!

OEDIPUS.   And I of dreadful hearing. Yet I must hear.

SHEPHERD.   If you must be told, then . . .

                                 They said it was Laïos' child;
But it is your wife who can tell you about that.

OEDIPUS.   My wife!—Did she give it to you?

SHEPHERD.   My lord, she did.

OEDIPUS.   Do you know why?

SHEPHERD.   I was told to get rid of it.

OEDIPUS.   Oh heartless mother!

SHEPHERD.   But in dread of prophecies . . .

OEDIPUS.   Tell me.

SHEPHERD.   It was said that the boy would kill his own father.

OEDIPUS.   Then why did you give him over to this old man?

SHEPHERD.   I pitied the baby, my King,
And I thought that this man would take him far away
To his own country.

                 He saved him—but for what a fate!
For if you are what this man says you are,
No man living is more wretched than Oedipus.

OEDIPUS.   Ah God!
It was true!

          All the prophecies!

                  —Now,
O Light, may I look on you for the last time!
I, Oedipus,
Oedipus, damned in his birth, in his marriage damned,
Damned in the blood he shed with his own hand!

                       [*He rushes into the palace.*]

ODE IV

CHORUS.   Alas for the seed of men.   [STROPHE 1]

What measure shall I give these generations
That breathe on the void and are void
And exist and do not exist?

Who bears more weight of joy
Than mass of sunlight shifting in images,
Or who shall make his thought stay on
That down time drifts away?

Your splendor is all fallen.

O naked brow of wrath and tears,
O change of Oedipus!
I who saw your days call no man blest—
Your great days like ghósts góne.

That mind was a strong bow.

Deep, how deep you drew it then, hard archer,
At a dim fearful range,

And brought dear glory down!

You overcame the stranger—
The virgin with her hooking lion claws—[43]
And though death sang, stood like a tower
To make pale Thebes take heart.

Fortress against our sorrow!

True king, giver of laws,
Majestic Oedipus!
No prince in Thebes had ever such renown,
No prince won such grace of power.

And now of all men ever known
Most pitiful is this man's story:
His fortunes are most changed, his state
Fallen to a low slave's
Ground under bitter fate.

O Oedipus, most royal one!
The great door that expelled you to the light[44]
Gave at night—ah, gave night to your glory:
As to the father, to the fathering son.

All understood too late.

How could that queen whom Laïos won,
The garden that he harrowed at his height,[45]
Be silent when that act was done?

But all eyes fail before time's eye,
All actions come to justice there.
Though never willed, though far down the deep past,
Your bed, your dread sirings,
Are brought to book at last.[46]

[43] The Sphinx, who had the face of a woman, the body of a lion, and the wings of a bird.
[44] Iokaste's womb.
[45] Another reference to Iokaste's womb and, by implication, to Iokaste herself.
[46] An allusion to the fates of Oedipus' children ("dread sirings"). His sons, Polyneikês and Etioklês, killed each other in battle, and his daughter Antigonê died tragically; the circumstances of her death are related in another of Sophocles' plays. A second daughter, Ismenê, seems never to have attained any significance.

Child by Laïos doomed to die,
Then doomed to lose that fortunate little death,
Would God you never took breath in this air
That with my wailing lips I take to cry:

For I weep the world's outcast.

I was blind, and now I can tell why:
Asleep, for you had given ease of breath
To Thebes, while the false years went by.

ÉXODOS

Enter, from the palace, SECOND MESSENGER.

SECOND MESSENGER.   Elders of Thebes,[47] most honored in this land,
What horrors are yours to see and hear, what weight
Of sorrow to be endured, if, true to your birth,
You venerate the line of Labdakos!
I think neither Istros nor Phasis, those great rivers,
Could purify this place of all the evil
It shelters now, or soon must bring to light—
Evil not done unconsciously, but willed.

The greatest griefs are those we cause ourselves.
CHORAGOS.   Surely, friend, we have grief enough already;
What new sorrow do you mean?
SECOND MESSENGER.   The Queen is dead.
CHORAGOS.   O miserable Queen! But at whose hand?
SECOND MESSENGER.   Her own.
The full horror of what happened you can not know,
For you did not see it; but I, who did, will tell you
As clearly as I can how she met her death.

When she had left us,
In passionate silence, passing through the court,
She ran to her apartment in the house,
Her hair clutched by the fingers of both hands.
She closed the doors behind her; then, by that bed
Where long ago the fatal son was conceived—
That son who should bring about his father's death—
We heard her call upon Laïos, dead so many years,
And heard her wail for the double fruit of her marriage,
A husband by her husband, children by her child.

Exactly how she died I do not know:
For Oedipus burst in moaning and would not let us
Keep vigil to the end: it was by him
As he stormed about the room that our eyes were caught.

47 The Chorus.

From one to another of us he went, begging a sword,
Hunting the wife who was not his wife, the mother
Whose womb had carried his own children and himself.
I do not know: it was none of us aided him,
But surely one of the gods was in control!
For with a dreadful cry
He hurled his weight, as though wrenched out of himself,
At the twin doors: the bolts gave, and he rushed in.
And there we saw her hanging, her body swaying
From the cruel cord she had noosed about her neck.
A great sob broke from him, heartbreaking to hear,
As he loosed the rope and lowered her to the ground.

I would blot out from my mind what happened next!
For the King ripped from her gown the golden brooches
That were her ornament, and raised them, and plunged them down
Straight into his own eyeballs, crying, 'No more,
No more shall you look on the misery about me,
The horrors of my own doing! Too long you have known
The faces of those whom I should never have seen,
Too long been blind to those for whom I was searching!
From this hour, go in darkness!' And as he spoke,
He struck at his eyes—not once, but many times;
And the blood spattered his beard,
Bursting from his ruined sockets like red hail.

So from the unhappiness of two this evil has sprung,
A curse on the man and woman alike. The old
Happiness of the house of Labdakos
Was happiness enough: where is it today?
It is all wailing and ruin, disgrace, death—all
The misery of mankind that has a name—
And it is wholly and for ever theirs.

CHORAGOS.   Is he in agony still? Is there no rest for him?
SECOND MESSENGER.   He is calling for someone to open the doors wide
So that all the children of Kadmos may look upon
His father's murderer, his mother's—no,
I can not say it!
                    And then he will leave Thebes,
Self-exiled, in order that the curse
Which he himself pronounced may depart from the house.
He is weak, and there is none to lead him,
So terrible is his suffering.
                    But you will see:
Look, the doors are opening; in a moment
You will see a thing that would crush a heart of stone.
            [*The central door is opened;* OEDIPUS, *blinded, is led in.*]
    CHORAGOS.   Dreadful indeed for men to see.
Never have my own eyes
Looked on a sight so full of fear.

Oedipus!
What madness came upon you, what daemon
Leaped on your life with heavier
Punishment than a mortal man can bear?
No: I can not even
Look at you, poor ruined one.
And I would speak, question, ponder,
If I were able. No.
You make me shudder.

    OEDIPUS. God.   God.
Is there a sorrow greater?
Where shall I find harbor in this world?
My voice is hurled far on a dark wind.
What has God done to me?

    CHORAGOS.   Too terrible to think of, or to see.

    OEDIPUS. O cloud of night,   [STROPHE 1]
Never to be turned away: night coming on,
I can not tell how: night like a shroud!

My fair winds brought me here.
                         O God. Again
The pain of the spikes where I had sight,
The flooding pain
Of memory, never to be gouged out.

    CHORAGOS.   This is not strange.
You suffer it all twice over, remorse in pain,
Pain in remorse.

    OEDIPUS. Ah dear friend   [ANTISTROPHE 1]
Are you faithful even yet, you alone?
Are you still standing near me, will you stay here,
Patient, to care for the blind?
                     The blind man!
Yet even blind I know who it is attends me,
By the voice's tone—
Though my new darkness hide the comforter.

    CHORAGOS. Oh fearful act!
What god was it drove you to rake black
Night across your eyes?

    OEDIPUS. Apollo. Apollo. Dear   [STROPHE 2]
Children, the god was Apollo.
He brought my sick, sick fate upon me.
But the blinding hand was my own!
How could I bear to see
When all my sight was horror everywhere?

CHORAGOS.   Everywhere; that is true.

OEDIPUS.   And now what is left?
Images? Love? A greeting even,
Sweet to the senses? Is there anything?
Ah, no, friends: lead me away.
Lead me away from Thebes.
                              Lead the great wreck
And hell of Oedipus, whom the gods hate.

CHORAGOS.   Your misery, you are not blind to that.
Would God you had never found it out!

[ANTISTROPHE 2]

OEDIPUS.   Death take the man who unbound
My feet on that hillside
And delivered me from death to life! What life?
If only I had died,
This weight of monstrous doom
Could not have dragged me and my darlings down.

CHORAGOS.   I would have wished the same.

OEDIPUS.   Oh never to have come here
With my father's blood upon me! Never
To have been the man they call his mother's husband!
Oh accurst! Oh child of evil,
To have entered that wretched bed—
                              the selfsame one!
More primal than sin itself, this fell to me.

CHORAGOS.   I do not know what words to offer you.
You were better dead than alive and blind.

OEDIPUS.   Do not counsel me any more. This punishment
That I have laid upon myself is just.
If I had eyes,
I do not know how I could bear the sight
Of my father, when I came to the house of Death,
Or my mother: for I have sinned against them both
So vilely that I could not make my peace
By strangling my own life.
                              Or do you think my children,
Born as they were born, would be sweet to my eyes?
Ah never, never! Nor this town with its high walls,
Nor the holy images of the gods.
                              For I,
Thrice miserable!—Oedipus, noblest of all the line
Of Kadmos, have condemned myself to enjoy
These things no more, by my own malediction
Expelling that man whom the gods declared
To be a defilement in the house of Laïos.
After exposing the rankness of my own guilt,
How could I look men frankly in the eyes?
No, I swear it,

If I could have stifled my hearing at its source,
I would have done it and made all this body
A tight cell of misery, blank to light and sound:
So I should have been safe in my dark mind
Beyond external evil.

                 Ah Kithairon!
Why did you shelter me? When I was cast upon you,
Why did I not die? Then I should never
Have shown the world my execrable birth.

Ah Polybos! Corinth, city that I believed
The ancient seat of my ancestors: how fair
I seemed, your child! And all the while this evil
Was cancerous within me!

                For I am sick
In my own being, sick in my origin.

O three roads, dark ravine, woodland and way
Where three roads met: you, drinking my father's blood,
My own blood, spilled by my own hand: can you remember
The unspeakable things I did there, and the things
I went on from there to do?

              O marriage, marriage!
The act that engendered me, and again the act
Performed by the son in the same bed—

                  Ah, the net
Of incest, mingling fathers, brothers, sons,
With brides, wives, mothers: the last evil
That can be known by men: no tongue can say
How evil!

       No. For the love of God, conceal me
Somewhere far from Thebes; or kill me; or hurl me
Into the sea, away from men's eyes for ever.
Come, lead me. You need not fear to touch me.
Of all men, I alone can bear this guilt. [*Enter* KREON.]
    CHORAGOS.   Kreon is here now. As to what you ask,
He may decide the course to take. He only
Is left to protect the city in your place.
    OEDIPUS.   Alas, how can I speak to him? What right have I
To beg his courtesy whom I have deeply wronged?
    KREON.[48]   I have not come to mock you, Oedipus,
Or to reproach you, either.
[*To* ATTENDANTS.]   —You, standing there:
If you have lost all respect for man's dignity,
At least respect the flame of Lord Helios:
Do not allow this pollution to show itself
Openly here, an affront to the earth

---

[48] Kreon acts as Regent of Thebes because Oedipus' sons are too young to rule.

And Heaven's rain and the light of day. No, take him
Into the house as quickly as you can.
For it is proper
That only the close kindred see his grief.

OEDIPUS.   I pray you in God's name, since your courtesy
Ignores my dark expectation, visiting
With mercy this man of all men most execrable:
Give me what I ask—for your good, not for mine.

KREON.   And what is it that you turn to me begging for?

OEDIPUS.   Drive me out of this country as quickly as may be
To a place where no human voice can ever greet me.

KREON.   I should have done that before now—only,
God's will had not been wholly revealed to me.

OEDIPUS.   But his command is plain: the parricide
Must be destroyed. I am that evil man.

KREON.   That is the sense of it, yes; but as things are,
We had best discover clearly what is to be done.

OEDIPUS.   You would learn more about a man like me?

KREON.   You are ready now to listen to the god.

OEDIPUS.   I will listen. But it is to you
That I must turn for help. I beg you, hear me.

The woman in there—
Give her whatever funeral you think proper:
She is your sister.
                    —But let me go, Kreon!
Let me purge my father's Thebes of the pollution
Of my living here, and go out to the wild hills,
To Kithairon, that has won such fame with me,
The tomb my mother and father appointed for me,
And let me die there, as they willed I should.
And yet I know
Death will not ever come to me through sickness
Or in any natural way: I have been preserved
For some unthinkable fate. But let that be.

As for my sons, you need not care for them.
They are men, they will find some way to live.
But my poor daughters, who have shared my table,
Who never before have been parted from their father—
Take care of them, Kreon; do this for me.
And will you let me touch them with my hands
A last time, and let us weep together?
Be kind, my lord,
Great prince, be kind!
                    Could I but touch them,
They would be mine again, as when I had my eyes.

                    [Enter ANTIGONE *and* ISMENE, *attended.*]

Ah, God!
Is it my dearest children I hear weeping?

Has Kreon pitied me and sent my daughters?

    KREON.   Yes, Oedipus: I knew that they were dear to you
In the old days, and know you must love them still.

    OEDIPUS.   May God bless you for this—and be a friendlier
Guardian to you than he has been to me!

Children, where are you?
Come quickly to my hands: they are your brother's—
Hands that have brought your father's once clear eyes
To this way of seeing—

                  Ah dearest ones,
I had neither sight nor knowledge then, your father
By the woman who was the source of his own life!
And I weep for you—having no strength to see you—,
I weep for you when I think of the bitterness
That men will visit upon you all your lives.
What homes, what festivals can you attend
Without being forced to depart again in tears?
And when you come to marriageable age,
Where is the man, my daughters, who would dare
Risk the bane that lies on all my children?
Is there any evil wanting? Your father killed
His father; sowed the womb of her who bore him;
Engendered you at the fount of his own existence!

That is what they will say of you.

                          Then, whom
Can you ever marry? There are no bridegrooms for you,
And your lives must wither away in sterile dreaming.

O Kreon, son of Menoikeus!
You are the only father my daughters have,
Since we, their parents, are both of us gone for ever.
They are your own blood: you will not let them
Fall into beggary and loneliness;
You will keep them from the miseries that are mine!
Take pity on them; see, they are only children,
Friendless except for you. Promise me this,
Great Prince, and give me your hand in token of it.

                      [KREON *clasps his right hand.*]

Children:
I could say much, if you could understand me,
But as it is, I have only this prayer for you:
Live where you can, be as happy as you can—
Happier, please God, than God has made your father.

    KREON.   Enough. You have wept enough. Now go within.

    OEDIPUS.   I must; but it is hard.

    KREON.   Time eases all things.

    OEDIPUS.   You know my mind, then?

KREON.   Say what you desire.

OEDIPUS.   Send me from Thebes!

KREON.   God grant that I may![49]

OEDIPUS.   But since God hates me . . .

KREON.   No, he will grant your wish.

OEDIPUS.   You promise?

KREON.   I can not speak beyond my knowledge.

OEDIPUS.   Then lead me in.

KREON.   Come now, and leave your children.

OEDIPUS.   No! Do not take them from me!

KREON.   Think no longer

That you are in command here, but rather think
How, when you were, you served your own destruction.

> [*Exeunt into the house all but the* CHORUS; *the*
> CHORAGOS *chants directly to the audience.*]

CHORAGOS.   Men of Thebes: look upon Oedipus.

This is the king who solved the famous riddle
And towered up, most powerful of men.
No mortal eyes but looked on him with envy,
Yet in the end ruin swept over him.

Let every man in mankind's frailty
Consider his last day; and let none
Presume on his good fortune until he find
Life, at his death, a memory without pain.

COMMENTARY

The plot of *Oedipus Rex* is at once the most ingenious and the most terrible that has ever been conceived. It can be thought of as a detective story in which the detective, secure in his own virtue and in the consciousness that he is doing his duty, undertakes to discover the identity of the person who has committed a crime of great seriousness and is forced by the evidence he turns up to recognize that the criminal is none other than himself. And more than this is in store for him. As he pursues his investigations further, he learns that the criminal act, because it was he who committed it, is immeasurably worse than at first it had seemed.

Summarized even in this abstract way, the story of Oedipus is calculated to disturb us in our deepest and most private emotions, for most of us live with the sense of a guilty secret, although what the secret is about we do not know. And of course the play haunts and disturbs us the more because of the peculiar heinousness of what Oedipus has done. He has committed not merely terrible crimes but terrible sins, violating not only the law of society but of the gods. And even the idea of sin does not comprehend the horror of a man's having killed his father and married his mother. These acts are, as we say, unthinkable; the human mind can do nothing with them.

[49] Kreon refuses to act until he knows the will of the gods in this matter.

Our disturbance is not lessened but increased by the consideration that Oedipus did not commit his awful acts by intention. Of all the circumstances of the hero's fate, this is the one that most teases, baffles, and terrifies. It is reasonable to say—it has been said—that Oedipus is not accountable for what he did, that he had not really incurred guilt in killing his father and marrying his mother because he had not meant to do these things; on the contrary, once he had heard the awful prophecy, he had bent all his effort toward not doing them. This exculpation of Oedipus is based upon Aristotle's doctrine, set forth in his *Ethics,* to which assent is given by law and morality throughout the Western world, that for an act to have ethical significance, for good or bad, the person who commits it must have done so with consciousness and will. It is in these terms that Oedipus argues for his blamelessness in *Oedipus at Colonus,* the play that Sophocles wrote thirty years later. Worn out with suffering and on the point of death, the aged Oedipus, in a moment of bitterness and self-pity, says that he should not have been adjudged guilty because he had had no intention of wrong-doing. But in *Oedipus Rex* he makes no such claim to innocence. He does not justify himself; his mind is wholly given over to horror and self-loathing. We feel this response to be appropriate. The rationality of Aristotle's doctrine of intention seems quite inapplicable to the emotion evoked by Oedipus' situation, which occurs at a depth to which reason cannot penetrate. It is from the disclosure of this primitive depth that the play derives its terrible power, leading us to recognize that a man may incur guilt, and of an ultimate kind, even though a rational ethic might pronounce him innocent; we are brought to confront the possibility that reason can be superseded by darker modes of judgment. The security that a rational ethic had seemed to afford is taken from us.

An engaging question often raised about *Oedipus Rex* is whether or not it is a tragedy of fate. Much ingenuity has been expended to show that it is not. Some critics feel that the play becomes less interesting and impressive if it is taken as a tragedy of fate, for the protagonist then lacks the dignity that we associate with the possession of free will; he becomes, as we say, a puppet in the hands of destiny. Those who hold this position believe that they have an ally in Aristotle, who, in his *Poetics,* says that the protagonist of a tragedy should be a man worthy of respect and admiration but having some discernible weakness or fault of character to which his tragic disaster may be attributed. In some important sense, that is, he is to be thought responsible for what befalls him.

Aristotle's prescription would certainly seem to be satisfied by the character of Oedipus. He is admirable for many qualities. He is wise and courageous; it was he who, when everyone else stood helpless before the Sphinx that ravaged Thebes, answered her riddle and destroyed her, thus freeing the land of which he then became the ruler. As a king he is virtuous and conscientious. To be sure, he is called *tyrannos,* which, although it is not to be translated as "tyrant," means a king who rules by his own power, as distinguished from *basileus,* a king by legal right. Yet he is in no way arbitrary or repressive; he admits his wife to equal rule with him and allows her brother Kreon to stand almost on a parity with the royal couple. As husband and father he is dutiful and loving. He is not lacking in piety; although he speaks contemptuously to the great seer Teiresias, the protégé of Apollo, he holds the gods in due awe and is quick to undertake what Apollo's oracle at Delphi tells him should be done to rid the city of plague.

One fault, however, Oedipus does have, that of pride, and he is quick to anger when his pride is offended. His slaying of his unknown father Laïos at the crossroads had been the outcome of this trait. And it is his choleric pride, amounting to arrogance, that prevents him from heeding any word of caution when he is pursuing his search for the killer of Laïos, with the result that he is forced to confront the truth that he himself is the killer—and, of course, something more than that.

Yet no matter how fully we take account of Oedipus's fault of character, we have no ground for saying that the tragic disaster is brought about by this personal flaw and not by the predestination announced in the prophecy. That the fault detonates the disaster is of course true, but the explosives have been laid by what, in the nature of the prophecy about Oedipus, we can only call fate. The young hero's hot-blooded response to Laïos' insult and show of violence did indeed lead him to kill *a man,* and, what is worse, a king; but it was the fated ignorance of his parenthood and the unsought but destined occasion of the meeting between father and son that led him to kill *his father.* Any other proud and hot-blooded man who had done what Oedipus did would have committed an act that was to be deplored and condemned: for Oedipus alone the act was immitigable, and the more so because it led to an act yet more horrifying, his marriage to his mother.

If we take the line that Oedipus brought about his tragedy by refusing to heed the advice to be cautious in his search for Laïos' killer, we find ourselves in the position of supposing that all would have been well if he had prudently given up his investigation and settled to live in contented ignorance with his wife and children in plague-ridden Thebes. Of course we can suppose no such thing. Nor would we have any satisfaction if any such thing came about. To be sure, we are impelled to cry out a warning to the impetuous man not to call upon *that* witness, not to ask *that* question; we are fearful of the moment when the full dreadful knowledge will come to him of who he is and what he has done. But we do not want Oedipus to remain oblivious of the truth about himself. An Oedipus who prudently gave up his search would be an object of condescension, even of contempt: the Oedipus who presses on to the conclusion that destroys him compels our awed respect.

In short, then, whatever it may also be, the story of Oedipus must certainly be called a tragedy of fate. Yet to say this is, after all, not to say much. Something of what must be added if we are to account for the peculiar power of *Oedipus Rex* is suggested by a comparison of the story of the play with a well-known tale of similar purport. In the city of Ispahan, in Persia, a certain man's servant came to him and said, "I was in the market place and there I saw Death and he made a threatening gesture to me." The man said, "Let us flee," and he and his servant set out posthaste for Samarra. No sooner had they entered that city than they encountered Death, to whom the man said, "Why did you threaten my servant in the market place in Ispahan?" Death replied, "My gesture was not one of threat but of surprise, for I had an appointment to meet you in Samarra, and I was surprised to learn, from seeing your servant, that you were still in Ispahan." In its barest outline, the story of Oedipus is no different from this—a man, fleeing his fate, encounters it. But the wry little parable of fatalism evokes no other response than an ironic shrug; the mind does not engage it, there is really nothing in the tale for the mind to engage. The implied generalization, that all men must submit to what is ordained for them, that some fulfil their fate by the very intention of evading it, may win from us a certain assent but not much interest. We respond very differently when a man such as Oedipus fulfils his fate by seeking to evade it—a man whose pride, courage, and intellect suggest an ideal of mankind, and whose particular destiny it is to experience on so great a scale the peculiarly human pain of remorse and self-reproach. The man who flees from Ispahan to Samarra is indeed without dignity, a mere puppet in the hands of destiny; the joke is on him, fate has made a fool of him. But Oedipus, who is unable to save himself by intelligence and right intention and who is subject to an order of things which does not proceed by human rules and is not susceptible to human understanding, is enhanced in stature by his doom.

Aristotle's *Poetics* is chiefly devoted to a discussion of tragedy, and it is obvious that among all the Athenian achievements in this genre the author gives his highest admiration to *Oedipus Rex*. One cannot resist the speculation that he held the play in especial regard because it so deeply challenges and so successfully baffles the rational intellect, of which he was the great exemplar, and that he loved this play because it proposed the existence of forces inscrutable to human reason. If his spirit was as large as his mind, he may well have found pleasure in contemplating an order that did not yield its secrets to the demands of rational intellect.

Oedipus at Colonus, the play that Sophocles wrote in the year of his death at the age of ninety, also speaks of an order that baffles reason. Oedipus is now very old; he has been wandering the earth, an outcast, attended only by his two daughters. Although he is feeble and foredone, his quickness to anger has not diminished, and now his rage is directed toward his two sons because they have permitted him to continue in the exile to which he had doomed himself. He is bitter at his fate and he insists on his blamelessness—he is not, it is plain, an endearing person. Yet word has gone out that the city will be blessed which gives this accursed outcast his last resting place and buries him with honor. And when death comes to him at Colonus, a suburb of Athens, it is not death as ordinary men know it, but apotheosis: by divine agency he is carried off from earth to live as a demigod. This end is not granted Oedipus in compensation for his suffering but in recognition of some power of his nature that approaches the divine. We are left to ponder how it is that this cursed man became a blessing and why this guilty man should have been so supremely rewarded.

THE

WILD

DUCK

H E N R I K   I B S E N

1 8 2 8 – 1 9 0 6

CHARACTERS

HAAKON WERLE, wholesale merchant and millowner
GREGERS WERLE, his son
OLD EKDAL
HJALMAR EKDAL, his son, a photographer
GINA EKDAL, Hjalmar's wife
HEDVIG, their daughter, aged fourteen
MRS. SØRBY, housekeeper for the elder Werle
RELLING, a doctor
MOLVIK, a former divinity student
GRAABERG, a bookkeeper
PETTERSEN, manservant to the elder Werle
JENSEN, a hired waiter
A FAT MAN
A BALD-HEADED MAN
A NEARSIGHTED MAN
SIX OTHER MEN, dinner guests at Werle's
OTHER HIRED SERVANTS

The first act takes place in WERLE's *house; the following four acts in* HJALMAR EKDAL's *studio.*

ACT I

At WERLE's *house. A richly and comfortably furnished study, with book-cases and upholstered furniture, a writing table, with papers and reports, in the middle of the floor, and green-shaded lamps softly illuminating the room. In the rear wall, open folding doors with curtains drawn back disclose a large, fashionable room, brightly lit by lamps and candelabra. In the right foreground of the study, a small private door leads to the offices. In the left foreground, a fireplace filled with glowing coals, and further back a double door to the dining room.*

WERLE's manservant, PETTERSEN, *in livery, and* JENSEN, *a hired waiter, in black, are straightening up the study. In the larger room two or three other hired waiters are moving about, putting things in order and lighting more candles. In from the dining room come laughter and the hum of many voices in conversation; a knife clinks upon a glass; silence; a toast is made; cries of "Bravo," and the hum of conversation resumes.*

PETTERSEN [*lighting a lamp by the fireplace and putting on the shade*]. Ah, you hear that, Jensen. Now the old boy's up on his feet, proposing a long toast to Mrs. Sørby.

JENSEN [*moving an armchair forward*]. Is it really true what people say, that there's something between them?

PETTERSEN. Lord knows.

JENSEN. I've heard he was a real goat in his day.

PETTERSEN. Could be.

JENSEN. But they say it's his son he's throwing this party for.

PETTERSEN. Yes. His son came home yesterday.

JENSEN. I never knew before that old Werle had any son.

PETTERSEN. Oh yes, he's got a son. But he spends all his time up at the works in Hoidal. He hasn't been in town all the years I've served in this house.

A HIRED WAITER [*in the door to the other room*]. Say, Pettersen, there's an old guy here who—

PETTERSEN [*muttering*]. What the hell—somebody coming now!

[*Old* EKDAL *appears from the right through the inner room. He is dressed in a shabby overcoat with a high collar, woolen gloves, and in his hand, a cane and a fur cap; under his arm is a bundle wrapped in brown paper. He has a dirty, reddish-brown wig and a little gray moustache.*]

PETTERSEN [*going toward him*]. Good Lord, what do *you* want in here?

EKDAL [*at the door*]. Just have to get into the office, Pettersen.

PETTERSEN. The office closed an hour ago, and—

EKDAL. Heard that one at the door, boy. But Graaberg's still in there. Be nice, Pettersen, and let me slip in that way. [*Pointing toward the private entrance.*] I've gone that way before.

PETTERSEN. All right, go ahead, then. [*Opens the door.*] But don't forget now—take the other way out; we have guests.

EKDAL. Got you—hmm! Thanks, Pettersen, good old pal! Thanks. [*To himself.*] Bonehead! [*He goes into the office;* PETTERSEN *shuts the door after him.*]

JENSEN. Is *he* on the office staff too?

PETTERSEN. No, he's just someone who does copying on the outside when it's needed. Still, in his time he was well up in the world, old Ekdal.

JENSEN. Yes, he looks like he's been a little of everything.

PETTERSEN. Oh yes. He was a lieutenant once, if you can imagine.

JENSEN. Good Lord—him a lieutenant!

PETTERSEN. So help me, he was. But then he went into the lumber business or something. They say he must have pulled some kind of dirty deal on the old man once, for the two of them were running the Hoidal works together then. Oh, I know good old Ekdal, all right. We've drunk many a schnapps and bottle of beer together over at Eriksen's.

JENSEN. He can't have much money for standing drinks.

PETTERSEN. My Lord, Jensen, you can bet it's me that stands the drinks. I always say a person ought to act refined toward quality that's come down in life.

JENSEN. Did he go bankrupt, then?

PETTERSEN. No, worse than that. He was sent to jail.

JENSEN. To jail!

PETTERSEN. Or maybe it was the penitentiary. [*Laughter from the dining room.*] Hist! They're leaving the table.

[*The dining room door is opened by a pair of servants inside.* MRS. SØRBY, *in conversation with two gentlemen, comes out. A moment later the rest of the guests follow, among them* WERLE. *Last of all come* HJALMAR EKDAL *and* GREGERS WERLE.]

MRS. SØRBY [*to the servant, in passing*]. Pettersen, will you have coffee served in the music room?

PETTERSEN. Yes, Mrs. Sørby.

[*She and the two gentlemen go into the inner room and exit to the right.* PETTERSEN *and* JENSEN *leave in the same way.*]

A FAT GUEST [*to a balding man*]. Phew! That dinner—that was a steep bit of work!

THE BALD-HEADED GUEST. Oh, with a little good will a man can do wonders in three hours.

THE FAT GUEST. Yes, but afterward, my dear fellow, afterward.

A THIRD GUEST. I hear we can sample coffee and liqueur in the music room.

THE FAT GUEST. Fine! Then perhaps Mrs. Sørby will play us a piece.

THE BALD-HEADED GUEST [*in an undertone*]. Just so Mrs. Sørby doesn't play us to pieces.

THE FAT GUEST. Oh, now really, Berta wouldn't punish her old friends, would she? [*They laugh and enter the inner room.*]

WERLE [*in a low, depressed tone*]. I don't think anyone noticed it, Gregers.

GREGERS. What?

WERLE. Didn't you notice it either?

GREGERS. What should I have noticed?

WERLE. We were thirteen at the table.

GREGERS. Really? Were we thirteen?

WERLE [*with a glance at* HJALMAR EKDAL]. Yes—our usual number is twelve. [*To the others.*] Be so kind, gentlemen. [*He and those remaining, excepting* HJALMAR *and* GREGERS, *go out to the rear and right.*]

HJALMAR [*who has heard the conversation*]. You shouldn't have sent me the invitation, Gregers.

GREGERS. What! The party's supposed to be for *me*. And then I'm not supposed to have my best and only friend—

HJALMAR. But I don't think your father likes it. Ordinarily I never come to this house.

GREGERS. So I hear. But I had to see you and talk with you, for I'm sure to be leaving soon again. Yes, we two old classmates, we've certainly drifted a long way apart. You know, we haven't seen each other now in sixteen—seventeen years.

HJALMAR. Has it been so long?

GREGERS. Yes, all of that. Well, how have you been? You look well. You're almost becoming stout.

HJALMAR. Hm, stout is hardly the word, though I probably look more of a man than I did then.

GREGERS. Yes, you do. The outer man hasn't suffered.

HJALMAR [*in a gloomier tone*]. Ah, but the inner man! Believe me, he has a different look. You know, of course, what misery we've been through, I and my family, since the last time the two of us met.

GREGERS [*dropping his voice*]. How's it going for your father now?

HJALMAR. Oh, Gregers, let's not talk about that. My poor, unhappy father naturally lives at home with me. He's got no one else in the whole world to turn to. But this all is so terribly hard for me to talk about, you know. Tell me, instead, how you've found life up at the mill.

GREGERS. Marvelously solitary, that's what—with a good chance to mull over a great many things. Come on, let's be comfortable. [*He sits in an armchair by the fire and urges* HJALMAR *down into another by its side.*]

HJALMAR [*emotionally*]. In any case, I'm grateful that you asked me here, Gregers, because it proves you no longer have anything against me.

GREGERS [*astonished*]. How could you think that I had anything against you?

HJALMAR. In those first years you did.

GREGERS. Which first years?

HJALMAR. Right after that awful misfortune. And it was only natural you should. It was just by a hair that your own father escaped being dragged into this—oh, this ugly business.

GREGERS. And that's why I had it in for you? Whoever gave you that idea?

HJALMAR. I know you did, Gregers; it was your father himself who told me.

GREGERS [*startled*]. Father! I see. Hm—is that why I never heard from you—not a single word?

HJALMAR. Yes.

GREGERS. Not even when you went out and became a photographer.

HJALMAR.   Your father said it wasn't worth writing you—about anything.

GREGERS [looking fixedly ahead].   No, no, maybe he was right there— But tell me, Hjalmar—do you find yourself reasonably content with things as they are?

HJALMAR [with a small sigh].   Oh, I suppose I do. What else can I say? At first, you can imagine, it was all rather strange for me. They were such completely different expectations that I came into. But then everything was so different. That immense, shattering misfortune for Father—the shame and the scandal, Gregers—

GREGERS [shaken].   Yes, yes. Of course.

HJALMAR.   I couldn't dream of going on with my studies; there wasn't a penny to spare. On the contrary, debts instead—mainly to your father, I think—

GREGERS.   Hm—

HJALMAR.   Anyway, I thought it was best to make a clean break—and cut all the old connections. It was your father especially who advised me to; and since he'd already been so helpful to me—

GREGERS.   He had?

HJALMAR.   Yes, you knew that, didn't you? Where could I get the money to learn photography and fit out a studio and establish myself? I can tell you, that all adds up.

GREGERS.   And all that Father paid for?

HJALMAR.   Yes, Gregers, didn't you know? I understood him to say that he'd written you about it.

GREGERS.   Not a word saying he was the one. Maybe he forgot. We've never exchanged anything but business letters. So that was Father, too—!

HJALMAR.   That's right. He never wanted people to know, but he was the one. And he was also the one who put me in a position to get married. Or perhaps—didn't you know that either?

GREGERS.   No, not at all. [Takes him by the arm.] But Hjalmar, I can't tell you how all this delights me—and disturbs me. Perhaps I've been unfair to my father—in certain ways. Yes, for all this does show good-heartedness, doesn't it? It's almost a kind of conscience—

HJALMAR.   Conscience?

GREGERS.   Yes, or whatever you want to call it. No, I can't tell you how glad I am to hear this about my father. So you're married, then, Hjalmar. That's further than I'll ever go. Well, I hope you're happy as a married man?

HJALMAR.   Oh, absolutely. She's as capable and fine a wife as any man could wish for. And she's not entirely without culture, either.

GREGERS [a bit surprised].   No, I'm sure she's not.

HJALMAR.   No. Life is a teacher, you see. Associating with me every day —and then there are one or two gifted people who visit us regularly. I can tell you, you wouldn't recognize Gina now.

GREGERS.   Gina?

HJALMAR.   Yes, Gregers, had you forgotten her name is Gina?

GREGERS.   Whose name is Gina? I haven't the faintest idea—

HJALMAR.   But don't you remember, she was here in this very house a while—in service?

GREGERS [looking at him].   You mean Gina Hansen—?

HJALMAR.   Yes, of course, Gina Hansen.

GREGERS.   Who was housekeeper for us that last year of Mother's illness?

HJALMAR.   Exactly. But my dear Gregers, I know for sure that your father wrote you about my marriage.

GREGERS [who has gotten up].   Yes, of course he did. But not that— [walks about the floor]. Yes, wait a minute—it may well be, now that I think of it. My father's letters are always so brief. [Sits on chair arm.] Listen, tell me, Hjalmar—this is interesting—how did you come to know Gina?—your wife, I mean.

HJALMAR.   Oh, it was all very simple. Gina didn't stay long here in the house; there was so much confusion—your mother's sickness and all. Gina couldn't stand it, so she just up and left. That was the year before your mother died—or maybe it was the same year.

GREGERS.   It was the same year. And I was up at the works at the time. But what then?

HJALMAR.   Well, then Gina lived at home with her mother, a Mrs. Hansen, a very capable, hardworking woman who ran a little restaurant. She also had a room for rent, a very pleasant, comfortable room.

GREGERS.   And you were lucky enough to find it?

HJALMAR.   Yes. Actually it was your father who suggested it to me. And it was there, you see—there that I really got to know Gina.

GREGERS.   And then your engagement followed?

HJALMAR.   Yes. Young people fall in love so easily—hm—

GREGERS [getting up and pacing about a little].   Tell me—when you became engaged—was it then that my father got you to—I mean, was it then that you started in learning photography?

HJALMAR.   That's right. I wanted to get on and set up a home as soon as possible, and both your father and I decided that this photography idea was the most feasible one. And Gina thought so too. Yes, and you see, there was another inducement, a lucky break, in that Gina had already taken up retouching.

GREGERS.   That worked out wonderfully all around.

HJALMAR [pleased, getting up].   Yes, isn't that so? Don't you think it's worked out wonderfully all around?

GREGERS.   Yes, I must say. My father has almost been a kind of providence to you.

HJALMAR [with feeling].   He didn't abandon his old friend's son in a time of need. You see, he does have a heart.

MRS. SØRBY [entering with WERLE on her arm].   No more nonsense, my dear Mr. Werle. You mustn't stay in there any longer, staring at all those lights; it's doing you no good.

WERLE [freeing his arm from hers and passing his hand over his eyes]. Yes, I guess you're right about that.

[PETTERSEN and JENSEN enter with trays.]

MRS. SØRBY [to the guests in the other room].   Gentlemen, please—if anyone wants a glass of punch, he must take the trouble to come in here.

THE FAT GUEST [comes over to MRS. SØRBY].   But really, is it true you've abolished our precious smoking privilege?

MRS. SØRBY.   Yes. Here in Mr. Werle's sanctum, it's forbidden.

THE BALD-HEADED GUEST. When did you pass these drastic amendments to the cigar laws, Mrs. Sørby?

MRS. SØRBY. After the last dinner—when there were certain persons here who let themselves exceed all limits.

THE BALD-HEADED GUEST. And my dear Berta, one isn't permitted to exceed the limits, even a little bit?

MRS. SØRBY. Not in any instance, Mr. Balle.

[*Most of the guests have gathered in the study; the waiters are proffering glasses of punch.*]

WERLE [*to* HJALMAR, *over by a table*]. What is it you're poring over, Ekdal?

HJALMAR. It's only an album, Mr. Werle.

THE BALD-HEADED GUEST [*who is wandering about*]. Ah, photographs! Yes, of course, that's just the thing for you.

THE FAT GUEST [*seated in an armchair*]. Haven't you brought along some of your own?

HJALMAR. No, I haven't.

THE FAT GUEST. You really should have. It's so good for the digestion to sit and look at pictures.

THE BALD-HEADED GUEST. And then it always adds a morsel to the entertainment, you know.

A NEARSIGHTED GUEST. And all contributions are gratefully received.

MRS. SØRBY. These gentlemen mean that if one's invited for dinner, one must also work for the food, Mr. Ekdal.

THE FAT GUEST. Where the larder's superior, *that* is pure joy.

THE BALD-HEADED GUEST. My Lord, it's all in the struggle for existence—

MRS. SØRBY. How right you are! [*They continue laughing and joking.*]

GREGERS [*quietly*]. You should talk with them, Hjalmar.

HJALMAR [*with a shrug*]. What could I talk about?

THE FAT GUEST. Don't you think, Mr. Werle, that Tokay compares favorably as a healthful drink for the stomach?

WERLE [*by the fireplace*]. The Tokay you had today I can vouch for in any case; it's one of the very, very finest years. But you recognized that well enough.

THE FAT GUEST. Yes, it had a remarkably delicate flavor.

HJALMAR [*tentatively*]. Is there some difference between the years?

THE FAT GUEST [*laughing*]. Oh, that's rich!

WERLE [*smiling*]. It certainly doesn't pay to offer you a noble wine.

THE BALD-HEADED GUEST. Tokay wines are like photographs, Mr. Ekdal—sunshine is of the essence. Isn't that true?

HJALMAR. Oh yes, light is very important.

MRS. SØRBY. Exactly the same as with court officials—who push for their place in the sun too, I hear.

THE BALD-HEADED GUEST. Ouch! That was a tired quip.

THE NEARSIGHTED GUEST. The lady's performing—

THE FAT GUEST. And at our expense. [*Frowning.*] Mrs. Sørby, Mrs. Sørby!

MRS. SØRBY. Yes, but it certainly is true now that the years can vary enormously. The old vintages are the finest.

THE NEARSIGHTED GUEST. Do you count me among the old ones?

MRS. SØRBY. Oh, far from it.

THE BALD-HEADED GUEST. Ha, you see! But what about *me*, Mrs. Sørby—?

THE FAT GUEST. Yes, and me! What years would you put us among?

MRS. SØRBY. I would put you all among the sweet years, gentlemen. [*She sips a glass of punch; the guests laugh and banter with her.*]

WERLE. Mrs. Sørby always finds a way out—when she wants to. Pass your glasses, gentlemen. Pettersen, take care of them. Gregers, I think we'll have a glass together. [GREGERS *does not stir.*] Won't you join us, Ekdal? I had no chance to remember you at the table.

[GRAABERG, *the bookkeeper, peers out from the door to the offices.*]

GRAABERG. Beg pardon, Mr. Werle, but I can't get out.

WERLE. What, are you locked in again?

GRAABERG. Yes, and Flakstad's left with the keys—

WERLE. Well, then, go through here.

GRAABERG. But there's someone else—

WERLE. All right, all right, both of you. Don't be shy.

[GRAABERG *and old* EKDAL *come out from the office.*]

WERLE [*involuntarily*]. Oh no!

[*The laughter and small talk die among the guests.* HJALMAR *starts at the sight of his father, sets down his glass, and turns away toward the fireplace.*]

EKDAL [*without looking up, but bowing slightly to each side and mumbling*]. Door locked. Door locked. Beg your pardon. [*He and* GRAABERG *exit in back to the right.*]

WERLE [*between his teeth*]. That damned Graaberg!

GREGERS [*with open mouth, staring at* HJALMAR]. But it couldn't have been—!

THE FAT GUEST. What's going on? Who was that?

GREGERS. Oh, no one. Only the bookkeeper and somebody else.

THE NEARSIGHTED GUEST [*to* HJALMAR]. Did *you* know him?

HJALMAR. I don't know—I didn't notice—

THE FAT GUEST [*getting up*]. What in thunder's wrong? [*He goes over to some others, who are talking.*]

MRS. SØRBY [*whispering to the waiter*]. Slip something to him outside, something really fine.

PETTERSEN [*nodding*]. I'll see to it. [*He goes out.*]

GREGERS [*in a shocked undertone*]. Then it really was him!

HJALMAR. Yes.

GREGERS. And yet you stood here and denied you knew him!

HJALMAR [*whispering fiercely*]. But how could I—!

GREGERS. Be recognized by your father?

HJALMAR [*painfully*]. Oh, if you were in my place, then—

[*The hushed conversations among the guests now mount into a forced joviality.*]

THE BALD-HEADED GUEST [*approaching* HJALMAR *and* GREGERS *amiably*]. Ah ha! You over here, polishing up old memories from your student years? Well? Won't you smoke, Mr. Ekdal? Have a light? Oh, that's right, we're not supposed to—

HJALMAR. Thanks, I couldn't—

THE FAT GUEST.   Haven't you got a neat little poem to recite for us, Mr. Ekdal? In times past you did that so nicely.

HJALMAR.   I'm afraid I can't remember any.

THE FAT GUEST.   Oh, that's a shame. Well, Balle, what can we find to do? [*The two men cross the floor into the other room and go out.*]

HJALMAR [*somberly*].   Gregers—I'm going! When a man's felt a terrible blow from fate—you understand. Say good night to your father for me.

GREGERS.   Yes, of course. Are you going straight home?

HJALMAR.   Yes, why?

GREGERS.   Well, I may pay you a visit later.

HJALMAR.   No, you mustn't. Not to my home. My house is a sad one, Gregers—especially after a brilliant occasion like this. We can always meet somewhere in town.

MRS. SØRBY [*who has approached; in a low voice*].   Are you going, Ekdal?

HJALMAR.   Yes.

MRS. SØRBY.   Greet Gina.

HJALMAR.   Thank you.

MRS. SØRBY.   And tell her I'll stop by to see her one day soon.

HJALMAR.   Yes. Thanks. [*To* GREGERS.] Stay here. I'd rather disappear without any fuss. [*He strolls around the floor, then into the other room and out to the right.*]

MRS. SØRBY [*quietly to the waiter, who has returned*].   Well, did the old man get something to take home?

PETTERSEN.   Sure. I slipped him a bottle of cognac.

MRS. SØRBY.   Oh, you could have found something better.

PETTERSEN.   Not at all, Mrs. Sørby. He knows nothing better than cognac.

THE FAT GUEST [*in the doorway, holding a score of music*].   How about the two of us playing something, Mrs. Sørby?

MRS. SØRBY.   All right. Let's.

[*The guests shout approval.* MRS. SØRBY *and the others exit right, through the inner room.* GREGERS *remains standing by the fireplace.* WERLE *looks for something on the writing table, seeming to wish that* GREGERS *would leave; when he fails to stir,* WERLE *crosses toward the door.*]

GREGERS.   Father, won't you wait a moment?

WERLE [*pausing*].   What is it?

GREGERS.   I must have a word with you.

WERLE.   Can't it wait till we're alone?

GREGERS.   No, it can't, because it just might occur that we never are alone.

WERLE [*coming closer*].   What does *that* mean?

[*Distant piano music is heard from the music room during the following conversation.*]

GREGERS.   How could anyone here let that family decay so pitifully?

WERLE.   You're referring to the Ekdals, no doubt.

GREGERS.   Yes, I mean the Ekdals. Lieutenant Ekdal was once so close to you.

WERLE.   Yes, worse luck, he was all too close; and for that I've paid a price these many years. He's the one I can thank for putting something of a blot on my good name and reputation.

GREGERS [*quietly*].   Was *he* really the only guilty one?

WERLE.   Who else do you mean!

GREGERS.   You and he were both in on buying that big stand of timber—

WERLE.   But it was Ekdal, wasn't it, who made the survey of the sections —that incompetent survey? He was the one who carried out all the illegal logging on state property. In fact, he was in charge of the whole operation up there. I had no idea of what Lieutenant Ekdal was getting into.

GREGERS.   Lieutenant Ekdal himself had no idea of what he was getting into.

WERLE.   Very likely. But the fact remains that he was convicted and I was acquitted.

GREGERS.   Yes, I'm aware that no proof was found.

WERLE.   Acquittal is acquittal. Why do you rake up this ugly old story that's given me gray hair before my time? Is this what you've been brooding about all those years up there? I can assure you, Gregers—here in town the whole business has been forgotten long ago—as far as I'm concerned.

GREGERS.   But that miserable Ekdal family!

WERLE.   Seriously, what would you have me do for these people? When Ekdal was let out, he was a broken man, beyond any help. There are people in this world who plunge to the bottom when they've hardly been winged, and they never come up again. Take my word for it, Gregers; I've done everything I could, short of absolutely compromising myself and arousing all kinds of suspicion and gossip—

GREGERS.   Suspicion—? So that's it.

WERLE.   I've gotten Ekdal copying jobs from the office, and I pay him much, much more than his work is worth—

GREGERS [*without looking at him*].   Hm. No doubt.

WERLE.   You're laughing? Maybe you think what I'm saying isn't true? There's certainly nothing to show in my books; I don't record such payments.

GREGERS [*with a cold smile*].   No. I'm sure that certain payments are best left unrecorded.

WERLE [*surprised*].   What do you mean by *that*?

GREGERS [*plucking up his courage*].   Did you record what it cost you to have Hjalmar Ekdal study photography?

WERLE.   I? Why should I?

GREGERS.   I know now it was you who paid for that. And now I know, too, that it was you who set him up so comfortably in business.

WERLE.   Well, and I suppose this still means that I've done nothing for the Ekdals! I can assure you, those people have already cost me enough expense.

GREGERS.   Have you recorded any of the expenses?

WERLE.   Why do you ask that?

GREGERS.   Oh, there are reasons. Listen, tell me—the time when you developed such warmth for your old friend's son—wasn't that just when he was planning to marry?

WERLE.   How the devil—how, after so many years, do you expect me—?

GREGERS.   You wrote me a letter then—a business letter, naturally; and in a postscript it said, brief as could be, that Hjalmar Ekdal had gotten married to a Miss Hansen.

WERLE.   Yes, that's right; that was her name.

GREGERS.   But you never said that this Miss Hansen was Gina Hansen—our former housekeeper.

WERLE [*with a derisive, yet uneasy laugh*].   No, it just never occurred to me that you'd be so very interested in our former housekeeper.

GREGERS.   I wasn't. But—[*dropping his voice*] there were others in the house who were quite interested in her.

WERLE.   What do you mean by that? [*Storming at him.*] You're not referring to me!

GREGERS [*quietly but firmly*].   Yes, I'm referring to you.

WERLE.   And you dare—! You have the insolence—! How could he, that ungrateful dog, that—photographer; how could he have the gall to make such insinuations?

GREGERS.   Hjalmar hasn't breathed a word of it. I don't think he has the shadow of a doubt about all this.

WERLE.   Then where did you get it from? Who could have said such a thing?

GREGERS.   My poor, unhappy mother said it—the last time I saw her.

WERLE.   Your mother! Yes, I might have guessed. She and you—you always stuck together. It was she who, right from the start, turned your mind against me.

GREGERS.   No. It was everything she had to suffer and endure until she broke down and died so miserably.

WERLE.   Oh, she had nothing to suffer and endure—no more, at least, than so many others. But you can't get anywhere with sick, high-strung people. I've certainly learned that. Now you're going around suspecting that sort of thing, digging up all manner of old rumors and slanders against your own father. Now listen, Gregers, I really think that at your age you could occupy yourself more usefully.

GREGERS.   Yes, all in due time.

WERLE.   Then your mind might be clearer than it seems to be now. What can it lead to, you up there at the works, slaving away year in and year out like a common clerk, never taking a penny over your month's salary. It's pure stupidity.

GREGERS.   Yes, if only I were so sure of that.

WERLE.   I understand you well enough. You want to be independent, without obligation to me. But here's the very opportunity for you to become independent, your own man in every way.

GREGERS.   So? And by what means—?

WERLE.   When I wrote you that it was essential you come to town now, immediately—hmm—

GREGERS.   Yes. What is it you really want of me? I've been waiting all day to find out.

WERLE.   I'm suggesting that you come into the firm as a partner.

GREGERS.   I! In your firm? As a partner?

WERLE.   Yes. It wouldn't mean we'd need to be together much. You could take over the offices here in town, and then I'd move up to the mill.

GREGERS.   You *would*?

WERLE.   Yes. You see, I can't take on work now the way I once could. I have to spare my eyes, Gregers; they're beginning to fail.

GREGERS. They've always been weak.

WERLE. Not like this. Besides—circumstances may make it desirable for me to live up there—at least for a while.

GREGERS. I never dreamed of anything like this.

WERLE. Listen, Gregers, there are so very many things that keep us apart, and yet, you know—we're father and son still. I think we should be able to reach some kind of understanding.

GREGERS. Just on the surface, is that what you mean?

WERLE. Well, at least that would be something. Think it over, Gregers. Don't you think it ought to be possible? Eh?

GREGERS [*looking at him coldly*]. There's something behind all this.

WERLE. How so?

GREGERS. It might be that somehow you're using me.

WERLE. In a relationship as close as ours, one can always be of use to the other.

GREGERS. Yes, so they say.

WERLE. I'd like to have you home with me now for a while. I'm a lonely man, Gregers; I've always felt lonely—all my life through, but particularly now when the years are beginning to press me. I need to have someone around—

GREGERS. You have Mrs. Sørby.

WERLE. Yes, I do—and she's become, you might say, almost indispensable. She's witty, even-tempered; she livens up the house—and that's what I need so badly.

GREGERS. Well, then, you've got everything the way you want it.

WERLE. Yes, but I'm afraid it can't go on. The world is quick to make inferences about a woman in her position. Yes, I was going to say, a man doesn't gain by it either.

GREGERS. Oh, when a man gives dinner parties like yours, he can certainly take a few risks.

WERLE. Yes, Gregers, but what about her? I'm afraid she won't put up with it much longer. And even if she did—even if, out of her feeling for me, she ignored the gossip and the backbiting and so on—do you still think, Gregers, you with your sharp sense of justice—

GREGERS [*cutting him off*]. Tell me short and sweet just one thing. Are you planning to marry her?

WERLE. And if I *were* planning such a thing—what then?

GREGERS. Yes, that's what I'm asking. What then?

WERLE. Would you be so irreconcilably set against it?

GREGERS. No, not at all. Not in any way.

WERLE. Well, I really didn't know whether, perhaps out of regard for your dead mother's memory—

GREGERS. I am not high-strung.

WERLE. Well, you may or may not be, but in any case you've taken a great load off my mind. I'm really very happy that I can count on your support in this.

GREGERS [*staring intently at him*]. Now I see how you want to use me.

WERLE. Use you! That's no way to talk!

GREGERS. Oh, let's not be squeamish in our choice of words. At least, not when it's man to man. [*He laughs brusquely.*] So that's it! That's why I—

damn it all!—had to make my personal appearance in town. On account of Mrs. Sørby, family life is in order in this house. Tableau of father with son! That's something new, all right!

WERLE.   How dare you speak in that tone!

GREGERS.   When has there ever been family life here? Never, as long as I can remember. But *now,* of course, there's need for a little of that. For who could deny what a fine impression it would make to hear that the son—on the wings of piety—came flying home to the aging father's wedding feast. What's left then of all the stories about what the poor dead woman suffered and endured? Not a scrap. Her own son ground them to dust.

WERLE.   Gregers—I don't think there's a man in this world you hate as much as me.

GREGERS.   I've seen you at too close quarters.

WERLE.   You've seen me with your mother's eyes. [*Dropping his voice.*] But you should remember that those eyes were—clouded at times.

GREGERS [*faltering*].   I know what you mean. But who bears the guilt for Mother's fatal weakness? You, and all those—! The last of them was that female that Hjalmar Ekdal was fixed up with when you had no more—ugh!

WERLE [*shrugs*].   Word for word, as if I were hearing your mother.

GREGERS [*paying no attention to him*].   . . . and there he sits right now, he with his great, guileless, childlike mind plunged in deception—living under the same roof with that creature, not knowing that what he calls home is built on a lie. [*Coming a step closer.*] When I look back on all you've done, it's as if I looked out over a battlefield with broken human beings on every side.

WERLE.   I almost think the gulf is too great between us.

GREGERS [*bows stiffly*].   So I've observed; therefore I'll take my hat and go.

WERLE.   You're going? Out of this house?

GREGERS.   Yes. Because now at least I can see a purpose to live for.

WERLE.   What purpose is that?

GREGERS.   You'd only laugh if you heard it.

WERLE.   A lonely man doesn't laugh so easily, Gregers.

GREGERS [*pointing toward the inner room*].   Look—your gentleman friends are playing blindman's buff with Mrs. Sørby. Good night and goodbye.

[*He goes out at the right rear. Laughter and joking from the company, which moves into view in the inner room.*]

WERLE [*muttering contemptuously after* GREGERS].   Huh! Poor fool—and he says he's not high-strung!

ACT II

HJALMAR EKDAL's *studio. The room, which is fairly spacious, appears to be a loft. To the right is a sloping roof with great panes of glass, half hidden by a blue curtain. In the far right corner is the entrance; nearer on the same side, a door to the living room. Similarly, at the left there are two doors, and between these an iron stove. At the back is a wide double door, designed to slide back to the sides. The studio is simply but comfortably furnished and decorated.*

Between the right-hand doors, slightly away from the wall, stands a sofa beside a table and some chairs; on the table is a lighted lamp with a shade; by the stove an old armchair. Photographic apparatus and equipment of various sorts are set up here and there in the room. At the left of the double doors stands a bookcase containing a few books, small boxes and flasks of chemicals, various tools, implements, and other objects. Photographs and such small articles as brushes, paper, and the like lie on the table.

  GINA EKDAL *sits on a chair by the table, sewing.* HEDVIG *sits on the sofa, hands shading her eyes, thumbs in her ears, reading a book.*

  GINA [*having glanced over several times at* HEDVIG, *as if with anxiety*]. Hedvig! [HEDVIG *does not hear.*]

  GINA [*louder*]. Hedvig!

  HEDVIG [*removing her hands and looking up*]. Yes, Mother?

  GINA. Hedvig, dear, you mustn't sit and read anymore.

  HEDVIG. Oh, but Mother, can't I please read a little longer? Just a little!

  GINA. No, no—you must set the book down. Your father doesn't like it; *he* never reads in the evening.

  HEDVIG [*closing the book*]. No, Daddy's no great one for reading.

  GINA [*lays her sewing aside and takes a pencil and a small notebook from the table*]. Do you remember how much we spent for butter today?

  HEDVIG. It was one sixty-five.

  GINA. That's right. [*Making a note.*] It's awful how much butter gets used in this house. And then so much for smoked sausage, and for cheese—let me see—[*making more notes*] and so much for ham—hmm. [*Adds.*] Yes, that adds right up to—

  HEDVIG. And then there's the beer.

  GINA. Yes, of course. [*Makes another note.*] It mounts up—but it can't be helped.

  HEDVIG. Oh, but you and I had no hot food for dinner, 'cause Daddy was out.

  GINA. No, and that's to the good. What's more, I also took in eight crowns fifty for photographs.

  HEDVIG. No! Was it that much?

  GINA. Exactly eight crowns fifty.

  [*Silence.* GINA *again picks up her sewing.* HEDVIG *takes paper and pencil and starts to draw, shading her eyes with her left hand.*]

  HEDVIG. Isn't it something to think that Daddy's at a big dinner party at old Mr. Werle's?

  GINA. You can't really say that he's at old Mr. Werle's. It was his son who sent him the invitation. [*After a pause.*] We have nothing to do with old Mr. Werle.

  HEDVIG. I can hardly wait for Daddy to come home. He promised he'd ask Mrs. Sørby about bringing me a treat.

  GINA. Yes, you can bet there are lots of treats to be had in *that* house.

  HEDVIG [*again drawing*]. Besides, I'm a little hungry, too.

  [*Old* EKDAL, *with a bundle of papers under his arm and another bundle in his coat pocket, comes in through the hall door.*]

  GINA. My, but you're late today, Grandfather.

EKDAL.   They'd locked the office. Had to wait for Graaberg. And then I had to go through—uhh.

GINA.   Did they give you something new to copy, Grandfather?

EKDAL.   This whole pile. Just look.

GINA.   That's fine.

HEDVIG.   And you've got a bundle in your pocket, too.

EKDAL.   Oh? Nonsense; that's nothing. [*Puts his cane away in the corner.*] Here's work for a good spell, Gina, this here. [*Pulls one of the double doors slightly open.*] Shh! [*Peers into the room a moment, then carefully closes the door again.*] He, he! They're sound asleep, the lot of them. And she's bedded down in the basket all on her own. He, he!

HEDVIG.   Are you sure she won't be cold in the basket, Grandpa?

EKDAL.   What a thought! Cold? In all that straw? [*Goes toward the farther door on the left.*] I'll find some matches in here, eh?

GINA.   The matches are on the bureau.

[EKDAL *goes into his room.*]

HEDVIG.   It's wonderful that Grandpa got all that copying to do.

GINA.   Yes, poor old Father; he'll earn himself a little pocket money.

HEDVIG.   And he also won't be able to sit the whole morning down in that horrid Mrs. Eriksen's café.

GINA.   That too, yes. [*A short silence.*]

HEDVIG.   Do you think they're still at the dinner table?

GINA.   Lord only knows; it may well be.

HEDVIG.   Just think, all the lovely food Daddy's eaten! I'm sure he'll be happy and content when he comes. Don't you think so, Mother?

GINA.   Of course. Imagine if we could tell him now that we'd rented out the room.

HEDVIG.   But that's not necessary tonight.

GINA.   Oh, it could well come in handy, you know. It's no good to us as it is.

HEDVIG.   No, I mean it's not necessary because tonight Daddy's feeling good. It's better we have news about the room some other time.

GINA [*looking over at her*].   Are you glad when you have something nice to tell your father when he comes home at night?

HEDVIG.   Yes, for things here are pleasanter then.

GINA [*reflecting*].   Well, there's something to that.

[Old EKDAL *comes in again and starts out through the nearer door to the left.*]

GINA [*half turning in her chair*].   Does Grandfather want something from the kitchen?

EKDAL.   I do, yes. Don't stir. [*He goes out.*]

GINA.   He never fusses with the fire out there. [*After a moment.*] Hedvig, go see what he's doing.

[EKDAL *reenters with a small jug of steaming water.*]

HEDVIG.   Are you after hot water, Grandpa?

EKDAL.   Yes, I am. Need it for something. Have to write, and the ink is caked thick as porridge—hmm.

GINA.   But you ought to have supper first, Grandfather. It's all set and waiting in there.

EKDAL. Never mind about the supper, Gina. Terribly busy, I tell you. I don't want anybody coming into my room—nobody. Hmm. [*He goes into his room.* GINA *and* HEDVIG *exchange glances.*]

GINA [*lowering her voice*]. Where do you figure he's gotten money?

HEDVIG. He must have got it from Graaberg.

GINA. Not a chance. Graaberg always sends the pay to me.

HEDVIG. Maybe he got a bottle somewhere on credit.

GINA. Poor Grandpa, no one'll give him credit.

[HJALMAR EKDAL, *wearing an overcoat and a gray felt hat, enters from the right.*]

GINA [*dropping her sewing and getting up*]. Ah, Hjalmar, here you are!

HEDVIG [*jumping up at the same time*]. At last you're home, Daddy!

HJALMAR [*putting his hat down*]. Yes, most of them were leaving.

HEDVIG. So early?

HJALMAR. Yes, it was only a dinner party. [*Starts to remove his overcoat.*]

GINA. Let me help you.

HEDVIG. Me too.

[*They take off his coat;* GINA *hangs it up on the rear wall.*]

HEDVIG. Were there many there, Daddy?

HJALMAR. Oh no, not many. We were some twelve, fourteen people at the table.

GINA. And you got to talk with every one of them?

HJALMAR. Oh yes, a little, though Gregers rather monopolized me.

GINA. Is Gregers as ugly as ever?

HJALMAR. Well, he doesn't look any better. Isn't the old man home?

HEDVIG. Yes, Grandpa's inside, writing.

HJALMAR. Did he say anything?

GINA. No, what should he say?

HJALMAR. Didn't he mention anything of—I thought I heard that he'd been with Graaberg. I'll go in and have a word with him.

GINA. No, no, don't bother.

HJALMAR. Why not? Did he say he wouldn't see me?

GINA. He doesn't want anyone in there this evening.

HEDVIG [*making signals*]. Uh—uh!

GINA [*not noticing*]. He's already been out here and gotten hot water.

HJALMAR. Aha! Is he—?

GINA. Yes, exactly.

HJALMAR. Good Lord, my poor old white-haired father! Well, let him be, enjoying life's pleasures as he may.

[*Old* EKDAL *in a bathrobe, smoking a pipe, enters from his room.*]

EKDAL. Home, eh? Thought it was your voice I heard.

HJALMAR. I just arrived.

EKDAL. You didn't see me at all, did you?

HJALMAR. No, but they said you'd been through—so I thought I'd follow after.

EKDAL. Hm, good of you, Hjalmar. Who were they, all those people?

HJALMAR. Oh, different sorts. There was Flor—he's at the court—and Balle and Kaspersen and, uh—I forget his name, but people at court, all of them—

EKDAL [*nodding*]. Listen to that, Gina! He travels only in the best circles.

GINA. Yes, it's real elegant in that house now.

HEDVIG. Did the court people sing, Daddy? Or give readings?

HJALMAR. No, they just babbled away. Of course they wanted *me* to recite for them, but I couldn't see that.

EKDAL. You couldn't see that, eh?

GINA. That you could easily have done.

HJALMAR. Never. One mustn't be a doormat for every passing foot. [*Walking about the room.*] At least, that's not my way.

EKDAL. No, no, that's not for Hjalmar.

HJALMAR. I don't know why I should always provide the entertainment, when I'm out in society so rarely. Let the others make an effort. There those fellows go from one banquet to the next, eating and drinking day in and day out. So let them do their tricks in return for all the good food they get.

GINA. But you didn't say that there?

HJALMAR [*humming*]. Um—um—um—they were told a thing or two.

EKDAL. Right to the nobility!

HJALMAR. I don't see why not. [*Casually.*] Later we had a little quibble about Tokay.

EKDAL. Tokay, you mean? That's a fine wine, that.

HJALMAR [*coming to a halt*]. On occasion. But I must tell you that not all years are equally good. Everything depends strictly on how much sun the grapes have had.

GINA. Really? Oh, Hjalmar, you know everything.

EKDAL. And they could argue about that?

HJALMAR. They tried to. But then they were informed that it's exactly the same with court officials. Among them as well, all years are not equally fine—it was said.

GINA. The things you think of!

EKDAL. He—he! So you served that up to them, eh?

HJALMAR. Smack between the eyes they got it.

EKDAL. Hear, Gina! He laid that one smack between the eyes of the nobility.

GINA. Just think, smack between the eyes.

HJALMAR. That's right. But I don't want a lot of talk about this. One doesn't speak of such things. Everything really went off in the most friendly spirit, naturally. They're all pleasant, genial people. How could I hurt their feelings? Never!

EKDAL. But smack between the eyes—

HEDVIG [*ingratiatingly*]. How nice to see you in evening clothes, Daddy. You look so well in them.

HJALMAR. Yes, don't you think so? And this one here really fits very well. It's almost as if it were made for me. A bit snug under the arms, maybe—help me, Hedvig. [*Takes off the coat.*] I'd rather wear my jacket. What did you do with my jacket, Gina?

GINA. Here it is. [*Brings the jacket and helps him into it.*]

HJALMAR. There! Now don't forget to give Molvik his coat back first thing in the morning.

GINA [*putting it away*]. I'll take care of it.

HJALMAR [*stretching*]. Ah, but this feels much more comfortable. This kind of free and easy dress suits my whole personality better. Don't you think so, Hedvig?

HEDVIG.   Yes, Daddy.

HJALMAR.   And when I pull my necktie out into a pair of flowing ends—so! Look! What then?

HEDVIG.   Yes, it goes so well with your moustache and your long, curly hair.

HJALMAR.   Curly? I wouldn't say it's that. I'd call it wavy.

HEDVIG.   Yes, but it *is* so curly.

HJALMAR.   No—wavy.

HEDVIG [*after a moment, tugs at his sleeve*].   Daddy!

HJALMAR.   What is it?

HEDVIG.   Oh, you know what.

HJALMAR.   No, I don't. Honestly.

HEDVIG [*laughing fretfully*].   Come on, Daddy, don't tease me any longer.

HJALMAR.   But what is it, then?

HEDVIG [*shaking him*].   Silly! Out with it, Daddy. You know—all the treats you promised me.

HJALMAR.   Oh—no! How did I ever forget that?

HEDVIG. · No, you can't fool me. Shame on you! Where have you hidden it?

HJALMAR.   So help me if I didn't forget. But wait a minute! I've got something else for you, Hedvig. [*Goes over and rummages in his coat pockets.*]

HEDVIG [*jumping and clapping her hands*].   Oh, Mother, Mother!

GINA.   You see, if you're only patient enough, then—

HJALMAR [*returning with a piece of paper*].   See, here we have it.

HEDVIG.   That? But that's just a piece of paper.

HJALMAR.   It's the bill of fare, the complete bill of fare. Here it says "menu"; that means "bill of fare."

HEDVIG.   Don't you have anything else?

HJALMAR.   I forgot to bring anything else, I tell you. But take my word for it: it's bad business, this doting on sugar candy. Now, if you'll sit down at the table and read the menu aloud, I'll describe for you just how each dish tasted. How's that, Hedvig?

HEDVIG [*swallowing her tears*].   Thanks. [*She sits, but does not read.* GINA *makes gestures at her, which* HJALMAR *notices.*]

HJALMAR [*pacing about the floor*].   What incredible things a family breadwinner is asked to remember; and if he forgets even the tiniest detail—immediately he's met with sour faces. Well he has to get used to that, too. [*Pauses at the stove beside* EKDAL.] Have you looked inside this evening, Father?

EKDAL.   Oh, that you can be sure of. She's gone into the basket.

HJALMAR.   No! Into the basket? Then she's begun to get used to it.

EKDAL.   Yes. You see, it was just as I predicted. But now there are some little things to do—

HJALMAR.   Some improvements, eh?

EKDAL.   But they've got to be done, you know.

HJALMAR.   All right, let's talk a bit about the improvements, Father. Come, we'll sit here on the sofa.

EKDAL.   Very good. Umm—think I'll fill my pipe first. Needs cleaning, too. Hmm. [*He goes into his room.*]

GINA [*smiling at* HJALMAR].   Clean his pipe!

HJALMAR.   Ah, now, Gina, let him be. Poor old derelict. Yes, the improvements—it's best we get those off our hands tomorrow.

GINA.   Tomorrow you won't have time, Hjalmar—

HEDVIG [*interrupting*].   Oh yes, he will, Mother!

GINA.   Remember those prints that need retouching. They've been called for so many times already.

HJALMAR.   Oh yes, those prints again. They'll be finished in no time. Did any new orders come in?

GINA.   No such luck. For tomorrow, I have nothing except those two portrait sittings you know about.

HJALMAR.   Nothing else? Ah, well, if people won't even try, then naturally—

GINA.   But what else can I do? I've put ads in the papers time and again.

HJALMAR.   Yes, ads, ads—you see what a help they are. And of course nobody's been to look at the spare room either?

GINA.   No, not yet.

HJALMAR.   That was to be expected. If one doesn't keep wide awake— Gina, you've simply got to pull yourself together.

HEDVIG [*going to him*].   Let me bring you your flute, Daddy.

HJALMAR.   No, no flute. I want no pleasures in this world. [*Pacing about.*] Ah, yes, work—I'll be deep in work tomorrow; there'll be no lack of *that*. I'll sweat and slave as long as my strength holds out—

GINA.   But Hjalmar dear, I didn't mean it that way.

HEDVIG.   Can't I get you a bottle of beer, then?

HJALMAR.   Absolutely not. There's nothing I need. [*Stopping.*] Beer? Did you say beer?

HEDVIG [*vivaciously*].   Yes, Daddy, lovely cool beer.

HJALMAR.   Well—if you really insist, I suppose you could bring in a bottle.

GINA.   Yes, do that. Then we'll have it cozy.

[HEDVIG *runs toward the kitchen door.* HJALMAR *by the stove stops her, gazes at her, clasps her about the head and hugs her to him.*]

HJALMAR.   Hedvig! Hedvig!

HEDVIG [*with tears of joy*].   Oh, my dearest Daddy!

HJALMAR.   No, don't call me that. There I sat, helping myself at a rich man's table, gorging myself with all good things—! I could at least have remembered—

GINA [*sitting at the table*].   Oh, nonsense, Hjalmar.

HJALMAR.   Yes, I could! But you mustn't be too hard on me. You both know I love you anyway.

HEDVIG [*throwing her arms around him*].   And we love you too, so much!

HJALMAR.   And if I should seem unreasonable at times, then—good Lord —remember that I am a man assailed by a host of cares. Ah, yes! [*Drying his eyes.*] No beer at a time like this. Bring me my flute. [HEDVIG *runs to the bookcase and fetches it.*] Thank you. There—so. With flute in hand, and you two close by me—ah!

[HEDVIG *sits at the table by* GINA, HJALMAR *walks back and forth, then forcefully begins to play a Bohemian folk dance, but in a slow elegiac tempo with sentimental intonation. After a moment he breaks off the melody and extends his left hand to* GINA.]

HJALMAR [*with feeling*].   So what if we skimp and scrape along under this roof, Gina—it's still our home. And I'll say this: it's good to be here. [*He starts playing again; immediately there comes a knock on the hall door.*]

GINA [*getting up*].   Shh, Hjalmar. I think someone's there.

HJALMAR [*returning the flute to the bookcase*].   What, again! [GINA *goes over and opens the door.*]

GREGERS WERLE [*out in the hallway*].   Excuse me—

GINA [*drawing back slightly*].   Oh!

GREGERS.   But doesn't Mr. Ekdal, the photographer, live here?

GINA.   Yes, that's right.

HJALMAR [*going toward the door*].   Gregers! Is it really you? Well, come right in.

GREGERS [*entering*].   I said I was going to drop in on you.

HJALMAR.   But tonight? Have you left the party?

GREGERS.   Left both party and family home. Good evening, Mrs. Ekdal. I don't know whether you recognize me?

GINA.   Oh yes. Young Mr. Werle is not so hard to recognize.

GREGERS.   No. I look like my mother, and you remember her, no doubt.

HJALMAR.   Did you say you'd left your home?

GREGERS.   Yes, I've moved into a hotel.

HJALMAR.   I see. Well, now that you've come, take off your things and sit down.

GREGERS.   Thank you. [*Removes his overcoat. He is dressed now in a simple grey suit of somewhat rustic cut.*]

HJALMAR.   Here, on the sofa. Make yourself at home.

[GREGERS *sits on the sofa,* HJALMAR *on a chair at the table.*]

GREGERS [*looking around*].   So this is where you work, then, Hjalmar. And you live here as well.

HJALMAR.   This is the studio, as you can see—

GINA.   There's more room in here, so we like it better.

HJALMAR.   We had a better place before; but this apartment has one great advantage: it has such wonderful adjoining rooms—

GINA.   And so we have a room on the other side of the hall that we can rent out.

GREGERS [*to* HJALMAR].   Ah, then you have lodgers, too.

HJALMAR.   No, not yet. It's not that easy, you know. One has to keep wide awake. [*To* HEDVIG.] But how about that beer?

[HEDVIG *nods and goes into the kitchen.*]

GREGERS.   So that's your daughter, then?

HJALMAR.   Yes, that's Hedvig.

GREGERS.   An only child?

HJALMAR.   She's the only one, yes. She's the greatest joy of our lives, and —[*lowering his voice*] also our deepest sorrow, Gregers.

GREGERS.   What do you mean?

HJALMAR.   Yes. You see, there's the gravest imminent danger of her losing her sight.

GREGERS.   Going blind!

HJALMAR. Yes. So far only the first signs are present, and things may go well for a while. All the same, the doctor has warned us. It will come inevitably.

GREGERS. What a dreadful misfortune! How did this happen?

HJALMAR [*sighing*]. Heredity, most likely.

GREGERS [*startled*]. Heredity?

GINA. Hjalmar's mother also had bad eyes.

HJALMAR. Yes, so my father says. I don't remember her.

GREGERS. Poor child. And how is she taking it?

HJALMAR. Oh, you can well imagine, we haven't the heart to tell her. She suspects nothing. She's carefree, gay, and singing like a tiny bird, she's fluttering into life's eternal night. [*Overcome.*] Oh, it's a brutal blow for me, Gregers. [HEDVIG *brings in beer and glasses on a tray, which she sets down on the table.*]

HJALMAR [*stroking her head*]. Thanks. Thanks, Hedvig.

[HEDVIG *puts her arms around his neck and whispers in his ear.*]

HJALMAR. No, No bread and butter now. [*Looking over.*] Or maybe Gregers will have a piece?

GREGERS [*making a gesture of refusal*]. No. No, thanks.

HJALMAR [*his tone still mournful*]. Well, you can bring in a little anyway. If you have a crust, that would be fine. And please, put enough butter on, too.

[HEDVIG *nods contentedly and returns to the kitchen.*]

GREGERS [*after following her with his eyes*]. In every other respect she looks so strong and healthy.

GINA. Yes, thank God, she's got nothing else wrong with her.

GREGERS. She'll certainly look like you when she grows up, Mrs. Ekdal. How old is she now?

GINA. Hedvig is almost fourteen exactly; her birthday's the day after tomorrow.

GREGERS. Rather tall for her age.

GINA. Yes, she's shot right up this past year.

GREGERS. Nothing like the growth of a child to show us how old we're getting. How long is it you've been married now?

GINA. We've been married now for—yes, near fifteen years.

GREGERS. No, truly! Has it been that long?

GINA [*looking at him, becoming wary*]. Yes, no doubt about it.

HJALMAR. That's right. Fifteen years, short a few months. [*Changing the subject.*] They must have been long years for you, Gregers, up there at the works.

GREGERS. They were long while I was living them—but now I scarcely know what became of the time.

[Old EKDAL *enters from his room, without his pipe, but with his old military cap on his head; his walk a bit unsteady.*]

EKDAL. There, now, Hjalmar. Now we can settle down and talk about that—umm. What was it again?

HJALMAR [*going toward him*]. Father, someone is here. Gregers Werle. I don't know if you remember him.

EKDAL [*regarding* GREGERS, *who has gotten up*]. Werle? That's the son, isn't it? What does he want with me?

HJALMAR. Nothing; it's me he's come to see.

EKDAL.   Well, then nothing's up, eh?

HJALMAB.   No, of course not.

EKDAL [*swinging his arms*].   It's not that I'm scared of anything, you know, but—

GREGERS [*going over to him*].   I just want to greet you from your old hunting grounds, Lieutenant Ekdal.

EKDAL.   Hunting grounds?

GREGERS.   Yes, up there around the Hoidal works.

EKDAL.   Oh, up there. Yes, I was well known there once.

GREGERS.   In those days you were a tremendous hunter.

EKDAL.   So I was. Still am, maybe. You're looking at my uniform. I ask nobody permission to wear it in here. As long as I don't walk in the streets with it— [HEDVIG *brings a plate of buttered bread, which she places on the table.*]

HJALMAR.   Sit down, Father, and have a glass of beer. Help yourself, Gregers.

[EKDAL *stumbles, muttering, over to the sofa.* GREGERS *sits on the chair nearest him,* HJALMAR *on the other side of* GREGERS. GINA *sits near the table and sews;* HEDVIG *stands beside her father.*]

GREGERS.   Do you remember, Lieutenant Ekdal, when Hjalmar and I would come up to visit you summers and at Christmas?

EKDAL.   Did you? No, no, no, I don't recall. But I'll tell you something: I've been a first-rate hunter. Bear— I've shot them, too. Shot nine in all.

GREGERS [*looking sympathetically at him*].   And now you hunt no more.

EKDAL.   Oh, I wouldn't say *that,* boy. Get some hunting in now and then. Yes, but not that kind there. The woods, you see—the woods, the woods— [*Drinks.*] How do the woods look up there?

GREGERS.   Not so fine as in your time. They've been cut into heavily.

EKDAL.   Cut into? [*More quietly, as if in fear.*] It's a dangerous business, that. It catches up with you. The woods take revenge.

HJALMAR [*filling his glass*].   Here, a little more, Father.

GREGERS.   How can a man like you—such an outdoorsman—live in the middle of a stuffy city, cooped up in these four walls?

EKDAL [*half laughs and glances at* HJALMAR].   Oh, it's not so bad here. Not bad at all.

GREGERS.   But all those other things, the very roots of your soul—that cool, sweeping breeze, that free life of the moors and forests, among the animals and birds—?

EKDAL [*smiling*].   Hjalmar, should we show him?

HJALMAR [*quickly and a bit embarrassed*].   No, no, Father, not tonight.

GREGERS.   What's that he wants to show me?

HJALMAR.   Oh, it's only a sort of—you can see it some other time.

GREGERS [*speaking again to* EKDAL].   Yes, my point was this, Lieutenant Ekdal, that now you might as well return with me to the works, for I'm sure to be leaving very soon. Without a doubt, you could get some copying to do up there; and here you've nothing in the world to stir your blood and make you happy.

EKDAL [*staring at him, astonished*].   I have nothing, nothing at all—!

GREGERS.   Of course you have Hjalmar, but then again, he has his own.

And a man like you, who's always felt himself so drawn to whatever is free and wild—

EKDAL [*striking the table*]. Hjalmar, now he's *got* to see it!

HJALMAR. But Father, is it worth it now? It's dark, you know—

EKDAL. Nonsense! There's moonlight. [*Getting up.*] I say he's got to see it. Let me by. Come and help me, Hjalmar!

HEDVIG. Oh yes, do that, Father!

HJALMAR [*getting up.*]. Well—all right.

GREGERS [*to* GINA]. What's this all about?

GINA. Oh, you really mustn't expect anything special.

[EKDAL *and* HJALMAR *have gone to the back wall to push aside the two halves of the double door;* HEDVIG *helps her grandfather, while* GREGERS *remains standing by the sofa and* GINA *sits, imperturbably sewing. The doorway opens on an extensive, irregular loft room with many nooks and corners, and two separate chimney shafts ascending through it. Clear moonlight streams through skylights into certain parts of the large room; others lie in deep shadow.*]

EKDAL [*to* GREGERS]. All the way over here, please.

GREGERS [*going over to them*]. What *is* it, then?

EKDAL. See for yourself—hmm.

HJALMAR [*somewhat self-conscious*]. All this belongs to Father, you understand.

GREGERS [*peering in at the doorway*]. So you keep poultry, Lieutenant Ekdal!

EKDAL. I'll say we keep poultry! They're roosting now; but you just ought to see our poultry by daylight!

HEDVIG. And then there's a—

EKDAL. Shh, shh—don't say anything yet.

GREGERS. And you've got pigeons too, I see.

EKDAL. Oh yes, it might just be we've got some pigeons. They have their nesting boxes up there under the eaves; pigeons like to perch high, you know.

HJALMAR. They're not ordinary pigeons, all of them.

EKDAL. Ordinary! No, I should say not! We have tumblers, and we have a couple of pouters also. But look here! Can you see that hutch over there by the wall?

GREGERS. Yes. What do you use that for?

EKDAL. The rabbits sleep there at night, boy.

GREGERS. Well, so you have rabbits too?

EKDAL. Yes, what the devil do you think we have but rabbits! He asks if we have rabbits, Hjalmar! Hmm! But now listen, this is really something! This is it! Out of the way, Hedvig. Stand right here—that's it—and look straight down there. Do you see a basket there with straw in it?

GREGERS. Yes, and there's a bird nesting in the basket.

EKDAL. Hmm! "A bird"—

GREGERS. Isn't it a duck?

EKDAL [*hurt*]. Yes, of course it's a duck.

HJALMAR. But what *kind* of duck?

HEDVIG. It's not just any old duck—

EKDAL. Shh!

GREGERS. And it's no exotic breed, either.

EKDAL.   No, Mr.—Werle, it's not any exotic breed—because it's a wild duck.

GREGERS.   No, is it really? A wild duck?

EKDAL.   Oh yes, that's what it is. That "bird" as you said—that's a wild duck. That's our wild duck, boy.

HEDVIG.   *My* wild duck—I own it.

GREGERS.   And it can survive up here indoors? And do well?

EKDAL.   You've got to understand, she's got a trough of water to splash around in.

HJALMAR.   Fresh water every other day.

GINA [*turning to* HJALMAR].   Hjalmar dear, it's freezing cold in here now.

EKDAL.   Hmm, let's close up, then. Doesn't pay to disturb their rest either. Lend a hand, Hedvig dear. [HJALMAR *and* HEDVIG *push the double doors together.*] Another time you can get a proper look at her. [*Sits in the armchair by the stove.*] Oh, they're most curious, the wild ducks, you know.

GREGERS.   But how did you capture it, Lieutenant Ekdal?

EKDAL.   Didn't capture it myself. There's a certain man here in town we can thank for it.

GREGERS [*starts slightly*].   That man—it wouldn't be my father?

EKDAL.   Exactly right—your father. Hmm.

HJALMAR.   It was odd you were able to guess that, Gregers.

GREGERS.   Well, you said before that you owed Father for so many different things, so I thought here too—

GINA.   But we didn't get the duck from Mr. Werle himself—

EKDAL.   We might just as well thank Haakon Werle for her anyhow, Gina. [*To* GREGERS.] He was out in his boat—follow me?—and he shot for her, but he sees so bad now, your father, that—hm—he only winged her.

GREGERS.   I see. She took some shot in her body.

HJALMAR.   Yes, some one, two—three pieces.

HEDVIG.   She got it under the wing, and so she couldn't fly.

GREGERS.   Ah, so she dived right for the bottom, eh?

EKDAL [*sleepily, with a thick voice*].   You can bet on that. They always do, the wild ducks—streak for the bottom, deep as they can get, boy—bite right into the weeds and sea moss—and all that devil's beard that grows down there. And then they never come up again.

GREGERS.   But Lieutenant Ekdal, *your* wild duck came up again.

EKDAL.   He had such a remarkably clever dog, your father. And that dog —he dove down and brought her up.

GREGERS [*turning to* HJALMAR].   And then you got her here.

HJALMAR.   Not directly. First she went home to your father's, but there she didn't do well, so Pettersen got his orders to put an end to her—

EKDAL [*half asleep*].   Hm—yes, Pettersen—that bonehead—

HJALMAR [*speaking more softly*].   That's the way we got her, you see. Father knows Pettersen a bit and when he heard all this about the wild duck, he arranged to have her handed over to us.

GREGERS.   And now she's absolutely thriving in that attic room.

HJALMAR.   Yes, it's incredible. She's gotten fat. I think she's been in there so long, too, that she's forgotten her old wild life, and that's what it all comes down to.

GREGERS. You're certainly right there, Hjalmar. Just don't let her ever catch sight of the sea and the sky— But I mustn't stay any longer, for I think your father's asleep.

HJALMAR. Oh, don't bother about that.

GREGERS. But incidentally—you said you had a room for rent, a free room?

HJALMAR. Yes. Why? Do you know someone, perhaps—?

GREGERS. Could I take that room?

HJALMAR. You?

GINA. No, not *you*, Mr. Werle—

GREGERS. Could I take the room? If so, I'll move in first thing in the morning.

HJALMAR. By all means, with the greatest pleasure—

GINA. No, but Mr. Werle, it's not at all the room for *you*.

HJALMAR. But Gina, how can you say that?

GINA. Oh, the room isn't large enough, or light enough, and—

GREGERS. That really doesn't matter, Mrs. Ekdal.

HJALMAR. I think it's a very pleasant room, and it's not badly furnished, either.

GINA. But remember those two who live right below.

GREGERS. What two are those?

GINA. Oh, one of them's been a private tutor—

HJALMAR. That's Molvik, from the university.

GINA. And then there's a doctor named Relling.

GREGERS. Relling? I know him somewhat. He practiced a while up in Hoidal.

GINA. They're a pretty wild pair, those fellows. They go out on the town evenings and then come home in the dead of night, and they're not always so—

GREGERS. One gets used to that soon enough. I'm hoping things will go for me the same as with the wild duck—

GINA. Well, I think you ought to sleep on it first, anyway.

GREGERS. You're not very anxious to have me in the house, Mrs. Ekdal.

GINA. Goodness, what makes you think that?

HJALMAR. Yes, Gina, this is really peculiar of you. [*To* GREGERS.] But tell me, do you expect to stay here in town till the first?

GREGERS [*putting on his overcoat*]. Yes, now I expect to stay on.

HJALMAR. But not at home with your father? What do you plan to do with yourself?

GREGERS. Yes, if I only knew that—then I'd be doing all right. But when one is cursed with being called Gregers—"Gregers"—and then "Werle" coming after—have you ever heard anything so disgusting?

HJALMAR. Oh, I don't agree at all.

GREGERS. Ugh! Phew! I feel I'd like to spit on any man with a name like that. But when one has to *live* with that curse of being called Gregers, as I do—

HJALMAR [*laughing*]. If you weren't Gregers Werle, who would you want to be?

GREGERS. If I could choose, above all else I'd like to be a clever dog.

GINA. A dog?

HEDVIG [*involuntarily*]. Oh no!

GREGERS. Yes. A really fantastic, clever dog, the kind that goes to the bottom after wild ducks when they dive under and bite fast into the weeds down in the mire.

HJALMAR. You know, Gregers—I can't follow a word you're saying.

GREGERS. Never mind. There's really nothing very remarkable in it. But tomorrow morning, early, I'll be moving in. [*To* GINA.] I won't be any trouble to you; I do everything for myself. [*To* HJALMAR.] The rest we can talk over tomorrow. Good night, Mrs. Ekdal. [*Nods to* HEDVIG.] Good night.

GINA. Good night, Mr. Werle.

HEDVIG. Good night.

HJALMAR [*who has lit a lamp*]. Just a minute. I'd better light your way; it's quite dark on the stairs.

[GREGERS *and* HJALMAR *go out through the hall.*]

GINA [*gazing into space, her sewing in her lap*]. Wasn't that a queer business, his wanting to be a dog?

HEDVIG. I'll tell you something, Mother—it seemed to me he meant something else by that.

GINA. What else could he mean?

HEDVIG. I don't know—but it was just as if he meant something else from what he said, all the time.

GINA. Do you think so? It was strange, all right.

HJALMAR [*coming back*]. The light was still lit. [*Putting out the lamp and setting it down.*] Ah, at last one can get a bite to eat. [*Beginning on the bread and butter.*] Well, now you see, Gina—if you simply keep wide awake, then—

GINA. What do you mean, wide awake?

HJALMAR. Well, it was lucky, then, that we got the room rented out for a while at last. And think—to a person like Gregers—a good old friend.

GINA. Yes. I don't know what to say. I don't.

HEDVIG. Oh, Mother, you'll see. It'll be fun.

HJALMAR. You really are peculiar. Before you were so eager to rent, and now you don't like it.

GINA. Yes, Hjalmar, if it could only have been somebody else. What do you think the old man will say?

HJALMAR. Old Werle? This doesn't concern him.

GINA. But you can sure bet that something has come up between them, since the son is moving out. You know how those two get along together.

HJALMAR. Yes, that may well be, but—

GINA. And now maybe the old man thinks it's you that's behind—

HJALMAR. He can think that as much as he likes! Old Werle has done a tremendous amount for me. God knows, I'm aware of that. But even so, I can't make myself eternally dependent on him.

GINA. But Hjalmar dear, that can have its effect on Grandfather. He may now lose that miserable little income he gets from Graaberg.

HJALMAR. I could almost say, so much the better! Isn't it rather humiliating for a man like me to see his gray-haired father go around like an outcast? But now time is gathering to a ripeness, I think. [*Takes another piece of bread and butter.*] Just as sure as I've got a mission in life, I'm going to carry it out!

HEDVIG. Oh yes, Daddy! Do!

GINA.   Shh! Don't wake him up.

HJALMAR [more quietly].   I will carry it out, I tell you. There will come a day when— And that's why it's good we got the room rented out, for now I'm more independently fixed. Any man must be that, who's got a mission in life. [Over by the armchair; emotionally.] Poor old white-haired Father—lean on your Hjalmar. He has broad shoulders—powerful shoulders, in any case. One fine day you'll wake up and— [To GINA.] You do believe that, don't you?

GINA [getting up].   Yes, of course I do. But first let's see about getting him to bed.

HJALMAR.   Yes, let's do that.

[Gently they lift up the old man.]

ACT III

HJALMAR EKDAL's studio. It is morning. Daylight streams through the large window in the sloping roof; the curtain is drawn back.

HJALMAR is sitting at the table, busy retouching a photograph; many other pictures lie in front of him. After a moment GINA, wearing a hat and coat, enters by the hall door; she has a covered basket on her arm.

HJALMAR.   Back so soon, Gina?

GINA.   Oh yes. Got to keep moving. [She sets the basket on a chair and takes her coat off.]

HJALMAR.   Did you look in on Gregers?

GINA.   Um-hm, I certainly did. Looks real nice in there. The moment he came, he got his room in beautiful shape.

HJALMAR.   Oh?

GINA.   Yes. He wanted to do everything himself, he said. So he starts building a fire in the stove, and the next thing he's closed down the damper so the whole room is full of smoke. Phew! What a stink, enough to—

HJALMAR.   Oh no!

GINA.   But that's not the best part! So then he wants to put it out, so he empties his whole water pitcher into the stove and now the floor's swimming in the worst muck.

HJALMAR.   That's a nuisance.

GINA.   I got the janitor's wife to come and scrub up after him, the pig; but it'll be unfit to live in till afternoon.

HJALMAR.   What's he doing with himself in the meantime?

GINA.   Thought he'd take a little walk, he said.

HJALMAR.   I was in to see him for a moment too—after you left.

GINA.   I heard that. You asked him for lunch.

HJALMAR.   Just the tiniest little midday snack, you understand. It's the very first day—we could hardly avoid it. You always have something in the house.

GINA.   I'll see what I can find.

HJALMAR.   But now don't make it too skimpy. Because Relling and Molvik are dropping in too, I think. I just met Relling on the stairs, you see, so of course I had to—

GINA.   Oh? Must we have those two also?

HJALMAR.   Good Lord, a couple of sandwiches more or less; what's the difference?

EKDAL [*opening his door and looking in*].   Say, listen, Hjalmar— [*Noticing* GINA.] Oh, well.

GINA.   Is there something Grandfather wants?

EKDAL.   Oh no. Let it be. Hmm. [*Goes in again.*]

GINA [*picking up the basket*].   Keep a sharp eye on him so he doesn't go out.

HJALMAR.   Oh yes, I'll do that. Listen, Gina, a little herring salad would be awfully good—because Relling and Molvik were out on a binge last night.

GINA.   Just so they don't come before I'm ready—

HJALMAR.   Not a chance. Take your time.

GINA.   That's fine, then—and meanwhile you can get a little work done.

HJALMAR.   Can't you see how I'm working! I'm working for all I'm worth.

GINA.   Because then you'll have *those* off your hands, you know. [*She carries the basket out to the kitchen.* HJALMAR *sits for a while, tinting the photograph in a glum and listless manner.*]

EKDAL [*peeks in, peers about the studio, and whispers*].   Are you busy, boy?

HJALMAR.   Of course. I'm sitting here struggling with these pictures—

EKDAL.   Oh well, don't bother. If you're so busy, then— Hm! [*He reenters his room, leaving the door ajar.*]

HJALMAR [*continues for a moment in silence, then puts down the brush and goes over to the door*].   Father, are *you* busy?

EKDAL [*grumbling from within*].   When you're busy—I'm busy too. Huh!

HJALMAR.   Yes, of course. [*Returns to his work.*]

EKDAL [*a moment later, coming in again*].   Hm. Well, now, Hjalmar, I'm really not *that* busy.

HJALMAR.   I thought you had copying to do.

EKDAL.   Oh, the devil! Can't he, Graaberg, wait a day or two? I'm sure it's no matter of life or death.

HJALMAR.   No, and you're no slave, either.

EKDAL.   And then there was that other business inside—

HJALMAR.   Yes, that's just it. Maybe you want to go in? Shall I open it up for you?

EKDAL.   Wouldn't be a bad idea, really.

HJALMAR [*getting up*].   And then we'd have *that* off our hands.

EKDAL.   Yes, exactly. And it has to be ready first thing tomorrow. But it *is* tomorrow, isn't it?

HJALMAR.   It certainly is tomorrow.

[HJALMAR *and* EKDAL *each push back one of the double doors. Within, morning sunlight shines through the skylights. A few doves fly back and forth; others perch, cooing, on the rafters. Chickens cackle now and then from back in the loft.*]

HJALMAR.   There, now you can get in, Father.

EKDAL [*going in*].   Aren't you coming along?

HJALMAR. Well, you know what—I almost think— [*Sees* GINA *in the kitchen doorway.*] I? No, I haven't the time; I've got to work. But that means our new mechanism—

[*He pulls a cord; inside a curtain descends, its lower portion composed of a strip of old sailcloth, the upper part being a piece of worn-out fishnetting. By this means, the floor of the loft is rendered invisible.*]

HJALMAR [*returning to the table*]. That's that. Now at last I can work in peace for a while.

GINA. Is he in there, romping around again?

HJALMAR. Isn't that better than having him run down to Mrs. Eriksen's? [*Sitting.*] Is there anything you want? You look so—

GINA. I only wanted to ask, do you think we can set the lunch table in here?

HJALMAR. Well, we haven't any portraits scheduled that early, have we?

GINA. No. I don't expect anybody except that couple who want to be taken together.

HJALMAR. Why the devil can't they be taken together some other day?

GINA. Now, Hjalmar dear, I've got them booked for during your midday nap.

HJALMAR. Well, that's fine, then. So we'll eat in here.

GINA. All right. But there's no hurry about setting the table, you can certainly use it a while longer.

HJALMAR. Oh, it's obvious I'm using the table as much as I can!

GINA. Because then you'll be free later on, you know.

[*She goes back into the kitchen. A short pause.*]

EKDAL [*at the door to the loft, behind the net*]. Hjalmar!

HJALMAR. Well?

EKDAL. 'Fraid we'll have to move the water trough after all.

HJALMAR. Yes, that's what I've been saying all along.

EKDAL. Hm—hm—hm. [*Disappears from the doorway.*]

[HJALMAR *works a bit, glances toward the loft, and half rises.* HEDVIG *enters from the kitchen.*]

HJALMAR [*hurriedly sitting again*]. What do you want?

HEDVIG. I was just coming in to you, Father.

HJALMAR [*after a moment*]. You seem to be kind of snooping around. Are you checking up, maybe?

HEDVIG. No, not at all.

HJALMAR. What's Mother doing out there now?

HEDVIG. Oh, she's half through the herring salad. [*Going over to the table.*] Don't you have some little thing I could help you with, Daddy?

HJALMAR. Oh no. It's better just to leave me alone with all this—so long as my strength holds out. Nothing to worry about, Hedvig—if only your father can keep his health—

HEDVIG. Oh, Daddy, no. That's horrid; you mustn't talk like that. [*She wanders about a little, stops by the loft doorway, and looks in.*]

HJALMAR. What's he trying to do now?

HEDVIG. It must be a new pathway up to the water trough.

HJALMAR. He can't possibly rig that up on his own! And I'm condemned to sit here—!

HEDVIG [going to him].   Let me take the brush, Daddy. I know I can.

HJALMAR.   Oh, nonsense, you'll only ruin your eyes.

HEDVIG.   No such thing. Give me the brush.

HJALMAR [getting up].   Well, it'll only be for a minute or two.

HEDVIG.   Pooh! How could that hurt me? [Takes the brush.] There now. [Sitting.] And here's one to go by.

HJALMAR.   But don't ruin your eyes! Hear me? I won't take the blame; you can take the blame yourself—you hear me?

HEDVIG [at work retouching].   Yes, yes, sure I will.

HJALMAR.   You're wonderfully clever, Hedvig. Just for a couple of minutes now.

[He slips around the edge of the curtain into the loft. HEDVIG sits at her work. HJALMAR and EKDAL are heard arguing inside.]

HJALMAR [appearing behind the net].   Hedvig, just hand me the pliers from the shelf. And the chisel, please. [Turning, over his shoulder.] Yes, now you'll see, Father. Will you give me a chance to show you the way I mean! [HEDVIG fetches the desired tools from the bookcase and passes them in to him.] Ah, thanks. See, dear, it was a good thing I came. [He vanishes from the doorway; sounds of carpentry and bantering are heard. HEDVIG remains, looking in at them. A moment later, a knock at the hall door; she fails to notice it.]

GREGERS [bareheaded, and without his overcoat, enters, hesitating slightly at the door].   Hm—

HEDVIG [turning and going toward him].   Good morning. Please come in.

GREGERS.   Thanks. [Looking at the loft.] You seem to have workmen in the house.

HEDVIG.   No, that's only Father and Grandfather. I'll go tell them.

GREGERS.   No, no, don't bother. I'd rather wait a bit. [He sits on the sofa.]

HEDVIG.   It's so messy here— [Starts to remove the photographs.]

GREGERS.   Oh, they can stay. Are those some pictures that have to be finished?

HEDVIG.   Yes, it's a little job I'm helping Daddy with.

GREGERS.   Please don't let me disturb you.

HEDVIG.   All right. [She gathers her materials around her and sets to work again; GREGERS meanwhile regards her in silence.]

GREGERS.   Did the wild duck sleep well last night?

HEDVIG.   Yes, I'm sure she did, thanks.

GREGERS [turning toward the loft].   It looks so very different by daylight than it did by moonlight.

HEDVIG.   Yes, it can change so completely. In the morning it looks different from in the afternoon; and when it rains it's different from when it's clear.

GREGERS.   Have you noticed that?

HEDVIG.   Sure. You can't help it.

GREGERS.   And do you like it in there with the wild duck, too?

HEDVIG.   Yes, whenever I can be there—

GREGERS.   But of course you don't have much free time; you do go to school, don't you?

HEDVIG.   No, not any more. Daddy's afraid I'll hurt my eyes.

GREGERS.   Oh. Then he reads to you himself.

HEDVIG. Daddy's promised to read to me, but he hasn't found time for that yet.

GREGERS. But isn't there anyone else to help you a little?

HEDVIG. Sure, there's Mr. Molvik, but he isn't always exactly, really—well—

GREGERS. He gets drunk, eh?

HEDVIG. He *certainly* does.

GREGERS. Well, then you do have time to yourself. And inside—I'll bet in there it's just like a world of its own—am I right?

HEDVIG. Oh, completely! And then there are so many wonderful things.

GREGERS. Really?

HEDVIG. Yes, big cupboards with books in them; and lots of the books have pictures.

GREGERS. Ah!

HEDVIG. And then there's an old cabinet with drawers and compartments, and a huge clock with figures that are supposed to come out. But the clock doesn't go any more.

GREGERS. Even time doesn't exist in there—with the wild duck.

HEDVIG. Yes. And then there's an old watercolor set and things like that. And then all the books.

GREGERS. And of course you read the books?

HEDVIG. Oh yes, whenever I can. But they're mostly in English, and I don't understand that. But then I look at the pictures. There's one just enormous book called *Harryson's History of London*; it must be a hundred years old, and it's got ever so many pictures in it. At the front there's a picture of Death with an hourglass and a girl. I think that's horrible. But then there are all the other pictures of churches and castles and streets and great ships sailing on the ocean.

GREGERS. But tell me, where did all these rare things come from!

HEDVIG. Oh, an old sea captain lived here once, and he brought them home. They called him "the flying Dutchman"—and that's the strangest thing, because he wasn't a Dutchman at all.

GREGERS. No?

HEDVIG. No. But then he didn't come back finally, and he left all these things behind.

GREGERS. Listen, tell me—when you sit in there and look at pictures, don't you ever want to go out and see the real world all for yourself?

HEDVIG. No, never! I'm going to stay at home always and help Daddy and Mother.

GREGERS. You mean finishing photographs?

HEDVIG. No, not just that. Most of all, I'd like to learn how to engrave pictures like those in the English books.

GREGERS. Hm. What does your father say to that?

HEDVIG. I don't think he likes it. Daddy's so funny about such things. Just think, he talks about me learning basket-making and wickerwork! But I don't see anything in *that*.

GREGERS. Oh no, I don't either.

HEDVIG. But Daddy's right when he says that if I'd learned how to make baskets, I could have made the new basket for the wild duck.

GREGERS. You could have, yes—and that really was up to you.

HEDVIG. Yes, because it's *my* wild duck.

GREGERS. Yes, of course it is.

HEDVIG. Uh-huh, I own it. But Daddy and Grandpa can borrow it as much as they want.

GREGERS. Oh? What do they do with it?

HEDVIG. Oh, they look after it and build things for it and so on.

GREGERS. I can well imagine. The wild duck rules supreme in there, doesn't she?

HEDVIG. Yes, she does, and that's because she's a real wild bird. And then it's so sad for her; the poor thing has no one to turn to.

GREGERS. No family, like the rabbits—

HEDVIG. No. Even the chickens have all the others that they were baby chicks with, but she's so completely apart from any of her own. So you see, everything is so really mysterious about the wild duck. There's no one who knows her, and no one who knows where she's come from, either.

GREGERS. And actually, she's been in the depths of the sea.

HEDVIG [*glances at him, suppresses a smile, and asks*]. Why did you say "depths of the sea"?

GREGERS. What else should I say?

HEDVIG. You could have said "bottom of the sea"—or "the ocean's bottom"?

GREGERS. But couldn't I just as well say "depths of the sea"?

HEDVIG. Sure. But to me it sounds so strange when someone else says "depths of the sea."

GREGERS. But why? Tell me why?

HEDVIG. No, I won't. It's something so stupid.

GREGERS. It couldn't be. Now tell me why you smiled.

HEDVIG. That was because always, when all of a sudden—in a flash—I happen to think of that in there, it always seems to me that the whole room and everything in it is called "the depths of the sea"! But that's all so stupid.

GREGERS. Don't you dare say that.

HEDVIG. Oh yes, because it's only an attic.

GREGERS. Are you so sure of that?

HEDVIG [*astonished*]. That it's an attic!

GREGERS. Yes. Do you know that for certain?

[HEDVIG, *speechless, stares at him open-mouthed.* GINA *enters from the kitchen with a tablecloth.*]

GREGERS [*getting up*]. I'm afraid I've come too early for you.

GINA. Oh, you can find yourself a spot; it's almost ready now. Clear the table, Hedvig.

[HEDVIG *puts away the materials; during the following dialogue, she and* GINA *set the table.* GREGERS *settles in the armchair and pages through an album.*]

GREGERS. I hear you can retouch photographs, Mrs. Ekdal.

GINA [*with a side-glance*]. Um-hm, so I can.

GREGERS. That's really very lucky.

GINA. Why "lucky"?

GREGERS. With Hjalmar a photographer, I mean.

HEDVIG. Mother can take pictures, too.

GINA.   Oh yes, I even got lessons in that.

GREGERS.   So we might say it's you who runs the business.

GINA.   Yes, when my husband hasn't the time himself—

GREGERS.   He finds himself so taken up with his old father, I suppose.

GINA.   Yes, and then a man like Hjalmar shouldn't have to go snapping pictures of every Tom, Dick and Harry.

GREGERS.   I agree; but once he's chosen this line of work, then—

GINA.   Mr. Werle, you must realize that my husband is not just any old photographer.

GREGERS.   Well, naturally; but even so—

[*A shot is fired in the loft.*]

GREGERS [*jumping up*].   What's that!

HEDVIG.   They go hunting.

GREGERS.   What! [*Going to the loft doorway.*] Have you gone hunting, Hjalmar?

HJALMAR [*behind the net*].   Are you here? I didn't realize; I was so occupied—[*To* HEDVIG.] And you, you didn't tell us. [*Comes into the studio.*]

GREGERS.   Do you go shooting in the loft?

HJALMAR [*producing a double-barreled pistol*].   Oh, only with this here.

GINA.   Yes, some day you and Grandfather'll have an accident with that there gun.

HJALMAR [*annoyed*].   I believe I've remarked that this type of firearm is called a pistol.

GINA.   I don't see that that makes it any better.

GREGERS.   So you've turned out a "hunter" as well, Hjalmar?

HJALMAR.   Just a little rabbit hunt, now and then. It's mainly for Father's sake, you understand.

GINA.   Men are so funny, really; they've always got to have their little diversities.

HJALMAR [*angrily*].   That's right, yes—they always have to have their little diversions.

GINA.   Yes, that's just what I was saying.

HJALMAR.   Oh, well! [*To* GREGERS.] So that's it, and then we're very lucky in the way the loft is placed—nobody can hear us when we're shooting. [*Puts the pistol on the highest bookshelf.*] Don't touch the pistol, Hedvig! One barrel's still loaded, don't forget.

GREGERS [*peering through the netting*].   You've got a hunting rifle too, I see.

HJALMAR.   Yes, that's Father's old rifle. It won't shoot any more; something's gone wrong with the lock. But it's a lot of fun to have anyway, because we can take it all apart and clean it and grease it and put it together again— Of course, it's mostly Father who fools around with that sort of thing.

HEDVIG [*crossing to* GREGERS].   Now you can really see the wild duck.

GREGERS.   I was just now looking at her. She seems to drag one wing a little.

HJALMAR.   Well, no wonder; she took a bad wound.

GREGERS.   And then she limps a little. Isn't that so?

HJALMAR.   Maybe just a tiny bit.

HEDVIG.   Yes, that was the foot the dog bit her in.

HJALMAR. But she hasn't a thing wrong with her otherwise; and that's simply remarkable when you think that she's had a charge of shot in her and been held by the teeth of a dog—

GREGERS [*with a glance at* HEDVIG]. And been in the depths of the sea—so long.

HEDVIG [*smiling*]. Yes.

GINA [*arranging the table*]. Oh, that sacred duck—there's fuss enough made over her.

HJALMAR. Hm. Are you nearly ready?

GINA. Yes, right away. Hedvig, now you can come and help me.

[GINA *and* HEDVIG *exit into the kitchen.*]

HJALMAR [*in an undertone*]. I don't think it's so good that you stand there, watching my father. He doesn't like it. [GREGERS *comes away from the loft doorway.*] And it's better, too, that I close up before the others come. [*Shooing away the menagerie with his hands.*] Hssh! Hssh! Go 'way now! [*With this he raises the curtain and draws the double doors together.*] I invented these contraptions myself. It's really great fun to have such things around to take care of and fix when they get out of whack. And besides, it's absolutely necessary, you know; Gina doesn't go for rabbits and chickens out here in the studio.

GREGERS. Of course not. And I suppose it *is* your wife who manages here?

HJALMAR. My general rule is to delegate the routine matters to her, and that leaves me free to retire to the living room to think over more important things.

GREGERS. And what sort of things are these, Hjalmar?

HJALMAR. I've been wondering why you haven't asked me that before. Or maybe you haven't heard about my invention.

GREGERS. Invention? No.

HJALMAR. Oh? Then you haven't? Well, no, up there in that waste and wilderness—

GREGERS. Then you've really invented something!

HJALMAR. Not completely invented it yet, but I'm getting very close. You must realize that when I decided to dedicate my life to photography, it wasn't my idea to spend time taking pictures of a lot of nobodies.

GREGERS. Yes, that's what your wife was just now saying.

HJALMAR. I swore that if I devoted my powers to the craft, I would then exalt it to such heights that it would become both an art and a science. That's when I decided on this amazing invention.

GREGERS. And what does this invention consist of? What's its purpose?

HJALMAR. Yes, Gregers, you mustn't ask for details like that yet. It takes time, you know. And you mustn't think it's vanity that's driving me, either. I'm certainly not working for myself. Oh no, it's my life's work that stands before me day and night.

GREGERS. What life's work is that?

HJALMAR. Remember the silver-haired old man?

GREGERS. Your poor father. Yes, but actually what can you do for him?

HJALMAR. I can raise his self-respect from the dead—by restoring the Ekdal name to dignity and honor.

GREGERS.   So that's your life's work.

HJALMAR.   Yes. I am going to rescue that shipwrecked man. That's just what he suffered—shipwreck—when the storm broke over him. When all those harrowing investigations took place, he wasn't himself anymore. That pistol, there—the one we use to shoot rabbits with—it's played a part in the tragedy of the Ekdals.

GREGERS.   Pistol! Oh?

HJALMAR.   When he was sentenced and facing prison, he had that pistol in his hand—

GREGERS.   You mean he—!

HJALMAR.   Yes. But he didn't dare. He was a coward. That shows how broken and degraded he'd become by then. Can you picture it? He, a soldier, a man who'd shot nine bears and was directly descended from two lieutenant colonels—I mean, one after the other, of course. Can you picture it, Gregers?

GREGERS.   Yes, I can picture it very well.

HJALMAR.   Well, I can't. And then that pistol intruded on our family history once again. When he was under lock and key, dressed like a common prisoner—oh, those were agonizing times for me, you can imagine. I kept the shades of both my windows drawn. When I looked out, I saw the sun shining the same as ever. I couldn't understand it. I saw the people going along the street, laughing and talking of trivial things. I couldn't understand it. I felt all creation should be standing still, like during an eclipse.

GREGERS.   I felt that way when my mother died.

HJALMAR.   During one of those times Hjalmar Ekdal put a pistol to his own breast.

GREGERS.   You were thinking of—

HJALMAR.   Yes.

GREGERS.   But you didn't shoot?

HJALMAR.   No. In that critical moment I won a victory over myself. I stayed alive. But you can bet it takes courage to choose life in those circumstances.

GREGERS.   Well, that depends on your point of view.

HJALMAR.   Oh, absolutely. But it was all for the best, because now I've nearly finished my invention; and then Dr. Relling thinks, just as I do, that they'll let Father wear his uniform again. That's the only reward I'm after.

GREGERS.   So it's really the uniform that he—?

HJALMAR.   Yes, that's what he really hungers and craves for. You've no idea how that makes my heart ache. Every time we throw a little family party—like my birthday, or Gina's, or whatever—then the old man comes in, wearing that uniform from his happier days. But if there's even a knock at the door, he goes scuttering back in his room fast as the old legs will carry him. You see, he doesn't dare show himself to strangers. What a heartrending spectacle for a son!

GREGERS.   Approximately when do you think the invention will be finished?

HJALMAR.   Oh, good Lord, don't hold me to a timetable. An invention, that's something you can hardly dictate to. It depends a great deal on inspiration, on a sudden insight—and it's nearly impossible to say in advance when that will occur.

GREGERS. But it *is* making progress?

HJALMAR. Of course it's making progress. Every single day I think about my invention. I'm brimming with it. Every afternoon, right after lunch, I lock myself in the living room where I can meditate in peace. But it's no use driving me; it simply won't work. Relling says so too.

GREGERS. And you don't think all those contraptions in the loft distract you and scatter your talents?

HJALMAR. No, no, no, on the contrary. You mustn't say that. I can't always go around here, brooding over the same nerve-racking problems. I need some diversion to fill in the time. You see, inspiration, the moment of insight—when that comes, nothing can stop it.

GREGERS. My dear Hjalmar, I suspect you've got a bit of the wild duck in you.

HJALMAR. Of the wild duck? What do you mean?

GREGERS. You've plunged to the bottom and clamped hold of the seaweed.

HJALMAR. I suppose you mean that near-fatal shot that brought down Father—and me as well?

GREGERS. Not quite that. I wouldn't say you're wounded; but you're wandering in a poisonous swamp, Hjalmar. You've got an insidious disease in your system, and so you've gone to the bottom to die in the dark.

HJALMAR. Me? Die in the dark! You know what, Gregers—you'll really have to stop that talk.

GREGERS. But never mind. I'm going to raise you up again. You know, I've found my purpose in life, too. I found it yesterday.

HJALMAR. Yes, that may well be; but you can just leave me out of it. I can assure you that—apart from my quite understandable melancholy—I'm as well off as any man could wish to be.

GREGERS. And your thinking so is part of the sickness.

HJALMAR. Gregers, you're my old friend—please—don't talk any more about sickness and poison. I'm not used to that kind of conversation. In my house nobody talks to me about ugly things.

GREGERS. That's not hard to believe.

HJALMAR. Yes, because it isn't good for me. And there's no swamp air here, as you put it. In a poor photographer's house, life is cramped; I know that. My lot is a poor one—but, you know, I'm an inventor. And I'm the family breadwinner, too. *That's* what sustains me through all the pettiness. Ah, here they come with the lunch.

[GINA *and* HEDVIG *bring in bottles of beer, a decanter of brandy, glasses, and the like. At the same time,* RELLING *and* MOLVIK *enter from the hall.*

Neither wears a hat or overcoat; MOLVIK *is dressed in black.*]

GINA [*setting things down on the table*]. Well, the two of them—right on time.

RELLING. Molvik was positive he could smell that herring salad, and there was just no holding him back. 'Morning for the second time, Ekdal.

HJALMAR. Gregers, I'd like you to meet Mr. Molvik. And Dr.—ah, but don't you know Relling?

GREGERS. Yes, slightly.

RELLING. Well, Mr. Werle junior. Yes, we've had a few run-ins together up at the Hoidal works. You've just moved in, haven't you?

GREGERS.   I moved in this morning.

RELLING.   And Molvik and I live downstairs; so you're not very far from a doctor and a priest, if you ever have need of such.

GREGERS.   Thanks; that could happen. After all, we had thirteen at the table last night.

HJALMAR.   Oh, don't start in on ugly subjects again!

RELLING.   You don't have to worry, Hjalmar; Lord knows this doesn't involve you.

HJALMAR.   I hope not, for my family's sake. But let's sit down and eat and drink and be merry.

GREGERS.   Shouldn't we wait for your father?

HJALMAR.   No, he'll have his lunch sent in to him later. Come now!

[*The men sit at the table, eating and drinking.* GINA *and* HEDVIG *go in and out, serving the food.*]

RELLING.   Last night Molvik was tight as a tick, Mrs. Ekdal.

GINA.   Oh? Last night again?

RELLING.   Didn't you hear him when I finally brought him home?

GINA.   No, can't say I did.

RELLING.   That's lucky—because Molvik was revolting last night.

GINA.   Is that so, Molvik?

MOLVIK.   Let's draw a veil over last night's activities. They have no bearing on my better self.

RELLING [*to* GREGERS].   All of a sudden he's possessed by an impulse; and then I have to take him out on a bat. You see, Mr. Molvik is demonic.

GREGERS.   Demonic?

RELLING.   Molvik is demonic, yes.

GREGERS.   Hm.

RELLING.   And demonic natures aren't made to go through life on the straight and narrow; they've got to take detours every so often. Well—and you're still sticking it out there at that dark, hideous mill.

GREGERS.   I've stuck it out till now.

RELLING.   And did you ever collect on that "summons" you were going around with?

GREGERS.   Summons? [*Understanding him.*] Oh, that.

HJALMAR.   Were you serving summonses, Gregers?

GREGERS.   Nonsense.

RELLING.   Oh, but he was, definitely. He was going around to all the farms and cabins with copies of something he called "Summons to the Ideal."

GREGERS.   I was young then.

RELLING.   You're right, there. You were very young. And that summons to the ideal—it wasn't ever honored during my time up there.

GREGERS.   Nor later, either.

RELLING.   Well, I guess you've learned enough to cut down your expectations a bit.

GREGERS.   Never—when I meet a man who's a real man.

HJALMAR.   Yes, that seems quite reasonable to me. A little butter, Gina.

RELLING.   And then a piece of pork for Molvik.

MOLVIK.   Ugh, no pork!

[*There is a knock at the loft door.*]

HJALMAR. Open it, Hedvig; Father wants to get out.

[HEDVIG *goes to open the door a little; old* EKDAL *enters with a fresh rabbit skin. He closes the door after him.*]

EKDAL. Good morning, gentlemen. Good hunting today. Shot a big one.

HJALMAR. And you went ahead and skinned it without waiting for me!

EKDAL. Salted it, too. It's nice tender meat, this rabbit meat. And it's so sweet. Tastes like sugar. Enjoy your food, gentlemen! [*He goes into his room.*]

MOLVIK [*getting up*]. Pardon—I, I can't—got to go downstairs right—

RELLING. Drink soda water, man!

MOLVIK [*rushing out the hall door*]. Ugh—ugh!

RELLING [*to* HJALMAR]. Let's empty a glass to the old hunter.

HJALMAR [*clinking glasses with him*]. Yes, to the gallant sportsman on the brink of the grave.

RELLING. To the old, gray-haired— [*Drinks.*] Tell me something, is it gray hair he's got, or is it white?

HJALMAR. It's really a little of both. But as a matter of fact, he's scarcely got a hair on his head.

RELLING. Well, fake hair will take you through life, good as any. You know, Ekdal, you're really a very lucky man. You have your high mission in life to fight for—

HJALMAR. And I am fighting for it, too.

RELLING. And then you've got this clever wife of yours, padding around in her slippers and waggling her hips and keeping you neat and cozy.

HJALMAR. Yes, Gina—[*nodding at her*] you're a good companion for life's journey, you are.

GINA. Oh, don't sit there deprecating me.

RELLING. And what about your Hedvig, Ekdal?

HJALMAR [*stirred*]. My child, yes! My child above all. Hedvig, come here to me. [*Caresses her head.*] What day is tomorrow, dear?

HEDVIG [*shaking him*]. Oh, don't talk about it, Daddy!

HJALMAR. It's like a knife turning in my heart when I think how bare it's all going to be, just the tiniest celebration out in the loft—

HEDVIG. Oh, but that will be just wonderful!

RELLING. And wait till that marvelous invention comes to the world, Hedvig!

HJALMAR. Ah, yes—then you'll see! Hedvig, I've resolved to make your future secure. As long as you live, you'll live in style. I'll assure you of something, one way or another. That will be the poor inventor's sole reward.

HEDVIG [*whispering with her arms around his neck*]. Oh, you dear, dear Daddy!

RELLING [*to* GREGERS]. Well, now, isn't it good for a change to be sitting around a well-spread table in a happy family circle?

HJALMAR. Yes, I really prize these hours around the table.

GREGERS. I, for my part, don't thrive in marsh gas.

RELLING. Marsh gas?

HJALMAR. Oh, don't start that rubbish again!

GINA. Lord knows there isn't any marsh gas here, Mr. Werle; every blessed day I air the place out.

GREGERS [*leaving the table*]. You can't air out the stench I mean.

HJALMAR. Stench!

GINA.   What about that, Hjalmar!

RELLING.   Beg pardon—but it wouldn't be you who brought that stench in with you from the mines up there?

GREGERS.   It's just like you to call what I'm bringing into this house a stench.

RELLING [*crossing over to him*].   Listen, Mr. Werle junior, I've got a strong suspicion that you're still going around with the uncut version of that "Summons to the Ideal" in your back pocket.

GREGERS.   I've got it written in my heart.

RELLING.   I don't care where the devil you've got it; I wouldn't advise you to play process-server here as long as I'm around.

GREGERS.   And what if I do anyway?

RELLING.   Then you'll go head first down the stairs, that's what.

HJALMAR [*getting up*].   Come, now, Relling!

GREGERS.   Yes, just throw me out—

GINA [*coming between them*].   You can't do that, Relling. But I'll tell you this, Mr. Werle—that you, who made all that mess with your stove, have no right to come to me talking about smells.

[*A knock at the hall door.*]

HEDVIG.   Mother, somebody's knocking.

GINA.   I'll go—[*She crosses and opens the door, gives a start, shudders and shrinks back.*] Uff! Oh no!

[*Old* WERLE, *in a fur coat, steps into the room.*]

WERLE.   Excuse me, but I think my son is living in this house.

GINA [*catching her breath*].   Yes.

HJALMAR [*coming closer*].   If Mr. Werle will be so good as to—

WERLE.   Thanks, I'd just like to talk with my son.

GREGERS.   Yes, why not? Here I am.

WERLE.   I'd like to talk with you in your room.

GREGERS.   In my room—fine—[*Starts in.*]

GINA.   No. Good Lord, that's in no condition for—

WERLE.   Well, out in the hall, then. This is just between us.

HJALMAR.   You can talk here, Mr. Werle. Come into the living room, Relling.

[HJALMAR *and* RELLING *go out to the right;* GINA *takes* HEDVIG *with her into the kitchen.*]

GREGERS [*after a brief interval*].   Well, now it's just the two of us.

WERLE.   You dropped a few remarks last night—And since you've now taken a room with the Ekdals, I must assume that you're planning something or other against me.

GREGERS.   I'm planning to open Hjalmar Ekdal's eyes. He's going to see his situation just as it is—that's all.

WERLE.   Is *that* the mission in life you talked about yesterday?

GREGERS.   Yes. You haven't left me any other.

WERLE.   Am I the one that spoiled your mind, Gregers?

GREGERS.   You've spoiled my entire life. I'm not thinking of all that with Mother. But you're the one I can thank for my going around, whipped and driven by this guilt-ridden conscience.

WERLE.   Ah, it's your conscience that's gone bad.

GREGERS.   I should have taken a stand against you when the trap was laid for Lieutenant Ekdal. I should have warned him, for I had a pretty good idea what was coming off.

WERLE.   Yes, you really should have spoken up then.

GREGERS.   I didn't dare; I was so cowed and frightened. I was unspeakably afraid of you—both then and for a long time after.

WERLE.   That fright seems to be over now.

GREGERS.   It is, luckily. The harm done to old Ekdal, both by me and—others, can never be undone; but Hjalmar I can free from all the lies and evasions that are smothering him here.

WERLE.   You believe you'd be doing him good by that?

GREGERS.   That's what I believe.

WERLE.   Maybe you think Ekdal's the kind of man who'll thank you for that friendly service?

GREGERS.   Yes! He *is* that kind of man.

WERLE.   Hmm—we'll see.

GREGERS.   And besides—if I'm ever to go on living, I'll have to find a cure for my sick conscience.

WERLE.   It'll never be sound. Your conscience has been sickly from childhood. It's an inheritance from your mother, Gregers—the only inheritance she left you.

GREGERS [*with a wry half-smile*].   You've never been able to accept the fact, have you, that you calculated wrong when you thought she'd bring you a fortune?

WERLE.   Let's not get lost in irrelevancies. Then you're still intent on this goal of putting Ekdal on what you suppose is the right track?

GREGERS.   Yes, I'm intent on that.

WERLE.   Well, then I could have saved myself the walk up here. For there's no point in asking if you'll move back home with me?

GREGERS.   No.

WERLE.   And you won't come into the business either?

GREGERS.   No.

WERLE.   Very well. But since I'm now planning a second marriage, the estate, of course, will be divided between us.

GREGERS [*quickly*].   No, I don't want that.

WERLE.   You don't want it?

GREGERS.   No, I wouldn't dare, for the sake of my conscience.

WERLE [*after a pause*].   You going back to the works again?

GREGERS.   No. I consider that I've retired from your service.

WERLE.   But what are you going to do, then?

GREGERS.   Simply carry out my life's mission; nothing else.

WERLE.   Yes, but afterwards? What will you live on?

GREGERS.   I have some of my salary put aside.

WERLE.   Yes, that won't last long!

GREGERS.   I think it will last my time.

WERLE.   What do you mean by that?

GREGERS.   I'm not answering any more.

WERLE.   Good-bye then, Gregers.

GREGERS.   Good-bye.

[*Old* WERLE *goes out.*]

HJALMAR [*peering out*].   Has he gone?

GREGERS. Yes.

[HJALMAR *and* RELLING *come in.* GINA *and* HEDVIG *also return from the kitchen.*]

RELLING. There's one lunch gone to the dogs.

GREGERS. Put your things on, Hjalmar; you've got to take a long walk with me.

HJALMAR. Yes, gladly. What did your father want? Was it anything to do with me?

GREGERS. Just come. We have some things to talk over. I'll go and get my coat. [*He leaves by the hall door.*]

GINA. You mustn't go out with him, Hjalmar.

RELLING. No, don't go. Stay where you are.

HJALMAR [*getting his hat and overcoat*]. But why? When a childhood friend feels a need to open his mind to me in private—

RELLING. But damn it all! Can't you see the man's mad, crazy, out of his skull!

GINA. Yes, that's the truth, if you'd listen. His mother, off and on, had those same conniption fits.

HJALMAR. That's just why he needs a friend's watchful eye on him. [*To* GINA.] Be sure dinner's ready in plenty of time. See you later. [*Goes out the hall door.*]

RELLING. It's really a shame that fellow didn't go straight to hell down one of the Hoidal mines.

GINA. Mercy—why do you say that?

RELLING [*muttering*]. Oh, I've got my reasons.

GINA. Do you think Gregers Werle is really crazy?

RELLING. No, worse luck. He's no crazier than most people. But he's got a disease in his system all the same.

GINA. What is it that's wrong with him?

RELLING. All right, I'll tell you, Mrs. Ekdal. He's suffering from an acute case of moralistic fever.

GINA. Moralistic fever?

HEDVIG. Is that a kind of disease?

RELLING. Oh yes, it's a national disease, but it only breaks out now and then. [*Nodding to* GINA.] Thanks for lunch. [*He goes out through the hall door.*]

GINA [*walking restlessly around the room*]. Ugh, that Gregers Werle— he was always a cold fish.

HEDVIG [*standing by the table, looking searchingly at her*]. This is all so strange to me.

ACT IV

HJALMAR EKDAL's *studio. A photograph has just been taken; a portrait camera covered with a cloth, a stand, a couple of chairs, a console table, among other things, stand well out in the room. Late afternoon light; it is near sunset; somewhat later it begins to grow dark.*

GINA *is standing in the hall doorway with a plate-holder and a wet photographic plate in her hand, talking with someone outside.*

GINA.   Yes, that's definite. When I promise something, I keep my word. On Monday the first dozen will be ready. Good-bye. Good-bye. [*Footsteps are heard descending the stairs.* GINA *closes the door, puts the plate into the holder, and slips both back into the covered camera.*]

HEDVIG [*coming in from the kitchen*].   Are they gone?

GINA [*tidying up*]. Yes, thank goodness, at last I'm rid of them.

HEDVIG.   But why do you suppose Daddy isn't home yet?

GINA.   Are you sure he's not below with Relling?

HEDVIG.   No, he's not there. I ran down the back stairs just now and asked.

GINA.   And his dinner's standing and getting cold, too.

HEDVIG.   Just imagine—Daddy's always sure to be on time for dinner.

GINA.   Oh, he'll be right along, you'll see.

HEDVIG.   Oh, I wish he would come! Everything's so funny around here.

GINA [*calling out*].   There he is!

[HJALMAR *comes in by the hall door.*]

HEDVIG [*running toward him*].   Daddy! Oh, we've waited ages for you!

GINA [*eyeing him*].   You've been out pretty long, Hjalmar.

HJALMAR [*without looking at her*].   I've been a while, yes. [*He takes off his overcoat.* GINA *and* HEDVIG *start to help him; he waves them away.*]

GINA.   Did you eat with Werle, maybe?

HJALMAR [*hanging his coat up*].   No.

GINA [*going toward the kitchen*].   I'll bring your dinner in, then.

HJALMAR.   No, the dinner can wait. I don't want to eat now.

HEDVIG [*coming closer*].   Don't you feel well, Daddy?

HJALMAR.   Well? Oh yes, well enough. We had an exhausting walk, Gregers and I.

GINA.   You shouldn't do that, Hjalmar; you're not used to it.

HJALMAR.   Hm. There are a lot of things a man's got to get used to in this world. [*Walking about the room a bit.*] Did anyone come while I was out?

GINA.   No one but that engaged couple.

HJALMAR.   No new orders?

GINA.   No, not today.

HEDVIG.   You'll see, there'll be some tomorrow, Daddy.

HJALMAR.   I certainly hope so, because tomorrow I'm going to throw myself into my work—completely.

HEDVIG.   Tomorrow! But don't you remember what day tomorrow is?

HJALMAR.   Oh yes, that's right. Well, the day after tomorrow, then. From now on, I'm doing everything myself; I just want to be left alone with all the work.

GINA.   But Hjalmar, what's the point of that? It'll only make your life miserable. Let me handle the photographing, and then you'll be free to work on the invention.

HEDVIG.   And free for the wild duck, Daddy—and for all the chickens and rabbits—

HJALMAR.   Don't talk to me about that rubbish! Starting tomorrow I shall never again set foot in that loft.

HEDVIG. Yes, but Daddy, you promised me tomorrow there'd be a celebration.

HJALMAR. Hm, that's true. Well, the day after, then. That infernal wild duck—I'd almost like to wring its neck!

HEDVIG [*crying out*]. The wild duck!

GINA. What an idea!

HEDVIG [*shaking him*]. Yes, but Daddy—it's my wild duck!

HJALMAR. That's why I won't do it. I haven't the heart—for your sake, Hedvig, I haven't the heart. But deep inside me I feel I ought to. I shouldn't tolerate under my roof a creature that's been in that man's hands.

GINA. My goodness, just because Grandfather got her from that worthless Pettersen—

HJALMAR [*pacing the floor*]. There are certain standards—what should I call them—ideal standards, let's say—certain claims on us that a man can't put aside without damaging his soul.

HEDVIG [*following him*]. But think—the wild duck—the poor wild duck!

HJALMAR [*stopping*]. You heard me say I'd spare it—for your sake. It won't be hurt, not a hair on its—well, anyway, I'll spare it. There are more important matters to settle. But Hedvig, now you better get out for your afternoon walk; it's already pretty dark for you.

HEDVIG. No, I don't want to go out now.

HJALMAR. Yes, go on. You seem to be blinking your eyes so. All these fumes in here aren't good for you; the air here under this roof is bad.

HEDVIG. All right, then, I'll run down the back stairs and take a little walk. My coat and hat? Oh, they're in my room. Daddy—promise you won't hurt the wild duck while I'm out.

HJALMAR. There won't be a feather ruffled on its head. [*Drawing her to him.*] You and I, Hedvig—we two! Now run along, dear.

[HEDVIG *nods to her parents and goes out through the kitchen.*]

HJALMAR [*walking around without looking up*]. Gina.

GINA. Yes?

HJALMAR. From tomorrow on—or let's say the day after tomorrow—I'd prefer to keep the household accounts myself.

GINA. You want to keep the household accounts, too?

HJALMAR. Yes, or budget the income, in any case.

GINA. Lord love us, there's nothing to that.

HJALMAR. One wouldn't think so. It seems to me you can make our money stretch remarkably far. [*Stopping and looking at her.*] How *is* that?

GINA. Hedvig and I, we don't need much.

HJALMAR. Is it true that Father gets such good pay for the copying he does for Werle?

GINA. I don't know how good it is. I don't know rates for such things.

HJALMAR. Well, what does he get, just roughly? Tell me!

GINA. It's never the same. I suppose it's roughly what he costs us, with a little pocket money thrown in.

HJALMAR. What he costs us! That's something you've never told me before!

GINA. No, I never could. You were always so happy thinking he got everything from you.

HJALMAR.   And instead it comes from Mr. Werle.

GINA.   Oh, but he's got plenty to spare, that one.

HJALMAR.   Let's have the lamp lit!

GINA [*lighting it*].   And then we can't know if it really is the old man; it could well be Graaberg—

HJALMAR.   Why try to put me off with Graaberg?

GINA.   No, I don't know. I just thought—

HJALMAR.   Hm!

GINA.   You know it wasn't me that got Grandfather the copying. It was Berta, that time she came here.

HJALMAR.   Your voice sounds so shaky.

GINA [*putting the shade on the lamp*].   It does?

HJALMAR.   And then your hands are trembling. Or aren't they?

GINA [*firmly*].   Say it straight out, Hjalmar. What is it he's gone and said about me?

HJALMAR.   Is it true—can it possibly be that—that there was some kind of involvement between you and Mr. Werle while you were in service there?

GINA.   That's not true. Not then, there wasn't. Werle was after me, all right. And his wife thought there was something to it, and she made a big fuss and bother, and she roasted me coming and going, she did—so I quit.

HJALMAR.   But then what!

GINA.   Yes, so then I went home. And Mother—well, she wasn't all you took her to be, Hjalmar; she ran on telling me one thing and another, because Werle was a widower by then.

HJALMAR.   Yes. And then!

GINA.   Well, you might as well know it all. He didn't give up till he had his way.

HJALMAR [*with a clap of his hands*].   And this is the mother of my child! How could you keep that hidden from me!

GINA.   Yes, I did the wrong thing; I really should have told you long ago.

HJALMAR.   Right at the start, you mean—so I could have known what sort you are.

GINA.   But would you have married me anyway?

HJALMAR.   How can you think that?

GINA.   No. But that's why I didn't dare say anything then. Because I'd come to be so terribly in love with you, as you know. And then how could I make myself utterly miserable—

HJALMAR [*walking about*].   And this is my Hedvig's mother! And then to know that everything I see around me—[*kicking at a table*] my whole home —I owe to a favored predecessor. Ah, that charmer Werle!

GINA.   Do you regret the fourteen, fifteen years we've lived together?

HJALMAR [*stopping in front of her*].   Tell me—don't you every day, every hour, regret this spider web of deception you've spun around me? Answer me that! Don't you really go around in a torment of remorse?

GINA.   Hjalmar dear, I've got so much to think about just with the housework and the day's routine—

HJALMAR.   Then you never turn a critical eye on your past!

GINA.   No. Good Lord, I'd almost forgotten that old affair.

HJALMAR. Oh, this dull, unfeeling content! To me there's something outrageous about it. Just think—not one regret!

GINA. But Hjalmar, tell me now—what would have happened to you if you hadn't found a wife like me?

HJALMAR. Like you—!

GINA. Yes, because I've always been a bit more hard-headed and resourceful than you. Well, of course I'm a couple of years older.

HJALMAR. What would have happened to me?

GINA. You were pretty bad off at the time you met me; you can't deny that.

HJALMAR. "Pretty bad off" you call it. Oh, you have no idea what a man goes through when he's deep in misery and despair—especially a man of my fiery temperament.

GINA. No, that may be. And I shouldn't say nothing about it, either, because you turned out such a good-hearted husband as soon as you got a house and home—and now we've made it so snug and cozy here, and pretty soon both Hedvig and I could begin spending a little on food and clothes.

HJALMAR. In the swamp of deception, yes.

GINA. Ugh, that disgusting creature, tracking his way through our house!

HJALMAR. I also thought this home was a good place to be. That was a pipe dream. Now where can I find the buoyancy I need to carry my invention into reality? Maybe it'll die with me; and then it'll be your past, Gina, that killed it.

GINA [close to tears]. No, you mustn't ever say such things, Hjalmar. All my days I've only wanted to do what's best for you!

HJALMAR. I wonder—what happens now to the breadwinner's dream? When I lay in there on the sofa pondering my invention, I had a hunch it would drain my last bit of strength. I sensed that the day I took the patent in my hand—that would be the day of—departure. And it was my dream that then you would go on as the departed inventor's prosperous widow.

GINA [drying her eyes]. No, don't say that, Hjalmar. Lord knows I never want to see the day I'm a widow.

HJALMAR. Oh, what does it matter? Everything's over and done with now. Everything!

[GREGERS cautiously opens the hall door and looks in.]

GREGERS. May I come in?

HJALMAR. Yes, do.

GREGERS [advancing with a beaming countenance, hands outstretched as if to take theirs]. Now, you dear people—! [Looks from one to the other, then whispers to HJALMAR.] But isn't it done, then?

HJALMAR [resoundingly]. It's done.

GREGERS. It is?

HJALMAR. I've just known the bitterest hour of my life.

GREGERS. But also the most exalted, I think.

HJALMAR. Well, anyway, it's off our hands for the moment.

GINA. God forgive you, Mr. Werle.

GREGERS [with great surprise]. But I don't understand this.

HJALMAR. What don't you understand?

GREGERS.   With this great rapport—the kind that forges a whole new way of life—a life, a companionship in truth with no more deception—

HJALMAR.   Yes, I know, I know all that.

GREGERS.   I was really positive that when I came through that door I'd be met by a transfigured light in both your faces. And what do I see instead but this gloomy, heavy, dismal—

GINA.   How true. [*She removes the lampshade.*]

GREGERS.   You don't want to understand me, Mrs. Ekdal. No, no, you'll need time—— But you yourself, Hjalmar? You must have gained a sense of high purpose out of this great unburdening.

HJALMAR.   Yes, naturally. That is—more or less.

GREGERS.   Because there's nothing in the world that compares with showing mercy to a sinner and lifting her up in the arms of love.

HJALMAR.   Do you think a man can recover so easily from the bitter cup I've just emptied!

GREGERS.   Not an ordinary man, no. But a man like you—!

HJALMAR.   Good Lord, yes, I know that. But you mustn't be driving me, Gregers. You see, these things take time.

GREGERS.   You've *lots* of the wild duck in you, Hjalmar.

[RELLING *has entered through the hall door.*]

RELLING.   Aha! The wild duck's flying again, eh?

HJALMAR.   Yes, the wounded trophy of old Werle's hunt.

RELLING.   Old Werle? Is it him you're talking about?

HJALMAR.   Him and—all of us.

RELLING [*under his breath to* GREGERS].   The devil take you!

HJALMAR.   What'd you say?

RELLING.   I merely expressed my heartfelt desire that this quack would cut out for home. If he stays here, he's just the man to ruin you both.

GREGERS.   They won't be ruined, Mr. Relling. Regarding Hjalmar, I'll say nothing. We know him. But she, too, surely, in the depths of her being, has something authentic, something sincere.

GINA [*near tears*].   Well, if I *was* that, why didn't you leave me alone?

RELLING [*to* GREGERS].   Would it be nosy to ask what you're really trying to do in this house?

GREGERS.   I want to establish a true marriage.

RELLING.   Then you don't think Ekdal's marriage is good enough as it is?

GREGERS.   It's about as good a marriage as most, unfortunately. But it isn't yet a *true* marriage.

HJALMAR.   You don't believe in ideals in life, Relling.

RELLING.   Nonsense, sonny boy! Excuse me, Mr. Werle, but how many—in round numbers—how many "true marriages" have you seen in your time?

GREGERS.   I believe I've hardly seen a single one.

RELLING.   And I likewise.

GREGERS.   But I've seen innumerable marriages of the opposite kind. And I've had a chance to see at close range what such a marriage can destroy in two people.

HJALMAR.   A man's whole moral foundation can crumble under his feet; that's the dreadful thing.

RELLING.   Well, I've never really exactly been married, so I'm no judge of these things. But I do know this, that the child is part of the marriage too. And you've got to leave the child in peace.

HJALMAR.   Ah, Hedvig! My poor Hedvig!

RELLING.   Yes, you'll please see that Hedvig's left out of it. You're both grown people; you're free, God knows, to slop up your private lives all you want. But I tell you, you've got to be careful with Hedvig, or else you might do her some serious harm.

HJALMAR.   Harm!

RELLING.   Yes, or she could do harm to herself—and possibly others as well.

GINA.   But how can you know that, Relling?

HJALMAR.   There's no immediate threat to her eyes, is there?

RELLING.   This has nothing to do with her eyes. Hedvig's arrived at a difficult age. She's open to all kinds of erratic ideas.

GINA.   You know—she is at that! She's begun to fool around something awful with the fire in the kitchen stove. She calls it playing house afire. I'm often scared she *will* set the house on fire.

RELLING.   See what I mean? I knew it.

GREGERS [*to* RELLING].   But how do you explain something like that?

RELLING [*brusquely*].   Her voice is changing, junior.

HJALMAR.   As long as the child has *me*! As long as I'm above the sod.

[*A knock is heard at the door.*]

GINA.   Shh, Hjalmar, someone's in the hall. [*Calling out.*] Come on in!

[MRS. SØRBY, *wearing street clothes, enters.*]

MRS. SØRBY.   Good evening!

GINA [*going toward her*].   Is it you, Berta!

MRS. SØRBY.   Oh yes, it's me. But perhaps I came at an awkward time?

HJALMAR.   Oh, not at all; a messenger from *that* house—

MRS. SØRBY [*to* GINA].   As a matter of fact, I'd hoped that I wouldn't find your menfolk in at this hour, so I ran over just to have a word with you and say good-bye.

GINA.   Oh? Are you going away?

MRS. SØRBY.   Yes, tomorrow, early—up to Hoidal. Mr. Werle left this afternoon. [*Casually to* GREGERS.] He sends his regards.

GINA.   Just think!

HJALMAR.   So Mr. Werle has left? And you're following him?

MRS. SØRBY.   Yes, what do you say to that, Ekdal?

HJALMAR.   I say watch out.

GREGERS.   Let me explain. My father is marrying Mrs. Sørby.

HJALMAR.   He's marrying her!

GINA.   Oh, Berta, it's come at last!

RELLING [*his voice quavering slightly*].   This really can't be true.

MRS. SØRBY.   Yes, my dear Relling, it's completely true.

RELLING.   You want to marry again?

MRS. SØRBY.   Yes, so it seems. Werle has gotten a special license, and we're going to have a very quiet wedding up at the works.

GREGERS.   So I ought to wish you happiness, like a good stepson.

MRS. SØRBY.   Thank you, if you really mean it. I'm hoping it will bring us happiness, both Werle and me.

RELLING.   That's a reasonable hope. Mr. Werle never gets drunk—as far as *I* know; and he's certainly not given to beating up his wives the way the late horse doctor did.

MRS. SØRBY.   Oh, now let Sørby rest in peace. He did have some worthy traits, you know.

RELLING.   Old Werle's traits are worth rather more, I'll bet.

MRS. SØRBY.   At least he hasn't wasted the best that's in him. Any man who does *that* has to take the consequences.

RELLING.   Tonight I'm going out with Molvik.

MRS. SØRBY.   You shouldn't, Relling. Don't do it—for my sake.

RELLING.   What else is left? [*To* HJALMAR.] If you'd care to, you could come too.

GINA.   No, thanks. Hjalmar never goes dissipating.

HJALMAR [*in an angry undertone*].   Can't you keep quiet!

RELLING.   Good-bye, Mrs.—Werle. [*He goes out the hall door.*]

GREGERS [*to* MRS SØRBY].   It would seem that you and Dr. Relling know each other quite intimately.

MRS. SØRBY.   Yes, we've known each other for many years. At one time something might have developed between us.

GREGERS.   It was certainly lucky for you that it didn't.

MRS. SØRBY.   Yes, that's true enough. But I've always been wary of following my impulses. After all, a woman can't just throw herself away.

GREGERS.   Aren't you even a little bit afraid that I'll drop my father a hint about this old friendship?

MRS. SØRBY.   You can be sure I've told him myself.

GREGERS.   Oh?

MRS. SØRBY.   Your father knows every last scrap of gossip that holds any grain of truth about me. I told him all of those things; it was the first thing I did when he made his intentions clear.

GREGERS.   Then I think you're more frank than most people.

MRS. SØRBY.   I've always been frank. In the long run, it's the best thing for us women to be.

HJALMAR.   What do you say to that, Gina?

GINA.   Oh, women are all so different. Some live one way and some live another.

MRS. SØRBY.   Well, Gina, I do think it's wisest to handle things as I have. And Werle, for his part, hasn't held back anything either. Really, it's this that's brought us so close together. Now he can sit and talk to me as freely as a child. He's never had that chance before. He, a healthy, vigorous man, had to spend his whole youth and all his best years hearing nothing but sermons on his sins. And generally those sermons were aimed at the most imaginary failings—at least from what *I* could see.

GINA.   Yes, that's just as true as you say.

GREGERS.   If you women are going to explore this subject, I'd better leave.

MRS. SØRBY.   You can just as well stay, for that matter; I won't say another word. But I did want you to understand that I haven't done anything sly or in any way underhanded. I suppose it looks like I've had quite a nice piece of luck, and that's true enough, up to a point. But, anyway, what I mean is that I'll not be taking any more than I give. One thing I'll never do is desert him.

And I can be useful to him and care for him now better than anyone else after he's helpless.

HJALMAR.   After he's helpless?

GREGERS [to MRS. SØRBY].   All right, don't talk about that here.

MRS. SØRBY.   No need to hide it any longer, much as he'd like to. He's going blind.

HJALMAR [astounded].   He's going blind? But that's peculiar. Is he going blind too?

GINA.   Lots of people do.

MRS. SØRBY.   And you can imagine what that means for a businessman. Well, I'll try to make my eyes do for his as well as I can. But I mustn't stay any longer; I've so much to take care of now. Oh yes, I was supposed to tell you this, Ekdal—that if there's anything Werle can do for you, please just get in touch with Graaberg.

GREGERS.   That offer Hjalmar Ekdal will certainly decline.

MRS. SØRBY.   Come, now, I don't think that in the past he's—

GINA.   No, Berta, Hjalmar doesn't need to take anything from Mr. Werle now.

HJALMAR [slowly and ponderously].   Would you greet your future husband from me and say that I intend very shortly to call on his bookkeeper, Graaberg—

GREGERS.   What! Is that what you want?

HJALMAR.   To call on his bookkeeper Graaberg, as I said, to request an itemized account of what I owe his employer. I shall repay this debt of honor— [Laughs.] That's a good name for it, "debt of honor"! But never mind. I shall repay every penny of it, with five percent interest.

GINA.   But Hjalmar dear, God knows we don't have the money for that.

HJALMAR.   Will you tell your husband-to-be that I'm working away relentlessly at my invention. Would you tell him that what keeps by spirits up through this grueling ordeal is the desire to be quit of a painful burden of debt. That's why I'm making my invention. The entire proceeds will be devoted to shedding my monetary ties with your imminent partner.

MRS. SØRBY.   Something has really happened in this house.

HJALMAR.   Yes, it certainly has.

MRS. SØRBY.   Well, good-bye, then. I still have a little more to talk about with you, Gina, but that can keep till another time. Good-bye.

[HJALMAR and GREGERS silently nod; GINA accompanies MRS. SØRBY to the door.]

HJALMAR.   Not across the threshold, Gina!

[MRS. SØRBY leaves; GINA closes the door behind her.]

HJALMAR.   There, now, Gregers—now I've got that pressing debt off my hands.

GREGERS.   You will soon, anyway.

HJALMAR.   I believe my attitude could be called correct.

GREGERS.   You're the man I always thought you were.

HJALMAR.   In certain circumstances it's impossible not to feel the summons of the ideal. As the family provider, you know, I've got to writhe and groan beneath it. Believe you me, it's really no joke for a man without means to try and pay off a long-standing debt over which the dust of oblivion, so to speak, had fallen. But it's got to be, all the same; my human self demands its rights.

GREGERS [*laying one hand on his shoulder*]. Ah, Hjalmar—wasn't it a good thing I came?

HJALMAR. Yes.

GREGERS. Getting a clear picture of the whole situation—wasn't that a good thing?

HJALMAR [*a bit impatiently*]. Of course it was good. But there's one thing that irks my sense of justice.

GREGERS. What's that?

HJALMAR. It's the fact that—oh, I don't know if I dare speak so freely about your father.

GREGERS. Don't hold back on my account.

HJALMAR. Well, uh—you see, I find something so irritating in the idea that I'm not the one, he's the one who's going to have the true marriage.

GREGERS. How can you say such a thing!

HJALMAR. But it's true. Your father and Mrs. Sørby are entering a marriage based on complete trust, one that's wholehearted and open on both sides. They haven't bottled up any secrets from each other; there isn't any reticence between them; they've declared—if you'll permit me—a mutual forgiveness of sins.

GREGERS. All right. So what?

HJALMAR. Yes, but that's the whole thing, then. You said yourself that the reason for all these difficulties was the founding of a true marriage.

GREGERS. But that marriage is a very different sort, Hjalmar. You certainly wouldn't compare either you or her with those two—well, you know what I mean.

HJALMAR. Still, I can't get over the idea that there's something in all this that violates my sense of justice. It really seems as if there's no just order to the universe.

GINA. Good Lord, Hjalmar, you mustn't say such things.

GREGERS. Hm, let's not start on that question.

HJALMAR. But then, on the other hand, I can definitely make out what seems to be the meticulous hand of fate. He's going blind.

GINA. Oh, that's not for sure.

HJALMAR. That is indisputable. Anyway, we oughtn't to doubt it, because it's precisely this fact that reveals the just retribution. Years back he abused the blind faith of a fellow human being—

GREGERS. I'm afraid he's done that to many others.

HJALMAR. And now a pitiless, mysterious something comes and claims the old man's eyes in return.

GINA. What a horrible thing to say! It really frightens me.

HJALMAR. It's useful sometimes to go down deep into the night side of existence.

[HEDVIG, *in her hat and coat, comes in, happy and breathless, through the hall door.*]

GINA. Back so soon?

HEDVIG. Yes, I got tired of walking, and it was just as well, 'cause then I met someone down at the door.

HJALMAR. That must have been Mrs. Sørby.

HEDVIG. Yes.

HJALMAR [*pacing back and forth*]. I hope that's the last time you'll see her.

[*Silence.* HEDVIG *glances timidly from one to the other, as if trying to read their feelings.*]

HEDVIG [*coaxingly, as she approaches*]. Daddy.

HJALMAR. Well—what is it, Hedvig?

HEDVIG. Mrs. Sørby brought along something for me.

HJALMAR [*stopping*]. For you?

HEDVIG. Yes. It's something meant for tomorrow.

GINA. Berta's always brought some little gift for your birthday.

HJALMAR. What is it?

HEDVIG. No, you can't know that yet, because Mother has to bring it to me in bed first thing in the morning.

HJALMAR. Oh, all this conspiracy that I'm left out of!

HEDVIG [*hurriedly*]. Oh, you can see it all right. It's a big letter. [*She takes the letter out of her coat pocket.*]

HJALMAR. A letter, too?

HEDVIG. Well, it's only the letter. I guess the rest will come later. But just think—a letter! I've never gotten a real letter before. And on the outside there, it says "Miss." [*She reads.*] "Miss Hedvig Ekdal." Just think—that's me.

HJALMAR. Let me see the letter.

HEDVIG [*handing it over*]. See, there.

HJALMAR. That's old Werle's writing.

GINA. Are you positive, Hjalmar?

HJALMAR. See for yourself.

GINA. Oh, how would I know?

HJALMAR. Hedvig, mind if I open the letter—and read it?

HEDVIG. Sure. If you want to, go right ahead.

GINA. No, not tonight, Hjalmar. It's meant for tomorrow.

HEDVIG [*softly*]. Oh, won't you let him read it! It's got to be something good, and then Daddy'll be happy and things will be pleasant again.

HJALMAR. May I open it, then?

HEDVIG. Yes, please do, Daddy. It'll be fun to find out what it is.

HJALMAR. Good. [*He opens the envelope, takes out a sheet of paper, and reads it through with growing bewilderment.*] Now what's this all about?

GINA. But what does it say?

HEDVIG. Oh yes, Daddy—tell us!

HJALMAR. Be quiet. [*He reads it through once more, turns pale, then speaks with evident restraint.*] This is a deed of gift, Hedvig.

HEDVIG. Honestly? What am I getting?

HJALMAR. Read for yourself.

[HEDVIG *goes over to the lamp and reads for a moment.*]

HJALMAR [*clenching his fists, in almost a whisper*]. The eyes! The eyes—and now that letter!

HEDVIG [*interrupting her reading*]. Yes, but I think the gift is for Grandfather.

HJALMAR [*taking the letter from her*]. Gina—do you understand this?

GINA.   I know nothing at all about it. Just tell me.

HJALMAR.   Mr. Werle writes Hedvig to say that her old grandfather needn't trouble himself any longer with copying work, but that henceforth he can draw one hundred crowns a month from the office—

GREGERS.   Aha!

HEDVIG.   One hundred crowns, Mother! I read that.

GINA.   That'll be nice for Grandfather.

HJALMAR.   One hundred crowns, as long as he needs it. That means till death, of course.

GINA.   Well, then he's provided for, poor dear.

HJALMAR.   But there's more. You didn't read far enough, Hedvig. Afterwards this gift passes over to you.

HEDVIG.   To me! All of it?

HJALMAR.   You're assured the same income for the rest of your life, he writes. Hear that, Gina?

GINA.   Yes, of course I heard.

HEDVIG.   Imagine me getting all that money! [*Shaking* HJALMAR.] Daddy, Daddy, aren't you glad?

HJALMAR [*disengaging himself*].   Glad! [*Walking about the room.*] Ah, what vistas—what perspectives it offers me. Hedvig is the one, she's the one he remembers so bountifully.

GINA.   Of course, because it's Hedvig's birthday.

HEDVIG.   And anyway, you'll have it, Daddy. You know that I'll give all the money to you and Mother.

HJALMAR.   To Mother, yes! There we have it.

GREGERS.   Hjalmar, this is a trap that's been set for you.

HJALMAR.   You think it could be another trap?

GREGERS.   When he was here this morning, he said, "Hjalmar Ekdal is not the man you think he is."

HJALMAR.   Not the man—!

GREGERS.   "You'll find that out," he said.

HJALMAR.   Find out if I could be bought off for a price, eh—!

HEDVIG.   But Mother, what's this all about?

GINA.   Go and take your things off.

[HEDVIG, *close to tears, goes out the kitchen door.*]

GREGERS.   Yes, Hjalmar—now we'll see who's right, he or I.

HJALMAR [*slowly tearing the paper in half and putting both pieces on the table*].   That is my answer.

GREGERS.   What I expected.

HJALMAR [*going over to* GINA, *who is standing by the stove, and speaking quietly*].   And now no more pretenses. If that thing between you and him was all over when you—came to be so terribly in love with me, as you put it—then why did he give us the means to get married?

GINA.   Maybe he thought he could come and go here.

HJALMAR.   Is that all? Wasn't he afraid of a certain possibility?

GINA.   I don't know what you mean.

HJALMAR.   I want to know if—your child has the right to live under my roof.

GINA [*draws herself up, her eyes flashing*].   And you can ask that?

HJALMAR.   Just answer me this: does Hedvig belong to me—or—? Well!

GINA [*regarding him with chill defiance*].   I don't know.

HJALMAR [*with a slight quaver*].   You don't know!

GINA.   How would *I* know that? A woman of my sort—

HJALMAR [*softly, turning from her*].   Then I have nothing more to do in this house.

GREGERS.   You must think about this, Hjalmar.

HJALMAR [*putting on his overcoat*].   There's nothing to think about for a man like me.

GREGERS.   Oh, there's so very much to think about. You three have got to stay together if you're ever going to win through to a self-sacrificial, forgiving spirit.

HJALMAR.   I don't want that. Never, never! My hat! [*Takes his hat.*] My home is down in ruins around me. [*Breaks into tears.*] Gregers, I have no child!

HEDVIG [*who has opened the kitchen door*].   What are you saying! [*Running toward him.*] Daddy, Daddy!

GINA.   Now look!

HJALMAR.   Don't come near me, Hedvig! Keep away. I can't bear seeing you. Oh, the eyes! Good-bye. [*Starts for the door.*]

HEDVIG [*clinging fast to him and shrieking*].   Oh no! Oh no! Don't leave me.

GINA [*crying out*].   Watch the child, Hjalmar. Watch the child!

HJALMAR.   I won't. I can't. I've got to get out—away from all this! [*He tears himself loose from* HEDVIG *and goes out through the hall door.*]

HEDVIG [*with desperate eyes*].   He's left us, Mother! He's left us! He'll never come back again!

GINA.   Now don't cry, Hedvig. Daddy's coming back.

HEDVIG [*throws herself, sobbing, on the sofa*].   No, no, he'll never come home to us again.

GREGERS.   Will you believe I've wanted everything for the best, Mrs. Ekdal?

GINA.   Yes, I think I believe that—but God have mercy on you all the same.

HEDVIG [*lying on the sofa*].   I think I'll die from all this. What did I do to him? Mother, you've got to make him come home!

GINA.   Yes, yes, yes, just be calm, and I'll step out and look for him. [*Putting on her coat.*] Maybe he's gone down to Relling's. But now don't you lie there, wailing away. Will you promise?

HEDVIG [*sobbing convulsively*].   Yes, I'll be all right—if only Daddy comes back.

GREGERS [*to* GINA, *about to leave*].   Wouldn't it be better, though, to let him fight through his painful battle first?

GINA.   Oh, he can do that later. First of all, we've got to comfort the child. [*She goes out the hall door.*]

HEDVIG [*sitting up and drying her tears*].   Now you have to tell me what it's all about. Why does Daddy not want to see me any more?

GREGERS.   That's something you mustn't ask until you're big and grown-up.

HEDVIG [*catching her breath*].   But I can't go on being so horribly unhappy till I'm big and grown-up. I bet I know what it is. Perhaps I'm really not Daddy's child.

GREGERS [*disturbed*].   How could that ever be?

HEDVIG.   Mother could have found me. And now maybe Daddy's found out. I've read about these things.

GREGERS.   Well, but if that was the—

HEDVIG.   Yes, I think he could love me even so. Or maybe more. The wild duck was sent us as a present too, and I'm terribly fond of it, all the same.

GREGERS [*divertingly*].   Of course, the wild duck, that's true. Let's talk a bit about the wild duck, Hedvig.

HEDVIG.   The poor wild duck. He can't bear to see her again, either. Imagine, he wanted to wring her neck!

GREGERS.   Oh, he certainly wouldn't do that.

HEDVIG.   No, but that's what he said. And I think it was awful for Daddy to say, because each night I make a prayer for the wild duck and ask that she be delivered from death and everything evil.

GREGERS [*looking at her*].   Do you always say your prayers at night?

HEDVIG.   Uh-huh.

GREGERS.   Who taught you that?

HEDVIG.   I taught myself, and that was once when Daddy was so sick and had leeches on his neck, and then he said he was in the jaws of death.

GREGERS.   Oh yes?

HEDVIG.   So I said a prayer for him when I went to bed. And I've kept it up ever since.

GREGERS.   And now you pray for the wild duck, too?

HEDVIG.   I thought it was best to put the wild duck in, because she was ailing so at the start.

GREGERS.   Do you say morning prayers, too?

HEDVIG.   No, not at all.

GREGERS.   Why not morning prayers as well?

HEDVIG.   In the morning it's light, and so there's nothing more to be afraid of.

GREGERS.   And the wild duck you love so much—your father wants to wring her neck.

HEDVIG.   No. He said it would be the best thing for him if he did, but for my sake he would spare her; and that was good of Daddy.

GREGERS [*coming closer*].   But what if you now, of your own free will, sacrificed the wild duck for *his* sake.

HEDVIG [*springing up*].   The wild duck!

GREGERS.   What if you, in a sacrificing spirit, gave up the dearest thing you own and know in the whole world?

HEDVIG.   Do you think that would help?

GREGERS.   Try it, Hedvig.

HEDVIG [*softly, with shining eyes*].   Yes, I'll try it.

GREGERS.   And the strength of mind, do you think you have it?

HEDVIG.   I'll ask Grandpa to shoot the wild duck for me.

GREGERS.   Yes, do that. But not a word to your mother about all this!

HEDVIG.   Why not?

GREGERS.   She doesn't understand us.

HEDVIG.   The wild duck? I'll try it tomorrow, early.

[GINA *comes in through the hall door.*]

HEDVIG [*going toward her*].   Did you find him, Mother?

GINA.   No. But I heard he'd looked in downstairs and gotten Relling along.

GREGERS.   Are you sure of that?

GINA.   Yes, I asked the janitor's wife. And Molvik was with them, she said.

GREGERS.   And this, right when his mind needs nothing so much as to wrestle in solitude—!

GINA [*taking off her coat*].   Oh, men are strange ones, they are. God knows where Relling has led him! I ran over to Mrs. Eriksen's café, but they weren't there.

HEDVIG [*struggling with her tears*].   Oh, what if he never comes back again!

GREGERS.   He *will* come back. I'll get a message to him tomorrow, and then you'll see just how quick he comes. Believe that, Hedvig, and sleep well. Good night. [*He goes out the hall door.*]

HEDVIG [*throwing herself, sobbing, into* GINA's *arms*].   Mother, Mother!

GINA [*pats her on the back and sighs*].   Ah, me, Relling was right. That's the way it goes when these crazy people come around, summoning up their ideals.

ACT V

HJALMAR EKDAL's *studio. A cold, gray morning light filters in; wet snow lies on the huge panes of the skylight.* GINA, *wearing a pinafore, comes in from the kitchen, carrying a feather duster and a cleaning cloth, and makes for the living room door. At the same moment* HEDVIG *rushes in from the hallway.*

GINA [*stopping*].   Well?

HEDVIG.   You know, Mother, I'm pretty sure he's down at Relling's—

GINA.   There, you see!

HEDVIG.   'Cause the janitor's wife said she heard Relling had two others with him when he came in last night.

GINA.   That's about what I thought.

HEDVIG.   But it's still no good if he won't come up to us.

GINA.   At least I can go down there and talk with him.

[EKDAL, *in dressing gown and slippers, smoking a pipe, appears in the doorway to his room.*]

EKDAL.   Say, Hjalmar— Isn't Hjalmar home?

GINA.   No, he's gone out, I guess.

EKDAL.   So early? In a raging blizzard like this? Oh, well, never mind; I'll take my morning walk alone, that's all.

[*He pulls the loft door ajar,* HEDVIG *helping him. He goes in; she closes up after him.*]

HEDVIG [*lowering her voice*].   Just think, Mother, when Grandpa finds out that Daddy's leaving us.

GINA. Go on, Grandpa won't hear anything of the kind. It was a real stroke of providence he wasn't here yesterday in all that racket.

HEDVIG. Yes, but—

[GREGERS *comes in the hall entrance.*]

GREGERS. Well? Had any reports on him?

GINA. He should be down at Relling's, they tell me.

GREGERS. With Relling! Did he really go out with those fellows?

GINA. Apparently.

GREGERS. Yes, but he who needed so much to be alone to pull himself together—!

GINA. Yes, just as you say.

[RELLING *enters from the hall.*]

HEDVIG [*going toward him*]. Is Daddy with you?

GINA [*simultaneously*]. Is he there?

RELLING. Yes, of course he is.

HEDVIG. And you never told us!

RELLING. Oh, I'm a beast. But first of all, I had that other beast to manage—you know, the demonic one, him—and then, next, I fell so sound asleep that—

GINA. What's Hjalmar been saying today?

RELLING. He's said absolutely nothing.

HEDVIG. Hasn't he talked at all?

RELLING. Not a blessed word.

GREGERS. No, no, I can well understand that.

GINA. But what's he doing, then?

RELLING. He's laid out on the sofa, snoring.

GINA. Oh? Yes, Hjalmar's great at snoring.

HEDVIG. He's asleep? Can he sleep?

RELLING. Well, so it seems.

GREGERS. It's conceivable—when all that strife of spirit has torn him.

GINA. And then he's never been used to roaming around the streets at night.

HEDVIG. Maybe it's a good thing that he's getting some sleep, Mother.

GINA. I think so too. But then it's just as well we don't rouse him too soon. Thanks a lot, Relling. Now I've got to clean and straighten up here a bit, and then— Come and help me, Hedvig.

[GINA *and* HEDVIG *disappear into the living room.*]

GREGERS [*turning to* RELLING]. Have you an explanation for the spiritual upheaval taking place within Hjalmar Ekdal?

RELLING. For the life of me, I can't remember any spiritual upheaval in him.

GREGERS. What! At a time of crisis like this, when his life has been recast? How can you believe that a rare personality like Hjalmar—?

RELLING. Pah! Personality—him! If he's ever had a tendency toward anything so abnormal as what you call personality, it was ripped up, root and vine, by the time he was grown, and that's a fact.

GREGERS. That's rather surprising—with all the loving care he had as a child.

RELLING. From those two warped, hysterical maiden aunts, you mean?

GREGERS. I want to tell you they were women who always lived up to the highest ideals—yes, now of course you'll start mocking me again.

RELLING. No, I'm hardly in a mood for that. Besides, I'm well informed here; he's regurgitated any amount of rhetoric about his "twin soul-mothers." I really don't believe he has much to thank them for. Ekdal's misfortune is that in his circle he's always been taken for a shining light—

GREGERS. And isn't he, perhaps, exactly that? In his heart's core, I mean?

RELLING. I've never noticed anything of the kind. His father thinks so—but that's nothing; the old lieutenant's been a fool all his life.

GREGERS. He has, all his life, been a man with a childlike awareness; and that's something you just don't understand.

RELLING. Oh, sure! But back when our dear, sweet Hjalmar became a student of sorts, right away he got taken up by his classmates as the great beacon of the future. Oh, he was good-looking, the lout—pink and white—just the way little moon-eyed girls like boys. And then he had that excitable manner and that heart-winning tremor in his voice, and he was so cute and clever at declaiming other people's poems and ideas—

GREGERS [indignantly]. Is it Hjalmar Ekdal you're speaking of that way?

RELLING. Yes, with your permission. That's an inside look at him, this idol you're groveling in front of.

GREGERS. I really didn't think I was utterly blind.

RELLING. Well, you're not far from it. Because you're a sick man, you are. You know that.

GREGERS. There you're right.

RELLING. Oh yes. Your case has complications. First there's this virulent moralistic fever; and then something worse—you keep going off in deliriums of hero worship; you always have to have something to admire that's outside of yourself.

GREGERS. Yes, I certainly have to look for it outside myself.

RELLING. But you're so woefully wrong about these great miraculous beings you think you see and hear around you. You've simply come back to a squatter's cabin with your summons to the ideal; there's nobody solvent here.

GREGERS. If you've got no higher estimate of Hjalmar Ekdal than this, how can you ever enjoy seeing him day after day?

RELLING. Good Lord, I *am* supposed to be some kind of doctor, I'm ashamed to say. Well, then I ought to look after the poor sick people I live with.

GREGERS. Oh, come! Is Hjalmar Ekdal sick, too?

RELLING. Most of the world is sick, I'm afraid.

GREGERS. And what's your prescription for Hjalmar?

RELLING. My standard one. I try to keep up the vital lie in him.

GREGERS. The vital—lie? I don't think I heard—

RELLING. Oh yes, I said the vital lie. The vital lie, don't you see—that's the animating principle of life.

GREGERS. May I ask what kind of lie has infected Hjalmar?

RELLING. No, thanks, I don't betray secrets like that to quacks. You'd just be able to damage him all the more for me. My method is tested, though. I've also used it on Molvik. I made him "demonic." That was my remedy for him.

GREGERS.   Then he isn't demonic?

RELLING.   What the devil does it mean to be demonic? That's just some hogwash I thought up to keep life going in him. If I hadn't done that, the poor innocent mutt would have given in years ago to self-contempt and despair. And then take the old lieutenant! But he really discovered his own cure himself.

GREGERS.   Lieutenant Ekdal? How so?

RELLING.   Well, what do you think of this bear hunter going into a dark loft to stalk rabbits? There isn't a happier sportsman in the world than the old man when he's prowling around in that junkyard. Those four or five dried-out Christmas trees he's got—to him they're like all the green forests of Hoidal; the hens and the rooster—they're the game birds up in the fir tops; and the rabbits hopping across the floor—they're the bears that call up his youth again, out in the mountain air.

GREGERS.   Poor, unhappy old Ekdal, yes. He certainly had to pare down his early ideals.

RELLING.   While I remember it, Mr. Werle junior—don't use that exotic word *ideals*. Not when we've got a fine native word—*lies*.

GREGERS.   You're implying the two have something in common?

RELLING.   Yes, about like typhus and typhoid fever.

GREGERS.   Dr. Relling, I won't rest till I've gotten Hjalmar out of your clutches.

RELLING.   So much the worse for him. Deprive the average man of his vital lie, and you've robbed him of happiness as well. [*To* HEDVIG, *entering from the living room.*] Well, little wild-duck mother, now I'll go down and see if Papa's still lying and pondering his marvelous invention. [*He goes out the hall door.*]

GREGERS [*approaching* HEDVIG].   I can see by your face that it isn't done.

HEDVIG.   What? Oh, about the wild duck. No.

GREGERS.   Your courage failed you when the time came to act, I suppose.

HEDVIG.   No, it's not exactly that. But when I woke up this morning early and thought of what we talked about, then it seemed so strange to me.

GREGERS.   Strange?

HEDVIG.   Yes, I don't know— Last night, right at the time, there was something so beautiful about it, but after I'd slept and then thought it over, it didn't seem like so much.

GREGERS.   Ah, no, you couldn't grow up here without some taint in you.

HEDVIG.   I don't care about that; if only Daddy would come up, then—

GREGERS.   Oh, if only your eyes were really open to what makes life worth living—if only you had the true, joyful, courageous spirit of self-sacrifice, *then* you'd see him coming up to you. But I still have faith in you. [*He goes out the hall door.*]

[HEDVIG *wanders across the room, then starts into the kitchen. At that moment a knock comes on the loft door,* HEDVIG *goes over and opens it a space;* EKDAL *slips out, and she slides it shut again.*]

EKDAL.   Hm, a morning walk alone is no fun at all.

HEDVIG.   Don't you want to go hunting, Grandpa?

EKDAL.   The weather's no good for hunting. Awfully dark in there; you can hardly see ahead of you.

HEDVIG.   Don't you ever want to shoot at anything but rabbits?

EKDAL.   Aren't rabbits good enough, eh?

HEDVIG.   Yes, but the wild duck, say?

EKDAL.   Ha, ha! You're afraid I'll shoot the wild duck for you? Never in this world, dear. Never!

HEDVIG.   No, you couldn't do that. It must be hard to shoot wild ducks.

EKDAL.   Couldn't? I certainly could!

HEDVIG.   How would you go about it, Grandpa?—I don't mean with *my* wild duck, but with others.

EKDAL.   I'd be sure to shoot them in the breast, understand; that's the safest. And then they've got to be shot *against* the feathers, you see—not *with* the feathers.

HEDVIG.   They die then, Grandpa?

EKDAL.   Oh yes, they do indeed—if you shoot them right. Well, got to go in and clean up. Hm—you understand—hm. [*He goes into his room.*]

[HEDVIG *waits a moment, glances at the living room door, goes to the bookcase, stands on tiptoe, takes down the double-barreled pistol from the shelf and looks at it.* GINA, *with duster and cloth, comes in from the living room.* HEDVIG *hastily sets down the pistol, unnoticed.*]

GINA.   Don't mess with your father's things, Hedvig.

HEDVIG [*leaving the bookcase*].   I was just straightening up a little.

GINA.   Go out in the kitchen instead and make sure the coffee's still hot; I'll take a tray along to him when I go down.

[HEDVIG *goes out;* GINA *begins to dust and clean up the studio. After a moment the hall door is cautiously opened, and* HJALMAR *peers in. He wears his overcoat, but no hat. He is unwashed, with tousled, unruly hair; his eyes are dull and inert.*]

GINA [*standing rooted with duster in hand, looking at him*].   Don't tell me, Hjalmar—are you back after all?

HJALMAR [*steps in and answers in a thick voice*].   I'm back—but only for one moment.

GINA.   Oh yes, I'm sure of that. But my goodness—what a sight you are!

HJALMAR.   Sight?

GINA.   And then your good winter coat! Well, it's done for.

HEDVIG [*at the kitchen door*].   Mother, should I— [*Seeing* HJALMAR, *giving a squeal of delight, and running toward him.*] Oh, Daddy, Daddy!

HJALMAR [*turning from her and waving her off*].   Get away! Get away! [*To* GINA.] Make her get away from me, will you!

GINA [*in an undertone*].   Go in the living room, Hedvig.

[HEDVIG *silently goes out.*]

HJALMAR [*with a busy air, pulling out the table drawer*].   I must have my books along. Where are my books?

GINA.   What books?

HJALMAR.   My scientific works, of course—the technical journals I use for my invention.

GINA [*looking over the bookshelves*].   Are these them, the ones without covers?

HJALMAR.   Yes, exactly.

GINA [*putting a stack of booklets on the table.*]   Could I get Hedvig to cut the pages for you?

HJALMAR.   Nobody has to cut pages for me. [*A short silence.*]

GINA.   Then it's definite that you're moving out, Hjalmar?

HJALMAR [*rummaging among the books*].   Yes, that would seem to me self-evident.

GINA.   I see.

HJALMAR.   How could I go on here and have my heart shattered every hour of the day!

GINA.   God forgive you for thinking so badly of me.

HJALMAR.   Show me proof—

GINA.   I think *you're* the one to show proof.

HJALMAR.   After your kind of past? There are certain standards—I'd like to call them ideal standards—

GINA.   But Grandfather? What'll happen to him, poor dear?

HJALMAR.   I know my duty; that helpless old soul leaves with me. I'm going downtown and make arrangements—hm—[*Hesitantly.*] Did anybody find my hat on the stairs?

GINA.   No. Have you lost your hat?

HJALMAR.   I had it on, naturally, when I came in last night; I'm positive of that. But today I couldn't find it.

GINA.   My Lord, where did you go with those two stumblebums?

HJALMAR.   Oh, don't bother me with petty questions. Do you think I'm in a mood to remember details?

GINA.   I just hope you didn't catch cold, Hjalmar. [*She goes out into the kitchen.*]

HJALMAR [*muttering to himself in exasperation, as he empties the table drawer*].   You're a sneak, Relling! A barbarian, that's what! Oh, snake in the grass! If I could just get someone to strangle you! [*He puts some old letters to one side, discovers the torn deed of the day before, picks it up and examines the pieces. He hurriedly puts them down as* GINA *enters.*]

GINA. [*setting a breakfast tray on the table*].   Here's a drop of something hot, if you care for it. And there's some bread and butter and a little salt meat.

HJALMAR [*glancing at the tray*].   Salt meat? Never under this roof! Of course I haven't enjoyed going without food for nearly twenty-four hours; but that doesn't matter— My notes! My unfinished memoirs! Where can I find my journal and my important papers? [*Opens the living room door, then draws back.*] There she is again!

GINA.   Well, goodness, the child has to be somewhere.

HJALMAR.   Come out. [*He stands aside, and* HEDVIG, *terrified comes into the studio.*]

HJALMAR [*with his hand on the doorknob, says to* GINA].   These last moments I'm spending in my former home, I'd like to be free from intruders— [*Goes into the living room.*]

HEDVIG [*rushing to her mother, her voice hushed and trembling*].   Does he mean me?

GINA.   Stay in the kitchen, Hedvig. Or, no—go into your own room instead. [*Speaking to* HJALMAR *as she goes in to him.*] Just a minute, Hjalmar. Don't muss up the bureau like that; I know where everything is. [HEDVIG *stands for a moment as if frozen by fright and bewilderment, biting her lips to keep the tears back; then she clenches her fists convulsively.*]

HEDVIG [*softly*]. The wild duck. [*She steals over and takes the pistol from the shelf, sets the loft door ajar, slips in and draws the door shut after her.* HJALMAR *and* GINA *start arguing in the living room.*]

HJALMAR [*re-enters with some notebooks and old loose papers, which he lays on the table*]. Oh, what good is that traveling bag! I've got a thousand things to take with me.

GINA [*following with the traveling bag*]. So leave everything else for the time being, and just take a shirt and a pair of shorts with you.

HJALMAR. Phew! These agonizing preparations! [*Takes off his overcoat and throws it on the sofa.*]

GINA. And there's your coffee getting cold, too.

HJALMAR. Hm. [*Unthinkingly takes a sip and then another.*]

GINA. The hardest thing for you will be to find another room like that, big enough for all the rabbits.

HJALMAR. What! Do I have to take all the rabbits with me, too?

GINA. Yes, Grandfather couldn't live without the rabbits, I'm sure.

HJALMAR. He's simply got to get used to it. The joys of life *I* have to renounce are higher than rabbits.

GINA [*dusting the bookcase*]. Should I put your flute in the traveling bag?

HJALMAR. No. No flute for me. But give me the pistol!

GINA. You want your pistol along?

HJALMAR. Yes. My loaded pistol.

GINA [*looking for it*]. It's gone. He must have taken it inside.

HJALMAR. Is he in the loft?

GINA. Of course he's in the loft.

HJALMAR. Hm—lonely old man. [*He takes a piece of bread and butter, eats it, and finishes the cup of coffee.*]

GINA. Now if we only hadn't rented the room, you could have moved in there.

HJALMAR. I should stay on under the same roof as—! Never! Never!

GINA. But couldn't you put up in the living room just for a day or two? You've got everything you need in there.

HJALMAR. Never within these walls!

GINA. Well, how about down with Relling and Molvik?

HJALMAR. Don't mention those barbarians' names! I can almost lose my appetite just thinking about them. Oh no, I've got to go out in sleet and snow —tramp from house to house and seek shelter for Father and me.

GINA. But you haven't any hat, Hjalmar! You've lost your hat.

HJALMAR. Oh, those two vermin, wallowing in sin! The hat will have to be bought. [*Taking another piece of bread and butter.*] Someone's got to make arrangements. I certainly don't intend to risk my life. [*Looking for something on the tray.*]

GINA. What are you looking for?

HJALMAR. Butter.

GINA. Butter's coming right up. [*Goes into the kitchen.*]

HJALMAR [*calling after her.*] Oh, never mind; I can just as easily eat dry bread.

GINA [*bringing in a butter dish*].   Look. It's fresh today. [*She passes him another cup of coffee. He sits on the sofa, spreads more butter on the bread, eats and drinks a moment in silence.*]

HJALMAR.   Could I—without being annoyed by anybody—anybody at all —put up in the living room just for a day or two?

GINA.   Yes, of course you could, if you want to.

HJALMAR.   Because I can't see any possibility of getting all Father's things out in one trip.

GINA.   And then there's this, too, that you've first got to tell him you're not living with us any longer.

HJALMAR [*pushing the coffee cup away*].   That too, yes. All these intricate affairs to unravel. I've got to clear my thinking; I need a breathing spell; I can't shoulder all these burdens in one day.

GINA.   No, and not when the weather's like it is out.

HJALMAR [*picking up* WERLE's *letter*].   I see this letter's still kicking around.

GINA.   Yes, *I* haven't touched it.

HJALMAR.   This trash is nothing to me—

GINA.   Well, I'm not going to use it for anything.

HJALMAR.   All the same, there's no point in throwing it around helter-skelter. In all the confusion of my moving, it could easily—

GINA.   I'll take good care of it, Hjalmar.

HJALMAR.   First and foremost, the deed of gift is Father's; it's really his affair whether or not he wants to use it.

GINA [*sighing*].   Yes, poor old Father—

HJALMAR.   Just for safety's sake—where would I find some paste?

GINA [*going to the bookcase*].   Here's the pastepot.

HJALMAR.   And then a brush.

GINA.   Here's a brush, too. [*Bringing both.*]

HJALMAR [*taking a pair of scissors*].   A strip of paper down the back, that's all. [*Cutting and pasting.*] Far be it from me to take liberties with another's property—least of all, a penniless old man's. No, nor with—the other person's. There, now. Let it lie a while. And when it's dry, then take it away. I don't want to set eyes on that document again. Ever!

[GREGERS *enters from the hall.*]

GREGERS [*somewhat surprised*].   What? Are you lounging in here, Hjalmar?

HJALMAR [*springing up*].   I was overcome by fatigue.

GREGERS.   Still, you've had breakfast, I see.

HJALMAR.   The body makes its claims now and then too.

GREGERS.   What have you decided to do?

HJALMAR.   For a man like me there's only one way open. I'm in the process of assembling my most important things. But that takes time, don't you know.

GINA [*a bit impatient*].   Should I get the room ready for you, or should I pack your bag?

HJALMAR [*after a vexed glance at* GREGERS].   Pack—and get the room ready!

GINA [*taking the traveling bag*]. All right, then I'll put in the shirt and the rest. [*She goes into the living room, shutting the door behind her.*]

GREGERS [*after a short silence*]. I never dreamed that things would end like this. Is it really necessary for you to leave house and home?

HJALMAR [*pacing restlessly about*]. What would you have me do? I wasn't made to be unhappy, Gregers. I've got to have it snug and secure and peaceful around me.

GREGERS. But why can't you, then? Give it a try. Now I'd say you have solid ground to build on—so make a fresh start. And don't forget you have your invention to live for, too.

HJALMAR. Oh, don't talk about the invention. That seems such a long way off.

GREGERS. Oh?

HJALMAR. Good Lord, yes. What would you really have me invent? Other people have invented so much already. It gets more difficult every day—

GREGERS. And you've put so much work in it.

HJALMAR. It was that dissolute Relling who got me started.

GREGERS. Relling?

HJALMAR. Yes, he was the one who first made me aware that I had a real talent for inventing something in photography.

GREGERS. Aha—that was Relling!

HJALMAR. Oh, I was so blissfully happy as a result. Not so much from the invention itself, but because Hedvig believed in it—believed in it with all the power and force of a child's mind. Yes, in other words, fool that I am, I've gone around imagining that she believed in it.

GREGERS. You can't really think that Hedvig could lie to you!

HJALMAR. Now I can think anything. It's Hedvig that ruins it all. She's managed to blot the sun right out of my life.

GREGERS. Hedvig! You mean Hedvig? How could she ever do that?

HJALMAR [*without answering*]. How inexpressibly I loved that child! How inexpressibly happy I was whenever I came home to my poor rooms and she came flying to meet me with those sweet, fluttering eyes. I was so unspeakably fond of her—and so I dreamed and deluded myself into thinking that she, too, was fond of me beyond words.

GREGERS. Can you call *that* just a delusion?

HJALMAR. How can I tell? I can't get anything out of Gina; and besides, she has no feeling at all for the ideal phase of these complications. But with you, Gregers, I feel impelled to open my mind. There's this horrible doubt— maybe Hedvig never really, truly has loved me.

GREGERS. She may perhaps give you proof that she has. [*Listening.*] What's that? I thought I heard the wild duck cry.

HJALMAR. The duck's quacking. Father's in the loft.

GREGERS. Is he? [*His face radiates joy.*] I tell you, you may yet have proof that your poor, misjudged Hedvig loves you!

HJALMAR. Oh, what proof could she give me? I don't dare hope to be reassured from that quarter.

GREGERS. Hedvig's completely free of deceit.

HJALMAR. Oh, Gregers, that's just what I can't be sure of. Who knows what Gina and this Mrs. Sørby have whispered and gossiped about in all the times they've sat here? And Hedvig uses her ears, you know. Maybe the deed of gift wasn't such a surprise, after all. In fact, I seemed to get that impression.

GREGERS.   What is this spirit that's gotten into you?

HJALMAR.   I've had my eyes opened. Just wait—you'll see; the deed of gift is only the beginning. Mrs. Sørby has always cared a lot for Hedvig, and now she has the power to do what she wants for the child. They can take her away from me any time they like.

GREGERS.   You're the last person in the world Hedvig would leave.

HJALMAR.   Don't be too sure of that. If they stand beckoning her with all they have—? Oh, I who've loved her so inexpressibly! I who'd find my highest joy in taking her tenderly by the hand and leading her as one leads a child terrified of the dark through a huge, empty room! I can feel it now with such gnawing certainty; the poor photographer up in this attic has never meant much to her. She's merely been clever to keep on a good footing with him till the right time came.

GREGERS.   You really don't believe that, Hjalmar.

HJALMAR.   The worst thing is precisely that I don't know what to believe —that I'll never know. But can you honestly doubt that it's just what I'm saying? [*With a bitter laugh.*] Ah, you're just too idealistic, my dear Gregers! Suppose the others come with their hands full of riches and call out to the child: Leave him. Life waits for you here with us—

GREGERS [*quickly*].   Yes, then what?

HJALMAR.   If I asked her then: Hedvig, are you willing to give up life for me? [*Laughs derisively.*] Yes, thanks—you'd hear all right what answer I'd get!

[*A pistol shot is heard in the loft.*]

GREGERS [*with a shout of joy*].   Hjalmar!

HJALMAR.   Hear that. He's got to go hunting as well.

GINA [*coming in*].   Oh, Hjalmar, it sounds like Grandfather's shooting up the loft by himself.

HJALMAR.   I'll take a look—

GREGERS [*animated and exalted*].   Wait now! Do you know what that was?

HJALMAR.   Of course I know.

GREGERS.   No, you don't know. But *I* do. That was the proof!

HJALMAR.   What proof?

GREGERS.   That was a child's sacrifice. She's had your father shoot the wild duck.

HJALMAR.   Shoot the wild duck!

GINA.   No, really—!

HJALMAR.   What for?

GREGERS.   She wanted to sacrifice to you the best thing she had in the world, because she thought then you'd have to love her again.

HJALMAR [*stirred, gently*].   Ah, that child!

GINA.   Yes, the things she thinks of!

GREGERS.   She only wants your love again, Hjalmar; she felt she couldn't live without it.

GINA [*struggling with tears*].   There you are, Hjalmar.

HJALMAR.   Gina, where's she gone?

GINA [*sniffling*].   Poor thing. I guess she's out in the kitchen.

HJALMAR [*going over and flinging the kitchen door open*].   Hedvig, come! Come here to me! [*Looking about.*] No, she's not there.

GINA.   Then she's in her own little room.

HJALMAR [*out of sight*].   No, she's not there either. [*Coming back in.*] She may have gone out.

GINA.   Yes, you didn't want her around anywhere in the house.

HJALMAR.   Oh, if only she comes home soon—so I can just let her know—! Things will work out now, Gregers—for now I really believe we can start life over again.

GREGERS [*quietly*].   I knew it; through the child everything rights itself.

[EKDAL *appears at the door to his room; he is in full uniform and is absorbed in buckling his sword.*]

HJALMAR [*astonished*].   Father! Are you there?

GINA.   Were you out gunning in your room?

EKDAL [*approaching angrily*].   So you've been hunting alone, eh, Hjalmar?

HJALMAR [*baffled and anxious*].   Then it wasn't you who fired a shot in the loft?

EKDAL.   Me, shoot? Hm!

GREGERS [*shouting to* HJALMAR].   She's shot the wild duck herself!

HJALMAR.   What is all this! [*Rushes to the loft doors, throws them open, looks in and cries:*] Hedvig!

GINA [*running to the door*].   Lord, what now!

HJALMAR [*going in*].   She's lying on the floor!

GINA [*simultaneously*].   Hedvig! [*Going into the loft.*] No, no, no!

EKDAL.   Ha, ha! So she's a hunter, too.

[HJALMAR, GINA, *and* GREGERS *carry* HEDVIG *into the studio; her right hand hangs down and her fingers curve tightly about the pistol.*]

HJALMAR [*distraught*].   The pistol's gone off. She's wounded herself. Call for help! Help!

GINA [*running into the hall and calling downstairs*].   Relling! Relling! Dr. Relling, come up as quick as you can!

EKDAL [*hushed*].   The woods take revenge.

HJALMAR [*on his knees by her*].   She's just coming to now. She's coming to now—oh yes, yes.

GINA [*who has returned*].   Where is she wounded? I can't see anything—

[RELLING *hurries in, and right after him,* MOLVIK, *who is without vest or tie, his dress coat open.*]

RELLING.   What's up here?

GINA.   They say Hedvig shot herself.

HJALMAR.   Come here and help.

RELLING.   Shot herself! [*He shoves the table to one side and begins to examine her.*]

HJALMAR [*kneeling still, looking anxiously up at him*].   It can't be serious? Huh, Relling? She's hardly bleeding. It can't be serious?

RELLING.   How did this happen?

HJALMAR.   Oh, how do I know—

GINA.   She wanted to shoot the wild duck.

RELLING.   The wild duck?

HJALMAR.   The pistol must have gone off.

RELLING.   Hm. I see.

EKDAL.   The woods take revenge. But I'm not scared, even so. [*He goes into the loft, shutting the door after him.*]

HJALMAR.   But Relling—why don't you say something?

RELLING.   You can see for yourself that Hedvig is dead.

GINA [*breaking into tears*].   Oh, my child, my child!

GREGERS [*hoarsely*].   In the depths of the sea—

HJALMAR [*jumping up*].   No, no she *must* live! Oh, in God's name, Relling—just for a moment—just enough so I can tell her how inexpressibly I loved her all the time!

RELLING.   It's reached the heart. Internal hemorrhage. She died on the spot.

HJALMAR.   And I drove her from me like an animal! And she crept terrified into the loft and died out of love for me. [*Sobbing.*] Never to make it right again! Never to let her know—! [*Clenching his fists and crying to heaven.*] Oh, you up there—if you *do* exist. Why have you done this to me!

GINA.   Hush, hush, you mustn't carry on like that. We just didn't deserve to keep her, I guess.

MOLVIK.   The child isn't dead; she sleepeth.

RELLING.   Rubbish!

HJALMAR [*becoming calm, going over to the sofa to stand, arms folded, looking at* HEDVIG].   There she lies, so stiff and still.

RELLING [*trying to remove the pistol*].   She holds it so tight, so tight.

GINA.   No, no, Relling, don't break her grip. Let the gun be.

HJALMAR.   She should have it with her.

GINA.   Yes, let her. But the child shouldn't lie displayed out here. She ought to go into her own little room, she should. Give me a hand, Hjalmar.

[HJALMAR *and* GINA *lift* HEDVIG *between them.*]

HJALMAR [*as they carry her off*].   Oh, Gina, Gina, how can you bear it!

GINA.   We must try to help each other. For now she belongs to us both, you know.

MOLVIK [*outstretching his arms and mumbling*].   Praise be to God. Dust to dust, dust to dust—

RELLING [*in a whisper*].   Shut up, you fool; you're drunk.

[HJALMAR *and* GINA *carry the body out through the kitchen door.* RELLING *closes it after them.* MOLVIK *steals out the hall door.*]

RELLING [*going over to* GREGERS].   Nobody's ever going to sell me the idea that this was an accident.

GREGERS [*who has stood in a convulsive fit of horror*].   Who can say how this awful thing happened?

RELLING.   There are powder burns on her blouse. She must have aimed the pistol point-blank at her breast and fired.

GREGERS.   Hedvig did not die in vain. Did you notice how grief freed the greatness in him?

RELLING.   The grief of death brings out greatness in almost everyone. But how long do you think this glory will last with *him*?

GREGERS.   I should think it would last and grow all his life.

RELLING.   In less than a year little Hedvig will be nothing more to him than a pretty theme for recitations.

GREGERS.   You dare say that about Hjalmar Ekdal!

RELLING.   We'll be lectured on this when the first grass shows on her grave. Then you can hear him spewing out phrases about "the child torn too soon from her father's heart," and you'll have your chance to watch him souse himself in conceit and self-pity. Wait and see.

GREGERS.   If you're right, and I'm wrong, then life isn't worth living.

RELLING.   Oh, life would be good in spite of all, if we only could have some peace from these damned shysters who come badgering us poor people with their "summons to the ideal."

GREGERS [staring straight ahead].   In that case, I'm glad my destiny is what it is.

RELLING.   Beg pardon—but what is your destiny?

GREGERS [about to leave].   To be the thirteenth man at the table.

RELLING.   Oh, the hell you say.

SIX CHARACTERS
IN SEARCH
OF AN AUTHOR
A Comedy in the Making

LUIGI PIRANDELLO
1867–1936

CHARACTERS OF THE COMEDY IN THE MAKING

THE FATHER
THE MOTHER
THE STEPDAUGHTER

THE SON
MADAME PACE
THE BOY } *These two do*
THE CHILD } *not speak*

ACTORS OF THE COMPANY

THE MANAGER
LEADING LADY
LEADING MAN
SECOND LADY LEAD
L'INGÉNUE
JUVENILE LEAD

OTHER ACTORS AND ACTRESSES
PROPERTY MAN
PROMPTER
MACHINIST
MANAGER'S SECRETARY
DOORKEEPER
SCENE SHIFTERS

Daytime: The Stage of a Theater

ACT I

N.B. *The Comedy is without acts or scenes. The performance is interrupted once, without the curtain being lowered, when the* MANAGER *and the chief characters withdraw to arrange the scenario. A second interruption of the action takes place when, by mistake, the stage hands let the curtain down.*

The spectators will find the curtain raised and the stage as it usually is during the daytime. It will be half dark, and empty, so that from the beginning the public may have the impression of an impromptu performance.

PROMPTER's box and a small table and chair for the MANAGER.

Two other small tables and several chairs scattered about as during rehearsals.

The ACTORS *and* ACTRESSES *of the company enter from the back of the stage:*

First one, then another, then two together: nine or ten in all. They are about to rehearse a Pirandello play: Mixing It Up. Some of the company move off towards their dressing rooms. The PROMPTER *who has the "book" under his arm, is waiting for the* MANAGER *in order to begin the rehearsal.*

The ACTORS *and* ACTRESSES, *some standing, some sitting, chat and smoke. One perhaps reads a paper; another cons his part.*

Finally, the MANAGER *enters and goes to the table prepared for him. His* SECRETARY *brings him his mail, through which he glances. The* PROMPTER *takes his seat, turns on a light, and opens the "book."*

THE MANAGER [*throwing a letter down on the table*]. I can't see. [*To* PROPERTY MAN.] Let's have a little light, please!

PROPERTY MAN. Yes sir, yes, at once. [*A light comes down on to the stage.*]

THE MANAGER [*clapping his hands*]. Come along! Come along! Second act of *Mixing It Up*. [*Sits down.*]

[*The* ACTORS *and* ACTRESSES *go from the front of the stage to the wings, all except the three who are to begin the rehearsal.*]

THE PROMPTER [*reading the "book"*]. "Leo Gala's house. A curious room serving as dining-room and study."

THE MANAGER [*to* PROPERTY MAN]. Fix up the old red room.

PROPERTY MAN [*noting it down*]. Red set. All right!

THE PROMPTER [*continuing to read from the "book"*]. "Table already laid and writing desk with books and papers. Bookshelves. Exit rear to Leo's bedroom. Exit left to kitchen. Principal exit to right."

THE MANAGER [*energetically*]. Well, you understand: The principal exit over there; here the kitchen. [*Turning to* ACTOR *who is to play the part of Socrates.*] You make your entrances and exits here. [*To* PROPERTY MAN.] The baize doors at the rear, and curtains.

PROPERTY MAN [*noting it down*]. Right-o!

PROMPTER [*reading as before*]. "When the curtain rises, Leo Gala, dressed in cook's cap and apron is busy beating an egg in a cup. Philip, also dressed as a cook, is beating another egg. Guido Venanzi is seated and listening."

LEADING MAN [*to* MANAGER]. Excuse me, but must I absolutely wear a cook's cap?

THE MANAGER [*annoyed*].   I imagine so. It says so there anyway. [*Pointing to the "book."*]

LEADING MAN.   But it's ridiculous!

THE MANAGER.   Ridiculous? Ridiculous? Is it my fault if France won't send us any more good comedies, and we are reduced to putting on Pirandello's works, where nobody understands anything, and where the author plays the fool with us all? [*The* ACTORS *grin. The* MANAGER *goes to* LEADING MAN *and shouts.*] Yes sir, you put on the cook's cap and beat eggs. Do you suppose that with all this egg-beating business you are on an ordinary stage? Get that out of your head. You represent the shell of the eggs you are beating! [*Laughter and comments among the* ACTORS.] Silence! and listen to my explanations, please! [*To* LEADING MAN.] "The empty form of reason without the fullness of instinct, which is blind"—You stand for reason, your wife is instinct. It's a mixing up of the parts, according to which you who act your own part become the puppet of yourself. Do you understand?

LEADING MAN.   I'm hanged if I do.

THE MANAGER.   Neither do I. But let's get on with it. It's sure to be a glorious failure anyway. [*Confidentially.*] But I say, please face three-quarters. Otherwise, what with the abstruseness of the dialogue, and the public that won't be able to hear you, the whole thing will go to hell. Come on! come on!

PROMPTER.   Pardon sir, may I get into my box? There's a bit of a draught.

THE MANAGER.   Yes, yes, of course!

[*At this point, the* DOORKEEPER *has entered from the stage door and advances towards the* MANAGER's *table, taking off his braided cap. During this manœuver, the* SIX CHARACTERS *enter, and stop by the door at back of stage, so that when the* DOORKEEPER *is about to announce their coming to the* MANAGER, *they are already on the stage. A tenuous light surrounds them, almost as if irradiated by them—the faint breath of their fantastic reality.*

This light will disappear when they come forward towards the ACTORS. *They preserve, however, something of the dream lightness in which they seem almost suspended; but this does not detract from the essential reality of their forms and expressions.*

He who is known as the FATHER *is a man of about 50: hair, reddish in color, thin at the temples; he is not bald, however; thick moustaches, falling over his still fresh mouth, which often opens in an empty and uncertain smile. He is fattish, pale; with an especially wide forehead. He has blue, oval-shaped eyes, very clear and piercing. Wears light trousers and a dark jacket. He is alternately mellifluous and violent in his manner.*

The MOTHER *seems crushed and terrified as if by an intolerable weight of shame and abasement. She is dressed in modest black and wears a thick widow's veil of crêpe. When she lifts this, she reveals a wax-like face. She always keeps her eyes downcast.*

The STEPDAUGHTER *is dashing, almost impudent, beautiful. She wears mourning too, but with great elegance. She shows contempt for the timid half-frightened manner of the wretched* BOY (*14 years old, and also dressed in black*); *on the other hand, she displays a lively tenderness for her little sister, the* CHILD (*about four*), *who is dressed in white, with a black silk sash at the waist.*

The SON (*22*) *tall, severe in his attitude of contempt for the* FATHER, *supercilious and indifferent to the* MOTHER. *He looks as if he had come on the stage against his will.*]

DOORKEEPER [*cap in hand*]. Excuse me, sir . . .

THE MANAGER [*rudely*]. Eh? What is it?

DOORKEEPER [*timidly*]. These people are asking for you, sir.

THE MANAGER [*furious*]. I am rehearsing, and you know perfectly well no one's allowed to come in during rehearsals! [*Turning to the* CHARACTERS.] Who are you, please? What do you want?

THE FATHER [*coming forward a little, followed by the others who seem embarrassed*]. As a matter of fact . . . we have come here in search of an author. . . .

THE MANAGER [*half angry, half amazed*]. An author? What author?

THE FATHER. Any author, sir.

THE MANAGER. But there's no author here. We are not rehearsing a new piece.

THE STEPDAUGHTER [*vivaciously*]. So much the better, so much the better! We can be your new piece.

AN ACTOR [*coming forward from the others*]. Oh, do you hear that?

THE FATHER [*to* STEPDAUGHTER]. Yes, but if the author isn't here . . . [*to* MANAGER.] . . . unless you would be willing . . .

THE MANAGER. You are trying to be funny.

THE FATHER. No, for Heaven's sake, what are you saying? We bring you a drama, sir.

THE STEPDAUGHTER. We may be your fortune.

THE MANAGER. Will you oblige me by going away? We haven't time to waste with mad people.

THE FATHER [*mellifluously*]. Oh sir, you know well that life is full of infinite absurdities, which, strangely enough, do not even need to appear plausible, since they are true.

THE MANAGER. What the devil is he talking about?

THE FATHER. I say that to reverse the ordinary process may well be considered a madness: that is, to create credible situations, in order that they may appear true. But permit me to observe that if this be madness, it is the sole *raison d'être* of your profession, gentlemen. [*The* ACTORS *look hurt and perplexed.*]

THE MANAGER [*getting up and looking at him*]. So our profession seems to you one worthy of madmen then?

THE FATHER. Well, to make seem true that which isn't true . . . without any need . . . for a joke as it were . . . Isn't that your mission, gentlemen: to give life to fantastic characters on the stage?

THE MANAGER [*interpreting the rising anger of the* COMPANY]. But I would beg you to believe, my dear sir, that the profession of the comedian is a noble one. If today, as things go, the playwrights give us stupid comedies to play and puppets to represent instead of men, remember we are proud to have given life to immortal works here on these very boards! [*The* ACTORS, *satisfied, applaud their* MANAGER.]

THE FATHER [*interrupting furiously*]. Exactly, perfectly, to living beings more alive than those who breathe and wear clothes: being less real perhaps, but truer! I agree with you entirely. [*The* ACTORS *look at one another in amazement.*]

THE MANAGER.   But what do you mean? Before, you said . . .

THE FATHER.   No, excuse me, I meant it for you, sir, who were crying out that you had no time to lose with madmen, while no one better than yourself knows that nature uses the instrument of human fantasy in order to pursue her high creative purpose.

THE MANAGER.   Very well—but where does all this take us?

THE FATHER.   Nowhere! It is merely to show you that one is born to life in many forms, in many shapes, as tree, or as stone, as water, as butterfly, or as woman. So one may also be born a character in a play.

THE MANAGER [*with feigned comic dismay*].   So you and these other friends of yours have been born characters?

THE FATHER.   Exactly, and alive as you see! [MANAGER *and* ACTORS *burst out laughing.*]

THE FATHER [*hurt*].   I am sorry you laugh, because we carry in us a drama, as you can guess from this woman here veiled in black.

THE MANAGER [*losing patience at last and almost indignant*].   Oh, chuck it! Get away please! Clear out of here! [*To* PROPERTY MAN.] For Heaven's sake, turn them out!

THE FATHER [*resisting*].   No, no, look here, we . . .

THE MANAGER [*roaring*].   We come here to work, you know.

LEADING ACTOR.   One cannot let oneself be made such a fool of.

THE FATHER [*determined, coming forward*].   I marvel at your incredulity, gentlemen. Are you not accustomed to see the characters created by an author spring to life in yourselves and face each other? Just because there is no "book" [*pointing to the* PROMPTER's *box.*] which contains us, you refuse to believe . . .

THE STEPDAUGHTER [*advances towards* MANAGER, *smiling and coquettish*]. Believe me, we are really six most interesting characters, sir; side-tracked however.

THE FATHER.   Yes, that is the word! [*To* MANAGER *all at once.*] In the sense, that is, that the author who created us alive no longer wished, or was no longer able, materially to put us into a work of art. And this was a real crime, sir; because he who has had the luck to be born a character can laugh even at death. He cannot die. The man, the writer, the instrument of the creation will die, but his creation does not die. And to live for ever, it does not need to have extraordinary gifts or to be able to work wonders. Who was Sancho Panza? Who was Don Abbondio? Yet they live eternally because—live germs as they were—they had the fortune to find a fecundating matrix, a fantasy which could raise and nourish them: make them live for ever!

THE MANAGER.   That is quite all right. But what do you want here, all of you?

THE FATHER.   We want to live.

THE MANAGER [*ironically*].   For Eternity?

THE FATHER.   No, sir, only for a moment . . . in you.

AN ACTOR.   Just listen to him!

LEADING LADY.   They want to live, in us! . . .

JUVENILE LEAD [*pointing to the* STEPDAUGHTER]. I've no objection, as far as that one is concerned!

THE FATHER.   Look here! Look here! The comedy has to be made. [*To the* MANAGER.] But if you and your actors are willing, we can soon concert it among ourselves.

THE MANAGER [*annoyed*].   But what do you want to concert? We don't go in for concerts here. Here we play dramas and comedies!

THE FATHER.   Exactly! That is just why we have come to you.

THE MANAGER.   And where is the "book"?

THE FATHER.   It is in us! [*The* ACTORS *laugh*.] The drama is in us, and we are the drama. We are impatient to play it. Our inner passion drives us on to this.

THE STEPDAUGHTER [*disdainful, alluring, treacherous, full of impudence*]. My passion, sir! Ah, if you only knew! My passion for him! [*Points to the* FATHER *and makes a pretence of embracing him. Then she breaks out into a loud laugh*.]

THE FATHER [*angrily*].   Behave yourself! And please don't laugh in that fashion.

THE STEPDAUGHTER.   With your permission, gentlemen, I, who am a two months' orphan, will show you how I can dance and sing. [*Sings and then dances* "Prenez garde à Tchou-Tchin-Tchou."]

> Les chinois sont un peuple malin,
> De Shanghaï à Pékin,
> Ils ont mis des écriteaux partout:
> Prenez garde à Tchou-Tchin-Tchou.[1]

ACTORS *and* ACTRESSES.   Bravo! Well done! Tip-top!

THE MANAGER.   Silence! This isn't a café concert, you know! [*Turning to the* FATHER *in consternation*.] Is she mad?

THE FATHER.   Mad? No, she's worse than mad.

THE STEPDAUGHTER [*to* MANAGER].   Worse? Worse? Listen! Stage this drama for us at once! Then you will see that at a certain moment I . . . when this little darling here . . . [*Takes the* CHILD *by the hand and leads her to the* MANAGER.] Isn't she a dear? [*Takes her up and kisses her.*] Darling! Darling! [*Puts her down again and adds feelingly.*] Well, when God suddenly takes this dear little child away from that poor mother there; and this imbecile here [*seizing hold of the* BOY *roughly and pushing him forward*] does the stupidest things, like the fool he is, you will see me run away. Yes, gentlemen, I shall be off. But the moment hasn't arrived yet. After what has taken place between him and me [*indicates the* FATHER *with a horrible wink*] I can't remain any longer in this society, to have to witness the anguish of this mother here for that fool . . . [*Indicates the* SON.] Look at him! Look at him! See how indifferent, how frigid he is, because he is the legitimate son. He despises me, despises him [*pointing to the* BOY], despises this baby here; because . . . we are bastards. [*Goes to the* MOTHER *and embraces her.*] And he doesn't want to recognize her as his mother —she who is the common mother of us all. He looks down upon her as if she were only the mother of us three bastards. Wretch! [*She says all this very*

---

[1] The Chinese are clever people,
From Shanghai to Peking,
They've put billboards everywhere:
Hearken to Tchou-Tchin-Tchou.
(French ditty)

rapidly, excitedly. At the word "bastards" she raises her voice, and almost spits out the final "Wretch!"]

THE MOTHER [to the MANAGER, in anguish]. In the name of these two little children, I beg you . . . [She grows faint and is about to fall.] Oh God!

THE FATHER [coming forward to support her as do some of the ACTORS]. Quick a chair, a chair for this poor widow!

THE ACTORS. Is it true? Has she really fainted?

THE MANAGER. Quick, a chair! Here!

[One of the ACTORS brings a chair, the others proffer assistance. The MOTHER tries to prevent the FATHER from lifting the veil which covers her face.]

THE FATHER. Look at her! Look at her!

THE MOTHER. No, stop; stop it please!

THE FATHER [raising her veil]. Let them see you!

THE MOTHER [rising and covering her face with her hands, in desperation]. I beg you, sir, to prevent this man from carrying out his plan which is loathsome to me.

THE MANAGER [dumbfounded]. I don't understand at all. What is the situation? Is this lady your wife? [To the FATHER.]

THE FATHER. Yes, gentlemen: my wife!

THE MANAGER. But how can she be a widow if you are alive? [The ACTORS find relief for their astonishment in a loud laugh.]

THE FATHER. Don't laugh! Don't laugh like that, for Heaven's sake. Her drama lies just here in this: she has had a lover, a man who ought to be here.

THE MOTHER [with a cry]. No! No!

THE STEPDAUGHTER. Fortunately for her, he is dead. Two months ago as I said. We are in mourning, as you see.

THE FATHER. He isn't here you see, not because he is dead. He isn't here —look at her a moment and you will understand—because her drama isn't a drama of the love of two men for whom she was incapable of feeling anything except possibly a little gratitude—gratitude not for me but for the other. She isn't a woman, she is a mother, and her drama—powerful sir, I assure you—lies, as a matter of fact, all in these four children she has had by two men.

THE MOTHER. I had them? Have you got the courage to say that I wanted them? [To the COMPANY.] It was his doing. It was he who gave me that other man, who forced me to go away with him.

THE STEPDAUGHTER. It isn't true.

THE MOTHER [startled]. Not true, isn't it?

THE STEPDAUGHTER. No, it isn't true, it just isn't true.

THE MOTHER. And what can you know about it?

THE STEPDAUGHTER. It isn't true. Don't believe it. [To MANAGER] Do you know why she says so? For that fellow there. [Indicates the SON.] She tortures herself, destroys herself on account of the neglect of that son there; and she wants him to believe that if she abandoned him when he was only two years old, it was because he [indicates the FATHER] made her do so.

THE MOTHER [vigorously]. He forced me to it, and I call God to witness it. [To the MANAGER.] Ask him [indicates the FATHER] if it isn't true. Let him speak. You [to DAUGHTER] are not in a position to know anything about it.

THE STEPDAUGHTER. I know you lived in peace and happiness with my father while he lived. Can you deny it?

THE MOTHER.   No, I don't deny it . . .

THE STEPDAUGHTER.   He was always full of affection and kindness for you.
[*To the* BOY, *angrily*.] It's true, isn't it? Tell them! Why don't you speak, you
little fool?

THE MOTHER.   Leave the poor boy alone. Why do you want to make me
appear ungrateful, daughter? I don't want to offend your father. I have answered
him that I didn't abandon my house and my son through any fault of mine,
nor from any wilful passion.

THE FATHER.   It is true. It was my doing.

LEADING MAN [*to the* COMPANY].   What a spectacle!

LEADING LADY.   We are the audience this time.

JUVENILE LEAD.   For once, in a way.

THE MANAGER [*beginning to get really interested*].   Let's hear them out.
Listen!

THE SON.   Oh yes, you're going to hear a fine bit now. He will talk to you
of the Demon of Experiment.

THE FATHER.   You are a cynical imbecile. I've told you so already a hundred times. [*To the* MANAGER.] He tries to make fun of me on account of this
expression which I have found to excuse myself with.

THE SON [*with disgust*].   Yes, phrases! phrases!

THE FATHER.   Phrases! Isn't everyone consoled when faced with a trouble
or fact he doesn't understand, by a word, some simple word, which tells us
nothing and yet calms us?

THE STEPDAUGHTER.   Even in the case of remorse. In fact, especially then.

THE FATHER.   Remorse? No, that isn't true. I've done more than use words
to quieten the remorse in me.

THE STEPDAUGHTER.   Yes, there was a bit of money too. Yes, yes, a bit of
money. There were the hundred lire he was about to offer me in payment,
gentlemen. . . . [*Sensation of horror among the* ACTORS.]

THE SON [*to the* STEPDAUGHTER].   This is vile.

THE STEPDAUGHTER.   Vile? There they were in a pale blue envelope on a
little mahogany table in the back of Madame Pace's shop. You know Madame
Pace—one of those ladies who attract poor girls of good family into their
ateliers, under the pretext of their selling *robes et manteaux.*[2]

THE SON.   And he thinks he has bought the right to tyrannize over us all
with those hundred lire he was going to pay; but which, fortunately—note this,
gentlemen—he had no chance of paying.

THE STEPDAUGHTER.   It was a near thing, though, you know! [*Laughs
ironically*.]

THE MOTHER [*protesting*].   Shame, my daughter, shame!

THE STEPDAUGHTER.   Shame indeed! This is my revenge! I am dying to
live that scene. . . . The room . . . I see it . . . Here is the window with the
mantles exposed, there the divan, the looking-glass, a screen, there in front of
the window the little mahogany table with the blue envelope containing one
hundred lire. I see it. I see it. I could take hold of it . . . But you, gentlemen,
you ought to turn your backs now: I am almost nude, you know. But I don't
blush: I leave that to him [*indicating the* FATHER].

2 (French) Dresses and coats.

THE MANAGER. I don't understand this at all.

THE FATHER. Naturally enough. I would ask you, sir, to exercise your authority a little here, and let me speak before you believe all she is trying to blame me with. Let me explain.

THE STEPDAUGHTER. Ah yes, explain it in your own way.

THE FATHER. But don't you see that the whole trouble lies here. In words, words. Each one of us has within him a whole world of things, each man of us his own special world. And how can we ever come to an understanding if I put in the words I utter the sense and value of things as I see them; while you who listen to me must inevitably translate them according to the conception of things each one of you has within himself. We think we understand each other, but we never really do. Look here! This woman [*indicating the* MOTHER] takes all my pity for her as a specially ferocious form of cruelty.

THE MOTHER. But you drove me away.

THE FATHER. Do you hear her? I drove her away! She believes I really sent her away.

THE MOTHER. You know how to talk, and I don't; but, believe me, sir [*to* MANAGER], after he had married me . . . who knows why? . . . I was a poor insignificant woman . . .

THE FATHER. But, good Heaven! it was just for your humility that I married you. I loved this simplicity in you. [*He stops when he sees she makes signs to contradict him, opens his arms wide in sign of desperation, seeing how hopeless it is to make himself understood.*] You see she denies it. Her mental deafness, believe me, is phenomenal, the limit [*touches his forehead*]: deaf, deaf, mentally deaf! She has plenty of feeling. Oh yes, a good heart for the children; but the brain—deaf, to the point of desperation—!

THE STEPDAUGHTER. Yes, but ask him how his intelligence has helped us.

THE FATHER. If we could see all the evil that may spring from good, what should we do? [*At this point the* LEADING LADY *who is biting her lips with rage at seeing the* LEADING MAN *flirting with the* STEPDAUGHTER, *comes forward and says to the* MANAGER]

LEADING LADY. Excuse me, but are we going to rehearse today?

MANAGER. Of course, of course; but let's hear them out.

JUVENILE LEAD. This is something quite new.

L'INGÉNUE. Most interesting!

LEADING LADY. Yes, for the people who like that kind of thing. [*Casts a glance at* LEADING MAN.]

THE MANAGER [*to* FATHER]. You must please explain yourself quite clearly. [*Sits down.*]

THE FATHER. Very well then: listen! I had in my service a poor man, a clerk, a secretary of mine, full of devotion, who became friends with her. [*Indicating the* MOTHER.] They understood one another, were kindred souls in fact, without, however, the least suspicion of any evil existing. They were incapable even of thinking of it.

THE STEPDAUGHTER. So he thought of it—for them!

THE FATHER. That's not true. I meant to do good to them—and to myself, I confess, at the same time. Things had come to the point that I could not say a word to either of them without their making a mute appeal, one to the other, with their eyes. I could see them silently asking each other how I was to be kept in countenance, how I was to be kept quiet. And this, believe me, was just about enough of itself to keep me in a constant rage, to exasperate me beyond measure.

THE MANAGER. And why didn't you send him away then—this secretary of yours?

THE FATHER. Precisely what I did, sir. And then I had to watch this poor woman drifting forlornly about the house like an animal without a master, like an animal one has taken in out of pity.

THE MOTHER. Ah yes! . . .

THE FATHER [*suddenly turning to the* MOTHER]. It's true about the son anyway, isn't it?

THE MOTHER. He took my son away from me first of all.

THE FATHER. But not from cruelty. I did it so that he should grow up healthy and strong by living in the country.

THE STEPDAUGHTER [*pointing to him ironically*]. As one can see.

THE FATHER [*quickly*]. Is it my fault if he has grown up like this? I sent him to a wet nurse in the country, a peasant, as *she* did not seem to me strong enough, though she is of humble origin. That was, anyway, the reason I married her. Unpleasant all this may be, but how can it be helped? My mistake possibly, but there we are! All my life I have had these confounded aspirations towards a certain moral sanity. [*At this point the* STEPDAUGHTER *bursts out into a noisy laugh.*] Oh, stop it! Stop it! I can't stand it.

THE MANAGER. Yes, please stop it, for Heaven's sake.

THE STEPDAUGHTER. But imagine moral sanity from him, if you please— the client of certain ateliers like that of Madame Pace!

THE FATHER. Fool! That is the proof that I am a man! This seeming contradiction, gentlemen, is the strongest proof that I stand here a live man before you. Why, it is just for this very incongruity in my nature that I have had to suffer what I have. I could not live by the side of that woman [*indicating the* MOTHER] any longer; but not so much for the boredom she inspired me with as for the pity I felt for her.

THE MOTHER. And so he turned me out—.

THE FATHER. —well provided for! Yes, I sent her to that man, gentlemen . . . to let her go free of me.

THE MOTHER. And to free himself.

THE FATHER. Yes, I admit it. It was also a liberation for me. But great evil has come of it. I meant well when I did it; and I did it more for her sake than mine. I swear it. [*Crosses his arms on his chest; then turns suddenly to the* MOTHER.] Did I ever lose sight of you until that other man carried you off to another town, like the angry fool he was? And on account of my pure interest in you . . . my pure interest, I repeat, that had no base motive in it . . . I watched with the tenderest concern the new family that grew up around her. She can bear witness to this. [*Points to the* STEPDAUGHTER.]

THE STEPDAUGHTER. Oh yes, that's true enough. When I was a kiddie, so so high, you know, with plaits over my shoulders and knickers longer than my skirts, I used to see him waiting outside the school for me to come out. He came to see how I was growing up.

THE FATHER. This is infamous, shameful!

THE STEPDAUGHTER. No. Why?

THE FATHER. Infamous! Infamous! [*Then excitedly to* MANAGER, *explaining*.] After she [*indicating* MOTHER] went away, my house seemed suddenly empty. She was my incubus, but she filled my house. I was like a dazed fly alone in the empty rooms. This boy here [*indicating the* SON] was educated away from home, and when he came back, he seemed to me to be no more mine. With no mother to stand between him and me, he grew up entirely for himself, on his own, apart, with no tie of intellect or affection binding him to me. And then—strange but true—I was driven, by curiosity at first and then by some tender sentiment, towards her family, which had come into being through my will. The thought of her began gradually to fill up the emptiness I felt all around me. I wanted to know if she were happy in living out the simple daily duties of life. I wanted to think of her as fortunate and happy because far away from the complicated torments of my spirit. And so, to have proof of this, I used to watch that child coming out of school.

THE STEPDAUGHTER. Yes, yes. True. He used to follow me in the street and smiled at me, waved his hand, like this. I would look at him with interest, wondering who he might be. I told my mother, who guessed at once. [*The* MOTHER *agrees with a nod*.] Then she didn't want to send me to school for some days; and when I finally went back, there he was again—looking so ridiculous—with a paper parcel in his hands. He came close to me, caressed me, and drew out a fine straw hat from the parcel, with a bouquet of flowers—all for me!

THE MANAGER. A bit discursive this, you know!

THE SON [*contemptuously*]. Literature! Literature!

THE FATHER. Literature indeed! This is life, this is passion!

THE MANAGER. It may be, but it won't act.

THE FATHER. I agree. This is only the part leading up. I don't suggest this should be staged. She [*pointing to the* STEPDAUGHTER], as you see, is no longer the flapper with plaits down her back—.

THE STEPDAUGHTER. —and the knickers showing below the skirt!

THE FATHER. The drama is coming now, sir; something new, complex, most interesting.

THE STEPDAUGHTER. As soon as my father died . . .

THE FATHER. —there was absolute misery for them. They came back here, unknown to me. Through her stupidity! [*Pointing to the* MOTHER.] It is true she can barely write her own name; but she could anyhow have got her daughter to write to me that they were in need. . . .

THE MOTHER. And how was I to divine all this sentiment in him?

THE FATHER. That is exactly your mistake, never to have guessed any of my sentiments.

THE MOTHER. After so many years apart, and all that had happened . . .

THE FATHER. Was it my fault if that fellow carried you away? It happened quite suddenly; for after he had obtained some job or other, I could find no trace of them; and so, not unnaturally, my interest in them dwindled. But the drama culminated unforeseen and violent on their return, when I was impelled by my miserable flesh that still lives . . . Ah! what misery, what wretchedness is that of the man who is alone and disdains debasing *liaisons*! Not old enough to do without women, and not young enough to go and look for one without shame. Misery? It's worse than misery; it's a horror; for no woman can any longer give him love; and when a man feels this . . . One ought to do without, you say? Yes, yes, I know. Each of us when he appears before his fellows is clothed in a certain dignity. But every man knows what unconfessable things pass within the secrecy of his own heart. One gives way to the temptation, only to rise from it again, afterwards, with a great eagerness to reestablish one's dignity, as if it were a tombstone to place on the grave of one's shame, and a monument to hide and sign the memory of our weaknesses. Everybody's in the same case. Some folks haven't the courage to say certain things, that's all!

THE STEPDAUGHTER. All appear to have the courage to do them though.

THE FATHER. Yes, but in secret. Therefore, you want more courage to say these things. Let a man but speak these things out, and folks at once label him a cynic. But it isn't true. He is like all the others, better indeed, because he isn't afraid to reveal with the light of the intelligence the red shame of human bestiality on which most men close their eyes so as not to see it. Woman—for example, look at her case! She turns tantalizing inviting glances on you. You seize her. No sooner does she feel herself in your grasp than she closes her eyes. It is the sign of her mission, the sign by which she says to man: "Blind yourself, for I am blind."

THE STEPDAUGHTER. Sometimes she can close them no more: when she no longer feels the need of hiding her shame to herself, but dry-eyed and dispassionately, sees only that of the man who has blinded himself without love. Oh, all these intellectual complications make me sick, disgust me—all his philosophy that uncovers the beast in man, and then seeks to save him, excuse him . . . I can't stand it, sir. When a man seeks to "simplify" life bestially, throwing aside every relic of humanity, every chaste aspiration, every pure feeling, all sense of ideality, duty, modesty, shame . . . then nothing is more revolting and nauseous than a certain kind of remorse—crocodiles' tears, that's what it is.

THE MANAGER. Let's come to the point. This is only discussion.

THE FATHER. Very good, sir! But a fact is like a sack which won't stand up when it is empty. In order that it may stand up, one has to put into it the reason and sentiment which have caused it to exist. I couldn't possibly know that after the death of that man, they had decided to return here, that they were in misery, and that she [*pointing to the* MOTHER] had gone to work as a modiste, and at a shop of the type of that of Madame Pace.

THE STEPDAUGHTER. A real high-class modiste, you must know, gentlemen. In appearance, she works for the leaders of the best society; but she arranges matters so that these elegant ladies serve her purpose . . . without prejudice to other ladies who are . . . well . . . only so so.

THE MOTHER. You will believe me, gentlemen, that it never entered my mind that the old hag offered me work because she had her eye on my daughter.

THE STEPDAUGHTER. Poor mamma! Do you know, sir, what that woman did when I brought her back the work my mother had finished? She would point out to me that I had torn one of my frocks, and she would give it back to my mother to mend. It was I who paid for it, always I; while this poor creature here believed she was sacrificing herself for me and these two children here, sitting up at night sewing Madame Pace's robes.

THE MANAGER. And one day you met there . . .

THE STEPDAUGHTER. Him, him. Yes, sir, an old client. There's a scene for you to play! Superb!

THE FATHER. She, the Mother arrived just then . . .

THE STEPDAUGHTER [*treacherously*]. Almost in time!

THE FATHER [*crying out*]. No, in time! in time! Fortunately I recognized her . . . in time. And I took them back home with me to my house. You can imagine now her position and mine: she, as you see her; and I who cannot look her in the face.

THE STEPDAUGHTER. Absurd! How can I possibly be expected—after that —to be a modest young miss, a fit person to go with his confounded aspirations for "a solid moral sanity"?

THE FATHER. For the drama lies all in this—in the conscience that I have, that each one of us has. We believe this conscience to be a single thing, but it is many-sided. There is one for this person, and another for that. Diverse consciences. So we have this illusion of being one person for all, of having a personality that is unique in all our acts. But it isn't true. We perceive this when, tragically perhaps, in something we do, we are, as it were, suspended, caught up in the air on a kind of hook. Then we perceive that all of us was not in that act, and that it would be an atrocious injustice to judge us by that action alone, as if all our existence were summed up in that one deed. Now do you understand the perfidy of this girl? She surprised me in a place, where she ought not to have known me, just as I could not exist for her; and she now seeks to attach to me a reality such as I could never suppose I should have to assume for her in a shameful and fleeting moment of my life. I feel this above all else. And the drama, you will see, acquires a tremendous value from this point. Then there is the position of the others . . . his . . . [*Indicating the* SON.]

THE SON [*shrugging his shoulders scornfully*]. Leave me alone! I don't come into this.

THE FATHER. What? You don't come into this?

THE SON. I've got nothing to do with it, and don't want to have; because you know well enough I wasn't made to be mixed up in all this with the rest of you.

THE STEPDAUGHTER. We are only vulgar folk! He is the fine gentleman. You may have noticed, Mr. Manager, that I fix him now and again with a look of scorn while he lowers his eyes—for he knows the evil he has done me.

THE SON [*scarcely looking at her*]. I?

THE STEPDAUGHTER. You! you! I owe my life on the streets to you. Did you or did you not deny us, with your behavior, I won't say the intimacy of home, but even that mere hospitality which makes guests feel at their ease? We were intruders who had come to disturb the kingdom of your legitimacy. I should like to have you witness, Mr. Manager, certain scenes between him and me. He says I have tyrannized over everyone. But it was just his behavior which made me insist on the reason for which I had come into the house—this reason he calls "vile"—into his house, with my mother who is his mother too. And I came as mistress of the house.

THE SON. It's easy for them to put me always in the wrong. But imagine, gentlemen, the position of a son, whose fate it is to see arrive one day at his home a young woman of impudent bearing, a young woman who inquires for his father, with whom who knows what business she has. This young man has then to witness her return bolder than ever, accompanied by that child there. He is obliged to watch her treat his father in an equivocal and confidential manner. She asks money of him in a way that lets one suppose he must give it her, *must*, do you understand, because he has every obligation to do so.

THE FATHER.   But I have, as a matter of fact, this obligation. I owe it to your mother.

THE SON.   How should I know? When had I ever seen or heard of her? One day there arrive with her [*indicating* STEPDAUGHTER] that lad and this baby here. I am told: "This is *your* mother too, you know." I divine from her manner [*indicating* STEPDAUGHTER *again*] why it is they have come home. I had rather not say what I feel and think about it. I shouldn't even care to confess to myself. No action can therefore be hoped for from me in this affair. Believe me, Mr. Manager, I am an "unrealized" character, dramatically speaking; and I find myself not at all at ease in their company. Leave me out of it I beg you.

THE FATHER.   What? It is just because you are so that . . .

THE SON.   How do you know what I am like? When did you ever bother your head about me?

THE FATHER.   I admit it. I admit it. But isn't that a situation in itself? This aloofness of yours which is so cruel to me and to your mother, who returns home and sees you almost for the first time grown up, who doesn't recognize you but knows you are her son . . . [*Pointing out the* MOTHER *to the* MANAGER.] See, she's crying!

THE STEPDAUGHTER [*angrily, stamping her foot*].   Like a fool!

THE FATHER [*indicating* STEPDAUGHTER].   She can't stand him you know. [*Then referring again to the* SON.] He says he doesn't come into the affair, whereas he is really the hinge of the whole action. Look at that lad who is always clinging to his mother, frightened and humiliated. It is on account of this fellow here. Possibly his situation is the most painful of all. He feels himself a stranger more than the others. The poor little chap feels mortified, humiliated at being brought into a home out of charity as it were. [*In confidence.*] He is the image of his father. Hardly talks at all. Humble and quiet.

THE MANAGER.   Oh, we'll cut him out. You've no notion what a nuisance boys are on the stage . . .

THE FATHER.   He disappears soon, you know. And the baby too. She is the first to vanish from the scene. The drama consists finally in this: when that mother re-enters my house, her family born outside of it, and shall we say superimposed on the original, ends with the death of the little girl, the tragedy of the boy and the flight of the elder daughter. It cannot go on, because it is foreign to its surroundings. So after much torment, we three remain: I, the mother, that son. Then, owing to the disappearance of that extraneous family, we too find ourselves strange to one another. We find we are living in an atmosphere of mortal desolation which is the revenge, as he [*indicating* SON] scornfully said of the Demon of Experiment, that unfortunately hides in me. Thus, sir, you see when faith is lacking, it becomes impossible to create certain states of happiness, for we lack the necessary humility. Vaingloriously, we try to substitute ourselves for this faith, creating thus for the rest of the world a reality which we believe after this fashion, while, actually, it doesn't exist. For each one of us has his own reality to be respected before God, even when it is harmful to one's very self.

THE MANAGER.   There is something in what you say. I assure you all this interests me very much. I begin to think there's the stuff for a drama in all this, and not a bad drama either.

THE STEPDAUGHTER [*coming forward*].   When you've got a character like me.

THE FATHER [*shutting her up, all excited to learn the decision of the* MANAGER].   You be quiet!

THE MANAGER [*reflecting, heedless of interruption*].   It's new . . . hem . . . yes . . .

THE FATHER.   Absolutely new!

THE MANAGER.   You've got a nerve though, I must say, to come here and fling it at me like this . . .

THE FATHER.   You will understand, sir, born as we are for the stage . . .

THE MANAGER.   Are you amateur actors then?

THE FATHER.   No, I say born for the stage, because . . .

THE MANAGER.   Oh, nonsense. You're an old hand, you know.

THE FATHER.   No sir, no. We act that rôle for which we have been cast, that rôle which we are given in life. And in my own case, passion itself, as usually happens, becomes a trifle theatrical when it is exalted.

THE MANAGER.   Well, well, that will do. But you see, without an author . . . I could give you the address of an author if you like.

THE FATHER.   No, no. Look here! You must be the author.

THE MANAGER.   I? What are you talking about?

THE FATHER.   Yes, you! Why not?

THE MANAGER.   Because I have never been an author: that's why.

THE FATHER.   Then why not turn author now? Everybody does it. You don't want any special qualities. Your task is made much easier by the fact that we are all here alive before you . . .

THE MANAGER.   It won't do.

THE FATHER.   What? When you see us live our drama . . .

THE MANAGER.   Yes, that's all right. But you want someone to write it.

THE FATHER.   No, no. Someone to take it down, possibly, while we play it, scene by scene! It will be enough to sketch it out at first, and then try it over.

THE MANAGER.   Well . . . I am almost tempted. It's a bit of an idea. One might have a shot at it.

THE FATHER.   Of course. You'll see what scenes will come out of it. I can give you one, at once . . .

THE MANAGER.   By Jove, it tempts me. I'd like to have a go at it. Let's try it out. Come with me to my office. [*Turning to the* ACTORS.] You are at liberty for a bit, but don't stop out of the theater for long. In a quarter of an hour, twenty minutes, all back here again! [*To the* FATHER.] We'll see what can be done. Who knows if we don't get something really extraordinary out of it?

THE FATHER.   There's no doubt about it. They [*indicating the* CHARACTERS.] had better come with us too, hadn't they?

THE MANAGER.   Yes, yes. Come on! come on! [*Moves away and then turning to the* ACTORS.] Be punctual, please! [MANAGER *and the* SIX CHARACTERS *cross the stage and go off. The other* ACTORS *remain, looking at one another in astonishment.*]

LEADING MAN.   Is he serious? What the devil does he want to do?

JUVENILE LEAD.   This is rank madness.

THIRD ACTOR.   Does he expect to knock up a drama in five minutes?

JUVENILE LEAD.   Like the improvisers!

LEADING LADY.   If he thinks I'm going to take part in a joke like this . . .

JUVENILE LEAD.   I'm out of it anyway.

FOURTH ACTOR.   I should like to know who they are. [*Alludes to* CHARACTERS.]

THIRD ACTOR.   What do you suppose? Madmen or rascals!

JUVENILE LEAD.   And he takes them seriously!

L'INGÉNUE.   Vanity! He fancies himself as an author now.

LEADING MAN.   It's absolutely unheard of. If the stage has come to this . . . well I'm . . .

FIFTH ACTOR.   It's rather a joke.

THIRD ACTOR.   Well, we'll see what's going to happen next.

[*Thus talking, the* ACTORS *leave the stage; some going out by the little door at the back; others retiring to their dressing-rooms.*

The curtain remains up.

The action of the play is suspended for twenty minutes.]

ACT II

The stage call-bells ring to warn the company that the play is about to begin again.

THE STEPDAUGHTER *comes out of the* MANAGER's *office along with the* CHILD *and the* BOY. *As she comes out of the office, she cries:* Nonsense! Nonsense! Do it yourselves! I'm not going to mix myself up in this mess. [*Turning to the* CHILD *and coming quickly with her on to the stage.*] Come on, Rosetta, let's run!

[*The* BOY *follows them slowly, remaining a little behind and seeming perplexed.*]

THE STEPDAUGHTER [*stops, bends over the* CHILD *and takes the latter's face between her hands*]. My little darling! You're frightened, aren't you? You don't know where you are, do you? [*Pretending to reply to a question of the* CHILD.] What is the stage? It's a place, baby, you know, where people play at being serious, a place where they act comedies. We've got to act a comedy now, dead serious, you know; and you're in it also, little one. [*Embraces her, pressing the little head to her breast, and rocking the* CHILD *for a moment.*] Oh darling, darling, what a horrid comedy you've got to play! What a wretched part they've found for you! A garden . . . a fountain . . . look . . . just suppose, kiddie, it's here. Where, you say? Why, right here in the middle. It's all pretence you know. That's the trouble, my pet: it's all make-believe here. It's better to imagine it though, because if they fix it up for you, it'll only be painted cardboard, painted cardboard for the rockery, the water, the plants . . . Ah, but I think a baby like this one would sooner have a make-believe fountain than a real one, so she could play with it. What a joke it'll be for the others! But for you, alas! not quite such a joke: you who are real, baby dear, and really play by a real fountain that is big and green and beautiful, with ever so many bamboos around it that are reflected in the water, and a whole lot of little ducks swimming about . . . No, Rosetta, no, your mother doesn't bother about you on account of that wretch of a son there. I'm in the devil of a temper, and as for that lad . . . [*Seizes* BOY *by the arm to force him to take one of his hands out of his pockets.*] What have you got there? What are you hiding? [*Pulls his hand out of his pocket, looks into it and catches the glint of a revolver.*] Ah, where did you get this? [*The* BOY, *very pale in the face, looks at her, but does not answer.*] Idiot! If I'd been in your place, instead of killing myself, I'd have shot one of those two, or both of them: father and son.

[*The* FATHER *enters from the office, all excited from his work. The* MANAGER *follows him.*]

THE FATHER.   Come on, come on, dear! Come here for a minute! We've arranged everything. It's all fixed up.

THE MANAGER [*also excited*].   If you please, young lady, there are one or two points to settle still. Will you come along?

THE STEPDAUGHTER [*following him towards the office*].   Ouff! what's the good, if you've arranged everything.

[*The* FATHER, MANAGER *and* STEPDAUGHTER *go back into the office again* (*off*) *for a moment. At the same time, the* SON, *followed by the* MOTHER, *comes out.*]

THE SON [*looking at the three entering office*].   Oh this is fine, fine! And to think I can't even get away!

[*The* MOTHER *attempts to look at him, but lowers her eyes immediately when he turns away from her. She then sits down. The* BOY *and the* CHILD *approach her. She casts a glance again at the* SON, *and speaks with humble tones, trying to draw him into conversation.*]

THE MOTHER.   And isn't my punishment the worst of all? [*Then seeing from the* SON'S *manner that he will not bother himself about her.*] My God! Why are you so cruel? Isn't it enough for one person to support all this torment? Must you then insist on others seeing it also?

THE SON [*half to himself, meaning the* MOTHER *to hear, however*].   And they want to put it on the stage! If there was at least a reason for it! He thinks he has got at the meaning of it all. Just as if each one of us in every circumstance of life couldn't find his own explanation of it! [*Pauses.*] He complains he was discovered in a place where he ought not to have been seen, in a moment of his life which ought to have remained hidden and kept out of the reach of convention which he has to maintain for other people. And what about my case? Haven't I had to reveal what no son ought ever to reveal: how father and mother live and are man and wife for themselves quite apart from that idea of father and mother which we give them? When this idea is revealed, our life is then linked at one point only to that man and that woman; and as such it should shame them, shouldn't it?

[*The* MOTHER *hides her face in her hands. From the dressing-rooms and the little door at the back of the stage the* ACTORS *and* STAGE MANAGER *return, followed by the* PROPERTY MAN, *and the* PROMPTER. *At the same moment, the* MANAGER *comes out of his office, accompanied by the* FATHER *and the* STEP-DAUGHTER.]

THE MANAGER.   Come on, come on, ladies and gentlemen! Heh! you there, machinist!

MACHINIST.   Yes sir?

THE MANAGER.   Fix up the white parlor with the floral decorations. Two wings and a drop with a door will do. Hurry up!

[*The* MACHINIST *runs off at once to prepare the scene, and arranges it while the* MANAGER *talks with the* STAGE MANAGER, *the* PROPERTY MAN, *and the* PROMPTER *on matters of detail.*]

THE MANAGER [*to* PROPERTY MAN].   Just have a look, and see if there isn't a sofa or divan in the wardrobe . . .

PROPERTY MAN.   There's the green one.

THE STEPDAUGHTER.   No, no! Green won't do. It was yellow, ornamented with flowers—very large! and most comfortable!

PROPERTY MAN.   There isn't one like that.

THE MANAGER.   It doesn't matter. Use the one we've got.

THE STEPDAUGHTER.   Doesn't matter? It's most important!

THE MANAGER.   We're only trying it now. Please don't interfere. [*To* PROPERTY MAN.] See if we've got a shop window—long and narrowish.

THE STEPDAUGHTER.   And the little table! The little mahogany table for the pale blue envelope!

PROPERTY MAN [*to* MANAGER].   There's that little gilt one.

THE MANAGER.   That'll do fine.

THE FATHER.   A mirror.

THE STEPDAUGHTER.   And the screen! We must have a screen. Otherwise how can I manage?

PROPERTY MAN.   That's all right, Miss. We've got any amount of them.

THE MANAGER [*to the* STEPDAUGHTER].   We want some clothes pegs too, don't we?

THE STEPDAUGHTER.   Yes, several, several!

THE MANAGER.   See how many we've got and bring them all.

PROPERTY MAN.   All right!

[*The* PROPERTY MAN *hurries off to obey his orders. While he is putting the things in their places, the* MANAGER *talks to the* PROMPTER *and then with the* CHARACTERS *and the* ACTORS.]

THE MANAGER [*to* PROMPTER].   Take your seat. Look here: this is the outline of the scenes, act by act. [*Hands him some sheets of paper.*] And now I'm going to ask you to do something out of the ordinary.

PROMPTER.   Take it down in shorthand?

THE MANAGER [*pleasantly surprised*].   Exactly! Can you do shorthand?

PROMPTER.   Yes, a little.

MANAGER.   Good! [*Turning to a stage hand.*] Go and get some paper from my office, plenty, as much as you can find.

[*The* STAGE HAND *goes off, and soon returns with a handful of paper which he gives to the* PROMPTER.]

THE MANAGER [*to* PROMPTER].   You follow the scenes as we play them, and try to get the points down, at any rate the most important ones. [*Then addressing the* ACTORS.] Clear the stage, ladies and gentlemen! Come over here [*pointing to the Left*] and listen attentively.

LEADING LADY.   But, excuse me, we . . .

THE MANAGER [*guessing her thought*].   Don't worry! You won't have to improvise.

LEADING MAN.   What have we to do then?

THE MANAGER.   Nothing. For the moment you just watch and listen. Everybody will get his part written out afterwards. At present we're going to try the thing as best we can. They're going to act now.

THE FATHER [*as if fallen from the clouds into the confusion of the stage*]. We? What do you mean, if you please, by a rehearsal?

THE MANAGER.   A rehearsal for them. [*Points to the* ACTORS.]

THE FATHER.   But since we are the characters . . .

THE MANAGER.   All right: "characters" then, if you insist on calling your-selves such. But here, my dear sir, the characters don't act. Here the actors do the acting. The characters are there, in the "book"—[*pointing towards* PROMPTER's *box*] when there is a "book"!

THE FATHER.   I won't contradict you; but excuse me, the actors aren't the characters. They want to be, they pretend to be, don't they? Now if these gentlemen here are fortunate enough to have us alive before them . . .

THE MANAGER.   Oh this is grand! You want to come before the public yourselves then?

THE FATHER.   As we are . . .

THE MANAGER.   I can assure you it would be a magnificent spectacle!

LEADING MAN.   What's the use of us here anyway then?

THE MANAGER.   You're not going to pretend that you can act? It makes me laugh! [*The* ACTORS *laugh*.] There, you see, they are laughing at the notion. But, by the way, I must cast the parts. That won't be difficult. They cast them-selves. [*To the* SECOND LADY LEAD.] You play the Mother. [*To the* FATHER.] We must find her a name.

THE FATHER.   Amalia, sir.

THE MANAGER.   But that is the real name of your wife. We don't want to call her by her real name.

THE FATHER.   Why ever not, if it is her name? . . . Still, perhaps, if that lady must . . . [*makes a slight motion of the hand to indicate the* SECOND LADY LEAD]. I see this woman here [*means the* MOTHER] as Amalia. But do as you like. [*Gets more and more confused*.] I don't know what to say to you. Already, I begin to hear my own words ring false, as if they had another sound . . .

THE MANAGER.   Don't you worry about it. It'll be our job to find the right tones. And as for her name, if you want her Amalia, Amalia it shall be; and if you don't like it, we'll find another! For the moment though, we'll call the characters in this way: [*to the* JUVENILE LEAD] You are the Son; [*to the* LEADING LADY] You naturally are the Stepdaughter . . .

THE STEPDAUGHTER [*excitedly*].   What? what? I, that woman there? [*Bursts out laughing*.]

THE MANAGER [*angry*].   What is there to laugh at?

LEADING LADY [*indignant*].   Nobody has ever dared to laugh at me. I insist on being treated with respect; otherwise I go away.

THE STEPDAUGHTER.   No, no, excuse me . . . I am not laughing at you . . .

THE MANAGER [*to* STEPDAUGHTER].   You ought to feel honored to be played by . . .

LEADING LADY [*at once, contemptuously*].   "That woman there" . . .

THE STEPDAUGHTER.   But I wasn't speaking of you, you know. I was speaking of myself—whom I can't see at all in you! That is all. I don't know . . . but . . . you . . . aren't in the least like me . . .

THE FATHER. True. Here's the point. Look here, sir, our temperaments, our souls . . .

THE MANAGER. Temperament, soul, be hanged. Do you suppose the spirit of the piece is in you? Nothing of the kind!

THE FATHER. What, haven't we our own temperaments, our own souls?

THE MANAGER. Not at all. Your soul or whatever you like to call it takes shape here. The actors give body and form to it, voice and gesture. And my actors—I may tell you—have given expression to much more lofty material than this little drama of yours, which may or may not hold up on the stage. But if it does, the merit of it, believe me, will be due to my actors.

THE FATHER. I don't dare contradict you, sir; but, believe me, it is a terrible suffering for us who are as we are, with these bodies of ours, these features to see . . .

THE MANAGER [cutting him short and out of patience]. Good heavens! The make-up will remedy all that, man, the make-up . . .

THE FATHER. Maybe. But the voice, the gestures . . .

THE MANAGER. Now, look here! On the stage, you as yourself, cannot exist. The actor here acts you, and that's an end to it!

THE FATHER. I understand. And now I think I see why our author who conceived us as we are, all alive, didn't want to put us on the stage after all. I haven't the least desire to offend your actors. Far from it! But when I think that I am to be acted by . . . I don't know by whom . . .

LEADING MAN [on his dignity]. By me, if you've no objection!

THE FATHER [humbly, mellifluously]. Honored, I assure you, sir. [Bows.] Still, I must say that try as this gentleman may, with all his good will and wonderful art, to absorb me into himself . . .

LEADING MAN. Oh chuck it! "Wonderful art!" Withdraw that, please!

THE FATHER. The performance he will give, even doing his best with make-up to look like me . . .

LEADING MAN. It will certainly be a bit difficult! [The ACTORS laugh.]

THE FATHER. Exactly! It will be difficult to act me as I really am. The effect will be rather—apart from the make-up—according as to how he supposes I am, as he senses me—if he does sense me—and not as I inside of myself feel myself to be. It seems to me then that account should be taken of this by everyone whose duty it may become to criticize us . . .

THE MANAGER. Heavens! The man's starting to think about the critics now! Let them say what they like. It's up to us to put on the play if we can. [Looking around.] Come on! come on! Is the stage set? [To the ACTORS and CHARACTERS.] Stand back—stand back! Let me see, and don't let's lose any more time! [To the STEPDAUGHTER.] Is it all right as it is now?

THE STEPDAUGHTER. Well, to tell the truth, I don't recognize the scene.

THE MANAGER. My dear lady, you can't possibly suppose that we can construct that shop of Madame Pace piece by piece here? [To the FATHER.] You said a white room with flowered wall paper, didn't you?

THE FATHER. Yes.

THE MANAGER. Well then. We've got the furniture right more or less. Bring that little table a bit further forward. [The stage hands obey the order. To

PROPERTY MAN.] You go and find an envelope, if possible, a pale blue one; and give it to that gentleman. [*Indicates the* FATHER.]

PROPERTY MAN.   An ordinary envelope?

MANAGER AND FATHER.   Yes, yes, an ordinary envelope.

PROPERTY MAN.   At once, sir. [*Exit.*]

THE MANAGER.   Ready, everyone! First scene—the Young Lady. [*The* LEADING LADY *comes forward.*] No, no, you must wait. I meant her. [*Indicating the* STEPDAUGHTER] You just watch—

THE STEPDAUGHTER [*adding at once*].   How I shall play it, how I shall live it! . . .

LEADING LADY [*offended*].   I shall live it also, you may be sure, as soon as I begin!

THE MANAGER [*with his hands to his head*].   Ladies and gentlemen, if you please! No more useless discussions! Scene I: the young lady with Madame Pace: Oh! [*Looks around as if lost.*] And this Madame Pace, where is she?

THE FATHER.   She isn't with us, sir.

THE MANAGER.   Then what the devil's to be done?

THE FATHER.   But she is alive too.

THE MANAGER.   Yes, but where is she?

THE FATHER.   One minute. Let me speak! [*Turning to the* ACTRESSES.] If these ladies would be so good as to give me their hats for a moment . . .

THE ACTRESSES [*half-surprised, half-laughing, in chorus*].   What?
Why?
Our hats?
What does he say?

THE MANAGER.   What are you going to do with the ladies' hats? [*The* ACTORS *laugh.*]

THE FATHER.   Oh nothing. I just want to put them on these pegs for a moment. And one of the ladies will be so kind as to take off her mantle . . .

THE ACTORS.   Oh, what d'you think of that?
Only the mantle?
He must be mad.

SOME ACTRESSES.   But why?
Mantles as well?

THE FATHER.   To hang them up here for a moment. Please be so kind, will you?

THE ACTRESSES [*taking off their hats, one or two also their cloaks, and going to hang them on the racks*].   After all, why not?
There you are!
This is really funny.
We've got to put them on show.

THE FATHER.   Exactly; just like that, on show.

THE MANAGER.   May we know why?

THE FATHER.   I'll tell you. Who knows if, by arranging the stage for her, she does not come here herself, attracted by the very articles of her trade? [*Inviting the* ACTORS *to look towards the exit at back of stage.*] Look! Look!

[*The door at the back of stage opens and* MADAME PACE *enters and takes a few steps forward. She is a fat, oldish woman with puffy oxygenated hair. She is rouged and powdered, dressed with a comical elegance in black silk. Round*

her waist is a long silver chain from which hangs a pair of scissors. The STEP-
DAUGHTER *runs over to her at once amid the stupor of the* ACTORS.]

THE STEPDAUGHTER [*turning towards her*].   There she is! There she is!

THE FATHER [*radiant*].   It's she! I said so, didn't I? There she is!

THE MANAGER [*conquering his surprise, and then becoming indignant*].
What sort of a trick is this?

LEADING MAN [*almost at the same time*].   What's going to happen next?

JUVENILE LEAD.   Where does *she* come from?

L'INGÉNUE.   They've been holding her in reserve, I guess.

LEADING LADY.   A vulgar trick!

THE FATHER [*dominating the protests*].   Excuse me, all of you! Why are
you so anxious to destroy in the name of a vulgar, commonplace sense of truth,
this reality which comes to birth attracted and formed by the magic of the stage
itself, which has indeed more right to live here than you, since it is much truer
than you—if you don't mind my saying so? Which is the actress among you
who is to play Madame Pace? Well, here is Madame Pace herself. And you
will allow, I fancy, that the actress who acts her will be less true than this
woman here, who is herself in person. You see my daughter recognized her and
went over to her at once. Now you're going to witness the scene.

[*But the scene between the* STEPDAUGHTER *and* MADAME PACE *has already
begun despite the protest of the* ACTORS *and the reply of the* FATHER. *It has
begun quietly, naturally, in a manner impossible for the stage. So when the*
ACTORS, *called to attention by the* FATHER, *turn round and see* MADAME PACE,
who has placed one hand under the STEPDAUGHTER's *chin to raise her head, they
observe her at first with great attention, but hearing her speak in an unintel-
ligible manner their interest begins to wane.*]

THE MANAGER.   Well? well?

LEADING MAN.   What does she say?

LEADING LADY.   One can't hear a word.

JUVENILE LEAD.   Louder! Louder please!

THE STEPDAUGHTER [*leaving* MADAME PACE, *who smiles a Sphinx-like smile,
and advancing towards the* ACTORS].   Louder? Louder? What are you talking
about? These aren't matters which can be shouted at the top of one's voice. If
I have spoken them out loud, it was to shame him and have my revenge.
[*Indicates the* FATHER.] But for Madame it's quite a different matter.

THE MANAGER.   Indeed? indeed? But here, you know, people have got to
make themselves heard, my dear. Even we who are on the stage can't hear you.
What will it be when the public's in the theater? And anyway, you can very
well speak up now among yourselves, since we shan't be present to listen to you
as we are now. You've got to pretend to be alone in a room at the back of a shop
where no one can hear you.

[*The* STEPDAUGHTER *coquettishly and with a touch of malice makes a sign
of disagreement two or three times with her finger.*]

THE MANAGER.   What do you mean by no?

THE STEPDAUGHTER [*sotto voce, mysteriously*].   There's someone who will
hear us if she [*indicating* MADAME PACE] speaks out loud.

THE MANAGER [*in consternation*].   What? Have you got someone else to
spring on us now? [*The* ACTORS *burst out laughing.*]

THE FATHER.   No, no sir. She is alluding to me. I've got to be here—there behind that door, in waiting; and Madame Pace knows it. In fact, if you will allow me, I'll go there at once, so I can be quite ready. [*Moves away.*]

THE MANAGER [*stopping him*]. No! wait! wait! We must observe the conventions of the theater. Before you are ready . . .

THE STEPDAUGHTER [*interrupting him*]. No, get on with it at once! I'm just dying, I tell you, to act this scene. If he's ready, I'm more than ready.

THE MANAGER [*shouting*]. But, my dear young lady, first of all, we must have the scene between you and this lady . . . [*Indicates* MADAME PACE.] Do you understand? . . .

THE STEPDAUGHTER. Good Heavens! She's been telling me what you know already: that mamma's work is badly done again, that the material's ruined; and that if I want her to continue to help us in our misery I must be patient . . .

MADAME PACE [*coming forward with an air of great importance*]. Yes indeed, sir, I no wanta take advantage of her, I no wanta be hard . . .

[*Note:* MADAME PACE *is supposed to talk in a jargon half Italian, half English.*]

THE MANAGER [*alarmed*]. What? What? she talks like that? [*The* ACTORS *burst out laughing again.*]

THE STEPDAUGHTER [*also laughing*]. Yes, yes, that's the way she talks, half English, half Italian! Most comical it is!

MADAME PACE. Itta seem not verra polite gentlemen laugha atta me eef I trya best speaka English.

THE MANAGER. *Diamine!*[3] Of course! Of course! Let her talk like that! Just what we want. Talk just like that, Madame, if you please! The effect will be certain. Exactly what was wanted to put a little comic relief into the crudity of the situation. Of course she talks like that! Magnificent!

THE STEPDAUGHTER. Magnificent? Certainly! When certain suggestions are made to one in language of that kind, the effect is certain, since it seems almost a joke. One feels inclined to laugh when one hears her talk about an "old signore" "who wanta talka nicely with you." Nice old signore, eh, Madame?

MADAME PACE. Not so old, my dear, not so old! And even if you no lika him, he won't make any scandal!

THE MOTHER [*jumping up amid the amazement and consternation of the* ACTORS, *who had not been noticing her. They move to restrain her*]. You old devil! You murderess!

THE STEPDAUGHTER [*running over to calm her* MOTHER]. Calm yourself, mother, calm yourself! Please don't . . .

THE FATHER [*going to her also at the same time*]. Calm yourself! Don't get excited! Sit down now!

THE MOTHER. Well then, take that woman away out of my sight!

THE STEPDAUGHTER [*to the* MANAGER]. It is impossible for my mother to remain here.

THE FATHER [*to the* MANAGER]. They can't be here together. And for this reason, you see: that woman there was not with us when we came . . . If they are on together, the whole thing is given away inevitably, as you see.

THE MANAGER. It doesn't matter. This is only a first rough sketch—just to get an idea of the various points of the scene, even confusedly . . . [*Turning*

---

[3] (Italian) The deuce!

to the MOTHER *and leading her to her chair.*] Come along, my dear lady, sit down now, and let's get on with the scene . . .

[*Meanwhile, the* STEPDAUGHTER, *coming forward again, turns to* MADAME PACE.]

THE STEPDAUGHTER.   Come on, Madame, come on!

MADAME PACE [*offended*].   No, no, *grazie*.[4] I not do anything witha your mother present.

THE STEPDAUGHTER.   Nonsense! Introduce this "old signore" who wants to talk nicely to me. [*Addressing the company imperiously.*] We've got to do this scene one way or another, haven't we? Come on! [*To* MADAME PACE.] You can go!

MADAME PACE.   Ah yes! I go'way! I go'way! Certainly! [*Exit furious.*]

THE STEPDAUGHTER [*to the* FATHER]. Now you make your entry. No, you needn't go over here. Come here. Let's suppose you've already come in. Like that, yes! I'm here with bowed head, modest like. Come on! Out with your voice! Say "Good morning, Miss" in that peculiar tone, that special tone . . .

THE MANAGER.   Excuse me, but are you the Manager, or am I? [*To the* FATHER, *who looks undecided and perplexed.*] Get on with it, man! Go down there to the back of the stage. You needn't go off. Then come right forward here.

[*The* FATHER *does as he is told, looking troubled and perplexed at first. But as soon as he begins to move, the reality of the action affects him, and he begins to smile and to be more natural. The* ACTORS *watch intently.*]

THE MANAGER [*sotto voce, quickly to the* PROMPTER *in his box*]. Ready! ready? Get ready to write now.

THE FATHER [*coming forward and speaking in a different tone*]. Good afternoon, Miss!

THE STEPDAUGHTER [*head bowed down slightly, with restrained disgust*]. Good afternoon!

THE FATHER [*looks under her hat which partly covers her face. Perceiving she is very young, he makes an exclamation, partly of surprise, partly of fear lest he compromise himself in a risky adventure.*] Ah . . . but . . . ah . . . I say . . . this is not the first time that you have come here, is it?

THE STEPDAUGHTER [*modestly*].   No sir.

THE FATHER.   You've been here before, eh? [*Then seeing her nod agreement.*] More than once? [*Waits for her to answer, looks under her hat, smiles, and then says.*] Well then, there's no need to be so shy, is there? May I take off your hat?

THE STEPDAUGHTER [*anticipating him and with veiled disgust*]. No sir . . . I'll do it myself. [*Takes it off quickly.*]

[*The* MOTHER, *who watches the progress of the scene with the* SON *and the other two* CHILDREN, *who cling to her, is on thorns; and follows with varying expressions of sorrow, indignation, anxiety, and horror the words and actions of the other two. From time to time she hides her face in her hands and sobs.*]

THE MOTHER.   Oh, my God, my God!

THE FATHER [*playing his part with a touch of gallantry*]. Give it to me! I'll put it down. [*Takes hat from her hands.*] But a dear little head like yours

---

4 (Italian) Thank you (with the implication, as frequently in English, that what is offered is not really desirable).

ought to have a smarter hat. Come and help me choose one from the stock, won't you?

L'INGÉNUE [*interrupting*].   I say . . . those are our hats you know.

THE MANAGER [*furious*].   Silence! silence! Don't try and be funny, if you please . . . We're playing the scene now I'd have you notice. [*To the* STEP-DAUGHTER.] Begin again, please!

THE STEPDAUGHTER [*continuing*].   No thank you, sir.

THE FATHER.   Oh, come now. Don't talk like that. You must take it. I shall be upset if you don't. There are some lovely little hats here; and then— Madame will be pleased. She expects it, anyway, you know.

THE STEPDAUGHTER.   No, no! I couldn't wear it!

THE FATHER.   Oh, you're thinking about what they'd say at home if they saw you come in with a new hat? My dear girl, there's always a way round these little matters, you know.

THE STEPDAUGHTER [*all keyed up*].   No, it's not that. I couldn't wear it because I am . . . as you see . . . you might have noticed . . . [*Showing her black dress.*]

THE FATHER.   . . . in mourning! Of course: I beg your pardon: I'm frightfully sorry . . .

THE STEPDAUGHTER [*forcing herself to conquer her indignation and nausea*]. Stop! Stop! It's I who must thank you. There's no need for you to feel mortified or specially sorry. Don't think any more of what I've said. [*Tries to smile.*] I must forget that I am dressed so . . .

THE MANAGER [*interrupting and turning to the* PROMPTER].   Stop a minute! Stop! Don't write that down. Cut out that last bit. [*Then to the* FATHER *and the* STEPDAUGHTER.] Fine! It's going fine! [*To the* FATHER *only.*] And now you can go on as we arranged. [*To the* ACTORS.] Pretty good that scene, where he offers her the hat, eh?

THE STEPDAUGHTER.   The best's coming now. Why can't we go on?

THE MANAGER.   Have a little patience! [*To the* ACTORS.] Of course, it must be treated rather lightly.

LEADING MAN.   Still, with a bit of go in it!

LEADING LADY.   Of course! It's easy enough! [*To the* LEADING MAN.] Shall you and I try it now?

LEADING MAN.   Why, yes! I'll prepare my entrance. [*Exit in order to make his entrance.*]

THE MANAGER [*to the* LEADING LADY].   See here! The scene between you and Madame Pace is finished. I'll have it written out properly after. You remain here . . . oh, where are you going?

LEADING LADY.   One minute. I want to put my hat on again. [*Goes over to hat-rack and puts her hat on her head.*]

THE MANAGER.   Good! You stay here with your head bowed down a bit.

THE STEPDAUGHTER.   But she isn't dressed in black.

LEADING LADY.   But I shall be, and much more effectively than you.

THE MANAGER [*to* STEPDAUGHTER].   Be quiet please, and watch! You'll be able to learn something. [*Clapping his hands.*] Come on! come on! Entrance, please!

[*The door at rear of stage opens, and the* LEADING MAN *enters with the lively manner of an old gallant. The rendering of the scene by the* ACTORS *from the very first words is seen to be quite a different thing, though it has not in any way the air of a parody. Naturally, the* STEPDAUGHTER *and the* FATHER, *not being able to recognize themselves in the* LEADING LADY *and the* LEADING MAN, *who deliver their words in different tones and with a different psychology, express, sometimes with smiles, sometimes with gestures, the impression they receive.]*

LEADING MAN. Good afternoon, Miss . . .

THE FATHER [*at once unable to contain himself*]. No! no!

[*The* STEPDAUGHTER *noticing the way the* LEADING MAN *enters, bursts out laughing.*]

THE MANAGER [*furious*]. Silence! And you please just stop that laughing. If we go on like this, we shall never finish.

THE STEPDAUGHTER. Forgive me, sir, but it's natural enough. This lady [*indicating* LEADING LADY] stands there still; but if she is supposed to be me, I can assure you that if I heard anyone say "Good afternoon" in that manner and in that tone, I should burst out laughing as I did.

THE FATHER. Yes, yes, the manner, the tone . . .

THE MANAGER. Nonsense! Rubbish! Stand aside and let me see the action.

LEADING MAN. If I've got to represent an old fellow who's coming into a house of an equivocal character . . .

THE MANAGER. Don't listen to them, for Heaven's sake! Do it again! It goes fine. [*Waiting for the* ACTORS *to begin again.*] Well?

LEADING MAN. Good afternoon, Miss.

LEADING LADY. Good afternoon.

LEADING MAN [*imitating the gesture of the* FATHER *when he looked under the hat, and then expressing quite clearly first satisfaction and then fear*]. Ah, but . . . I say . . . this is not the first time that you have come here, is it?

THE MANAGER. Good, but not quite so heavily. Like this. [*Acts himself.*] "This isn't the first time that you have come here" . . . [*To the* LEADING LADY.] And you say: "No, sir."

LEADING LADY. No, sir.

LEADING MAN. You've been here before, more than once.

THE MANAGER. No, no, stop! Let her nod "yes" first. "You've been here before, eh?" [*The* LEADING LADY *lifts up her head slightly and closes her eyes as though in disgust. Then she inclines her head twice.*]

THE STEPDAUGHTER [*unable to contain herself*]. Oh my God! [*Puts a hand to her mouth to prevent herself from laughing.*]

THE MANAGER [*turning round*]. What's the matter?

THE STEPDAUGHTER. Nothing, nothing!

THE MANAGER [*to* LEADING MAN]. Go on!

LEADING MAN. You've been here before, eh? Well then, there's no need to be so shy, is there? May I take off your hat?

[*The* LEADING MAN *says this last speech in such a tone and with such gestures that the* STEPDAUGHTER, *though she has her hand to her mouth, cannot keep from laughing.*]

LEADING LADY [*indignant*]. I'm not going to stop here to be made a fool of by that woman there.

LEADING MAN. Neither am I! I'm through with it!

THE MANAGER [*shouting to* STEPDAUGHTER].   Silence! for once and all, I tell you!

THE STEPDAUGHTER.   Forgive me! forgive me!

THE MANAGER.   You haven't any manners: that's what it is! You go too far.

THE FATHER [*endeavoring to intervene*].   Yes, it's true, but excuse her . . .

THE MANAGER.   Excuse what? It's absolutely disgusting.

THE FATHER.   Yes, sir, but believe me, it has such a strange effect when . . .

THE MANAGER.   Strange? Why strange? Where is it strange?

THE FATHER.   No, sir; I admire your actors—this gentleman here, this lady; but they are certainly not us!

THE MANAGER.   I should hope not. Evidently they cannot be you, if they are actors.

THE FATHER.   Just so: actors! Both of them act our parts exceedingly well. But, believe me, it produces quite a different effect on us. They want to be us, but they aren't, all the same.

THE MANAGER.   What is it then anyway?

THE FATHER.   Something that is . . . that is theirs—and no longer ours . . .

THE MANAGER.   But naturally, inevitably. I've told you so already.

THE FATHER.   Yes, I understand . . . I understand . . .

THE MANAGER.   Well then, let's have no more of it! [*Turning to the* ACTORS.] We'll have the rehearsals by ourselves, afterwards, in the ordinary way. I never could stand rehearsing with the author present. He's never satisfied! [*Turning to the* FATHER *and* STEPDAUGHTER.] Come on! Let's get on with it again; and try and see if you can't keep from laughing.

THE STEPDAUGHTER.   Oh, I shan't laugh any more. There's a nice little bit coming for me now: you'll see.

THE MANAGER.   Well then: when she says "Don't think any more of what I've said. I must forget, etc.," you [*addressing the* FATHER] come in sharp with "I understand, I understand"; and then you ask her . . .

THE STEPDAUGHTER [*interrupting*].   What?

THE MANAGER.   Why she is in mourning.

THE STEPDAUGHTER.   Not at all! See here: when I told him that it was useless for me to be thinking about my wearing mourning, do you know how he answered me? "Ah well," he said, "then let's take off this little frock."

THE MANAGER.   Great! Just what we want, to make a riot in the theater!

THE STEPDAUGHTER.   But it's the truth!

THE MANAGER.   What does that matter? Acting is our business here. Truth up to a certain point, but no further.

THE STEPDAUGHTER.   What do you want to do then?

THE MANAGER.   You'll see, you'll see! Leave it to me.

THE STEPDAUGHTER.   No sir! What you want to do is to piece together a little romantic sentimental scene out of my disgust, out of all the reasons, each more cruel and viler than the other, why I am what I am. He is to ask me why I'm in mourning; and I'm to answer with tears in my eyes, that it is just two months since papa died. No sir, no! He's got to say to me; as he did say: "Well, let's take off this little dress at once." And I; with my two months' mourning in my heart, went there behind that screen, and with these fingers tingling with shame . . .

THE MANAGER [*running his hands through his hair*]. For Heaven's sake! What are you saying?

THE STEPDAUGHTER [*crying out excitedly*]. The truth! The truth!

THE MANAGER. It may be. I don't deny it, and I can understand all your horror; but you must surely see that you can't have this kind of thing on the stage. It won't go.

THE STEPDAUGHTER. Not possible, eh? Very well! I'm much obliged to you —but I'm off!

THE MANAGER. Now be reasonable! Don't lose your temper!

THE STEPDAUGHTER. I won't stop here! I won't! I can see you've fixed it all up with him in your office. All this talk about what is possible for the stage . . . I understand! He wants to get at his complicated "cerebral drama," to have his famous remorses and torments acted; but I want to act my part, *my part!*

THE MANAGER [*annoyed, shaking his shoulders*]. Ah! Just *your* part! But, if you will pardon me, there are other parts than yours: his [*indicating the* FATHER] and hers! [*Indicating the* MOTHER.] On the stage you can't have a character becoming too prominent and overshadowing all the others. The thing is to pack them all into a neat little framework and then act what is actable. I am aware of the fact that everyone has his own interior life which he wants very much to put forward. But the difficulty lies in this fact: to set out just so much as is necessary for the stage, taking the other characters into consideration, and at the same time hint at the unrevealed interior life of each. I am willing to admit, my dear young lady, that from your point of view it would be a fine idea if each character could tell the public all his troubles in a nice monologue or a regular one-hour lecture. [*Good-humoredly.*] You must restrain yourself, my dear, and in your own interest, too; because this fury of yours, this exaggerated disgust you show, may make a bad impression, you know. After you have confessed to me that there were others before him at Madame Pace's and more than once . . .

THE STEPDAUGHTER [*bowing her head, impressed*]. It's true. But remember those others mean him for me all the same.

THE MANAGER [*not understanding*]. What? The others? What do you mean?

THE STEPDAUGHTER. For one who has gone wrong, sir, he who was responsible for the first fault is responsible for all that follow. He is responsible for my faults, was, even before I was born. Look at him, and see if it isn't true!

THE MANAGER. Well, well! And does the weight of so much responsibility seem nothing to you? Give him a chance to act it, to get it over!

THE STEPDAUGHTER. How? How can he act all his "noble remorses" all his "moral torments," if you want to spare him the horror of being discovered one day—after he had asked her what he did ask her—in the arms of her, that already fallen woman, that child, sir, that child he used to watch come out of school? [*She is moved.*]

[*The* MOTHER *at this point is overcome with emotion, and breaks out into a fit of crying. All are touched. A long pause.*]

THE STEPDAUGHTER [*as soon as the* MOTHER *becomes a little quieter, adds resolutely and gravely*]. At present, we are unknown to the public. Tomorrow, you will act us as you wish, treating us in your own manner. But do you really want to see drama, do you want to see it flash out as it really did?

THE MANAGER. Of course! That's just what I do want, so I can use as much of it as is possible.

THE STEPDAUGHTER. Well then, ask that Mother there to leave us.

THE MOTHER [*changing her low plaint into a sharp cry*]. No! No! Don't permit it, sir, don't permit it!

THE MANAGER. But it's only to try it.

THE MOTHER. I can't bear it. I can't.

THE MANAGER. But since it has happened already . . . I don't understand!

THE MOTHER. It's taking place now. It happens all the time. My torment isn't a pretended one. I live and feel every minute of my torture. Those two children there—have you heard them speak? They can't speak any more. They cling to me to keep my torment actual and vivid for me. But for themselves, they do not exist, they aren't any more. And she [*indicating* STEPDAUGHTER] has run away, she has left me, and is lost. If I now see her here before me, it is only to renew for me the tortures I have suffered for her too.

THE FATHER. The eternal moment! She [*indicating the* STEPDAUGHTER] is here to catch me, fix me, and hold me eternally in the stocks for that one fleeting and shameful moment of my life. She can't give it up! And you, sir, cannot either fairly spare me it.

THE MANAGER. I never said I didn't want to act it. It will form, as a matter of fact, the nucleus of the whole first act right up to her surprise. [*Indicating the* MOTHER.]

THE FATHER. Just so! This is my punishment: the passion in all of us that must culminate in her final cry.

THE STEPDAUGHTER. I can hear it still in my ears. It's driven me mad, that cry!—You can put me on as you like; it doesn't matter. Fully dressed, if you like—provided I have at least the arm bare; because, standing like this [*she goes close to the* FATHER *and leans her head on his breast*] with my head so, and my arms round his neck, I saw a vein pulsing in my arm here; and then, as if that live vein had awakened disgust in me, I closed my eyes like this, and let my head sink on his breast. [*Turning to the* MOTHER.] Cry out, mother! Cry out! [*Buries head in the* FATHER's *breast, and with her shoulders raised as if to prevent her hearing the cry, adds in tones of intense emotion.*] Cry out as you did then!

THE MOTHER [*coming forward to separate them*]. No! My daughter, my daughter! [*And after having pulled her away from him.*] You brute! you brute! She is my daughter! Don't you see she's my daughter?

THE MANAGER [*walking backwards towards footlights*]. Fine! fine! Damned good! And then, of course—curtain!

THE FATHER [*going towards him excitedly*]. Yes, of course, because that's the way it really happened.

THE MANAGER [*convinced and pleased*]. Oh, yes, no doubt about it. Curtain here, curtain!

[*At the reiterated cry of the* MANAGER, *the* MACHINIST *lets the curtain down, leaving the* MANAGER *and the* FATHER *in front of it before the footlights.*]

THE MANAGER. The darned idiot! I said "curtain" to show the act should end there, and he goes and lets it down in earnest. [*To the* FATHER, *while he pulls the curtain back to go on to the stage again.*] Yes, yes, it's all right. Effect certain! That's the right ending. I'll guarantee the first act at any rate.

ACT III

When the curtain goes up again, it is seen that the stage hands have shifted the bit of scenery used in the last part, and have rigged up instead at the back of the stage a drop, with some trees, and one or two wings. A portion of a fountain basin is visible. The MOTHER *is sitting on the Right with the two children by her side. The* SON *is on the same side, but away from the others. He seems bored, angry, and full of shame. The* FATHER *and the* STEPDAUGHTER *are also seated towards the Right front. On the other side (Left) are the* ACTORS, *much in the positions they occupied before the curtain was lowered. Only the* MANAGER *is standing up in the middle of the stage, with his hand closed over his mouth in the act of meditating.*

THE MANAGER [*shaking his shoulders after a brief pause*]. Ah yes: the second act! Leave it to me, leave it all to me as we arranged, and you'll see! It'll go fine!

THE STEPDAUGHTER. Our entry into his house [*indicates the* FATHER] in spite of him . . . [*indicates the* SON].

THE MANAGER [*out of patience*]. Leave it to me. I tell you!

THE STEPDAUGHTER. Do let it be clear, at any rate, that it is in spite of my wishes.

THE MOTHER [*from her corner, shaking her head*]. For all the good that's come of it . . .

THE STEPDAUGHTER [*turning towards her quickly*]. It doesn't matter. The more harm done us, the more remorse for him.

THE MANAGER [*impatiently*]. I understand! Good Heavens! I understand! I'm taking it into account.

THE MOTHER [*supplicatingly*]. I beg you, sir, to let it appear quite plain that for conscience' sake I did try in every way . . .

THE STEPDAUGHTER [*interrupting indignantly and continuing for the* MOTHER]. . . . to pacify me, to dissuade me from spiting him. [*To* MANAGER.] Do as she wants: satisfy her, because it is true! I enjoy it immensely. Anyhow, as you can see, the meeker she is, the more she tries to get at his heart, the more distant and aloof does he become.

THE MANAGER. Are we going to begin this second act or not?

THE STEPDAUGHTER. I'm not going to talk any more now. But I must tell you this: you can't have the whole action take place in the garden, as you suggest. It isn't possible!

THE MANAGER. Why not?

THE STEPDAUGHTER. Because he [*indicates the* SON *again*] is always shut up alone in his room. And then there's all the part of that poor dazed-looking boy there which takes place indoors.

THE MANAGER. Maybe! On the other hand, you will understand—we can't change scenes three or four times in one act.

THE LEADING MAN. They used to once.

THE MANAGER. Yes, when the public was up to the level of that child there.

THE LEADING LADY. It makes the illusion easier.

THE FATHER [*irritated*]. The illusion! For Heaven's sake, don't say illusion. Please don't use that word, which is particularly painful for us.

THE MANAGER [*astounded*]. And why, if you please?

THE FATHER. It's painful, cruel, really cruel; and you ought to understand that.

THE MANAGER. But why? What ought we to say then? The illusion, I tell you sir, which we've got to create for the audience . . .

THE LEADING MAN. With our acting.

THE MANAGER. The illusion of a reality.

THE FATHER. I understand; but you, perhaps, do not understand us. Forgive me! You see . . . here for you and your actors, the thing is only—and rightly so . . . a kind of game . . .

THE LEADING LADY [*interrupting indignantly*]. A game! We're not children here, if you please! We are serious actors.

THE FATHER. I don't deny it. What I mean is the game, or play, of your art, which has to give, as the gentleman says, a perfect illusion of reality.

THE MANAGER. Precisely——!

THE FATHER. Now, if you consider the fact that we [*indicates himself and the other five* CHARACTERS], as we are, have no other reality outside of this illusion . . .

THE MANAGER [*astonished, looking at his* ACTORS, *who are also amazed*]. And what does that mean?

THE FATHER [*after watching them for a moment with a wan smile*]. As I say, sir, that which is a game of art for you is our sole reality. [*Brief pause. He goes a step or two nearer the* MANAGER *and adds*] But not only for us, you know, by the way. Just you think it over well. [*Looks him in the eyes.*] Can you tell me who you are?

THE MANAGER [*perplexed, half smiling.*] What? Who am I? I am myself.

THE FATHER. And if I were to tell you that that isn't true, because you are I? . . .

THE MANAGER. I should say you were mad——! [*The* ACTORS *laugh.*]

THE FATHER. You're quite right to laugh: because we are all making believe here. [*To the* MANAGER.] And you can therefore object that it's only for a joke that that gentleman there [*indicates the* LEADING MAN], who naturally is himself, has to be me, who am on the contrary myself—this thing you see here. You see I've caught you in a trap! [*The* ACTORS *laugh.*]

THE MANAGER [*annoyed*]. But we've had all this over once before. Do you want to begin again?

THE FATHER. No, no! that wasn't my meaning! In fact, I should like to request you to abandon this game of art [*looking at the* LEADING LADY *as if anticipating her*] which you are accustomed to play here with your actors, and to ask you seriously once again: who are you?

THE MANAGER [*astonished and irritated, turning to his* ACTORS]. If this fellow here hasn't got a nerve! A man who calls himself a character comes and asks me who I am!

THE FATHER [*with dignity, but not offended*]. A character, sir, may always ask a man who he is. Because a character has really a life of his own, marked with his especial characteristics; for which reason he is always "somebody." But a man—I'm not speaking of you now—may very well be "nobody."

THE MANAGER. Yes, but you are asking these questions of me, the boss, the manager! Do you understand?

THE FATHER. But only in order to know if you, as you really are now, see yourself as you once were with all the illusions that were yours then, with all the things both inside and outside of you as they seemed to you—as they were then indeed for you. Well, sir, if you think of all those illusions that mean nothing to you now, of all those things which don't even *seem* to you to exist any more, while once they *were* for you, don't you feel that—I won't say these boards—but the very earth under your feet is sinking away from you when you reflect that in the same way this *you* as you feel it today—all this present reality of yours—is fated to seem a mere illusion to you tomorrow?

THE MANAGER [*without having understood much, but astonished by the specious argument*]. Well, well! And where does all this take us anyway?

THE FATHER. Oh, nowhere! It's only to show you that if we [*indicating the* CHARACTERS] have no other reality beyond illusion, you too must not count overmuch on your reality as you feel it today, since, like that of yesterday, it may prove an illusion for you tomorrow.

THE MANAGER [*determining to make fun of him*]. Ah, excellent! Then you'll be saying next that you, with this comedy of yours that you brought here to act, are truer and more real than I am.

THE FATHER [*with the greatest seriousness*]. But of course; without doubt!

THE MANAGER. Ah, really?

THE FATHER. Why, I thought you'd understand that from the beginning.

THE MANAGER. More real than I?

THE FATHER. If your reality can change from one day to another . . .

THE MANAGER. But everyone knows it can change. It is always changing, the same as anyone else's.

THE FATHER [*with a cry*]. No, sir, not ours! Look here! That is the very difference! Our reality doesn't change: it can't change! It can't be other than what it is, because it is already fixed for ever. It's terrible. Ours is an immutable reality which should make you shudder when you approach us if you are really conscious of the fact that your reality is a mere transitory and fleeting illusion, taking this form today and that tomorrow, according to the conditions, according to your will, your sentiments, which in turn are controlled by an intellect that shows them to you today in one manner and tomorrow . . . who knows how? . . . Illusions of reality represented in this fatuous comedy of life that never ends, nor can ever end! Because if tomorrow it were to end . . . then why, all would be finished.

THE MANAGER. Oh for God's sake, will you *at least* finish with this philosophizing and let us try and shape this comedy which you yourself have brought me here? You argue and philosophize a bit too much, my dear sir. You know you seem to me almost, almost . . . [*Stops and looks him over from head to foot.*] Ah, by the way, I think you introduced yourself to me as a—what shall . . . we say—a "character," created by an author who did not afterwards care to make a drama of his own creations.

THE FATHER.   It is the simple truth, sir.

THE MANAGER.   Nonsense! Cut that out, please! None of us believes it, because it isn't a thing, as you must recognize yourself, which one can believe seriously. If you want to know, it seems to me you are trying to imitate the manner of a certain author whom I heartily detest—I warn you—although I have unfortunately bound myself to put on one of his works. As a matter of fact, I was just starting to rehearse it, when you arrived. [*Turning to the* ACTORS.] And this is what we've gained—out of the frying-pan into the fire!

THE FATHER.   I don't know to what author you may be alluding, but believe me I feel what I think; and I seem to be philosophizing only for those who do not think what they feel, because they blind themselves with their own sentiment. I know that for many people this self-blinding seems much more "human"; but the contrary is really true. For man never reasons so much and becomes so introspective as when he suffers; since he is anxious to get at the cause of his sufferings, to learn who has produced them, and whether it is just or unjust that he should have to bear them. On the other hand, when he is happy, he takes his happiness as it comes and doesn't analyze it, just as if happiness were his right. The animals suffer without reasoning about their sufferings. But take the case of a man who suffers and begins to reason about it. Oh no! it can't be allowed! Let him suffer like an animal, and then—ah yes, he is "human!"

THE MANAGER.   Look here! Look here! You're off again, philosophizing worse than ever.

THE FATHER.   Because I suffer, sir! I'm not philosophizing: I'm crying aloud the reason of my sufferings.

THE MANAGER [*makes brusque movement as he is taken with a new idea*]. I should like to know if anyone has ever heard of a character who gets right out of his part and perorates and speechifies as you do. Have you ever heard of a case? I haven't.

THE FATHER.   You have never met such a case, sir, because authors, as a rule, hide the labor of their creations. When the characters are really alive before their author, the latter does nothing but follow them in their action, in their words, in the situations which they suggest to him; and he has to will them the way they will themselves—for there's trouble if he doesn't. When a character is born, he acquires at once such an independence, even of his own author, that he can be imagined by everybody even in many other situations where the author never dreamed of placing him; and so he acquires for himself a meaning which the author never thought of giving him.

THE MANAGER.   Yes, yes, I know this.

THE FATHER.   What is there then to marvel at in us? Imagine such a misfortune for characters as I have described to you: to be born of an author's fantasy, and be denied life by him; and then answer me if these characters left alive, and yet without life, weren't right in doing what they did do and are doing now, after they have attempted everything in their power to persuade him to give them their stage life. We've all tried him in turn, I, she [*indicating the* STEPDAUGHTER] and she [*indicating the* MOTHER].

THE STEPDAUGHTER.   It's true. I too have sought to tempt him, many, many times, when he has been sitting at his writing table, feeling a bit melancholy, at the twilight hour. He would sit in his armchair too lazy to switch on the light, and all the shadows that crept into his room were full of our presence coming to tempt him. [*As if she saw herself still there by the writing table, and was annoyed by the presence of the* ACTORS.] Oh, if you would only go away, go away and leave us alone—mother here with that son of hers—I with that Child —that Boy there always alone—and then I with him—[*just hints at the* FATHER] —and then I alone, alone . . . in those shadows! [*Makes a sudden movement as if in the vision she has of herself illuminating those shadows she wanted to seize hold of herself.*]Ah! my life! my life! Oh, what scenes we proposed to him —and I tempted him more than any of the others!

THE FATHER.   Maybe. But perhaps it was your fault that he refused to give us life: because you were too insistent, too troublesome.

THE STEPDAUGHTER.   Nonsense! Didn't he make me so himself? [*Goes close to the* MANAGER *to tell him as if in confidence.*] In my opinion he abandoned us in a fit of depression, of disgust for the ordinary theater as the public knows it and likes it.

THE SON.   Exactly what it was, sir; exactly that!

THE FATHER.   Not at all! Don't believe it for a minute. Listen to me! You'll be doing quite right to modify, as you suggest, the excesses both of this girl here, who wants to do too much, and of this young man, who won't do anything at all.

THE SON.   No, nothing!

THE MANAGER.   You too get over the mark occasionally, my dear sir, if I may say so.

THE FATHER.   I? When? Where?

THE MANAGER.   Always! Continuously! Then there's this insistence of yours in trying to make us believe you are a character. And then too, you must really argue and philosophize less, you know, much less.

THE FATHER.   Well, if you want to take away from me the possibility of representing the torment of my spirit which never gives me peace, you will be suppressing me: that's all. Every true man, sir, who is a little above the level of the beasts and plants does not live for the sake of living, without knowing how to live; but he lives so as to give a meaning and a value of his own to life. For me this is *everything*. I cannot give up this, just to represent a mere fact as she [*indicating the* STEPDAUGHTER] wants. It's all very well for her, since her "vendetta" lies in the "fact." I'm not going to do it. It destroys my *raison d'être*.

THE MANAGER.   Your *raison d'être*! Oh, we're going ahead fine! First she starts off, and then you jump in. At this rate, we'll never finish.

THE FATHER.   Now, don't be offended. Have it your own way—provided, however, that within the limits of the parts you assign us each one's sacrifice isn't too great.

THE MANAGER.   You've got to understand that you can't go on arguing at your own pleasure. Drama is action, sir, action and not confounded philosophy.

THE FATHER.   All right. I'll do just as much arguing and philosophizing as everybody does when he is considering his own torments.

THE MANAGER.   If the drama permits! But for Heaven's sake, man, let's get along and come to the scene.

THE STEPDAUGHTER.   It seems to me we've got too much action with our coming into his house. [*Indicating* FATHER.] You said, before, you couldn't change the scene every five minutes.

THE MANAGER.   Of course not. What we've got to do is to combine and group up all the facts in one simultaneous, close-knit action. We can't have it as you want, with your little brother wandering like a ghost from room to room, hiding behind doors and meditating a project which—what did you say it did to him?

THE STEPDAUGHTER.   Consumes him, sir, wastes him away!

THE MANAGER.   Well, it may be. And then at the same time, you want the little girl there to be playing in the garden . . . one in the house, and the other in the garden: isn't that it?

THE STEPDAUGHTER.   Yes, in the sun, in the sun! That is my only pleasure: to see her happy and careless in the garden after the misery and squalor of the horrible room where we all four slept together. And I had to sleep with her—I, do you understand?—with my vile contaminated body next to hers with her folding me fast in her loving little arms. In the garden, whenever she spied me, she would run to take me by the hand. She didn't care for the big flowers, only the little ones; and she loved to show me them and pet me.

THE MANAGER.   Well then, we'll have it in the garden. Everything shall happen in the garden; and we'll group the other scenes there. [*Calls a stage hand.*] Here, a back-cloth with trees and something to do as a fountain basin. [*Turning around to look at the back of the stage.*] Ah, you've fixed it up. Good! [*To the* STEPDAUGHTER.] This is just to give an idea, of course. The boy, instead of hiding behind the doors, will wander about here in the garden, hiding behind the trees. But it's going to be rather difficult to find a child to do that scene with you where she shows you the flowers. [*Turning to the* YOUTH.] Come forward a little, will you please? Let's try it now! Come along! come along! [*Then seeing him come shyly forward, full of fear and looking lost.*] It's a nice business, this lad here. What's the matter with him? We'll have to give him a word or two to say. [*Goes close to him, puts a hand on his shoulders, and leads him behind one of the trees.*] Come on! come on! Let me see you a little! Hide here . . . yes, like that. Try and show your head just a little as if you were looking for someone . . . [*Goes back to observe the effect, when the* BOY *at once goes through the action.*] Excellent! fine! [*Turning to the* STEPDAUGHTER.] Suppose the little girl there were to surprise him as he looks round, and run over to him, so we could give him a word or two to say?

THE STEPDAUGHTER.   It's useless to hope he will speak, as long as that fellow there is here . . . [*Indicates the* SON.] You must send him away first.

THE SON [*jumping up*].   Delighted! delighted! I don't ask for anything better. [*Begins to move away.*]

THE MANAGER [*at once stopping him*].   No! No! Where are you going? Wait a bit!

[*The* MOTHER *gets up alarmed and terrified at the thought the he is really about to go away. Instinctively she lifts her arms to prevent him, without, however, leaving her seat.*]

THE SON [*to* MANAGER *who stops him*].   I've got nothing to do with this affair. Let me go please! Let me go!

THE MANAGER.   What do you mean by saying you've got nothing to do with this?

THE STEPDAUGHTER [*calmly, with irony*].   Don't bother to stop him: he won't go away.

THE FATHER. He has to act the terrible scene in the garden with his mother.

THE SON [*suddenly resolute and with dignity*]. I shall act nothing at all. I've said so from the very beginning. [*To the* MANAGER.] Let me go!

THE STEPDAUGHTER [*going over to the* MANAGER]. Allow me? [*Puts down the* MANAGER'S *arm, which is restraining the* SON.] Well, go away then, if you want to! [*The* SON *looks at her with contempt and hatred. She laughs and says.*] You see, he can't, he can't go away! He is obliged to stay here, indissolubly bound to the chain. If I, who fly off when that happens which has to happen, because I can't bear him—if I am still here and support that face and expression of his, you can well imagine that he is unable to move. He has to remain here, has to stop with that nice father of his, and that mother whose only son he is. [*Turning to the* MOTHER.] Come on, mother, come along! [*Turning to the* MANAGER *to indicate her.*] You see, she was getting up to keep him back. [*To the* MOTHER, *beckoning her with her hand.*] Come on! come on! [*Then to the* MANAGER.] You can imagine how little she wants to show these actors of yours what she really feels; but so eager is she to get near him that . . . There, you see? She is willing to act her part. [*And in fact, the* MOTHER *approaches him; and as soon as the* STEPDAUGHTER *has finished speaking, opens her arms to signify that she consents.*]

THE SON [*suddenly*]. No! no! I can't go away, then I'll stop here; but I repeat: I act nothing!

THE FATHER [*to the* MANAGER *excitedly*]. You can force him, sir.

THE SON. Nobody can force me.

THE FATHER. I can.

THE STEPDAUGHTER. Wait a minute, wait . . . First of all, the baby has to go to the fountain . . . [*Runs to take the* CHILD *and leads her to the fountain.*]

THE MANAGER. Yes, yes of course; that's it. Both at the same time.

[*The* SECOND LADY LEAD *and the* JUVENILE LEAD *at this point separate themselves from the group of* ACTORS. *One watches the* MOTHER *attentively; the other moves about studying the movements and manner of the* SON, *whom he will have to act.*]

THE SON [*to the* MANAGER]. What do you mean by both at the same time? It isn't right. There was no scene between me and her. [*Indicates the* MOTHER.] Ask her how it was!

THE MOTHER. Yes, it's true. I had come into his room . . .

THE SON. Into my room, do you understand? Nothing to do with the garden.

THE MANAGER. It doesn't matter. Haven't I told you we've got to group the action?

THE SON [*observing the* JUVENILE LEAD *studying him*]. What do you want?

THE JUVENILE LEAD. Nothing! I was just looking at you.

THE SON [*turning towards the* SECOND LADY LEAD]. Ah! she's at it too: to re-act her part [*indicating the* MOTHER]!

THE MANAGER. Exactly! And it seems to me that you ought to be grateful to them for their interest.

THE SON. Yes, but haven't you yet perceived that it isn't possible to live in front of a mirror which not only freezes us with the image of ourselves, but throws our likeness back at us with a horrible grimace?

THE FATHER.   That is true, absolutely true. You must see that.

THE MANAGER [to the SECOND LADY LEAD and the JUVENILE LEAD].   He's right! Move away from them!

THE SON.   Do as you like. I'm out of this!

THE MANAGER.   Be quiet, you, will you? And let me hear your mother! [To the MOTHER.] You were saying you had entered . . .

THE MOTHER.   Yes, into his room, because I couldn't stand it any longer. I went to empty my heart to him of all the anguish that tortures me . . . But as soon as he saw me come in . . .

THE SON.   Nothing happened! There was no scene. I went away, that's all! I don't care for scenes!

THE MOTHER.   It's true, true. That's how it was.

THE MANAGER.   Well now, we've got to do this bit between you and him. It's indispensable.

THE MOTHER.   I'm ready . . . when you are ready. If you could only find a chance for me to tell him what I feel here in my heart.

THE FATHER [going to SON in a great rage].   You'll do this for your mother, for your mother, do you understand?

THE SON [quite determined].   I do nothing!

THE FATHER [taking hold of him and shaking him].   For God's sake, do as I tell you! Don't you hear your mother asking you for a favor? Haven't you even got the guts to be a son?

THE SON [taking hold of the FATHER].   No! No! And for God's sake stop it, or else . . . [General agitation. The MOTHER, frightened, tries to separate them.]

THE MOTHER [pleading].   Please! please!

THE FATHER [not leaving hold of the SON].   You've got to obey, do you hear?

THE SON [almost crying from rage].   What does it mean, this madness you've got? [They separate.] Have you no decency, that you insist on showing everyone our shame? I won't do it! I won't! And I stand for the will of our author in this. He didn't want to put us on the stage, after all!

THE MANAGER.   Man alive! You came here . . .

THE SON [indicating the FATHER].   He did! I didn't!

THE MANAGER.   Aren't you here now?

THE SON.   It was his wish, and he dragged us along with him. He's told you not only the things that did happen, but also things that have never happened at all.

THE MANAGER.   Well, tell me then what did happen. You went out of your room without saying a word?

THE SON.   Without a word, so as to avoid a scene!

THE MANAGER.   And then what did you do?

THE SON.   Nothing . . . walking in the garden . . . [Hesitates for a moment with expression of gloom.]

THE MANAGER [coming closer to him, interested by his extraordinary reserve].   Well, well . . . walking in the garden . . .

THE SON [*exasperated*]. Why on earth do you insist? It's horrible! [*The* MOTHER *trembles, sobs, and looks towards the fountain.*]

THE MANAGER [*slowly observing the glance and turning towards the* SON *with increasing apprehension*]. The baby?

THE SON. There in the fountain . . .

THE FATHER [*pointing with tender pity to the* MOTHER]. She was following him at the moment . . .

THE SON. I ran over to her; I was jumping in to drag her out when I saw something that froze my blood . . . the boy there standing stock still, with eyes like a madman's, watching his little drowned sister, in the fountain! [*The* STEPDAUGHTER *bends over the fountain to hide the* CHILD. *She sobs.*] Then . . . [*A revolver shot rings out behind the trees where the* BOY *is hidden.*]

THE MOTHER [*with a cry of terror runs over in that direction together with several of the* ACTORS *amid general confusion*]. My son! My son! [*Then amid the cries and exclamations one hears her voice.*] Help! Help!

THE MANAGER [*pushing the* ACTORS *aside while they lift up the* BOY *and carry him off*]. Is he really wounded?

SOME ACTORS. He's dead! dead!

OTHER ACTORS. No, no, it's only make believe, it's only pretence!

THE FATHER [*with a terrible cry*]. Pretence? Reality, sir, reality!

THE MANAGER. Pretence? Reality? To hell with it all! Never in my life has such a thing happened to me. I've lost a whole day over these people, a whole day!

Curtain

COMMENTARY

The essence of the theatre, as everyone is quick to understand, is illusion. The theatre sets out to induce in an audience the belief that the things and events it presents are not what they are known to be. The man on the stage who wears a crown and a purple robe and stalks with so stately a tread is a salaried actor who will go home after the performance to a light supper, a glass of beer, and bed. The audience knows this to be so but consents to accept him as "the King" and it has appropriate emotions when, in the course of the play, his "sacred" person is assaulted. Of course these emotions are not the same as would be felt by actual loyal subjects witnessing an actual attempt upon the life of their ruler, but they are consonant with the actual situation and they are often intense.

The audience comes to the performance with good will toward the theatre's designs upon it, with every intention of submitting to such illusion as the theatre can produce. The theatre, for its part, undertakes to provide the audience with adequate ground for suspending or mitigating its ordinary common-sense knowledge. The range of means by which the theatre brings about a successful illusion is wide. It includes, among other things, the distance set between the audience and the actors, scenery and lighting-effects, costume and make-up, the mimetic skill of the actors, the kind of language the actors are given to speak. The number of such devices employed varies considerably from epoch to epoch. Some cultural periods require more of them, some less. Victorian audiences would have considered inadequate the bare stage with which the Elizabethans were quite content. In our own day, the theatre is eclectic in its modes of production, which sometimes are very elaborate, sometimes so sparse as to suggest that all the theatre needs in order to bring illusion into being is to show that it wishes to do so.

Yet in the degree that the theatre is devoted to illusion, it delights in destroying it, or in seeming to destroy it. The word *illusion* comes from the Latin word meaning "to mock" (*illudere*), which in turn comes from the word meaning "to play" (*ludere*), and a favorite activity of the theatre is to play with the idea of illusion itself, to mock the very thing it most tries to create—and the audience that accepts it. Sometimes, having brought the illusion into being, it seems to suggest that it has no belief whatever in its own creation.

An amusing example of this occurs far back in the history of the theatre. The ancient Athenian drama was sacred to the god Dionysus, and the only time plays were presented was at the festival in his honor. On these occasions the priest of the god's cult presided over the performance and sat in the audience in a place of honor close to the stage. In one of the comedies of Aristophanes, *The Frogs,* the chief character is the god himself; he is represented as an arrant coward, and at one point in the action, when threatened with a beating, the comic Dionysus runs from the stage toward the audience and throws himself at the feet of the presiding priest whose protection he claims. The priest would seem to have been visibly disconcerted by this unexpected turn of events, and the Dionysus-character mocked his blushes and other signs of embarrassment.

No doubt the audience found the episode especially funny, and in a way that was different from the other comic moments in the play. The sudden destruction of the assumptions that the spectators had been making, the unexpected mingling of the world of the stage with the world of actuality, surely delighted the Athenians as similar shocks to their expectation have delighted all audiences since. Nothing that the theatre does is more engaging than its disclosing its own theatricality, its opening to question the illusion it has contrived. When Hamlet discusses the art of acting with the strolling players who have come to Elsinore there is always a little stir of new attention in the audience as it receives this reminder that the Prince of Denmark is himself an actor, and the excitement increases when, in a succeeding scene, the players act before the royal court the beginning of a crude little drama called "The Murder of Gonzago." This play-within-a-play is much less "real" than the play that contains it and it is usually acted in a stilted, unrealistic manner to emphasize the difference. But it has the effect of recalling to us that *Hamlet* is itself "merely" a play. Part of our experience of *Hamlet* becomes the awareness of the theatre itself—and of the theatre's awareness of itself.

One reason why these awarenesses—ours of the theatre and the theatre's of itself—are so engaging is that they relate to a primitive tendency to question the reality of what is commonly accepted as reality, to speculate whether life itself is not an illusion. The tendency may justly be called primitive because it is so commonly observed in children, who often have moments of thinking that all that goes on around them is but a show devised (sometimes with the purpose of putting them to a "test") by some supernal agency. This supposition of the nonreality of the actual world is of great importance in philosophic thought. Plato conceived of all that we see and know as the simulacrum of a reality that is concealed from us, and the continued interest of philosophers in the question of whether what we know is consonant with what really is made possible Alfred North Whitehead's statement that all succeeding philosophy is but "a series of footnotes to Plato." That life is a dream has often been said. Sometimes life is spoken of as a game. It is also said to be a play, and this is perhaps the most common expression of the impulse to doubt life's literal reality. Jaques' famous speech in *As You Like It,* "All the world's a stage / And all the men and women merely players," sums up an idea that has established itself in our language—we naturally speak of the "part" a person "plays" in life or in some particular situation, and of the way in which he fulfills his "rôle." Indeed the very word *person* suggests the theatre, for the original meaning of the Latin word *persona* was the mask worn by the actors of antiquity.

Of all the theatre's many celebrations of its own mysterious power, of all the challenging comparisons it makes between its own reality and that of life, Pirandello's *Six Characters in Search of an Author* is the most elaborate and brilliant. It carries the fascinating contrivance of the play-within-a-play to the point where it becomes a play-about-a-play. One might say that its *dramatis personae* are the elements of the theatre itself, all of them, as the author himself observed, in conflict with one another. The Six Characters have been "rejected" by the author, or at least he has declared himself unwilling to present their drama. The director, who despises the plays of Pirandello which he is required to put on, consents, after some resistance, to show interest in the Characters, but he finds them difficult and eventually not very satisfactory. The actors who are to play the Characters are contemptuous of them and hostile to them, an attitude which is reciprocated by the Father and the Stepdaughter, both because the actors have no drama of their own and also because they falsify the essence of the characters they play. The illusion of the theatre is wholly negated: we are permitted—forced, indeed—to see the bare stage and the shabby "properties" that are used for its contrivance. Yet of course, in spite of the civil war taking place within it, the theater realizes its familiar purpose. We of the audience do indeed believe in the reality of the Characters who are said to have been denied their existence by the author; we are fascinated and distressed by their painful situation and shocked by its outcome. The theatre as Pirandello represents it is very much like life itself, always at odds with itself, always getting in its own way, yet always pursuing and, in the end, having its way.

It is, of course, life itself that the Characters hope that the theatre will give them, and they are not concerned with distinguishing between real life and theatrical life, between life as people and life as characters. "The drama is in us and we are the drama," says the Father. "We are impatient to play it. Our inner passion drives us on to this." The Father's speech confirms—in this most un-Aristotelian play—Aristotle's idea that a drama is not the representation of a person but of an action.

Yet there is a distinction to be observed among the various ways in which the Characters think about the possibility of their realization. The Father and the Stepdaughter are fierce and explicit in their demand that they be permitted to come into existence through the acting out of their drama. Painful and shameful as their fate is, they insist upon fulfilling and demonstrating it; they may be said to love it as the means by which they attain life—they *are* their fate, they are the drama it makes. The Son, however, wants no part of the drama in which he is inextricably, although marginally, involved. It can only distress and disgust him. He is, he says, an " 'unrealized' character" and wishes to remain just that. And we, aware of the pale, thin censoriousness and self-regard that make him stand aloof from his ill-fated family, agree with his estimate of the quality of his existence, except that we take him to be personally rather than dramatically unrealized: to us he seems fully projected as the dramatic representation of an unrealized person, one whose being is in the control of his personal deficiencies. His refusal to take part in the drama as a Character is tantamount to refusing to be what in colloquial speech we call a "real person," someone whose force or courage or definiteness we necessarily perceive. Yet, for all his objection to being implicated in the drama, and despite his repugnance to the family's fate, he has had to come to the theatre as part of the family; and when, in a moment of indignation, he says that he is leaving the situation from which he is so alienated, he does not go, he cannot go. Whatever his desire may be, he is bound to the family fate and has his part in its drama; against his will, he is *in* life even though he does not occupy much space in it.

As for the Mother, she is incapable of conceiving herself as dramatic. She is wholly committed to her motherly functions and feelings and for her such ideas as "fate" and "existence," let alone "drama," have no meaning. She cannot conceive them because to do so requires a double vision that she lacks: the ability to stand off from her function and feelings and observe them. The Father, the Stepdaughter—and even, in his own dim way, the Son—have this capacity; they "see themselves" and they put a value upon what they see. But the Mother, who cannot see herself, sets no value upon herself. It is not merely that, like the Son, she objects to being in this particular drama; the very idea of drama, since it involves observation and a degree of conceptualization, is offensive to her: it belittles the actuality of life. She is, Pirandello says in his Preface to the play, realized as Nature, while the Father and the Stepdaughter (and in some degree the Son) are realized as Mind.

In the preface Pirandello speaks of "the inherent tragic conflict between life (which is always moving and changing) and form (which fixes it, immutable)." The conflict is not only tragic but ironic, for the "form" that Pirandello conceives of as the antagonist of "life" would seem to be brought into being by life itself for the furtherance of life. (A similar idea is central to Thomas Mann's story, "Disorder and Early Sorrow" [pages 300 ff.].) The Characters exist, they live, by reason of their fixity and immutability: the word *character* derives from the Greek word meaning to engrave, and it suggests the quality of permanence. The Father and the Stepdaughter are committed to repeat the situation that pains and shames them; they cannot move beyond it, yet it is through this compulsive reliving of the past, which denies a future in which they might move and change, that they achieve their reality of existence, their life. Realized as Mind, they are fixed by the form appropriate to Mind, their idea of themselves. The Mother, realized as Nature, is fixed by the form appropriate to Nature, her instinctual blind devotion to her maternal function of bringing life into being and preserving it.

PART

2 FICTION

MY
KINSMAN,
MAJOR MOLINEUX

NATHANIEL HAWTHORNE

1 8 0 4 – 1 8 6 4

AFTER THE KINGS of Great Britain had assumed the right of appointing the colonial governors, the measures of the latter seldom met with the ready and generous approbation which had been paid to those of their predecessors, under the original charters. The people looked with most jealous scrutiny to the exercise of power which did not emanate from themselves, and they usually rewarded their rulers with slender gratitude for the compliances by which, in softening their instructions from beyond the sea, they had incurred the reprehension of those who gave them. The annals of Massachusetts Bay will inform us, that of six governors in the space of about forty years from the surrender of the old charter, under James II, two were imprisoned by a popular insurrection; a third, as Hutchinson[1] inclines to believe, was driven from the province by the whizzing of a musket-ball; a fourth, in the opinion of the same historian, was hastened to his grave by continual bickerings with the House of Representatives; and the remaining two, as well as their successors, till the Revolution, were favored with few and brief intervals of peaceful sway. The inferior members of the court party, in times of high political excitement, led scarcely a more desirable life. These remarks may serve

1 Thomas Hutchinson, *The History of the Colony and Province of Massachusetts Bay*, Boston, 1764.

as a preface to the following adventures, which chanced upon a summer night, not far from a hundred years ago.[2] The reader, in order to avoid a long and dry detail of colonial affairs, is requested to dispense with an account of the train of circumstances that had caused much temporary inflammation of the popular mind.

It was near nine o'clock of a moonlight evening, when a boat crossed the ferry with a single passenger, who had obtained his conveyance at that unusual hour by the promise of an extra fare. While he stood on the landing-place, searching in either pocket for the means of fulfilling his agreement, the ferryman lifted a lantern, by the aid of which, and the newly risen moon, he took a very accurate survey of the stranger's figure. He was a youth of barely eighteen years, evidently country-bred, and now, as it should seem, upon his first visit to town. He was clad in a coarse gray coat, well worn, but in excellent repair; his under garments[3] were durably constructed of leather, and fitted tight to a pair of serviceable and well-shaped limbs; his stockings of blue yarn were the incontrovertible work of a mother or a sister; and on his head was a three-cornered hat, which in its better days had perhaps sheltered the graver brow of the lad's father. Under his left arm was a heavy cudgel formed of an oak sapling, and retaining a part of the hardened root; and his equipment was completed by a wallet, not so abundantly stocked as to incommode the vigorous shoulders on which it hung. Brown, curly hair, well-shaped features, and bright, cheerful eyes were nature's gifts, and worth all that art could have done for his adornment.

The youth, one of whose names was Robin, finally drew from his pocket the half of a little province bill of five shillings, which, in the depreciation in that sort of currency, did but satisfy the ferryman's demand, with the surplus of a sexangular piece of parchment, valued at three pence. He then walked forward into the town, with as light a step as if his day's journey had not already exceeded thirty miles, and with as eager an eye as if he were entering London city, instead of the little metropolis of a New England colony. Before Robin had proceeded far, however, it occurred to him that he knew not whither to direct his steps; so he paused, and looked up and down the narrow street, scrutinizing the small and mean wooden buildings that were scattered on either side.

"This low hovel cannot be my kinsman's dwelling," thought he, "nor yonder old house, where the moonlight enters at the broken casement; and truly I see none hereabouts that might be worthy of him. It would have been wise to inquire my way of the ferryman, and doubtless he would have gone with me, and earned a shilling from the Major for his pains. But the next man I meet will do as well."

He resumed his walk, and was glad to perceive that the street now became wider, and the houses more respectable in their appearance. He soon discerned a figure moving on moderately in advance, and hastened his steps to overtake it. As Robin drew nigh, he saw that the passenger was a man in years, with a full periwig of gray hair, a wide-skirted coat of dark cloth, and silk stockings rolled above his knees. He carried a long and polished cane, which he struck down perpendicularly before him at every step; and at regular intervals he uttered two successive hems, of a peculiarly solemn and sepulchral intonation. Having made these observations, Robin laid hold of the skirt of the old man's coat, just when

[2] The story was written in 1828 or 1829.
[3] Knee breeches.

the light from the open door and windows of a barber's shop fell upon both their figures.

"Good evening to you, honored sir," said he, making a low bow, and still retaining his hold of the skirt. "I pray you tell me whereabouts is the dwelling of my kinsman, Major Molineux."

The youth's question was uttered very loudly; and one of the barbers, whose razor was descending on a well-soaped chin, and another who was dressing a Ramillies wig,[4] left their occupations, and came to the door. The citizen, in the mean time, turned a long-favored countenance upon Robin, and answered him in a tone of excessive anger and annoyance. His two sepulchral hems, however, broke into the very centre of his rebuke, with most singular effect, like a thought of the cold grave obtruding among wrathful passions.

"Let go my garment, fellow! I tell you, I know not the man you speak of. What! I have authority, I have—hem, hem—authority; and if this be the respect you show for your betters, your feet shall be brought acquainted with the stocks by daylight, tomorrow morning!"

Robin released the old man's skirt, and hastened away, pursued by an ill-mannered roar of laughter from the barber's shop. He was at first considerably surprised by the result of his question, but, being a shrewd youth, soon thought himself able to account for the mystery.

"This is some country representative," was his conclusion, "who has never seen the inside of my kinsman's door, and lacks the breeding to answer a stranger civilly. The man is old, or verily—I might be tempted to turn back and smite him on the nose. Ah, Robin, Robin! even the barber's boys laugh at you for choosing such a guide! You will be wiser in time, friend Robin."

He now became entangled in a succession of crooked and narrow streets, which crossed each other, and meandered at no great distance from the water-side. The smell of tar was obvious to his nostrils, the masts of vessels pierced the moonlight above the tops of the buildings, and the numerous signs, which Robin paused to read, informed him that he was near the centre of business. But the streets were empty, the shops were closed, and lights were visible only in the second stories of a few dwelling-houses. At length, on the corner of a narrow lane, through which he was passing, he beheld the broad countenance of a British hero swinging before the door of an inn,[5] whence proceeded the voices of many guests. The casement of one of the lower windows was thrown back, and a very thin curtain permitted Robin to distinguish a party at supper, round a well-furnished table. The fragrance of the good cheer steamed forth into the outer air, and the youth could not fail to recollect that the last remnant of his travelling stock of provision had yielded to his morning appetite, and that noon had found and left him dinnerless.

"Oh, that a parchment three-penny might give me a right to sit down at yonder table!" said Robin, with a sigh. "But the Major will make me welcome to the best of his victuals; so I will even step boldly in, and inquire my way to his dwelling."

He entered the tavern, and was guided by the murmur of voices and the

[4] A wig having a long plait behind tied with a bow at the top and the bottom.
[5] An inn would often be named after a famous personage, whose picture would appear on a sign projecting from above the main entry.

fumes of tobacco to the public-room. It was a long and low apartment, with oaken walls, grown dark in the continual smoke, and a floor which was thickly sanded, but of no immaculate purity. A number of persons—the larger part of whom appeared to be mariners, or in some way connected with the sea—occupied the wooden benches, or leather-bottomed chairs, conversing on various matters, and occasionally lending their attention to some topic of general interest. Three or four little groups were draining as many bowls of punch, which the West India trade had long since made a familiar drink in the colony. Others, who had the appearance of men who lived by regular and laborious handicraft, preferred the insulated bliss of an unshared potation, and became more taciturn under its influence. Nearly all, in short, evinced a predilection for the Good Creature[6] in some of its various shapes, for this is a vice to which, as Fast Day sermons of a hundred years ago will testify, we have a long hereditary claim. The only guests to whom Robin's sympathies inclined him were two or three sheepish countrymen, who were using the inn somewhat after the fashion of a Turkish caravansary;[7] they had gotten themselves into the darkest corner of the room, and heedless of the Nicotian[8] atmosphere, were supping on the bread of their own ovens, and the bacon cured in their own chimney-smoke. But though Robin felt a sort of brotherhood with these strangers, his eyes were attracted from them to a person who stood near the door, holding whispered conversation with a group of ill-dressed associates. His features were separately striking almost to grotesqueness, and the whole face left a deep impression on the memory. The forehead bulged out into a double prominence, with a vale between; the nose came boldly forth in an irregular curve, and its bridge was of more than a finger's breadth; the eyebrows were deep and shaggy, and the eyes glowed beneath them like fire in a cave.

While Robin deliberated of whom to inquire respecting his kinsman's dwelling, he was accosted by the innkeeper, a little man in a stained white apron, who had come to pay his professional welcome to the stranger. Being in the second generation from a French Protestant, he seemed to have inherited the courtesy of his parent nation; but no variety of circumstances was ever known to change his voice from the one shrill note in which he now addressed Robin.

"From the country, I presume, sir?" said he, with a profound bow. "Beg leave to congratulate you on your arrival, and trust you intend a long stay with us. Fine town here, sir, beautiful buildings, and much that may interest a stranger. May I hope for the honor of your commands in respect to supper?"

"The man sees a family likeness! the rogue has guessed that I am related to the Major!" thought Robin, who had hitherto experienced little superfluous civility.

All eyes were now turned on the country lad, standing at the door, in his worn three-cornered hat, gray coat, leather breeches, and blue yarn stockings, leaning on an oaken cudgel, and bearing a wallet on his back.

Robin replied to the courteous innkeeper, with such an assumption of con-

[6] Applied humorously to intoxicating liquor, but originally signifying that part of God's creation which ministers to the material comfort of man. See I Timothy 4:4, "Every creature of God is good."

[7] A public building in which travelers prepare and eat the food they have brought with them.

[8] Filled with tobacco smoke (from the name of Jacques Nicot, who introduced tobacco into France in 1560).

fidence as befitted the Major's relative. "My honest friend," he said, "I shall make it a point to patronize your house on some occasion, when"—here he could not help lowering his voice—"when I may have more than a parchment three-pence in my pocket. My present business," continued he, speaking with lofty confidence, "is merely to inquire my way to the dwelling of my kinsman, Major Molineux."

There was a sudden and general movement in the room, which Robin interpreted as expressing the eagerness of each individual to become his guide. But the innkeeper turned his eyes to a written paper on the wall, which he read, or seemed to read, with occasional recurrences to the young man's figure.

"What have we here?" said he, breaking his speech into little dry fragments. " 'Left the house of the subscriber, bounden servant,[9] Hezekiah Mudge,—had on, when he went away, gray coat, leather breeches, master's third-best hat. One pound currency reward to whosoever shall lodge him in any jail of the providence.' Better trudge, boy; better trudge!"

Robin had begun to draw his hand towards the lighter end of the oak cudgel, but a strange hostility in every countenance induced him to relinquish his purpose of breaking the courteous innkeeper's head. As he turned to leave the room, he encountered a sneering glance from the bold-featured personage whom he had before noticed; and no sooner was he beyond the door, than he heard a general laugh, in which the innkeeper's voice might be distinguished, like the dropping of small stones into a kettle.

"Now, is it not strange," thought Robin, with his usual shrewdness,—"is it not strange that the confession of an empty pocket should outweigh the name of my kinsman, Major Molineux? Oh, if I had one of those grinning rascals in the woods, where I and my oak sapling grew up together, I would teach him that my arm is heavy though my purse be light!"

On turning the corner of the narrow lane, Robin found himself in a spacious street, with an unbroken line of lofty houses on each side, and a steepled building at the upper end, whence the ringing of a bell announced the hour of nine. The light of the moon, and the lamps from the numerous shop-windows, discovered people promenading on the pavement, and amongst them Robin had hoped to recognize his hitherto inscrutable relative. The result of his former inquiries made him unwilling to hazard another, in a scene of such publicity, and he determined to walk slowly and silently up the street, thrusting his face close to that of every elderly gentleman, in search of the Major's lineaments. In his progress, Robin encountered many gay and gallant figures. Embroidered garments of showy colors, enormous periwigs, gold-laced hats, and silver-hilted swords glided past him and dazzled his optics. Travelled youths, imitators of the European fine gentlemen of the period, trod jauntily along, half dancing to the fashionable tunes which they hummed, and making poor Robin ashamed of his quiet and natural gait. At length, after many pauses to examine the gorgeous display of goods in the shop-windows, and after suffering some rebukes for the impertinence of his scrutiny into people's faces, the Major's kinsman found himself near the steepled building, still unsuccessful in his search. As yet, however, he had seen only one side of the thronged street; so Robin crossed, and continued the same

[9] An indentured servant, bound by contract to serve for a certain time before obtaining his freedom.

sort of inquisition down the opposite pavement, with stronger hopes than the philosopher seeking an honest man, but with no better fortune. He had arrived about midway towards the lower end, from which his course began, when he overheard the approach of some one who struck down a cane on the flag-stones at every step, uttering at regular intervals, two sepulchral hems.

"Mercy on us!" quoth Robin, recognizing the sound.

Turning a corner, which chanced to be close at his right hand, he hastened to pursue his researches in some other part of the town. His patience now was wearing low, and he seemed to feel more fatigue from his rambles since he crossed the ferry, than from his journey of several days on the other side. Hunger also pleaded loudly within him, and Robin began to balance the propriety of demand-ing, violently, and with lifted cudgel, the necessary guidance from the first soli-tary passenger whom he should meet. While a resolution to this effect was gain-ing strength, he entered a street of mean appearance, on either side of which a row of ill-built houses was straggling towards the harbor. The moonlight fell upon no passenger along the whole extent, but in the third domicile which Robin passed there was a half-opened door, and his keen glance detected a woman's garment within.

"My luck may be better here," said he to himself.

Accordingly, he approached the door, and beheld it shut closer as he did so; yet an open space remained, sufficing for the fair occupant to observe the stranger, without a corresponding display on her part. All that Robin could discern was a strip of scarlet petticoat, and the occasional sparkle of an eye, as if the moonbeams were trembling on some bright thing.

"Pretty mistress," for I may call her so with a good conscience, thought the shrewd youth, since I know nothing to the contrary,—"my sweet pretty mistress, will you be kind enough to tell me whereabouts I must seek the dwelling of my kinsman, Major Molineux?"

Robin's voice was plaintive and winning, and the female, seeing nothing to be shunned in the handsome country youth, thrust open the door, and came forth into the moonlight. She was a dainty little figure, with a white neck, round arms, and a slender waist, at the extremity of which her scarlet petticoat jutted out over a hoop, as if she were standing in a balloon. Moreover, her face was oval and pretty, her hair dark beneath the little cap, and her bright eyes possessed a sly freedom, which triumphed over those of Robin.

"Major Molineux dwells here," said this fair woman.

Now, her voice was the sweetest Robin had heard that night, yet he could not help doubting whether that sweet voice spoke Gospel truth. He looked up and down the mean street, and then surveyed the house before which they stood. It was a small, dark edifice of two stories, the second of which projected over the lower floor, and the front apartment had the aspect of a shop for petty commodi-ties.

"Now, truly, I am in luck," replied Robin, cunningly, "and so indeed is my kinsman, the Major, in having so pretty a housekeeper. But I prithee trouble him to step to the door; I will deliver him a message from his friends in the country, and then go back to my lodgings at the inn."

"Nay, the Major has been abed this hour or more," said the lady of the scarlet petticoat; "and it would be to little purpose to disturb him to-night, seeing his evening draught was of the strongest. But he is a kind-hearted man, and it would be as much as my life's worth to let a kinsman of his turn away from the door. You are the good old gentleman's very picture, and I could swear that was his rainy-weather hat. Also he has garments very much resembling those leather small-clothes. But come in, I pray, for I bid you hearty welcome in his name."

So saying, the fair and hospitable dame took our hero by the hand; and the touch was light, and the force was gentleness, and though Robin read in her eyes what he did not hear in her words, yet the slender-waisted woman in the scarlet petticoat proved stronger than the athletic country youth. She had drawn his half-willing footsteps nearly to the threshold, when the opening of a door in the neighborhood startled the Major's housekeeper, and, leaving the Major's kinsman, she vanished speedily into her own domicile. A heavy yawn preceded the appearance of a man, who, like the Moonshine of Pyramus and Thisbe,[10] carried a lantern, needlessly aiding his sister luminary in the heavens. As he walked sleepily up the street, he turned his broad, dull face on Robin, and displayed a long staff, spiked at the end.

"Home, vagabond, home!" said the watchman, in accents that seemed to fall asleep as soon as they were uttered. "Home, or we'll set you in the stocks by peep of day!"

"This is the second hint of the kind," thought Robin. "I wish they would end my difficulties, by setting me there to-night."

Nevertheless, the youth felt an instinctive antipathy towards the guardian of midnight order, which at first prevented him from asking his usual question. But just when the man was about to vanish behind the corner, Robin resolved not to lose the opportunity, and shouted lustily after him,—

"I say, friend! will you guide me to the house of my kinsman, Major Molineux?"

The watchman made no reply, but turned the corner and was gone; yet Robin seemed to hear the sound of drowsy laughter stealing along the solitary street. At that moment, also, a pleasant titter saluted him from the open window above his head; he looked up, and caught the sparkle of a saucy eye; a round arm beckoned to him, and next he heard light footsteps descending the staircase within. But Robin, being of the household of a New England clergyman, was a good youth, as well as a shrewd one; so he resisted temptation, and fled away.

He now roamed desperately, and at random, through the town, almost ready to believe that a spell was on him, like that by which a wizard of his country had once kept three pursuers wandering, a whole winter night, within twenty paces of the cottage which they sought. The streets lay before him, strange and desolate, and the lights were extinguished in almost every house. Twice, however, little parties of men, among whom Robin distinguished individuals in outlandish attire, came hurrying along; but, though on both occasions, they paused to address him, such intercourse did not at all enlighten his perplexity. They did but utter a few words in some language of which Robin knew nothing, and perceiving his inability to answer, bestowed a curse upon him in plain English and hastened away. Finally, the lad determined to knock at the door of every mansion that might appear worthy to be occupied by his kinsman, trusting that perseverance would

---

[10] In Shakespeare's *A Midsummer-Night's Dream*, Act V, Scene 1, a man with a lantern represents the moon in a comically inept performance of the tragic love story of Pyramus and Thisbe.

overcome the fatality that had hitherto thwarted him. Firm in this resolve, he was passing beneath the walls of a church, which formed the corner of two streets, when, as he turned into the shade of its steeple. he encountered a bulky stranger, muffled in a cloak. The man was proceeding with the speed of earnest business, but Robin planted himself full before him, holding the oak cudgel with both hands across his body as a bar to further passage.

"Halt, honest man, and answer me a question," said he, very resolutely. "Tell me, this instant, whereabouts is the dwelling of my kinsman, Major Molineux!"

"Keep your tongue between your teeth, fool, and let me pass!" said a deep, gruff voice, which Robin partly remembered. "Let me pass, or I'll strike you to the earth!"

"No, no, neighbor!" cried Robin, flourishing his cudgel, and then thrusting its larger end close to the man's muffled face. "No, no, I'm not the fool you take me for, nor do you pass till I have an answer to my question. Whereabouts is the dwelling of my kinsman, Major Molineux?"

The stranger, instead of attempting to force his passage, stepped back into the moonlight, unmuffled his face, and stared full into that of Robin.

"Watch here an hour, and Major Molineux will pass by," said he.

Robin gazed with dismay and astonishment on the unprecedented physiognomy of the speaker. The forehead with its double prominence, the broad hooked nose, the shaggy eyebrows, and fiery eyes were those which he had noticed at the inn, but the man's complexion had undergone a singular, or, more properly, a twofold change. One side of the face blazed an intense red, while the other was black as midnight, the division line being in the broad bridge of the nose; and a mouth which seemed to extend from ear to ear was black or red, in contrast to the color of the cheek. The effect was as if two individual devils, a fiend of fire and a fiend of darkness, had united themselves to form this infernal visage. The stranger grinned in Robin's face, muffled his party-colored features, and was out of sight in a moment.

"Strange things we travellers see!" ejaculated Robin.

He seated himself, however, upon the steps of the church-door, resolving to wait the appointed time for his kinsman. A few moments were consumed in philosophical speculations upon the species of man who had just left him; but having settled this point shrewdly, rationally, and satisfactorily, he was compelled to look elsewhere for his amusement. And first he threw his eyes along the street. It was of more respectable appearance than most of those into which he had wandered; and the moon, creating, like the imaginative power, a beautiful strangeness in familiar objects, gave something of romance to a scene that might not have possessed it in the light of day. The irregular and often quaint architecture of the houses, some of whose roofs were broken into numerous little peaks, while others ascended, steep and narrow, into a single point, and others again were square; the pure snow-white of some of their complexions, the aged darkness of others, and the thousand sparklings, reflected from bright substances in the walls of many; these matters engaged Robin's attention for a while, and then began to grow wearisome. Next he endeavored to define the forms of distant objects, starting away, with almost ghostly indistinctness, just as his eye appeared to grasp them; and finally he took a minute survey of an edifice which stood on the opposite side of the street, directly in front of the church-door, where he was stationed. It was a large, square mansion, distinguished from its neighbors by a balcony, which rested on tall pillars, and by an elaborate Gothic window, communicating therewith.

"Perhaps this is the very house I have been seeking," thought Robin.

Then he strove to speed away the time, by listening to a murmur which swept continually along the street, yet was scarcely audible, except to an unaccustomed ear like his; it was a low, dull, dreamy sound, compounded of many noises, each of which was at too great a distance to be separately heard. Robin marvelled at this snore of a sleeping town, and marvelled more whenever its continuity was broken by now and then a distant shout, apparently loud where it originated. But altogether it was a sleep-inspiring sound, and, to shake off its drowsy influence, Robin arose, and climbed a window-frame, that he might view the interior of the church. There the moonbeams came trembling in, and fell down upon the deserted pews, and extended along the quiet aisles. A fainter yet more awful radiance was hovering around the pulpit, and one solitary ray had dared to rest upon the open page of the great Bible. Had nature, in that deep hour, become a worshipper in the house which man had builded? Or was that heavenly light the visible sanctity of the place,—visible because no earthly and impure feet were within the walls? The scene made Robin's heart shiver with a sensation of loneliness stronger than he had ever felt in the remotest depths of his native woods; so he turned away and sat down again before the door. There were graves around the church, and now an uneasy thought obtruded into Robin's breast. What if the object of his search, which had been so often and so strangely thwarted, were all the time mouldering in his shroud? What if his kinsman should glide through yonder gate, and nod and smile to him in dimly passing by?

"Oh that any breathing thing were here with me!" said Robin.

Recalling his thoughts from this uncomfortable track, he sent them over forest, hill, and stream, and attempted to imagine how that evening of ambiguity and weariness had been spent by his father's household. He pictured them assembled at the door, beneath the tree, the great old tree, which had been spared for its huge twisted trunk and venerable shade, when a thousand leafy brethren fell. There, at the going down of the summer sun, it was his father's custom to perform domestic worship, that the neighbors might come and join with him like brothers of the family, and that the wayfaring man might pause to drink at that fountain, and keep his heart pure by freshening the memory of home. Robin distinguished the seat of every individual of the little audience; he saw the good man in the midst, holding the Scriptures in the golden light that fell from the western clouds; he beheld him close the book and all rise up to pray. He heard the old thanksgivings for daily mercies, the old supplications for their continuance, to which he had so often listened in weariness, but which were now among his dear remembrances. He perceived the slight inequality of his father's voice when he came to speak of the absent one; he noted how his mother turned her face to the broad and knotted trunk; how his elder brother scorned, because the beard was rough upon his upper lip, to permit his features to be moved; how the younger sister drew down a low hanging branch before her eyes; and how the little one of all, whose sports had hitherto broken the decorum of the scene, understood the prayer for her playmate, and burst into clamorous grief. Then he saw them go in at the door; and when Robin would have entered also, the latch tinkled into its place, and he was excluded from his home.

"Am I here, or there?" cried Robin, starting; for all at once, when his thoughts had become visible and audible in a dream, the long, wide, solitary street shone out before him.

He aroused himself, and endeavored to fix his attention steadily upon the large edifice which he had surveyed before. But still his mind kept vibrating between fancy and reality; by turns, the pillars of the balcony lengthened into the tall, bare stems of pines, dwindled down to human figures, settled again into their true shape and size, and then commenced a new succession of changes. For a single moment, when he deemed himself awake, he could have sworn that a visage—one which he seemed to remember, yet could not absolutely name as his kinsman's—was looking towards him from the Gothic window. A deeper sleep wrestled with and nearly overcame him, but fled at the sound of footsteps along the opposite pavement. Robin rubbed his eyes, discerned a man passing at the foot of the balcony, and addressed him in a loud, peevish, and lamentable cry.

"Hallo, friend! must I wait here all night for my kinsman, Major Molineux?"

The sleeping echoes awoke, and answered the voice; and the passenger, barely able to discern a figure sitting in the oblique shade of the steeple, traversed the street to obtain a nearer view. He was himself a gentleman in his prime, of open, intelligent, cheerful, and altogether prepossessing countenance. Perceiving a country youth, apparently homeless and without friends, he accosted him in a tone of real kindness, which had become strange to Robin's ears.

"Well, my good lad, why are you sitting here?" inquired he. "Can I be of service to you in any way?"

"I am afraid not, sir," replied Robin, despondingly; "yet I shall take it kindly, if you'll answer me a single question. I've been searching, half the night, for one Major Molineux; now, sir, is there really such a person in these parts, or am I dreaming?"

"Major Molineux! The name is not altogether strange to me," said the gentleman, smiling. "Have you any objection to telling me the nature of your business with him?"

Then Robin briefly related that his father was a clergyman, settled on a small salary, at a long distance back in the country, and that he and Major Molineux were brothers' children. The Major, having inherited riches, and acquired civil and military rank, had visited his cousin, in great pomp, a year or two before; had manifested much interest in Robin and an elder brother, and, being childless himself, had thrown out hints respecting the future establishment of one of them in life. The elder brother was destined to succeed to the farm which his father cultivated in the interval of sacred duties; it was therefore determined that Robin should profit by his kinsman's generous intentions, especially as he seemed to be rather the favorite, and was thought to possess other necessary endowments.

"For I have the name of being a shrewd youth," observed Robin, in this part of his story.

"I doubt not you deserve it," replied his new friend, good-naturedly; "but pray proceed."

"Well, sir, being nearly eighteen years old, and well grown, as you see," continued Robin, drawing himself up to his full height, "I thought it high time to begin in the world. So my mother and sister put me in handsome trim, and my father gave me half the remnant of his last year's salary, and five days ago I started for this place, to pay the Major a visit. But, would you believe it, sir! I crossed the ferry a little after dark, and have yet found nobody that would show me the way to his dwelling; only, an hour or two since, I was told to wait here, and Major Molineux would pass by."

"Can you describe the man who told you this?" inquired the gentleman.

"Oh, he was a very ill-favored fellow, sir," replied Robin, "with two great bumps on his forehead, a hook nose, fiery eyes; and, what struck me as the strangest, his face was of two different colors. Do you happen to know such a man, sir?"

"Not intimately," answered the stranger, "but I chanced to meet him a little time previous to your stopping me. I believe you may trust his word, and that the Major will very shortly pass through this street. In the mean time, as I have a singular curiosity to witness your meeting, I will sit down here upon the steps and bear you company."

He seated himself accordingly, and soon engaged his companion in animated discourse. It was but of brief continuance, however, for a noise of shouting, which had long been remotely audible, drew so much nearer that Robin inquired its cause.

"What may be the meaning of this uproar?" asked he. "Truly, if your town be always as noisy, I shall find little sleep while I am an inhabitant."

"Why, indeed, friend Robin, there do appear to be three or four riotous fellows abroad to-night," replied the gentleman. "You must not expect all the stillness of your native woods here in our streets. But the watch will shortly be at the heels of these lads and"—

"Ay, and set them in the stocks by peep of day," interrupted Robin, recollecting his own encounter with the drowsy lantern-bearer. "But, dear sir, if I may trust my ears, an army of watchmen would never make head against such a multitude of rioters. There were at least a thousand voices went up to make that one shout."

"May not a man have several voices, Robin, as well as two complexions?" said his friend.

"Perhaps a man may; but Heaven forbid that a woman should!" responded the shrewd youth, thinking of the seductive tones of the Major's housekeeper.

The sounds of a trumpet in some neighboring street now became so evident and continual, that Robin's curiosity was strongly excited. In addition to the shouts, he heard frequent bursts from many instruments of discord, and a wild and confused laughter filled up the intervals. Robin rose from the steps, and looked wistfully towards a point whither people seemed to be hastening.

"Surely some prodigious merry-making is going on," exclaimed he. "I have laughed very little since I left home, sir, and should be sorry to lose an opportunity. Shall we step round the corner by that darkish house, and take our share of the fun?"

"Sit down again, sit down, good Robin," replied the gentleman, laying his hand on the skirt of the gray coat. "You forget that we must wait here for your kinsman; and there is reason to believe that he will pass by, in the course of a very few moments."

The near approach of the uproar had now disturbed the neighborhood; windows flew open on all sides; and many heads, in the attire of the pillow, and confused by sleep suddenly broken, were protruded to the gaze of whoever had leisure to observe them. Eager voices hailed each other from house to house, all demanding the explanation, which not a soul could give. Half-dressed men hurried towards the unknown commotion, stumbling as they went over the stone steps that thrust themselves into the narrow foot-walk. The shouts, the laughter, and the tuneless bray, the antipodes of music, came onwards with increasing din, till scattered individuals, and then denser bodies, began to appear round a corner at the distance of a hundred yards.

"Will you recognize your kinsman, if he passes in this crowd?" inquired the gentleman.

"Indeed, I can't warrant it, sir; but I'll take my stand here, and keep a bright lookout," answered Robin, descending to the outer edge of the pavement.

A mighty stream of people now emptied into the street, and came rolling slowly towards the church. A single horseman wheeled the corner in the midst of them, and close behind him came a band of fearful wind-instruments, sending forth a fresher discord now that no intervening buildings kept it from the ear. Then a redder light disturbed the moonbeams, and a dense multitude of torches shone along the street, concealing, by their glare, whatever object they illuminated. The single horseman, clad in a military dress, and bearing a drawn sword, rode onward as the leader, and, by his fierce and variegated countenance, appeared like war personified; the red of one cheek was an emblem of fire and sword; the blackness of the other betokened the mourning that attends them. In his train were wild figures in the Indian dress, and many fantastic shapes without a model, giving the whole march a visionary air, as if a dream had broken forth from some feverish brain, and were sweeping visibly through the midnight streets. A mass of people, inactive, except as applauding spectators, hemmed the procession in; and several women ran along the sidewalk, piercing the confusion of heavier sounds with their shrill voices of mirth or terror.

"The double-faced fellow has his eye upon me," muttered Robin, with an indefinite but an uncomfortable idea that he was himself to bear a part in the pageantry.

The leader turned himself in the saddle, and fixed his glance full upon the country youth, as the steed went slowly by. When Robin had freed his eyes from those fiery ones, the musicians were passing before him, and the torches were close at hand; but the unsteady brightness of the latter formed a veil which he could not penetrate. The rattling of wheels over the stones sometimes found its way to his ear, and confused traces of a human form appeared at intervals, and then melted into the vivid light. A moment more, and the leader thundered a command to halt: the trumpets vomited a horrid breath, and then held their peace; the shouts and laughter of the people died away, and there remained only a universal hum, allied to silence. Right before Robin's eyes was an uncovered cart. There the torches blazed the brightest, there the moon shone out like day, and there, in tar-and-feathery dignity, sat his kinsman, Major Molineux!

He was an elderly man, of large and majestic person, and strong, square features, betokening a steady soul; but steady as it was, his enemies had found means to shake it. His face was pale as death, and far more ghastly; the broad forehead was contracted in his agony, so that his eyebrows formed one grizzled line; his eyes were red and wild, and the foam hung white upon his quivering lip. His whole frame was agitated by a quick and continual tremor, which his pride strove to quell, even in those circumstances of overwhelming humiliation.

But perhaps the bitterest pang of all was when his eyes met those of Robin; for he evidently knew him on the instant, as the youth stood witnessing the foul disgrace of a head grown gray in honor. They stared at each other in silence, and Robin's knees shook, and his hair bristled, with a mixture of pity and terror. Soon, however, a bewildering excitement began to seize upon his mind; the preceding adventures of the night, the unexpected appearance of the crowd, the torches, the confused din and the hush that followed, the spectre of his kinsman reviled by that great multitude,—all this, and, more than all, a perception of tremendous ridicule in the whole scene, affected him with a sort of mental inebriety. At that moment a voice of sluggish merriment saluted Robin's ears; he turned instinctively, and just behind the corner of the church stood the lantern-bearer, rubbing his eyes, and drowsily enjoying the lad's amazement. Then he heard a peal of laughter like the ringing of silvery bells; a woman twitched his arm, a saucy eye met his, and he saw the lady of the scarlet petticoat. A sharp, dry cachinnation appealed to his memory, and, standing on tiptoe in the crowd, with his white apron over his head, he beheld the courteous little innkeeper. And lastly, there sailed over the heads of the multitude a great, broad laugh, broken in the midst by two sepulchral hems; thus, "Haw, haw, haw,—hem, hem,—haw, haw, haw, haw!"

The sound proceeded from the balcony of the opposite edifice, and thither Robin turned his eyes. In front of the Gothic window stood the old citizen, wrapped in a wide gown, his gray periwig exchanged for a nightcap, which was thrust back from his forehead, and his silk stockings hanging about his legs. He supported himself on his polished cane in a fit of convulsive merriment, which manifested itself on his solemn old features like a funny inscription on a tombstone. Then Robin seemed to hear the voices of the barbers, of the guests of the inn, and of all who had made sport of him that night. The contagion was spreading among the multitude, when all at once, it seized upon Robin, and he sent forth a shout of laughter that echoed through the street,—every man shook his sides, every man emptied his lungs, but Robin's shout was the loudest there. The cloud-spirits peeped from their silvery islands, as the congregated mirth went roaring up the sky! The Man in the Moon heard the far bellow. "Oho," quoth he, "the old earth is frolicsome to-night!"

When there was a momentary calm in that tempestuous sea of sound, the leader gave the sign, the procession resumed its march. On they went, like fiends that throng in mockery around some dead potentate, mighty no more, but majestic still in his agony. On they went, in counterfeited pomp, in senseless uproar, in frenzied merriment, trampling all on an old man's heart. On swept the tumult, and left a silent street behind.

"Well, Robin, are you dreaming?" inquired the gentleman, laying his hand on the youth's shoulder.

Robin started, and withdrew his arm from the stone post to which he had instinctively clung, as the living stream rolled by him. His cheek was somewhat pale, and his eye not quite as lively as in the earlier part of the evening.

"Will you be kind enough to show me the way to the ferry?" said he, after a moment's pause.

"You have, then, adopted a new subject of inquiry?" observed his companion, with a smile.

"Why, yes, sir," replied Robin, rather dryly. "Thanks to you, and to my other friends, I have at last met my kinsman, and he will scarce desire to see my face again. I begin to grow weary of a town life, sir. Will you show me the way to the ferry?"

"No, my good friend Robin,—not to-night, at least," said the gentleman. "Some few days hence, if you wish it, I will speed you on your journey. Or, if you prefer to remain with us, perhaps, as you are a shrewd youth, you may rise in the world without the help of your kinsman, Major Molineux."

THE
DEATH
OF
IVAN ILYCH

LEO TOLSTOI
1828–1910

I

DURING AN INTERVAL in the Melvinski trial in the large building of the Law Courts, the members and public prosecutor met in Ivan Egorovich Shebek's private room, where the conversation turned on the celebrated Krasovski case. Fëdor Vasilievich warmly maintained that it was not subject to their jurisdiction, Ivan Egorovich maintained the contrary, while Peter Ivanovich, not having entered into the discussion at the start, took no part in it but looked through the *Gazette* which had just been handed in.

"Gentlemen," he said, "Ivan Ilych has died!"

"You don't say so!"

"Here, read it yourself," replied Peter Ivanovich, handing Fëdor Vasilievich the paper still damp from the press. Surrounded by a black border were the words: "Praskovya Fëdorovna Golovina, with profound sorrow, informs relatives and friends of the demise of her beloved husband Ivan Ilych Golovin, Member of the Court of Justice, which occurred on February the 4th of this year 1882. The funeral will take place on Friday at one o'clock in the afternoon."

Ivan Ilych had been a colleague of the gentlemen present and was liked by them all. He had been ill for some weeks with an illness said to be incurable.

His post had been kept open for him, but there had been conjectures that in case of his death Alexeev might receive his appointment, and that either Vinnikov or Shtabel would succeed Alexeev. So on receiving the news of Ivan Ilych's death the first thought of each of the gentlemen in that private room was of the changes and promotions it might occasion among themselves or their acquaintances.

"I shall be sure to get Shtabel's place or Vinnikov's," thought Fëdor Vasilievich. "I was promised that long ago, and the promotion means an extra eight hundred rubles a year for me besides the allowance."

"Now I must apply for my brother-in-law's transfer from Kaluga," thought Peter Ivanovich. "My wife will be very glad, and then she won't be able to say that I never do anything for her relations."

"I thought he would never leave his bed again," said Peter Ivanovich aloud. "It's very sad."

"But what really was the matter with him?"

"The doctors couldn't say—at least they could, but each of them said something different. When last I saw him I thought he was getting better."

"And I haven't been to see him since the holidays. I always meant to go."

"Had he any property?"

"I think his wife had a little—but something quite trifling."

"We shall have to go to see her, but they live so terribly far away."

"Far away from you, you mean. Everything's far away from your place."

"You see, he never can forgive my living on the other side of the river," said Peter Ivanovich, smiling at Shebek. Then, still talking of the distances between different parts of the city, they returned to the Court.

Besides considerations as to the possible transfers and promotions likely to result from Ivan Ilych's death, the mere fact of the death of a near acquaintance aroused, as usual, in all who heard of it the complacent feeling that, "it is he who is dead and not I."

Each one thought or felt, "Well, he's dead but I'm alive!" But the more intimate of Ivan Ilych's acquaintances, his so-called friends, could not help thinking also that they would now have to fulfil the very tiresome demands of propriety by attending the funeral service and paying a visit of condolence to the widow.

Fëdor Vasilievich and Peter Ivanovich had been his nearest acquaintances. Peter Ivanovich had studied law with Ivan Ilych and had considered himself to be under obligations to him.

Having told his wife at dinner-time of Ivan Ilych's death and of his conjecture that it might be possible to get her brother transferred to their circuit, Peter Ivanovich sacrificed his usual nap, put on his evening clothes, and drove to Ivan Ilych's house.

At the entrance stood a carriage and two cabs. Leaning against the wall in the hall downstairs near the cloak-stand was a coffin-lid covered with cloth of gold, ornamented with gold cord and tassels, that had been polished up with metal powder. Two ladies in black were taking off their fur cloaks. Peter Ivanovich recognized one of them as Ivan Ilych's sister, but the other was a stranger to him. His colleague Schwartz was just coming downstairs, but on seeing Peter Ivanovich enter he stopped and winked at him, as if to say: "Ivan Ilych has made a mess of things—not like you and me."

Schwartz's face with his Piccadilly whiskers[1] and his slim figure in evening dress, had as usual an air of elegant solemnity which contrasted with the playfulness of his character and had a special piquancy here, or so it seemed to Peter Ivanovich.

Peter Ivanovich allowed the ladies to precede him and slowly followed them upstairs. Schwartz did not come down but remained where he was, and Peter Ivanovich understood that he wanted to arrange where they should play bridge that evening. The ladies went upstairs to the widow's room, and Schwartz with seriously compressed lips but a playful look in his eyes, indicated by a twist of his eyebrows the room to the right where the body lay.

Peter Ivanovich, like everyone else on such occasions, entered feeling uncertain what he would have to do. All he knew was that at such times it is always safe to cross oneself. But he was not quite sure whether one should make obeisances while doing so. He therefore adopted a middle course. On entering the room he began crossing himself and made a slight movement resembling a bow. At the same time, as far as the motion of his head and arm allowed, he surveyed the room. Two young men—apparently nephews, one of whom was a high-school pupil—were leaving the room, crossing themselves as they did so. An old woman was standing motionless, and a lady with strangely arched eyebrows was saying something to her in a whisper. A vigorous, resolute Church Reader, in a frock-coat, was reading something in a loud voice with an expression that precluded any contradiction. The butler's assistant, Gerasim, stepping lightly in front of Peter Ivanovich, was strewing something on the floor. Noticing this, Peter Ivanovich was immediately aware of a faint odour of a decomposing body.

The last time he had called on Ivan Ilych, Peter Ivanovich had seen Gerasim in the study. Ivan Ilych had been particularly fond of him and he was performing the duty of a sick nurse.

Peter Ivanovich continued to make the sign of the cross slightly inclining his head in an intermediate direction between the coffin, the Reader, and the icons on the table in a corner of the room. Afterwards, when it seemed to him that this movement of his arm in crossing himself had gone on too long, he stopped and began to look at the corpse.

The dead man lay, as dead men always lie, in a specially heavy way, his rigid limbs sunk in the soft cushions of the coffin, with the head forever bowed on the pillow. His yellow waxen brow with bald patches over his sunken temples was thrust up in the way peculiar to the dead, the protruding nose seeming to press on the upper lip. He was much changed and had grown even thinner since Peter Ivanovich had last seen him, but, as is always the case with the dead, his face was handsomer and above all more dignified than when he was alive. The expression on the face said that what was necessary had been accomplished, and accomplished rightly. Besides this there was in that expression a reproach and a warning to the living. This warning seemed to Peter Ivanovich out of place, or at least not applicable to him. He felt a certain discomfort and so he hurriedly crossed himself once more and turned and went out of the door—too hurriedly and too regardless of propriety, as he himself was aware.

Schwartz was waiting for him in the adjoining room with legs spread wide

[1] Side whiskers.

apart and both hands toying with his top-hat behind his back. The mere sight of that playful, well-groomed, and elegant figure refreshed Peter Ivanovich. He felt that Schwartz was above all these happenings and would not surrender to any depressing influences. His very look said that this incident of a church service for Ivan Ilych could not be a sufficient reason for infringing the order of the session—in other words, that it would certainly not prevent his unwrapping a new pack of cards and shuffling them that evening while a footman placed four fresh candles on the table: in fact, that there was no reason for supposing that this incident would hinder their spending the evening agreeably. Indeed he said this in a whisper as Peter Ivanovich passed him, proposing that they should meet for a game at Fëdor Vasilievich's. But apparently Peter Ivanovich was not destined to play bridge that evening. Praskovya Fëdorovna (a short, fat woman who despite all efforts to the contrary had continued to broaden steadily from her shoulders downwards and who had the same extraordinarily arched eyebrows as the lady who had been standing by the coffin), dressed all in black, her head covered with lace, came out of her own room with some other ladies, conducted them to the room where the dead body lay, and said: "The service will begin immediately. Please go in."

Schwartz, making an indefinite bow, stood still, evidently neither accepting nor declining this invitation. Praskovya Fëdorovna, recognizing Peter Ivanovich, sighed, went close up to him, took his hand, and said: "I know you were a true friend to Ivan Ilych . . ." and looked at him awaiting some suitable response. And Peter Ivanovich knew that, just as it had been the right thing to cross himself in that room, so what he had to do here was to press her hand, sigh, and say, "Believe me. . . ." So he did all this and as he did it felt that the desired result had been achieved: that both he and she were touched.

"Come with me. I want to speak to you before it begins," said the widow. "Give me your arm."

Peter Ivanovich gave her his arm and they went to the inner rooms, passing Schwartz, who winked at Peter Ivanovich compassionately.

"That does for our bridge! Don't object if we find another player. Perhaps you can cut in when you do escape," said his playful look.

Peter Ivanovich sighed still more deeply and despondently, and Praskovya Fëdorovna pressed his arm gratefully. When they reached the drawing-room, upholstered in pink cretonne and lighted by a dim lamp, they sat down at the table—she on a sofa and Peter Ivanovich on a low pouffe, the springs of which yielded spasmodically under his weight. Praskovya Fëdorovna had been on the point of warning him to take another seat, but felt that such a warning was out of keeping with her present condition and so changed her mind. As he sat down on the pouffe Peter Ivanovich recalled how Ivan Ilych had arranged this room and had consulted him regarding this pink cretonne with green leaves. The whole room was full of furniture and knick-knacks, and on her way to the sofa the lace of the widow's black shawl caught on the carved edge of the table. Peter Ivanovich rose to detach it, and the springs of the pouffe, relieved of his weight, rose also and gave him a push. The widow began detaching her shawl herself, and Peter Ivanovich again sat down, suppressing the rebellious springs of the pouffe under him. But the widow had not quite freed herself and Peter Ivanovich got up again, and again the pouffe rebelled and even creaked. When this was all over she took out a clean cambric handkerchief and began to weep.

The episode with the shawl and the struggle with the pouffe had cooled Peter Ivanovich's emotions and he sat there with a sullen look on his face. This awkward situation was interrupted by Sokolov, Ivan Ilych's butler, who came to report that the plot in the cemetery that Praskovya Fëdorovna had chosen would cost two hundred rubles. She stopped weeping and, looking at Peter Ivanovich with the air of a victim, remarked in French that it was very hard for her. Peter Ivanovich made a silent gesture signifying his full conviction that it must indeed be so.

"Please smoke," she said in a magnanimous yet crushed voice, and turned to discuss with Sokolov the price of the plot for the grave.

Peter Ivanovich while lighting his cigarette heard her inquiring very circumstantially into the prices of different plots in the cemetery and finally decide which she would take. When that was done she gave instructions about engaging the choir. Sokolov then left the room.

"I look after everything myself," she told Peter Ivanovich, shifting the albums that lay on the table; and noticing that the table was endangered by his cigarette-ash, she immediately passed him an ash-tray, saying as she did so: "I consider it an affectation to say that my grief prevents my attending to practical affairs. On the contrary, if anything can—I won't say console me, but—distract me, it is seeing to everything concerning him." She again took out her handkerchief as if preparing to cry, but suddenly, as if mastering her feeling, she shook herself and began to speak calmly. "But there is something I want to talk to you about."

Peter Ivanovich bowed, keeping control of the springs of the pouffe, which immediately began quivering under him.

"He suffered terribly the last few days."

"Did he?" said Peter Ivanovich.

"Oh, terribly! He screamed unceasingly, not for minutes but for hours. For the last three days he screamed incessantly. It was unendurable. I cannot understand how I bore it; you could hear him three rooms off. Oh, what I have suffered!"

"Is it possible that he was conscious all that time?" asked Peter Ivanovich.

"Yes," she whispered. "To the last moment. He took leave of us a quarter of an hour before he died, and asked us to take Volodya away."

The thought of the sufferings of this man he had known so intimately, first as a merry little boy, then as a school-mate, and later as a grown-up colleague, suddenly struck Peter Ivanovich with horror, despite an unpleasant consciousness of his own and this woman's dissimulation. He again saw that brow, and that nose pressing down on the lip, and felt afraid for himself.

"Three days of frightful suffering and then death! Why, that might suddenly, at any time, happen to me," he thought, and for a moment felt terrified. But—he did not himself know how—the customary reflection at once occurred to him that this had happened to Ivan Ilych and not to him, and that it should not and could not happen to him, and to think that it could would be yielding to depression which he ought not to do, as Schwartz's expression plainly showed. After which reflection Peter Ivanovich felt reassured, and began to ask with interest about the details of Ivan Ilych's death, as though death was an accident natural to Ivan Ilych but certainly not to himself.

After many details of the really dreadful physical sufferings Ivan Ilych had endured (which details he learnt only from the effect those sufferings had produced on Praskovya Fëdorovna's nerves) the widow apparently found it necessary to get to business.

"Oh, Peter Ivanovich, how hard it is! How terribly, terribly hard!" and she again began to weep.

Peter Ivanovich sighed and waited for her to finish blowing her nose. When she had done so he said, "Believe me . . ." and she again began talking and brought out what was evidently her chief concern with him—namely, to question him as to how she could obtain a grant of money from the government on the occasion of her husband's death. She made it appear that she was asking Peter Ivanovich's advice about her pension, but he soon saw that she already knew about that to the minutest detail, more even than he did himself. She knew how much could be got out of the government in consequence of her husband's death, but wanted to find out whether she could not possibly extract something more. Peter Ivanovich tried to think of some means of doing so, but after reflecting for a while and, out of propriety, condemning the government for its niggardliness, he said he thought that nothing more could be got. Then she sighed and evidently began to devise means of getting rid of her visitor. Noticing this, he put out his cigarette, rose, pressed her hand, and went out into the anteroom.

In the dining-room where the clock stood that Ivan Ilych had liked so much and had bought at an antique shop, Peter Ivanovich met a priest and a few acquaintances who had come to attend the service, and he recognized Ivan Ilych's daughter, a handsome young woman. She was in black and her slim figure appeared slimmer than ever. She had a gloomy, determined, almost angry expression, and bowed to Peter Ivanovich as though he were in some way to blame. Behind her, with the same offended look, stood a wealthy young man, an examining magistrate, whom Peter Ivanovich also knew and who was her fiancé, as he had heard. He bowed mournfully to them and was about to pass into the death-chamber, when from under the stairs appeared the figure of Ivan Ilych's schoolboy son, who was extremely like his father. He seemed a little Ivan Ilych, such as Peter Ivanovich remembered when they studied law together. His tear-stained eyes had in them the look that is seen in the eyes of boys of thirteen or fourteen who are not pure-minded. When he saw Peter Ivanovich he scowled morosely and shamefacedly. Peter Ivanovich nodded to him and entered the death-chamber. The service began: candles, groans, incense, tears, and sobs. Peter Ivanovich stood looking gloomily down at his feet. He did not look once at the dead man, did not yield to any depressing influence, and was one of the first to leave the room. There was no one in the anteroom, but Gerasim darted out of the dead man's room, rummaged with his strong hands among the fur coats to find Peter Ivanovich's and helped him on with it.

"Well, friend Gerasim," said Peter Ivanovich, so as to say something. "It's a sad affair, isn't it?"

"It's God's will. We shall all come to it some day," said Gerasim, displaying his teeth—the even, white teeth of a healthy peasant—and, like a man in the thick of urgent work, he briskly opened the front door, called the coachman, helped Peter Ivanovich into the sledge, and sprang back to the porch as if in readiness for what he had to do next.

Peter Ivanovich found the fresh air particularly pleasant after the smell of incense, the dead body, and carbolic acid.

"Where to, sir?" asked the coachman.

"It's not too late even now. . . . I'll call round on Fëdor Vasilievich."

He accordingly drove there and found them just finishing the first rubber, so that it was quite convenient for him to cut in.

II

Ivan Ilych's life had been most simple and most ordinary and therefore most terrible.

He had been a member of the Court of Justice, and died at the age of forty-five. His father had been an official who after serving in various ministries and departments in Petersburg had made the sort of career which brings men to positions from which by reason of their long service they cannot be dismissed, though they are obviously unfit to hold any responsible position, and for whom therefore posts are especially created, which though fictitious carry salaries of from six to ten thousand rubles that are not fictitious, and in receipt of which they live on to a great age.

Such was the Privy Councillor and superfluous member of various superfluous institutions, Ilya Epimovich Golovin.

He had three sons, of whom Ivan Ilych was the second. The eldest son was following in his father's footsteps only in another department, and was already approaching that stage in the service at which a similar sinecure would be reached. The third son was a failure. He had ruined his prospects in a number of positions and was now serving in the railway department. His father and brothers, and still more their wives, not merely disliked meeting him, but avoided remembering his existence unless compelled to do so. His sister had married Baron Greff, a Petersburg official of her father's type. Ivan Ilych was *le phénix de la famille*[2] as people said. He was neither as cold and formal as his elder brother nor as wild as the younger, but was a happy mean between them—an intelligent, polished, lively and agreeable man. He had studied with his younger brother at the School of Law, but the latter had failed to complete the course and was expelled when he was in the fifth class. Ivan Ilych finished the course well. Even when he was at the School of Law he was just what he remained for the rest of his life: a capable, cheerful, good-natured, and sociable man, though strict in the fulfilment of what he considered to be his duty: and he considered his duty to be what was so considered by those in authority. Neither as a boy nor as a man was he a toady, but from early youth was by nature attracted to people of high station as a fly is drawn to the light, assimilating their ways and views of life and establishing friendly relations with them. All the enthusiasms of childhood and youth passed without leaving much trace on him; he succumbed to sensuality, to vanity, and latterly among the highest classes to

2 (French) The uniquely perfect member of the family (as the phoenix was supposed to be among birds, there being only one example of its species at any given time). In Tolstoi's work the upper-class Russian habit of interlarding conversation with French phrases often suggests a kind of genteel self-complacency.

liberalism, but always within limits which his instinct unfailingly indicated to him as correct.

At school he had done things which had formerly seemed to him very horrid and made him feel disgusted with himself when he did them; but when later on he saw that such actions were done by people of good position and that they did not regard them as wrong, he was able not exactly to regard them as right, but to forget about them entirely or not be at all troubled at remembering them.

Having graduated from the School of Law and qualified for the tenth rank of the civil service, and having received money from his father for his equipment, Ivan Ilych ordered himself clothes at Scharmer's, the fashionable tailor, hung a medallion inscribed *respice finem*[3] on his watch-chain, took leave of his professor and the prince who was patron of the school, had a farewell dinner with his comrades at Donon's first-class restaurant, and with his new and fashionable portmanteau, linen, clothes, shaving and other toilet appliances, and a travelling rug, all purchased at the best shops, he set off for one of the provinces where, through his father's influence, he had been attached to the Governor as an official for special service.

In the province Ivan Ilych soon arranged as easy and agreeable a position for himself as he had had at the School of Law. He performed his official tasks, made his career, and at the same time amused himself pleasantly and decorously. Occasionally he paid official visits to country districts, where he behaved with dignity both to his superiors and inferiors, and performed the duties entrusted to him, which related chiefly to the sectarians, with an exactness and incorruptible honesty of which he could not but feel proud.

In official matters, despite his youth and taste for frivolous gaiety, he was exceedingly reserved, punctilious, and even severe; but in society he was often amusing and witty, and always good-natured, correct in his manner, and *bon enfant*,[4] as the governor and his wife—with whom he was like one of the family—used to say of him.

In the province he had an affair with a lady who made advances to the elegant young lawyer, and there was also a milliner; and there were carousals with aides-de-camp who visited the district, and after-supper visits to a certain outlying street of doubtful reputation; and there was too some obsequiousness to his chief and even to his chief's wife, but all this was done with such a tone of good breeding that no hard names could be applied to it. It all came under the heading of the French saying: *"Il faut que jeunesse se passe."*[5] It was all done with clean hands, in clean linen, with French phrases, and above all among people of the best society and consequently with the approval of people of rank.

So Ivan Ilych served for five years and then came a change in his official life. The new and reformed judicial institutions were introduced, and new men were needed. Ivan Ilych became such a new man. He was offered the post of examining magistrate, and he accepted it though the post was in another

[3] (Latin) Think upon, or provide for, the end. Two meanings of *end*—immediate goals and death—should be noted.
[4] (French) Well-behaved towards his elders and superiors (literally, "good child").
[5] (French) A proverbial expression signifying that the sins of youth should be treated indulgently (literally, "youth must take its course").

province and obliged him to give up the connexions he had formed and to make new ones. His friends met to give him a send-off; they had a group-photograph taken and presented him with a silver cigarette-case, and he set off to his new post.

As examining magistrate Ivan Ilych was just as *comme il faut*[6] and decorous a man, inspiring general respect and capable of separating his official duties from his private life, as he had been when acting as an official on special service. His duties now as examining magistrate were far more interesting and attractive than before. In his former position it had been pleasant to wear an undress uniform made by Scharmer, and to pass through the crowd of petitioners and officials who were timorously awaiting an audience with the governor, and who envied him as with free and easy gait he went straight into his chief's private room to have a cup of tea and a cigarette with him. But not many people had then been directly dependent on him—only police officials and the sectarians when he went on special missions—and he liked to treat them politely, almost as comrades, as if he were letting them feel that he who had the power to crush them was treating them in this simple, friendly way. There were then but few such people. But now, as an examining magistrate, Ivan Ilych felt that everyone without exception, even the most important and self-satisfied, was in his power, and that he need only write a few words on a sheet of paper with a certain heading, and this or that important, self-satisfied person would be brought before him in the role of an accused person or a witness, and if he did not choose to allow him to sit down, would have to stand before him and answer his questions. Ivan Ilych never abused his power; he tried on the contrary to soften its expression, but the consciousness of it and of the possibility of softening its effect, supplied the chief interest and attraction of his office. In his work itself, especially in his examinations, he very soon acquired a method of eliminating all considerations irrelevant to the legal aspect of the case, and reducing even the most complicated case to a form in which it would be presented on paper only in its externals, completely excluding his personal opinion of the matter, while above all observing every prescribed formality. The work was new and Ivan Ilych was one of the first men to apply the new Code of 1864.[7]

On taking up the post of examining magistrate in a new town, he made new acquaintances and connexions, placed himself on a new footing, and assumed a somewhat different tone. He took up an attitude of rather dignified aloofness towards the provincial authorities, but picked out the best circle of legal gentlemen and wealthy gentry living in the town and assumed a tone of slight dissatisfaction with the government, of moderate liberalism, and of enlightened citizenship. At the same time, without at all altering the elegance of his toilet, he ceased shaving his chin and allowed his beard to grow as it pleased.

Ivan Ilych settled down very pleasantly in this new town. The society there, which inclined towards opposition to the Governor, was friendly, his salary was larger, and he began to play *vint* [a form of bridge], which he found added not a little to the pleasure of life, for he had a capacity for cards, played good-humouredly, and calculated rapidly and astutely, so that he usually won.

After living there for two years he met his future wife, Praskovya Fëdorovna

[6] (French) Proper, careful to observe the proprieties.
[7] Judicial proceedings were completely reformed after the emancipation of the serfs in 1861.

Mikhel, who was the most attractive, clever, and brilliant girl of the set in which he moved, and among other amusements and relaxations from his labours as examining magistrate, Ivan Ilych established light and playful relations with her.

While he had been an official on special service he had been accustomed to dance, but now as an examining magistrate it was exceptional for him to do so. If he danced now, he did it as if to show that though he served under the reformed order of things, and had reached the fifth official rank, yet when it came to dancing he could do it better than most people. So at the end of an evening he sometimes danced with Praskovya Fëdorovna, and it was chiefly during these dances that he captivated her. She fell in love with him. Ivan Ilych had at first no definite intention of marrying, but when the girl fell in love with him he said to himself: "Really, why shouldn't I marry?"

Praskovya Fëdorovna came of a good family, was not bad looking, and had some little property. Ivan Ilych might have aspired to a more brilliant match, but even this was good. He had his salary, and she, he hoped, would have an equal income. She was well connected, and was a sweet, pretty, and thoroughly correct young woman. To say that Ivan Ilych married because he fell in love with Praskovya Fëdorovna and found that she sympathized with his views of life would be as incorrect as to say that he married because his social circle approved of the match. He was swayed by both these considerations: the marriage gave him personal satisfaction, and at the same time it was considered the right thing by the most highly placed of his associates.

So Ivan Ilych got married.

The preparations for marriage and the beginning of married life, with its conjugal caresses, the new furniture, new crockery, and new linen, were very pleasant until his wife became pregnant—so that Ivan Ilych had begun to think that marriage would not impair the easy, agreeable, gay and always decorous character of his life, approved of by society and regarded by himself as natural, but would even improve it. But from the first months of his wife's pregnancy, something new, unpleasant, depressing, and unseemly, and from which there was no way of escape, unexpectedly showed itself.

His wife, without any reason—*de gaieté de cœur*[8] as Ivan Ilych expressed it to himself—began to disturb the pleasure and propriety of their life. She began to be jealous without any cause, expected him to devote his whole attention to her, found fault with everything, and made coarse and ill-mannered scenes.

At first Ivan Ilych hoped to escape from the unpleasantness of this state of affairs by the same easy and decorous relation to life that had served him heretofore: he tried to ignore his wife's disagreeable moods, continued to live in his usual easy and pleasant way, invited friends to his house for a game of cards, and also tried going out to his club or spending his evenings with friends. But one day his wife began upbraiding him so vigorously, using such coarse words, and continued to abuse him every time he did not fulfil her demands, so resolutely and with such evident determination not to give way till he submitted—that is, till he stayed at home and was bored just as she was—that he became alarmed. He now realized that matrimony—at any rate with Praskovya Fëdorovna—was not always conducive to the pleasures and amenities of life,

[8] (French) Out of mere wantonness.

but on the contrary often infringed both comfort and propriety, and that he must therefore entrench himself against such infringement. And Ivan Ilych began to seek for means of doing so. His official duties were the one thing that imposed upon Praskovya Fëdorovna, and by means of his official work and the duties attached to it he began struggling with his wife to secure his own independence.

With the birth of their child, the attempts to feed it and the various failures in doing so, and with the real and imaginary illnesses of mother and child, in which Ivan Ilych's sympathy was demanded but about which he understood nothing, the need of securing for himself an existence outside his family life became still more imperative.

As his wife grew more irritable and exacting and Ivan Ilych transferred the centre of gravity of his life more and more to his official work, so did he grow to like his work better and became more ambitious than before.

Very soon, within a year of his wedding, Ivan Ilych had realized that marriage, though it may add some comforts to life, is in fact a very intricate and difficult affair towards which in order to perform one's duty, that is, to lead a decorous life approved of by society, one must adopt a definite attitude just as towards one's official duties.

And Ivan Ilych evolved such an attitude towards married life. He only required of it those conveniences—dinner at home, housewife, and bed—which it could give him, and above all that propriety of external forms required by public opinion. For the rest he looked for light-hearted pleasure and propriety, and was very thankful when he found them, but if he met with antagonism and querulousness he at once retired into his separate fenced-off world of official duties, where he found satisfaction.

Ivan Ilych was esteemed a good official, and after three years was made Assistant Public Prosecutor. His new duties, their importance, the possibility of indicting and imprisoning anyone he chose, the publicity his speeches received, and the success he had in all these things, made his work still more attractive.

More children came. His wife became more and more querulous and ill-tempered, but the attitude Ivan Ilych had adopted towards his home life rendered him almost impervious to her grumbling.

After seven years' service in that town he was transferred to another province as Public Prosecutor. They moved, but were short of money and his wife did not like the place they moved to. Though the salary was higher the cost of living was greater, besides which two of their children died and family life became still more unpleasant for him.

Praskovya Fëdorovna blamed her husband for every inconvenience they encountered in their new home. Most of the conversations between husband and wife, especially as to the children's education, led to topics which recalled former disputes, and those disputes were apt to flare up again at any moment. There remained only those rare periods of amorousness which still came to them at times but did not last long. These were islets at which they anchored for a while and then again set out upon that ocean of veiled hostility which showed itself in their aloofness from one another. This aloofness might have grieved Ivan Ilych had he considered that it ought not to exist, but he now regarded the position as normal, and even made it the goal at which he aimed in family life. His aim was to free himself more and more from those unpleasantnesses and to give them a semblance of harmlessness and propriety. He attained this by spending less and less time with his family, and when obliged to be at home he tried to safeguard his position by the presence of outsiders. The chief thing however was that he had his official duties. The whole interest of his life now centred in the official world and that interest absorbed him. The consciousness of his power, being able to ruin anybody he wished to ruin, the importance, even the external dignity of his entry into court, or meetings with his subordinates, his success with superiors and inferiors, and above all his masterly handling of cases, of which he was conscious—all this gave him pleasure and filled his life, together with chats with his colleagues, dinners, and bridge. So that on the whole Ivan Ilych's life continued to flow as he considered it should do—pleasantly and properly.

So things continued for another seven years. His eldest daughter was already sixteen, another child had died, and only one son was left, a schoolboy and a subject of dissension. Ivan Ilych wanted to put him in the School of Law, but to spite him Praskovya Fëdorovna entered him at the High School. The daughter had been educated at home and had turned out well: the boy did not learn badly either.

III

So Ivan Ilych lived for seventeen years after his marriage. He was already a Public Prosecutor of long standing, and had declined several proposed transfers while awaiting a more desirable post, when an unanticipated and unpleasant occurrence quite upset the peaceful course of his life. He was expecting to be offered the post of presiding judge in a University town, but Happe somehow came to the front and obtained the appointment instead. Ivan Ilych became irritable, reproached Happe, and quarrelled both with him and with his immediate superiors—who became colder to him and again passed him over when other appointments were made.

This was in 1880, the hardest year of Ivan Ilych's life. It was then that it became evident on the one hand that his salary was insufficient for them to live on, and on the other that he had been forgotten, and not only this, but that what was for him the greatest and most cruel injustice appeared to others a quite ordinary occurrence. Even his father did not consider it his duty to help him. Ivan Ilych felt himself abandoned by everyone, and that they regarded his position with a salary of 3,500 rubles as quite normal and even fortunate. He alone knew that with the consciousness of the injustices done him, with his wife's incessant nagging, and with the debts he had contracted by living beyond his means, his position was far from normal.

In order to save money that summer he obtained leave of absence and went with his wife to live in the country at her brother's place.

In the country, without his work, he experienced *ennui* for the first time in his life, and not only *ennui* but intolerable depression, and he decided that it was impossible to go on living like that, and that it was necessary to take energetic measures.

Having passed a sleepless night pacing up and down the veranda, he decided to go to Petersburg and bestir himself, in order to punish those who had failed to appreciate him and to get transferred to another ministry.

Next day, despite many protests from his wife and her brother, he started for Petersburg with the sole object of obtaining a post with a salary of five thousand rubles a year. He was no longer bent on any particular department, or tendency, or kind of activity. All he now wanted was an appointment to another post with a salary of five thousand rubles, either in the administration, in the banks, with the railways, in one of the Empress Marya's Institutions,[9] or even in the customs—but it had to carry with it a salary of five thousand rubles and be in a ministry other than that in which they had failed to appreciate him.

And this quest of Ivan Ilych's was crowned with remarkable and un-expected success. At Kursk an acquaintance of his, F. I. Ilyin, got into the first-class carriage, sat down beside Ivan Ilych, and told him of a telegram just received by the Governor of Kursk announcing that a change was about to take place in the ministry: Peter Ivanovich was to be superseded by Ivan Semëno-vich.

The proposed change, apart from its significance for Russia, had a special significance for Ivan Ilych, because by bringing forward a new man, Peter Petrovich, and consequently his friend Zachar Ivanovich, it was highly favour-able for Ivan Ilych, since Zachar Ivanovich was a friend and colleague of his.

In Moscow this news was confirmed, and on reaching Petersburg Ivan Ilych found Zachar Ivanovich and received a definite promise of an appoint-ment in his former department of Justice.

A week later he telegraphed to his wife: "Zachar in Miller's place. I shall receive appointment on presentation of report."

Thanks to this change of personnel, Ivan Ilych had unexpectedly obtained an appointment in his former ministry which placed him two stages above his former colleagues besides giving him five thousand rubles salary and three thousand five hundred rubles for expenses connected with his removal. All his ill humour towards his former enemies and the whole department vanished, and Ivan Ilych was completely happy.

He returned to the country more cheerful and contented than he had been for a long time. Praskovya Fëdorovna also cheered up and a truce was arranged between them. Ivan Ilych told of how he had been fêted by everybody in Peters-burg, how all those who had been his enemies were put to shame and now fawned on him, how envious they were of his appointment, and how much everybody in Petersburg had liked him.

Praskovya Fëdorovna listened to all this and appeared to believe it. She did not contradict anything, but only made plans for their life in the town to which they were going. Ivan Ilych saw with delight that these plans were his plans, that he and his wife agreed, and that, after a stumble, his life was regaining its due and natural character of pleasant lightheartedness and de-corum.

Ivan Ilych had come back for a short time only, for he had to take up his new duties on the 10th of September. Moreover, he needed time to settle into the new place, to move all his belongings from the province, and to buy and

9 These were orphanage-schools for girls.

order many additional things: in a word, to make such arrangements as he had resolved on, which were almost exactly what Praskovya Fëdorovna too had decided on.

Now that everything had happened so fortunately, and that he and his wife were at one in their aims and moreover saw so little of one another, they got on together better than they had done since the first years of marriage. Ivan Ilych had thought of taking his family away with him at once, but the insistence of his wife's brother and her sister-in-law, who had suddenly become particularly amiable and friendly to him and his family, induced him to depart alone.

So he departed, and the cheerful state of mind induced by his success and by the harmony between his wife and himself, the one intensifying the other, did not leave him. He found a delightful house, just the thing both he and his wife had dreamt of. Spacious, lofty reception rooms in the old style, a convenient and dignified study, rooms for his wife and daughter, a study for his son—it might have been specially built for them. Ivan Ilych himself super-intended the arrangements, chose the wallpapers, supplemented the furniture (preferably with antiques which he considered particularly *comme il faut*), and supervised the upholstering. Everything progressed and progressed and ap-proached the ideal he had set himself: even when things were only half com-pleted they exceeded his expectations. He saw what a refined and elegant char-acter, free from vulgarity, it would all have when it was ready. On falling asleep he pictured to himself how the reception-room would look. Looking at the yet unfinished drawing-room he could see the fireplace, the screen, the what-not, the little chairs dotted here and there, the dishes and plates on the walls, and the bronzes, as they would be when everything was in place. He was pleased by the thought of how his wife and daughter, who shared his taste in this matter, would be impressed by it. They were certainly not expect-ing as much. He had been particularly successful in finding, and buying cheaply, antiques which gave a particularly aristocratic character to the whole place. But in his letters he intentionally understated everything in order to be able to surprise them. All this so absorbed him that his new duties—though he liked his official work—interested him less than he had expected. Sometimes he even had moments of absent-mindedness during the Court Sessions, and would con-sider whether he should have straight or curved cornices for his curtains. He was so interested in it all that he often did things himself, rearranging the furniture, or rehanging the curtains. Once when mounting a step-ladder to show the upholsterer, who did not understand, how he wanted the hangings draped, he made a false step and slipped, but being a strong and agile man he clung on and only knocked his side against the knob of the window frame. The bruised place was painful but the pain soon passed, and he felt particularly bright and well just then. He wrote: "I feel fifteen years younger." He thought he would have everything ready by September, but it dragged on till mid-October. But the result was charming not only in his eyes but to everyone who saw it.

In reality it was just what is usually seen in the houses of people of moder-ate means who want to appear rich, and therefore succeed only in resembling others like themselves: there were damasks, dark wood, plants, rugs, and dull and polished bronzes—all the things people of a certain class have in order to resemble other people of that class. His house was so like the others that it would never have been noticed, but to him it all seemed to be quite exceptional. He was very happy when he met his family at the station and brought them to the newly furnished house all lit up, where a footman in a white tie opened the door into the hall decorated with plants, and when they went on into the drawing-room and the study uttering exclamations of delight. He conducted them everywhere, drank in their praises eagerly, and beamed with pleasure. At tea that evening, when Praskovya Fëdorovna among other things asked him about his fall, he laughed and showed them how he had gone flying and had frightened the upholsterer.

"It's a good thing I'm a bit of an athlete. Another man might have been killed, but I merely knocked myself, just here; it hurts when it's touched, but it's passing off already—it's only a bruise."

So they began living in their new home—in which, as always happens, when they got thoroughly settled in they found they were just one room short—and with the increased income, which as always was just a little (some five hundred rubles) too little, but it was all very nice.

Things went particularly well at first, before everything was finally arranged and while something had still to be done: this thing bought, that thing ordered, another thing moved, and something else adjusted. Though there were some disputes between husband and wife, they were both so well satisfied and had so much to do that it all passed off without any serious quarrels. When nothing was left to arrange it became rather dull and something seemed to be lacking, but they were then making acquaintances, forming habits, and life was growing fuller.

Ivan Ilych spent his mornings at the law court and came home to dinner, and at first he was generally in a good humour, though he occasionally became irritable just on account of his house. (Every spot on the tablecloth or the upholstery, and every broken window-blind string, irritated him. He had devoted so much trouble to arranging it all that every disturbance of it distressed him.) But on the whole his life ran its course as he believed life should do: easily, pleasantly, and decorously.

He got up at nine, drank his coffee, read the paper, and then put on his undress uniform and went to the law courts. There the harness in which he worked had already been stretched to fit him and he donned it without a hitch: petitioners, inquiries at the chancery, the chancery itself, and the sittings public and administrative. In all this the thing was to exclude everything fresh and vital, which always disturbs the regular course of official business, and to admit only official relations with people, and then only on official grounds. A man would come, for instance, wanting some information. Ivan Ilych, as one in whose sphere the matter did not lie, would have nothing to do with him: but if the man had some business with him in his official capacity, something that could be expressed on officially stamped paper, he would do everything, positively everything he could within the limits of such relations, and in doing so would maintain the semblance of friendly human relations, that is, would observe the courtesies of life. As soon as the official relations ended, so did everything else. Ivan Ilych possessed this capacity to separate his real life from the official side of affairs and not mix the two, in the highest degree, and by long practice and natural aptitude had brought it to such a pitch that sometimes, in the manner of a virtuoso, he would even allow himself to let the human and official relations mingle. He let himself do this just because he felt that he could at any time he chose resume the strictly official attitude again and drop the human relation. And he did it all easily, pleasantly, correctly, and even artistically. In the intervals between the sessions he smoked, drank tea, chatted a little about politics, a little about general topics, a little about cards, but most of all about official appointments. Tired, but with the feelings of a virtuoso—one of the first violins who has played his part in an orchestra with precision—he would return home to find that his wife and daughter had been out paying calls, or had a visitor, and that his son had been to school, had done his homework with his tutor, and was duly learning what is taught at High Schools. Everything was as it should be. After dinner, if they had no visitors, Ivan Ilych sometimes read a book that was being much discussed at the time, and in the evening settled down to work, that is, read official papers, compared the depositions of witnesses, and noted paragraphs of the Code applying to them. This was neither dull nor amusing. It was dull when he might have been playing bridge, but if no bridge was available it was at any rate better than doing nothing or sitting with his wife. Ivan Ilych's chief pleasure was giving little dinners to which he invited men and women of good social position, and just as his drawing-room resembled all other drawing-rooms so did his enjoyable little parties resemble all other such parties.

Once they even gave a dance. Ivan Ilych enjoyed it and everything went off well, except that it led to a violent quarrel with his wife about the cakes and sweets. Praskovya Fëdorovna had made her own plans, but Ivan Ilych insisted on getting everything from an expensive confectioner and ordered too many cakes, and the quarrel occurred because some of those cakes were left over and the confectioner's bill came to forty-five rubles. It was a great and disagreeable quarrel. Praskovya Fëdorovna called him "a fool and an imbecile," and he clutched at his head and made angry allusions to divorce.

But the dance itself had been enjoyable. The best people were there, and Ivan Ilych had danced with Princess Trufonova, a sister of the distinguished founder of the Society "Bear my Burden."

The pleasures connected with his work were pleasures of ambition; his social pleasures were those of vanity; but Ivan Ilych's greatest pleasure was playing bridge. He acknowledged that whatever disagreeable incident happened in his life, the pleasure that beamed like a ray of light above everything else was to sit down to bridge with good players, not noisy partners, and of course to four-handed bridge (with five players it was annoying to have to stand out, though one pretended not to mind), to play a clever and serious game (when the cards allowed it) and then to have supper and drink a glass of wine. After a game of bridge, especially if he had won a little (to win a large sum was unpleasant), Ivan Ilych went to bed in specially good humour.

So they lived. They formed a circle of acquaintances among the best people and were visited by people of importance and by young folk. In their views as to their acquaintances, husband, wife and daughter were entirely agreed, and tacitly and unanimously kept at arm's length and shook off the shabby friends and relations who, with much show of affection, gushed into the drawing-room with its Japanese plates on the walls. Soon these shabby friends ceased to obtrude themselves and only the best people remained in the Golovins' set.

Young men made up to Lisa, and Petrishchev, an examining magistrate and

Dmitri Ivanovich Petrishchev's son and sole heir, began to be so attentive to her that Ivan Ilych had already spoken to Praskovya Fëdorovna about it, and considered whether they should not arrange a party for them, or get up some private theatricals.

So they lived, and all went well, without change, and life flowed pleasantly.

IV

They were all in good health. It could not be called ill health if Ivan Ilych sometimes said that he had a queer taste in his mouth and felt some discomfort in his left side.

But this discomfort increased and, though not exactly painful, grew into a sense of pressure in his side accompanied by ill humour. And his irritability became worse and worse and began to mar the agreeable, easy, and correct life that had established itself in the Golovin family. Quarrels between husband and wife became more and more frequent, and soon the ease and amenity disappeared and even the decorum was barely maintained. Scenes again became frequent, and very few of those islets remained on which husband and wife could meet without an explosion. Praskovya Fëdorovna now had good reason to say that her husband's temper was trying. With characteristic exaggeration she said he had always had a dreadful temper, and that it had needed all her good nature to put up with it for twenty years. It was true that now the quarrels were started by him. His bursts of temper always came just before dinner, often just as he began to eat his soup. Sometimes he noticed that a plate or dish was chipped, or the food was not right, or his son put his elbow on the table, or his daughter's hair was not done as he liked it, and for all this he blamed Praskovya Fëdorovna. At first she retorted and said disagreeable things to him, but once or twice he fell into such a rage at the beginning of dinner that she realized it was due to some physical derangement brought on by taking food, and so she restrained herself and did not answer, but only hurried to get the dinner over. She regarded this self-restraint as highly praiseworthy. Having come to the conclusion that her husband had a dreadful temper and made her life miserable, she began to feel sorry for herself, and the more she pitied herself the more she hated her husband. She began to wish he would die; yet she did not want him to die because then his salary would cease. And this irritated her against him still more. She considered herself dreadfully unhappy just because not even his death could save her, and though she concealed her exasperation, that hidden exasperation of hers increased his irritation also.

After one scene in which Ivan Ilych had been particularly unfair and after which he had said in explanation that he certainly was irritable but that it was due to his not being well, she said that if he was ill it should be attended to, and insisted on his going to see a celebrated doctor.

He went. Everything took place as he had expected and as it always does. There was the usual waiting and the important air assumed by the doctor, with which he was so familiar (resembling that which he himself assumed in court), and the sounding and listening, and the questions which called for answers that were foregone conclusions and were evidently unnecessary, and the look of importance which implied that "if only you put yourself in our hands we will arrange everything—we know indubitably how it has to be done, always in the same way for everybody alike." It was all just as it was in the law courts. The doctor put on just the same air towards him as he himself put on towards an accused person.

The doctor said that so-and-so indicated that there was so-and-so inside the patient, but if the investigation of so-and-so did not confirm this, then he must assume that and that. If he assumed that and that, then . . . and so on. To Ivan Ilych only one question was important: was his case serious or not? But the doctor ignored that inappropriate question. From his point of view it was not the one under consideration, the real question was to decide between a floating kidney, chronic catarrh, or appendicitis. It was not a question of Ivan Ilych's life or death, but one between a floating kidney and appendicitis. And that question the doctor solved brilliantly, as it seemed to Ivan Ilych, in favour of the appendix, with the reservation that should an examination of the urine give fresh indications the matter would be reconsidered. All this was just what Ivan Ilych had himself brilliantly accomplished a thousand times in dealing with men on trial. The doctor summed up just as brilliantly, looking over his spectacles triumphantly and even gaily at the accused. From the doctor's summing up Ivan Ilych concluded that things were bad, but that for the doctor, and perhaps for everybody else, it was a matter of indifference, though for him it was bad. And this conclusion struck him painfully, arousing in him a great feeling of pity for himself and of bitterness towards the doctor's indifference to a matter of such importance.

He said nothing of this, but rose, placed the doctor's fee on the table, and remarked with a sigh: "We sick people probably often put inappropriate questions. But tell me, in general, is this complaint dangerous, or not? . . ."

The doctor looked at him sternly over his spectacles with one eye, as if to say: "Prisoner, if you will not keep to the questions put to you, I shall be obliged to have you removed from the court."

"I have already told you what I consider necessary and proper. The analysis may show something more." And the doctor bowed.

Ivan Ilych went out slowly, seated himself disconsolately in his sledge, and drove home. All the way home he was going over what the doctor had said, trying to translate those complicated, obscure, scientific phrases into plain language and find in them an answer to the question: "Is my condition bad? Is it very bad? Or is there as yet nothing much wrong?" And it seemed to him that the meaning of what the doctor had said was that it was very bad. Everything in the streets seemed depressing. The cabmen, the houses, the passers-by, and the shops, were dismal. His ache, this dull gnawing ache that never ceased for a moment, seemed to have acquired a new and more serious significance from the doctor's dubious remarks. Ivan Ilych now watched it with a new and oppressive feeling.

He reached home and began to tell his wife about it. She listened, but in the middle of his account his daughter came in with her hat on, ready to go out with her mother. She sat down reluctantly to listen to this tedious story, but could not stand it long, and her mother too did not hear him to the end.

"Well, I am very glad," she said. "Mind now to take your medicine regularly. Give me the prescription and I'll send Gerasim to the chemist's." And she went to get ready to go out.

While she was in the room Ivan Ilych had hardly taken time to breathe, but he sighed deeply when she left it.

"Well," he thought, "perhaps it isn't so bad after all."

He began taking his medicine and following the doctor's directions, which had been altered after the examination of the urine. But then it happened that there was a contradiction between the indications drawn from the examination of the urine and the symptoms that showed themselves. It turned out that what was happening differed from what the doctor had told him, and that he had either forgotten, or blundered, or hidden something from him. He could not, however, be blamed for that, and Ivan Ilych still obeyed his orders implicitly and at first derived some comfort from doing so.

From the time of his visit to the doctor, Ivan Ilych's chief occupation was the exact fulfilment of the doctor's instructions regarding hygiene and the taking of medicine, and the observation of his pain and his excretions. His chief interests came to be people's ailments and people's health. When sickness, deaths, or recoveries were mentioned in his presence, especially when the illness resembled his own, he listened with agitation which he tried to hide, asked questions, and applied what he heard to his own case.

The pain did not grow less, but Ivan Ilych made efforts to force himself to think that he was better. And he could do this so long as nothing agitated him. But as soon as he had any unpleasantness with his wife, any lack of success in his official work, or held bad cards at bridge, he was at once acutely sensible of his disease. He had formerly borne such mischances, hoping soon to adjust what was wrong, to master it and attain success, or make a grand slam. But now every mischance upset him and plunged him into despair. He would say to himself: "There now, just as I was beginning to get better and the medicine had begun to take effect, comes this accursed misfortune, or unpleasantness. . . ." And he was furious with the mishap, or with the people who were causing the unpleasantness and killing him, for he felt that this fury was killing him but could not restrain it. One would have thought that it should have been clear to him that this exasperation with circumstances and people aggravated his illness, and that he ought therefore to ignore unpleasant occurrences. But he drew the very opposite conclusion: he said that he needed peace, and he watched for everything that might disturb it and became irritable at the slightest infringement of it. His condition was rendered worse by the fact that he read medical books and consulted doctors. The progress of his disease was so gradual that he could deceive himself when comparing one day with another—the difference was so slight. But when he consulted the doctors it seemed to him that he was getting worse, and even very rapidly. Yet despite this he was continually consulting them.

That month he went to see another celebrity, who told him almost the same as the first had done but put his questions rather differently, and the interview with this celebrity only increased Ivan Ilych's doubts and fears. A friend of a friend of his, a very good doctor, diagnosed his illness again quite differently from the others, and though he predicted recovery, his questions and suppositions bewildered Ivan Ilych still more and increased his doubts. A homoeopathist diagnosed the disease in yet another way, and prescribed medicine which Ivan Ilych took secretly for a week. But after a week, not feeling any improvement and having lost confidence both in the former doctor's treatment and in this one's, he became still more despondent. One day a lady acquaintance mentioned a cure effected by a wonder-working icon. Ivan Ilych caught himself listening attentively and beginning to believe that it had occurred. This incident alarmed him. "Has my mind really weakened to such an extent?" he asked himself. "Nonsense! It's all rubbish. I mustn't give way to nervous fears but having chosen a doctor must keep strictly to his treatment. That is what I will do. Now it's all settled. I won't think about it, but will follow the treatment seriously till summer, and then we shall see. From now there must be no more of this wavering!" This was easy to say but impossible to carry out. The pain in his side oppressed him and seemed to grow worse and more incessant, while the taste in his mouth grew stranger and stranger. It seemed to him that his breath had a disgusting smell, and he was conscious of a loss of appetite and strength. There was no deceiving himself: something terrible, new, and more important than anything before in his life, was taking place within him of which he alone was aware. Those about him did not understand or would not understand it, but thought everything in the world was going on as usual. That tormented Ivan Ilych more than anything. He saw that his household, especially his wife and daughter who were in a perfect whirl of visiting, did not understand anything of it and were annoyed that he was so depressed and so exacting, as if he were to blame for it. Though they tried to disguise it he saw that he was an obstacle in their path, and that his wife had adopted a definite line in regard to his illness and kept to it regardless of anything he said or did. Her attitude was this: "You know," she would say to her friends, "Ivan Ilych can't do as other people do, and keep to the treatment prescribed for him. One day he'll take his drops and keep strictly to his diet and go to bed in good time, but the next day unless I watch him he'll suddenly forget his medicine, eat sturgeon—which is forbidden—and sit up playing cards till one o'clock in the morning."

"Oh, come, when was that?" Ivan Ilych would ask in vexation. "Only once at Peter Ivanovich's."

"And yesterday with Shebek."

"Well, even if I hadn't stayed up, this pain would have kept me awake."

"Be that as it may you'll never get well like that, but will always make us wretched."

Praskovya Fëdorovna's attitude to Ivan Ilych's illness, as she expressed it both to others and to him, was that it was his own fault and was another of the annoyances he caused her. Ivan Ilych felt that this opinion escaped her involuntarily—but that did not make it easier for him.

At the law courts too, Ivan Ilych noticed, or thought he noticed, a strange attitude towards himself. It sometimes seemed to him that people were watching him inquisitively as a man whose place might soon be vacant. Then again, his friends would suddenly begin to chaff him in a friendly way about his low spirits, as if the awful, horrible, and unheard-of thing that was going on within him, incessantly gnawing at him and irresistibly drawing him away, was a very agreeable subject for jests. Schwartz in particular irritated him by his jocularity, vivacity, and *savoir-faire*, which reminded him of what he himself had been ten years ago.

Friends came to make up a set and they sat down to cards. They dealt, bending the new cards to soften them, and he sorted the diamonds in his hand and found he had seven. His partner said "No trumps" and supported him with two diamonds. What more could be wished for? It ought to be jolly and lively. They would make a grand slam. But suddenly Ivan Ilych was conscious of that gnawing pain, that taste in his mouth, and it seemed ridiculous that in such circumstances he should be pleased to make a grand slam.

He looked at his partner Mikhail Mikhaylovich, who rapped the table with his strong hand and instead of snatching up the tricks pushed the cards courteously and indulgently towards Ivan Ilych that he might have the pleasure of gathering them up without the trouble of stretching out his hand for them. "Does he think I am too weak to stretch out my arm?" thought Ivan Ilych, and forgetting what he was doing he over-trumped his partner, missing the grand slam by three tricks. And what was most awful of all was that he saw how upset Mikhail Mikhaylovich was about it but did not himself care. And it was dreadful to realize why he did not care.

They all saw that he was suffering, and said: "We can stop if you are tired. Take a rest." Lie down? No, he was not at all tired, and he finished the rubber. All were gloomy and silent. Ivan Ilych felt that he had diffused this gloom over them and could not dispel it. They had supper and went away, and Ivan Ilych was left alone with the consciousness that his life was poisoned and was poisoning the lives of others, and that this poison did not weaken but penetrated more and more deeply into his whole being.

With this consciousness, and with physical pain besides that terror, he must go to bed, often to lie awake the greater part of the night. Next morning he had to get up again, dress, go to the law courts, speak, and write; or if he did not go out, spend at home those twenty-four hours a day each of which was a torture. And he had to live thus all alone on the brink of an abyss, with no one who understood or pitied him.

V

So one month passed and then another. Just before the New Year his brother-in-law came to town and stayed at their house. Ivan Ilych was at the law courts and Praskovya Fëdorovna had gone shopping. When Ivan Ilych came home and entered his study he found his brother-in-law there—a healthy, florid man—unpacking his portmanteau himself. He raised his head on hearing Ivan Ilych's footsteps and looked up at him for a moment without a word. That stare told Ivan Ilych everything. His brother-in-law opened his mouth to utter an exclamation of surprise but checked himself, and that action confirmed it all.

"I have changed, eh?"

"Yes, there is a change."

And after that, try as he would to get his brother-in-law to return to the subject of his looks, the latter would say nothing about it. Praskovya Fëdorovna came home and her brother went out to her. Ivan Ilych locked the door and began to examine himself in the glass, first full face, then in profile. He took up a portrait of himself taken with his wife, and compared it with what he saw in the glass. The change in him was immense. Then he bared his arms to the elbow, looked at them, drew the sleeves down again, sat down on an ottoman, and grew blacker than night.

"No, no, this won't do!" he said to himself, and jumped up, went to the table, took up some law papers and began to read them, but could not continue. He unlocked the door and went into the reception-room. The door leading to the drawing-room was shut. He approached it on tiptoe and listened.

"No, you are exaggerating!" Praskovya Fëdorovna was saying.

"Exaggerating! Don't you see it? Why, he's a dead man! Look at his eyes—there's no light in them. But what is it that is wrong with him?"

"No one knows. Nikolaevich [that was another doctor] said something, but I don't know what. And Leshchetitsky [this was the celebrated specialist] said quite the contrary . . ."

Ivan Ilych walked away, went to his own room, lay down, and began musing: "The kidney, a floating kidney." He recalled all the doctors had told him of how it detached itself and swayed about. And by an effort of imagination he tried to catch that kidney and arrest it and support it. So little was needed for this, it seemed to him. "No, I'll go to see Peter Ivanovich again." [That was the friend whose friend was a doctor.] He rang, ordered the carriage, and got ready to go.

"Where are you going, Jean?"[10] asked his wife, with a specially sad and exceptionally kind look.

This exceptionally kind look irritated him. He looked morosely at her.

"I must go to see Peter Ivanovich."

He went to see Peter Ivanovich, and together they went to see his friend, the doctor. He was in, and Ivan Ilych had a long talk with him.

Reviewing the anatomical and physiological details of what in the doctor's opinion was going on inside him, he understood it all.

There was something, a small thing, in the vermiform appendix. It might all come right. Only stimulate the energy of one organ and check the activity of another, then absorption would take place and everything would come right. He got home rather late for dinner, ate his dinner, conversed cheerfully, but could not for a long time bring himself to go back to work in his room. At last, however, he went to his study and did what was necessary, but the consciousness that he had put something aside—an important, intimate matter which he would revert to when his work was done—never left him. When he had finished his work he remembered that this intimate matter was the thought of his vermiform appendix. But he did not give himself up to it, and went to the drawing-room for tea. There were callers there, including the examining magistrate who was a desirable match for his daughter, and they were conversing, playing the piano, and singing. Ivan Ilych, as Praskovya Fëdorovna remarked, spent that evening more cheerfully than usual, but he never for a moment forgot that he had postponed the important matter of the appendix. At eleven o'clock he said good-night and went to his bedroom. Since his illness he had slept alone in a small room next to his study. He undressed and took up a novel by Zola, but instead of reading it fell into thought, and in his imagination that desired im-

[10] Praskovya Fëdorovna addresses her husband familiarly not by his Russian name but by its French equivalent.

provement in the vermiform appendix occurred. There was the absorption and evacuation and the re-establishment of normal activity. "Yes, that's it!" he said to himself. "One need only assist nature, that's all." He remembered his medicine, rose, took it, and lay down on his back watching for the beneficent action of the medicine and for it to lessen the pain. "I need only take it regularly and avoid all injurious influences. I am already feeling better, much better." He began touching his side: it was not painful to the touch. "There, I really don't feel it. It's much better already." He put out the light and turned on his side. . . . "The appendix is getting better, absorption is occurring." Suddenly he felt the old, familiar, dull, gnawing pain, stubborn and serious. There was the same familiar loathsome taste in his mouth. His heart sank and he felt dazed. "My God! My God!" he muttered. "Again, again! and it will never cease." And suddenly the matter presented itself in a quite different aspect. "Vermiform appendix! Kidney!" he said to himself. "It's not a question of appendix or kidney, but of life and . . . death. Yes, life was there and now it is going, going and I cannot stop it. Yes. Why deceive myself? Isn't it obvious to everyone but me that I'm dying, and that it's only a question of weeks, days . . . it may happen this moment. There was light and now there is darkness. I was here and now I'm going there! Where?" A chill came over him, his breathing ceased, and he felt only the throbbing of his heart.

"When I am not, what will there be? There will be nothing. Then where shall I be when I am no more? Can this be dying? No, I don't want to!" He jumped up and tried to light the candle, felt for it with trembling hands, dropped candle and candlestick on the floor, and fell back on his pillow.

"What's the use? It makes no difference," he said to himself, staring with wide-open eyes into the darkness. "Death. Yes, death. And none of them know or wish to know it, and they have no pity for me. Now they are playing." (He heard through the door the distant sound of a song and its accompaniment.) "It's all the same to them, but they will die too! Fools! I first, and they later, but it will be the same for them. And now they are merry . . . the beasts!"

Anger choked him and he was agonizingly, unbearably, miserable. "It is impossible that all men have been doomed to suffer this awful horror!" He raised himself.

"Something must be wrong. I must calm myself—must think it all over from the beginning." And he again began thinking. "Yes, the beginning of my illness: I knocked my side, but I was quite well that day and the next. It hurt a little, then rather more. I saw the doctor, then followed despondency and anguish, more doctors, and I drew nearer to the abyss. My strength grew less and I kept coming nearer and nearer, and now I have wasted away and there is no light in my eyes. I think of the appendix—but this is death! I think of mending the appendix, and all the while here is death! Can it really be death?" Again terror seized him and he gasped for breath. He leant down and began feeling for the matches, pressing with his elbow on the stand beside the bed. It was in the way and hurt him, he grew furious with it, pressed on it still harder, and upset it. Breathless and in despair he fell on his back, expecting death to come immediately.

Meanwhile the visitors were leaving. Praskovya Fëdorovna was seeing them off. She heard something fall and came in.

"What has happened?"

"Nothing. I knocked it over accidentally."

She went out and returned with a candle. He lay there panting heavily, like a man who has run a thousand yards, and stared upwards at her with a fixed look.

"What is it, Jean?"

"No . . . o . . . thing. I upset it." ("Why speak of it? She won't understand," he thought.)

And in truth she did not understand. She picked up the stand, lit his candle, and hurried away to see another visitor off. When she came back he still lay on his back, looking upwards.

"What is it? Do you feel worse?"

"Yes."

She shook her head and sat down.

"Do you know, Jean, I think we must ask Leshchetitsky to come and see you here."

This meant calling in the famous specialist, regardless of expense. He smiled malignantly and said "No." She remained a little longer and then went up to him and kissed his forehead.

While she was kissing him he hated her from the bottom of his soul and with difficulty refrained from pushing her away.

"Good-night. Please God you'll sleep."

"Yes."

VI

Ivan Ilych saw that he was dying, and he was in continual despair.

In the depth of his heart he knew he was dying, but not only was he not accustomed to the thought, he simply did not and could not grasp it.

The syllogism he had learnt from Kiezewetter's Logic: "Caius is a man, men are mortal, therefore Caius is mortal," had always seemed to him correct as applied to Caius, but certainly not as applied to himself. That Caius—man in the abstract—was mortal, was perfectly correct, but he was not Caius, not an abstract man, but a creature quite, quite separate from all others. He had been little Vanya, with a mamma and a papa, with Mitya and Volodya, with the toys, a coachman and a nurse, afterwards with Katenka and with all the joys, griefs, and delights of childhood, boyhood, and youth. What did Caius know of the smell of that striped leather ball Vanya had been so fond of? Had Caius kissed his mother's hand like that, and did the silk of her dress rustle so for Caius? Had he rioted like that at school when the pastry was bad? Had Caius been in love like that? Could Caius preside at a session as he did? "Caius really was mortal, and it was right for him to die; but for me, little Vanya, Ivan Ilych, with all my thoughts and emotions, it's altogether a different matter. It cannot be that I ought to die. That would be too terrible."

Such was his feeling.

"If I had to die like Caius, I should have known it was so. An inner voice would have told me so, but there was nothing of the sort in me and I and all my friends felt that our case was quite different from that of Caius. And now here it is!" he said to himself. "It can't be. It's impossible! But here it is. How is this? How is one to understand it?"

He could not understand it, and tried to drive this false, incorrect, morbid thought away and to replace it by other proper and healthy thoughts. But that thought, and not the thought only but the reality itself, seemed to come and confront him.

And to replace that thought he called up a succession of others, hoping to find in them some support. He tried to get back into the former current of thoughts that had once screened the thought of death from him. But strange to say, all that had formerly shut off, hidden, and destroyed, his consciousness of death, no longer had that effect. Ivan Ilych now spent most of his time in attempting to re-establish that old current. He would say to himself: "I will take up my duties again—after all I used to live by them." And banishing all doubts he would go to the law courts, enter into conversation with his colleagues, and sit carelessly as was his wont, scanning the crowd with a thoughtful look and leaning both his emaciated arms on the arms of his oak chair; bending over as usual to a colleague and drawing his papers nearer he would interchange whispers with him, and then suddenly raising his eyes and sitting erect would pronounce certain words and open the proceedings. But suddenly in the midst of those proceedings the pain in his side, regardless of the stage the proceedings had reached, would begin its own gnawing work. Ivan Ilych would turn his attention to it and try to drive the thought of it away, but without success. *It* would come and stand before him and look at him, and he would be petrified and the light would die out of his eyes, and he would again begin asking himself whether *It* alone was true. And his colleagues and subordinates would see with surprise and distress that he, the brilliant and subtle judge, was becoming confused and making mistakes. He would shake himself, try to pull himself together, manage somehow to bring the sitting to a close, and return home with the sorrowful consciousness that his judicial labours could not as formerly hide from him what he wanted them to hide, and could not deliver him from *It*. And what was worst of all was that *It* drew his attention to itself not in order to make him take some action but only that he should look at *It*, look it straight in the face: look at it and without doing anything, suffer inexpressibly.

And to save himself from this condition Ivan Ilych looked for consolations —new screens—and new screens were found and for a while seemed to save him, but then they immediately fell to pieces or rather became transparent, as if *It* penetrated them and nothing could veil *It*.

In these latter days he would go into the drawing-room he had arranged— that drawing-room where he had fallen and for the sake of which (how bitterly ridiculous it seemed) he had sacrificed his life—for he knew that his illness originated with that knock. He would enter and see that something had scratched the polished table. He would look for the cause of this and find that it was the bronze ornamentation of an album, that had got bent. He would take up the expensive album which he had lovingly arranged, and feel vexed with his daughter and her friends for their untidiness—for the album was torn here and there and some of the photographs turned upside down. He would put it carefully in order and bend the ornamentation back into position. Then it would occur to him to place all those things in another corner of the room, near the plants. He would call the footman, but his daughter or wife would come to help him. They would not agree, and his wife would contradict him, and he would dispute and grow angry. But that was all right, for then he did not think about *It. It* was invisible.

But then, when he was moving something himself, his wife would say: "Let the servants do it. You will hurt yourself again." And suddenly *It* would flash through the screen and he would see it. It was just a flash, and he hoped it would disappear, but he would involuntarily pay attention to his side. "It sits there as before, gnawing just the same!" And he could no longer forget *It,* but could distinctly see it looking at him from behind the flowers. "What is it all for?"

"It really is so! I lost my life over that curtain as I might have done when storming a fort. Is that possible? How terrible and how stupid. It can't be true! It can't, but it is."

He would go to his study, lie down, and again be alone with *It*: face to face with *It*. And nothing could be done with *It* except to look at it and shudder.

VII

How it happened it is impossible to say because it came about step by step, unnoticed, but in the third month of Ivan Ilych's illness, his wife, his daughter, his son, his acquaintances, the doctors, the servants, and above all he himself, were aware that the whole interest he had for other people was whether he would soon vacate his place, and at last release the living from the discomfort caused by his presence and be himself released from his sufferings.

He slept less and less. He was given opium and hypodermic injections of morphine, but this did not relieve him. The dull depression he experienced in a somnolent condition at first gave him a little relief, but only as something new, afterwards it became as distressing as the pain itself or even more so.

Special foods were prepared for him by the doctors' orders, but all those foods became increasingly distasteful and disgusting to him.

For his excretions also special arrangements had to be made, and this was a torment to him every time—a torment from the uncleanliness, the unseemliness, and the smell, and from knowing that another person had to take part in it.

But just through this most unpleasant matter, Ivan Ilych obtained comfort. Gerasim, the butler's young assistant, always came in to carry the things out. Gerasim was a clean, fresh peasant lad, grown stout on town food and always cheerful and bright. At first the sight of him, in his clean Russian peasant costume, engaged in that disgusting task embarrassed Ivan Ilych.

Once when he got up from the commode too weak to draw up his trousers, he dropped into a soft armchair and looked with horror at his bare, enfeebled thighs with the muscles so sharply marked on them.

Gerasim with a firm light tread, his heavy boots emitting a pleasant smell of tar and fresh winter air, came in wearing a clean Hessian apron, the sleeves of his print shirt tucked up over his strong bare young arms; and refraining from looking at his sick master out of consideration for his feelings, and restraining the joy of life that beamed from his face, he went up to the commode.

"Gerasim!" said Ivan Ilych in a weak voice.

Gerasim started, evidently afraid he might have committed some blunder, and with a rapid movement turned his fresh, kind, simple young face which just showed the first downy signs of a beard.

"Yes, sir?"

"That must be very unpleasant for you. You must forgive me. I am helpless."

"Oh, why, sir," and Gerasim's eyes beamed and he showed his glistening white teeth, "what's a little trouble? It's a case of illness with you, sir."

And his deft strong hands did their accustomed task, and he went out of the room stepping lightly. Five minutes later he as lightly returned.

Ivan Ilych was still sitting in the same position in the armchair.

"Gerasim," he said when the latter had replaced the freshly-washed utensil. "Please come here and help me." Gerasim went up to him. "Lift me up. It is hard for me to get up, and I have sent Dmitri away."

Gerasim went up to him, grasped his master with his strong arms deftly but gently, in the same way that he stepped—lifted him, supported him with one hand, and with the other drew up his trousers and would have set him down again, but Ivan Ilych asked to be led to the sofa. Gerasim, without an effort and without apparent pressure, led him, almost lifting him, to the sofa and placed him on it.

"Thank you. How easily and well you do it all!"

Gerasim smiled again and turned to leave the room. But Ivan Ilych felt his presence such a comfort that he did not want to let him go.

"One thing more, please move up that chair. No, the other one—under my feet. It is easier for me when my feet are raised."

Gerasim brought the chair, set it down gently in place, and raised Ivan Ilych's legs on to it. It seemed to Ivan Ilych that he felt better while Gerasim was holding up his legs.

"It's better when my legs are higher," he said. "Place that cushion under them."

Gerasim did so. He again lifted the legs and placed them, and again Ivan Ilych felt better while Gerasim held his legs. When he set them down Ivan Ilych fancied he felt worse.

"Gerasim," he said. "Are you busy now?"

"Not at all, sir," said Gerasim, who had learnt from the townfolk how to speak to gentlefolk.

"What have you still to do?"

"What have I to do? I've done everything except chopping the logs for tomorrow."

"Then hold my legs up a bit higher, can you?"

"Of course I can. Why not?" And Gerasim raised his master's legs higher and Ivan Ilych thought that in that position he did not feel any pain at all.

"And how about the logs?"

"Don't trouble about that, sir. There's plenty of time."

Ivan Ilych told Gerasim to sit down and hold his legs, and began to talk to him. And strange to say it seemed to him that he felt better while Gerasim held his legs up.

After that Ivan Ilych would sometimes call Gerasim and get him to hold his legs on his shoulders, and he liked talking to him. Gerasim did it all easily, willingly, simply, and with a good nature that touched Ivan Ilych. Health, strength, and vitality in other people were offensive to him, but Gerasim's strength and vitality did not mortify but soothed him.

What tormented Ivan Ilych most was the deception, the lie, which for some reason they all accepted, that he was not dying but was simply ill, and that he only need keep quiet and undergo a treatment and then something very good would result. He however knew that do what they would nothing would come of it, only still more agonizing suffering and death. This deception tortured him—their not wishing to admit what they all knew and what he knew, but wanting to lie to him concerning his terrible condition, and wishing and forcing him to participate in that lie. Those lies—lies enacted over him on the eve of his death and destined to degrade this awful, solemn act to the level of their visitings, their curtains, their sturgeon for dinner—were a terrible agony for Ivan Ilych. And strangely enough, many times when they were going through their antics over him he had been within a hairbreadth of calling out to them: "Stop lying! You know and I know that I am dying. Then at least stop lying about it!" But he had never had the spirit to do it. The awful, terrible act of his dying was, he could see, reduced by those about him to the level of a casual, unpleasant, and almost indecorous incident (as if someone entered a drawing-room diffusing an unpleasant odour) and this was done by that very decorum which he had served all his life long. He saw that no one felt for him, because no one even wished to grasp his position. Only Gerasim recognized it and pitied him. And so Ivan Ilych felt at ease only with him. He felt comforted when Gerasim supported his legs (sometimes all night long) and refused to go to bed, saying: "Don't you worry, Ivan Ilych. I'll get sleep enough later on," or when he suddenly became familiar and exclaimed: "If you weren't sick it would be another matter, but as it is, why should I grudge a little trouble?" Gerasim alone did not lie; everything showed that he alone understood the facts of the case and did not consider it necessary to disguise them, but simply felt sorry for his emaciated and enfeebled master. Once when Ivan Ilych was sending him away he even said straight out: "We shall all of us die, so why should I grudge a little trouble?"—expressing the fact that he did not think his work burdensome, because he was doing it for a dying man and hoped someone would do the same for him when his time came.

Apart from this lying, or because of it, what most tormented Ivan Ilych was that no one pitied him as he wished to be pitied. At certain moments after prolonged suffering he wished most of all (though he would have been ashamed to confess it) for someone to pity him as a sick child is pitied. He longed to be petted and comforted. He knew he was an important functionary, that he had a beard turning grey, and that therefore what he longed for was impossible, but still he longed for it. And in Gerasim's attitude towards him there was something akin to what he wished for, and so that attitude comforted him. Ivan Ilych wanted to weep, wanted to be petted and cried over, and then his colleague Shebek would come, and instead of weeping and being petted,

Ivan Ilych would assume a serious, severe, and profound air, and by force of habit would express his opinion on a decision of the Court of Cassation and would stubbornly insist on that view. This falsity around him and within him did more than anything else to poison his last days.

VIII

It was morning. He knew it was morning because Gerasim had gone, and Peter the footman had come and put out the candles, drawn back one of the curtains, and begun quietly to tidy up. Whether it was morning or evening, Friday or Sunday, made no difference, it was all just the same: the gnawing, unmitigated, agonizing pain, never ceasing for an instant, the consciousness of life inexorably waning but not yet extinguished, the approach of that ever dreaded and hateful Death which was the only reality, and always the same falsity. What were days, weeks, hours, in such a case?

"Will you have some tea, sir?"

"He wants things to be regular, and wishes the gentlefolk to drink tea in the morning," thought Ivan Ilych, and only said "No."

"Wouldn't you like to move onto the sofa, sir?"

"He wants to tidy up the room, and I'm in the way. I am uncleanliness and disorder," he thought, and said only:

"No, leave me alone."

The man went on bustling about. Ivan Ilych stretched out his hand. Peter came up, ready to help.

"What is it, sir?"

"My watch."

Peter took the watch which was close at hand and gave it to his master.

"Half-past eight. Are they up?"

"No, sir, except Vladimir Ivanich" (the son) "who has gone to school. Praskovya Fëdorovna ordered me to wake her if you asked for her. Shall I do so?"

"No, there's no need to." "Perhaps I'd better have some tea," he thought, and added aloud: "Yes, bring me some tea."

Peter went to the door, but Ivan Ilych dreaded being left alone. "How can I keep him here? Oh yes, my medicine." "Peter, give me my medicine." "Why not? Perhaps it may still do me some good." He took a spoonful and swallowed it. "No, it won't help. It's all tomfoolery, all deception," he decided as soon as he became aware of the familiar, sickly, hopeless taste. "No, I can't believe in it any longer. But the pain, why this pain? If it would only cease just for a moment!" And he moaned. Peter turned towards him. "It's all right. Go and fetch me some tea."

Peter went out. Left alone Ivan Ilych groaned not so much with pain, terrible though that was, as from mental anguish. Always and for ever the same, always these endless days and nights. If only it would come quicker! If only *what* would come quicker? Death, darkness? . . . No, no! Anything rather than death!

When Peter returned with the tea on a tray, Ivan Ilych stared at him for a time in perplexity, not realizing who and what he was. Peter was disconcerted by that look and his embarrassment brought Ivan Ilych to himself.

"Oh, tea! All right, put it down. Only help me to wash and put on a clean shirt."

And Ivan Ilych began to wash. With pauses for rest, he washed his hands and then his face, cleaned his teeth, brushed his hair, and looked in the glass. He was terrified by what he saw, especially by the limp way in which his hair clung to his pallid forehead.

While his shirt was being changed he knew that he would be still more frightened at the sight of his body, so he avoided looking at it. Finally he was ready. He drew on a dressing-gown, wrapped himself in a plaid, and sat down in the armchair to take his tea. For a moment he felt refreshed, but as soon as he began to drink the tea he was again aware of the same taste, and the pain also returned. He finished it with an effort, and then lay down stretching out his legs, and dismissed Peter.

Always the same. Now a spark of hope flashes up, then a sea of despair rages, and always pain; always pain, always despair, and always the same. When alone he had a dreadful and distressing desire to call someone, but he knew beforehand that with others present it would be still worse. "Another dose of morphine—to lose consciousness. I will tell him, the doctor, that he must think of something else. It's impossible, impossible, to go on like this."

An hour and another pass like that. But now there is a ring at the door bell. Perhaps it's the doctor? It is. He comes in fresh, hearty, plump, and cheerful, with that look on his face that seems to say: "There now, you're in a panic about something, but we'll arrange it all for you directly!" The doctor knows this expression is out of place here, but he has put it on once for all and can't take it off—like a man who has put on a frock-coat in the morning to pay a round of calls.

The doctor rubs his hands vigorously and reassuringly.

"Brr! How cold it is! There's such a sharp frost; just let me warm myself!" he says, as if it were only a matter of waiting till he was warm, and then he would put everything right.

"Well now, how are you?"

Ivan Ilych feels that the doctor would like to say: "Well, how are your affairs?" but that even he feels that this would not do, and says instead: "What sort of a night have you had?"

Ivan Ilych looks at him as much as to say: "Are you really never ashamed of lying?" But the doctor does not wish to understand this question, and Ivan Ilych says: "Just as terrible as ever. The pain never leaves me and never subsides. If only something . . ."

"Yes, you sick people are always like that. . . . There, now I think I am warm enough. Even Praskovya Fëdorovna, who is so particular, could find no fault with my temperature. Well, now I can say good-morning," and the doctor presses his patient's hand.

Then, dropping his former playfulness, he begins with a most serious face to examine the patient, feeling his pulse and taking his temperature, and then begins the sounding and auscultation.

Ivan Ilych knows quite well and definitely that all this is nonsense and pure deception, but when the doctor, getting down on his knee, leans over him, putting the ear first higher than lower, and performs various gymnastic movements over him with a significant expression on his face, Ivan Ilych submits to it all as he used to submit to the speeches of the lawyers, though he knew very well that they were all lying and why they were lying.

The doctor, kneeling on the sofa, is still sounding him when Praskovya Fëdorovna's silk dress rustles at the door and she is heard scolding Peter for not having let her know of the doctor's arrival.

She comes in, kisses her husband, and at once proceeds to prove that she has been up a long time already, and only owing to a misunderstanding failed to be there when the doctor arrived.

Ivan Ilych looks at her, scans her all over, sets against her the whiteness and plumpness and cleanness of her hands and neck, the gloss of her hair, and the sparkle of her vivacious eyes. He hates her with his whole soul. And the thrill of hatred he feels for her makes him suffer from her touch.

Her attitude towards him and his disease is still the same. Just as the doctor had adopted a certain relation to his patient which he could not abandon, so had she formed one towards him—that he was not doing something he ought to do and was himself to blame, and that she reproached him lovingly for this —and she could not now change that attitude.

"You see he doesn't listen to me and doesn't take his medicine at the proper time. And above all he lies in a position that is no doubt bad for him—with his legs up."

She described how he made Gerasim hold his legs up.

The doctor smiled with a contemptuous affability that said: "What's to be done? These sick people do have foolish fancies of that kind, but we must forgive them."

When the examination was over the doctor looked at his watch, and then Praskovya Fëdorovna announced to Ivan Ilych that it was of course as he pleased, but she had sent today for a celebrated specialist who would examine him and have a consultation with Michael Danilovich (their regular doctor).

"Please don't raise any objections. I am doing this for my own sake," she said ironically, letting it be felt that she was doing it all for his sake and only said this to leave him no right to refuse. He remained silent, knitting his brows. He felt that he was so surrounded and involved in a mesh of falsity that it was hard to unravel anything.

Everything she did for him was entirely for her own sake, and she told him she was doing for herself what she actually was doing for herself, as if that was so incredible that he must understand the opposite.

At half-past eleven the celebrated specialist arrived. Again the sounding began and the significant conversations in his presence and in another room, about the kidneys and the appendix, and the questions and answers, with such an air of importance that again, instead of the real question of life and death which now alone confronted him, the question arose of the kidney and appendix which were not behaving as they ought to and would now be attacked by Michael Danilovich and the specialist and forced to mend their ways.

The celebrated specialist took leave of him with a serious though not hopeless look, and in reply to the timid question Ivan Ilych, with eyes glistening with fear and hope, put to him as to whether there was a chance of recovery, said that he could not vouch for it but there was a possibility. The look of hope with which Ivan Ilych watched the doctor out was so pathetic that Praskovya Fëdorovna, seeing it, even wept as she left the room to hand the doctor his fee.

The gleam of hope kindled by the doctor's encouragement did not last long. The same room, the same pictures, curtains, wall-paper, medicine bottles, were all there, and the same aching suffering body, and Ivan Ilych began to moan. They gave him a subcutaneous injection and he sank into oblivion.

It was twilight when he came to. They brought him his dinner and he swallowed some beef tea with difficulty, and then everything was the same again and night was coming on.

After dinner, at seven o'clock, Praskovya Fëdorovna came into the room in evening dress, her full bosom pushed up by her corset, and with traces of powder on her face. She had reminded him in the morning that they were going to the theatre. Sarah Bernhardt was visiting the town and they had a box, which he had insisted on their taking. Now he had forgotten about it and her toilet offended him, but he concealed his vexation when he remembered that he had himself insisted on their securing a box and going because it would be an instructive and aesthetic pleasure for the children.

Praskovya Fëdorovna came in, self-satisfied but yet with a rather guilty air. She sat down and asked how he was, but, as he saw, only for the sake of asking and not in order to learn about it, knowing that there was nothing to learn—and then went on to what she really wanted to say: that she would not on any account have gone but that the box had been taken and Helen and their daughter were going, as well as Petrishchev (the examining magistrate, their daughter's fiancé) and that it was out of the question to let them go alone; but that she would have much preferred to sit with him for a while; and he must be sure to follow the doctor's orders while she was away.

"Oh, and Fëdor Petrovich" (the fiancé) "would like to come in. May he? And Lisa?"

"All right."

Their daughter came in in full evening dress, her fresh young flesh exposed (making a show of that very flesh which in his own case caused so much suffering), strong, healthy, evidently in love, and impatient with illness, suffering, and death, because they interfered with her happiness.

Fëdor Petrovich came in too, in evening dress, his hair curled *à la Capoul*,[11] a tight stiff collar round his long sinewy neck, an enormous white shirt-front and narrow black trousers tightly stretched over his strong thighs. He had one white glove tightly drawn on, and was holding his opera hat in his hand.

Following him the schoolboy crept in unnoticed, in a new uniform, poor little fellow, and wearing gloves. Terribly dark shadows showed under his eyes, the meaning of which Ivan Ilych knew well.

His son had always seemed pathetic to him, and now it was dreadful to see the boy's frightened look of pity. It seemed to Ivan Ilych that Vasya was the only one besides Gerasim who understood and pitied him.

They all sat down and again asked how he was. A silence followed. Lisa asked her mother about the opera-glasses, and there was an altercation between mother and daughter as to who had taken them and where they had been put. This occasioned some unpleasantness.

[11] A rather elaborate men's hair style named after Victor Capoul (1839–1924), a brilliant French singer.

Fëdor Petrovich inquired of Ivan Ilych whether he had ever seen Sarah Bernhardt. Ivan Ilych did not at first catch the question, but then replied: "No, have you seen her before?"

"Yes, in *Adrienne Lecouvreur*."[12]

Praskovya Fëdorovna mentioned some rôles in which Sarah Bernhardt was particularly good. Her daughter disagreed. Conversation sprang up as to the elegance and realism of her acting—the sort of conversation that is always repeated and is always the same.

In the midst of the conversation Fëdor Petrovich glanced at Ivan Ilych and became silent. Ivan Ilych was staring with glittering eyes straight before him, evidently indignant with them. This had to be rectified, but it was impossible to do so. The silence had to be broken, but for a time no one dared to break it and they all became afraid that the conventional deception would suddenly become obvious and the truth become plain to all. Lisa was the first to pluck up courage and break that silence, but by trying to hide what everybody was feeling, she betrayed it.

"Well, if we are going it's time to start," she said, looking at her watch, a present from her father, and with a faint and significant smile at Fëdor Petrovich relating to something known only to them. She got up with a rustle of her dress.

They all rose, said good-night, and went away.

When they had gone it seemed to Ivan Ilych that he felt better; the falsity had gone with them. But the pain remained—that same pain and that same fear that made everything monotonously alike, nothing harder and nothing easier. Everything was worse.

Again minute followed minute and hour followed hour. Everything remained the same and there was no cessation. And the inevitable end of it all became more and more terrible.

"Yes, send Gerasim here," he replied to a question Peter asked.

IX

His wife returned late at night. She came in on tiptoe, but he heard her, opened his eyes, and made haste to close them again. She wished to send Gerasim away and to sit with him herself, but he opened his eyes and said: "No, go away."

"Are you in great pain?"

"Always the same."

"Take some opium."

He agreed and took some. She went away.

Till about three in the morning he was in a state of stupefied misery. It seemed to him that he and his pain were being thrust into a narrow, deep black sack, but though they were pushed further and further in they could not be pushed to the bottom. And this, terrible enough in itself, was accompanied by suffering. He struggled but yet co-operated. And suddenly he broke through, fell, and regained consciousness. Gerasim was sitting at the foot of the bed

---

12 A French tragedy by Scribe and Legouvé (1849) on the death of the celebrated eighteenth-century actress named in the title. The play provided Sarah Bernhardt with one of her most famous parts.

dozing quietly, while he himself lay with his emaciated stockinged legs resting on Gerasim's shoulders; the same shaded candle was there and the same unceasing pain.

"Go away, Gerasim," he whispered.

"It's all right, sir. I'll stay a while."

"No. Go away."

He removed his legs from Gerasim's shoulders, turned sideways onto his arm, and felt sorry for himself. He only waited till Gerasim had gone into the next room and then restrained himself no longer but wept like a child. He wept on account of his helplessness, his terrible loneliness, the cruelty of man, the cruelty of God, and the absence of God.

"Why hast Thou done all this? Why hast Thou brought me here? Why, why dost Thou torment me so terribly?"

He did not expect an answer and yet wept because there was no answer and could be none. The pain again grew more acute, but he did not stir and did not call. He said to himself: "Go on! Strike me! But what is it for? What have I done to Thee? What is it for?"

Then he grew quiet and not only ceased weeping but even held his breath and became all attention. It was as though he were listening not to an audible voice but to the voice of his soul, to the current of thoughts arising within him.

"What is it you want?" was the first clear conception capable of expression in words, that he heard.

"What do you want? What do you want?" he repeated to himself.

"What do I want? To live and not to suffer," he answered.

And again he listened with such concentrated attention that even his pain did not distract him.

"To live? How?" asked his inner voice.

"Why, to live as I used to—well and pleasantly."

"As you lived before, well and pleasantly?" the voice repeated.

And in imagination he began to recall the best moments of his pleasant life. But strange to say none of those best moments of his pleasant life now seemed at all what they had then seemed—none of them except the first recollections of childhood. There, in childhood, there had been something really pleasant with which it would be possible to live if it could return. But the child who had experienced that happiness existed no longer, it was like a reminiscence of somebody else.

As soon as the period began which had produced the present Ivan Ilych, all that had then seemed joys now melted before his sight and turned into something trivial and often nasty.

And the further he departed from childhood and the nearer he came to the present the more worthless and doubtful were the joys. This began with the School of Law. A little that was really good was still found there—there was light-heartedness, friendship, and hope. But in the upper classes there had already been fewer of such good moments. Then during the first years of his official career, when he was in the service of the Governor, some pleasant moments again occurred: they were the memories of love for a woman. Then all became confused and there was still less of what was good; later on again there was still less that was good, and the further he went the less there was. His marriage, a mere accident, then the disenchantment that followed it, his wife's bad breath and the sensuality and hypocrisy: then that deadly official life and those preoccupations about money, a year of it, and two, and ten, and twenty, and always the same thing. And the longer it lasted the more deadly it became. "It is as if I had been going downhill while I imagined I was going up. And that is really what it was. I was going up in public opinion, but to the same extent life was ebbing away from me. And now it is all done and there is only death."

"Then what does it mean? Why? It can't be that life is so senseless and horrible. But if it really has been so horrible and senseless, why must I die and die in agony? There is something wrong!"

"Maybe I did not live as I ought to have done," it suddenly occurred to him. "But how could that be, when I did everything properly?" he replied, and immediately dismissed from his mind this, the sole solution of all the riddles of life and death, as something quite impossible.

"Then what do you want now? To live? Live how? Live as you lived in the law courts when the usher proclaimed 'The judge is coming!' The judge is coming, the judge!" he repeated to himself. "Here he is, the judge. But I am not guilty!" he exclaimed angrily. "What is it for?" And he ceased crying, but turning his face to the wall continued to ponder on the same question: Why, and for what purpose, is there all this horror? But however much he pondered he found no answer. And whenever the thought occurred to him, as it often did, that it all resulted from his not having lived as he ought to have done, he at once recalled the correctness of his whole life and dismissed so strange an idea.

X

Another fortnight passed. Ivan Ilych now no longer left his sofa. He would not lie in bed but lay on the sofa, facing the wall nearly all the time. He suffered ever the same unceasing agonies and in his loneliness pondered always on the same insoluble question: "What is this? Can it be that it is Death?" And the inner voice answered: "Yes, it is Death."

"Why these sufferings?" And the voice answered, "For no reason—they just are so." Beyond and besides this there was nothing.

From the very beginning of his illness, ever since he had first been to see the doctor, Ivan Ilych's life had been divided between two contrary and alternating moods: now it was despair and the expectation of this uncomprehended and terrible death, and now hope and an intently interested observation of the functioning of his organs. Now before his eyes there was only a kidney or an intestine that temporarily evaded its duty, and now only that incomprehensible and dreadful death from which it was impossible to escape.

These two states of mind had alternated from the very beginning of his illness, but the further it progressed the more doubtful and fantastic became the conception of the kidney, and the more real the sense of impending death.

He had but to call to mind what he had been three months before and what he was now, to call to mind with what regularity he had been going downhill, for every possibility of hope to be shattered.

Latterly during that loneliness in which he found himself as he lay facing the back of the sofa, a loneliness in the midst of a populous town and surrounded by numerous acquaintances and relations but that yet could not have been more complete anywhere—either at the bottom of the sea or under the earth—during that terrible loneliness Ivan Ilych had lived only in memories of the past. Pictures of his past rose before him one after another. They always began with what was nearest in time and then went back to what was the most remote—to his childhood—and rested there. If he thought of the stewed prunes that had been offered him that day, his mind went back to the raw shrivelled French plums of his childhood, their peculiar flavour and the flow of saliva when he sucked their stones, and along with the memory of that taste came a whole series of memories of those days: his nurse, his brother, and their toys. "No, I mustn't think of that. . . . It is too painful," Ivan Ilych said to himself, and brought himself back to the present—to the button on the back of the sofa and the creases in its morocco. "Morocco is expensive, but it does not wear well: there had been a quarrel about it. It was a different kind of quarrel and a different kind of morocco that time when we tore father's portfolio and were punished, and Mamma brought us some tarts. . . . " And again his thoughts dwelt on his childhood, and again it was painful and he tried to banish them and fix his mind on something else.

Then again together with that chain of memories another series passed through his mind—of how his illness had progressed and grown worse. There also the further back he looked the more life there had been. There had been more of what was good in life and more of life itself. The two merged together. "Just as the pain went on getting worse and worse, so my life grew worse and worse," he thought. "There is one bright spot there at the back, at the beginning of life, and afterwards all becomes blacker and blacker and proceeds more and more rapidly—in inverse ratio to the square of the distance from death," thought Ivan Ilych. And the example of a stone falling downwards with increasing velocity entered his mind. Life, a series of increasing sufferings, flies further and further towards its end—the most terrible suffering. "I am flying. . . ." He shuddered, shifted himself, and tried to resist, but was already aware that resistance was impossible, and again with eyes weary of gazing but unable to cease seeing what was before them, he stared at the back of the sofa and waited —awaiting that dreadful fall and shock and destruction.

"Resistance is impossible!" he said to himself. "If I could only understand what it is all for! But that too is impossible. An explanation would be possible if it could be said that I have not lived as I ought to. But it is impossible to say that," and he remembered all the legality, correctitude, and propriety of his life. "That at any rate can certainly not be admitted," he thought, and his lips smiled ironically as if someone could see that smile and be taken in by it. "There is no explanation! Agony, death . . . What for?"

XI

Another two weeks went by in this way and during that fortnight an event occurred that Ivan Ilych and his wife had desired. Petrishchev formally proposed. It happened in the evening. The next day Praskovya Fëdorovna came into her husband's room considering how best to inform him of it, but that very night there had been a fresh change for the worse in his condition. She found him still lying on the sofa but in a different position. He lay on his back, groaning and staring fixedly in front of him.

She began to remind him of his medicines, but he turned his eyes toward her with such a look that she did not finish what she was saying; so great an animosity, to her in particular, did that look express.

"For Christ's sake let me die in peace!" he said.

She would have gone away, but just then their daughter came in and went up to say good morning. He looked at her as he had done at his wife, and in reply to her inquiry about his health said dryly that he would soon free them all of himself. They were both silent and after sitting with him for a while went away.

"Is it our fault?" Lisa said to her mother. "It's as if we were to blame! I am sorry for papa, but why should we be tortured?"

The doctor came at his usual time. Ivan Ilych answered "Yes" and "No," never taking his angry eyes from him, and at last said: "You know you can do nothing for me, so leave me alone."

"We can ease your sufferings."

"You can't even do that. Let me be."

The doctor went into the drawing-room and told Praskovya Fëdorovna that the case was very serious and that the only resource left was opium to allay her husband's sufferings, which must be terrible.

It was true, as the doctor said, that Ivan Ilych's physical sufferings were terrible, but worse than the physical sufferings were his mental sufferings, which were his chief torture.

His mental sufferings were due to the fact that that night, as he looked at Gerasim's sleepy, good-natured face with its prominent cheek-bones, the question suddenly occurred to him: "What if my whole life has really been wrong?"

It occurred to him that what had appeared perfectly impossible before, namely that he had not spent his life as he should have done, might after all be true. It occurred to him that his scarcely perceptible attempts to struggle against what was considered good by the most highly placed people, those scarcely noticeable impulses which he had immediately suppressed, might have been the real thing, and all the rest false. And his professional duties and the whole arrangement of his life and of his family, and all his social and official interests, might all have been false. He tried to defend all those things to himself and suddenly felt the weakness of what he was defending. There was nothing to defend.

"But if that is so," he said to himself, "and I am leaving this life with the consciousness that I have lost all that was given me and it is impossible to rectify it—what then?"

He lay on his back and began to pass his life in review in quite a new way. In the morning when he saw first his footman, then his wife, then his daughter, and then the doctor, their every word and movement confirmed to him the awful truth that had been revealed to him during the night. In them he saw himself—all that for which he had lived—and saw clearly that it was not real at all, but a terrible and huge deception which had hidden both life and death. This consciousness intensified his physical suffering tenfold. He groaned and tossed about, and pulled at his clothing which choked and stifled him. And he hated them on that account.

He was given a large dose of opium and became unconscious, but at noon his sufferings began again. He drove everybody away and tossed from side to side.

His wife came to him and said:

"Jean, my dear, do this for me. It can't do any harm and often helps. Healthy people often do it."

He opened his eyes wide.

"What? Take communion? Why? It's unnecessary! However . . ."

She began to cry.

"Yes, do, my dear. I'll send for our priest. He is such a nice man."

"All right. Very well," he muttered.

When the priest came and heard his confession, Ivan Ilych was softened and seemed to feel a relief from his doubts and consequently from his sufferings, and for a moment there came a ray of hope. He again began to think of the vermiform appendix and the possibility of correcting it. He received the sacrament with tears in his eyes.

When they laid him down again afterwards he felt a moment's ease, and the hope that he might live awoke in him again. He began to think of the operation that had been suggested to him. "To live! I want to live!" he said to himself.

His wife came to congratulate him after his communion, and when uttering the usual conventional words she added:

"You feel better, don't you?"

Without looking at her he said "Yes."

Her dress, her figure, the expression of her face, the tone of her voice, all revealed the same thing. "This is wrong, it is not as it should be. All you have lived for and still live for is falsehood and deception, hiding life and death from you." And as soon as he admitted that thought, his hatred and his agonizing physical suffering again sprang up, and with that suffering a consciousness of the unavoidable, approaching end. And to this was added a new sensation of grinding shooting pain and a feeling of suffocation.

The expression of his face when he uttered that "yes" was dreadful. Having uttered it, he looked her straight in the eyes, turned on his face with a rapidity extraordinary in his weak state and shouted:

"Go away! Go away and leave me alone!"

XII

From that moment the screaming began that continued for three days, and was so terrible that one could not hear it through two closed doors without horror. At the moment he answered his wife he realized that he was lost, that there was no return, that the end had come, the very end, and his doubts were still unsolved and remained doubts.

"Oh! Oh! Oh!" he cried in various intonations. He had begun by screaming "I won't!" and continued screaming on the letter O.

For three whole days, during which time did not exist for him, he struggled in that black sack into which he was being thrust by an invisible, resistless force.

He struggled as a man condemned to death struggles in the hands of the executioner, knowing that he cannot save himself. And every moment he felt that despite all his efforts he was drawing nearer and nearer to what terrified him. He felt that his agony was due to his being thrust into that black hole and still more to his not being able to get right into it. He was hindered from getting into it by his conviction that his life had been a good one. That very justification of his life held him fast and prevented his moving forward, and it caused him most torment of all.

Suddenly some force struck him in the chest and side, making it still harder to breathe, and he fell through the hole and there at the bottom was a light. What had happened to him was like the sensation one sometimes experiences in a railway carriage when one thinks one is going backwards while one is really going forwards and suddenly becomes aware of the real direction.

"Yes, it was all not the right thing," he said to himself, "but that's no matter. It can be done. But what *is* the right thing?" he asked himself, and suddenly grew quiet.

This occurred at the end of the third day, two hours before his death. Just then his schoolboy son had crept softly in and gone up to the bedside. The dying man was still screaming and waving his arms. His hand fell on the boy's head, and the boy caught it, pressed it to his lips, and began to cry.

At that very moment Ivan Ilych fell through and caught sight of the light, and it was revealed to him that though his life had not been what it should have been, this could still be rectified. He asked himself, "What *is* the right thing?" and grew still, listening. Then he felt that someone was kissing his hand. He opened his eyes, looked at his son, and felt sorry for him. His wife came up to him and he glanced at her. She was gazing at him open-mouthed, with undried tears on her nose and cheek and a despairing look on her face. He felt sorry for her too.

"Yes, I am making them wretched," he thought. "They are sorry, but it will be better for them when I die." He wished to say this but had not the strength to utter it. "Besides, why speak? I must act," he thought. With a look at his wife he indicated his son and said: "Take him away . . . sorry for him . . . sorry for you too. . . ." He tried to add, "forgive me," but said "forgo" and waved his hand, knowing that He whose understanding mattered would understand.

And suddenly it grew clear to him that what had been oppressing him and would not leave him was dropping away at once from two sides, from ten sides, and from all sides. He was sorry for them, he must act so as not to hurt them and free himself from these sufferings. "How good and how simple!" he thought. "And the pain?" he asked himself. "What has become of it? Where are you, pain?"

He turned his attention to it.

"Yes, here it is. Well, what of it? Let the pain be."

"And death . . . where is it?"

He sought his former accustomed fear of death and did not find it. "Where is it? What death?" There was no fear because there was no death.

In place of death there was light.

"So that's what it is!" he suddenly exclaimed aloud. "What joy!"

To him all this happened in a single instant, and the meaning of that instant did not change. For those present his agony continued for another two hours. Something rattled in his throat, his emaciated body twitched, then the gasping and rattle became less and less frequent.

"It is finished!" said someone near him.

He heard these words and repeated them in his soul.

"Death is finished," he said to himself. "It is no more!"

He drew in a breath, stopped in the midst of a sigh, stretched out, and died.

THE PUPIL

HENRY JAMES
1843-1916

I

THE POOR YOUNG MAN hesitated and procrastinated: it cost him such an effort to broach the subject of terms, to speak of money to a person who spoke only of feelings and, as it were, of the aristocracy. Yet he was unwilling to take leave, treating his engagement as settled, without some more conventional glance in that direction than he could find an opening for in the manner of the large affable lady who sat there drawing a pair of soiled *gants de Suède*[1] through a fat jewelled hand and, at once pressing and gliding, repeated over and over everything but the thing he would have liked to hear. He would have liked to hear the figure of his salary; but just as he was nervously about to sound that note the little boy came back—the little boy Mrs. Moreen had sent out of the room to fetch her fan. He came back without the fan, only with the casual observation that he couldn't find it. As he dropped this cynical confession he looked straight and hard at the candidate for the honour of taking his education in hand. This personage reflected somewhat grimly that the first thing he

1 (French) Suede gloves (literally, Swedish gloves).

should have to teach his little charge would be to appear to address himself to his mother when he spoke to her—especially not to make her such an improper answer as that.

When Mrs. Moreen bethought herself of this pretext for getting rid of their companion Pemberton supposed it was precisely to approach the delicate subject of his remuneration. But it had been only to say some things about her son that it was better a boy of eleven shouldn't catch. They were extravagantly to his advantage save when she lowered her voice to sigh, tapping her left side familiarly, "And all overclouded by *this,* you know; all at the mercy of a weakness—!" Pemberton gathered that the weakness was in the region of the heart. He had known the poor child was not robust: this was the basis on which he had been invited to treat, through an English lady, an Oxford acquaintance, then at Nice, who happened to know both his needs and those of the amiable American family looking out for something really superior in the way of a resident tutor.

The young man's impression of his prospective pupil, who had come into the room as if to see for himself the moment Pemberton was admitted, was not quite the soft solicitation the visitor had taken for granted. Morgan Moreen was somehow sickly without being "delicate," and that he looked intelligent—it is true Pemberton wouldn't have enjoyed his being stupid—only added to the suggestion that, as with his big mouth and big ears he really couldn't be called pretty, he might too utterly fail to please. Pemberton was modest, was even timid; and the chance that his small scholar would prove cleverer than himself had quite figured, to his anxiety, among the dangers of an untried experiment. He reflected, however, that these were risks one had to run when one accepted a position, as it was called, in a private family; when as yet one's university honours had, pecuniarily speaking, remained barren. At any rate when Mrs. Moreen got up as to intimate that, since it was understood he would enter upon his duties within the week she would let him off now, he succeeded, in spite of the presence of the child, in squeezing out a phrase about the rate of payment. It was not the fault of the conscious smile which seemed a reference to the lady's expensive identity, it was not the fault of this demonstration, which had, in a sort, both vagueness and point, if the allusion didn't sound rather vulgar. This was exactly because she became still more gracious to reply: "Oh I can assure you that all that will be quite regular."

Pemberton only wondered, while he took up his hat, what "all that" was to amount to—people had such different ideas. Mrs. Moreen's words, however, seemed to commit the family to a pledge definite enough to elicit from the child a strange little comment in the shape of the mocking foreign ejaculation "Oh la-la!"

Pemberton, in some confusion, glanced at him as he walked slowly to the window with his back turned, his hands in his pockets and the air in his elderly shoulders of a boy who didn't play. The young man wondered if he should be able to teach him to play, though his mother had said it would never do and that this was why school was impossible. Mrs. Moreen exhibited no discomfiture; she only continued blandly: "Mr. Moreen will be delighted to meet your wishes. As I told you, he has been called to London for a week. As soon as he comes back you shall have it out with him."

This was so frank and friendly that the young man could only reply, laughing as his hostess laughed: "Oh I don't imagine we shall have much of a battle."

"They'll give you anything you like," the boy remarked unexpectedly, returning from the window. "We don't mind what anything costs—we live awfully well."

"My darling, you're too quaint!" his mother exclaimed, putting out to caress him a practised but ineffectual hand. He slipped out of it, but looked with intelligent innocent eyes at Pemberton, who had already had time to notice that from one moment to the other his small satiric face seemed to change its time of life. At this moment it was infantine, yet it appeared also to be under the influence of curious intuitions and knowledges. Pemberton rather disliked precocity and was disappointed to find gleams of it in a disciple not yet in his teens. Nevertheless he divined on the spot that Morgan wouldn't prove a bore. He would prove on the contrary a source of agitation. This idea held the young man, in spite of a certain repulsion.

"You pompous little person! We're not extravagant!" Mrs. Moreen gaily protested, making another unsuccessful attempt to draw the boy to her side. "You must know what to expect," she went on to Pemberton.

"The less you expect the better!" her companion interposed. "But we *are* people of fashion."

"Only so far as *you* make us so!" Mrs. Moreen tenderly mocked. "Well then, on Friday—don't tell me you're superstitious—and mind you don't fail us. Then you'll see us all. I'm so sorry the girls are out. I guess you'll like the girls. And, you know, I've another son, quite different from this one."

"He tries to imitate me," Morgan said to their friend.

"He tries? Why he's twenty years old!" cried Mrs. Moreen.

"You're very witty," Pemberton remarked to the child—a proposition his mother echoed with enthusiasm, declaring Morgan's sallies to be the delight of the house.

The boy paid no heed to this; he only enquired abruptly of the visitor, who was surprised afterwards that he hadn't struck him as offensively forward: "Do you *want* very much to come?"

"Can you doubt it after such a description of what I shall hear?" Pemberton replied. Yet he didn't want to come at all; he was coming because he had to go somewhere, thanks to the collapse of his fortune at the end of a year abroad spent on the system of putting his scant patrimony into a single full wave of experience. He had had his full wave but couldn't pay the score at his inn. Moreover he had caught in the boy's eyes the glimpse of a far-off appeal.

"Well, I'll do the best I can for you," said Morgan; with which he turned away again. He passed out of one of the long windows; Pemberton saw him go and lean on the parapet of the terrace. He remained there while the young man took leave of his mother, who, on Pemberton's looking as if he expected a farewell from him, interposed with: "Leave him, leave him; he's so strange!" Pemberton supposed her to fear something he might say. "He's a genius—you'll love him," she added. "He's much the most interesting person in the family." And before he could invent some civility to oppose to this she wound up with: "But we're all good, you know!"

"He's a genius—you'll love him!" were words that recurred to our aspirant before the Friday, suggesting among many things that geniuses were not invariably loveable. However, it was all the better if there was an element that would make tutorship absorbing: he had perhaps taken too much for granted it would only disgust him. As he left the villa after his interview he looked up at the balcony and saw the child leaning over it. "We shall have great larks!" he called up.

Morgan hung fire a moment and then gaily returned: "By the time you come back I shall have thought of something witty!"

This made Pemberton say to himself: "After all he's rather nice."

II

On the Friday he saw them all, as Mrs. Moreen had promised, for her husband had come back and the girls and the other son were at home. Mr. Moreen had a white moustache, a confiding manner and, in his buttonhole, the ribbon of a foreign order—bestowed, as Pemberton eventually learned, for services. For what services he never clearly ascertained: this was a point—one of a large number—that Mr. Moreen's manner never confided. What it emphatically did confide was that he was even more a man of the world than you might first make out. Ulick, the firstborn, was in visible training for the same profession—under the disadvantage as yet, however, of a buttonhole but feebly floral and a moustache with no pretensions to type. The girls had hair and figures and manners and small fat feet, but had never been out alone. As for Mrs. Moreen Pemberton saw on a nearer view that her elegance was intermittent and her parts didn't always match. Her husband, as she had promised, met with enthusiasm Pemberton's ideas in regard to a salary. The young man had endeavoured to keep these stammerings modest, and Mr. Moreen made it no secret that *he* found them wanting in "style." He further mentioned that he aspired to be intimate with his children, to be their best friend, and that he was always looking out for them. That was what he went off for, to London and other places—to look out; and this vigilance was the theory of life, as well as the real occupation, of the whole family. They all looked out, for they were very frank on the subject of its being necessary. They desired it to be understood that they were earnest people, and also that their fortune, though quite adequate for earnest people, required the most careful administration. Mr. Moreen, as the parent bird, sought sustenance for the nest. Ulick invoked support mainly at the club, where Pemberton guessed that it was usually served on green cloth.[2] The girls used to do up their hair and their frocks themselves, and our young man felt appealed to to be glad, in regard to Morgan's education, that, though it must naturally be of the best, it didn't cost too much. After a little he *was* glad, forgetting at times his own needs in the interest inspired by the child's character and culture and the pleasure of making easy terms for him.

During the first weeks of their acquaintance Morgan had been as puzzling as a page in an unknown language—altogether different from the obvious little Anglo-Saxons who had misrepresented childhood to Pemberton. Indeed the whole mystic volume in which the boy had been amateurishly bound demanded some practice in translation. Today, after a considerable interval, there is something phantasmagoric, like a prismatic reflexion or a serial novel, in Pemberton's memory of the queerness of the Moreens. If it were not for a few tangible tokens—a lock of Morgan's hair cut by his own hand, and the half-dozen letters

[2] An allusion to gambling (gambling tables are covered in green felt).

received from him when they were disjoined—the whole episode and the figures peopling it would seem too inconsequent for anything but dreamland. Their supreme quaintness was their success—as it appeared to him for a while at the time; since he had never seen a family so brilliantly equipped for failure. Wasn't it success to have kept him so hatefully long? Wasn't it success to have drawn him in that first morning at déjeuner,[3] the Friday he came—it was enough to *make* one superstitious—so that he utterly committed himself, and this not by calculation or on a signal, but from a happy instinct which made them, like a band of gipsies, work so neatly together? They amused him as much as if they had really been a band of gipsies. He was still young and had not seen much of the world—his English years had been properly arid; therefore the reversed conventions of the Moreens—for they had *their* desperate proprieties—struck him as topsy-turvy. He had encountered nothing like them at Oxford; still less had any such note been struck to his younger American ear during the four years at Yale in which he had richly supposed himself to be reacting against a Puritan strain. The reaction of the Moreens, at any rate, went ever so much further. He had thought himself very sharp that first day in hitting them all off in his mind with the "cosmopolite" label. Later it seemed feeble and colourless—confessedly helplessly provisional.

He yet when he first applied it felt a glow of joy—for an instructor he was still empirical—rise from the apprehension that living with them would really be to see life. Their sociable strangeness was an intimation of that—their chatter of tongues, their gaiety and good humour, their infinite dawdling (they were always getting themselves up, but it took for ever, and Pemberton had once found Mr. Moreen shaving in the drawing-room), their French, their Italian and, cropping up in the foreign fluencies, their cold tough slices of American. They lived on maccaroni and coffee—they had these articles prepared in perfection—but they knew recipes for a hundred other dishes. They overflowed with music and song, were always humming and catching each other up, and had a sort of professional acquaintance with Continental cities. They talked of "good places" as if they had been pickpockets or strolling players. They had at Nice a villa, a carriage, a piano and a banjo, and they went to official parties. They were a perfect calendar of the "days" of their friends, which Pemberton knew them, when they were indisposed, to get out of bed to go to, and which made the week larger than life when Mrs. Moreen talked of them with Paula and Amy. Their initiations gave their new inmate at first an almost dazzling sense of culture. Mrs. Moreen had translated something at some former period —an author whom it made Pemberton feel *borné*[4] never to have heard of. They could imitate Venetian and sing Neapolitan, and when they wanted to say something very particular communicated with each other in an ingenious dialect of their own, an elastic spoken cipher which Pemberton at first took for some *patois*[5] of one of their countries, but which he "caught on to" as he would not have grasped provincial development of Spanish or German.

"It's the family language—Ultramoreen," Morgan explained to him drolly enough; but the boy rarely condescended to use it himself, though he dealt in colloquial Latin as if he had been a little prelate.

Among all the "days" with which Mrs. Moreen's memory was taxed she

[3] (French) Breakfast.
[4] (French) Limited, parochial.
[5] (French) Provincial dialect.

managed to squeeze in one of her own, which her friends sometimes forgot. But the house drew a frequented air from the number of fine people who were freely named there and from several mysterious men with foreign titles and English clothes whom Morgan called the Princes and who, on sofas with the girls, talked French very loud—though sometimes with some oddity of accent —as if to show they were saying nothing improper. Pemberton wondered how the Princes could ever propose in that tone and so publicly: he took for granted cynically that this was what was desired of them. Then he recognised that even for the chance of such an advantage Mrs. Moreen would never allow Paula and Amy to receive alone. These young ladies were not at all timid, but it was just the safeguards that made them so candidly free. It was a houseful of Bohemians who wanted tremendously to be Philistines.

In one respect, however, certainly, they achieved no rigour—they were wonderfully amiable and ecstatic about Morgan. It was a genuine tenderness, an artless admiration, equally strong in each. They even praised his beauty, which was small, and were as afraid of him as if they felt him of finer clay. They spoke of him as a little angel and a prodigy—they touched on his want of health with long, vague faces. Pemberton feared at first an extravagance that might make him hate the boy, but before this happened he had become extravagant himself. Later, when he had grown rather to hate the others, it was a bribe to patience for him that they were at any rate nice about Morgan, going on tiptoe if they fancied he was showing symptoms, and even giving up somebody's "day" to procure him a pleasure. Mixed with this too was the oddest wish to make him independent, as if they had felt themselves not good enough for him. They passed him over to the new member of their circle very much as if wishing to force some charity of adoption on so free an agent and get rid of their own charge. They were delighted when they saw Morgan take so to his kind playfellow, and could think of no higher praise for the young man. It was strange how they contrived to reconcile the appearance, and indeed the essential fact, of adoring the child with their eagerness to wash their hands of him. Did they want to get rid of him before he should find them out? Pemberton was finding them out month by month. The boy's fond family, however this might be, turned their backs with exaggerated delicacy, as if to avoid the reproach of interfering. Seeing in time how little he had in common with them— it was by *them* he first observed it; they proclaimed it with complete humility— his companion was moved to speculate on the mysteries of transmission, the far jumps of heredity. Where this detachment from most of the things they represented had come from was more than an observer could say—it certainly had burrowed under two or three generations.

As for Pemberton's own estimate of his pupil, it was a good while before he got the point of view, so little had he been prepared for it by the smug young barbarians to whom the tradition of tutorship, as hitherto revealed to him, had been adjusted. Morgan was scrappy and surprising, deficient in many properties supposed common to the *genus* and abounding in others that were the portion only of the supernaturally clever. One day his friend made a great stride: it cleared up the question to perceive that Morgan *was* supernaturally clever and that, though the formula was temporarily meagre, this would be the only assumption on which one could successfully deal with him. He had the general quality of a child for whom life had not been simplified by school, a kind of homebred sensibility which might have been bad for himself but was charming for others, and a whole range of refinement and perception—little musical vibrations as taking as picked-up airs—begotten by wandering about Europe at the tail of his migratory tribe. This might not have been an education to recommend in advance, but its results with so special a subject were as appreciable as the marks on a piece of fine porcelain. There was at the same time in him a small strain of stoicism, doubtless the fruit of having had to begin early to bear pain, which counted for pluck and made it of less consequence that he might have been thought at school rather a polyglot little beast. Pemberton indeed quickly found himself rejoicing that school was out of the question: in any million of boys it was probably good for all but one, and Morgan was that millionth. It would have made him comparative and superior—it might have made him really require kicking. Pemberton would try to be school himself—a bigger seminary than five hundred grazing donkeys, so that, winning no prizes, the boy would remain unconscious and irresponsible and amusing—amusing, because, though life was already intense in his childish nature, freshness still made there a strong draught for jokes. It turned out that even in the still air of Morgan's various disabilities jokes flourished greatly. He was a pale lean acute undeveloped little cosmopolite, who liked intellectual gymnastics and who also, as regards the behaviour of mankind, had noticed more things than you might suppose, but who nevertheless had his proper playroom of superstitions, where he smashed a dozen toys a day.

III

At Nice once, toward evening, as the pair rested in the open air after a walk, and looked over the sea at the pink western lights, he said suddenly to his comrade: "Do you like it, you know—being with us all in this intimate way?"

"My dear fellow, why should I stay if I didn't?"

"How do I know you'll stay? I'm almost sure you won't, very long."

"I hope you don't mean to dismiss me," said Pemberton.

Morgan debated, looking at the sunset. "I think if I did right I ought to."

"Well, I know I'm supposed to instruct you in virtue; but in that case don't do right."

"You're very young—fortunately," Morgan went on, turning to him again.

"Oh yes, compared with you!"

"Therefore it won't matter so much if you do lose a lot of time."

"That's the way to look at it," said Pemberton accommodatingly.

They were silent a minute; after which the boy asked: "Do you like my father and my mother very much?"

"Dear me, yes. Charming people."

Morgan received this with another silence; then unexpectedly, familiarly, but at the same time affectionately, he remarked: "You're a jolly old humbug!"

For a particular reason the words made our young man change colour. The boy noticed in an instant that he had turned red, whereupon he turned red himself and pupil and master exchanged a longish glance in which there was a consciousness of many more things than are usually touched upon, even tacitly, in such a relation. It produced for Pemberton an embarrassment; it raised in a shadowy form a question—this was the first glimpse of it—destined to play a singular and, as he imagined, owing to the altogether peculiar conditions, an unprecedented part in his intercourse with his little companion. Later, when he found himself talking with the youngster in a way in which few youngsters could ever have been talked with, he thought of that clumsy moment on the bench at Nice as the dawn of an understanding that had broadened. What had added to the clumsiness then was that he thought it his duty to declare to Morgan that he might abuse him, Pemberton, as much as he liked, but must never abuse his parents. To this Morgan had the easy retort that he hadn't dreamed of abusing them; which appeared to be true: it put Pemberton in the wrong.

"Then why am I a humbug for saying *I* think them charming?" the young man asked, conscious of a certain rashness.

"Well—they're not your parents."

"They love you better than anything in the world—never forget that," said Pemberton.

"Is that why you like them so much?"

"They're very kind to me," Pemberton replied evasively.

"You *are* a humbug!" laughed Morgan passing an arm into his tutor's. He leaned against him looking off at the sea again and swinging his long thin legs.

"Don't kick my shins," said Pemberton while he reflected "Hang it, I can't complain of them to the child!"

"There's another reason too," Morgan went on, keeping his legs still.

"Another reason for what?"

"Besides their not being your parents."

"I don't understand you," said Pemberton.

"Well, you will before long. All right!"

He did understand fully before long, but he made a fight even with himself before he confessed it. He thought it the oddest thing to have a struggle with the child about. He wondered he didn't hate the hope of the Moreens for bringing the struggle on. But by the time it began any such sentiment for that scion was closed to him. Morgan was a special case, and to know him was to accept him on his own odd terms. Pemberton had spent his aversion to special cases before arriving at knowledge. When at last he did arrive his quandary was great. Against every interest he had attached himself. They would have to meet things together. Before they went home that evening at Nice the boy had said, clinging to his arm:

"Well, at any rate you'll hang on to the last."

"To the last?"

"Till you're fairly beaten."

"*You* ought to be fairly beaten!" cried the young man, drawing him closer.

IV

A year after he had come to live with them Mr. and Mrs. Moreen suddenly gave up the villa at Nice. Pemberton had got used to suddenness, having seen it practised on a considerable scale during two jerky little tours—one in

Switzerland the first summer, and the other late in the winter, when they all ran down to Florence and then, at the end of ten days, liking it much less than they had intended, straggled back in mysterious depression. They had returned to Nice "for ever," as they said; but this didn't prevent their squeezing, one rainy muggy May night, into a second-class railway-carriage—you could never tell by which class they would travel—where Pemberton helped them to stow away a wonderful collection of bundles and bags. The explanation of this manœuvre was that they had determined to spend the summer "in some bracing place"; but in Paris they dropped into a small furnished apartment—a fourth floor in a third-rate avenue, where there was a smell on the staircase and the *portier*[6] was hateful—and passed the next four months in blank indigence.

The better part of this baffled sojourn was for the preceptor and his pupil, who, visiting the Invalides[7] and Notre Dame, the Conciergerie[8] and all the museums, took a hundred remunerative rambles. They learned to know their Paris, which was useful, for they came back another year for a longer stay, the general character of which in Pemberton's memory today mixes pitiably and confusedly with that of the first. He sees Morgan's shabby knickerbockers—the everlasting pair that didn't match his blouse and that as he grew longer could only grow faded. He remembers the particular holes in his three or four pair of coloured stockings.

Morgan was dear to his mother, but he never was better dressed than was absolutely necessary—partly, no doubt, by his own fault, for he was as indifferent to his appearance as a German philosopher. "My dear fellow, you *are* coming to pieces," Pemberton would say to him in sceptical remonstrance; to which the child would reply, looking at him serenely up and down: "My dear fellow, so are you! I don't want to cast you in the shade." Pemberton could have no rejoinder for this—the assertion so closely represented the fact. If however the deficiencies of his own wardrobe were a chapter by themselves he didn't like his little charge to look too poor. Later he used to say "Well, if we're poor, why, after all, shouldn't we look it?" and he consoled himself with thinking there was something rather elderly and gentlemanly in Morgan's disrepair—it differed from the untidiness of the urchin who plays and spoils his things. He could trace perfectly the degrees by which, in proportion as her little son confined himself to his tutor for society, Mrs. Moreen shrewdly forbore to renew his garments. She did nothing that didn't show, neglected him because he escaped notice, and then, as he illustrated this clever policy, discouraged at home his public appearances. Her position was logical enough—those members of her family who did show had to be showy.

During this period and several others Pemberton was quite aware of how he and his comrade might strike people; wandering languidly through the Jardin des Plantes[9] as if they had nowhere to go, sitting on the winter days in the galleries of the Louvre, so splendidly ironical to the homeless, as if for the

6 (French) Doorkeeper and janitor.

7 The *Hôtel des Invalides* was founded as a military hospital. It now contains the imposing tomb of Napoleon and a military museum.

8 The old prison of the *Palais de Justice*, chiefly notable to tourists for its use as a place of execution during the Reign of Terror.

9 A large botanical garden, containing also a museum and a small zoo.

advantage of the *calorifère*.[10] They joked about it sometimes: it was the sort of joke that was perfectly within the boy's compass. They figured themselves as part of the vast vague hand-to-mouth multitude of the enormous city and pretended they were proud of their position in it—it showed them "such a lot of life" and made them conscious of a democratic brotherhood. If Pemberton couldn't feel a sympathy in destitution with his small companion—for after all Morgan's fond parents would never have let him really suffer—the boy would at least feel it with him, so it came to the same thing. He used sometimes to wonder what people would think they were—to fancy they were looked askance at, as if it might be a suspected case of kidnapping. Morgan wouldn't be taken for a young patrician with a preceptor—he wasn't smart enough; though he might pass for his companion's sickly little brother. Now and then he had a five-franc piece, and except once, when they bought a couple of lovely neckties, one of which he made Pemberton accept, they laid it out scientifically in old books. This was sure to be a great day, always spent on the quays, in a rummage of the dusty boxes that garnish the parapets.[11] Such occasions helped them to live, for their books ran low very soon after the beginning of their acquaintance. Pemberton had a good many in England, but he was obliged to write to a friend and ask him kindly to get some fellow to give him something for them.

If they had to relinquish that summer the advantage of the bracing climate the young man couldn't but suspect this failure of the cup when at their very lips to have been the effect of a rude jostle of his own. This had represented his first blow-out, as he called it, with his patrons; his first successful attempt —though there was little other success about it—to bring them to a consideration of his impossible position. As the ostensible eve of a costly journey the moment had struck him as favourable to an earnest protest, the presentation of an ultimatum. Ridiculous as it sounded, he had never yet been able to compass an uninterrupted private interview with the elder pair or with either of them singly. They were always flanked by their elder children, and poor Pemberton usually had his own little charge at his side. He was conscious of its being a house in which the surface of one's delicacy got rather smudged; nevertheless he had preserved the bloom of his scruple against announcing to Mr. and Mrs. Moreen with publicity that he shouldn't be able to go on longer without a little money. He was still simple enough to suppose Ulick and Paula and Amy might not know that since his arrival he had only had a hundred and forty francs; and he was magnanimous enough to wish not to compromise their parents in their eyes. Mr. Moreen now listened to him, as he listened to every one and to every thing, like a man of the world, and seemed to appeal to him— though not of course too grossly—to try and be a little more of one himself. Pemberton recognised in fact the importance of the character—from the advantage it gave Mr. Moreen. He was not even confused or embarrassed, whereas the young man in his service was more so than there was any reason for. Neither was he surprised—at least any more than a gentleman had to be who freely confessed himself a little shocked—though not perhaps strictly at Pemberton.

[10] (French) Hot-air stove.
[11] The booksellers' movable stalls, set up on parapets along the Seine.

"We must go into this, mustn't we, dear?" he said to his wife. He assured his young friend that the matter should have his very best attention; and he melted into space as elusively as if, at the door, he were taking an inevitable but deprecatory precedence. When, the next moment, Pemberton found himself alone with Mrs. Moreen it was to hear her say "I see, I see"—stroking the roundness of her chin and looking as if she were only hesitating between a dozen easy remedies. If they didn't make their push Mr. Moreen could at least disappear for several days. During his absence his wife took up the subject again spontaneously, but her contribution to it was merely that she had thought all the while they were getting on so beautifully. Pemberton's reply to this revelation was that unless they immediately put down something on account he would leave them on the spot and for ever. He knew she would wonder how he would get away, and for a moment expected her to enquire. She didn't, for which he was almost grateful to her, so little was he in a position to tell.

"You won't, you *know* you won't—you're too interested," she said. "You *are* interested, you know you are, you dear kind man!" She laughed with almost condemnatory archness, as if it were a reproach—though she wouldn't insist; and flirted a soiled pocket-handkerchief at him.

Pemberton's mind was fully made up to take his step the following week. This would give him time to get an answer to a letter he had dispatched to England. If he did in the event nothing of the sort—that is if he stayed another year and then went away only for three months—it was not merely because before the answer to his letter came (most unsatisfactory when it did arrive) Mr. Moreen generously counted out to him, and again with the sacrifice to "form" of a marked man of the world, three hundred francs in elegant ringing gold. He was irritated to find that Mrs. Moreen was right, that he couldn't at the pinch bear to leave the child. This stood out clearer for the very reason that, the night of his desperate appeal to his patrons, he had seen fully for the first time where he was. Wasn't it another proof of the success with which those patrons practised their arts that they had managed to avert for so long the illuminating flash? It descended on our friend with a breadth of effect which perhaps would have struck a spectator as comical, after he had returned to his little servile room, which looked into a close court where a bare dirty opposite wall took, with the sound of shrill clatter, the reflexion of lighted back windows. He had simply given himself away to a band of adventurers. The idea, the word itself, wore a romantic horror for him—he had always lived on such safe lines. Later it assumed a more interesting, almost a soothing, sense: it pointed a moral, and Pemberton could enjoy a moral. The Moreens were adventurers not merely because they didn't pay their debts, because they lived on society, but because their whole view of life, dim and confused and instinctive, like that of clever colour-blind animals, was speculative and rapacious and mean. Oh they were "respectable," and that only made them more *immondes!*[12] The young man's analysis, while he brooded, put it at last very simply—they were adventurers because they were toadies and snobs. That was the completest account of them—it was the law of their being. Even when this truth became vivid to their ingenuous inmate he remained unconscious of how much his mind had been prepared for it by the extraordinary little boy who had now

12 (French) Impure, morally detestable.

become such a complication in his life. Much less could he then calculate on the information he was still to owe the extraordinary little boy.

V

But it was during the ensuing time that the real problem came up—the problem of how far it was excusable to discuss the turpitude of parents with a child of twelve, of thirteen, of fourteen. Absolutely inexcusable and quite impossible it of course at first appeared; and indeed the question didn't press for some time after Pemberton had received his three hundred francs. They produced a temporary lull, a relief from the sharpest pressure. The young man frugally amended his wardrobe and even had a few francs in his pocket. He thought the Moreens looked at him as if he were almost too smart, as if they ought to take care not to spoil him. If Mr. Moreen hadn't been such a man of the world he would perhaps have spoken of the freedom of such neckties on the part of a subordinate. But Mr. Moreen was always enough a man of the world to let things pass—he had certainly shown that. It was singular how Pemberton guessed that Morgan, though saying nothing about it, knew something had happened. But three hundred francs, especially when one owed money, couldn't last for ever; and when the treasure was gone—the boy knew when it had failed —Morgan did break ground. The party had returned to Nice at the beginning of the winter, but not to the charming villa. They went to an hotel, where they stayed three months, and then moved to another establishment, explaining that they had left the first because, after waiting and waiting, they couldn't get the rooms they wanted. These apartments, the rooms they wanted, were generally very splendid; but fortunately they never *could* get them—fortunately, I mean, for Pemberton, who reflected always that if they had got them there would have been a still scanter educational fund. What Morgan said at last was said suddenly, irrelevantly, when the moment came, in the middle of a lesson, and consisted of the apparently unfeeling words: "You ought to *filer,* you know—you really ought."

Pemberton stared. He had learnt enough French slang from Morgan to know that to *filer* meant to cut sticks. "Ah my dear fellow, don't turn me off!"

Morgan pulled a Greek lexicon toward him—he used a Greek-German— to look out a word, instead of asking it of Pemberton. "You can't go on like this, you know."

"Like what, my boy?"

"You know they don't pay you up," said Morgan, blushing and turning his leaves.

"Don't pay me?" Pemberton stared again and feigned amazement. "What on earth put that into your head?"

"It has been there a long time," the boy replied rummaging his book.

Pemberton was silent, then he went on: "I say, what are you hunting for? They pay me beautifully."

"I'm hunting for the Greek for awful whopper," Morgan dropped.

"Find that rather for gross impertinence and disabuse your mind. What do I want of money?"

"Oh that's another question!"

Pemberton wavered—he was drawn in different ways. The severely correct thing would have been to tell the boy that such a matter was none of his business and bid him go on with his lines. But they were really too intimate for that; it was not the way he was in the habit of treating him; there had been no reason it should be. On the other hand Morgan had quite lighted on the truth —he really shouldn't be able to keep it up much longer; therefore why not let him know one's real motive for forsaking him? At the same time it wasn't decent to abuse to one's pupil the family of one's pupil; it was better to misrepresent than to do that. So in reply to his comrade's last exclamation he just declared, to dismiss the subject, that he had received several payments.

"I say—I say!" the boy ejaculated, laughing.

"That's all right," Pemberton insisted. "Give me your written rendering."

Morgan pushed a copybook across the table, and he began to read the page, but with something running in his head that made it no sense. Looking up after a minute or two he found the child's eyes fixed on him and felt in them something strange. Then Morgan said: "I'm not afraid of the stern reality."

"I haven't yet seen the thing you *are* afraid of—I'll do you that justice!"

This came out with a jump—it was perfectly true—and evidently gave Morgan pleasure. "I've thought of it a long time," he presently resumed.

"Well, don't think of it any more."

The boy appeared to comply, and they had a comfortable and even an amusing hour. They had a theory that they were very thorough, and yet they seemed always to be in the amusing part of lessons, the intervals between the dull dark tunnels, where there were waysides and jolly views. Yet the morning was brought to a violent end by Morgan's suddenly leaning his arms on the table, burying his head in them and bursting into tears: at which Pemberton was the more startled that, as it then came over him, it was the first time he had ever seen the boy cry and that the impression was consequently quite awful.

The next day, after much thought, he took a decision and, believing it to be just, immediately acted on it. He cornered Mr. and Mrs. Moreen again and let them know that if on the spot they didn't pay him all they owed him he wouldn't only leave their house but would tell Morgan exactly what had brought him to it.

"Oh you *haven't* told him?" cried Mrs. Moreen with a pacifying hand on her well-dressed bosom.

"Without warning you? For what do you take me?" the young man returned.

Mr. and Mrs. Moreen looked at each other; he could see that they appreciated, as tending to their security, his superstition of delicacy, and yet that there was a certain alarm in their relief. "My dear fellow," Mr. Moreen demanded, "what use *can* you have, leading the quiet life we all do, for such a lot of money?"—a question to which Pemberton made no answer, occupied as he was in noting that what passed in the mind of his patrons was something like: "Oh then, if we've felt that the child, dear little angel, has judged us and how he regards us, and we haven't been betrayed, he must have guessed—and in short it's *general!*" an inference that rather stirred up Mr. and Mrs. Moreen, as Pemberton had desired it should. At the same time, if he had supposed his threat would do something towards bringing them round, he was disappointed to find them taking for granted—how vulgar their perception *had* been!—that he had already given them away. There was a mystic uneasiness in their parental breasts, and that had been the inferior sense of it. None the less, however, his threat did touch them; for if they had escaped it was only to meet a new danger. Mr. Moreen appealed to him, on every precedent, as a man of the world; but his wife had recourse, for the first time since his domestication with them, to a fine *hauteur*, reminding him that a devoted mother, with her child, had arts that protected her against gross misrepresentation.

"I should misrepresent you grossly if I accused you of common honesty!" our friend replied; but as he closed the door behind him sharply, thinking he had not done himself much good, while Mr. Moreen lighted another cigarette, he heard his hostess shout after him more touchingly:

"Oh you do, you *do,* put the knife to one's throat!"

The next morning, very early, she came to his room. He recognised her knock, but had no hope she brought him money; as to which he was wrong, for she had fifty francs in her hand. She squeezed forward in her dressing-gown, and he received her in his own, between his bath-tub and his bed. He had been tolerably schooled by this time to the "foreign ways" of his hosts. Mrs. Moreen was ardent, and when she was ardent she didn't care what she did; so she now sat down on his bed, his clothes being on the chairs, and, in her preoccupation, forgot, as she glanced round, to be ashamed of giving him such a horrid room. What Mrs. Moreen's ardour now bore upon was the design of persuading him that in the first place she was very good-natured to bring him fifty francs, and that in the second, if he would only see it, he was really too absurd to expect to be *paid.* Wasn't he paid enough without perpetual money—wasn't he paid by the comfortable luxurious home he enjoyed with them all, without a care, an anxiety, a solitary want? Wasn't he sure of his position, and wasn't that everything to a young man like him, quite unknown, with singularly little to show, the ground of whose exorbitant pretensions it had never been easy to discover? Wasn't he paid above all by the sweet relation he had established with Morgan —quite ideal as from master to pupil—and by the simple privilege of knowing and living with so amazingly gifted a child; than whom really (and she meant literally what she said) there was no better company in Europe? Mrs. Moreen herself took to appealing to him as a man of the world; she said "Voyons, mon cher,"[13] and "My dear man, look here now"; and urged him to be reasonable, putting it before him that it was truly a chance for him. She spoke as if, according as he *should* be reasonable, he would prove himself worthy to be her son's tutor and of the extraordinary confidence they had placed in him.

After all, Pemberton reflected, it was only a difference of theory and the theory didn't matter much. They had hitherto gone on that of remunerated, as now they would go on that of gratuitous, service; but why should they have so many words about it? Mrs. Moreen at all events continued to be convincing; sitting there with her fifty francs she talked and reiterated as women reiterate, and bored and irritated him, while he leaned against the wall with his hands in the pockets of his wrapper, drawing it together round his legs and looking over the head of his visitor at the grey negations of his window. She wound up with saying: "You see I bring you a definite proposal."

[13] (French) Practically the equivalent of Mrs. Moreen's following sentence in English.

"A definite proposal?"

"To make our relations regular, as it were—to put them on a comfortable footing."

"I see—it's a system," said Pemberton. "A kind of organised blackmail."

Mrs. Moreen bounded up, which was exactly what he wanted. "What do you mean by that?"

"You practise on one's fears—one's fears about the child if one should go away."

"And pray what would happen to him in that event?" she demanded with majesty.

"Why he'd be alone with *you*."

"And pray with whom *should* a child be but with those whom he loves most?"

"If you think that, why don't you dismiss me?"

"Do you pretend he loves you more than he loves *us*?" cried Mrs. Moreen.

"I think he ought to. I make sacrifices for him. Though I've heard of those *you* make I don't see them."

Mrs. Moreen stared a moment; then with emotion she grasped her inmate's hand. "*Will* you make it—the sacrifice?"

He burst out laughing. "I'll see. I'll do what I can. I'll stay a little longer. Your calculation's just—I *do* hate intensely to give him up; I'm fond of him and he thoroughly interests me, in spite of the inconvenience I suffer. You know my situation perfectly. I haven't a penny in the world and, occupied as you see me with Morgan, am unable to earn money."

Mrs. Moreen tapped her undressed arm with her folded banknote. "Can't you write articles? Can't you translate as I do?"

"I don't know about translating; it's wretchedly paid."

"I'm glad to earn what I can," said Mrs. Moreen with prodigious virtue.

"You ought to tell me who you do it for." Pemberton paused a moment, and she said nothing; so he added: "I've tried to turn off some little sketches, but the magazines won't have them—they're declined with thanks."

"You see then you're not such a phœnix,"[14] his visitor pointedly smiled—"to pretend to abilities you're sacrificing for our sake."

"I haven't time to do things properly," he ruefully went on. Then as it came over him that he was almost abjectly good-natured to give these explanations he added: "If I stay on longer it must be on one condition—that Morgan shall know distinctly on what footing I am."

Mrs. Moreen demurred. "Surely you don't want to show off to a child?"

"To show *you* off, do you mean?"

Again she cast about, but this time it was to produce a still finer flower. "And *you* talk of blackmail!"

"You can easily prevent it," said Pemberton.

"And *you* talk of practising on fears!" she bravely pushed on.

"Yes, there's no doubt I'm a great scoundrel."

His patroness met his eyes—it was clear she was in straits. Then she thrust out her money at him. "Mr. Moreen desired me to give you this on account."

"I'm much obliged to Mr. Moreen, but we *have* no account."

"You won't take it?"

14 In the sense of one of unequalled excellence.

"That leaves me more free," said Pemberton.

"To poison my darling's mind?" groaned Mrs. Moreen.

"Oh your darling's mind—!" the young man laughed.

She fixed him a moment, and he thought she was going to break out tormentedly, pleadingly: "For God's sake, tell me what *is* in it!" But she checked this impulse—another was stronger. She pocketed the money—the crudity of the alternative was comical—and swept out of the room with the desperate concession: "You may tell him any horror you like!"

VI

A couple of days after this, during which he had failed to profit by so free a permission, he had been for a quarter of an hour walking with his charge in silence when the boy became sociable again with the remark: "I'll tell you how I know it; I know it through Zénobie."

"Zénobie? Who in the world is *she?*"

"A nurse I used to have—ever so many years ago. A charming woman. I liked her awfully, and she liked me."

"There's no accounting for tastes. What is it you know through her?"

"Why what their idea is. She went away because they didn't fork out. She did like me awfully, and she stayed two years. She told me all about it—that at last she could never get her wages. As soon as they saw how much she liked me they stopped giving her anything. They thought she'd stay for nothing—just *because,* don't you know?" And Morgan had a queer little conscious lucid look. "She did stay ever so long—as long as she could. She was only a poor girl. She used to send money to her mother. At last she couldn't afford it any longer, and went away in a fearful rage one night—I mean of course in a rage against *them*. She cried over me tremendously, she hugged me nearly to death. She told me all about it," the boy repeated. "She told me it was their idea. So I guessed, ever so long ago, that they have had the same idea with you."

"Zénobie was very sharp," said Pemberton. "And she made you so."

"Oh that wasn't Zénobie; that was nature. And experience!" Morgan laughed.

"Well, Zénobie was a part of your experience."

"Certainly I was a part of hers, poor dear!" the boy wisely sighed. "And I'm part of yours."

"A very important part. But I don't see how you know I've been treated like Zénobie."

"Do you take me for the biggest dunce you've known?" Morgan asked. "Haven't I been conscious of what we've been through together?"

"What we've been through?"

"Our privations—our dark days."

"Oh our days have been bright enough."

Morgan went on in silence for a moment. Then he said: "My dear chap, you're a hero!"

"Well, you're another!" Pemberton retorted.

"No I'm not, but I ain't a baby. I won't stand it any longer. You must get some occupation that pays. I'm ashamed, I'm ashamed!" quavered the boy with a ring of passion, like some high silver note from a small cathedral chorister, that deeply touched his friend.

"We ought to go off and live somewhere together," the young man said.

"I'll go like a shot if you'll take me."

"I'd get some work that would keep us both afloat," Pemberton continued.

"So would I. Why shouldn't *I* work? I ain't such a beastly little muff[15] as *that* comes to."

"The difficulty is that your parents wouldn't hear of it. They'd never part with you; they worship the ground you tread on. Don't you see the proof of it?" Pemberton developed. "They don't dislike me; they wish me no harm; they're very amiable people, but they're perfectly ready to expose me to any awkwardness in life for your sake."

The silence in which Morgan received his fond sophistry struck Pemberton somehow as expressive. After a moment the child repeated: "You *are* a hero!" Then he added: "They leave me with you altogether. You've all the responsibility. They put me off on you from morning till night. Why then should they object to my taking up with you completely? I'd help you."

"They're not particularly keen about my being helped, and they delight in thinking of you as *theirs*. They're tremendously proud of you."

"I'm not proud of *them*. But you know that," Morgan returned.

"Except for the little matter we speak of they're charming people," said Pemberton, not taking up the point made for his intelligence, but wondering greatly at the boy's own, and especially at this fresh reminder of something he had been conscious of from the first—the strangest thing in his friend's large little composition, a temper, a sensibility, even a private ideal, which made him as privately disown the stuff his people were made of. Morgan had in secret a small loftiness which made him acute about betrayed meanness; as well as a critical sense for the manners immediately surrounding him that was quite without precedent in a juvenile nature, especially when one noted that it had not made this nature "old-fashioned," as the word is of children—quaint or wizened or offensive. It was as if he had been a little gentleman and had paid the penalty by discovering that he was the only such person in his family. This comparison didn't make him vain, but it could make him melancholy and a trifle austere. While Pemberton guessed at these dim young things, shadows of shadows, he was partly drawn on and partly checked, as for a scruple, by the charm of attempting to sound the little cool shallows that were so quickly growing deeper. When he tried to figure to himself the morning twilight of childhood, so as to deal with it safely, he saw it was never fixed, never arrested, that ignorance, at the instant he touched it, was already flushing faintly into knowledge, that there was nothing that at a given moment you could say an intelligent child didn't know. It seemed to him that he himself knew too much to imagine Morgan's simplicity and too little to disembroil his tangle.

The boy paid no heed to his last remark; he only went on: "I'd have spoken to them about their idea, as I call it, long ago, if I hadn't been sure what they'd say."

"And what would they say?"

15 (Colloquial) One who is awkward or stupid.

"Just what they said about what poor Zénobie told me—that it was a horrid dreadful story, that they had paid her every penny they owed her."

"Well, perhaps they had," said Pemberton.

"Perhaps they've paid you!"

"Let us pretend they have, and *n'en parlons plus*."[16]

"They accused her of lying and cheating"—Morgan stuck to historic truth. "That's why I don't want to speak to them."

"Lest they should accuse me too?" To this Morgan made no answer, and his companion, looking down at him—the boy turned away his eyes, which had filled—saw that he couldn't have trusted himself to utter. "You're right. Don't worry them," Pemberton pursued. "Except for that, they *are* charming people."

"Except for *their* lying and *their* cheating?"

"I say—I say!" cried Pemberton, imitating a little tone of the lad's which was itself an imitation.

"We must be frank, at the last; we *must* come to an understanding," said Morgan with the importance of the small boy who lets himself think he is arranging great affairs—almost playing at shipwreck or at Indians. "I know all about everything."

"I dare say your father has his reasons," Pemberton replied, but too vaguely, as he was aware.

"For lying and cheating?"

"For saving and managing and turning his means to the best account. He has plenty to do with his money. You're an expensive family."

"Yes, I'm very expensive," Morgan concurred in a manner that made his preceptor burst out laughing.

"He's saving for *you*," said Pemberton. "They think of you in everything they do."

"He might, while he's about it, save a little—" The boy paused, and his friend waited to hear what. Then Morgan brought out oddly: "A little reputation."

"Oh there's plenty of that. That's all right!"

"Enough of it for the people they know, no doubt. The people they know are awful."

"Do you mean the princes? We mustn't abuse the princes."

"Why not? They haven't married Paula—they haven't married Amy. They only clean out Ulick."

"You *do* know everything!" Pemberton declared.

"No I don't after all. I don't know what they live on, or how they live, or *why* they live! What have they got and how did they get it? Are they rich, are they poor, or have they a *modeste aisance*?[17] Why are they always chivey-ing[18] me about—living one year like ambassadors and the next like paupers? Who are they, anyway, and what are they? I've thought of all that—I've thought of a lot of things. They're so beastly worldly. That's what I hate most—oh I've *seen* it! All they care about is to make an appearance and to pass for something or

---

[16] (French) Let's not say any more about it.
[17] An income leaving them in moderately easy circumstances.
[18] (British colloquialism) Chasing, harassing.

other. What the dickens do they want to pass for? What *do* they, Mr. Pemberton?"

"You pause for a reply," said Pemberton, treating the question as a joke, yet wondering too and greatly struck with his mate's intense if imperfect vision. "I haven't the least idea."

"And what good does it do? Haven't I seen the way people treat them—the 'nice' people, the ones they want to know? They'll take anything from them—they'll lie down and be trampled on. The nice ones hate that—they just sicken them. You're the only really nice person we know."

"Are you sure? They don't lie down for me!"

"Well, you shan't lie down for them. You've got to go—that's what you've got to do," said Morgan.

"And what will become of you?"

"Oh I'm growing up. I shall get off before long. I'll see you later."

"You had better let me finish you," Pemberton urged, lending himself to the child's strange superiority.

Morgan stopped in their walk, looking up at him. He had to look up much less than a couple of years before—he had grown, in his loose leanness, so long and high. "Finish me?" he echoed.

"There are such a lot of jolly things we can do together yet. I want to turn you out—I want you to do me credit."

Morgan continued to look at him. "To give you credit—do you mean?"

"My dear fellow, you're too clever to live."

"That's just what I'm afraid you think. No, no; it isn't fair—I can't endure it. We'll separate next week. The sooner it's over the sooner to sleep."

"If I hear of anything—any other chance—I promise to go," Pemberton said.

Morgan consented to consider this. "But you'll be honest," he demanded; "you won't pretend you haven't heard?"

"I'm much more likely to pretend I have."

"But what can you hear of, this way, stuck in a hole with us? You ought to be on the spot, to go to England—you ought to go to America."

"One would think you were *my* tutor!" said Pemberton.

Morgan walked on and after a little had begun again: "Well, now that you know I know and that we look at the facts and keep nothing back—it's much more comfortable, isn't it?"

"My dear boy, it's so amusing, so interesting, that it will surely be quite impossible for me to forego such hours as these."

This made Morgan stop once more. "You *do* keep something back. Oh you're not straight—I am!"

"How am I not straight?"

"Oh you've got your idea!"

"My idea?"

"Why that I probably shan't make old—make older—bones, and that you can stick it out till I'm removed."

"You *are* too clever to live!" Pemberton repeated.

"I call it a mean idea," Morgan pursued. "But I shall punish you by the way I hang on."

"Look out or I'll poison you!" Pemberton laughed.

"I'm stronger and better every year. Haven't you noticed that there hasn't been a doctor near me since you came?"

"*I'm* your doctor," said the young man, taking his arm and drawing him tenderly on again.

Morgan proceeded and after a few steps gave a sigh of mingled weariness and relief. "Ah now that we look at the facts it's all right!"

VII

They looked at the facts a good deal after this; and one of the first consequences of their doing so was that Pemberton stuck it out, in his friends parlance, for the purpose. Morgan made the facts so vivid and so droll, and at the same time so bald and so ugly, that there was fascination in talking them over with him, just as there would have been heartlessness in leaving him alone with them. Now that the pair had such perceptions in common it was useless for them to pretend they didn't judge such people; but the very judgement and the exchange of perceptions created another tie. Morgan had never been so interesting as now that he himself was made plainer by the sidelight of these confidences. What came out in it most was the small fine passion of his pride. He had plenty of that, Pemberton felt—so much that one might perhaps wisely wish for it some early bruises. He would have liked his people to have a spirit and had waked up to the sense of their perpetually eating humble-pie. His mother would consume any amount, and his father would consume even more than his mother. He had a theory that Ulick had wriggled out of an "affair" at Nice: there had once been a flurry at home, a regular panic, after which they all went to bed and took medicine, not to be accounted for on any other supposition. Morgan had a romantic imagination, fed by poetry and history, and he would have liked those who "bore his name"—as he used to say to Pemberton with the humour that made his queer delicacies manly—to carry themselves with an air. But their one idea was to get in with people who didn't want them and to take snubs as if they were honourable scars. Why people didn't want them more he didn't know—that was people's own affair; after all they weren't superficially repulsive, they were a hundred times cleverer than most of the dreary grandees, the "poor swells" they rushed about Europe to catch up with. "After all they *are* amusing—they are!" he used to pronounce with the wisdom of the ages. To which Pemberton always replied: "Amusing—the great Moreen troupe? Why they're altogether delightful; and if it weren't for the hitch that you and I (feeble performers!) make in the *ensemble* they'd carry everything before them."

What the boy couldn't get over was the fact that this particular blight seemed, in a tradition of self-respect, so undeserved and so arbitrary. No doubt people had a right to take the line they liked, but why should *his* people have liked the line of pushing and toadying and lying and cheating? What had their forefathers—all decent folk, so far as he knew—done to them, or what had *he* done to them? Who had poisoned their blood with the fifth-rate social ideal, the fixed idea of making smart acquaintances and getting into the *monde chic*,[19] especially when it was foredoomed to failure and exposure? They showed so what they were after; that was what made the people they wanted not want *them*. And never a wince for dignity, never a throb of shame at looking each other in the face, never any independence or resentment or disgust. If his father or his brother would only knock some one down once or twice a year! Clever as they were they never guessed the impression they made. They were good-natured, yes—as good-natured as Jews at the doors of clothing-shops! But was that the model one wanted one's family to follow? Morgan had dim memories of an old grandfather, the maternal, in New York, whom he had been taken across the ocean at the age of five to see: a gentleman with a high neck-cloth and a good deal of pronunciation, who wore a dress-coat in the morning, which made one wonder what he wore in the evening, and had, or was supposed to have, "property" and something to do with the Bible Society. It couldn't have been but that *he* was a good type. Pemberton himself remembered Mrs. Clancy, a widowed sister of Mr. Moreen's, who was as irritating as a moral tale and had paid a fortnight's visit to the family at Nice shortly after he came to live with them. She was "pure and refined," as Amy said over the banjo, and had the air of not knowing what they meant when they talked, and of keeping something rather important back. Pemberton judged that what she kept back was an approval of many of their ways; therefore it was to be supposed that she too was of a good type, and that Mr. and Mrs. Moreen and Ulick and Paula and Amy might easily have been of a better one if they would.

But that they wouldn't was more and more perceptible from day to day. They continued to "chivey," as Morgan called it, and in due time became aware of a variety of reasons for proceeding to Venice. They mentioned a great many of them—they were always strikingly frank and had the brightest friendly chatter, at the late foreign breakfast in especial, before the ladies had made up their faces, when they leaned their arms on the table, had something to follow the *demi-tasse,* and, in the heat of familiar discussion as to what they "really ought" to do, fell inevitably into the languages in which they could *tutoyer*.[20] Even Pemberton liked them then; he could endure even Ulick when he heard him give his little flat voice for the "sweet sea-city." That was what made him have a sneaking kindness for them—that they were so out of the workaday world and kept him so out of it. The summer had waned when, with cries of ecstasy, they all passed out on the balcony that overhung the Grand Canal.[21] The sunsets then were splendid and the Dorringtons had arrived. The Dorringtons were the only reason they hadn't talked of at breakfast; but the reasons they didn't talk of at breakfast always came out in the end. The Dorringtons on the other hand came out very little; or else when they did they stayed—as was natural—for hours, during which periods Mrs. Moreen and the girls sometimes called at their hotel (to see if they had returned) as many as three times running. The gondola was for the ladies, as in Venice too there were "days," which Mrs. Moreen knew in their order an hour after she arrived. She immediately took one herself, to which the Dorringtons never came, though on a

[19] Fashionable society.
[20] Languages in which a distinction between formal and informal modes of address permits a clear expression of intimacy through the choice of the familiar (informal) form (French *tutoyer:* to address by the informal pronoun *tu,* not the formal *vous*).
[21] The family has now arrived in Venice, the "sweet sea-city."

certain occasion when Pemberton and his pupil were together at Saint Mark's
—where, taking the best walks they had ever had and haunting a hundred
churches, they spent a great deal of time—they saw the old lord turn up with
Mr. Moreen and Ulick, who showed him the dim basilica as if it belonged to
them. Pemberton noted how much less, among its curiosities, Lord Dorrington
carried himself as a man of the world; wondering too whether, for such services,
his companions took a fee from him. The autumn at any rate waned, the Dorringtons departed, and Lord Verschoyle, the eldest son, had proposed neither for
Amy nor for Paula.

One sad November day, while the wind roared round the old palace and
the rain lashed the lagoon, Pemberton, for exercise and even somewhat for
warmth—the Moreens were horribly frugal about fires; it was a cause of suffering to their inmate—walked up and down the big bare *sala*[22] with his pupil.
The scagliola[23] floor was cold, the high battered casements shook in the storm,
and the stately decay of the place was unrelieved by a particle of furniture.
Pemberton's spirits were low, and it came over him that the fortune of the
Moreens was now even lower. A blast of desolation, a portent of disgrace and
disaster, seemed to draw through the comfortless hall. Mr. Moreen and Ulick
were in the Piazza, looking out for something, strolling drearily, in mackintoshes,
under the arcades; but still, in spite of mackintoshes, unmistakeable men of
the world. Paula and Amy were in bed—it might have been thought they were
staying there to keep warm. Pemberton looked askance at the boy at his side, to
see to what extent he was conscious of these dark omens. But Morgan, luckily
for him, was now mainly conscious of growing taller and stronger and indeed
of being in his fifteenth year. This fact was intensely interesting to him and
the basis of a private theory—which, however, he had imparted to his tutor—that
in a little while he should stand on his own feet. He considered that the situation would change—that in short he should be "finished," grown up, producible
in the world of affairs and ready to prove himself of sterling ability. Sharply
as he was capable at times of analysing, as he called it, his life, there were happy
hours when he remained, as he also called it—and as the name, really, of their
right ideal—"jolly" superficial; the proof of which was his fundamental assumption that he should presently go to Oxford, to Pemberton's college, and aided
and abetted by Pemberton, do the most wonderful things. It depressed the
young man to see how little in such a project he took account of ways and
means: in other connexions he mostly kept to the measure. Pemberton tried to
imagine the Moreens at Oxford and fortunately failed; yet unless they were to
adopt it as a residence there would be no *modus vivendi*[24] for Morgan. How
could he live without an allowance, and where was the allowance to come from?
He, Pemberton, might live on Morgan; but how could Morgan live on *him*?
What was to become of him anyhow? Somehow the fact that he was a big boy
now, with better prospects of health, made the question of his future more
difficult. So long as he was markedly frail the great consideration he inspired
seemed enough of an answer to it. But at the bottom of Pemberton's heart was
the recognition of his probably being strong enough to live and not yet strong
enough to struggle or to thrive. Morgan himself at any rate was in the first

[22] (Italian) The reception hall.
[23] Plasterwork imitating marble.
[24] The term has ironical force here.

flush of the rosiest consciousness of adolescence, so that the beating of the tempest seemed to him after all but the voice of life and the challenge of fate. He had on his shabby little overcoat, with the collar up, but was enjoying his walk.

It was interrupted at last by the appearance of his mother at the end of the *sala*. She beckoned him to come to her, and while Pemberton saw him, complaisant, pass down the long vista and over the damp false marble, he wondered what was in the air. Mrs. Moreen said a word to the boy and made him go into the room she had quitted. Then, having closed the door after him, she directed her steps swiftly to Pemberton. There *was* something in the air, but his wildest flight of fancy wouldn't have suggested what it proved to be. She signified that she had made a pretext to get Morgan out of the way, and then she enquired—without hesitation—if the young man could favour her with the loan of three louis. While, before bursting into a laugh, he stared at her with surprise, she declared that she was awfully pressed for the money; she was desperate for it—it would save her life.

"Dear lady, *c'est trop fort!*"[25] Pemberton laughed in the manner and with the borrowed grace of idiom that marked the best colloquial, the best anecdotic, moments of his friends themselves. "Where in the world do you suppose I should get three louis, *du train dont vous allez?*"[26]

"I thought you worked—wrote things. Don't they pay you?"

"Not a penny."

"Are you such a fool as to work for nothing?"

"You ought surely to know that."

Mrs. Moreen stared, then she coloured a little. Pemberton saw she had quite forgotten the terms—if "terms" they could be called—that he had ended by accepting from herself; they had burdened her memory as little as her conscience. "Oh yes, I see what you mean—you've been very nice about that; but why drag it in so often?" She had been perfectly urbane with him ever since the rough scene of explanation in his room the morning he made her accept *his* "terms"—the necessity of his making his case known to Morgan. She had felt no resentment after seeing there was no danger Morgan would take the matter up with her. Indeed, attributing this immunity to the good taste of his influence with the boy, she had once said to Pemberton "My dear fellow, it's an immense comfort you're a gentleman." She repeated this in substance now. "Of course you're a gentleman—that's a bother the less!" Pemberton reminded her that he had not "dragged in" anything that wasn't already in as much as his foot was in his shoe; and she also repeated her prayer that, somewhere and somehow, he would find her sixty francs. He took the liberty of hinting that if he could find them it wouldn't be to lend them to *her*—as to which he consciously did himself injustice, knowing that if he had them he would certainly put them at her disposal. He accused himself, at bottom and not unveraciously, of a fantastic, a demoralised sympathy with her. If misery made strange bedfellows it also made strange sympathies. It was moreover a part of the abasement of living with such people that one had to make vulgar retorts, quite out of one's own tradition of good manners. "Morgan, Morgan, to what pass have I come for you?" he

25 (French) It's too bad; that is, I'm sorry.
26 (French) The way you go on.

groaned while Mrs. Moreen floated voluminously down the *sala* again to liberate the boy, wailing as she went that everything was too odious.

Before their young friend was liberated there came a thump at the door communicating with the staircase, followed by the apparition of a dripping youth who poked in his head. Pemberton recognised him as the bearer of a telegram and recognised the telegram as addressed to himself. Morgan came back as, after glancing at the signature—that of a relative in London—he was reading the words: "Found jolly job for you, engagement to coach opulent youth on own terms. Come at once." The answer happily was paid and the messenger waited. Morgan, who had drawn near, waited too and looked hard at Pemberton; and Pemberton, after a moment, having met his look, handed him the telegram. It was really by wise looks—they knew each other so well now—that, while the telegraph-boy, in his waterproof cape, made a great puddle on the floor, the thing was settled between them. Pemberton wrote the answer with a pencil against the frescoed wall, and the messenger departed. When he had gone the young man explained himself.

"I'll make a tremendous charge; I'll earn a lot of money in a short time, and we'll live on it."

"Well, I hope the opulent youth will be a dismal dunce—he probably will," Morgan parenthesised—"and keep you a long time a-hammering of it in."

"Of course the longer he keeps me the more we shall have for our old age."

"But suppose *they* don't pay you!" Morgan awfully suggested.

"Oh there are not two such—!" but Pemberton pulled up; he had been on the point of using too invidious a term. Instead of this he said "Two such fatalities."

Morgan flushed—the tears came to his eyes. "*Dites toujours*[27] two such rascally crews!" Then in a different tone he added: "Happy opulent youth!"

"Not if he's a dismal dunce."

"Oh they're happier then. But you can't have everything, can you?" the boy smiled.

Pemberton held him fast, hands on his shoulders—he had never loved him so. "What will become of *you,* what will you do?" He thought of Mrs. Moreen, desperate for sixty francs.

"I shall become an *homme fait.*"[28] And then as if he recognised all the bearings of Pemberton's allusion: "I shall get on with them better when you're not here."

"Ah don't say that—it sounds as if I set you against them!"

"You do—the sight of you. It's all right; you know what I mean. I shall be beautiful. I'll take their affairs in hand; I'll marry my sisters."

"You'll marry yourself!" joked Pemberton; as high, rather tense pleasantry would evidently be the right, or the safest, tone for their separation.

It was, however, not purely in this strain that Morgan suddenly asked: "But I say—how will you get to your jolly job? You'll have to telegraph to the opulent youth for money to come on."

Pemberton bethought himself. "They won't like that, will they?"

"Oh look out for them!"

27 (French) Say what you intended to.
28 (French) A grown-up man.

Then Pemberton brought out his remedy. "I'll go to the American Consul; I'll borrow some money of him—just for the few days, on the strength of the telegram."

Morgan was hilarious. "Show him the telegram—then collar the money and stay!"

Pemberton entered into the joke sufficiently to reply that for Morgan he was really capable of that; but the boy, growing more serious, and to prove he hadn't meant what he said, not only hurried him off to the Consulate—since he was to start that evening, as he had wired to his friend—but made sure of their affair by going with him. They splashed through the tortuous perforations and over the humpbacked bridges, and they passed through the Piazza, where they saw Mr. Moreen and Ulick go into a jeweller's shop. The Consul proved accommodating—Pemberton said it wasn't the letter, but Morgan's grand air—and on their way back they went into Saint Mark's for a hushed ten minutes. Later they took up and kept up the fun of it to the very end; and it seemed to Pemberton a part of that fun that Mrs. Moreen, who was very angry when he had announced her his intention, should charge him, grotesquely and vulgarly and in reference to the loan she had vainly endeavoured to effect, with bolting lest they should "get something out" of him. On the other hand he had to do Mr. Moreen and Ulick the justice to recognise that when on coming in *they* heard the cruel news they took it like perfect men of the world.

VIII

When he got at work with the opulent youth, who was to be taken in hand for Balliol,[29] he found himself unable to say if this aspirant had really such poor parts or if the appearance were only begotten of his own long association with an intensely living little mind. From Morgan he heard half a dozen times: the boy wrote charming young letters, a patchwork of tongues, with indulgent postscripts in the family Volapuk[30] and, in little squares and rounds and crannies of the text, the drollest illustrations—letters that he was divided between the impulse to show his present charge as a vain, a wasted incentive, and the sense of something in them that publicity would profane. The opulent youth went up in due course and failed to pass; but it seemed to add to the presumption that brilliancy was not expected of him all at once that his parents, condoning the lapse, which they good-naturedly treated as little as possible as if it were Pemberton's, should have sounded the rally again, begged the young coach to renew the siege.

The young coach was now in a position to lend Mrs. Moreen three louis, and he sent her a post-office order even for a larger amount. In return for this favour he received a frantic scribbled line from her: "Implore you to come back instantly—Morgan dreadfully ill." They were on the rebound, once more in Paris—often as Pemberton had seen them depressed he had never seen them crushed—and communication was therefore rapid. He wrote to the boy to ascer-

[29] A college of Oxford University.
[30] One of the artificially constructed international languages, combining elements from a number of tongues.

tain the state of his health, but awaited the answer in vain. He accordingly, after three days, took an abrupt leave of the opulent youth and, crossing the Channel, alighted at the small hotel, in the quarter of the Champs Elysées,[31] of which Mrs. Moreen had given him the address. A deep if dumb dissatisfaction with this lady and her companions bore him company: they couldn't be vulgarly honest, but they could live at hotels, in velvety *entresols*,[32] amid a smell of burnt pastilles, surrounded by the most expensive city in Europe. When he had left them in Venice it was with an irrepressible suspicion that something was going to happen; but the only thing that could have taken place was again their masterly retreat. "How is he? where is he?" he asked of Mrs. Moreen; but before she could speak these questions were answered by the pressure round his neck of a pair of arms, in shrunken sleeves, which still were capable of an effusive young foreign squeeze.

"Dreadfully ill—I don't see it!" the young man cried. And then to Morgan: "Why on earth didn't you relieve me? Why didn't you answer my letter?"

Mrs. Moreen declared that when she wrote he was very bad, and Pemberton learned at the same time from the boy that he had answered every letter he had received. This led to the clear inference that Pemberton's note had been kept from him so that the game to be practised should not be interfered with. Mrs. Moreen was prepared to see the fact exposed, as Pemberton saw the moment he faced her that she was prepared for a good many other things. She was prepared above all to maintain that she had acted from a sense of duty, that she was enchanted she had got him over, whatever they might say, and that it was useless of him to pretend he didn't know in all his bones that his place at such a time was with Morgan. He had taken the boy away from them and now had no right to abandon him. He had created for himself the gravest responsibilities and must at least abide by what he had done.

"Taken him away from you?" Pemberton exclaimed indignantly.

"Do it—do it for pity's sake; that's just what I want. I can't stand *this*—and such scenes. They're awful frauds—poor dears!" These words broke from Morgan, who had intermitted his embrace, in a key which made Pemberton turn quickly to him and see that he had suddenly seated himself, was breathing in great pain and was very pale.

"*Now* do you say he's not in a state, my precious pet?" shouted his mother, dropping on her knees before him with clasped hands, but touching him no more than if he had been a gilded idol. "It will pass—it's only for an instant; but don't say such dreadful things!"

"I'm all right—all right," Morgan panted to Pemberton, whom he sat looking up at with a strange smile, his hands resting on either side on the sofa.

"Now do you pretend I've been dishonest, that I've deceived?" Mrs. Moreen flashed at Pemberton as she got up.

"It isn't *he* says it, it's I!" the boy returned, apparently easier but sinking back against the wall; while his restored friend, who had sat down beside him, took his hand and bent over him.

"Darling child, one does what one can; there are so many things to consider," urged Mrs. Moreen. "It's his *place*—his only place. You see *you* think it is now."

[31] An expensive district.
[32] Mezzanine rooms.

"Take me away—take me away," Morgan went on, smiling to Pemberton with his white face.

"Where shall I take you, and how—oh *how*, my boy?" the young man stammered, thinking of the rude way in which his friends in London held that, for his convenience, with no assurance of prompt return, he had thrown them over; of the just resentment with which they would already have called in a successor, and of the scant help to finding fresh employment that resided for him in the grossness of his having failed to pass his pupil.

"Oh we'll settle that. You used to talk about it," said Morgan. "If we can only go all the rest's a detail."

"Talk about it as much as you like, but don't think you can attempt it. Mr. Moreen would never consent—it would be so *very* hand-to-mouth," Pemberton's hostess beautifully explained to him. Then to Morgan she made it clearer: "It would destroy our peace, it would break our hearts. Now that he's back it will be all the same again. You'll have your life, your work and your freedom, and we'll all be happy as we used to be. You'll bloom and grow perfectly well, and we won't have any more silly experiments, will we? They're too absurd. It's Mr. Pemberton's place—every one in his place. You in yours, your papa in his, me in mine—*n'est-ce pas, chéri?*[33] We'll all forget how foolish we've been and have lovely times."

She continued to talk and to surge vaguely about the little draped stuffy salon while Pemberton sat with the boy, whose colour gradually came back; and she mixed up her reasons, hinting that there were going to be changes, that the other children might scatter (who knew?—Paula had her ideas) and that then it might be fancied how much the poor old parent-birds would want the little nestling. Morgan looked at Pemberton, who wouldn't let him move; and Pemberton knew exactly how he felt at hearing himself called a little nestling. He admitted that he had had one or two bad days, but he protested afresh against the wrong of his mother's having made them the ground of an appeal to poor Pemberton. Poor Pemberton could laugh now, apart from the comicality of Mrs. Moreen's mustering so much philosophy for her defence—she seemed to shake it out of her agitated petticoats, which knocked over the light gilt chairs—so little did their young companion, *marked,* unmistakeably marked at the best, strike him as qualified to repudiate any advantage.

He himself was in for it at any rate. He should have Morgan on his hands again indefinitely; though indeed he saw the lad had a private theory to produce which would be intended to smooth this down. He was obliged to him for it in advance; but the suggested amendment didn't keep his heart rather from sinking, any more than it prevented him from accepting the prospect on the spot, with some confidence moreover that he should do so even better if he could have a little supper. Mrs. Moreen threw out more hints about the changes that were to be looked for, but she was such a mixture of smiles and shudders—she confessed she was very nervous—that he couldn't tell if she were in high feather or only in hysterics. If the family was really at last going to pieces why shouldn't she recognise the necessity of pitching Morgan into some sort of lifeboat? This presumption was fostered by the fact that they were established in luxurious quarters in the capital of pleasure; that was exactly where they naturally *would*

33 (French) Isn't that right, dear?

be established in view of going to pieces. Moreover didn't she mention that Mr. Moreen and the others were enjoying themselves at the opera with Mr. Granger, and wasn't *that* also precisely where one would look for them on the eve of a smash? Pemberton gathered that Mr. Granger was a rich vacant American—a big bill with a flourishy heading and no items; so that one of Paula's "ideas" was probably that this time she hadn't missed fire—by which straight shot indeed she would have shattered the general cohesion. And if the cohesion was to crumble what would become of poor Pemberton? He felt quite enough bound up with them to figure to his alarm as a dislodged block in the edifice.

It was Morgan who eventually asked if no supper had been ordered for him; sitting with him below, later, at the dim delayed meal, in the presence of a great deal of corded green plush, a plate of ornamental biscuit and an aloofness marked on the part of the waiter. Mrs. Moreen had explained that they had been obliged to secure a room for the visitor out of the house; and Morgan's consolation—he offered it while Pemberton reflected on the nastiness of lukewarm sauces—proved to be, largely, that this circumstance would facilitate their escape. He talked of their escape—recurring to it often afterwards—as if they were making up a "boy's book" together. But he likewise expressed his sense that there was something in the air, that the Moreens couldn't keep it up much longer. In point of fact, as Pemberton was to see, they kept it up for five or six months. All the while, however, Morgan's contention was designed to cheer him. Mr. Moreen and Ulick, whom he had met the day after his return, accepted that return like perfect men of the world. If Paula and Amy treated it even with less formality an allowance was to be made for them, inasmuch as Mr. Granger hadn't come to the opera after all. He had only placed his box at their service, with a bouquet for each of the party; there was even one apiece, embittering the thought of his profusion, for Mr. Moreen and Ulick. "They're all like that," was Morgan's comment; "at the very last, just when we think we've landed them they're back in the deep sea!"

Morgan's comments in the days were more and more free; they even included a large recognition of the extraordinary tenderness with which he had been treated while Pemberton was away. Oh yes, they couldn't do enough to be nice to him, to show him they had him on their mind and make up for his loss. That was just what made the whole thing so sad and caused him to rejoice after all in Pemberton's return—he had to keep thinking of their affection less, had less sense of obligation. Pemberton laughed out at this last reason, and Morgan blushed and said "Well, dash it, you know what I mean." Pemberton knew perfectly what he meant; but there were a good many things that—dash it too!—it didn't make any clearer. This episode of his second sojourn in Paris stretched itself out wearily, with their resumed readings and wanderings and maunderings, their potterings on the quays, their hauntings of the museums, their occasional lingerings in the Palais Royal[34] when the first sharp weather came on and there was a comfort in warm emanations, before Chevet's wonderful succulent window. Morgan wanted to hear all about the opulent youth—he took an immense interest in him. Some of the details of his opulence—Pemberton could spare him none of them—evidently fed the boy's appreciation of all his friend had given up to come back to him; but in addition to the greater reci-

[34] A palace now occupied by the Council of State and the *Théâtre Français,* and containing shops.

procity established by that heroism he had always his little brooding theory, in which there was a frivolous gaiety too, that their long probation was drawing to a close. Morgan's conviction that the Moreens couldn't go on much longer kept pace with the unexpected impetus with which, from month to month, they did go on. Three weeks after Pemberton had rejoined them they went on to another hotel, a dingier one than the first; but Morgan rejoiced that his tutor had at least still not sacrificed the advantage of a room outside. He clung to the romantic utility of this when the day, or rather the night, should arrive for their escape.

For the first time, in this complicated connexion, our friend felt his collar gall him. It was, as he had said to Mrs. Moreen in Venice, *trop fort*[35]—everything was *trop fort*. He could neither really throw off his blighting burden nor find in it the benefit of a pacified conscience or of a rewarded affection. He had spent all the money accruing to him in England, and he saw his youth going and that he was getting nothing back for it. It was all very well of Morgan to count it for reparation that he should now settle on him permanently—there was an irritating flaw in such a view. He saw what the boy had in his mind; the conception that as his friend had had the generosity to come back he must show his gratitude by giving him his life. But the poor friend didn't desire the gift—what could he do with Morgan's dreadful little life? Of course at the same time that Pemberton was irritated he remembered the reason, which was very honourable to Morgan and which dwelt simply in his making one so forget that he was no more than a patched urchin. If one dealt with him on a different basis one's misadventures were one's own fault. So Pemberton waited in a queer confusion of yearning and alarm for the catastrophe which was held to hang over the house of Moreen, of which he certainly at moments felt the symptoms brush his cheek and as to which he wondered much in what form it would find its liveliest effect.

Perhaps it would take the form of sudden dispersal—a frightened *sauve qui peut*,[36] a scuttling into selfish corners. Certainly they were less elastic than of yore; they were evidently looking for something they didn't find. The Dorringtons hadn't re-appeared, the princes had scattered; wasn't that the beginning of the end? Mrs. Moreen had lost her reckoning of the famous "days"; her social calendar was blurred—it had turned its face to the wall. Pemberton suspected that the great, the cruel discomfiture had been the unspeakable behaviour of Mr. Granger, who seemed not to know what he wanted, or, what was much worse, what *they* wanted. He kept sending flowers, as if to bestrew the path of his retreat, which was never the path of a return. Flowers were all very well, but—Pemberton could complete the proposition. It was now positively conspicuous that in the long run the Moreens were a social failure; so that the young man was almost grateful the run had not been short. Mr. Moreen indeed was still occasionally able to get away on business and, what was more surprising, was likewise able to get back. Ulick had no club, but you couldn't have discovered it from his appearance, which was as much as ever that of a person looking at life from the window of such an institution; therefore Pemberton was doubly surprised at an answer he once heard him make his mother in the desperate tone of a man familiar with the worst privations. Her question Pemberton had

35 (French) Too much to stand, too painful.
36 (French) Everyone for himself.

not quite caught; it appeared to be an appeal for a suggestion as to whom they might get to take Amy. "Let the Devil take her!" Ulick snapped; so that Pemberton could see that they had not only lost their amiability but had ceased to believe in themselves. He could also see that if Mrs. Moreen was trying to get people to take her children she might be regarded as closing the hatches for the storm. But Morgan would be the last she would part with.

One winter afternoon—it was a Sunday—he and the boy walked far together in the Bois de Boulogne.[37] The evening was so splendid, the cold lemon-coloured sunset so clear, the stream of carriages and pedestrians so amusing and the fascination of Paris so great, that they stayed out later than usual and became aware that they should have to hurry home to arrive in time for dinner. They hurried accordingly, arm-in-arm, good humoured and hungry, agreeing that there was nothing like Paris after all and that after everything too that had come and gone they were not yet sated with innocent pleasures. When they reached the hotel they found that, though scandalously late, they were in time for all the dinner they were likely to sit down to. Confusion reigned in the apartments of the Moreens—very shabby ones this time, but the best in the house —and before the interrupted service of the table, with objects displaced almost as if there had been a scuffle and a great wine-stain from an overturned bottle, Pemberton couldn't blink the fact that there had been a scene of the last proprietary firmness. The storm had come—they were all seeking refuge. The hatches were down, Paula and Amy were invisible—they had never tried the most casual art upon Pemberton, but he felt they had enough of an eye to him not to wish to meet him as young ladies whose frocks had been confiscated— and Ulick appeared to have jumped overboard. The host and his staff, in a word, had ceased to "go on" at the pace of their guests, and the air of embarrassed detention, thanks to a pile of gaping trunks in the passage, was strangely commingled with the air of indignant withdrawal.

When Morgan took all this in—and he took it in very quickly—he coloured to the roots of his hair. He had walked from his infancy among difficulties and dangers, but he had never seen a public exposure. Pemberton noticed in a second glance at him that the tears had rushed into his eyes and that they were tears of a new and untasted bitterness. He wondered an instant, for the boy's sake, whether he might successfully pretend not to understand. Not successfully, he felt, as Mr. and Mrs. Moreen, dinnerless by their extinguished hearth, rose before him in their little dishonoured salon, casting about with glassy eyes for the nearest port in such a storm. They were not prostrate but were horribly white, and Mrs. Moreen had evidently been crying. Pemberton quickly learned however that her grief was not for the loss of her dinner, much as she usually enjoyed it, but the fruit of a blow that struck even deeper, as she made all haste to explain. He would see for himself, so far as that went, how the great change had come, the dreadful bolt had fallen, and how they would now all have to turn themselves about. Therefore cruel as it was to them to part with their darling she must look to him to carry a little further the influence he had so fortunately acquired with the boy—to induce his young charge to follow him into some modest retreat. They depended on him—that was the fact—to take their delightful child temporarily under his protection: it would leave Mr.

[37] A large park, with woods and lakes.

Moreen and herself so much more free to give the proper attention (too little, alas! had been given) to the readjustment of their affairs.

"We trust you—we feel we *can*," said Mrs. Moreen, slowly rubbing her plump white hands and looking with compunction hard at Morgan, whose chin, not to take liberties, her husband stroked with a tentative paternal forefinger.

"Oh yes—we feel that we *can*. We trust Mr. Pemberton fully, Morgan," Mr. Moreen pursued.

Pemberton wondered again if he might pretend not to understand; but everything good gave way to the intensity of Morgan's understanding. "Do you mean he may take me to live with him for ever and ever?" cried the boy. "May take me away, away anywhere he likes?"

"For ever and ever? *Comme vous-y-allez!*"[38] Mr. Moreen laughed indulgently. "For as long as Mr. Pemberton may be so good."

"We've struggled, we've suffered," his wife went on; "but you've made him so your own that we've already been through the worst of the sacrifice."

Morgan had turned away from his father—he stood looking at Pemberton with a light in his face. His sense of shame for their common humiliated state had dropped; the case had another side—the thing was to clutch at *that*. He had a moment of boyish joy, scarcely mitigated by the reflexion that with this unexpected consecration of his hope—too sudden and too violent; the turn taken was away from a *good* boy's book—the "escape" was left on their hands. The boyish joy was there an instant, and Pemberton was almost scared at the rush of gratitude and affection that broke through his first abasement. When he stammered "My dear fellow, what do you say to *that?*" how could one not say something enthusiastic? But there was more need for courage at something else that immediately followed and that made the lad sit down quickly on the nearest chair. He had turned quite livid and had raised his hand to his left side. They were all three looking at him, but Mrs. Moreen suddenly bounded forward. "Ah his darling little heart!" she broke out; and this time, on her knees before him and without respect for the idol, she caught him ardently in her arms. "You walked him too far, you hurried him too fast!" she hurled over her shoulder at Pemberton. Her son made no protest, and the next instant, still holding him, she sprang up with her face convulsed and with the terrified cry "Help, help! he's going, he's gone!" Pemberton saw with equal horror, by Morgan's own stricken face, that he was beyond their wildest recall. He pulled him half out of his mother's hands, and for a moment, while they held him together, they looked all their dismay into each other's eyes. "He couldn't stand it with his weak organ," said Pemberton—"the shock, the whole scene, the violent emotion."

"But I thought he *wanted* to go to you!" wailed Mrs. Moreen.

"I *told* you he didn't, my dear," her husband made answer. Mr. Moreen was trembling all over and was in his way as deeply affected as his wife. But after the very first he took his bereavement as a man of the world.

38 (French) How you go on!

THE
SECRET SHARER

JOSEPH CONRAD
1857–1924

I

ON MY RIGHT HAND there were lines of fishing-stakes resembling a mysterious system of half-submerged bamboo fences, incomprehensible in its division of the domain of tropical fishes, and crazy of aspect as if abandoned for ever by some nomad tribe of fishermen now gone to the other end of the ocean; for there was no sign of human habitation as far as the eye could reach. To the left a group of barren islets, suggesting ruins of stone walls, towers, and blockhouses, had its foundations set in a blue sea that itself looked solid, so still and stable did it lie below my feet; even the track of light from the westering sun shone smoothly, without that animated glitter which tells of an imperceptible ripple. And when I turned my head to take a parting glance at the tug which had just left us anchored outside the bar, I saw the straight line of the flat shore joined to the stable sea, edge to edge, with a perfect and unmarked closeness, in one levelled floor half brown, half blue under the enormous dome of the sky. Corresponding in their insignificance to the islets of the sea, two small clumps of trees, one on each side of the only fault in the impeccable joint, marked the mouth of the river Meinam[1] we had just left on the first preparatory stage of our homeward journey;

[1] Flowing past Bangkok into the Gulf of Siam.

and, far back on the inland level, a larger and loftier mass, the grove surrounding the great Paknam pagoda, was the only thing on which the eye could rest from the vain task of exploring the monotonous sweep of the horizon. Here and there gleams as of a few scattered pieces of silver marked the windings of the great river; and on the nearest of them, just within the bar, the tug steaming right into the land became lost to my sight, hull and funnel and masts, as though the impassive earth had swallowed her up without an effort, without a tremor. My eye followed the light cloud of her smoke, now here, now there, above the plain, according to the devious curves of the stream, but always fainter and farther away, till I lost it at last behind the mitre-shaped hill of the great pagoda. And then I was left alone with my ship, anchored at the head of the Gulf of Siam.

She floated at the starting-point of a long journey, very still in an immense stillness, the shadows of her spars flung far to the eastward by the setting sun. At that moment I was alone on her decks. There was not a sound in her—and around us nothing moved, nothing lived, not a canoe on the water, not a bird in the air, not a cloud in the sky. In this breathless pause at the threshold of a long passage we seemed to be measuring our fitness for a long and arduous enterprise, the appointed task of both our existences to be carried out, far from all human eyes, with only sky and sea for spectators and for judges.

There must have been some glare in the air to interfere with one's sight, because it was only just before the sun left us that my roaming eyes made out beyond the highest ridge of the principal islet of the group something which did away with the solemnity of perfect solitude. The tide of darkness flowed on swiftly; and with tropical suddenness a swarm of stars came out above the shadowy earth, while I lingered yet, my hand resting lightly on my ship's rail as if on the shoulder of a trusted friend. But, with all that multitude of celestial bodies staring down at one, the comfort of quiet communion with her was gone for good. And there were also disturbing sounds by this time—voices, footsteps forward; the steward flitted along the maindeck, a busily ministering spirit; a hand-bell tinkled urgently under the poopdeck. . . .

I found my two officers waiting for me near the supper table, in the lighted cuddy. We sat down at once, and as I helped the chief mate, I said:

"Are you aware that there is a ship anchored inside the islands? I saw her mastheads above the ridge as the sun went down."

He raised sharply his simple face, overcharged by a terrible growth of whisker, and emitted his usual ejaculations: "Bless my soul, sir! You don't say so!"

My second mate was a round-cheeked, silent young man, grave beyond his years, I thought; but as our eyes happened to meet I detected a slight quiver on his lips. I looked down at once. It was not my part to encourage sneering on board my ship. It must be said, too, that I knew very little of my officers. In consequence of certain events of no particular significance, except to myself, I had been appointed to the command only a fortnight before. Neither did I know much of the hands forward. All these people had been together for eighteen months or so, and my position was that of the only stranger on board. I mention this because it has some bearing on what is to follow. But what I felt most was my being a stranger to the ship; and if all the truth must be told, I was somewhat of a stranger to myself. The youngest man on board (barring the second mate), and untried as yet by a position of the fullest responsibility, I was willing to take the adequacy of the others for granted. They had simply to be equal to their tasks; but I wondered how far I should turn out faithful to that ideal conception of one's own personality every man sets up for himself secretly.

Meantime the chief mate, with an almost visible effect of collaboration on the part of his round eyes and frightful whiskers, was trying to evolve a theory of the anchored ship. His dominant trait was to take all things into earnest consideration. He was of a painstaking turn of mind. As he used to say, he "liked to account to himself" for practically everything that came in his way, down to a miserable scorpion he had found in his cabin a week before. The why and the wherefore of that scorpion—how it got on board and came to select his room rather than the pantry (which was a dark place and more what a scorpion would be partial to), and how on earth it managed to drown itself in the inkwell of his writing-desk—had exercised him infinitely. The ship within the islands was much more easily accounted for; and just as we were about to rise from table he made his pronouncement. She was, he doubted not, a ship from home lately arrived. Probably she drew too much water to cross the bar except at the top of spring tides. Therefore she went into that natural harbor to wait for a few days in preference to remaining in an open roadstead.

"That's so," confirmed the second mate, suddenly, in his slightly hoarse voice. "She draws over twenty feet. She's the Liverpool ship *Sephora* with a cargo of coal. Hundred and twenty-three days from Cardiff."

We looked at him in surprise.

"The tugboat skipper told me when he came on board for your letters, sir," explained the young man. "He expects to take her up the river the day after tomorrow."

After thus overwhelming us with the extent of his information he slipped out of the cabin. The mate observed regretfully that he "could not account for that young fellow's whims." What prevented him telling us all about it at once, he wanted to know.

I detained him as he was making a move. For the last two days the crew had had plenty of hard work, and the night before they had very little sleep. I felt painfully that I—a stranger—was doing something unusual when I directed him to let all hands turn in without setting an anchor-watch. I proposed to keep on deck myself till one o'clock or thereabouts. I would get the second mate to relieve me at that hour.

"He will turn out the cook and the steward at four," I concluded, "and then give you a call. Of course at the slightest sign of any sort of wind we'll have the hands up and make a start at once."

He concealed his astonishment. "Very well, sir." Outside the cuddy he put his head in the second mate's door to inform him of my unheard-of caprice to take a five hours' anchor-watch on myself. I heard the other raise his voice incredulously—"What? The Captain himself?" Then a few more murmurs, a door closed, then another. A few moments later I went on deck.

My strangeness, which had made me sleepless, had prompted that unconventional arrangement, as if I had expected in those solitary hours of the night to get on terms with the ship of which I knew nothing, manned by men of whom I knew very little more. Fast alongside a wharf, littered like any ship in port with a tangle of unrelated things, invaded by unrelated shore people, I had hardly seen her yet properly. Now, as she lay cleared for sea, the stretch of her main-deck seemed to me very fine under the stars. Very fine, very roomy for her size, and very inviting. I descended the poop and paced the waist, my mind picturing to myself the coming passage through the Malay Archipelago, down the Indian Ocean, and up the Atlantic. All its phases were familiar enough to me, every characteristic, all the alternatives which were likely to face me on the high seas—everything! . . . except the novel responsibility of command. But I took heart from the reasonable thought that the ship was like other ships, the men like other men, and that the sea was not likely to keep any special surprises expressly for my discomfiture.

Arrived at that comforting conclusion, I bethought myself of a cigar and went below to get it. All was still down there. Everybody at the after end of the ship was sleeping profoundly. I came out again on the quarter-deck, agreeably at ease in my sleeping-suit on that warm breathless night, barefooted, a glowing cigar in my teeth, and, going forward, I was met by the profound silence of the fore end of the ship. Only as I passed the door of the forecastle I heard a deep, quiet, trustful sigh of some sleeper inside. And suddenly I rejoiced in the great security of the sea as compared with the unrest of the land, in my choice of that untempted life presenting no disquieting problems, invested with an elementary moral beauty by the absolute straightforwardness of its appeal and by the singleness of its purpose.

The riding-light in the fore-rigging burned with a clear, untroubled, as if symbolic, flame, confident and bright in the mysterious shades of the night. Passing on my way aft along the other side of the ship, I observed that the rope side-ladder, put over, no doubt, for the master of the tug when he came to fetch away our letters, had not been hauled in as it should have been. I became annoyed at this, for exactitude in small matters is the very soul of discipline. Then I reflected that I had myself peremptorily dismissed my officers from duty, and by my own act had prevented the anchor-watch being formally set and things properly attended to. I asked myself whether it was wise ever to interfere with the established routine of duties even from the kindest of motives. My action might have made me appear eccentric. Goodness only knew how that absurdly whiskered mate would "account" for my conduct, and what the whole ship thought of that informality of their new captain. I was vexed with myself.

Not from compunction certainly, but, as it were mechanically, I proceeded to get the ladder in myself. Now a side-ladder of that sort is a light affair and comes in easily, yet my vigorous tug, which should have brought it flying on board, merely recoiled upon my body in a totally unexpected jerk. What the devil! . . . I was so astounded by the immovableness of that ladder that I remained stock-still, trying to account for it to myself like that imbecile mate of mine. In the end, of course, I put my head over the rail.

The side of the ship made an opaque belt of shadow on the darkling glassy shimmer of the sea. But I saw at once something elongated and pale floating very close to the ladder. Before I could form a guess a faint flash of phosphorescent light, which seemed to issue suddenly from the naked body of a man, flickered in the sleeping water with the elusive, silent play of summer lightning in a night sky. With a gasp I saw revealed to my stare a pair of feet, the long legs, a broad livid back immersed right up to the neck in a greenish cadaverous glow. One hand, awash, clutched the bottom rung of the ladder. He was complete but for the head. A headless corpse! The cigar dropped out of my gaping mouth with a tiny plop and a short hiss quite audible in the absolute stillness of all things under heaven. At that I suppose he raised up his face, a dimly pale oval in the shadow of the ship's side. But even then I could only barely make out down there the shape of his black-haired head. However, it was enough for the horrid, frost-bound sensation which had gripped me about the chest to pass off. The moment of vain exclamations was past, too. I only climbed on the spare spar and leaned over the rail as far as I could, to bring my eyes nearer to that mystery floating alongside.

As he hung by the ladder, like a resting swimmer, the sea-lightning played about his limbs at every stir; and he appeared in it ghastly, silvery, fish-like. He remained as mute as a fish, too. He made no motion to get out of the water, either. It was inconceivable that he should not attempt to come on board, and strangely troubling to suspect that perhaps he did not want to. And my first words were prompted by just that troubled incertitude.

"What's the matter?" I asked in my ordinary tone, speaking down to the face upturned exactly under mine.

"Cramp," it answered, no louder. Then slightly anxious, "I say, no need to call any one."

"I was not going to," I said.

"Are you alone on deck?"

"Yes."

I had somehow the impression that he was on the point of letting go the ladder to swim away beyond my ken—mysterious as he came. But, for the moment, this being appearing as if he had risen from the bottom of the sea (it was certainly the nearest land to the ship) wanted only to know the time. I told him. And he, down there, tentatively:

"I suppose your captain's turned in?"

"I am sure he isn't," I said.

He seemed to struggle with himself, for I heard something like the low, bitter murmur of doubt. "What's the good?" His next words came out with a hesitating effort.

"Look here, my man. Could you call him out quietly?"

I thought the time had come to declare myself.

"I am the captain."

I heard a "By Jove!" whispered at the level of the water. The phosphorescence flashed in the swirl of the water all about his limbs, his other hand seized the ladder.

"My name's Leggatt."

The voice was calm and resolute. A good voice. The self-possession of that man had somehow induced a corresponding state in myself. It was very quietly that I remarked:

"You must be a good swimmer."

"Yes. I've been in the water practically since nine o'clock. The question for me now is whether I am to let go this ladder and go on swimming till I sink from exhaustion, or—to come on board here."

I felt this was no mere formula of desperate speech, but a real alternative in the view of a strong soul. I should have gathered from this that he was young; indeed, it is only the young who are ever confronted by such clear issues. But at the time it was pure intuition on my part. A mysterious communication was established already between us two—in the face of that silent, darkened tropical sea. I was young, too; young enough to make no comment. The man in the water began suddenly to climb up the ladder, and I hastened away from the rail to fetch some clothes.

Before entering the cabin I stood still, listening in the lobby at the foot of the stairs. A faint snore came through the closed door of the chief mate's room. The second mate's door was on the hook, but the darkness in there was absolutely soundless. He, too, was young and could sleep like a stone. Remained the steward, but he was not likely to wake up before he was called. I got a sleeping-suit out of my room and, coming back on deck, saw the naked man from the sea sitting on the main-hatch, glimmering white in the darkness, his elbows on his knees and his head in his hands. In a moment he had concealed his damp body in a sleeping-suit of the same grey-stripe pattern as the one I was wearing and followed me like my double on the poop. Together we moved right aft, barefooted, silent.

"What is it?" I asked in a deadened voice, taking the lighted lamp out of the binnacle, and raising it to his face.

"An ugly business."

He had rather regular features; a good mouth; light eyes under somewhat heavy, dark eyebrows; a smooth, square forehead; no growth on his cheeks; a small, brown moustache, and a well-shaped, round chin. His expression was concentrated, meditative, under the inspecting light of the lamp I held up to his face; such as a man thinking hard in solitude might wear. My sleeping-suit was just right for his size. A well-knit young fellow of twenty-five at most. He caught his lower lip with the edge of white, even teeth.

"Yes," I said, replacing the lamp in the binnacle. The warm, heavy tropical night closed upon his head again.

"There's a ship over there," he murmured.

"Yes, I know. The *Sephora*. Did you know of us?"

"Hadn't the slightest idea. I am the mate of her——" He paused and corrected himself. "I should say I was."

"Aha! Something wrong?"

"Yes. Very wrong indeed. I've killed a man."

"What do you mean? Just now?"

"No, on the passage. Weeks ago. Thirty-nine south. When I say a man——"

"Fit of temper," I suggested, confidently.

The shadowy, dark head, like mine, seemed to nod imperceptibly above the ghostly grey of my sleeping-suit. It was, in the night, as though I had been faced by my own reflection in the depths of a sombre and immense mirror.

"A pretty thing to have to own up to for a Conway[2] boy," murmured my double, distinctly.

"You're a Conway boy?"

"I am," he said, as if startled. Then, slowly . . . "Perhaps you too——"

It was so; but being a couple of years older I had left before he joined. After a quick interchange of dates a silence fell; and I thought suddenly of my absurd mate with his terrific whiskers and the "Bless my soul—you don't say so" type of intellect. My double gave me an inkling of his thoughts by saying: "My father's a parson in Norfolk. Do you see me before a judge and jury on

2 A British merchant marine training ship.

that charge? For myself I can't see the necessity. There are fellows that an angel from heaven—— And I am not that. He was one of those creatures that are just simmering all the time with a silly sort of wickedness. Miserable devils that have no business to live at all. He wouldn't do his duty and wouldn't let anybody else do theirs. But what's the good of talking! You know well enough the sort of ill-conditioned snarling cur——"

He appealed to me as if our experiences had been as identical as our clothes. And I knew well enough the pestiferous danger of such a character where there are no means of legal repression. And I knew well enough also that my double there was no homicidal ruffian. I did not think of asking him for details, and he told me the story roughly in brusque, disconnected sentences. I needed no more. I saw it all going on as though I were myself inside that other sleeping-suit.

"It happened while we were setting a reefed foresail, at dusk. Reefed fore-sail! You understand the sort of weather. The only sail we had left to keep the ship running; so you may guess what it had been like for days. Anxious sort of job, that. He gave me some of his cursed insolence at the sheet. I tell you I was overdone with this terrific weather that seemed to have no end to it. Terrific, I tell you—and a deep ship. I believe the fellow himself was half crazed with funk. It was no time for gentlemanly reproof, so I turned round and felled him like an ox. He up and at me. We closed just as an awful sea made for the ship. All hands saw it coming and took to the rigging, but I had him by the throat, and went on shaking him like a rat, the men above us yelling, 'Look out! look out!'" Then a crash as if the sky had fallen on my head. They say that for over ten minutes hardly anything was to be seen of the ship—just the three masts and a bit of the forecastle head and of the poop all awash driving along in a smother of foam. It was a miracle that they found us, jammed together behind the forebits. It's clear that I meant business, because I was holding him by the throat still when they picked us up. He was black in the face. It was too much for them. It seems they rushed us aft together, gripped as we were, screaming 'Murder!' like a lot of luna-tics, and broke into the cuddy. And the ship running for her life, touch and go all the time, any minute her last in a sea fit to turn your hair grey only a-looking at it. I understand that the skipper, too, started raving like the rest of them. The man had been deprived of sleep for more than a week, and to have this sprung on him at the height of a furious gale nearly drove him out of his mind. I wonder they didn't fling me overboard after getting the carcass of their precious ship-mate out of my fingers. They had rather a job to separate us, I've been told. A sufficiently fierce story to make an old judge and a respectable jury sit up a bit. The first thing I heard when I came to myself was the maddening howling of that endless gale, and on that the voice of the old man. He was hanging on to my bunk, staring into my face out of his sou'wester.

"'Mr. Leggatt, you have killed a man. You can act no longer as chief mate of this ship.'"

His care to subdue his voice made it sound monotonous. He rested a hand on the end of the skylight to steady himself with, and all that time did not stir a limb, so far as I could see. "Nice little tale for a quiet tea-party," he concluded in the same tone.

One of my hands, too, rested on the end of the sky-light; neither did I stir a limb, so far as I knew. We stood less than a foot from each other. It occurred to me that if old "Bless my soul—you don't say so" were to put his head up the companion and catch sight of us, he would think he was seeing double, or imagine himself come upon a scene of weird witchcraft; the strange captain having a quiet confabulation by the wheel with his own grey ghost. I became very much concerned to prevent anything of the sort. I heard the other's soothing undertone.

"My father's a parson in Norfolk," it said. Evidently he had forgotten he had told me this important fact before. Truly a nice little tale.

"You had better slip down into my stateroom now," I said, moving off stealthily. My double followed my movements; our bare feet made no sound; I let him in, closed the door with care, and, after giving a call to the second mate, returned on deck for my relief.

"Not much sign of any wind yet," I remarked when he approached.

"No, sir. Not much," he assented, sleepily, in his hoarse voice, with just enough deference, no more, and barely suppressing a yawn.

"Well, that's all you have to look out for. You have got your orders."

"Yes, sir."

I paced a turn or two on the poop and saw him take up his position face forward with his elbow in the ratlines of the mizzen-rigging before I went below. The mate's faint snoring was still going on peacefully. The cuddy lamp was burning over the table on which stood a vase with flowers, a polite attention from the ship's provision merchant—the last flowers we should see for the next three months at the very least. Two bunches of bananas hung from the beam symmetrically, one on each side of the rudder-casing. Everything was as before in the ship—except that two of her captain's sleeping-suits were simultaneously in use, one motionless in the cuddy, the other keeping very still in the captain's stateroom.

It must be explained here that my cabin had the form of the capital letter L, the door being within the angle and opening into the short part of the letter. A couch was to the left, the bed-place to the right; my writing-desk and the chronometers' table faced the door. But any one opening it, unless he stepped right inside, had no view of what I call the long (or vertical) part of the letter. It contained some lockers surmounted by a bookcase; and a few clothes, a thick jacket or two, caps, oilskin coat, and such like, hung on hooks. There was at the bottom of that part a door opening into my bath-room, which could be entered also directly from the saloon. But that way was never used.

The mysterious arrival had discovered the advantage of this particular shape. Entering my room, lighted strongly by a big bulkhead lamp swung on gimbals above my writing-desk, I did not see him anywhere till he stepped out quietly from behind the coats hung in the recessed part.

"I heard somebody moving about, and went in there at once," he whispered.

I, too, spoke under my breath.

"Nobody is likely to come in here without knocking and getting permission."

He nodded. His face was thin and the sunburn faded, as though he had been ill. And no wonder. He had been, I heard presently, kept under arrest in his cabin for nearly seven weeks. But there was nothing sickly in his eyes or in his expression. He was not a bit like me, really; yet, as we stood leaning over my bed-place, whispering side by side, with our dark heads together and our backs to the door, anybody bold enough to open it stealthily would have been treated to the uncanny sight of a double captain busy talking in whispers with his other self.

"But all this doesn't tell me how you came to hang on to our side-ladder," I inquired, in the hardly audible murmurs we used, after he had told me something more of the proceedings on board the *Sephora* once the bad weather was over.

"When we sighted Java Head I had had time to think all those matters out several times over. I had six weeks of doing nothing else, and with only an hour or so every evening for a tramp on the quarter-deck."

He whispered, his arms folded on the side of my bed-place, staring through the open port. And I could imagine perfectly the manner of this thinking out—a stubborn if not a steadfast operation; something of which I should have been perfectly incapable.

"I reckoned it would be dark before we closed with the land," he continued, so low that I had to strain my hearing, near as we were to each other, shoulder touching shoulder almost. "So I asked to speak to the old man. He always seemed very sick when he came to see me—as if he could not look me in the face. You know, that foresail saved the ship. She was too deep to have run long under bare poles. And it was I that managed to set it for him. Anyway, he came. When I had him in my cabin—he stood by the door looking at me as if I had the halter round my neck already—I asked him right away to leave my cabin door unlocked at night while the ship was going through Sunda Straits. There would be the Java coast within two or three miles, off Angier Point. I wanted nothing more. I've had a prize for swimming my second year in the Conway."

"I can believe it," I breathed out.

"God only knows why they locked me in every night. To see some of their faces you'd have thought they were afraid I'd go about at night strangling people. Am I a murdering brute? Do I look it? By Jove! if I had been he wouldn't have trusted himself like that into my room. You'll say I might have chucked him aside and bolted out, there and then—it was dark already. Well, no. And for the same reason I wouldn't think of trying to smash the door. There would have been a rush to stop me at the noise, and I did not mean to get into a confounded scrimmage. Somebody else might have got killed—for I would not have broken out only to get chucked back, and I did not want any more of that work. He refused, looking more sick than ever. He was afraid of the men, and also of that old second mate of his who had been sailing with him for years—a grey-headed old humbug; and his steward, too, had been with him devil knows how long—seventeen years or more—a dogmatic sort of loafer who hated me like poison, just because I was the chief mate. No chief mate ever made more than one voyage in the *Sephora*, you know. Those two old chaps ran the ship. Devil only knows what the skipper wasn't afraid of (all his nerve went to pieces altogether in that hellish spell of bad weather we had)—of what the law would do to him—of his wife, perhaps. Oh, yes! she's on board. Though I don't think she would have meddled. She would have been only too glad to have me out of the ship in any way. The 'brand of Cain'[3] business, don't you see. That's all right. I was ready enough to go off wandering on the face of the earth—and that was price enough to pay for an Abel of that sort. Anyhow, he wouldn't listen to me. 'This thing must take its course. I represent the law here.' He was shaking like a leaf. 'So you won't?' 'No!' 'Then

[3] After killing Abel, Cain is condemned to wander the earth as a fugitive and vagabond, but the Lord puts a mark on his forehead so that no one will kill him. (See Genesis 4 : 12–15).

I hope you will be able to sleep on that,' I said, and turned my back on him. 'I wonder that *you* can,' cries he, and locks the door.

"Well, after that, I couldn't. Not very well. That was three weeks ago. We have had a slow passage through the Java Sea; drifted about Carimata for ten days. When we anchored here they thought, I suppose, it was all right. The nearest land (and that's five miles) is the ship's destination; the consul would soon set about catching me; and there would have been no object in bolting to these islets there. I don't suppose there's a drop of water on them. I don't know how it was, but to-night that steward, after bringing me my supper, went out to let me eat it, and left the door unlocked. And I ate it—all there was, too. After I had finished I strolled out on the quarter-deck. I don't know that I meant to do anything. A breath of fresh air was all I wanted, I believe. Then a sudden temptation came over me. I kicked off my slippers and was in the water before I had made up my mind fairly. Somebody heard the splash and they raised an awful hullabaloo. 'He's gone! Lower the boats! He's committed suicide! No, he's swimming.' Certainly I was swimming. It's not so easy for a swimmer like me to commit suicide by drowning. I landed on the nearest islet before the boat left the ship's side. I heard them pulling about in the dark, hailing, and so on, but after a bit they gave up. Everything quieted down and the anchorage became as still as death. I sat down on a stone and began to think. I felt certain they would start searching for me at daylight. There was no place to hide on those stony things— and if there had been, what would have been the good? But now I was clear of that ship, I was not going back. So after a while I took off all my clothes, tied them up in a bundle with a stone inside, and dropped them in the deep water on the outer side of that islet. That was suicide enough for me. Let them think what they liked, but I didn't mean to drown myself. I meant to swim till I sank— but that's not the same thing. I struck out for another of these little islands, and it was from that one that I first saw your riding-light. Something to swim for. I went on easily, and on the way I came upon a flat rock a foot or two above water. In the daytime, I dare say, you might make it out with a glass from your poop. I scrambled up on it and rested myself for a bit. Then I made another start. That last spell must have been over a mile."

His whisper was getting fainter and fainter, and all the time he stared straight out through the port-hole, in which there was not even a star to be seen. I had not interrupted him. There was something that made comment impossible in his narrative, or perhaps in himself; a sort of feeling, a quality, which I can't find a name for. And when he ceased, all I found was a futile whisper: "So you swam for our light?"

"Yes—straight for it. It was something to swim for. I couldn't see any stars low down because the coast was in the way, and I couldn't see the land, either. The water was like glass. One might have been swimming in a confounded thousand-feet deep cistern with no place for scrambling out anywhere; but what I didn't like was the notion of swimming round and round like a crazed bullock before I gave out; and as I didn't mean to go back . . . No. Do you see me being hauled back, stark naked, off one of these little islands by the scruff of the neck and fighting like a wild beast? Somebody would have got killed for certain, and I did not want any of that. So I went on. Then your ladder——"

"Why didn't you hail the ship?" I asked, a little louder.

He touched my shoulder lightly. Lazy footsteps came right over our heads and stopped. The second mate had crossed from the other side of the poop and might have been hanging over the rail, for all we knew.

"He couldn't hear us talking—could he?" My double breathed into my very ear, anxiously.

His anxiety was an answer, a sufficient answer, to the question I had put to him. An answer containing all the difficulty of that situation. I closed the port hole quietly, to make sure. A louder word might have been overheard.

"Who's that?" he whispered then.

"My second mate. But I don't know much more of the fellow than you do."

And I told him a little about myself. I had been appointed to take charge while I least expected anything of the sort, not quite a fortnight ago. I didn't know either the ship or the people. Hadn't had the time in port to look about me or size anybody up. And as to the crew, all they knew was that I was appointed to take the ship home. For the rest, I was almost as much of a stranger on board as himself, I said. And at the moment I felt it most acutely. I felt that it would take very little to make me a suspect person in the eyes of the ship's company.

He had turned about meantime; and we, the two strangers in the ship, faced each other in identical attitudes.

"Your ladder——" he murmured, after a silence. "Who'd have thought of finding a ladder hanging over at night in a ship anchored out here! I felt just then a very unpleasant faintness. After the life I've been leading for nine weeks, anybody would have got out of condition. I wasn't capable of swimming round as far as your rudder-chains. And, lo and behold! there was a ladder to get hold of. After I gripped it I said to myself, 'What's the good?' When I saw a man's head looking over I thought I would swim away presently and leave him shouting—in whatever language it was. I didn't mind being looked at. I—I liked it. And then you speaking to me so quietly—as if you had expected me—made me hold on a little longer. It had been a confounded lonely time—I don't mean while swimming. I was glad to talk a little to somebody that didn't belong to the *Sephora*. As to asking for the captain, that was a mere impulse. It could have been no use, with all the ship knowing about me and the other people pretty certain to be round here in the morning. I don't know—I wanted to be seen, to talk with somebody, before I went on. I don't know what I would have said. . . . 'Fine night, isn't it?' or something of the sort."

"Do you think they will be round here presently?" I asked with some incredulity.

"Quite likely," he said, faintly.

He looked extremely haggard all of a sudden. His head rolled on his shoulders.

"H'm. We shall see then. Meantime get into that bed," I whispered. "Want help? There."

It was a rather high bed-place with a set of drawers underneath. This amazing swimmer really needed the lift I gave him by seizing his leg. He tumbled in, rolled over on his back, and flung one arm across his eyes. And then, with his face nearly hidden, he must have looked exactly as I used to look in that bed. I gazed upon my other self for a while before drawing across carefully the two green serge curtains which ran on a brass rod. I thought for a moment of pinning them together for greater safety, but I sat down on the couch, and once there I felt unwilling to rise and hunt for a pin. I would do it in a moment. I was extremely tired, in a peculiarly intimate way, by the strain of stealthiness, by the effort of whispering and the general secrecy of this excitement. It was three o'clock by now and I had been on my feet since nine, but I was not sleepy; I could not have gone to sleep. I sat there, fagged out, looking at the curtains, trying to clear my mind of the confused sensation of being in two places at once, and greatly bothered by an exasperating knocking in my head. It was a relief to discover suddenly that it was not in my head at all, but on the outside of the door. Before I could collect myself the words "Come in" were out of my mouth, and the steward entered with a tray, bringing in my morning coffee. I had slept, after all, and I was so frightened that I shouted, "This way! I am here, steward," as though he had been miles away. He put down the tray on the table next the couch and only then said, very quietly, "I can see you are here, sir." I felt him give me a keen look, but I dared not meet his eyes just then. He must have wondered why I had drawn the curtains of my bed before going to sleep on the couch. He went out, hooking the door open as usual.

I heard the crew washing decks above me. I knew I would have been told at once if there had been any wind. Calm, I thought, and I was doubly vexed. Indeed, I felt dual more than ever. The steward reappeared suddenly in the doorway. I jumped up from the couch so quickly that he gave a start.

"What do you want here?"

"Close your port, sir—they are washing decks."

"It is closed," I said, reddening.

"Very well, sir." But he did not move from the doorway and returned my stare in an extraordinary, equivocal manner for a time. Then his eyes wavered, all his expression changed, and in a voice unusually gentle, almost coaxingly:

"May I come in to take the empty cup away, sir?"

"Of course!" I turned my back on him while he popped in and out. Then I unhooked and closed the door and even pushed the bolt. This sort of thing could not go on very long. The cabin was as hot as an oven, too. I took a peep at my double, and discovered that he had not moved, his arm was still over his eyes; but his chest heaved; his hair was wet; his chin glistened with perspiration. I reached over him and opened the port.

"I must show myself on deck," I reflected.

Of course, theoretically, I could do what I liked, with no one to say nay to me within the whole circle of the horizon; but to lock my cabin door and take the key away I did not dare. Directly I put my head out of the companion I saw the group of my two officers, the second mate barefooted, the chief mate in long india-rubber boots, near the break of the poop, and the steward half-way down the poop-ladder talking to them eagerly. He happened to catch sight of me and dived, the second ran down on the main-deck shouting some order or other, and the chief mate came to meet me, touching his cap.

There was a sort of curiosity in his eye that I did not like. I don't know whether the steward had told them that I was "queer" only, or downright drunk, but I know the man meant to have a good look at me. I watched him coming with a smile which, as he got into point-blank range, took effect and froze his very whiskers. I did not give him time to open his lips.

"Square the yards by lifts and braces before the hands go to breakfast."

It was the first particular order I had given on board that ship; and I stayed on deck to see it executed, too. I had felt the need of asserting myself without loss of time. That sneering young cub got taken down a peg or two on that occasion, and I also seized the opportunity of having a good look at the face of every foremast man as they filed past me to go to the after braces. At breakfast time, eating nothing myself, I presided with such frigid dignity that the two mates were only too glad to escape from the cabin as soon as decency permitted; and all the time the dual working of my mind distracted me almost to the point of insanity. I was constantly watching myself, my secret self, as dependent on my actions as my own personality, sleeping in that bed, behind that door which faced me as I sat at the head of the table. It was very much like being mad, only it was worse because one was aware of it.

I had to shake him for a solid minute, but when at last he opened his eyes it was in the full possession of his senses, with an inquiring look.

"All's well so far," I whispered. "Now you must vanish into the bath-room."

He did so, as noiseless as a ghost, and then I rang for the steward, and facing him boldly, directed him to tidy up my stateroom while I was having my bath—"and be quick about it." As my tone admitted of no excuses, he said, "Yes, sir," and ran off to fetch his dust-pan and brushes. I took a bath and did most of my dressing, splashing, and whistling softly for the steward's edification, while the secret sharer of my life stood drawn up bolt upright in that little space, his face looking very sunken in daylight, his eyelids lowered under the stern, dark line of his eyebrows drawn together by a slight frown.

When I left him there to go back to my room the steward was finishing dusting. I sent for the mate and engaged him in some insignificant conversation. It was, as it were, trifling with the terrific character of his whiskers; but my object was to give him an opportunity for a good look at my cabin. And then I could at last shut, with a clear conscience, the door of my stateroom and get my double back into the recessed part. There was nothing else for it. He had to sit still on a small folding stool, half smothered by the heavy coats hanging there. We listened to the steward going into the bath-room out of the saloon, filling the water-bottles there, scrubbing the bath, setting things to rights, whisk, bang, clatter—out again into the saloon—turn the key—click. Such was my scheme for keeping my second self invisible. Nothing better could be contrived under the circumstances. And there we sat; I at my writing-desk ready to appear busy with some papers, he behind me out of sight of the door. It would not have been prudent to talk in daytime; and I could not have stood the excitement of that queer sense of whispering to myself. Now and then, glancing over my shoulder, I saw him far back there, sitting rigidly on the low stool, his bare feet close together, his arms folded, his head hanging on his breast—and perfectly still. Anybody would have taken him for me.

I was fascinated by it myself. Every moment I had to glance over my shoulder. I was looking at him when a voice outside the door said:

"Beg pardon, sir."

"Well!" . . . I kept my eyes on him, and so when the voice outside the door announced, "There's a ship's boat coming our way, sir," I saw him give a start—the first movement he had made for hours. But he did not raise his bowed head.

"All right. Get the ladder over."

I hesitated. Should I whisper something to him? But what? His immobility seemed to have been never disturbed. What could I tell him he did not know already? . . . Finally I went on deck.

II

The skipper of the *Sephora* had a thin red whisker all round his face, and the sort of complexion that goes with hair of that colour; also the particular, rather smeary shade of blue in the eyes. He was not exactly a showy figure; his shoulders were high, his stature but middling—one leg slightly more bandy than the other. He shook hands, looking vaguely around. A spiritless tenacity was his main characteristic, I judged. I behaved with a politeness which seemed to disconcert him. Perhaps he was shy. He mumbled to me as if he were ashamed of what he was saying; gave his name (it was something like Archbold—but at this distance of years I hardly am sure), his ship's name, and a few other particulars of that sort, in the manner of a criminal making a reluctant and doleful confession. He had had terrible weather on the passage out—terrible—terrible—wife aboard, too.

By this time we were seated in the cabin and the steward brought in a tray with a bottle and glasses. "Thanks! No." Never took liquor. Would have some water, though. He drank two tumblerfuls. Terrible thirsty work. Ever since daylight had been exploring the islands round his ship.

"What was that for—fun?" I asked, with an appearance of polite interest.

"No!" He sighed. "Painful duty."

As he persisted in his mumbling and I wanted my double to hear every word, I hit upon the notion of informing him that I regretted to say I was hard of hearing.

"Such a young man, too!" he nodded, keeping his smeary blue, unintelligent eyes fastened upon me. "What was the cause of it—some disease?" he inquired, without the least sympathy and as if he thought that, if so, I'd got no more than I deserved.

"Yes; disease," I admitted in a cheerful tone which seemed to shock him. But my point was gained, because he had to raise his voice to give me his tale. It is not worth while to record that version. It was just over two months since all this had happened, and he had thought so much about it that he seemed completely muddled as to its bearings, but still immensely impressed.

"What would you think of such a thing happening on board your own ship? I've had the *Sephora* for these fifteen years. I am a well-known shipmaster."

He was densely distressed—and perhaps I should have sympathised with him if I had been able to detach my mental vision from the unsuspected sharer of my cabin as though he were my second self. There he was on the other side of the bulkhead, four or five feet from us, no more, as we sat in the saloon. I looked politely at Captain Archbold (if that was his name), but it was the other I saw, in a grey sleeping-suit, seated on a low stool, his bare feet close together, his arms folded, and every word said between us falling into the ears of his dark head bowed on his chest.

"I have been at sea now, man and boy, for seven-and-thirty years, and I've never heard of such a thing happening in an English ship. And that it should be my ship. Wife on board, too."

I was hardly listening to him.

"Don't you think," I said, "that the heavy sea which, you told me, came aboard just then might have killed the man? I have seen the sheer weight of a sea kill a man very neatly, by simply breaking his neck."

"Good God!" he uttered, impressively, fixing his smeary blue eyes on me. "The sea! No man killed by the sea ever looked like that." He seemed positively scandalised at my suggestion. And as I gazed at him, certainly not prepared for anything original on his part, he advanced his head close to mine and thrust his tongue out at me so suddenly that I couldn't help starting back.

After scoring over my calmness in this graphic way he nodded wisely. If I had seen the sight, he assured me, I would never forget it as long as I lived. The weather was too bad to give the corpse a proper sea burial. So next day at dawn they took it up on the poop, covering its face with a bit of bunting; he read a short prayer, and then, just as it was, in its oilskins and long boots, they launched it amongst those mountainous seas that seemed ready every moment to swallow up the ship herself and the terrified lives on board of her.

"That reefed foresail saved you," I threw in.

"Under God—it did," he exclaimed fervently. "It was by a special mercy, I firmly believe, that it stood some of those hurricane squalls."

"It was the setting of that sail which——" I began.

"God's own hand in it," he interrupted me. "Nothing less could have done it. I don't mind telling you that I hardly dared give the order. It seemed impossible that we could touch anything without losing it, and then our last hope would have been gone."

The terror of that gale was on him yet. I let him go on for a bit, then said, casually—as if returning to a minor subject:

"You were very anxious to give up your mate to the shore people, I believe?"

He was. To the law. His obscure tenacity on that point had in it something incomprehensible and a little awful; something, as it were, mystical, quite apart from his anxiety that he should not be suspected of "countenancing any doings of that sort." Seven-and-thirty virtuous years at sea, of which over twenty of immaculate command, and the last fifteen in the *Sephora*, seemed to have laid him under some pitiless obligation.

"And you know," he went on, groping shamefacedly amongst his feelings, "I did not engage that young fellow. His people had some interest with my owners. I was in a way forced to take him on. He looked very smart, very gentlemanly, and all that. But do you know—I never liked him, somehow. I am a plain man. You see, he wasn't exactly the sort for the chief mate of a ship like the *Sephora*."

I had become so connected in thought and impressions with the secret sharer of my cabin that I felt as if I, personally, were being given to understand that I, too, was not the sort that would have done for the chief mate of a ship like the *Sephora*. I had no doubt of it in my mind.

"Not at all the style of man. You understand," he insisted, superfluously, looking hard at me.

I smiled urbanely. He seemed at a loss for a while.

"I suppose I must report a suicide."

"Beg pardon?"

"Sui-cide! That's what I'll have to write to my owners directly I get in."

"Unless you manage to recover him before to-morrow," I assented, dispassionately. . . . "I mean, alive."

He mumbled something which I really did not catch, and I turned my ear to him in a puzzled manner. He fairly bawled:

"The land—I say, the mainland is at least seven miles off my anchorage."

"About that."

My lack of excitement, of curiosity, of surprise, of any sort of pronounced interest, began to arouse his distrust. But except for the felicitous pretense of deafness I had not tried to pretend anything. I had felt utterly incapable of playing the part of ignorance properly, and therefore was afraid to try. It is also certain that he had brought some ready-made suspicions with him, and that he viewed my politeness as a strange and unnatural phenomenon. And yet how else could I have received him? Not heartily! That was impossible for psychological reasons, which I need not state here. My only object was to keep off his inquiries. Surlily? Yes, but surliness might have provoked a point-blank question. From its novelty to him and from its nature, punctilious courtesy was the manner best calculated to restrain the man. But there was the danger of his breaking through my defense bluntly. I could not, I think, have met him by a direct lie, also for psychological (not moral) reasons. If he had only known how afraid I was of his putting my feeling of identity with the other to the test! But, strangely enough—(I thought of it only afterwards)—I believe that he was not a little disconcerted by the reverse side of that weird situation, by something in me that reminded him of the man he was seeking—suggested a mysterious similitude to the young fellow he had distrusted and disliked from the first.

However that might have been, the silence was not very prolonged. He took another oblique step.

"I reckon I had no more than a two-mile pull to your ship. Not a bit more."

"And quite enough, too, in this awful heat," I said.

Another pause full of mistrust followed. Necessity, they say, is mother of invention, but fear, too, is not barren of ingenious suggestions. And I was afraid he would ask me point-blank for news of my other self.

"Nice little saloon, isn't it?" I remarked, as if noticing for the first time the way his eyes roamed from one closed door to the other. "And very well fitted out, too. Here, for instance," I continued, reaching over the back of my seat negligently and flinging the door open, "is my bath-room."

He made an eager movement, but hardly gave it a glance. I got up, shut the door of the bath-room, and invited him to have a look round, as if I were very proud of my accommodation. He had to rise and be shown round, but he went through the business without any raptures whatever.

"And now we'll have a look at my stateroom," I declared, in a voice as loud as I dared to make it, crossing the cabin to the starboard side with purposely heavy steps.

He followed me in and gazed around. My intelligent double had vanished. I played my part.

"Very convenient—isn't it?"

"Very nice. Very comf . . ." He didn't finish and went out brusquely as if to escape from some unrighteous wiles of mine. But it was not to be. I had been too frightened not to feel vengeful; I felt I had him on the run, and I meant to keep him on the run. My polite insistence must have had something menacing in it, because he gave in suddenly. And I did not let him off a single item; mate's room, pantry, storerooms, the very sail-locker which was also under the poop—he had to look into them all. When at last I showed him out on the quarter-deck he drew a long, spiritless sigh, and mumbled dismally that he must really be going back to his ship now. I desired my mate, who had joined us, to see to the captain's boat.

The man of whiskers gave a blast on the whistle which he used to wear hanging round his neck, and yelled, "*Sephora's* away!" My double down there in my cabin must have heard, and certainly could not feel more relieved than I. Four fellows came running out from somewhere forward and went over the side, while my own men, appearing on deck too, lined the rail. I escorted my visitor to the gangway ceremoniously, and nearly overdid it. He was a tenacious beast. On the very ladder he lingered, and in that unique, guiltily conscientious manner of sticking to the point:

"I say . . . you . . . you don't think that——"

I covered his voice loudly:

"Certainly not. . . . I am delighted. Goodby."

I had an idea of what he meant to say, and just saved myself by the privilege of defective hearing. He was too shaken generally to insist, but my mate, close witness of that parting, looked mystified and his face took on a thoughtful cast. As I did not want to appear as if I wished to avoid all communication with my officers, he had the opportunity to address me.

"Seems a very nice man. His boat's crew told our chaps a very extraordinary story, if what I am told by the steward is true. I suppose you had it from the captain, sir?"

"Yes. I had a story from the captain."

"A very horrible affair—isn't it, sir?"

"It is."

"Beats all these tales we hear about murders in Yankee ships."

"I don't think it beats them. I don't think it resembles them in the least."

"Bless my soul—you don't say so! But of course I've no acquaintance whatever with American ships, not I, so I couldn't go against your knowledge. It's horrible enough for me. . . . But the queerest part is that those fellows seemed to have some idea the man was hidden aboard here. They had really. Did you ever hear of such a thing?"

"Preposterous—isn't it?"

We were walking to and fro athwart the quarterdeck. No one of the crew forward could be seen (the day was Sunday), and the mate pursued:

"There was some little dispute about it. Our chaps took offense. 'As if we would harbor a thing like that,' they said. 'Wouldn't you like to look for him in our coal-hole?' Quite a tiff. But they made it up in the end. I suppose he did drown himself. Don't you, sir?"

"I don't suppose anything."

"You have no doubt in the matter, sir?"

"None whatever."

I left him suddenly. I felt I was producing a bad impression, but with my double down there it was most trying to be on deck. And it was almost as trying to be below. Altogether a nerve-trying situation. But on the whole I felt less torn in two when I was with him. There was no one in the whole ship whom I dared take into my confidence. Since the hands had got to know his story, it would have been impossible to pass him off for any one else, and an accidental discovery was to be dreaded now more than ever. . . .

The steward being engaged in laying the table for dinner, we could talk only with our eyes when I first went down. Later in the afternoon we had a cautious try at whispering. The Sunday quietness of the ship was against us; the stillness of air and water around her was against us; the elements, the men were against us—everything was against us in our secret partnership; time itself—for this could not go on forever. The very trust in Providence was, I suppose, denied to his guilt. Shall I confess that this thought cast me down very much? And as to the chapter of accidents which counts for so much in the book of success, I could only hope that it was closed. For what favorable accident could be expected?

"Did you hear everything?" were my first words as soon as we took up our position side by side, leaning over my bed-place.

He had. And the proof of it was his earnest whisper, "The man told you he hardly dared to give the order."

I understood the reference to be to that saving foresail.

"Yes. He was afraid of it being lost in the setting."

"I assure you he never gave the order. He may think he did, but he never gave it. He stood there with me on the break of the poop after the maintopsail blew away, and whimpered about our last hope—positively whimpered about it and nothing else—and the night coming on! To hear one's skipper go on like that in such weather was enough to drive any fellow out of his mind. It worked me up into a sort of desperation. I just took it into my own hands and went away from him, boiling, and—— But what's the use telling you? *You* know! . . . Do you think that if I had not been pretty fierce with them I should have got the men to do anything? Not it! The bo's'n perhaps? Perhaps! It wasn't a heavy sea—it was a sea gone mad! I suppose the end of the world will be something like that; and a man may have the heart to see it coming once and be done with it—but to have to face it day after day—— I don't blame anybody. I was precious little better than the rest. Only—I was an officer of that old coal-wagon, anyhow——"

"I quite understand," I conveyed that sincere assurance into his ear. He was out of breath with whispering; I could hear him pant slightly. It was all very simple. The same strung-up force which had given twenty-four men a chance, at least, for their lives, had, in a sort of recoil, crushed an unworthy mutinous existence.

But I had no leisure to weigh the merits of the matter—footsteps in the saloon, a heavy knock. "There's enough wind to get under way with, sir." Here was the call of a new claim upon my thoughts and even upon my feelings.

"Turn the hands up," I cried through the door. "I'll be on deck directly."

I was going out to make the acquaintance of my ship. Before I left the cabin our eyes met—the eyes of the only two strangers on board. I pointed to the recessed part where the little camp-stool awaited him and laid my finger on my lips. He made a gesture—somewhat vague—a little mysterious, accompanied by a faint smile, as if of regret.

This is not the place to enlarge upon the sensations of a man who feels for the first time a ship move under his feet to his own independent word. In my case they were not unalloyed. I was not wholly alone with my command; for there was that stranger in my cabin. Or rather, I was not completely and wholly with her. Part of me was absent. That mental feeling of being in two places at once affected me physically as if the mood of secrecy had penetrated my very soul. Before an hour had elapsed since the ship had begun to move, having occasion to ask the mate (he stood by my side) to take a compass bearing of the Pagoda, I caught myself reaching up to his ear in whispers. I say I caught myself, but enough had escaped to startle the man. I can't describe it otherwise than by saying that he shied. A grave, preoccupied manner, as though he were in possession of some perplexing intelligence, did not leave him henceforth. A little later I moved away from the rail to look at the compass with such a stealthy gait that the helmsman noticed it—and I could not help noticing the unusual roundness of his eyes. These are trifling instances, though it's to no commander's advantage to be suspected of ludicrous eccentricities. But I was also more seriously affected. There are to a seaman certain words, gestures, that should in given conditions come as naturally, as instinctively as the winking of a menaced eye. A certain order should spring on to his lips without thinking; a certain sign should get itself made, so to speak, without reflection. But all unconscious alertness had abandoned me. I had to make an effort of will to recall myself back (from the cabin) to the conditions of the moment. I felt that I was appearing an irresolute commander to those people who were watching me more or less critically.

And, besides, there were the scares. On the second day out, for instance, coming off the deck in the afternoon (I had straw slippers on my bare feet) I stopped at the open pantry door and spoke to the steward. He was doing something there with his back to me. At the sound of my voice he nearly jumped out of his skin, as the saying is, and incidentally broke a cup.

"What on earth's the matter with you?" I asked, astonished.

He was extremely confused. "Beg your pardon, sir. I made sure you were in your cabin."

"You see I wasn't."

"No, sir. I could have sworn I had heard you moving in there not a moment ago. It's most extraordinary . . . very sorry, sir."

I passed on with an inward shudder. I was so identified with my secret double that I did not even mention the fact in those scanty, fearful whispers we exchanged. I suppose he had made some slight noise of some kind or other. It would have been miraculous if he hadn't at one time or another. And yet, haggard as he appeared, he looked always perfectly self-controlled, more than calm—almost invulnerable. On my suggestion he remained almost entirely in the bathroom, which, upon the whole, was the safest place. There could be really no shadow of an excuse for any one ever wanting to go in there, once the steward had done with it. It was a very tiny place. Sometimes he reclined on the floor, his legs bent, his head sustained on one elbow. At others I would find him on the campstool, sitting in his grey sleeping-suit and with his cropped dark hair like a patient, unmoved convict. At night I would smuggle him into my bed-place, and we would whisper together, with the regular footfalls of the officer of the watch passing and repassing over our heads. It was an infinitely miserable time. It was lucky that some tins of fine preserves were stowed in a locker in my stateroom; hard bread I could always get hold of; and so he lived on stewed chicken, paté de foie gras, asparagus, cooked oysters, sardines—on all sorts of abominable sham delicacies out of tins. My early morning coffee he always drank; and it was all I dared do for him in that respect.

Every day there was the horrible maneuvering to go through so that my room and then the bath-room should be done in the usual way. I came to hate the sight of the steward, to abhor the voice of that harmless man. I felt that it was he who would bring on the disaster of discovery. It hung like a sword over our heads.

The fourth day out, I think (we were then working down the east side of the Gulf of Siam, tack for tack, in light winds and smooth water)—the fourth day, I say, of this miserable juggling with the unavoidable, as we sat at our evening meal, that man, whose slightest movement I dreaded, after putting down the dishes ran up on deck busily. This could not be dangerous. Presently he came down again; and then it appeared that he had remembered a coat of mine which I had thrown over a rail to dry after having been wetted in a shower which had passed over the ship in the afternoon. Sitting stolidly at the head of the table I became terrified at the sight of the garment on his arm. Of course he made for my door. There was no time to lose.

"Steward," I thundered. My nerves were so shaken that I could not govern my voice and conceal my agitation. This was the sort of thing that made my terrifically whiskered mate tap his forehead with his forefinger. I had detected him using that gesture while talking on deck with a confidential air to the carpenter. It was too far to hear a word, but I had no doubt that this pantomime could only refer to the strange new captain.

"Yes, sir," the pale-faced steward turned resignedly to me. It was this maddening course of being shouted at, checked without rhyme or reason, arbitrarily chased out of my cabin, suddenly called into it, sent flying out of his pantry on incomprehensible errands, that accounted for the growing wretchedness of his expression.

"Where are you going with that coat?"

"To your room, sir."

"Is there another shower coming?"

"I'm sure I don't know, sir. Shall I go up again and see, sir?"

"No! never mind."

My object was attained, as of course my other self in there would have heard everything that passed. During this interlude my two officers never raised their eyes off their respective plates; but the lip of that confounded cub, the second mate, quivered visibly.

I expected the steward to hook my coat on and come out at once. He was very slow about it; but I dominated my nervousness sufficiently not to shout after him. Suddenly I became aware (it could be heard plainly enough) that the fellow for some reason or other was opening the door of the bath-room. It was the end. The place was literally not big enough to swing a cat in. My voice died in my throat and I went stony all over. I expected to hear a yell of surprise and terror, and made a movement, but had not the strength to get on my legs. Everything remained still. Had my second self taken the poor wretch by the throat? I don't know what I could have done next moment if I had not seen the steward come out of my room, close the door, and then stand quietly by the sideboard.

"Saved," I thought. "But, no! Lost! Gone! He was gone!"

I laid my knife and fork down and leaned back in my chair. My head swam.

After a while, when sufficiently recovered to speak in a steady voice, I instructed my mate to put the ship round at eight o'clock himself.

"I won't come on deck," I went on. "I think I'll turn in, and unless the wind shifts I don't want to be disturbed before midnight. I feel a bit seedy."

"You did look middling bad a little while ago," the chief mate remarked without showing any great concern.

They both went out, and I stared at the steward clearing the table. There was nothing to be read on that wretched man's face. But why did he avoid my eyes I asked myself. Then I thought I should like to hear the sound of his voice.

"Steward!"

"Sir!" Startled as usual.

"Where did you hang up that coat?"

"In the bath-room, sir." The usual anxious tone. "It's not quite dry yet, sir."

For some time longer I sat in the cuddy. Had my double vanished as he had come? But of his coming there was an explanation, whereas his disappearance would be inexplicable. . . . I went slowly into my dark room, shut the door, lighted the lamp, and for a time dared not turn round. When at last I did I saw him standing bolt-upright in the narrow recessed part. It would not be true to say I had a shock, but an irresistible doubt of his bodily existence flitted through my mind. Can it be, I asked myself, that he is not visible to other eyes than mine? It was like being haunted. Motionless, with a grave face, he raised his hands slightly at me in a gesture which meant clearly, "Heavens! what a narrow escape!" Narrow indeed. I think I had come creeping quietly as near insanity as any man who has not actually gone over the border. That gesture restrained me, so to speak.

The mate with the terrific whiskers was now putting the ship on the other tack. In the moment of profound silence which follows upon the hands going to their stations I heard on the poop his raised voice: "Hard alee!" and the distant shout of the order repeated on the maindeck. The sails, in that light breeze, made but a faint fluttering noise. It ceased. The ship was coming round slowly; I held my breath in the renewed stillness of expectation; one wouldn't have thought that there was a single living soul on her decks. A sudden brisk shout, "Mainsail haul!" broke the spell, and in the noisy cries and rush overhead of the men running away with the main-brace we two, down in my cabin, came together in our usual position by the bed-place.

He did not wait for my question. "I heard him fumbling here and just managed to squat myself down in the bath," he whispered to me. "The fellow only opened the door and put his arm in to hang the coat up. All the same——"

"I never thought of that," I whispered back, even more appalled than before at the closeness of the shave, and marvelling at that something unyielding in his character which was carrying him through so finely. There was no agitation in his whisper. Whoever was being driven distracted, it was not he. He was sane. And the proof of his sanity was continued when he took up the whispering again.

"It would never do for me to come to life again."

It was something that a ghost might have said. But what he was alluding to was his old captain's reluctant admission of the theory of suicide. It would obviously serve his turn—if I had understood at all the view which seemed to govern the unalterable purpose of his action.

"You must maroon me as soon as ever you can get amongst these islands off the Cambodge[4] shore," he went on.

"Maroon you! We are not living in a boy's adventure tale," I protested. His scornful whispering took me up.

"We aren't indeed! There's nothing of a boy's tale in this. But there's nothing else for it. I want no more. You don't suppose I am afraid of what can be done to me? Prison or gallows or whatever they may please. But you don't see me coming back to explain such things to an old fellow in a wig and twelve respectable tradesmen, do you? What can they know whether I am guilty or not—or of *what* I am guilty, either? That's my affair. What does the Bible say? 'Driven off the face of the earth.' Very well. I am off the face of the earth now. As I came at night so I shall go."

"Impossible!" I murmured. "You can't."

"Can't? . . . Not naked like a soul on the Day of Judgment. I shall freeze on to this sleeping-suit. The Last Day is not yet—and . . . you have understood thoroughly. Didn't you?"

I felt suddenly ashamed of myself. I may say truly that I understood—and my hesitation in letting that man swim away from my ship's side had been a mere sham sentiment, a sort of cowardice.

"It can't be done now till next night," I breathed out. "The ship is on the off-shore tack and the wind may fail us."

"As long as I know that you understand," he whispered. "But of course you do. It's a great satisfaction to have got somebody to understand. You seem to have been there on purpose." And in the same whisper, as if we two whenever we talked had to say things to each other which were not fit for the world to hear, he added, "It's very wonderful."

We remained side by side talking in our secret way—but sometimes silent or just exchanging a whispered word or two at long intervals. And as usual he stared through the port. A breath of wind came now and again into our faces. The ship might have been moored in dock, so gently and on an even keel she slipped through the water, that did not murmur even at our passage, shadowy and silent like a phantom sea.

At midnight I went on deck, and to my mate's great surprise put the ship round on the other tack. His terrible whiskers flitted round me in silent criticism. I certainly should not have done it if it had been only a question of getting out of that sleepy gulf as quickly as possible. I believe he told the second mate, who relieved him, that it was a great want of judgment. The other only yawned. That intolerable cub shuffled about so sleepily and lolled against the rails in such a slack, improper fashion that I came down on him sharply.

"Aren't you properly awake yet?"

"Yes, sir! I am awake."

"Well, then, be good enough to hold yourself as if you were. And keep a look-out. If there's any current we'll be closing with some islands before daylight."

The east side of the gulf is fringed with islands, some solitary, others in groups. On the blue background of the high coast they seem to float on silvery patches of calm water, arid and grey, or dark green and rounded like clumps of

[4] The French name of Cambodia. The story takes place when France controlled Indochina.

evergreen bushes, with the larger ones, a mile or two long, showing the outlines of ridges, ribs of grey rock under the dank mantle of matted leafage. Unknown to trade, to travel, almost to geography, the manner of life they harbour is an unsolved secret. There must be villages—settlements of fishermen at least—on the largest of them, and some communication with the world is probably kept up by native craft. But all that forenoon, as we headed for them, fanned along by the faintest of breezes, I saw no sign of man or canoe in the field of the telescope I kept on pointing at the scattered group.

At noon I gave no orders for a change of course, and the mate's whiskers became much concerned and seemed to be offering themselves unduly to my notice. At last I said:

"I am going to stand right in. Quite in—as far as I can take her."

The stare of extreme surprise imparted an air of ferocity also to his eyes, and he looked truly terrific for a moment.

"We're not doing well in the middle of the gulf," I continued casually. "I am going to look for the land breezes to-night."

"Bless my soul! Do you mean, sir, in the dark amongst the lot of all them islands and reefs and shoals?"

"Well—if there are any regular land breezes at all on this coast one must get close inshore to find them, mustn't one?"

"Bless my soul!" he exclaimed again under his breath. All that afternoon he wore a dreamy, contemplative appearance which in him was a mark of perplexity. After dinner I went into my stateroom as if I meant to take some rest. There we two bent our dark heads over a half-unrolled chart lying on my bed.

"There," I said. "It's got to be Koh-ring. I've been looking at it ever since sunrise. It has got two hills and a low point. It must be inhabited. And on the coast opposite there is what looks like the mouth of a biggish river—with some town, no doubt, not far up. It's the best chance for you that I can see."

"Anything. Koh-ring let it be."

He looked thoughtfully at the chart as if surveying chances and distances from a lofty height—and following with his eyes his own figure wandering on the blank land of Cochin-China,[5] and then passing off that piece of paper clean out of sight into uncharted regions. And it was as if the ship had two captains to plan her course for her. I had been so worried and restless running up and down that I had not had the patience to dress that day. I had remained in my sleeping-suit, with straw slippers and a soft floppy hat. The closeness of the heat in the gulf had been most oppressive, and the crew were used to see me wandering in that airy attire.

"She will clear the south point as she heads now," I whispered into his ear. "Goodness only knows when, though, but certainly after dark. I'll edge her in to half a mile, as far as I may be able to judge in the dark——"

"Be careful," he murmured, warningly—and I realised suddenly that all my future, the only future for which I was fit, would perhaps go irretrievably to pieces in any mishap to my first command.

I could not stop a moment longer in the room. I motioned him to get out of sight and made my way on the poop. That unplayful cub had the watch. I walked up and down for a while thinking things out, then beckoned him over.

[5] A colony of French Indochina from 1862 to 1948; now a part of South Vietnam.

"Send a couple of hands to open the two quarterdeck ports," I said, mildly. He actually had the impudence, or else so forgot himself in his wonder at such an incomprehensible order, as to repeat:

"Open the quarter-deck ports! What for, sir?"

"The only reason you need concern yourself about is because I tell you to do so. Have them opened wide and fastened properly."

He reddened and went off, but I believe made some jeering remark to the carpenter as to the sensible practice of ventilating a ship's quarter-deck. I know he popped into the mate's cabin to impart the fact to him because the whiskers came on deck, as it were by chance, and stole glances at me from below—for signs of lunacy or drunkenness, I suppose.

A little before supper, feeling more restless than ever, I rejoined, for a moment, my second self. And to find him sitting so quietly was surprising, like something against nature, inhuman.

I developed my plan in a hurried whisper.

"I shall stand in as close as I dare and then put her round. I will presently find means to smuggle you out of here into the sail-locker, which communicates with the lobby. But there is an opening, a sort of square for hauling the sails out, which gives straight on the quarter-deck and which is never closed in fine weather, so as to give air to the sails. When the ship's way is deadened in stays and all the hands are aft at the main-braces you will have a clear road to slip out and get overboard through the open quarter-deck port. I've had them both fastened up. Use a rope's end to lower yourself into the water so as to avoid a splash—you know. It could be heard and cause some beastly complication."

He kept silent for a while, then whispered, "I understand."

"I won't be there to see you go," I began with an effort. "The rest . . . I only hope I have understood, too."

"You have. From first to last"—and for the first time there seemed to be a faltering, something strained in his whisper. He caught hold of my arm, but the ringing of the supper bell made me start. He didn't, though; he only released his grip.

After supper I didn't come below again till well past eight o'clock. The faint, steady breeze was loaded with dew; and the wet, darkened sails held all there was of propelling power in it. The night, clear and starry, sparkled darkly, and the opaque, lightless patches shifting slowly against the low stars were the drifting islets. On the port bow there was a big one more distant and shadowily imposing by the great space of sky it eclipsed.

On opening the door I had a back view of my very own self looking at a chart. He had come out of the recess and was standing near the table.

"Quite dark enough," I whispered.

He stepped back and leaned against my bed with a level, quiet glance. I sat on the couch. We had nothing to say to each other. Over our heads the officer of the watch moved here and there. Then I heard him move quickly. I knew what that meant. He was making for the companion; and presently his voice was outside my door.

"We are drawing in pretty fast, sir. Land looks rather close."

"Very well," I answered. "I am coming on deck directly."

I waited till he was gone out of the cuddy, then rose. My double moved too.

The time had come to exchange our last whispers, for neither of us was ever to hear each other's natural voice.

"Look here!" I opened a drawer and took out three sovereigns. "Take this anyhow. I've got six and I'd give you the lot, only I must keep a little money to buy some fruit and vegetables for the crew from native boats as we go through Sunda Straits."

He shook his head.

"Take it," I urged him, whispering desperately. "No one can tell what——"

He smiled and slapped meaningly the only pocket of the sleeping-jacket. It was not safe, certainly. But I produced a large old silk handkerchief of mine, and tying the three pieces of gold in a corner, pressed it on him. He was touched, I suppose, because he took it at last and tied it quickly round his waist under the jacket, on his bare skin.

Our eyes met; several seconds elapsed, till, our glances still mingled, I extended my hand and turned the lamp out. Then I passed through the cuddy, leaving the door of my room wide open. . . . "Steward!"

He was still lingering in the pantry in the greatness of his zeal, giving a rub-up to a plated cruet stand the last thing before going to bed. Being careful not to wake up the mate, whose room was opposite, I spoke in an undertone.

He looked round anxiously. "Sir."

"Can you get me a little hot water from the galley?"

"I am afraid, sir, the galley fire's been out for some time now."

"Go and see."

He flew up the stairs.

"Now," I whispered, loudly, into the saloon—too loudly, perhaps, but I was afraid I couldn't make a sound. He was by my side in an instant—the double captain slipped past the stairs—through a tiny dark passage . . . a sliding door. We were in the sail-locker, scrambling on our knees over the sails. A sudden thought struck me. I saw myself wandering barefooted, bareheaded, the sun beating on my dark poll. I snatched off my floppy hat and tried hurriedly in the dark to ram it on my other self. He dodged and fended off silently. I wonder what he thought had come to me before he understood and suddenly desisted. Our hands met gropingly, lingered united in a steady, motionless clasp for a second. . . . No word was breathed by either of us when they separated.

I was standing quietly by the pantry door when the steward returned.

"Sorry, sir. Kettle barely warm. Shall I light the spirit-lamp?"

"Never mind."

I came out on deck slowly. It was now a matter of conscience to shave the land as close as possible—for now he must go overboard whenever the ship was put in stays. Must! There could be no going back for him. After a moment I walked over to leeward and my heart flew into my mouth at the nearness of the land on the bow. Under any other circumstances I would not have held on a minute longer. The second mate had followed me anxiously.

I looked on till I felt I could command my voice.

"She will weather," I said then in a quiet tone.

"Are you going to try that, sir?" he stammered out incredulously.

I took no notice of him and raised my tone just enough to be heard by the helmsman.

"Keep her good full."

"Good full, sir."

The wind fanned my cheek, the sails slept, the world was silent. The strain of watching the dark loom of the land grow bigger and denser was too much for me. I had shut my eyes—because the ship must go closer. She must! The stillness was intolerable. Were we standing still?

When I opened my eyes the second view started my heart with a thump. The black southern hill of Koh-ring seemed to hang right over the ship like a towering fragment of the everlasting night. On that enormous mass of blackness there was not a gleam to be seen, not a sound to be heard. It was gliding irresistibly towards us and yet seemed already within reach of the hand. I saw the vague figures of the watch grouped in the waist, gazing in awed silence.

"Are you going on, sir?" inquired an unsteady voice at my elbow.

I ignored it. I had to go on.

"Keep her full. Don't check her way. That won't do now," I said warningly.

"I can't see the sails very well," the helmsman answered me, in strange, quavering tones.

Was she close enough? Already she was, I won't say in the shadow of the land, but in the very blackness of it, already swallowed up as it were, gone too close to be recalled, gone from me altogether.

"Give the mate a call," I said to the young man who stood at my elbow as still as death. "And turn all hands up."

My tone had a borrowed loudness reverberated from the height of the land. Several voices cried out together: "We are all on deck, sir."

Then stillness again, with the great shadow gliding closer, towering higher, without a light, without a sound. Such a hush had fallen on the ship that she might have been a bark of the dead floating in slowly under the very gate of Erebus.[6]

"My God! Where are we?"

It was the mate moaning at my elbow. He was thunderstruck, and as it were deprived of the moral support of his whiskers. He clapped his hands and absolutely cried out, "Lost!"

"Be quiet," I said, sternly.

He lowered his tone, but I saw the shadowy gesture of his despair. "What are we doing here?"

"Looking for the land wind."

He made as if to tear his hair, and addressed me recklessly.

"She will never get out. You have done it, sir. I knew it'd end in something like this. She will never weather, and you are too close now to stay. She'll drift ashore before she's round. O my God!"

I caught his arm as he was raising it to batter his poor devoted head, and shook it violently.

"She's ashore already," he wailed, trying to tear himself away.

"Is she? . . . Keep good full there!"

"Good full, sir," cried the helmsman in a frightened, thin child-like voice.

I hadn't let go the mate's arm and went on shaking it. "Ready about, do you hear? You go forward"—shake—"and stop there"—shake—"and hold your noise"—

6 In Greek mythology, the son of Chaos and the brother of Night, hence, darkness personified.

shake—"and see these head-sheets properly overhauled"—shake, shake—shake.

And all the time I dared not look towards the land lest my heart should fail me. I released my grip at last and he ran forward as if fleeing for dear life.

I wondered what my double there in the sail-locker thought of this commotion. He was able to hear everything—and perhaps he was able to understand why, on my conscience, it had to be thus close—no less. My first order "Hard alee!" re-echoed ominously under the towering shadow of Koh-ring as if I had shouted in a mountain gorge. And then I watched the land intently. In that smooth water and light wind it was impossible to feel the ship coming-to. No! I could not feel her. And my second self was making now ready to slip out and lower himself overboard. Perhaps he was gone already . . . ?

The great black mass brooding over our very mastheads began to pivot away from the ship's side silently. And now I forgot the secret stranger ready to depart, and remembered only that I was a total stranger to the ship. I did not know her. Would she do it? How was she to be handled?

I swung the mainyard and waited helplessly. She was perhaps stopped, and her very fate hung in the balance, with the black mass of Koh-ring like the gate of the everlasting night towering over her taffrail. What would she do now? Had she way on her yet? I stepped to the side swiftly, and on the shadowy water I could see nothing except a faint phosphorescent flash revealing the glassy smoothness of the sleeping surface. It was impossible to tell—and I had not learned yet the feel of my ship. Was she moving? What I needed was something easily seen, a piece of paper, which I could throw overboard and watch. I had nothing on me. To run down for it I didn't dare. There was no time. All at once my strained, yearning stare distinguished a white object floating within a yard of the ship's side. White on the black water. A phosphorescent flash passed under it. What was that thing? . . . I recognised my own floppy hat. It must have fallen off his head . . . and he didn't bother. Now I had what I wanted—the saving mark for my eyes. But I hardly thought of my other self, now gone from the ship, to be hidden for ever from all friendly faces, to be a fugitive and a vagabond on the earth, with no brand of the curse on his sane forehead to stay a slaying hand . . . too proud to explain.

And I watched the hat—the expression of my sudden pity for his mere flesh. It had been meant to save his homeless head from the dangers of the sun. And now—behold—it was saving the ship, by serving me for a mark to help out the ignorance of my strangeness. Ha! It was drifting forward, warning me just in time that the ship had gathered sternway.

"Shift the helm," I said in a low voice to the seaman standing still like a statue.

The man's eyes glistened wildly in the binnacle light as he jumped round to the other side and spun round the wheel.

I walked to the break of the poop. On the overshadowed deck all hands stood by the forebraces waiting for my order. The stars ahead seemed to be gliding from right to left. And all was so still in the world that I heard the quiet remark, "She's round," passed in a tone of intense relief between two seamen.

"Let go and haul."

The foreyards ran round with a great noise, amidst cheery cries. And now the frightful whiskers made themselves heard giving various orders. Already the ship was drawing ahead. And I was alone with her. Nothing! no one in the world should stand now between us, throwing a shadow on the way of silent knowledge and mute affection, the perfect communion of a seaman with his first command.

Walking to the taffrail, I was in time to make out, on the very edge of a darkness thrown by a towering black mass like the very gateway of Erebus—yes, I was in time to catch an evanescent glimpse of my white hat left behind to mark the spot where the secret sharer of my cabin and of my thoughts, as though he were my second self, had lowered himself into the water to take his punishment: a free man, a proud swimmer striking out for a new destiny.

THE DEAD

JAMES JOYCE
1882–1941

Lily, the caretaker's daughter, was literally run off her feet. Hardly had she brought one gentleman into the little pantry behind the office on the ground floor and helped him off with his overcoat than the wheezy hall-door bell clanged again and she had to scamper along the bare hallway to let in another guest. It was well for her she had not to attend to the ladies also. But Miss Kate and Miss Julia had thought of that and had converted the bathroom upstairs into a ladies' dressing-room. Miss Kate and Miss Julia were there, gossiping and laughing and fussing, walking after each other to the head of the stairs, peering down over the banisters and calling down to Lily to ask her who had come.

It was always a great affair, the Misses Morkan's annual dance. Everybody who knew them came to it, members of the family, old friends of the family, the members of Julia's choir, any of Kate's pupils that were grown up enough, and even some of Mary Jane's pupils too. Never once had it fallen flat. For years and years it had gone off in splendid style, as long as anyone could remember; ever since Kate and Julia, after the death of their brother Pat, had left the house in Stoney Batter and taken Mary Jane, their only niece, to live with them in the dark, gaunt house on Usher's Island, the upper part of which they had rented from Mr. Fulham, the corn-factor on the ground floor. That was a good thirty years ago if it was a day. Mary Jane, who was then a little girl in short clothes, was now the main prop of the household, for she had the organ in Haddington Road. She had been through the Academy and gave a pupils' concert every year in the upper room of the Antient Concert Rooms. Many of her pupils belonged to the better-class families on the Kingstown and Dalkey line. Old as they were, her aunts also did their share. Julia, though she was quite grey, was still the leading soprano in Adam and Eve's, and Kate, being too feeble to go about much, gave music lessons to beginners on the old square piano in the back room. Lily, the caretaker's daughter, did housemaid's work for them. Though their life was modest, they believed in eating well; the best of everything: diamond-bone sirloins, three shilling tea and the best bottled stout. But Lily seldom made a mistake in the orders, so that she got on well with her three mistresses. They were fussy, that was all. But the only thing they would not stand was back answers.

Of course, they had good reason to be fussy on such a night. And then it was long after ten o'clock and yet there was no sign of Gabriel and his wife. Besides they were dreadfully afraid that Freddy Malins might turn up screwed. They would not wish for worlds that any of Mary Jane's pupils should see him under the influence; and when he was like that it was sometimes very hard to manage him. Freddy Malins always came late, but they wondered what could be keeping Gabriel: and that was what brought them every two minutes to the banisters to ask Lily had Gabriel or Freddy come.

"O, Mr. Conroy," said Lily to Gabriel when she opened the door for him, "Miss Kate and Miss Julia thought you were never coming. Good-night, Mrs. Conroy."

"I'll engage they did," said Gabriel, "but they forget that my wife here takes three mortal hours to dress herself."

He stood on the mat, scraping the snow from his goloshes, while Lily led his wife to the foot of the stairs and called out:

"Miss Kate, here's Mrs. Conroy."

Kate and Julia came toddling down the dark stairs at once. Both of them kissed Gabriel's wife, said she must be perished alive, and asked was Gabriel with her.

"Here I am as right as the mail, Aunt Kate! Go on up. I'll follow," called out Gabriel from the dark.

He continued scraping his feet vigorously while the three women went upstairs, laughing, to the ladies' dressing-room. A light fringe of snow lay like a cape on the shoulders of his overcoat and like toecaps on the toes of his goloshes; and, as the buttons of his overcoat slipped with a squeaking noise through the snow-stiffened frieze, a cold, fragrant air from out-of-doors escaped from crevices and folds.

"Is it snowing again, Mr. Conroy?" asked Lily.

She had preceded him into the pantry to help him off with his overcoat. Gabriel smiled at the three syllables she had given his surname and glanced at her. She was a slim, growing girl, pale in complexion and with hay-coloured hair. The gas in the pantry made her look still paler. Gabriel had known her when she was a child and used to sit on the lowest step nursing a rag doll.

"Yes, Lily," he answered, "and I think we're in for a night of it."

He looked up at the pantry ceiling, which was shaking with the stamping and shuffling of feet on the floor above, listened for a moment to the piano and then glanced at the girl, who was folding his overcoat carefully at the end of a shelf.

"Tell me, Lily," he said in a friendly tone, "do you still go to school?"

"O no, sir," she answered. "I'm done schooling this year and more."

"O, then," said Gabriel gaily, "I suppose we'll be going to your wedding one of these fine days with your young man, eh?"

The girl glanced back at him over her shoulder and said with great bitterness:

"The men that is now is only all palaver and what they can get out of you."

Gabriel coloured, as if he felt he had made a mistake and, without looking at her, kicked off his goloshes and flicked actively with his muffler at his patent-leather shoes.

He was a stout, tallish young man. The high colour of his cheeks pushed upwards even to his forehead, where it scattered itself in a few formless patches of pale red; and on his hairless face there scintillated restlessly the polished lenses and the bright gilt rims of the glasses which screened his delicate and restless eyes. His glossy black hair was parted in the middle and brushed in a long curve behind his ears where it curled slightly beneath the groove left by his hat.

When he had flicked lustre into his shoes he stood up and pulled his waist-coat down more tightly on his plump body. Then he took a coin rapidly from his pocket.

"O Lily," he said, thrusting it into her hands, "it's Christmas-time, isn't it? Just . . . here's a little. . . ."

He walked rapidly towards the door.

"O no, sir!" cried the girl, following him. "Really, sir, I wouldn't take it."

"Christmas-time! Christmas-time!" said Gabriel, almost trotting to the stairs and waving his hand to her in deprecation.

The girl, seeing that he had gained the stairs, called out after him:

"Well, thank you, sir."

He waited outside the drawing-room door until the waltz should finish, listening to the skirts that swept against it and to the shuffling of feet. He was still discomposed by the girl's bitter and sudden retort. It had cast a gloom over him which he tried to dispel by arranging his cuffs and the bows of his tie. He then took from his waistcoat pocket a little paper and glanced at the headings he had made for his speech. He was undecided about the lines from Robert Browning, for he feared they would be above the heads of his hearers. Some quotation that they would recognise from Shakespeare or from the Melodies[1] would be better. The indelicate clacking of the men's heels and the shuffling of their soles reminded him that their grade of culture differed from his. He would only make himself ridiculous by quoting poetry to them which they could not understand. They would think that he was airing his superior education. He would fail with them just as he had failed with the girl in the pantry. He had taken up a wrong tone. His whole speech was a mistake from first to last, an utter failure.

Just then his aunts and his wife came out of the ladies' dressing-room. His aunts were two small, plainly dressed old women. Aunt Julia was an inch or so the taller. Her hair, drawn low over the tops of her ears, was grey; and grey also, with darker shadows, was her large flaccid face. Though she was stout in build and

___

[1] The *Irish Melodies* of Thomas Moore (1779–1852).

stood erect, her slow eyes and parted lips gave her the appearance of a woman who did not know where she was or where she was going. Aunt Kate was more vivacious. Her face, healthier than her sister's, was all puckers and creases, like a shrivelled red apple, and her hair, braided in the same old-fashioned way, had not lost its ripe nut colour.

They both kissed Gabriel frankly. He was their favourite nephew, the son of their dead elder sister, Ellen, who had married T. J. Conroy of the Port and Docks.

"Gretta tells me you're not going to take a cab back to Monkstown to-night, Gabriel," said Aunt Kate.

"No," said Gabriel, turning to his wife, "we had quite enough of that last year, hadn't we? Don't you remember, Aunt Kate, what a cold Gretta got out of it? Cab windows rattling all the way, and the east wind blowing in after we passed Merrion. Very jolly it was. Gretta caught a dreadful cold."

Aunt Kate frowned severely and nodded her head at every word.

"Quite right, Gabriel, quite right," she said. "You can't be too careful."

"But as for Gretta there," said Gabriel, "she'd walk home in the snow if she were let."

Mrs. Conroy laughed.

"Don't mind him, Aunt Kate," she said. "He's really an awful bother, what with green shades for Tom's eyes at night and making him do the dumb-bells, and forcing Eva to eat the stirabout.[2] The poor child! And she simply hates the sight of it! . . . O, but you'll never guess what he makes me wear now!"

She broke out into a peal of laughter and glanced at her husband, whose admiring and happy eyes had been wandering from her dress to her face and hair. The two aunts laughed heartily, too, for Gabriel's solicitude was a standing joke with them.

"Goloshes!" said Mrs. Conroy. "That's the latest. Whenever it's wet underfoot I must put on my goloshes. To-night even, he wanted me to put them on, but I wouldn't. The next thing he'll buy me will be a diving suit."

Gabriel laughed nervously and patted his tie reassuringly, while Aunt Kate nearly doubled herself, so heartily did she enjoy the joke. The smile soon faded from Aunt Julia's face and her mirthless eyes were directed towards her nephew's face. After a pause she asked:

"And what are goloshes, Gabriel?"

"Goloshes, Julia!" exclaimed her sister. "Goodness me, don't you know what goloshes are? You wear them over your . . . over your boots, Gretta, isn't it?"

"Yes," said Mrs. Conroy. "Guttapercha[3] things. We both have a pair now. Gabriel says everyone wears them on the Continent."

"O, on the Continent," murmured Aunt Julia, nodding her head slowly.

Gabriel knitted his brows and said, as if he were slightly angered:

"It's nothing very wonderful, but Gretta thinks it very funny because she says the word reminds her of Christy Minstrels."[4]

"But tell me, Gabriel," said Aunt Kate, with brisk tact. "Of course, you've seen about the room. Gretta was saying . . ."

"O, the room is all right," replied Gabriel. "I've taken one in the Gresham."

2 Oatmeal or other porridge.
3 A gray to brown tough substance resembling rubber.
4 A troupe of American Negro minstrels organized about 1860 by Edwin P. Christy.

"To be sure," said Aunt Kate, "by far the best thing to do. And the children, Gretta, you're not anxious about them?"

"O, for one night," said Mrs. Conroy. "Besides, Bessie will look after them."

"To be sure," said Aunt Kate again. "What a comfort it is to have a girl like that, one you can depend on! There's that Lily, I'm sure I don't know what has come over her lately. She's not the girl she was at all."

Gabriel was about to ask his aunt some questions on this point, but she broke off suddenly to gaze after her sister, who had wandered down the stairs and was craning her neck over the banisters.

"Now, I ask you," she said almost testily, "where is Julia going? Julia! Julia! Where are you going?"

Julia, who had gone half way down one flight, came back and announced blandly:

"Here's Freddy."

At the same moment a clapping of hands and a final flourish of the pianist told that the waltz had ended. The drawing-room door was opened from within and some couples came out. Aunt Kate drew Gabriel aside hurriedly and whispered into his ear:

"Slip down, Gabriel, like a good fellow and see if he's all right, and don't let him up if he's screwed. I'm sure he's screwed. I'm sure he is."

Gabriel went to the stairs and listened over the banisters. He could hear two persons talking in the pantry. Then he recognised Freddy Malins' laugh. He went down the stairs noisily.

"It's such a relief," said Aunt Kate to Mrs. Conroy, "that Gabriel is here. I always feel easier in my mind when he's here. . . . Julia, there's Miss Daly and Miss Power will take some refreshment. Thanks for your beautiful waltz, Miss Daly. It made lovely time."

A tall wizen-faced man, with a stiff grizzled moustache and swarthy skin, who was passing out with his partner, said:

"And may we have some refreshment, too, Miss Morkan?"

"Julia," said Aunt Kate summarily, "and here's Mr. Browne and Miss Furlong. Take them in, Julia, with Miss Daly and Miss Power."

"I'm the man for the ladies," said Mr. Browne, pursing his lips until his moustache bristled and smiling in all his wrinkles. "You know, Miss Morkan, the reason they are so fond of me is—"

He did not finish his sentence, but, seeing that Aunt Kate was out of earshot, at once led the three young ladies into the back room. The middle of the room was occupied by two square tables placed end to end, and on these Aunt Julia and the caretaker were straightening and smoothing a large cloth. On the sideboard were arrayed dishes and plates, and glasses and bundles of knives and forks and spoons. The top of the closed square piano served also as a sideboard for viands and sweets. At a smaller sideboard in one corner two young men were standing, drinking hop-bitters.

Mr. Browne led his charges thither and invited them all, in jest, to some ladies' punch, hot, strong and sweet. As they said they never took anything strong, he opened three bottles of lemonade for them. Then he asked one of the young men to move aside, and taking hold of the decanter, filled out for himself a goodly measure of whisky. The young men eyed him respectfully while he took a trial sip.

"God help me," he said, smiling, "it's the doctor's orders."

His wizened face broke into a broader smile, and the three young ladies laughed in musical echo to his pleasantry, swaying their bodies to and fro, with nervous jerks of their shoulders. The boldest said:

"O, now, Mr. Browne, I'm sure the doctor never ordered anything of the kind."

Mr. Browne took another sip of his whisky and said, with sidling mimicry:

"Well, you see, I'm like the famous Mrs. Cassidy, who is reported to have said: 'Now, Mary Grimes, if I don't take it, make me take it, for I feel I want it.'"

His hot face had leaned forward a little too confidentially and he had assumed a very low Dublin accent so that the young ladies, with one instinct, received his speech in silence. Miss Furlong, who was one of Mary Jane's pupils, asked Miss Daly what was the name of the pretty waltz she had played; and Mr. Browne, seeing that he was ignored, turned promptly to the two young men who were more appreciative.

A red-faced young woman, dressed in pansy, came into the room, excitedly clapping her hands and crying:

"Quadrilles! Quadrilles!"

Close on her heels came Aunt Kate, crying:

"Two gentlemen and three ladies, Mary Jane!"

"O, here's Mr. Bergin and Mr. Kerrigan," said Mary Jane. "Mr. Kerrigan, will you take Miss Power? Miss Furlong, may I get you a partner, Mr. Bergin. O, that'll just do now."

"Three ladies, Mary Jane," said Aunt Kate.

The two young gentlemen asked the ladies if they might have the pleasure, and Mary Jane turned to Miss Daly.

"O, Miss Daly, you're really awfully good, after playing for the last two dances, but really we're so short of ladies to-night."

"I don't mind in the least, Miss Morkan."

"But I've a nice partner for you, Mr. Bartell D'Arcy, the tenor. I'll get him to sing later on. All Dublin is raving about him."

"Lovely voice, lovely voice!" said Aunt Kate.

As the piano had twice begun the prelude to the first figure Mary Jane led her recruits quickly from the room. They had hardly gone when Aunt Julia wandered slowly into the room, looking behind her at something.

"What is the matter, Julia?" asked Aunt Kate anxiously. "Who is it?"

Julia, who was carrying in a column of table-napkins, turned to her sister and said, simply, as if the question had surprised her:

"It's only Freddy, Kate, and Gabriel with him."

In fact right behind her Gabriel could be seen piloting Freddy Malins across the landing. The latter, a young man of about forty, was of Gabriel's size and build, with very round shoulders. His face was fleshy and pallid, touched with colour only at the thick hanging lobes of his ears and at the wide wings of his nose. He had coarse features, a blunt nose, a convex and receding brow, tumid and protruded lips. His heavy-lidded eyes and the disorder of his scanty hair made him look sleepy. He was laughing heartily in a high key at a story which he had been telling Gabriel on the stairs and at the same time rubbing the knuckles of his left fist backwards and forwards into his left eye.

"Good-evening, Freddy," said Aunt Julia.

Freddy Malins bade the Misses Morkan good-evening in what seemed an offhand fashion by reason of the habitual catch in his voice and then, seeing that Mr. Browne was grinning at him from the sideboard, crossed the room on rather shaky legs and began to repeat in an undertone the story he had just told to Gabriel.

"He's not so bad, is he?" said Aunt Kate to Gabriel.

Gabriel's brows were dark but he raised them quickly and answered:

"O, no, hardly noticeable."

"Now, isn't he a terrible fellow!" she said. "And his poor mother made him take the pledge on New Year's Eve. But come on, Gabriel, into the drawing-room."

Before leaving the room with Gabriel she signalled to Mr. Browne by frowning and shaking her forefinger in warning to and fro. Mr. Browne nodded in answer and, when she had gone, said to Freddy Malins:

"Now, then, Teddy, I'm going to fill you out a good glass of lemonade just to buck you up."

Freddy Malins, who was nearing the climax of his story, waved the offer aside impatiently but Mr. Browne, having first called Freddy Malins' attention to a disarray in his dress, filled out and handed him a full glass of lemonade. Freddy Malins' left hand accepted the glass mechanically, his right hand being engaged in the mechanical readjustment of his dress. Mr. Browne, whose face was once more wrinkling with mirth, poured out for himself a glass of whisky while Freddy Malins exploded, before he had well reached the climax of his story, in a kink of high-pitched bronchitic laughter and, setting down his untasted and overflowing glass, began to rub the knuckles of his left fist backwards and forwards into his left eye, repeating words of his last phrase as well as his fit of laughter would allow him.

. . . .

Gabriel could not listen while Mary Jane was playing her Academy piece, full of runs and difficult passages, to the hushed drawing-room. He liked music but the piece she was playing had no melody for him and he doubted whether it had any melody for the other listeners, though they had begged Mary Jane to play something. Four young men, who had come from the refreshment-room to stand in the doorway at the sound of the piano, had gone away quietly in couples after a few minutes. The only persons who seemed to follow the music were Mary Jane herself, her hands racing along the key-board or lifted from it at the pauses like those of a priestess in momentary imprecation, and Aunt Kate standing at her elbow to turn the page.

Gabriel's eyes, irritated by the floor, which glittered with beeswax under the heavy chandelier, wandered to the wall above the piano. A picture of the balcony scene in *Romeo and Juliet* hung there and beside it was a picture of the two murdered princes in the Tower which Aunt Julia had worked in red, blue and brown wools when she was a girl. Probably in the school they had gone to as girls that kind of work had been taught for one year. His mother had worked for him as a birthday present a waistcoat of purple tabinet,[5] with little foxes' heads upon it, lined with brown satin and having round mulberry buttons. It was strange that his mother had had no musical talent though Aunt Kate used to call her the brains

[5] A watered fabric of silk and wool resembling poplin.

carrier of the Morkan family. Both she and Julia had always seemed a little proud of their serious and matronly sister. Her photograph stood before the pierglass. She held an open book on her knees and was pointing out something in it to Constantine who, dressed in a man-o'-war suit, lay at her feet. It was she who had chosen the names of her sons for she was very sensible of the dignity of family life. Thanks to her, Constantine was now senior curate in Balbriggan and, thanks to her, Gabriel himself had taken his degree in the Royal University. A shadow passed over his face as he remembered her sullen opposition to his marriage. Some slighting phrases she had used still rankled in his memory; she had once spoken of Gretta as being country cute and that was not true of Gretta at all. It was Gretta who had nursed her during all her last long illness in their house at Monkstown.

He knew that Mary Jane must be near the end of her piece for she was playing again the opening melody with runs of scales after every bar and while he waited for the end the resentment died down in his heart. The piece ended with a trill of octaves in the treble and a final deep octave in the bass. Great applause greeted Mary Jane as, blushing and rolling up her music nervously, she escaped from the room. The most vigorous clapping came from the four young men in the doorway who had gone away to the refreshment-room at the beginning of the piece but had come back when the piano had stopped.

Lancers were arranged. Gabriel found himself partnered with Miss Ivors. She was a frank-mannered talkative young lady, with a freckled face and prominent brown eyes. She did not wear a low-cut bodice and the large brooch which was fixed in the front of her collar bore on it an Irish device and motto.

When they had taken their places she said abruptly:

"I have a crow to pluck with you."

"With me?" said Gabriel.

She nodded her head gravely.

"What is it?" asked Gabriel, smiling at her solemn manner.

"Who is G. C.?" answered Miss Ivors, turning her eyes upon him.

Gabriel coloured and was about to knit his brows, as if he did not understand, when she said bluntly:

"O, innocent Amy! I have found out that you write for *The Daily Express.* Now, aren't you ashamed of yourself?"

"Why should I be ashamed of myself?" asked Gabriel, blinking his eyes and trying to smile.

"Well, I'm ashamed of you," said Miss Ivors frankly. "To say you'd write for a paper like that. I didn't think you were a West Briton."[6]

A look of perplexity appeared on Gabriel's face. It was true that he wrote a literary column every Wednesday in *The Daily Express,* for which he was paid fifteen shillings. But that did not make him a West Briton surely. The books he received for review were almost more welcome than the paltry cheque. He loved to feel the covers and turn over the pages of newly printed books. Nearly every day when his teaching in the college was ended he used to wander down the quays to the second-hand booksellers, to Hickey's on Bachelor's Walk, to Webb's or Massey's on Aston's Quay, or to O'Clohissey's in the by-street. He did not know how to meet her charge. He wanted to say that literature was above politics. But

[6] An Irishman devoted to the English interest.

they were friends of many years' standing and their careers had been parallel, first at the University and then as teachers: he could not risk a grandiose phrase with her. He continued blinking his eyes and trying to smile and murmured lamely that he saw nothing political in writing reviews of books.

When their turn to cross had come he was still perplexed and inattentive. Miss Ivors promptly took his hand in a warm grasp and said in a soft friendly tone:

"Of course, I was only joking. Come, we cross now."

When they were together again she spoke of the University question and Gabriel felt more at ease. A friend of hers had shown her his review of Browning's poems. That was how she had found out the secret: but she liked the review immensely. Then she said suddenly:

"O, Mr. Conroy, will you come for an excursion to the Aran Isles this summer? We're going to stay there a whole month. It will be splendid out in the Atlantic. You ought to come. Mr. Clancy is coming, and Mr. Kilkelly and Kathleen Kearney. It would be splendid for Gretta too if she'd come. She's from Connacht, isn't she?"

"Her people are," said Gabriel shortly.

"But you will come, won't you?" said Miss Ivors, laying her warm hand eagerly on his arm.

"The fact is," said Gabriel, "I have just arranged to go——"

"Go where?" asked Miss Ivors.

"Well, you know, every year I go for a cycling tour with some fellows and so——"

"But where?" asked Miss Ivors.

"Well, we usually go to France or Belgium or perhaps Germany," said Gabriel awkwardly.

"And why do you go to France and Belgium," said Miss Ivors, "instead of visiting your own land?"

"Well," said Gabriel, "it's partly to keep in touch with the languages and partly for a change."

"And haven't you your own language to keep in touch with—Irish?" asked Miss Ivors.

"Well," said Gabriel, "if it comes to that, you know, Irish is not my language."

Their neighbours had turned to listen to the cross-examination. Gabriel glanced right and left nervously and tried to keep his good humour under the ordeal which was making a blush invade his forehead.

"And haven't you your own land to visit," continued Miss Ivors, "that you know nothing of, your own people, and your own country?"

"O, to tell you the truth," retorted Gabriel suddenly, "I'm sick of my own country, sick of it!"

"Why?" asked Miss Ivors.

Gabriel did not answer for his retort had heated him.

"Why?" repeated Miss Ivors.

They had to go visiting together and, as he had not answered her, Miss Ivors said warmly:

"Of course, you've no answer."

Gabriel tried to cover his agitation by taking part in the dance with great energy. He avoided her eyes for he had seen a sour expression on her face. But when they met in the long chain he was surprised to feel his hand firmly pressed. She looked at him from under her brows for a moment quizzically until he smiled. Then, just as the chain was about to start again, she stood on tiptoe and whispered into his ear:

"West Briton!"

When the lancers were over Gabriel went away to a remote corner of the room where Freddy Malin's mother was sitting. She was a stout feeble old woman with white hair. Her voice had a catch in it like her son's and she stuttered slightly. She had been told that Freddy had come and that he was nearly all right. Gabriel asked her whether she had had a good crossing. She lived with her married daughter in Glasgow and came to Dublin on a visit once a year. She answered placidly that she had had a beautiful crossing and that the captain had been most attentive to her. She spoke also of the beautiful house her daughter kept in Glasgow, and of all the friends they had there. While her tongue rambled on Gabriel tried to banish from his mind all memory of the unpleasant incident with Miss Ivors. Of course the girl or woman, or whatever she was, was an enthusiast but there was a time for all things. Perhaps he ought not to have answered her like that. But she had no right to call him a West Briton before people, even in joke. She had tried to make him ridiculous before people, heckling him and staring at him with her rabbit's eyes.

He saw his wife making her way towards him through the waltzing couples. When she reached him she said into his ear:

"Gabriel, Aunt Kate wants to know won't you carve the goose as usual. Miss Daly will carve the ham and I'll do the pudding."

"All right," said Gabriel.

"She's sending in the younger ones first as soon as this waltz is over so that we'll have the table to ourselves."

"Were you dancing?" asked Gabriel.

"Of course I was. Didn't you see me? What row had you with Molly Ivors?"

"No row. Why? Did she say so?"

"Something like that. I'm trying to get that Mr. D'Arcy to sing. He's full of conceit, I think."

"There was no row," said Gabriel moodily, "only she wanted me to go for a trip to the west of Ireland and I said I wouldn't."

His wife clasped her hands excitedly and gave a little jump.

"O, do go, Gabriel," she cried. "I'd love to see Galway again."

"You can go if you like," said Gabriel coldly.

She looked at him for a moment, then turned to Mrs. Malins and said:

"There's a nice husband for you, Mrs. Malins."

While she was threading her way back across the room Mrs. Malins, without adverting to the interruption, went on to tell Gabriel what beautiful places there were in Scotland and beautiful scenery. Her son-in-law brought them every year to the lakes and they used to go fishing. Her son-in-law was a splendid fisher. One day he caught a beautiful big fish and the man in the hotel cooked it for their dinner.

Gabriel hardly heard what she said. Now that supper was coming near he began to think again about his speech and about the quotation. When he saw Freddy Malins coming across the room to visit his mother Gabriel left the chair free for him and retired into the embrasure of the window. The room had already cleared and from the back room came the clatter of plates and knives. Those who still remained in the drawing-room seemed tired of dancing and were conversing quietly in little groups. Gabriel's warm trembling fingers tapped the cold pane of the window. How cool it must be outside! How pleasant it would be to walk out alone, first along by the river and then through the park! The snow would be lying on the branches of the trees and forming a bright cap on the top of the Wellington Monument. How much more pleasant it would be there than at the supper-table!

He ran over the headings of his speech: Irish hospitality, sad memories, the Three Graces,[7] Paris,[8] the quotation from Browning. He repeated to himself a phrase he had written in his review: "One feels that one is listening to a thought-tormented music." Miss Ivors had praised the review. Was she sincere? Had she really any life of her own behind all her propagandism? There had never been any ill-feeling between them until that night. It unnerved him to think that she would be at the supper-table, looking up at him while he spoke with her critical quizzing eyes. Perhaps she would not be sorry to see him fail in his speech. An idea came into his mind and gave him courage. He would say, alluding to Aunt Kate and Aunt Julia: "Ladies and Gentlemen, the generation which is now on the wane among us may have had its faults but for my part I think it had certain qualities of hospitality, of humour, of humanity, which the new and very serious and hypereducated generation that is growing up around us seems to me to lack." Very good: that was one for Miss Ivors. What did he care that his aunts were only two ignorant old women?

A murmur in the room attracted his attention. Mr. Browne was advancing from the door, gallantly escorting Aunt Julia, who leaned upon his arm, smiling and hanging her head. An irregular musketry of applause escorted her also as far as the piano and then, as Mary Jane seated herself on the stool, and Aunt Julia, no longer smiling, half turned so as to pitch her voice fairly into the room, gradually ceased. Gabriel recognised the prelude. It was that of an old song of Aunt Julia's—*Arrayed for the Bridal*. Her voice, strong and clear in tone, attacked with great spirit the runs which embellish the air and though she sang very rapidly she did not miss even the smallest of the grace notes. To follow the voice, without looking at the singer's face, was to feel and share the excitement of swift and secure flight. Gabriel applauded loudly with all the others at the close of the song and loud applause was borne in from the invisible supper-table. It sounded so genuine that a little colour struggled into Aunt Julia's face as she bent to replace in the music-stand the old leather-bound song-book that had her initials on the cover. Freddy Malins, who had listened with his head perched sideways to hear her better, was still applauding when everyone else had ceased and talking animatedly to his mother who nodded her head gravely and slowly in acquiescence. At last, when he could clap no more, he stood up suddenly and hurried across the room to Aunt Julia whose hand he seized and held in both his hands, shaking it when words failed him or the catch in his voice proved too much for him.

"I was just telling my mother," he said, "I never heard you sing so well, never. No, I never heard your voice so good as it is to-night. Now! Would you believe

---

[7] In Roman mythology, goddesses who embodied beauty and charm.
[8] In Greek legend, the son of Priam, king of Troy, and through his abduction of Helen, the cause of the Trojan War.

that now? That's the truth. Upon my word and honour that's the truth. I never heard your voice sound so fresh and so . . . so clear and fresh, never."

Aunt Julia smiled broadly and murmured something about compliments as she released her hand from his grasp. Mr. Browne extended his open hand towards her and said to those who were near him in the manner of a showman introducing a prodigy to an audience:

"Miss Julia Morkan, my latest discovery!"

He was laughing very heartily at this himself when Freddy Malins turned to him and said:

"Well, Browne, if you're serious you might make a worse discovery. All I can say is I never heard her sing half so well as long as I am coming here. And that's the honest truth."

"Neither did I," said Mr. Browne. "I think her voice has greatly improved."

Aunt Julia shrugged her shoulders and said with meek pride:

"Thirty years ago I hadn't a bad voice as voices go."

"I often told Julia," said Aunt Kate emphatically, "that she was simply thrown away in that choir. But she never would be said by me."

She turned as if to appeal to the good sense of the others against a refractory child while Aunt Julia gazed in front of her, a vague smile of reminiscence playing on her face.

"No," continued Aunt Kate, "she wouldn't be said or led by anyone, slaving there in that choir night and day, night and day. Six o'clock on Christmas morning! And all for what?"

"Well, isn't it for the honour of God, Aunt Kate?" asked Mary Jane, twisting round on the piano-stool and smiling.

Aunt Kate turned fiercely on her niece and said:

"I know all about the honour of God, Mary Jane, but I think it's not at all honourable for the pope to turn out the women out of the choirs that have slaved there all their lives and put little whipper-snappers of boys over their heads. I suppose it is for the good of the Church if the pope does it. But it's not just, Mary Jane, and it's not right."

She had worked herself into a passion and would have continued in defence of her sister for it was a sore subject with her but Mary Jane, seeing that all the dancers had come back, intervened pacifically:

"Now, Aunt Kate, you're giving scandal to Mr. Browne who is of the other persuasion."

Aunt Kate turned to Mr. Browne, who was grinning at this allusion to his religion, and said hastily:

"O, I don't question the pope's being right. I'm only a stupid old woman and I wouldn't presume to do such a thing. But there's such a thing as common everyday politeness and gratitude. And if I were in Julia's place I'd tell that Father Healey straight up to his face . . ."

"And besides, Aunt Kate," said Mary Jane, "we really are all hungry and when we are hungry we are all very quarrelsome."

"And when we are thirsty we are also quarrelsome," added Mr. Browne.

"So that we had better go to supper," said Mary Jane, "and finish the discussion afterwards."

On the landing outside the drawing-room Gabriel found his wife and Mary Jane trying to persuade Miss Ivors to stay for supper. But Miss Ivors, who had put on her hat and was buttoning her cloak, would not stay. She did not feel in the least hungry and she had already overstayed her time.

"But only for ten minutes, Molly," said Mrs. Conroy. "That won't delay you."

"To take a pick itself," said Mary Jane, "after all your dancing."

"I really couldn't," said Miss Ivors.

"I am afraid you didn't enjoy yourself at all," said Mary Jane hopelessly.

"Ever so much, I assure you," said Miss Ivors, "but you really must let me run off now."

"But how can you get home?" asked Mrs. Conroy.

"O, it's only two steps up the quay."

Gabriel hesitated a moment and said:

"If you will allow me, Miss Ivors, I'll see you home if you are really obliged to go."

But Miss Ivors broke away from them.

"I won't hear of it," she cried. "For goodness' sake go in to your suppers and don't mind me. I'm quite well able to take care of myself."

"Well, you're the comical girl, Molly," said Mrs. Conroy frankly.

"*Beannacht libh*,"[9] cried Miss Ivors, with a laugh, as she ran down the staircase.

Mary Jane gazed after her, a moody puzzled expression on her face, while Mrs. Conroy leaned over the banisters to listen for the hall-door. Gabriel asked himself was he the cause of her abrupt departure. But she did not seem to be in ill humour: she had gone away laughing. He stared blankly down the staircase.

At the moment Aunt Kate came toddling out of the supper-room, almost wringing her hands in despair.

"Where is Gabriel?" she cried. "Where on earth is Gabriel? There's everyone waiting in there, stage to let, and nobody to carve the goose!"

"Here I am, Aunt Kate!" cried Gabriel, with sudden animation, "ready to carve a flock of geese, if necessary."

A fat brown goose lay at one end of the table and at the other end, on a bed of creased paper strewn with sprigs of parsley, lay a great ham, stripped of its outer skin and peppered over with crust crumbs, a neat paper frill round its shin and beside this was a round of spiced beef. Between these rival ends ran parallel lines of side-dishes: two little minsters of jelly, red and yellow; a shallow dish full of blocks of blancmange and red jam, a large green leaf-shaped dish with a stalk-shaped handle, on which lay bunches of purple raisins and peeled almonds, a companion dish on which lay a solid rectangle of Smyrna figs, a dish of custard topped with grated nutmeg, a small bowl full of chocolates and sweets wrapped in gold and silver papers and a glass vase in which stood some tall celery stalks. In the centre of the table there stood, as sentries to a fruit-stand which upheld a pyramid of oranges and American apples, two squat old-fashioned decanters of cut glass, one containing port and the other dark sherry. On the closed square piano a pudding in a huge yellow dish lay in waiting and behind it were three squads of bottles of stout and ale and minerals, drawn up according to the colours of their uniforms, the first two black, with brown and red labels, the third and smallest squad white, with transverse green sashes.

Gabriel took his seat boldly at the head of the table and, having looked to the

[9] (Irish) Blessings be with you (a form of leave-taking).

edge of the carver, plunged his fork firmly into the goose. He felt quite at ease now for he was an expert carver and liked nothing better than to find himself at the head of a well-laden table.

"Miss Furlong, what shall I send you?" he asked. "A wing or a slice of the breast?"

"Just a small slice of the breast."

"Miss Higgins, what for you?"

"O, anything at all, Mr. Conroy."

While Gabriel and Miss Daly exchanged plates of goose and plates of ham and sliced beef Lily went from guest to guest with a dish of hot floury potatoes wrapped in a white napkin. This was Mary Jane's idea and she had also suggested apple sauce for the goose but Aunt Kate had said that plain roast goose without any apple sauce had always been good enough for her and she hoped she might never eat worse. Mary Jane waited on her pupils and saw that they got the best slices and Aunt Kate and Aunt Julia opened and carried across from the piano bottles of stout and ale for the gentlemen and bottles of minerals for the ladies. There was a great deal of confusion and laughter and noise, the noise of orders and counter-orders, of knives and forks, of corks and glass-stoppers. Gabriel began to carve second helpings as soon as he had finished the first round without serving himself. Everyone protested loudly so that he compromised by taking a long draught of stout for he had found the carving hot work. Mary Jane settled down quietly to her supper but Aunt Kate and Aunt Julia were still toddling round the table, walking on each other's heels, getting in each other's way and giving each other unheeded orders. Mr. Browne begged of them to sit down and eat their suppers and so did Gabriel but they said there was time enough, so that, at last, Freddy Malins stood up and, capturing Aunt Kate, plumped her down on her chair amid general laughter.

When everyone had been well served Gabriel said, smiling:

"Now, if anyone wants a little more of what vulgar people call stuffing let him or her speak."

A chorus of voices invited him to begin his own supper and Lily came forward with three potatoes which she had reserved for him.

"Very well," said Gabriel amiably, as he took another preparatory draught, "kindly forget my existence, ladies and gentlemen, for a few minutes."

He set to his supper and took no part in the conversation with which the table covered Lily's removal of the plates. The subject of talk was the opera company which was then at the Theatre Royal. Mr. Bartell D'Arcy, the tenor, a dark-complexioned young man with a smart moustache, praised very highly the leading contralto of the company but Miss Furlong thought she had a rather vulgar style of production. Freddy Malins said there was a Negro chieftain singing in the second part of the Gaiety pantomime who had one of the finest tenor voices he had ever heard.

"Have you heard him?" he asked Mr. Bartell D'Arcy across the table.

"No," answered Mr. Bartell D'Arcy carelessly.

"Because," Freddy Malins explained, "now I'd be curious to hear your opinion of him. I think he has a grand voice."

"It takes Teddy to find out the really good things," said Mr. Browne familiarly to the table.

"And why couldn't he have a voice too?" asked Freddy Malins sharply. "Is it because he's only a black?"

Nobody answered this question and Mary Jane led the table back to the legitimate opera. One of her pupils had given her a pass for *Mignon*. Of course it was very fine, she said, but it made her think of poor Georgina Burns. Mr. Browne could go back farther still, to the old Italian companies that used to come to Dublin—Tietjens, Ilma de Murzka, Campanini, the great Trebelli, Giuglini, Ravelli, Aramburo. Those were the days, he said, when there was something like singing to be heard in Dublin. He told too of how the top gallery of the old Royal used to be packed night after night, of how one night an Italian tenor had sung five encores to *Let me like a Soldier fall*, introducing a high C every time and of how the gallery boys would sometimes in their enthusiasm unyoke the horses from the carriage of some great *prima donna* and pull her themselves through the streets to her hotel. Why did they never play the grand old operas now, he asked, *Dinorah, Lucrezia Borgia?* Because they could not get the voices to sing them: that was why.

"O, well," said Mr. Bartell D'Arcy, "I presume there are as good singers to-day as there were then."

"Where are they?" asked Mr. Browne defiantly.

"In London, Paris, Milan," said Mr. Bartell D'Arcy warmly. "I suppose Caruso, for example, is quite as good, if not better than any of the men you have mentioned."

"Maybe so," said Mr. Browne. "But I may tell you I doubt it strongly."

"O, I'd give anything to hear Caruso sing," said Mary Jane.

"For me," said Aunt Kate, who had been picking a bone, "there was only one tenor. To please me, I mean. But I suppose none of you ever heard of him."

"Who was he, Miss Morkan?" asked Mr. Bartell D'Arcy politely.

"His name," said Aunt Kate, "was Parkinson. I heard him when he was in his prime and I think he had then the purest tenor voice that was ever put into a man's throat."

"Strange," said Mr. Bartell D'Arcy. "I never even heard of him."

"Yes, yes, Miss Morkan is right," said Mr. Browne. "I remember hearing of old Parkinson but he's too far back for me."

"A beautiful, pure, sweet, mellow English tenor," said Aunt Kate with enthusiasm.

Gabriel having finished, the huge pudding was transferred to the table. The clatter of forks and spoons began again. Gabriel's wife served out spoonfuls of the pudding and passed the plates down the table. Midway down they were held up by Mary Jane, who replenished them with raspberry or orange jelly or with blancmange and jam. The pudding was of Aunt Julia's making and she received praises for it from all quarters. She herself said that it was not quite brown enough.

"Well, I hope, Miss Morkan," said Mr. Browne, "that I'm brown enough for you because, you know, I'm all brown."

All the gentlemen, except Gabriel, ate some of the pudding out of compliment to Aunt Julia. As Gabriel never ate sweets the celery had been left for him. Freddy Malins also took a stalk of celery and ate it with his pudding. He had been told that celery was a capital thing for the blood and he was just then under doctor's care. Mrs. Malins, who had been silent all through the supper, said that her son was going down to Mount Melleray in a week or so. The table then spoke of

Mount Melleray, how bracing the air was down there, how hospitable the monks were and how they never asked for a penny-piece from their guests.

"And do you mean to say," asked Mr. Browne incredulously, "that a chap can go down there and put up there as if it were a hotel and live on the fat of the land and then come away without paying anything?"

"O, most people give some donation to the monastery when they leave," said Mary Jane.

"I wish we had an institution like that in our Church," said Mr. Browne candidly.

He was astonished to hear that the monks never spoke, got up at two in the morning and slept in their coffins. He asked what they did it for.

"That's the rule of the order," said Aunt Kate firmly.

"Yes, but why?" asked Mr. Browne.

Aunt Kate repeated that it was the rule, that was all. Mr. Browne still seemed not to understand. Freddy Malins explained to him, as best he could, that the monks were trying to make up for the sins committed by all the sinners in the outside world. The explanation was not very clear for Mr. Browne grinned and said:

"I like that idea very much but wouldn't a comfortable spring bed do them as well as a coffin?"

"The coffin," said Mary Jane, "is to remind them of their last end."

As the subject had grown lugubrious it was buried in a silence of the table during which Mrs. Malins could be heard saying to her neighbour in an indistinct undertone:

"They are very good men, the monks, very pious men."

The raisins and almonds and figs and apples and oranges and chocolates and sweets were now passed about the table and Aunt Julia invited all the guests to have either port or sherry. At first Mr. Bartell D'Arcy refused to take either but one of his neighbours nudged him and whispered something to him upon which he allowed his glass to be filled. Gradually as the last glasses were being filled the conversation ceased. A pause followed, broken only by the noise of the wine and by unsettlings of chairs. The Misses Morkan, all three, looked down at the tablecloth. Someone coughed once or twice and then a few gentlemen patted the table gently as a signal for silence. The silence came and Gabriel pushed back his chair and stood up.

The patting at once grew louder in encouragement and then ceased altogether. Gabriel leaned his ten trembling fingers on the tablecloth and smiled nervously at the company. Meeting a row of upturned faces he raised his eyes to the chandelier. The piano was playing a waltz tune and he could hear the skirts sweeping against the drawing-room door. People, perhaps, were standing in the snow on the quay outside, gazing up at the lighted windows and listening to the waltz music. The air was pure there. In the distance lay the park where the trees were weighted with snow. The Wellington Monument wore a gleaming cap of snow that flashed westward over the white field of Fifteen Acres.

He began:

"Ladies and Gentlemen,

"It has fallen to my lot this evening, as in years past, to perform a very pleasing task but a task for which I am afraid my poor powers as a speaker are all too inadequate."

"No, no!" said Mr. Browne.

"But, however that may be, I can only ask you to-night to take the will for the deed and to lend me your attention for a few moments while I endeavour to express to you in words what my feelings are on this occasion.

"Ladies and Gentlemen, it is not the first time that we have gathered together under this hospitable roof, around this hospitable board. It is not the first time that we have been the recipients—or perhaps, I had better say, the victims— of the hospitality of certain good ladies."

He made a circle in the air with his arm and paused. Everyone laughed or smiled at Aunt Kate and Aunt Julia and Mary Jane who all turned crimson with pleasure. Gabriel went on more boldly:

"I feel more strongly with every recurring year that our country has no tradition which does it so much honour and which it should guard so jealously as that of its hospitality. It is a tradition that is unique as far as my experience goes (and I have visited not a few places abroad) among the modern nations. Some would say, perhaps, that with us it is rather a failing than anything to be boasted of. But granted even that, it is, to my mind, a princely failing, and one that I trust will long be cultivated among us. Of one thing, at least, I am sure. As long as this one roof shelters the good ladies aforesaid—and I wish from my heart it may do so for many and many a long year to come—the tradition of genuine warm-hearted courteous Irish hospitality, which our forefathers have handed down to us and which we in turn must hand down to our descendants, is still alive among us."

A hearty murmur of assent ran round the table. It shot through Gabriel's mind that Miss Ivors was not there and that she had gone away discourteously: and he said with confidence in himself:

"Ladies and Gentlemen,

"A new generation is growing up in our midst, a generation actuated by new ideas and new principles. It is serious and enthusiastic for these new ideas and its enthusiasm, even when it is misdirected, is, I believe, in the main sincere. But we are living in a sceptical and, if I may use the phrase, a thought-tormented age: and sometimes I fear that this new generation, educated or hypereducated as it is, will lack those qualities of humanity, of hospitality, of kindly humour which belonged to an older day. Listening tonight to the names of all those great singers of the past it seemed to me, I must confess, that we were living in a less spacious age. Those days might, without exaggeration, be called spacious days: and if they are gone beyond recall let us hope, at least, that in gatherings such as this we shall still speak of them with pride and affection, still cherish in our hearts the memory of those dead and gone great ones whose fame the world will not willingly let die."

"Hear, hear!" said Mr. Browne loudly.

"But yet," continued Gabriel, his voice falling into a softer inflection, "there are always in gatherings such as this sadder thoughts that will recur to our minds: thoughts of the past, of youth, of changes, of absent faces that we miss here to-night. Our path through life is strewn with many such sad memories: and were we to brood upon them always we could not find the heart to go on bravely with our work among the living. We have all of us living duties and living affections which claim, and rightly claim, our strenuous endeavours.

"Therefore, I will not linger on the past. I will not let any gloomy moralising intrude upon us here tonight. Here we are gathered together for a brief moment from the bustle and rush of our everyday routine. We are met here as friends, in the spirit of good-fellowship, as colleagues, also to a certain extent, in the true spirit of *camaraderie*, and as the guests of—what shall I call them?—the Three Graces of the Dublin musical world."

The table burst into applause and laughter at this allusion. Aunt Julia vainly asked each of her neighbours in turn to tell her what Gabriel had said.

"He says we are the Three Graces, Aunt Julia," said Mary Jane.

Aunt Julia did not understand but she looked up, smiling, at Gabriel, who continued in the same vein:

"Ladies and Gentlemen,

"I will not attempt to play tonight the part that Paris played on another occasion. I will not attempt to choose between them.[10] The task would be an invidious one and one beyond my poor powers. For when I view them in turn, whether it be our chief hostess herself, whose good heart, whose too good heart, has become a byword with all who know her, or her sister, who seems to be gifted with perennial youth and whose singing must have been a surprise and a revelation to us all tonight, or, last but not least, when I consider our youngest hostess, talented, cheerful, hard-working and the best of nieces, I confess, Ladies and Gentlemen, that I do not know to which of them I should award the prize."

Gabriel glanced down at his aunts and, seeing the large smile on Aunt Julia's face and the tears which had risen to Aunt Kate's eyes, hastened to his close. He raised his glass of port gallantly, while every member of the company fingered a glass expectantly, and said loudly:

"Let us toast them all three together. Let us drink to their health, wealth, long life, happiness and prosperity and may they long continue to hold the proud and self-won position which they hold in their profession and the position of honour and affection which they hold in our hearts."

All the guests stood up, glass in hand, and turning towards the three seated ladies, sang in unison, with Mr. Brown as leader:

"For they are jolly gay fellows,
For they are jolly gay fellows,
For they are jolly gay fellows,
Which nobody can deny."

Aunt Kate was making frank use of her handkerchief and even Aunt Julia seemed moved. Freddy Malins beat time with his pudding-fork and the singers turned towards one another, as if in melodious conference, while they sang with emphasis:

"Unless he tells a lie,
Unless he tells a lie,"

Then, turning once more towards their hostesses, they sang:

"For they are jolly gay fellows,
For they are jolly gay fellows,
For they are jolly gay fellows,
Which nobody can deny."

[10] The "judgment of Paris" involved not the Graces, but three goddesses, Hera, Aphrodite, and Athene. Paris was asked to choose the fairest.

The acclamation which followed was taken up beyond the door of the supper-room by many of the other guests and renewed time after time, Freddy Malins acting as officer with his fork on high.

The piercing morning air came into the hall where they were standing so that Aunt Kate said:

"Close the door, somebody. Mrs. Malins will get her death of cold."

"Browne is out there, Aunt Kate," said Mary Jane.

"Browne is everywhere," said Aunt Kate, lowering her voice.

Mary Jane laughed at her tone.

"Really," she said archly, "he is very attentive."

"He has been laid on here like the gas," said Aunt Kate in the same tone, "all during the Christmas."

She laughed herself this time good-humouredly and then added quickly:

"But tell him to come in, Mary Jane, and close the door. I hope to goodness he didn't hear me."

At that moment the hall-door was opened and Mr. Browne came in from the doorstep, laughing as if his heart would break. He was dressed in a long green overcoat with mock astrakhan cuffs and collar and wore on his head an oval fur cap. He pointed down the snow-covered quay from where the sound of shrill prolonged whistling was borne in.

"Teddy will have all the cabs in Dublin out," he said.

Gabriel advanced from the little pantry behind the office, struggling into his overcoat and, looking round the hall, said:

"Gretta not down yet?"

"She's getting on her things, Gabriel," said Aunt Kate.

"Who's playing up there?" asked Gabriel.

"Nobody. They're all gone."

"O no, Aunt Kate," said Mary Jane. "Bartell D'Arcy and Miss O'Callaghan aren't gone yet."

"Someone is fooling at the piano anyhow," said Gabriel.

Mary Jane glanced at Gabriel and Mr. Browne and said with a shiver:

"It makes me feel cold to look at you two gentlemen muffled up like that. I wouldn't like to face your journey home at this hour."

"I'd like nothing better this minute," said Mr. Browne stoutly, "than a rattling fine walk in the country or a fast drive with a good spanking goer between the shafts."

"We used to have a very good horse and trap at home," said Aunt Julia sadly.

"The never-to-be-forgotten Johnny," said Mary Jane, laughing.

Aunt Kate and Gabriel laughed too.

"Why, what was wonderful about Johnny?" asked Mr. Browne.

"The late lamented Patrick Morkan, our grandfather, that is," explained Gabriel, "commonly known in his later years as the old gentleman, was a glue-boiler."

"O, now, Gabriel," said Aunt Kate, laughing, "he had a starch mill."

"Well, glue or starch," said Gabriel, "the old gentleman had a horse by the name of Johnny. And Johnny used to work in the old gentleman's mill, walking round and round in order to drive the mill. That was all very well; but now comes the tragic part about Johnny. One fine day the old gentleman thought he'd like to drive out with the quality to a military review in the park."

"The Lord have mercy on his soul," said Aunt Kate compassionately.

"Amen," said Gabriel. "So the old gentleman, as I said, harnessed Johnny and put on his very best tall hat and his very best stock collar and drove out in grand style from his ancestral mansion somewhere near Back Lane, I think."

Everyone laughed, even Mrs. Malins, at Gabriel's manner and Aunt Kate said:

"O, now, Gabriel, he didn't live in Back Lane, really. Only the mill was there."

"Out from the mansion of his forefathers," continued Gabriel, "he drove with Johnny. And everything went on beautifully until Johnny came in sight of King Billy's statue: and whether he fell in love with the horse King Billy sits on or whether he thought he was back again in the mill, anyhow he began to walk round the statue."

Gabriel paced in a circle round the hall in his goloshes amid the laughter of the others.

"Round and round he went," said Gabriel, "and the old gentleman, who was a very pompous old gentleman, was highly indignant. 'Go on, sir! What do you mean, sir? Johnny! Johnny! Most extraordinary conduct! Can't understand the horse!'"

The peal of laughter which followed Gabriel's imitation of the incident was interrupted by a resounding knock at the hall door. Mary Jane ran to open it and let in Freddy Malins. Freddy Malins, with his hat well back on his head and his shoulders humped with cold, was puffing and steaming after his exertions.

"I could only get one cab," he said.

"O, we'll find another along the quay," said Gabriel.

"Yes," said Aunt Kate. "Better not keep Mrs. Malins standing in the draught."

Mrs. Malins was helped down the front steps by her son and Mr. Browne and, after many manœuvres, hoisted into the cab. Freddy Malins clambered in after her and spent a long time settling her on the seat, Mr. Browne helping him with advice. At last she was settled comfortably and Freddy Malins invited Mr. Browne into the cab. There was a good deal of confused talk, and then Mr. Browne got into the cab. The cabman settled his rug over his knees, and bent down for the address. The confusion grew greater and the cabman was directed differently by Freddy Malins and Mr. Browne, each of whom had his head out through a window of the cab. The difficulty was to know where to drop Mr. Browne along the route, and Aunt Kate, Aunt Julia and Mary Jane helped the discussion from the doorstep with cross-directions and contradictions and abundance of laughter. As for Freddy Malins he was speechless with laughter. He popped his head in and out of the window every moment to the great danger of his hat, and told his mother how the discussion was progressing, till at last Mr. Browne shouted to the bewildered cabman above the din of everybody's laughter:

"Do you know Trinity College?"

"Yes, sir," said the cabman.

"Well, drive bang up against Trinity College gates," said Mr. Browne, "and then we'll tell you where to go. You understand now?"

"Yes, sir," said the cabman.

"Make like a bird for Trinity College."

"Right, sir," said the cabman.

The horse was whipped up and the cab rattled off along the quay amid a chorus of laughter and adieus.

Gabriel had not gone to the door with the others. He was in a dark part of the hall gazing up the staircase. A woman was standing near the top of the first flight, in the shadow also. He could not see her face but he could see the terra-cotta and salmon-pink panels of her skirt which the shadow made appear black and white. It was his wife. She was leaning on the banisters, listening to something. Gabriel was surprised at her stillness and strained his ear to listen also. But he could hear little save the noise of laughter and dispute on the front steps, a few chords struck on the piano and a few notes of a man's voice singing.

He stood still in the gloom of the hall, trying to catch the air that the voice was singing and gazing up at his wife. There was grace and mystery in her attitude as if she were a symbol of something. He asked himself what is a woman standing on the stairs in the shadow, listening to distant music, a symbol of. If he were a painter he would paint her in that attitude. Her blue felt hat would show off the bronze of her hair against the darkness and the dark panels of her skirt would show off the light ones. *Distant Music* he would call the picture if he were a painter.

The hall-door was closed; and Aunt Kate, Aunt Julia and Mary Jane came down the hall, still laughing.

"Well, isn't Freddy terrible?" said Mary Jane. "He's really terrible."

Gabriel said nothing but pointed up the stairs towards where his wife was standing. Now that the hall-door was closed the voice and the piano could be heard more clearly. Gabriel held up his hand for them to be silent. The song seemed to be in the old Irish tonality and the singer seemed uncertain both of his words and of his voice. The voice, made plaintive by distance and by the singer's hoarseness, faintly illuminated the cadence of the air with words expressing grief:

> "O, the rain falls on my heavy locks
> And the dew wets my skin,
> My babe lies cold . . ."

"O," exclaimed Mary Jane. "It's Bartell D'Arcy singing and he wouldn't sing all the night. O, I'll get him to sing a song before he goes."

"O, do, Mary Jane," said Aunt Kate.

Mary Jane brushed past the others and ran to the staircase, but before she reached it the singing stopped and the piano was closed abruptly.

"O, what a pity!" she cried. "Is he coming down, Gretta?"

Gabriel heard his wife answer yes and saw her come down towards them. A few steps behind her were Mr. Bartell D'Arcy and Miss O'Callaghan.

"O, Mr. D'Arcy," cried Mary Jane, "it's downright mean of you to break off like that when we were all in raptures listening to you."

"I have been at him all the evening," said Miss O'Callaghan, "and Mrs. Conroy, too, and he told us he had a dreadful cold and couldn't sing."

"O, Mr. D'Arcy," said Aunt Kate, "now that was a great fib to tell."

"Can't you see that I'm as hoarse as a crow?" said Mr. D'Arcy roughly.

He went into the pantry hastily and put on his overcoat. The others, taken aback by his rude speech, could find nothing to say. Aunt Kate wrinkled her brows and made signs to the others to drop the subject. Mr. D'Arcy stood swathing his neck carefully and frowning.

"It's the weather," said Aunt Julia, after a pause.

"Yes, everybody has colds," said Aunt Kate readily, "everybody."

"They say," said Mary Jane, "we haven't had snow like it for thirty years; and I read this morning in the newspapers that the snow is general all over Ireland."

"I love the look of snow," said Aunt Julia sadly.

"So do I," said Miss O'Callaghan. "I think Christmas is never really Christmas unless we have the snow on the ground."

"But poor Mr. D'Arcy doesn't like the snow," said Aunt Kate, smiling.

Mr. D'Arcy came from the pantry, fully swathed and buttoned, and in a repentant tone told them the history of his cold. Everyone gave him advice and said it was a great pity and urged him to be very careful of his throat in the night air. Gabriel watched his wife, who did not join in the conversation. She was standing right under the dusty fanlight and the flame of the gas lit up the rich bronze of her hair, which he had seen her drying at the fire a few days before. She was in the same attitude and seemed unaware of the talk about her. At last she turned towards them and Gabriel saw that there was colour on her cheeks and that her eyes were shining. A sudden tide of joy went leaping out of his heart.

"Mr. D'Arcy," she said, "what is the name of that song you were singing?"

"It's called *The Lass of Aughrim*," said Mr. D'Arcy, "but I couldn't remember it properly. Why? Do you know it?"

"*The Lass of Aughrim*," she repeated. "I couldn't think of the name."

"It's a very nice air," said Mary Jane. "I'm sorry you were not in voice tonight."

"Now, Mary Jane," said Aunt Kate, "don't annoy Mr. D'Arcy. I won't have him annoyed."

Seeing that all were ready to start she shepherded them to the door, where good-night was said:

"Well, good-night, Aunt Kate, and thanks for the pleasant evening."

"Good-night, Gabriel. Good-night, Gretta!"

"Good-night, Aunt Kate, and thanks ever so much. Good-night, Aunt Julia."

"O, good-night. Gretta, I didn't see you."

"Good-night, Mr. D'Arcy. Good-night, Miss O'Callaghan."

"Good-night, Miss Morkan."

"Good-night, again."

"Good-night, all. Safe home."

"Good-night. Good-night."

The morning was still dark. A dull, yellow light brooded over the houses and the river; and the sky seemed to be descending. It was slushy underfoot; and only streaks and patches of snow lay on the roofs, on the parapets of the quay and on the area railings. The lamps were still burning redly in the murky air and, across the river, the palace of the Four Courts stood out menacingly against the heavy sky.

She was walking on before him with Mr. Bartell D'Arcy, her shoes in a brown parcel tucked under one arm and her hands holding her skirt up from the slush. She had no longer any grace of attitude, but Gabriel's eyes were still bright with happiness. The blood went bounding along his veins; and the thoughts went rioting through his brain, proud, joyful, tender, valorous.

She was walking on before him so lightly and so erect that he longed to run after her noiselessly, catch her by the shoulders and say something foolish and affectionate into her ear. She seemed to him so frail that he longed to defend her against something and then to be alone with her. Moments of their secret life together burst like stars upon his memory. A heliotrope envelope was lying beside his breakfast-cup and he was caressing it with his hand. Birds were twittering in the ivy and the sunny web of the curtain was shimmering along the floor: he could not eat for happiness. They were standing on the crowded platform and he was placing a ticket inside the warm palm of her glove. He was standing with her in the cold, looking in through a grated window at a man making bottles in a roaring furnace. It was very cold. Her face, fragrant in the cold air, was quite close to his; and suddenly he called out to the man at the furnace:

"Is the fire hot, sir?"

But the man could not hear with the noise of the furnace. It was just as well. He might have answered rudely.

A wave of yet more tender joy escaped from his heart and went coursing in warm flood along his arteries. Like the tender fire of stars moments of their life together, that no one knew of or would ever know of, broke upon and illumined his memory. He longed to recall to her those moments, to make her forget the years of their dull existence together and remember only their moments of ecstasy. For the years, he felt, had not quenched his soul or hers. Their children, his writing, her household cares had not quenched all their souls' tender fire. In one letter that he had written to her then he had said: "Why is it that words like these seem to me so dull and cold? Is it because there is no word tender enough to be your name?"

Like distant music these words that he had written years before were borne towards him from the past. He longed to be alone with her. When the others had gone away, when he and she were in the room in the hotel, then they would be alone together. He would call her softly:

"Gretta!"

Perhaps she would not hear at once: she would be undressing. Then something in his voice would strike her. She would turn and look at him. . . .

At the corner of Winetavern Street they met a cab. He was glad of its rattling noise as it saved him from conversation. She was looking out of the window and seemed tired. The others spoke only a few words, pointing out some building or street. The horse galloped along wearily under the murky morning sky, dragging his old rattling box after his heels, and Gabriel was again in a cab with her, galloping to catch the boat, galloping to their honeymoon.

As the cab drove across O'Connell Bridge Miss O'Callaghan said:

"They say you never cross O'Connell Bridge without seeing a white horse."

"I see a white man this time," said Gabriel.

"Where?" asked Mr. Bartell D'Arcy.

Gabriel pointed to the statue, on which lay patches of snow. Then he nodded familiarly to it and waved his hand.

"Good-night, Dan," he said gaily.

When the cab drew up before the hotel, Gabriel jumped out and, in spite of Mr. Bartell D'Arcy's protest, paid the driver. He gave the man a shilling over his fare. The man saluted and said:

"A prosperous New Year to you, sir."

"The same to you," said Gabriel cordially.

She leaned for a moment on his arm in getting out of the cab and while standing at the curbstone, bidding the others good-night. She leaned lightly on his arm, as lightly as when she had danced with him a few hours before. He had felt proud and happy then, happy that she was his, proud of her grace and wifely carriage. But now, after the kindling again of so many memories, the first touch of her body, musical and strange and perfumed, sent through him a keen pang of lust. Under cover of her silence he pressed her arm closely to his side; and, as they stood at the hotel door, he felt that they had escaped from their lives and duties, escaped from home and friends and run away together with wild and radiant hearts to a new adventure.

An old man was dozing in a great hooded chair in the hall. He lit a candle in the office and went before them to the stairs. They followed him in silence, their feet falling in soft thuds on the thickly carpeted stairs. She mounted the stairs behind the porter, her head bowed in the ascent, her frail shoulders curved as with a burden, her skirt tightly about her. He could have flung his arms about her hips and held her still, for his arms were trembling with desire to seize her and only the stress of his nails against the palms of his hands held the wild impulse of his body in check. The porter halted on the stairs to settle his guttering candle. They halted, too, on the steps below him. In the silence Gabriel could hear the falling of the molten wax into the tray and the thumping of his own heart against his ribs.

The porter led them along a corridor and opened a door. Then he set his unstable candle down on a toilet-table and asked at what hour they were to be called in the morning.

"Eight," said Gabriel.

The porter pointed to the tap of the electric-light and began a muttered apology, but Gabriel cut him short.

"We don't want any light. We have light enough from the street. And I say," he added, pointing to the candle, "you might remove that handsome article, like a good man."

The porter took up his candle again, but slowly, for he was surprised by such a novel idea. Then he mumbled good-night and went out. Gabriel shot the lock to.

A ghastly light from the street lamp lay in a long shaft from one window to the door. Gabriel threw his overcoat and hat on a couch and crossed the room toward the window. He looked down into the street in order that his emotion might calm a little. Then he turned and leaned against a chest of drawers with his back to the light. She had taken off her hat and cloak and was standing before a large swinging mirror, unhooking her waist. Gabriel paused for a few moments, watching her, and then said:

"Gretta!"

She turned away from the mirror slowly and walked along the shaft of light towards him. Her face looked so serious and weary that the words would not pass Gabriel's lips. No, it was not the moment yet.

"You looked tired," he said.

"I am a little," she answered.

"You don't feel ill or weak?"

"No, tired: that's all."

She went on to the window and stood there, looking out. Gabriel waited again and then fearing that diffidence was about to conquer him, he said abruptly:

"By the way, Gretta!"

"What is it?"

"You know that poor fellow Malins?" he said quickly.

"Yes. What about him?"

"Well, poor fellow, he's a decent sort of chap, after all," continued Gabriel in a false voice. "He gave me back that sovereign I lent him, and I didn't expect it, really. It's a pity he wouldn't keep away from that Browne, because he's not a bad fellow, really."

He was trembling now with annoyance. Why did she seem so abstracted? He did not know how he could begin. Was she annoyed, too, about something? If she would only turn to him or come to him of her own accord! To take her as she was would be brutal. No, he must see some ardour in her eyes first. He longed to be master of her strange mood.

"When did you lend him the pound?" she asked, after a pause.

Gabriel strove to restrain himself from breaking out into brutal language about the sottish Malins and his pound. He longed to cry to her from his soul, to crush her body against his, to overmaster her. But he said:

"Oh, at Christmas, when he opened that little Christmas-card shop in Henry Street."

He was in such a fever of rage and desire that he did not hear her come from the window. She stood before him for an instant, looking at him strangely. Then, suddenly raising herself on tiptoe and resting her hands lightly on his shoulders, she kissed him.

"You are a very generous person, Gabriel," she said.

Gabriel, trembling with delight at her sudden kiss and at the quaintness of her phrase, put his hands on her hair and began smoothing it back, scarcely touching it with his fingers. The washing had made it fine and brilliant. His heart was brimming over with happiness. Just when he was wishing for it she had come to him of her own accord. Perhaps her thoughts had been running with his. Perhaps she had felt the impetuous desire that was in him, and then the yielding mood had come upon her. Now that she had fallen to him so easily, he wondered why he had been so diffident.

He stood, holding her head between his hands. Then, slipping one arm swiftly about her body and drawing her towards him, he said softly:

"Gretta, dear, what are you thinking about?"

She did not answer nor yield wholly to his arm. He said again, softly:

"Tell me what it is, Gretta. I think I know what is the matter. Do I know?"

She did not answer at once. Then she said in an outburst of tears:

"O, I am thinking about that song, *The Lass of Aughrim*."

She broke loose from him and ran to the bed and, throwing her arms across the bed-rail, hid her face. Gabriel stood stock-still for a moment in astonishment and then followed her. As he passed in the way of the cheval-glass he caught sight of himself in full length, his broad, well-filled shirt front, the face whose expression always puzzled him when he saw it in a mirror, and his glimmering gilt-rimmed eyeglasses. He halted a few paces from her and said:

"What about the song? Why does that make you cry?"

She raised her head from her arms and dried her eyes with the back of her hand like a child. A kinder note than he had intended went into his voice.

"Why, Gretta?" he asked.

"I am thinking about a person long ago who used to sing that song."

"And who was the person long ago?" asked Gabriel, smiling.

"It was a person I used to know in Galway when I was living with my grandmother," she said.

The smile passed away from Gabriel's face. A dull anger began to gather again at the back of his mind and the dull fires of his lust began to glow angrily in his veins.

"Someone you were in love with?" he asked ironically.

"It was a young boy I used to know," she answered, "named Michael Furey. He used to sing that song, *The Lass of Aughrim*. He was very delicate."

Gabriel was silent. He did not wish her to think that he was interested in this delicate boy.

"I can see him so plainly," she said, after a moment. "Such eyes as he had: big, dark eyes! And such an expression in them—an expression!"

"O, then, you are in love with him?" said Gabriel.

"I used to go out walking with him," she said, "when I was in Galway."

A thought flew across Gabriel's mind.

"Perhaps that was why you wanted to go to Galway with that Ivors girl?" he said coldly.

She looked at him and asked in surprise:

"What for?"

Her eyes made Gabriel feel awkward. He shrugged his shoulders and said:

"How do I know? To see him, perhaps."

She looked away from him along the shaft of light towards the window in silence.

"He is dead," she said at length. "He died when he was only seventeen. Isn't it a terrible thing to die so young as that?"

"What was he?" asked Gabriel, still ironically.

"He was in the gasworks," she said.

Gabriel felt humiliated by the failure of his irony and by the evocation of this figure from the dead, a boy in the gasworks. While he had been full of memories of their secret life together, full of tenderness and joy and desire, she had been comparing him in her mind with another. A shameful consciousness of his own person assailed him. He saw himself as a ludicrous figure, acting as a pennyboy[11] for his aunts, a nervous, well-meaning sentimentalist, orating to vulgarians and idealising his own clownish lusts, the pitiable fatuous fellow he had caught a glimpse of in the mirror. Instinctively he turned his back more to the light lest she might see the shame that burned upon his forehead.

He tried to keep up his tone of cold interrogation, but his voice when he spoke was humble and indifferent.

"I suppose you were in love with this Michael Furey, Gretta," he said.

"I was great with him at that time," she said.

Her voice was veiled and sad. Gabriel, feeling now how vain it would be to try to lead her whither he had purposed, caressed one of her hands and said, also sadly:

"And what did he die of so young, Gretta? Consumption, was it?"

---

11 A boy who haunts cattle markets in the hope of being employed as a drover at a penny per beast.

"I think he died for me," she answered.

A vague terror seized Gabriel at this answer, as if, at that hour when he had hoped to triumph, some impalpable and vindictive being was coming against him, gathering forces against him in its vague world. But he shook himself free of it with an effort of reason and continued to caress her hand. He did not question her again, for he felt that she would tell him of herself. Her hand was warm and moist: it did not respond to his touch, but he continued to caress it just as he had caressed her first letter to him that spring morning.

"It was in the winter," she said, "about the beginning of the winter when I was going to leave my grandmother's and come up here to the convent. And he was ill at the time in his lodgings in Galway and wouldn't be let out, and his people in Oughterard were written to. He was in decline, they said, or something like that. I never knew rightly."

She paused for a moment and sighed.

"Poor fellow," she said. "He was very fond of me and he was such a gentle boy. We used to go out together, walking, you know, Gabriel, like the way they do in the country. He was going to study singing only for his health. He had a very good voice, poor Michael Furey."

"Well; and then?" asked Gabriel.

"And then when it came to the time for me to leave Galway and come up to the convent he was much worse and I wouldn't be let see him so I wrote him a letter saying I was going up to Dublin and would be back in the summer, and hoping he would be better then."

She paused for a moment to get her voice under control, and then went on:

"Then the night before I left, I was in my grandmother's house in Nuns' Island, packing up, and I heard gravel thrown up against the window. The window was so wet I couldn't see, so I ran downstairs as I was and slipped out the back into the garden and there was the poor fellow at the end of the garden, shivering."

"And did you not tell him to go back?" asked Gabriel.

"I implored of him to go home at once and told him he would get his death in the rain. But he said he did not want to live. I can see his eyes as well as well! He was standing at the end of the wall where there was a tree."

"And did he go home?" asked Gabriel.

"Yes, he went home. And when I was only a week in the convent he died and he was buried in Oughterard, where his people came from. O, the day I heard that, that he was dead!"

She stopped, choking with sobs, and, overcome by emotion, flung herself face downward on the bed, sobbing in the quilt. Gabriel held her hand for a moment longer, irresolutely, and then, shy of intruding on her grief, let it fall gently and walked quietly to the window.

She was fast asleep.

Gabriel, leaning on his elbow, looked for a few moments unresentfully on her tangled hair and half-open mouth, listening to her deep-drawn breath. So she had had that romance in her life: a man had died for her sake. It hardly pained him now to think how poor a part he, her husband, had played in her life. He watched her while she slept, as though he and she had never lived together as man and wife. His curious eyes rested long upon her face and on her hair: and, as he thought of what she must have been then, in that time of her first girlish beauty, a strange, friendly pity for her entered his soul. He did not like to say even to himself that her face was no longer beautiful, but he knew that it was no longer the face for which Michael Furey had braved death.

Perhaps she had not told him all the story. His eyes moved to the chair over which she had thrown some of her clothes. A petticoat string dangled to the floor. One boot stood upright, its limp upper fallen down: the fellow of it lay upon its side. He wondered at his riot of emotions of an hour before. From what had it proceeded? From his aunt's supper, from his own foolish speech, from the wine and dancing, the merry-making when saying good-night in the hall, the pleasure of the walk along the river in the snow. Poor Aunt Julia! She, too, would soon be a shade with the shade of Patrick Morkan and his horse. He had caught that haggard look upon her face for a moment when she was singing *Arrayed for the Bridal*. Soon, perhaps, he would be sitting in that same drawing-room, dressed in black, his silk hat on his knees. The blinds would be drawn down and Aunt Kate would be sitting beside him, crying and blowing her nose and telling him how Julia had died. He would cast about in his mind for some words that might console her, and would find only lame and useless ones. Yes, yes: that would happen very soon.

The air of the room chilled his shoulders. He stretched himself cautiously along under the sheets and lay down beside his wife. One by one, they were all becoming shades. Better pass boldly into that other world, in the full glory of some passion, than fade and wither dismally with age. He thought of how she who lay beside him had locked in her heart for so many years that image of her lover's eyes when he had told her that he did not wish to live.

Generous tears filled Gabriel's eyes. He had never felt like that himself towards any woman, but he knew that such a feeling must be love. The tears gathered more thickly in his eyes and in the partial darkness he imagined he saw the form of a young man standing under a dripping tree. Other forms were near. His soul had approached that region where dwell the vast hosts of the dead. He was conscious of, but could not apprehend, their wayward and flickering existence. His own identity was fading out into a grey impalpable world: the solid world itself, which these dead had one time reared and lived in, was dissolving and dwindling.

A few light taps upon the pane made him turn to the window. It had begun to snow again. He watched sleepily the flakes, silver and dark, falling obliquely against the lamplight. The time had come for him to set out on his journey westward. Yes, the newspapers were right, snow was general all over Ireland. It was falling on every part of the dark central plain, on the treeless hills, falling softly upon the Bog of Allen and, farther westward, softly falling into the dark mutinous Shannon waves. It was falling, too, upon every part of the lonely churchyard on the hill where Michael Furey lay buried. It lay thickly drifted on the crooked crosses and headstones, on the spears of the little gate, on the barren thorns. His soul swooned slowly as he heard the snow falling faintly through the universe and faintly falling, like the descent of their last end, upon all the living and the dead.

COMMENTARY

" 'He died when he was only seventeen!' " says Gretta Conroy when she tells her husband about Michael Furey. " 'Isn't it a terrible thing to die so young as that?' " But no reader will give the answer that Gretta seems to expect from her husband. No reader upon whom the story has had its intended effect can fail to know that it is better to have died as Michael Furey died than to have lived after the fashion of Gabriel Conroy and all the other guests at the Christmas party. And this is the answer that Gabriel Conroy does indeed give when he lies down beside his sleeping wife. "Better pass boldly into that other world," he thinks, "in the full glory of some passion, than fade and wither dismally with age." The title of the story, we eventually understand, refers less to Michael Furey than to Gabriel Conroy, to the guests at the Christmas party, to all the people of Ireland as Conroy now perceives them. They, although still breathing, are the truly dead, and young Michael Furey, if only because he exists as he does in the minds of Gretta and Gabriel Conroy, is alive, a clearly defined personal entity, a strong energy.

"The Dead" is the last, the longest, and the most complex of the stories of James Joyce's first volume of fiction, *Dubliners*. Of this book Joyce said, "My intention was to write a chapter of the moral history of my country and I chose Dublin for the scene because the city seemed to me the centre of paralysis." What Joyce had in mind when he spoke of "paralysis" is suggested by an incident in "The Dead," Aunt Julia's singing. For a fleeting moment there is a remission of the "paralysis," for the old lady sings surprisingly well, and we are told that "to follow the voice was to feel and share the excitement of swift and secure flight." *The excitement of swift and secure flight:* here is life as the poets wish it to be, as we all at some time imagine it possibly can be. But in quoting the sentence, I have omitted a qualifying clause. The whole sentence reads: "To follow the voice, without looking at the singer's face, was to feel and share the excitement of swift and secure flight." If one did look at her face, Joyce is telling us, one saw the approach of death and the limitation of mind and spirit that marks not Aunt Julia alone but all the relatives and friends who are gathered around her. One saw the poverty of experience and passion, of gaiety, wit, intelligence—the death-in-life of a narrow, provincial existence.

Joyce writes of his own nation and city with passionate particularity. But when we consider the very high place that "The Dead" has been given in the canon of modern literature, and the admiration it has won from readers of the most diverse backgrounds, we must say that Joyce has written a chapter in the moral history not only of his own country but of the whole modern western world. Gabriel Conroy's plight, his sense that he has been overtaken by death-in-life, is shared by many in our time: it is one of the characteristics of modern society that an ever-growing number of people are not content to live by habit and routine and by the unquestioning acceptance of the circumstances into which they have been born. They believe they have the right to claim for themselves pleasure, or power, or dignity, or fullness of experience; a prerogative which in former times was exercised by relatively few people, usually members of the privileged classes, and which now seems available to many people regardless of class. Yet almost in the degree that modern man feels free to assert the personal claims which are the expression of a heightened sense of individuality, he seems to fall prey to that peculiarly modern disorder so often remarked by novelists, psychologists, and sociologists—an uncertainty about who the person is who makes the claims, a diminished sense of his personal identity.

Identity is the word that Gabriel Conroy uses when he thinks about death: he sees "his own identity . . . fading out into a grey impalpable world." And his imagination of death provides the image of his life. All through the evening his identity had been fading out into the grey impalpable world of his aunts' party. All through his youth and his early middle-age his identity had been fading out into the grey impalpable world of Dublin society.

It is sometimes said that Gabriel Conroy is what James Joyce would have been, or what he supposed he would have been, if he had not fled Dublin at the age of twenty, with no resources but his talent and his youth, risking privation for the sake of achievement and fame. And certainly the juxtaposition of the author and his character helps us understand Gabriel Conroy. Joyce was one of an old and rare species of man: he was a genius, with all the stubborn resistance and courage, all the strong sense of identity, by which, in addition to great gifts, genius is defined. Gabriel Conroy is one of a new, and very numerous, kind of man whose large demand upon life is supported neither by native gift nor moral energy. He has the knowledge of excellence but cannot achieve it for himself; he admires distinction and cannot attain it.

Poor Conroy's deficiency manifests itself most saliently and sadly in his relation to his wife. Gretta is a person of rather considerable distinction; among the guests at the party she is the only woman who possesses beauty, charm, and temperament. She is vivacious and spirited, and, as her evocation of the dead Michael Furey suggests, she has a capacity for intense feeling. To this endowment her husband responds with admiration and love, but he has the dim, implicit knowledge that he cannot match it with qualities of his own. When his wife tells him the story of her girlhood romance, his inarticulate self-knowledge is suddenly made explicit and devastating. The sharp clarity with which Michael Furey has remained in Gretta's consciousness, his embodiment of will and passion, make plain to Gabriel Conroy how fully he himself has succumbed to his aunts' impalpable grey world of habit, respectability, and mediocrity.

The literary means by which Joyce represents the world of Conroy's friends and relatives are striking in their subtlety and diversity. If Joyce has an opinion about the people who gather at the old aunts'—and we know he has—he does not express it overtly. At times he seems to subordinate his own judgment to theirs, as when he gravely tells us about the serving maid Lily that she "seldom made a mistake in the orders, so that she got on well with her three mistresses. They were fussy, that was all. But the only thing they would not stand was back answers." Now and then he seems to yield to the spirit of the party and uses a prose which, in a fatigued way, takes on something of the consciously fanciful humor of Dickens in his scenes of jollification: "On the closed square piano a pudding in a huge yellow dish lay in waiting and behind it were three squads of bottles of stout and ale and minerals, drawn up according to the colours of their uniforms, the first two black, with brown and red labels, the third and smallest squad white, with transverse green sashes." For the most part, however, the tone of the prose is neutral and a little naive, as if Joyce has no point of view of his own, or as if he were saying that he has no wish to judge, let alone to blame—for how can one blame the dead for being dead?

Nothing could be more brilliant and subtle, or humane, than Joyce's management of his own—and our—relation to Gabriel Conroy. All the details of Conroy's behavior at the party contribute to our perception of his second-rateness. But we are never invited to despise him, we are never permitted to triumph over him. Joyce spares him nothing in making us aware of his mediocrity: we know all about his nervous desire to be liked and approved, his wish to be thought superior, his fear of asserting whatever superiority he may actually have, his lack of intellectual and emotional courage, his sulky resentment when he feels slighted, his easy sentimentality. But at the same time Joyce does not obscure Conroy's genuine intention of kindness, his actual considerateness, his demand upon himself that he be large-minded and generous. And he protects Conroy from our ultimate contempt by making plain the extent of his fairly accurate self-knowledge; there is little we discern to Conroy's discredit that the unhappy man does not himself know and deplore.

But self-knowledge cannot save Conroy from being the kind of man he is, and when we try to say what that kind is, we are bound to think of his commitment to galoshes. In the British Isles, much more than in America, the wearing of galoshes and rubbers is regarded as an excessive and rather foolish caution about one's health. The fact that Conroy makes such a great thing of wearing them himself and urges them on his wife—but on the night of the party she defies him—puts him in almost too obvious contrast with Michael Furey, who had died from standing in the rain to bid his love farewell. It is Conroy's sense of his vulnerability, his uneasy feeling that almost every situation is a threat, that makes him what he is. He has no valid reason to think that the servant girl is really angry with him; when she responds to his remark about her getting married, her "great bitterness" is directed not at him but at the conditions of her life, yet Conroy feels that "he had made a mistake," that he had "failed" with her, and he is extravagantly distressed. He is equally self-conscious and timorous in his half-flirtatious dispute with Miss Ivors, feeling that the nature of their relation makes it impossible for him to "risk a grandiose phrase with her." He does indeed achieve a moment of dignity when he is moved by desire for his wife, but even here he protects himself, resolving to postpone his wooing until he is certain of being fully responded to. And when he does at last speak, it is to make an irrelevant and banal remark that quite belies his emotion.

Conroy's own last adverse judgment on himself is extreme—he sees himself as "a ludicrous figure, acting as a pennyboy for his aunts, a nervous, well-meaning sentimentalist, orating to vulgarians and idealising his own clownish lusts, the pitiable fatuous fellow he had caught a glimpse of in the mirror." This extravagance of self-contempt is not only the outcome of self-knowledge; it is also the expression of Conroy's self-pity, an emotion which we are taught to despise. But Joyce does not despise it and he does not permit us to despise it. As Conroy lies in defeat and meditation beside his sleeping wife, his evocation of the sadness of life under the dominion of death is the climax of his self-pity, yet when his commiseration with himself reaches this point of intensity, the author's own emotion is seen to be in active accord with it. This sudden identification of the author with his character is one of the most striking and effective elements of the story. Joyce feels exactly what Conroy feels about the sadness of human life, its terrible nearness to death, and the *waste* that every life is; he directs no irony upon Conroy's grief but makes Conroy's suffering his own, with no reservations whatever. At several points in the story he has clearly regarded Conroy's language, or the tone of his thoughts, as banal, or vulgar, or sentimental. But as the story approaches its conclusion, it becomes impossible for us to know whose language we are hearing, Conroy's or the author's, or to whose tone of desperate sorrow we are responding. It is as if Joyce, secure in his genius and identity, were saying that under the aspect of the imagination of death and of death-in-life there is no difference between him and the mediocre, sentimental man of whom he has been writing.

DISORDER AND EARLY SORROW

THOMAS MANN
1875–1955

THE PRINCIPAL DISH at dinner had been croquettes made of turnip greens. So there follows a trifle,[1] concocted out of those dessert powders we use nowadays,[2] that taste like almond soap. Xaver, the youthful manservant, in his outgrown striped jacket, white woollen gloves, and yellow sandals, hands it round, and the "big folk" take this opportunity to remind their father, tactfully, that company is coming today.

The "big folk" are two, Ingrid and Bert. Ingrid is brown-eyed, eighteen, and perfectly delightful. She is on the eve of her exams, and will probably pass them, if only because she knows how to wind masters, and even headmasters, round her finger. She does not, however, mean to use her certificate once she gets it; having leanings towards the stage, on the ground of her ingratiating smile, her equally ingratiating voice, and a marked and irresistible talent for burlesque. Bert is blond and seventeen. He intends to get done with school somehow, anyhow, and fling himself into the arms of life. He will be a dancer, or a cabaret actor, possibly even a waiter—but not a waiter anywhere else save at Cairo, the night-club, whither he has once already taken flight, at five in the morning, and been brought back

---

[1] A dessert, usually made with sponge cake and custard.
[2] The period of the ruinous inflation in Germany after World War I. Mann's story appeared in 1925.

crestfallen. Bert bears a strong resemblance to the youthful manservant. Xaver Kleinsgutl, of about the same age as himself; not because he looks common—in features he is strikingly like his father, Professor Cornelius—but by reason of an approximation of types, due in its turn to far-reaching compromises in matters of dress and bearing generally. Both lads wear their heavy hair very long on top, with a cursory parting in the middle, and give their heads the same characteristic toss to throw it off the forehead. When one of them leaves the house, by the garden gate, bareheaded in all weathers, in a blouse rakishly girt with a leather strap, and sheers off bent well over with his head on one side; or else mounts his push-bike—Xaver makes free with his employers', of both sexes, or even, in acutely irresponsible mood, with the Professor's own—Dr. Cornelius from his bedroom window cannot, for the life of him, tell whether he is looking at his son or his servant. Both, he thinks, look like young moujiks.[3] And both are impassioned cigarette-smokers, though Bert has not the means to compete with Xaver, who smokes as many as thirty a day of a brand named after a popular cinema star. The big folk call their father and mother the "old folk"—not behind their backs, but as a form of address and in all affection: "Hullo, old folks," they will say; though Cornelius is only forty-seven years old and his wife eight years younger. And the Professor's parents, who lead in his household the humble and hesitant life of the really old, are on the big folk's lips the "ancients." As for the "little folk," Ellie and Snapper, who take their meals upstairs with blue-faced Ann— so-called because of her prevailing facial hue—Ellie and Snapper follow their mother's example and address their father by his first name, Abel. Unutterably comic it sounds, in its pert, confiding familiarity; particularly on the lips, in the sweet accents, of five-year-old Eleanor, who is the image of Frau Cornelius's baby pictures and whom the Professor loves above everything else in the world.

"Darling old thing," says Ingrid affably, laying her large but shapely hand on his, as he presides in proper middle-class style over the family table, with her on his left and the mother opposite: "Parent mine, may I ever so gently jog your memory, for you have probably forgotten: this is the afternoon we were to have our little jollification, our turkey-trot with eats to match. You haven't a thing to do but just bear up and not funk it; everything will be over by nine o'clock."

"Oh—ah!" says Cornelius, his face falling. "Good!" he goes on, and nods his head to show himself in harmony with the inevitable. "I only meant—is this really the day? Thursday, yes. How time flies! Well, what time are they coming?"

"Half past four they'll be dropping in, I should say," answers Ingrid, to whom her brother leaves the major rôle in all dealings with the father. Upstairs, while he is resting, he will hear scarcely anything, and from seven to eight he takes his walk. He can slip out by the terrace if he likes.

"Tut!" says Cornelius deprecatingly, as who should say: "You exaggerate." But Bert puts in: "It's the one evening in the week Wanja doesn't have to play. Any other night he'd have to leave by half past six, which would be painful for all concerned."

Wanja is Ivan Herzl, the celebrated young leading man at the Stadttheater.[4] Bert and Ingrid are on intimate terms with him, they often visit him in his dressing-room and have tea. He is an artist of the modern school, who stands on the stage in strange and, to the professor's mind, utterly affected dancing attitudes,

---

[3] Russian peasants.
[4] The municipal theater in Munich.

and shrieks lamentably. To a professor of history, all highly repugnant; but Bert has entirely succumbed to Herzl's influence, blackens the lower rim of his eyelids—despite painful but fruitless scenes with the father—and with youthful carelessness of the ancestral anguish declares that not only will he take Herzl for his model if he becomes a dancer, but in case he turns out to be a waiter at the Cairo he means to walk precisely thus.

Cornelius slightly raises his brows and makes his son a little bow—indicative of the unassumingness and self-abnegation that befits his age. You could not call it a mocking bow or suggestive in any special sense. Bert may refer it to himself or equally to his so talented friend.

"Who else is coming?" next inquires the master of the house. They mention various people, names all more or less familiar, from the city, from the suburban colony, from Ingrid's school. They still have some telephoning to do, they say. They have to phone Max. This is Max Hergesell, an engineering student; Ingrid utters his name in the nasal drawl which according to her is the traditional intonation of all the Hergesells. She goes on to parody it in the most abandonedly funny and lifelike way, and the parents laugh until they nearly choke over the wretched trifle. For even in these times when something funny happens people have to laugh.

From time to time the telephone bell rings in the Professor's study, and the big folk run across, knowing it is their affair. Many people had to give up their telephones the last time the price rose, but so far the Corneliuses have been able to keep theirs, just as they have kept their villa, which was built before the war, by dint of the salary Cornelius draws as professor of history—a million marks, and more or less adequate to the chances and changes of post-war life. The house is comfortable, even elegant, though sadly in need of repairs that cannot be made for lack of materials, and at present disfigured by iron stoves with long pipes. Even so, it is still the proper setting of the upper middle class, though they themselves look odd enough in it, with their worn and turned clothing and altered way of life. The children, of course, know nothing else; to them it is normal and regular, they belong by birth to the "villa proletariat." The problem of clothing troubles them not at all. They and their like have evolved a costume to fit the time, by poverty out of taste for innovation: in summer it consists of scarcely more than a belted linen smock and sandals. The middle-class parents find things rather more difficult.

The big folk's table-napkins hang over their chair-backs, they talk with their friends over the telephone. These friends are the invited guests who have rung up to accept or decline or arrange; and the conversation is carried on in the jargon of the clan, full of slang and high spirits, of which the old folk understand hardly a word. These consult together meantime about the hospitality to be offered to the impending guests. The Professor displays a middle-class ambitiousness: he wants to serve a sweet—or something that looks like a sweet—after the Italian salad and brownbread sandwiches. But Frau Cornelius says that would be going too far. The guests would not expect it, she is sure—and the big folk, returning once more to their trifle, agree with her.

The mother of the family is of the same general type as Ingrid, though not so tall. She is languid; the fantastic difficulties of the housekeeping have broken and worn her. She really ought to go and take a cure,[5] but feels incapable; the

[5] A rest cure, a visit to a spa.

floor is always swaying under her feet, and everything seems upside down. She speaks of what is uppermost in her mind: the eggs, they simply must be bought today. Six thousand marks apiece they are, and just so many are to be had on this one day of the week at one single shop fifteen minutes' journey away. Whatever else they do, the big folk must go and fetch them immediately after luncheon, with Danny, their neighbour's son, who will soon be calling for them; and Xaver Kleinsgutl will don civilian garb and attend his young master and mistress. For no single household is allowed more than five eggs a week; therefore the young people will enter the shop singly, one after another, under assumed names, and thus wring twenty eggs from the shopkeeper for the Cornelius family. This enterprise is the sporting event of the week for all participants, not excepting the moujik Kleinsgutl, and most of all for Ingrid and Bert, who delight in misleading and mystifying their fellow-men and would revel in the performance even if it did not achieve one single egg. They adore impersonating fictitious characters; they love to sit in a bus and carry on long lifelike conversations in a dialect which they otherwise never speak, the most commonplace dialogue about politics and people and the price of food, while the whole bus listens open-mouthed to this incredibly ordinary prattle, though with a dark suspicion all the while that something is wrong somewhere. The conversation waxes ever more shameless, it enters into revolting detail about these people who do not exist. Ingrid can make her voice sound ever so common and twittering and shrill as she impersonates a shop-girl with an illegitimate child, said child being a son with sadistic tendencies, who lately out in the country treated a cow with such unnatural cruelty that no Christian could have borne to see it. Bert nearly explodes at her twittering, but restrains himself and displays a grisly sympathy; he and the unhappy shop-girl entering into a long, stupid, depraved, and shuddery conversation over the particular morbid cruelty involved; until an old gentleman opposite, sitting with his ticket folded between his index finger and his seal ring, can bear it no more and makes public protest against the nature of the themes these young folk are discussing with such particularity. He uses the Greek plural: "themata." Whereat Ingrid pretends to be dissolving in tears, and Bert behaves as though his wrath against the old gentleman was with difficulty being held in check and would probably burst out before long. He clenches his fists, he gnashes his teeth, he shakes from head to foot; and the unhappy old gentleman, whose intentions had been of the best, hastily leaves the bus at the next stop.

Such are the diversions of the big folk. The telephone plays a prominent part in them: they ring up any and everybody—members of government, opera singers, dignitaries of the Church—in the character of shop assistants, or perhaps as Lord or Lady Doolittle. They are only with difficulty persuaded that they have the wrong number. Once they emptied their parents' card-tray[6] and distributed its contents among the neighbours' letter-boxes, wantonly, yet not without enough impish sense of the fitness of things to make it highly upsetting. God only knowing why certain people should have called where they did.

Xaver comes in to clear away, tossing the hair out of his eyes. Now that he has taken off his gloves you can see the yellow chain-ring[7] on his left hand. And as

[6] A tray on which visitors had left calling cards.
[7] A wrist chain, something like an identification chain or charm bracelet, worn by young men of bohemian tendencies at this time. It sometimes conveyed a slight hint of effeminacy.

the Professor finishes his watery eight-thousand-mark beer and lights a cigarette, the little folk can be heard scrambling down the stair, coming, by established custom, for their after-dinner call on Father and Mother. They storm the dining-room, after a struggle with the latch clutched by both pairs of little hands at once; their clumsy small feet twinkle over the carpet, in red felt slippers with the socks falling down on them. With prattle and shoutings each makes for his own place: Snapper to Mother, to climb on her lap, boast of all he has eaten, and thump his fat little tum; Ellie to her Abel, so much hers because she is so very much his; because she consciously luxuriates in the deep tenderness—like all deep feeling, concealing a melancholy strain—with which he holds her small form embraced; in the love in his eyes as he kisses her little fairy hand or the sweet brow with its delicate tracery of tiny blue veins.

The little folk look like each other, with the strong undefined likeness of brother and sister. In clothing and haircut they are twins. Yet they are sharply distinguished after all, and quite on sex lines. It is a little Adam and a little Eve. Not only is Snapper the sturdier and more compact, he appears consciously to emphasize his four-year-old masculinity in speech, manner, and carriage, lifting his shoulders and letting the little arms hang down quite like a young American athlete, drawing down his mouth when he talks and seeking to give his voice a gruff and forthright ring. But all this masculinity is the result of effort rather than natively his. Born and brought up in these desolate, distracted times, he has been endowed by them with an unstable and hypersensitive nervous system and suffers greatly under life's disharmonies. He is prone to sudden anger and outbursts of bitter tears, stamping his feet at every trifle; for this reason he is his mother's special nursling and care. His round, round eyes are chestnut brown and already inclined to squint, so that he will need glasses in the near future. His little nose is long, the mouth small—the father's nose and mouth they are, more plainly than ever since the Professor shaved his pointed beard and goes smooth-faced. The pointed beard had become impossible—even professors must make some concession to the changing times.

But the little daughter sits on her father's knee, his Eleonorchen,[8] his little Eve, so much more gracious a little being, so much sweeter-faced than her brother—and he holds his cigarette away from her while she fingers his glasses with her dainty wee hands. The lenses are divided for reading and distance, and each day they tease her curiosity afresh.

At bottom he suspects that his wife's partiality may have a firmer basis than his own: that Snapper's refractory masculinity perhaps is solider stuff than his own little girl's more explicit charm and grace. But the heart will not be commanded, that he knows; and once and for all his heart belongs to the little one, as it has since the day she came, since the first time he saw her. Almost always when he holds her in his arms he remembers that first time: remembers the sunny room in the Women's Hospital, where Ellie first saw the light, twelve years after Bert was born. He remembers how he drew near, the mother smiling the while, and cautiously put aside the canopy of the diminutive bed that stood beside the large one. There lay the little miracle among the pillows: so well formed, so encompassed, as it were, with the harmony of sweet proportions, with little hands that even then, though so much tinier, were beautiful as now; with

[8] Affectionate diminutive form of Eleanor, "little Eleanor."

wide-open eyes blue as the sky and brighter than the sunshine—and almost in that very second he felt himself captured and held fast. This was love at first sight, love everlasting: a feeling unknown, unhoped for, unexpected—in so far as it could be a matter of conscious awareness; it took entire possession of him, and he understood, with joyous amazement, that this was for life.

But he understood more. He knows, does Dr. Cornelius, that there is something not quite right about this feeling, so unaware, so undreamed of, so involuntary. He has a shrewd suspicion that it is not by accident it has so utterly mastered him and bound itself up with his existence; that he had—even subconsciously—been preparing for it, or, more precisely, been prepared for it. There is, in short, something in him which at a given moment was ready to issue in such a feeling; and this something, highly extraordinary to relate, is his essence and quality as a professor of history. Dr. Cornelius, however, does not actually say this, even to himself; he merely realizes it, at odd times, and smiles a private smile. He knows that history professors do not love history because it is something that comes to pass, but only because it is something that *has* come to pass; that they hate a revolution like the present one because they feel it is lawless, incoherent, irrelevant—in a word, unhistoric; that their hearts belong to the coherent, disciplined, historic past. For the temper of timelessness, the temper of eternity—thus the scholar communes with himself when he takes his walk by the river before supper—that temper broods over the past; and it is a temper much better suited to the nervous system of a history professor than are the excesses of the present. The past is immortalized; that is to say, it is dead; and death is the root of all godliness and all abiding significance. Dr. Cornelius, walking alone in the dark, has a profound insight into this truth. It is this conservative instinct of his, his sense of the eternal, that has found in his love for his little daughter a way to save itself from the wounding inflicted by the times. For father love, and a little child on its mother's breast—are not these timeless, and thus very, very holy and beautiful? Yet Cornelius, pondering there in the dark, descries something not perfectly right and good in his love. Theoretically, in the interests of science, he admits it to himself. There is something ulterior about it, in the nature of it; that something is hostility, hostility against the history of to-day, which is still in the making and thus not history at all, in behalf of the genuine history that has already happened—that is to say, death. Yes, passing strange though all this is, yet it is true; true in a sense, that is. His devotion to this priceless little morsel of life and new growth has something to do with death, it clings to death as against life; and that is neither right nor beautiful—in a sense. Though only the most fanatical asceticism could be capable, on no other ground than such casual scientific perception, of tearing this purest and most precious of feelings out of his heart.

He holds his darling on his lap and her slim rosy legs hang down. He raises his brows as he talks to her, tenderly, with a half-teasing note of respect, and listens enchanted to her high, sweet little voice calling him Abel. He exchanges a look with the mother, who is caressing her Snapper and reading him a gentle lecture. He must be more reasonable, he must learn self-control; today again, under the manifold exasperations of life, he has given way to rage and behaved like a howling dervish. Cornelius casts a mistrustful glance at the big folk now and then, too; he thinks it not unlikely they are not unaware of those scientific preoccupations of his evening walks. If such be the case they do not show it. They stand there leaning their arms on their chair-backs and with a benevolence not untinctured with irony look on at the parental happiness.

The children's frocks are of a heavy, brick-red stuff, embroidered in modern "arty" style. They once belonged to Ingrid and Bert and are precisely alike, save that little knickers come out beneath Snapper's smock. And both have their hair bobbed. Snapper's is a streaky blond, inclined to turn dark. It is bristly and sticky and looks for all the world like a droll, badly fitting wig. But Ellie's is chestnut brown, glossy and fine as silk, as pleasing as her whole little personality. It covers her ears—and these ears are not a pair, one of them being the right size, the other distinctly too large. Her father will sometimes uncover this little abnormality and exclaim over it as though he had never noticed it before, which both makes Ellie giggle and covers her with shame. Her eyes are now golden brown, set far apart and with sweet gleams in them—such a clear and lovely look! The brows above are blond; the nose still unformed, with thick nostrils and almost circular holes; the mouth large and expressive, with a beautifully arching and mobile upper lip. When she laughs, dimples come in her cheeks and she shows her teeth like loosely strung pearls. So far she has lost but one tooth, which her father gently twisted out with his handkerchief after it had grown very wobbling. During this small operation she had paled and trembled very much. Her cheeks have the softness proper to her years, but they are not chubby; indeed, they are rather concave, due to her facial structure, with its somewhat prominent jaw. On one, close to the soft fall of her hair, is a downy freckle.

Ellie is not too well pleased with her looks—a sign that already she troubles about such things. Sadly she thinks it is best to admit it once for all, her face is "homely"; though the rest of her, "on the other hand," is not bad at all. She loves expressions like "on the other hand"; they sound choice and grown-up to her, and she likes to string them together, one after the other: "very likely," "probably," "after all." Snapper is self-critical too, though more in the moral sphere: he suffers from remorse for his attacks of rage and considers himself a tremendous sinner. He is quite certain that heaven is not for such as he; he is sure to go to "the bad place" when he dies, and no persuasions will convince him to the contrary—as that God sees the heart and gladly makes allowances. Obstinately he shakes his head, with the comic, crooked little peruke,[9] and vows there is no place for him in heaven. When he has a cold he is immediately quite choked with mucus; rattles and rumbles from top to toe if you even look at him; his temperature flies up at once and he simply puffs. Nursy is pessimistic on the score of his constitution: such fat-blooded children as he might get a stroke any minute. Once she even thought she saw the moment at hand: Snapper had been in one of his berserker rages, and in the ensuing fit of penitence stood himself in the corner with his back to the room. Suddenly Nursy noticed that his face had gone all blue, far bluer, even, than her own. She raised the alarm, crying out that the child's all too rich blood had at length brought him to his final hour; and Snapper, to his vast astonishment, found himself, so far from being rebuked for evil-doing, encompassed in tenderness and anxiety—until it turned out that his colour was not caused by apoplexy but by the distempering on the nursery wall, which had come off on his tear-wet face.

Nursy has come downstairs too, and stands by the door, sleek-haired, owl-

[9] A wig.

eyed, with her hands folded over her white apron, and a severely dignified manner born of her limited intelligence. She is very proud of the care and training she gives her nurslings and declares that they are "enveloping wonderfully." She has had seventeen suppurated teeth lately removed from her jaws and been measured for a set of symmetrical yellow ones in dark rubber gums; these now embellish her peasant face. She is obsessed with the strange conviction that these teeth of hers are the subject of general conversation, that, as it were, the sparrows on the housetops chatter of them. "Everybody knows I've had a false set put in," she will say; "there has been a great deal of foolish talk about them." She is much given to dark hints and veiled innuendo: speaks, for instance, of a certain Dr. Bleifuss, whom every child knows, and "there are even some in the house who pretend to be him." All one can do with talk like this is charitably to pass it over in silence. But she teaches the children nursery rhymes: gems like:

> "Puff, puff, here comes the train!
> Puff, puff, toot, toot,
> Away it goes again,"

Or that gastronomical jingle, so suited, in its sparseness, to the times, and yet seemingly with a blitheness of its own:

> "Monday we begin the week,
> Tuesday there's a bone to pick.
> Wednesday we're half way through,
> Thursday what a great to-do!
> Friday we eat what fish we're able,
> Saturday we dance round the table.
> Sunday brings us pork and greens—
> Here's a feast for kings and queens!"

Also a certain four-line stanza with a romantic appeal, unutterable and unuttered:

> "Open the gate, open the gate
> And let the carriage drive in.
> Who is it in the carriage sits?
> A lordly sir with golden hair."

Or, finally that ballad about golden-haired Marianne who sat on a, sat on a, sat on a stone, and combed out her, combed out her, combed out her hair; and about blood-thirsty Rudolph, who pulled out a, pulled out a, pulled out a knife— and his ensuing direful end. Ellie enunciates all these ballads charmingly, with her mobile little lips, and sings them in her sweet little voice—much better than Snapper. She does everything better than he does, and he pays her honest admiration and homage and obeys her in all things except when visited by one of his attacks. Sometimes she teaches him, instructs him upon the birds in the picture-book and tells him their proper names: "This is a chaffinch, Buddy, this is a bullfinch, this is a cowfinch." He has to repeat them after her. She gives him medical instruction too, teaches him the names of diseases, such as infammation of the lungs, infammation of the blood, infammation of the air. If he does not pay attention and cannot say the words after her, she stands him in the corner. Once she even boxed his ears, but was so ashamed that she stood herself in the corner for a long time. Yes, they are fast friends, two souls with but a single thought, and have all their adventures in common. They come home from a walk and relate as with one voice that they have seen two moollies and a teeny-weenty baby calf. They are on familiar terms with the kitchen, which consists of Xaver and the ladies Hinterhofer, two sisters once of the lower middle class who, in these evil days, are reduced to living *"au pair"*[10] as the phrase goes and officiating as cook and housemaid for their board and keep. The little ones have a feeling that Xaver and the Hinterhofers are on much the same footing with their father and mother as they are themselves. At least sometimes, when they have been scolded, they go downstairs and announce that the master and mistress are cross. But playing with the servants lacks charm compared with the joys of playing upstairs. The kitchen could never rise to the height of the games their father can invent. For instance, there is "four gentlemen taking a walk." When they play it Abel will crook his knees until he is the same height with themselves and go walking with them, hand in hand. They never get enough of this sport; they could walk round and round the dining-room a whole day on end, five gentlemen in all, counting the diminished Abel.

Then there is the thrilling cushion game. One of the children, usually Ellie, seats herself, unbeknownst to Abel, in his seat at table. Still as a mouse she awaits his coming. He draws near with his head in the air, descanting in loud, clear tones upon the surpassing comfort of his chair; and sits down on top of Ellie. "What's this, what's this?" says he. And bounces about, deaf to the smothered giggles exploding behind him. "Why have they put a cushion in my chair? And what a queer, hard, awkward-shaped cushion it is!" he goes on. "Frightfully uncomfortable to sit on!" And keeps pushing and bouncing about more and more on the astonishing cushion and clutching behind him into the rapturous giggling and squeaking, until at last he turns round, and the game ends with a magnificent climax of discovery and recognition. They might go through all this a hundred times without diminishing by an iota its power to thrill.

Today is no time for such joys. The imminent festivity disturbs the atmosphere, and besides there is work to be done, and, above all, the eggs to be got. Ellie has just time to recite "Puff, puff," and Cornelius to discover that her ears are not mates, when they are interrupted by the arrival of Danny, come to fetch Bert and Ingrid. Xaver, meantime, has exchanged his striped livery for an ordinary coat, in which he looks rather rough-and-ready, though as brisk and attractive as ever. So then Nursy and the children ascend to the upper regions, the Professor withdraws to his study to read, as always after dinner, and his wife bends her energies upon the sandwiches and salad that must be prepared. And she has another errand as well. Before the young people arrive she has to take her shopping-basket and dash into town on her bicycle, to turn into provisions a sum of money she has in hand, which she dares not keep lest it lose all value.

Cornelius reads, leaning back in his chair, with his cigar between his middle and index finger. First he reads Macaulay[11] on the origin of the English public debt at the end of the seventeenth century; then an article in a French periodical on the rapid increase in the Spanish debt towards the end of the sixteenth. Both these for his lecture on the morrow. He intends to compare the astonishing

[10] (French) Without pay; working in return for room and board.
[11] Thomas Babington, Baron Macaulay (1800–1859), English historian, writer, and statesman.

prosperity which accompanied the phenomenon in England with its fatal effects a hundred years earlier in Spain, and to analyse the ethical and psychological grounds of the difference in results. For that will give him a chance to refer back from the England of William III, which is the actual subject in mind, to the time of Philip II and the Counter-Reformation,[12] which is his own special field. He has already written a valuable work on this period; it is much cited and got him his professorship. While his cigar burns down and gets strong, he excogitates a few pensive sentences in a key of gentle melancholy, to be delivered before his class next day: about the practically hopeless struggle carried on by the belated Philip against the whole trend of history: against the new, the kingdom-disrupting power of the Germanic ideal of freedom and individual liberty. And about the persistent, futile struggle of the aristocracy, condemned by God and rejected of man, against the forces of progress and change. He savours his sentences; keeps on polishing them while he puts back the books he has been using; then goes upstairs for the usual pause in his day's work, the hour with drawn blinds and closed eyes, which he so imperatively needs. But today, he recalls, he will rest under disturbed conditions, amid the bustle of preparations for the feast. He smiles to find his heart giving a mild flutter at the thought. Disjointed phrases on the theme of black-clad Philip and his times mingle with a confused consciousness that they will soon be dancing down below. For five minutes or so he falls asleep.

As he lies and rests he can hear the sound of the garden gate and the repeated ringing at the bell. Each time a little pang goes through him, of excitement and suspense, at the thought that the young people have begun to fill the floor below. And each time he smiles at himself again—though even his smile is slightly nervous, is tinged with the pleasurable anticipations people always feel before a party. At half past four—it is already dark—he gets up and washes at the washstand. The basin has been out of repair for two years. It is supposed to tip, but has broken away from its socket on one side and cannot be mended because there is nobody to mend it; neither replaced because no shop can supply another. So it has to be hung up above the vent and emptied by lifting in both hands and pouring out the water. Cornelius shakes his head over this basin, as he does several times a day—whenever, in fact, he has occasion to use it. He finishes his toilet with care, standing under the ceiling light to polish his glasses till they shine. Then he goes downstairs.

On his way to the dining-room he hears the gramophone already going, and the sound of voices. He puts on a polite, society air; at his tongue's end is the phrase he means to utter: "Pray don't let me disturb you," as he passes directly into the dining-room for his tea. "Pray don't let me disturb you"—it seems to him precisely the *mot juste*; towards the guests cordial and considerate, for himself a very bulwark.

The lower floor is lighted up, all the bulbs in the chandelier are burning save one that has burned out. Cornelius pauses on a lower step and surveys the entrance hall. It looks pleasant and cosy in the bright light, with its copy of Marées[13] over the brick chimney-piece, its wainscoted walls—wainscoted in soft wood—and red-carpeted floor, where the guests stand in groups, chatting, each with his tea-cup and slice of bread-and-butter spread with anchovy paste. There

12 The Catholic reaction to the Protestant Reformation (16th century).
13 Hans von Marées (1837–1887), German Romantic painter.

is a festal haze, faint scents of hair and clothing and human breath come to him across the room, it is all characteristic and familiar and highly evocative. The door into the dressing-room is open, guests are still arriving.

A large group of people is rather bewildering at first sight. The Professor takes in only the general scene. He does not see Ingrid, who is standing just at the foot of the steps, in a dark silk frock with a pleated collar falling softly over the shoulders, and bare arms. She smiles up at him, nodding and showing her lovely teeth.

"Rested?" she asks, for his private ear. With a quite unwarranted start he recognizes her, and she presents some of her friends.

"May I introduce Herr Zuber?" she says. "And this is Fräulein Plaichinger."

Herr Zuber is insignificant. But Fräulein Plaichinger is a perfect Germania, blond and voluptuous, arrayed in floating draperies. She has a snub nose, and answers the Professor's salutation in the high, shrill pipe so many stout women have.

"Delighted to meet you," he says. "How nice of you to come! A classmate of Ingrid's, I suppose?"

And Herr Zuber is a golfing partner of Ingrid's. He is in business; he works in his uncle's brewery. Cornelius makes a few jokes about the thinness of the beer and professes to believe that Herr Zuber could easily do something about the quality if he would. "But pray don't let me disturb you," he goes on, and turns towards the dining-room.

"There comes Max," says Ingrid. "Max, you sweep, what do you mean by rolling up at this time of day?" For such is the way they talk to each other, offensively to an older ear; of social forms, of hospitable warmth, there is no faintest trace. They all call each other by their first names.

A young man comes up to them out of the dressing-room and makes his bow; he has an expanse of white shirt-front and a little black string tie. He is as pretty as a picture, dark, with rosy cheeks, clean-shaven of course, but with just a sketch of side-whisker. Not a ridiculous or flashy beauty, not like a gypsy fiddler, but just charming to look at, in a winning, well-bred way, with kind dark eyes. He even wears his dinner-jacket a little awkwardly.

"Please don't scold me, Cornelia," he says; "it's the idiotic lectures." And Ingrid presents him to her father as Herr Hergesell.

Well, and so this is Herr Hergesell. He knows his manners, does Herr Hergesell, and thanks the master of the house quite ingratiatingly for his invitation as they shake hands. "I certainly seem to have missed the bus," says he jocosely. "Of course I have lectures today up to four o'clock; I would have; and after that I had to go home to change." Then he talks about his pumps, with which he has just been struggling in the dressing-room.

"I brought them with me in a bag," he goes on. "Mustn't tramp all over the carpet in our brogues—it's not done. Well, I was ass enough not to fetch along a shoe-horn, and I find I simply can't get in! What a sell! They are the tightest I've ever had, the numbers don't tell you a thing, and all the leather today is just cast iron. It's not leather at all. My poor finger"—he confidingly displays a reddened digit and once more characterizes the whole thing as a "sell," and a putrid sell into the bargain. He really does talk just as Ingrid said he did, with a peculiar nasal drawl, not affectedly in the least, but merely because that is the way of all the Hergesells.

Dr. Cornelius says it is very careless of them not to keep a shoe-horn in the cloak-room and displays proper sympathy with the mangled finger. "But now you *really* must not let me disturb you any longer," he goes on. "*Auf wiedersehen!*" And he crosses the hall into the dining-room.

There are guests there too, drinking tea; the family table is pulled out. But the Professor goes at once to his own little upholstered corner with the electric light bulb above it—the nook where he usually drinks his tea. His wife is sitting there talking with Bert and two other young men, one of them Herzl, whom Cornelius knows and greets; the other a typical "Wandervogel"[14] named Möller, a youth who obviously neither owns nor cares to own the correct evening dress of the middle classes (in fact, there is no such thing any more), nor to ape the manners of a gentleman (and, in fact, there is no such thing any more either). He has a wilderness of hair, horn spectacles, and a long neck, and wears golf stockings and a belted blouse. His regular occupation, the Professor learns, is banking, but he is by way of being an amateur folk-lorist and collects folk-songs from all localities and in all languages. He sings them, too, and at Ingrid's command has brought his guitar; it is hanging in the dressing-room in an oilcloth case. Herzl, the actor, is small and slight, but he has a strong growth of black beard, as you can tell by the thick coat of powder on his cheeks. His eyes are larger than life, with a deep and melancholy glow. He has put on rouge besides the powder— those dull carmine high-lights on the cheeks can be nothing but a cosmetic. "Queer," thinks the Professor. "You would think a man would be one thing or the other—not melancholic and use face paint at the same time. It's a psychological contradiction. How can a melancholy man rouge? But here we have a perfect illustration of the abnormality of the artist soul-form. It can make possible a contradiction like this—perhaps it even consists in the contradiction. All very interesting—and no reason whatever for not being polite to him. Politeness is a primitive convention—and legitimate. . . . Do take some lemon, Herr Hofschauspieler!"[15]

Court actors and court theatres—there are no such things any more, really. But Herzl relishes the sound of the title, notwithstanding he is a revolutionary artist. This must be another contradiction inherent in his soul-form; so, at least, the Professor assumes, and he is probably right. The flattery he is guilty of is a sort of atonement for his previous hard thoughts about the rouge.

"Thank you so much—it's really too good of you, sir," says Herzl, quite embarrassed. He is so overcome that he almost stammers; only his perfect enunciation saves him. His whole bearing towards his hostess and the master of the house is exaggeratedly polite. It is almost as though he had a bad conscience in respect of his rouge; as though an inward compulsion had driven him to put it on, but now, seeing it through the Professor's eyes, he disapproves of it himself, and thinks, by an air of humility towards the whole of unrouged society, to mitigate its effect.

They drink their tea and chat: about Möller's folk-songs, about Basque folk-songs and Spanish folk-songs; from which they pass to the new production of *Don Carlos*[16] at the Stadttheater, in which Herzl plays the title-role. He talks about his

14 (German) Literally, bird of passage: someone with no fixed status.
15 (German) Court actor.
16 Play by Johann Christoph Friedrich von Schiller (1759–1805).

own rendering of the part and says he hopes his conception of the character has unity. They go on to criticize the rest of the cast, the setting, and the production as a whole; and Cornelius is struck, rather painfully, to find the conversation trending towards his own special province, back to Spain and the Counter-Reformation. He has done nothing at all to give it this turn, he is perfectly innocent, and hopes it does not look as though he had sought an occasion to play the professor. He wonders, and falls silent, feeling relieved when the little folk come up to the table. Ellie and Snapper have on their blue velvet Sunday frocks; they are permitted to partake in the festivities up to bed-time. They look shy and large-eyed as they say how-do-you-do to the strangers and, under pressure, repeat their names and ages. Herr Möller does nothing but gaze at them solemnly, but Herzl is simply ravished. He rolls his eyes up to heaven and puts his hands over his mouth; he positively blesses them. It all, no doubt, comes from his heart, but he is so addicted to theatrical methods of making an impression and getting an effect that both words and behaviour ring frightfully false. And even his enthusiasm for the little folk looks too much like part of his general craving to make up for the rouge on his cheeks.

The tea-table has meanwhile emptied of guests, and dancing is going on in the hall. The children run off, the Professor prepares to retire. "Go and enjoy yourselves," he says to Möller and Herzl, who have sprung from their chairs as he rises from his. They shake hands and he withdraws into his study, his peaceful kingdom, where he lets down the blinds, turns on the desk lamp, and sits down to his work.

It is work which can be done, if necessary, under disturbed conditions: nothing but a few letters and a few notes. Of course, Cornelius's mind wanders. Vague impressions float through it: Herr Hergesell's refractory pumps, the high pipe in that plump body of the Plaichinger female. As he writes, or leans back in his chair and stares into space, his thoughts go back to Herr Möller's collection of Basque folk-songs, to Herzl's posings and humility, to "his" Carlos and the court of Philip II. There is something strange, he thinks, about conversations. They are so ductile, they will flow of their own accord in the direction of one's dominating interest. Often and often he has seen this happen. And while he is thinking, he is listening to the sounds next door—rather subdued, he finds them. He hears only voices, no sound of footsteps. The dancers do not glide or circle round the room; they merely walk about over the carpet, which does not hamper their movements in the least. Their way of holding each other is quite different and strange, and they move to the strains of the gramophone, to the weird music of the new world. He concentrates on the music and makes out that it is a jazz-band record, with various percussion instruments and the clack and clatter of castanets, which, however, are not even faintly suggestive of Spain, but merely jazz like the rest. No, not Spain. . . . His thoughts are back at their old round.

Half an hour goes by. It occurs to him it would be no more than friendly to go and contribute a box of cigarettes to the festivities next door. Too bad to ask the young people to smoke their own—though they have probably never thought of it. He goes into the empty dining-room and takes a box from his supply in the cupboard: not the best ones, nor yet the brand he himself prefers, but a certain long, thin kind he is not averse to getting rid of—after all, they are nothing but youngsters. He takes the box into the hall, holds it up with a smile, and deposits it on the mantel-shelf. After which he gives a look round and returns to his own room.

There comes a lull in dance and music. The guests stand about the room in groups or round the table at the window or are seated in a circle by the fireplace. Even the built-in stairs, with their worn velvet carpet, are crowded with young folk as in an amphitheatre: Max Hergesell is there, leaning back with one elbow on the step above and gesticulating with his free hand as he talks to the shrill, voluptuous Plaichinger. The floor of the hall is nearly empty, save just in the centre: there, directly beneath the chandelier, the two little ones in their blue velvet frocks clutch each other in an awkward embrace and twirl silently round and round, oblivious of all else. Cornelius, as he passes, strokes their hair, with a friendly word; it does not distract them from their small solemn preoccupation. But at his own door he turns to glance round and sees young Hergesell push himself off the stair by his elbow—probably because he noticed the Professor. He comes down into the arena, takes Ellie out of her brother's arms, and dances with her himself. It looks very comic, without the music, and he crouches down just as Cornelius does when he goes walking with the four gentlemen, holding the fluttered Ellie as though she were grown up and taking little "shimmying" steps. Everybody watches with huge enjoyment, the gramophone is put on again, dancing becomes general. The Professor stands and looks, with his hand on the door-knob. He nods and laughs; when he finally shuts himself into his study the mechanical smile still lingers on his lips.

Again he turns over pages by his desk lamp, takes notes, attends to a few simple matters. After a while he notices that the guests have forsaken the entrance hall for his wife's drawing-room, into which there is a door from his own study as well. He hears their voices and the sounds of a guitar being tuned. Herr Möller, it seems, is to sing—and does so. He twangs the strings of his instrument and sings in a powerful bass a ballad in a strange tongue, possibly Swedish. The Professor does not succeed in identifying it, though he listens attentively to the end, after which there is great applause. The sound is deadened by the portière that hangs over the dividing door. The young bank-clerk begins another song. Cornelius goes softly in.

It is half-dark in the drawing-room; the only light is from the shaded standard lamp, beneath which Möller sits, on the divan, with his legs crossed, picking his strings. His audience is grouped easily about; as there are not enough seats, some stand, and more, among them many young ladies, are simply sitting on the floor with their hands clasped round their knees or even with their legs stretched out before them. Hergesell sits thus, in his dinner-jacket, next the piano, with Fräulein Plaichinger beside him. Frau Cornelius is holding both children on her lap as she sits in her easy-chair opposite the singer. Snapper, the Bœotian,[17] begins to talk loud and clear in the middle of the song and has to be intimidated with hushings and finger-shakings. Never, never would Ellie allow herself to be guilty of such conduct. She sits there daintily erect and still on her mother's knee. The Professor tries to catch her eye and exchange a private signal with his little girl; but she does not see him. Neither does she seem to be looking at the singer. Her gaze is directed lower down.

[17] Dullard, clown; derived from the proverbial rusticity of the inhabitants of the ancient Greek city of Boeotia.

Möller sings the "joli tambour":[18]

"Sire, mon roi, donnez-moi votre fille—"

They are all enchanted. "How good!" Hergesell is heard to say, in the odd, nasally condescending Hergesell tone. The next one is a beggar ballad, to a tune composed by young Möller himself; it elicits a storm of applause:

"Gypsy lassie a-goin' to the fair,
Huzza!
Gypsy laddie a-goin' to be there—
Huzza, diddlety umpty dido!"

Laughter and high spirits, sheer reckless hilarity, reigns after this jovial ballad. "Frightfully good!" Hergesell comments again, as before. Follows another popular song, this time a Hungarian one; Möller sings it in its own outlandish tongue, and most effectively. The Professor applauds with ostentation. It warms his heart and does him good, this outcropping of artistic, historic, and cultural elements all amongst the shimmying. He goes up to young Möller and congratulates him, talks about the songs and their sources, and Möller promises to lend him a certain annotated book of folk-songs. Cornelius is the more cordial because all the time, as fathers do, he has been comparing the parts and achievements of this young stranger with those of his own son, and being gnawed by envy and chagrin. This young Möller, he is thinking, is a capable bank-clerk (though about Möller's capacity he knows nothing whatever) and has this special gift besides, which must have taken talent and energy to cultivate. "And here is my poor Bert, who knows nothing and can do nothing and thinks of nothing except playing the clown, without even talent for that!" He tries to be just; he tells himself that, after all, Bert has innate refinement; that probably there is a good deal more to him than there is to the successful Möller; that perhaps he has even something of the poet in him, and his dancing and table-waiting are due to mere boyish folly and the distraught times. But paternal envy and pessimism win the upper hand; when Möller begins another song, Dr. Cornelius goes back to his room.

He works as before, with divided attention, at this and that, while it gets on for seven o'clock. Then he remembers a letter he may just as well write, a short letter and not very important, but letter-writing is wonderful for the way it takes up the time, and it is almost half past when he has finished. At half past eight the Italian salad will be served; so now is the prescribed moment for the Professor to go out into the wintry darkness to post his letters and take his daily quantum of fresh air and exercise. They are dancing again, and he will have to pass through the hall to get his hat and coat; but they are used to him now, he need not stop and beg them not to be disturbed. He lays away his papers, takes up the letters he has written, and goes out. But he sees his wife sitting near the door of his room and pauses a little by her easy-chair.

She is watching the dancing. Now and then the big folk or some of their guests stop to speak to her; the party is at its height, and there are more onlookers than these two: blue-faced Ann is standing at the bottom of the stairs, in all the dignity of her limitations. She is waiting for the children, who simply cannot get their fill of these unwonted festivities, and watching over Snapper, lest his

[18] An old French folk song.

all too rich blood be churned to the danger-point by too much twirling round. And not only the nursery but the kitchen takes an interest: Xaver and the two ladies Hinterhofer are standing by the pantry door looking on with relish. Fräulein Walburga, the elder of the two sunken sisters (the culinary section—she objects to being called a cook), is a whimsical, good-natured sort, brown-eyed, wearing glasses with thick circular lenses; the nose-piece is wound with a bit of rag to keep it from pressing on her nose. Fräulein Cecilia is younger, though not so precisely young either. Her bearing is as self-assertive as usual, this being her way of sustaining her dignity as a former member of the middle class. For Fräulein Cecilia feels acutely her descent into the ranks of domestic service. She positively declines to wear a cap or other badge of servitude, and her hardest trial is on the Wednesday evening when she has to serve the dinner while Xaver has his after-noon out. She hands the dishes with averted face and elevated nose—a fallen queen; and so distressing is it to behold her degradation that one evening when the little folk happened to be at table and saw her they both with one accord burst into tears. Such anguish is unknown to young Xaver. He enjoys serving and does it with an ease born of practice as well as talent, for he was once a "piccolo."[19] But otherwise he is a thorough-paced good-for-nothing and windbag—with quite distinct traits of character of his own, as his long-suffering employers are always ready to concede, but perfectly impossible and a bag of wind for all that. One must just take him as he is, they think, and not expect figs from thistles. He is the child and product of the disrupted times, a perfect specimen of his genera-tion, follower of the revolution, Bolshevist sympathizer. The Professor's name for him is the "minute-man," because he is always to be counted on in any sudden crisis, if only it address his sense of humour or love of novelty, and will display therein amazing readiness and resource. But he utterly lacks a sense of duty and can as little be trained to the performance of the daily round and common task as some kinds of dog can be taught to jump over a stick. It goes so plainly against the grain that criticism is disarmed. One becomes resigned. On grounds that appealed to him as unusual and amusing he would be ready to turn out of his bed at any hour of the night. But he simply cannot get up before eight in the morning, he cannot do it, he will not jump over the stick. Yet all day long the evidence of this free and untrammelled existence, the sound of his mouth-organ, his joyous whistle, or his raucous but expressive voice lifted in song, rises to the hearing of the world above-stairs; and the smoke of his cigarettes fills the pantry. While the Hinterhofer ladies work he stands and looks on. Of a morning while the Professor is breakfasting, he tears the leaf off the study calendar—but does not lift a finger to dust the room. Dr. Cornelius has often told him to leave the calen-dar alone, for he tends to tear off two leaves at a time and thus to add to the general confusion. But young Xaver appears to find joy in this activity, and will not be deprived of it.

Again, he is fond of children, a winning trait. He will throw himself into games with the little folk in the garden, make and mend their toys with great ingenuity, even read aloud from their books—and very droll it sounds in his thick-lipped pronunciation. With his whole soul he loves the cinema; after an evening spent there he inclines to melancholy and yearning and talking to himself. Vague hopes stir in him that some day he may make his fortune in that gay world and

[19] Apprentice waiter in a restaurant.

belong to it by rights—hopes based on his shock of hair and his physical agility and daring. He likes to climb the ash tree in the front garden, mounting branch by branch to the very top and frightening everybody to death who sees him. Once there he lights a cigarette and smokes it as he sways to and fro, keeping a look-out for a cinema director who might chance to come along and engage him.

If he changed his striped jacket for mufti, he might easily dance with the others and no one would notice the difference. For the big folk's friends are rather anomalous in their clothing: evening dress is worn by a few, but it is by no means the rule. There is quite a sprinkling of guests, both male and female, in the same general style as Möller the ballad-singer. The Professor is familiar with the circumstances of most of this young generation he is watching as he stands beside his wife's chair; he has heard them spoken of by name. They are students at the high school or at the School of Applied Art; they lead, at least the masculine portion, that precarious and scrambling existence which is purely the product of the time. There is a tall, pale, spindling youth, the son of a dentist, who lives by speculation. From all the Professor hears, he is a perfect Aladdin. He keeps a car, treats his friends to champagne suppers, and showers presents upon them on every occasion, costly little trifles in mother-of-pearl and gold. So today he has brought gifts to the young givers of the feast: for Bert a gold lead-pencil, and for Ingrid a pair of earrings of barbaric size, great gold circlets that fortunately do not have to go through the little ear-lobe, but are fastened over it by means of a clip. The big folk come laughing to their parents to display these trophies; and the parents shake their heads even while they admire—Aladdin bowing over and over from afar.

The young people appear to be absorbed in their dancing—if the performance they are carrying out with so much still concentration can be called dancing. They stride across the carpet, slowly, according to some unfathomable prescript, strangely embraced; in the newest attitude, tummy advanced and shoulders high, waggling the hips. They do not get tired, because nobody could. There is no such thing as heightened colour or heaving bosoms. Two girls may dance together or two young men—it is all the same. They move to the exotic strains of the gramophone, played with the loudest needles to procure the maximum of sound: shimmies, fox-trots, one-steps, double foxes, African shimmies, Java dances, and Creole polkas, the wild musky melodies follow one another, now furious, now languishing, a monotonous Negro programme in unfamiliar rhythm, to a clacking, clashing, and strumming orchestral accompaniment.

"What is that record?" Cornelius inquires of Ingrid, as she passes him by in the arms of the pale young speculator, with reference to the piece then playing, whose alternate languors and furies he finds comparatively pleasing and showing a certain resourcefulness in detail.

"*Prince of Pappenheim*: 'Console thee, dearest child,'" she answers, and smiles pleasantly back at him with her white teeth.

The cigarette smoke wreathes beneath the chandelier. The air is blue with a festal haze compact of sweet and thrilling ingredients that stir the blood with memories of green-sick pains and are particularly poignant to those whose youth—like the Professor's own—has been over-sensitive. . . . The little folk are still on the floor. They are allowed to stop up until eight, so great is their delight in the party. The guests have got used to their presence; in their own way, they have their place in the doings of the evening. They have separated, anyhow: Snapper revolves all alone in the middle of the carpet, in his little blue velvet smock, while Ellie is running after one of the dancing couples, trying to hold the man fast by his coat. It is Max Hergesell and Fräulein Plaichinger. They dance well, it is a pleasure to watch them. One has to admit that these mad modern dances, when the right people dance them, are not so bad after all—they have something quite taking. Young Hergesell is a capital leader, dances according to rule, yet with individuality. So it looks. With what aplomb can he walk backwards—when space permits! And he knows how to be graceful standing still in a crowd. And his partner supports him well, being unsuspectedly lithe and buoyant, as fat people often are. They look at each other, they are talking, paying no heed to Ellie, though others are smiling to see the child's persistence. Dr. Cornelius tries to catch up his little sweetheart as she passes and draw her to him. But Ellie eludes him, almost peevishly; her dear Abel is nothing to her now. She braces her little arms against his chest and turns her face away with a persecuted look. Then escapes to follow her fancy once more.

The Professor feels an involuntary twinge. Uppermost in his heart is hatred for this party, with its power to intoxicate and estrange his darling child. His love for her—that not quite disinterested, not quite unexceptionable love of his—is easily wounded. He wears a mechanical smile, but his eyes have clouded, and he stares fixedly at a point in the carpet, between the dancers' feet.

"The children ought to go to bed," he tells his wife. But she pleads for another quarter of an hour; she has promised already, and they do love it so! He smiles again and shakes his head, stands so a moment and then goes across to the cloak-room, which is full of coats and hats and scarves and overshoes. He has trouble in rummaging out his own coat, and Max Hergesell comes out of the hall, wiping his brow.

"Going out, sir?" he asks, in Hergesellian accents, dutifully helping the older man on with his coat. "Silly business this, with my pumps," he says. "They pinch like hell. The brutes are simply too tight for me, quite apart from the bad leather. They press just here on the ball of my great toe"—he stands on one foot and holds the other in his hand—"it's simply unbearable. There's nothing for it but to take them off; my brogues will have to do the business. . . . Oh, let me help you, sir."

"Thanks," says Cornelius. "Don't trouble. Get rid of your own tormentors. . . . Oh, thanks very much!" For Hergesell has gone on one knee to snap the fasteners of his snow-boots.

Once more the Professor expresses his gratitude; he is pleased and touched by so much sincere respect and youthful readiness to serve. "Go and enjoy yourself," he counsels. "Change your shoes and make up for what you have been suffering. Nobody can dance in shoes that pinch. Good-bye, I must be off to get a breath of fresh air."

"I'm going to dance with Ellie now," calls Hergesell after him. "She'll be a first-rate dancer when she grows up, and that I'll swear to."

"Think so?" Cornelius answers, already half out. "Well, you are a connoisseur, I'm sure. Don't get curvature of the spine with stooping."

He nods again and goes. "Fine lad," he thinks as he shuts the door. "Student of engineering. Knows what he's bound for, got a good clear head, and so well set up and pleasant too." And again paternal envy rises as he compares his poor Bert's status with this young man's, which he puts in the rosiest light that his son's may look the darker. Thus he sets out on his evening walk.

He goes up the avenue, crosses the bridge, and walks along the bank on the other side as far as the next bridge but one. The air is wet and cold, with a little snow now and then. He turns up his coat-collar and slips the crook of his cane over the arm behind his back. Now and then he ventilates his lungs with a long deep breath of the night air. As usual when he walks, his mind reverts to his professional preoccupations, he thinks about his lectures and the things he means to say tomorrow about Philip's struggle against the Germanic revolution, things steeped in melancholy and penetratingly just. Above all just, he thinks. For in one's dealings with the young it behooves one to display the scientific spirit, to exhibit the principles of enlightenment—not only for purposes of mental discipline, but on the human and individual side, in order not to wound them or indirectly offend their political sensibilities; particularly in these days, when there is so much tinder in the air, opinions are so frightfully split up and chaotic, and you may so easily incur attacks from one party or the other, or even give rise to scandal, by taking sides on a point of history. "And taking sides is unhistoric anyhow," so he muses. "Only justice, only impartiality is historic." And could not, properly considered, be otherwise. . . . For justice can have nothing of youthful fire and blithe, fresh, loyal conviction. It is by nature melancholy. And, being so, has secret affinity with the lost cause and the forlorn hope rather than with the fresh and blithe and loyal—perhaps this affinity is its very essence and without it it would not exist at all! . . . "And is there then no such thing as justice?" the Professor asks himself, and ponders the question so deeply that he absently posts his letters in the next box and turns round to go home. This thought of his is unsettling and disturbing to the scientific mind—but is it not after all itself scientific, psychological, conscientious, and therefore to be accepted without prejudice, no matter how upsetting? In the midst of which musings Dr. Cornelius finds himself back at his own door.

On the outer threshold stands Xaver, and seems to be looking for him.

"Herr Professor," says Xaver, tossing back his hair, "go upstairs to Ellie straight off. She's in a bad way."

"What's the matter?" asks Cornelius in alarm. "Is she ill?"

"No-o, not to say ill," answers Xaver. "She's just in a bad way and crying fit to bust her little heart. It's along o' that chap with the shirt-front that danced with her—Herr Hergesell. She couldn't be got to go upstairs peaceably, not at no price at all, and she's b'en crying bucketfuls."

"Nonsense," says the Professor, who has entered and is tossing off his things in the cloak-room. He says no more; opens the glass door and without a glance at the guests turns swiftly to the stairs. Takes them two at a time, crosses the upper hall and the small room leading into the nursery. Xaver follows at his heels, but stops at the nursery door.

A bright light still burns within, showing the gay frieze that runs all round the room, the large row of shelves heaped with a confusion of toys, the rocking-horse on his swaying platform, with red-varnished nostrils and raised hoofs. On the linoleum lie other toys—building blocks, railway trains, a little trumpet. The two white cribs stand not far apart, Ellie's in the window corner, Snapper's out in the room.

Snapper is asleep. He has said his prayers in loud, ringing tones, prompted by Nurse, and gone off at once into vehement, profound, and rosy slumber—from which a cannon-ball fired at close range could not rouse him. He lies with both fists flung back on the pillows on either side of the tousled head with its funny crooked little slumber-tossed wig.

A circle of females surrounds Ellie's bed: not only blue-faced Ann is there, but the Hinterhofer ladies too, talking to each other and to her. They make way as the Professor comes up and reveal the child sitting all pale among her pillows, sobbing and weeping more bitterly than he has ever seen her sob and weep in her life. Her lovely little hands lie on the coverlet in front of her, the nightgown with its narrow lace border has slipped down from her shoulder—such a thin, birdlike little shoulder—and the sweet head Cornelius loves so well, set on the neck like a flower on its stalk, her head is on one side, with the eyes rolled up to the corner between wall and ceiling above her head. For there she seems to envisage the anguish of her heart and even to nod to it—either on purpose or because her head wobbles as her body is shaken with the violence of her sobs. Her eyes rain down tears. The bow-shaped lips are parted, like a little *mater dolorosa's*,[20] and from them issue long, low wails that in nothing resemble the unnecessary and exasperating shrieks of a naughty child, but rise from the deep extremity of her heart and wake in the Professor's own a sympathy that is well-nigh intolerable. He has never seen his darling so before. His feelings find immediate vent in an attack on the ladies Hinterhofer.

"What about the supper?" he asks sharply. "There must be a great deal to do. Is my wife being left to do it alone?"

For the acute sensibilities of the former middle class this is quite enough. The ladies withdraw in righteous indignation, and Xaver Kleingutl jeers at them as they pass out. Having been born to low life instead of achieving it, he never loses a chance to mock at their fallen state.

"Childie, childie," murmurs Cornelius, and sitting down by the crib enfolds the anguished Ellie in his arms. "What is the trouble with my darling?"

She bedews his face with her tears.

"Abel . . . Abel . . ." she stammers between sobs. "Why—isn't Max—my brother? Max ought to be—my brother!"

Alas, alas! What mischance is this? Is this what the party has wrought, with its fatal atmosphere? Cornelius glances helplessly up at the blue-faced Ann standing there in all the dignity of her limitations with her hands before her on her apron. She purses up her mouth and makes a long face. "It's pretty young," she says, "for the female instincts to be showing up."

"Hold your tongue," snaps Cornelius, in his agony. He has this much to be thankful for, that Ellie does not turn from him now; she does not push him away as she did downstairs, but clings to him in her need, while she reiterates her absurd, bewildered prayer that Max might be her brother, or with a fresh burst of desire demands to be taken downstairs so that he can dance with her again. But Max, of course, is dancing with Fräulein Plaichinger, that behemoth who is his rightful partner and has every claim upon him; whereas Ellie—never, thinks the Professor, his heart torn with the violence of his pity, never has she looked so tiny and birdlike as now, when she nestles to him shaken with sobs and all unaware of what is happening in her little soul. No, she does not know. She does not comprehend that her suffering is on account of Fräulein Plaichinger, fat, overgrown, and utterly within her rights in dancing with Max Hergesell, whereas

[20] (Latin) Our Lady of Sorrow: applied to the Virgin Mary mourning for Christ.

Ellie may only do it once, by way of a joke, although she is incomparably the more charming of the two. Yet it would be quite mad to reproach young Hergesell with the state of affairs or to make fantastic demands upon him. No, Ellie's suffering is without help or healing and must be covered up. Yet just as it is without understanding, so it is also without restraint—and that is what makes it so horribly painful. Xaver and blue-faced Ann do not feel this pain, it does not affect them—either because of native callousness or because they accept it as the way of nature. But the Professor's fatherly heart is quite torn by it, and by a distressful horror of this passion, so hopeless and so absurd.

Of no avail to hold forth to poor Ellie on the subject of the perfectly good little brother she already has. She only casts a distraught and scornful glance over at the other crib, where Snapper lies vehemently slumbering, and with fresh tears calls again for Max. Of no avail either the promise of a long, long walk tomorrow, all five gentlemen, round and round the dining-room table; or a dramatic description of the thrilling cushion games they will play. No, she will listen to none of all this, nor to lying down and going to sleep. She will not sleep, she will sit bolt upright and suffer. . . . But on a sudden they stop and listen, Abel and Ellie; listen to something miraculous that is coming to pass, that is approaching by strides, two strides, to the nursery door, that now overwhelmingly appears. . . .

It is Xaver's work, not a doubt of that. He has not remained by the door where he stood to gloat over the ejection of the Hinterhofers. No, he has bestirred himself, taken a notion; likewise steps to carry it out. Downstairs he has gone, twitched Herr Hergesell's sleeve, and made a thick-lipped request. So here they both are. Xaver, having done his part, remains by the door; but Max Hergesell comes up to Ellie's crib; in his dinner-jacket, with his sketchy side-whisker and charming black eyes; obviously quite pleased with his rôle of swan knight[21] and fairy prince, as one who should say: "See, here am I, now all losses are restored and sorrows end!"

Cornelius is almost as much overcome as Ellie herself.

"Just look," he says feebly, "look who's here. This is uncommonly good of you, Herr Hergesell."

"Not a bit of it," says Hergesell. "Why shouldn't I come to say good-night to my fair partner?"

And he approaches the bars of the crib, behind which Ellie sits struck mute. She smiles blissfully through her tears. A funny, high little note that is half a sigh of relief comes from her lips, then she looks dumbly up at her swan knight with her golden-brown eyes—tear-swollen though they are, so much more beautiful than the fat Plaichinger's. She does not put up her arms. Her joy, like her grief, is without understanding; but she does not do that. The lovely little hands lie quiet on the coverlet, and Max Hergesell stands with his arms leaning over the rail as on a balcony.

"And now," he says smartly, "she need not 'sit the livelong night and weep upon her bed'!"[22] He looks at the Professor to make sure he is receiving due credit

[21] In Richard Wagner's opera *Lohengrin* (1847) the hero arrives in a boat drawn by swans to save Elsa of Brabant.

[22] Quoted from a lyric in Chapter 13 of *Wilhelm Meister's Apprenticeship,* a novel by Johann Wolfgang von Goethe (1749–1832). The lyric expresses the plight of a man on whom the suffering and guilt implicit in living are divinely imposed without his having chosen to undergo them.

for the quotation. "Ha ha!" he laughs, "she's beginning young. 'Console thee, dearest child!' Never mind, you're all right! Just as you are you'll be wonderful! You've only got to grow up. . . . And you'll lie down and go to sleep like a good girl, now I've come to say good-night? And not cry any more, little Lorelei?"[23]

Ellie looks up at him, transfigured. One birdlike shoulder is bare; the Professor draws the lace-trimmed nighty over it. There comes into his mind a sentimental story he once read about a dying child who longs to see a clown he had once, with unforgettable ecstasy, beheld in a circus. And they bring the clown to the bedside marvellously arrayed, embroidered before and behind with silver butterflies; and the child dies happy. Max Hergesell is not embroidered, and Ellie, thank God, is not going to die, she has only been "in a bad way." But, after all, the effect is the same. Young Hergesell leans over the bars of the crib and rattles on, more for the father's ear than the child's, but Ellie does not know that—and the father's feelings towards him are a most singular mixture of thankfulness, embarrassment, and hatred.

"Good night, little Lorelei," says Hergesell, and gives her his hand through the bars. Her pretty, soft, white little hand is swallowed up in the grasp of his big, strong, red one. "Sleep well," he says, "and sweet dreams! But don't dream about me—God forbid! Not at your age—ha ha!" And then the fairy clown's visit is at an end. Cornelius accompanies him to the door. "No, no, positively, no thanks called for, don't mention it," he large-heartedly protests; and Xaver goes downstairs with him, to help serve the Italian salad.

But Dr. Cornelius returns to Ellie, who is now lying down, with her cheek pressed into her flat little pillow.

"Well, wasn't that lovely?" he says as he smooths the covers. She nods, with one last little sob. For a quarter of an hour he sits beside her and watches while she falls asleep in her turn, beside the little brother who found the right way so much earlier than she. Her silky brown hair takes the enchanting fall it always does when she sleeps; deep, deep lie the lashes over the eyes that late so abundantly poured forth their sorrow; the angelic mouth with its bowed upper lip is peacefully relaxed and a little open. Only now and then comes a belated catch in her slow breathing.

And her small hands, like pink and white flowers, lie so quietly, one on the coverlet, the other on the pillow by her face—Dr. Cornelius, gazing, feels his heart melt with tenderness as with strong wine.

"How good," he thinks, "that she breathes in oblivion with every breath she draws! That in childhood each night is a deep wide gulf between one day and the next. Tomorrow, beyond all doubt, young Hergesell will be a pale shadow, powerless to darken her little heart. Tomorrow, forgetful of all but present joy, she will walk with Abel and Snapper, all five gentlemen, round and round the table, will play the ever-thrilling cushion game."

Heaven be praised for that!

[23] Legendary siren of the Rhine, whose beauty distracted sailors from the dangers of the surrounding cliffs and rocks.

DI GRASSO
A Tale of Odessa

ISAAC BABEL
1894–1939

I WAS FOURTEEN, and of the undauntable fellowship of dealers in theater tickets. My boss was a tricky customer with a permanently screwed-up eye and enormous silky handle bars; Nick Schwarz was his name. I came under his sway in that unhappy year when the Italian Opera flopped in Odessa.[1] Taking a lead from the critics on the local paper, our impresario decided not to import Anselmi and Tito Ruffo as guest artistes but to make do with a good stock company. For this he was sorely punished; he went bankrupt, and we with him. We were promised Chaliapin to straighten out our affairs, but Chaliapin wanted three thousand a performance; so instead we had the Sicilian tragedian Di Grasso with his troupe. They arrived at the hotel in peasant carts crammed with children, cats, cages in which Italian birds hopped and skipped. Casting an eye over this gypsy crew, Nick Schwarz opined:

"Children, this stuff won't sell."

When he had settled in, the tragedian made his way to the market with a bag. In the evening he arrived at the theater with another bag. Hardly fifty people had turned up. We tried selling tickets at half-price, but there were no takers.

[1] A city in the U.S.S.R.

That evening they staged a Sicilian folk drama, a tale as commonplace as the change from night to day and vice versa. The daughter of a rich peasant pledges her troth to a shepherd. She is faithful to him till one day there drives out from the city a young slicker in a velvet waistcoat. Passing the time of day with the new arrival, the maiden giggled in all the wrong places and fell silent when she shouldn't have. As he listened to them, the shepherd twisted his head this way and that like a startled bird. During the whole of the first act he kept flattening himself against walls, dashing off somewhere, his pants flapping, and on his return gazing wildly about.

"This stuff stinks," said Nick Schwarz in the intermission. "Only place it might go down is some dump like Kremenchug."

The intermission was designed to give the maiden time to grow ripe for betrayal. In the second act we just couldn't recognize her: she behaved insufferably, her thoughts were clearly elsewhere, and she lost no time in handing the shepherd back his ring. Thereupon he led her over to a poverty-stricken but brightly painted image of the Holy Virgin, and said in his Sicilian patois:

"Signora," said he in a low voice, turning away, "the Holy Virgin desires you to give me a hearing. To Giovanni, the fellow from the city, the Holy Virgin will grant as many women as he can cope with; but I need none save you. The Virgin Mary, our stainless intercessor, will tell you exactly the same thing if you ask Her."

The maiden stood with her back to the painted wooden image. As she listened she kept impatiently tapping her foot.

In the third act Giovanni, the city slicker, met his fate. He was having a shave at the village barber's, his powerful male legs thrust out all over the front of the stage. Beneath the Sicilian sun the pleats in his waistcoat gleamed. The scene represented a village fair. In a far corner stood the shepherd; silent he stood there amid the carefree crowd. First he hung his head; then he raised it, and beneath the weight of his attentive and burning gaze Giovanni started stirring and fidgeting in his barber chair, till pushing the barber aside he leaped to his feet. In a voice shaking with passion he demanded that the policeman should remove from the village square all persons of a gloomy and suspicious aspect. The shepherd—the part was played by Di Grasso himself—stood there lost in thought; then he gave a smile, soared into the air, sailed across the stage, plunged down on Giovanni's shoulders, and having bitten through the latter's throat, began, growling and squinting, to suck blood from the wound. Giovanni collapsed, and the curtain, falling noiselessly and full of menace, hid from us killed and killer. Waiting for no more, we dashed to the box office in Theater Lane, which was to open next day, Nick Schwarz beating the rest by a short neck. Came the dawn, and with it the *Odessa News* informed the few people who had been at the theater that they had seen the most remarkable actor of the century.

On this visit Di Grasso played *King Lear, Othello, Civil Death,* Turgenev's *The Parasite,* confirming with every word and every gesture that there is more justice in outbursts of noble passion than in all the joyless rules that run the world.

Tickets for these shows were snapped up at five times face value. Scouting round for ticket-traders, would-be purchasers found them at the inn, yelling their heads off, purple, vomiting a harmless sacrilege.

A pink and dusty sultriness was injected into Theater Lane. Shopkeepers in felt slippers bore green bottles of wine and barrels of olives out onto the pavement. In tubs outside the shops macaroni seethed in foaming water, and the steam from it melted in the distant skies. Old women in men's boots dealt in seashells and souvenirs, pursuing hesitant purchasers with loud cries. Moneyed Jews with beards parted down the middle and combed to either side would drive up to the Northern Hotel and tap discreetly on the doors of fat women with raven hair and little mustaches, Di Grasso's actresses. All were happy in Theater Lane; all, that is, save for one person. I was that person. In those days catastrophe was approaching me: at any moment my father might miss the watch I had taken without his permission and pawned to Nick Schwarz. Having had the gold turnip long enough to get used to it, and being a man who replaced tea as his morning drink by Bessarabian wine, Nick Schwarz, even with his money back, could still not bring himself to return the watch to me. Such was his character. And my father's character differed in no wise from his. Hemmed in by these two characters, I sorrowfully watched other people enjoying themselves. Nothing remained for me but to run away to Constantinople. I had made all the arrangements with the second engineer of the S.S. *Duke of Kent,* but before embarking on the deep I decided to say goodbye to Di Grasso. For the last time he was playing the shepherd who is swung aloft by an incomprehensible power. In the audience were all the Italian colony, with the bald but shapely consul at their head. There were fidgety Greeks and bearded externs with their gaze fastened fanatically upon some point invisible to all other mortals; there was the long-armed Utochkin. Nick Schwarz had even brought his missis, in a violet shawl with a fringe; a woman with all the makings of a grenadier she was, stretching right out to the steppes, and with a sleepy little crumpled face at the far end. When the curtain fell this face was drenched in tears.

"Now you see what love means," she said to Nick as they were leaving the theater.

Stomping ponderously, Madam Schwarz moved along Langeron Street; tears rolled from her fishlike eyes, and the shawl with the fringe shuddered on her obese shoulders. Dragging her mannish soles, rocking her head, she reckoned up, in a voice that made the street re-echo, the women who got on well with their husbands.

"'Ducky' they're called by their husbands; 'sweetypie' they're called . . ."

The cowed Nick walked along by his wife, quietly blowing on his silky mustaches. From force of habit I followed on behind, sobbing. During a momentary pause Madam Schwarz heard my sobs and turned around.

"See here," she said to her husband, her fisheyes agoggle, "may I not die a beautiful death if you don't give the boy his watch back!"

Nick froze, mouth agape; then came to and, giving me a vicious pinch, thrust the watch at me sideways.

"What can I expect of him," the coarse and tear-muffled voice of Madam Schwarz wailed disconsolately as it moved off into the distance, "what can I expect but beastliness today and beastliness tomorrow? I ask you, how long is a woman supposed to put up with it?"

They reached the corner and turned into Pushkin Street. I stood there clutching the watch, alone; and suddenly, with a distinctness such as I had never before experienced, I saw the columns of the Municipal Building soaring up into the heights, the gas-lit foliage of the boulevard, Pushkin's bronze head touched by the dim gleam of the moon; saw for the first time the things surrounding me as they really were: frozen in silence and ineffably beautiful.

COMMENTARY

One of the conventional ways of praising art is to associate it with the peaceful and "constructive" virtues and to put it at the furthest possible remove from violence. But artists themselves are not misled by this pious view of their enterprise. They know how often the act of creation is bound up with the aggressive impulses. And perhaps no one has made this knowledge quite so salient in his conception of art as Isaac Babel.

Babel was one of the very few writers of genius to develop under Soviet rule. For a short period after his work began to appear in the 1920's, his remarkable gifts were recognized and he enjoyed a measure of fame, but then he fell into disfavor with the regime and was accused of political crimes. Although never brought to trial, he was sent to a prison camp, where he died in 1939 or 1940.

The great—the crucial—experience of Babel's life was his service with a regiment of Cossacks in 1920 during a campaign of the terrible civil war that followed the Russian Revolution. To understand the meaning of this experience, we must know that Babel was a Jew and that no two peoples could be more completely and significantly antithetical to each other than the Jews of Eastern Europe and the Cossacks. The Jews conceived their ideal character to be intellectual, humane, and peaceable. The Cossacks were physical and violent, men of the body, the sword, and the horse. The relation between the two groups had long been extremely hostile. Each held the other in contempt, and the hatred between them was the more intense because the Czarist government of Russia had used Cossack troops in its systematic persecution of the Jews. Nothing, then, could have been more anomalous than that a Jew—and an intellectual and rather weakly Jew at that, a man "with spectacles on his nose and autumn in his heart," as Babel described himself—should ride and fight by the side of the Cossacks. It is clear from his superb stories about this experience—they were collected in a volume called *Red Cavalry*—that Babel wanted to eradicate from his temperament the quietism that had been instilled into it by his Jewish upbringing, and that it was for this reason that he undertook to share the Cossack life of physicality and violence, even of cruelty.

Babel's wish to model his behavior on that of his Cossack comrades was not easily attained. He found, as he said, that to face death was not so very hard, but that it was hard indeed to acquire what he called "the simplest of proficiencies—the ability to kill [one's] fellowmen." Much as he admired the grace and force of the Cossacks and the fierce directness with which they expressed their feelings, he could not rid himself of the pacific ideals of his Jewish heritage. But although the way of peace and the way of violence were always in conflict in his mind, it is plain that his interest was more engaged by the way of violence. It seemed to promise him a kind of liberation of spirit and his fulfilment as a man.

No less did it promise him liberation and fulfilment as a writer. Babel was intensely conscious of the problems of style, and whenever he talked about style he resorted to metaphors of physical violence. He spoke of prose as a series of military maneuvers executed by the "army of words, the army in which all kinds of weapons may be brought into play." He remarked that "there is no iron that can enter the human heart with such stupefying effect as a period placed at just the right moment." He thought that the essence of art was unexpectedness, a surprise attack upon the reader's habitual assumptions.

This conception of art as disciplined violence is the theme of what was to be the last story that Babel wrote. "Di Grasso" is composed in the intimate, colloquial, seemingly casual manner that Babel had made his own, and on first reading it may seem to be a very simple story, not much more than an anecdote. But Babel was anything but a simple man, and this story has all the subtlety and complexity that we might expect to find in a highly developed writer's apologia for his art, which in effect "Di Grasso" is.

An Italian theatrical company has come for a repertory season to Odessa, Russia's great Black Sea port, a city famous for its cosmopolitan interest in the arts of performance. The troupe's first performance begins in a most unpromising way, for the play is a dull provincial piece, the acting is ridden by cliché and convention. But then one moment brings to an end, and redeems, all the boredom—when the actor Di Grasso "gave a smile, soared into the air, sailed across the stage, plunged down on [the villain's] shoulders, and having bitten through the latter's throat, began, growling and squinting, to suck blood from the wound." Di Grasso is to go through a long repertory, and in all his performances he will "with every word and every gesture" confirm the idea that "there is more justice in outbursts of noble passion than in all the joyless rules that run the world." But although he plays Othello and King Lear, the nature of his genius is most forcibly suggested to the young protagonist of the story—whom we take to be a representation of Babel himself—not by his performance of these great rôles but by the absurd incident of physical violence in an inferior play.

What was it in that moment of melodramatic nonsense that enchanted the audience and became so memorable to the author? Certainly the sheer virtuosity of the leap is a decisive element—the actor's extraordinary ability to "soar into the air," to "sail across the stage," to do, or seem to do, what presumably cannot be done. Although the word *virtuosity* may indeed be used in praise, it may also be used with a contemptuous intention, to suggest mere technical skill, with, by implication, a paucity of spiritual or intellectual energy. Yet mere technical skill can delight us, as in the performance of jugglers, trapeze artists, and stage magicians. And an unusual degree of technical skill has the effect of enhancing or confirming the other qualities an artist may possess. Everyone who saw Nijinski perform believed him to be the greatest dancer of all time, and almost every account of his art makes reference to one extraordinary achievement—his power of levitation, his ability, like Di Grasso's, to soar into the air and sail across the stage. Those who saw him do this seem to have had an intimation of the possibility of freedom from the bondage of our human condition. It is no small idea for a leap to propose!

The naked ferocity that Di Grasso displays has an effect related to that of his astonishing leap—it, too, suggests the idea of a liberation. This, however, is a liberation not from the general human condition but from the constraints of society, from the dullness, the passivity, the acquiescence in which we live most of our lives.

But the intention of Babel's story goes beyond its celebration of the great murderous leap and its assertion that intensity, or "noble passion," is the very soul of art. Babel is concerned with the moral effect which may result from the kind of aesthetic experience he has described.

The wife of the ticket speculator would seem to be the least likely person in the world to exemplify the moral power that art can have. She is gross in manner, grotesque in appearance, and therefore she ought not, by conventional notions, be susceptible to the noble passions; and we may easily suppose that what susceptibility she does have will not last very long. Yet, if only for the moment, the great leap of Di Grasso and his display of ferocity bring to her mind ideas of love, tenderness, and generosity, and she turns upon her cadging husband in rage at his lack of all large-minded emotions. What is more, she recalls a particular instance of her husband's meanness that she will no longer put up with. Decency has become suddenly, if fleetingly, important to her—she knows that her husband has been keeping illicitly a watch that belongs to his young assistant's father; she insists that it be returned at once and she is not to be withstood.

The story might well have come to its end with this episode, but the final paragraph carries it to a further development of great charm and profundity. The young Babel—for at this point we can no longer doubt that the narrator is the author writing about himself in his youth—is freed from the anguish and fear caused by his being unable to regain possession of his father's watch, and now, all at once, he perceives the street in which he stands with "a distinctness such as [he] had never before experienced." Now, "for the first time," he sees the things around him "as they really were: frozen in silence and ineffably beautiful." His sudden unexpected relief from anxiety and wretchedness has brought about this almost mystical perception. An aesthetic experience has produced an act of moral decency; the act of moral decency becomes the cause of a transcendent experience. We can scarcely suppose that Babel was unaware of the irony implicit in the fact that the pure and peaceful contemplation described in the last paragraph of "Di Grasso" owed its existence to the violence of the actor's leap.

HILLS
LIKE
WHITE
ELEPHANTS

ERNEST HEMINGWAY

1898–1961

THE HILLS ACROSS THE VALLEY of the Ebro were long and white. On this side there was no shade and no trees and the station was between two lines of rails in the sun. Close against the side of the station there was the warm shadow of the building and a curtain, made of strings of bamboo beads, hung across the open door into the bar, to keep out flies. The American and the girl with him sat at a table in the shade, outside the building. It was very hot and the express from Barcelona would come in forty minutes. It stopped at this junction for two minutes and went on to Madrid.

"What should we drink?" the girl asked. She had taken off her hat and put it on the table.

"It's pretty hot," the man said.

"Let's drink beer."

"Doz cervezas," the man said into the curtain.

"Big ones?" a woman asked from the doorway.

"Yes. Two big ones."

The woman brought two glasses of beer and two felt pads. She put the felt pads and the beer glasses on the table and looked at the man and the girl. The girl was looking off at the line of hills. They were white in the sun and the country was brown and dry.

"They look like white elephants," she said.

"I've never seen one," the man drank his beer.

"No, you wouldn't have."

"I might have," the man said. "Just because you say I wouldn't have doesn't prove anything."

The girl looked at the bead curtain. "They've painted something on it," she said. "What does it say?"

"Anis del Toro. It's a drink."

"Could we try it?"

The man called "Listen" through the curtain. The woman came out from the bar.

"Four reales."

"We want two Anis del Toro."

"With water?"

"Do you want it with water?"

"I don't know," the girl said. "Is it good with water?"

"It's all right."

"You want them with water?" asked the woman.

"Yes, with water."

"It tastes like licorice," the girl said and put the glass down.

"That's the way with everything."

"Yes," said the girl. "Everything tastes of licorice. Especially all the things you've waited so long for, like absinthe."

"Oh, cut it out."

"You started it," the girl said. "I was being amused. I was having a fine time."

"Well, let's try to have a fine time."

"All right. I was trying. I said the mountains looked like white elephants. Wasn't that bright?"

"That was bright."

"I wanted to try this new drink. That's all we do, isn't it—look at things and try new drinks?"

"I guess so."

The girl looked across at the hills.

"They're lovely hills," she said. "They don't really look like white elephants. I just meant the coloring of their skin through the trees."

"Should we have another drink?"

"All right."

The warm wind blew the bead curtain against the table.

"The beer's nice and cool," the man said.

"It's lovely," the girl said.

"It's really an awfully simple operation, Jig," the man said. "It's not really an operation at all."

The girl looked at the ground the table legs rested on.

"I know you wouldn't mind it, Jig. It's really not anything. It's just to let the air in."

The girl did not say anything.

"I'll go with you and I'll stay with you all the time. They just let the air in and then it's all perfectly natural."

"Then what will we do afterward?"

"We'll be fine afterward. Just like we were before."

"What makes you think so?"

"That's the only thing that bothers us. It's the only thing that's made us unhappy."

The girl looked at the bead curtain, put her hand out and took hold of two of the strings of beads.

"And you think then we'll be all right and be happy."

"I know we will. You don't have to be afraid. I've known lots of people that have done it."

"So have I," said the girl. "And afterward they were all so happy."

"Well," the man said, "if you don't want to you don't have to. I wouldn't have you do it if you didn't want to. But I know it's perfectly simple."

"And you really want to?"

"I think it's the best thing to do. But I don't want you to do it if you don't really want to."

"And if I do it you'll be happy and things will be like they were and you'll love me?"

"I love you now. You know I love you."

"I know. But if I do it, then it will be nice again if I say things are like white elephants, and you'll like it?"

"I'll love it. I love it now but I just can't think about it. You know how I get when I worry."

"If I do it you won't ever worry?"

"I won't worry about that because it's perfectly simple."

"Then I'll do it. Because I don't care about me."

"What do you mean?"

"I don't care about me."

"Well, I care about you."

"Oh, yes. But I don't care about me. And I'll do it and then everything will be fine."

"I don't want you to do it if you feel that way."

The girl stood up and walked to the end of the station. Across, on the other side, were fields of grain and trees along the banks of the Ebro. Far away, beyond the river, were mountains. The shadow of a cloud moved across the field of grain and she saw the river through the trees.

"And we could have all this," she said. "And we could have everything and every day we make it more impossible."

"What did you say?"

"I said we could have everything."

"We can have everything."

" No, we can't."

"We can have the whole world."

"No, we can't."

"We can go everywhere."

"No, we can't. It isn't ours any more."

"It's ours."

"No, it isn't. And once they take it away, you never get it back."

"But they haven't taken it away."

"We'll wait and see."

"Come on back in the shade," he said. "You mustn't feel that way."

"I don't feel any way," the girl said. "I just know things."

"I don't want you to do anything that you don't want to do———"

"Nor that isn't good for me," she said. "I know. Could we have another beer?"

"All right. But you've got to realize———"

"I realize," the girl said. "Can't we maybe stop talking?"

They sat down at the table and the girl looked across at the hills on the dry side of the valley and the man looked at her and at the table.

"You've got to realize," he said, "that I don't want you to do it if you don't want to. I'm perfectly willing to go through with it if it means anything to you."

"Doesn't it mean anything to you? We could get along."

"Of course it does. But I don't want anybody but you. I don't want any one else. And I know it's perfectly simple."

"Yes, you know it's perfectly simple."

"It's all right for you to say that, but I do know it."

"Would you do something for me now?"

"I'd do anything for you."

"Would you please please please please please please please stop talking?"

He did not say anything but looked at the bags against the wall of the station. There were labels on them from all the hotels where they had spent nights.

"But I don't want you to," he said, "I don't care anything about it."

"I'll scream," said the girl.

The woman came out through the curtains with two glasses of beer and put them down on the damp felt pads. "The train comes in five minutes," he said.

"What did she say?" asked the girl.

"That the train is coming in five minutes."

The girl smiled brightly at the woman, to thank her.

"I'd rather take the bags over to the other side of the station," the man said. She smiled at him.

"All right. Then come back and we'll finish the beer."

He picked up the two heavy bags and carried them around the station to the other tracks. He looked up the tracks but could not see the train. Coming back, he walked through the barroom, where people waiting for the train were drinking. He drank an Anis at the bar and looked at the people. They were all waiting reasonably for the train. He went out through the bead curtain. She was sitting at the table and smiled at him.

"Do you feel better?" he asked.

"I feel fine," she said. "There's nothing wrong with me. I feel fine."

BARN
BURNING

WILLIAM FAULKNER

1 8 9 7 – 1 9 6 2

THE STORE IN WHICH the Justice of the Peace's court was sitting smelled of cheese. The boy, crouched on his nail keg at the back of the crowded room, knew he smelled cheese, and more: from where he sat he could see the ranked shelves close-packed with the solid, squat, dynamic shapes of tin cans whose labels his stomach read, not from the lettering which meant nothing to his mind but from the scarlet devils and the silver curve of fish—this, the cheese which he knew he smelled and the hermetic meat which his intestines believed he smelled coming in intermittent gusts momentary and brief between the other constant one, the smell and sense just a little of fear because mostly of despair and grief, the old fierce pull of blood. He could not see the table where the Justice sat and before which his father and his father's enemy (*our enemy* he thought in that despair; *ourn! mine and hisn both! He's my father!*) stood, but he could hear them, the two of them that is, because his father had said no word yet:

"But what proof have you, Mr. Harris?"

"I told you. The hog got into my corn. I caught it up and sent it back to him. He had no fence that would hold it. I told him so, warned him. The next time I put the hog in my pen. When he came to get it I gave him enough wire to patch up his pen. The next time I put the hog up and kept it. I rode down to his house and saw the wire I gave him still rolled on to the spool in his yard. I told him he could have the hog when he paid me a dollar pound fee. That evening a nigger came with the dollar and got the hog. He was a strange nigger. He said, 'He say to tell you wood and hay kin burn.' I said, 'What?' 'That whut he say to tell you,' the nigger said. 'Wood and hay kin burn.' That night my barn burned. I got the stock out but I lost the barn."

"Where is the nigger? Have you got him?"

"He was a strange nigger, I tell you. I don't know what became of him."

"But that's not proof. Don't you see that's not proof?"

"Get that boy up here. He knows." For a moment the boy thought too that the man meant his older brother until Harris said, "Not him. The little one. The boy," and, crouching, small for his age, small and wiry like his father, in patched and faded jeans even too small for him, with straight, uncombed, brown hair and eyes gray and wild as storm scud, he saw the men between himself and the table part and become a lane of grim faces, at the end of which he saw the Justice, a shabby, collarless, graying man in spectacles, beckoning him. He felt no floor under his bare feet; he seemed to walk beneath the palpable weight of the grim turning faces. His father, stiff in his black Sunday coat donned not for the trial but for the moving, did not even look at him. *He aims for me to lie,* he thought, again with that frantic grief and despair. *And I will have to do hit.*

"What's your name, boy?" the Justice said.

"Colonel Sartoris Snopes," the boy whispered.

"Hey?" the Justice said. "Talk louder. Colonel Sartoris? I reckon anybody named for Colonel Sartoris in this country can't help but tell the truth, can they?" The boy said nothing. *Enemy! Enemy!* he thought; for a moment he could not even see, could not see that the Justice's face was kindly nor discern that his voice was troubled when he spoke to the man named Harris: "Do you want me to question this boy?" But he could hear, and during those subsequent long seconds while there was absolutely no sound in the crowded little room save that of quiet and intent breathing it was as if he had swung outward at the end of a grape vine, over a ravine, and at the top of the swing had been caught in a prolonged instant of mesmerized gravity, weightless in time.

"No!" Harris said violently, explosively. "Damnation! Send him out of here!" Now time, the fluid world, rushed beneath him again, the voices coming to him again through the smell of cheese and sealed meat, the fear and despair and the old grief of blood:

"This case is closed. I can't find against you, Snopes, but I can give you advice. Leave this country and don't come back to it."

His father spoke for the first time, his voice cold and harsh, level, without emphasis: "I aim to. I don't figure to stay in a country among people who . . ." he said something unprintable and vile, addressed to no one.

"That'll do," the Justice said. "Take your wagon and get out of this country before dark. Case dismissed."

His father turned, and he followed the stiff black coat, the wiry figure walking a little stiffly from where a Confederate provost's man's musket ball had taken him in the heel on a stolen horse thirty years ago, followed the two backs now, since his older brother had appeared from somewhere in the crowd, no taller than the father but thicker, chewing tobacco steadily, between the two lines of grim-faced men and out of the store and across the worn gallery and down the sagging steps and among the dogs and half-grown boys in the mild May dust, where as he passed a voice hissed:

"Barn burner!"

Again he could not see, whirling; there was a face in a red haze, moon-like, bigger than the full moon, the owner of it half again his size, he leaping in the red haze toward the face, feeling no blow, feeling no shock when his head struck the earth, scrabbling up and leaping again, feeling no blow this time either and tasting no blood, scrabbling up to see the other boy in full flight and himself already leaping into pursuit as his father's hand jerked him back, the harsh, cold voice speaking above him: "Go get in the wagon."

It stood in a grove of locusts and mulberries across the road. His two hulking sisters in their Sunday dresses and his mother and her sister in calico and sunbonnets were already in it, sitting on and among the sorry residue of the dozen and more movings which even the boy could remember—the battered stove, the broken beds and chairs, the clock inlaid with mother-of-pearl, which would not run, stopped at some fourteen minutes past two o'clock of a dead and forgotten day and time, which had been his mother's dowry. She was crying, though when she saw him she drew her sleeve across her face and began to descend from the wagon. "Get back," the father said.

"He's hurt. I got to get some water and wash his . . ."

"Get back in the wagon," his father said. He got in too, over the tail-gate. His father mounted to the seat where the older brother already sat and struck the gaunt mules two savage blows with the peeled willow, but without heat. It was not even sadistic; it was exactly that same quality which in later years would cause his descendants to over-run the engine before putting a motor car into motion, striking and reining back in the same movement. The wagon went on, the store with its quiet crowd of grimly watching men dropped behind; a curve in the road hid it. *Forever* he thought. *Maybe he's done satisfied now, now that he has* . . . stopping himself, not to say it aloud even to himself. His mother's hand touched his shoulder.

"Does hit hurt?" she said.

"Naw," he said. "Hit don't hurt. Lemme be."

"Can't you wipe some of the blood off before hit dries?"

"I'll wash to-night," he said. "Lemme be, I tell you."

The wagon went on. He did not know where they were going. None of them ever did or ever asked, because it was always somewhere, always a house of sorts waiting for them a day or two days or even three days away. Likely his father had already arranged to make a crop on another farm before he . . . Again he had to stop himself. He (the father) always did. There was something about his wolflike independence and even courage when the advantage was at least neutral which impressed strangers, as if they got from his latent ravening ferocity not so much a sense of dependability as a feeling that his ferocious conviction in the rightness of his own actions would be of advantage to all whose interest lay with his.

That night they camped in a grove of oaks and beeches where a spring ran. The nights were still cool and they had a fire against it, of a rail lifted from a nearby fence and cut into lengths—a small fire, neat, niggard almost, a shrewd fire; such fires were his father's habit and custom always, even in freezing weather. Older, the boy might have remarked this and wondered why not a big one; why should not a man who had not only seen the waste and extravagance of war, but who had in his blood an inherent voracious prodigality with material not his own, have burned everything in sight? Then he might have gone a step farther and thought that that was the reason: that niggard blaze was the living fruit of nights passed during those four years in the woods hiding from all men, blue or gray, with his strings of horses (captured horses, he called them). And older still, he might have divined the true reason: that the element of fire spoke to some deep mainspring of his father's being, as the element of steel or of powder spoke to other men, as the one weapon for the preservation of integrity, else breath were not worth the breathing, and hence to be regarded with respect and used with discretion.

But he did not think this now and he had seen those same niggard blazes all his life. He merely ate his supper beside it and was already half asleep over his iron plate when his father called him, and once more he followed the stiff back, the stiff and ruthless limp, up the slope and on to the starlit road where, turning, he could see his father against the stars but without face or depth—a shape black, flat, and bloodless as though cut from tin in the iron folds of the frockcoat which had not been made for him, the voice harsh like tin and without heat like tin:

"You were fixing to tell them. You would have told him." He didn't answer. His father struck him with the flat of his hand on the side of the head, hard but without heat, exactly as he had struck the two mules at the store, exactly as he would strike either of them with any stick in order to kill a horse fly, his voice still without heat or anger: "You're getting to be a man. You got to learn. You got to learn to stick to your own blood or you ain't going to have any blood to stick to you. Do you think either of them, any man there this morning, would? Don't you know all they wanted was a chance to get at me because they knew I had them beat? Eh?" Later, twenty years later, he was to tell himself, "If I had said they wanted only truth, justice, he would have hit me again." But now he said nothing. He was not crying. He just stood there. "Answer me," his father said.

"Yes," he whispered. His father turned.

"Get on to bed. We'll be there to-morrow."

To-morrow they were there. In the early afternoon the wagon stopped before a paintless two-room house identical almost with the dozen others it had stopped before even in the boy's ten years, and again, as on the other dozen occasions, his mother and aunt got down and began to unload the wagon, although his two sisters and his father and brother had not moved.

"Likely hit ain't fitten for hawgs," one of the sisters said.

"Nevertheless, fit it will and you'll hog it and like it," his father said. "Get out of them chairs and help your Ma unload."

The two sisters got down, big, bovine, in a flutter of cheap ribbons; one of them drew from the jumbled wagon bed a battered lantern, the other a worn broom. His father handed the reins to the older son and began to climb stiffly over the wheel. "When they get unloaded, take the team to the barn and feed them." Then he said, and at first the boy thought he was still speaking to his brother: "Come with me."

"Me?" he said.

"Yes," his father said. "You."

"Abner," his mother said. His father paused and looked back—the harsh level stare beneath the shaggy, graying, irascible brows.

"I reckon I'll have a word with the man that aims to begin to-morrow owning me body and soul for the next eight months."

They went back up the road. A week ago—or before last night, that is— he would have asked where they were going, but not now. His father had struck him before last night but never before had he paused afterward to explain why; it was as if the blow and the following calm, outrageous voice still rang, reper- cussed, divulging nothing to him save the terrible handicap of being young, the light weight of his few years, just heavy enough to prevent his soaring free of the world as it seemed to be ordered but not heavy enough to keep him footed solid in it, to resist it and try to change the course of its events.

Presently he could see the grove of oaks and cedars and the other flowering trees and shrubs where the house would be, though not the house yet. They walked beside a fence massed with honeysuckle and Cherokee roses and came to a gate swinging open between two brick pillars, and now, beyond a sweep of drive, he saw the house for the first time and at that instant he forgot his father and the terror and despair both, and even when he remembered his father again (who had not stopped) the terror and despair did not return. Because, for all the twelve movings, they had sojourned until now in a poor country, a land of small farms and fields and houses, and he had never seen a house like this before. *Hit's big as a courthouse* he thought quietly, with a surge of peace and joy whose reason he could not have thought into words, being too young for that: *They are safe from him. People whose lives are a part of this peace and dignity are beyond his touch, he no more to them than a buzzing wasp: capable of stinging for a little moment but that's all; the spell of this peace and dignity rendering even the barns and stable and cribs which belong to it impervious to the puny flames he might contrive* . . . this, the peace and joy, ebbing for an instant as he looked again at the stiff black back, the stiff and implacable limp of the figure which was not dwarfed by the house, for the reason that it had never looked big anywhere and which now, again the serene columned back- drop, had more than ever that impervious quality of something cut ruthlessly from tin, depthless, as though, sidewise to the sun, it would cast no shadow. Watching him, the boy remarked the absolutely undeviating course which his father held and saw the stiff foot come squarely down in a pile of fresh drop- pings where a horse had stood in the drive and which his father could have avoided by a simple change of stride. But it ebbed only for a moment, though he could not have thought this into words either, walking on in the spell of the house, which he could even want but without envy, without sorrow, certainly never with that ravening and jealous rage which unknown to him walked in the ironlike black coat before him. *Maybe he will feel it too. Maybe it will even change him now from what maybe he couldn't help but be.*

They crossed the portico. Now he could hear his father's stiff foot as it came down on the boards with clocklike finality, a sound out of all proportion to the displacement of the body it bore and which was not dwarfed either by the white door before it, as though it had attained to a sort of vicious and raven- ing minimum not to be dwarfed by anything—the flat, wide, black hat, the formal coat of broadcloth which had once been black but which had now the friction-glazed greenish cast of the bodies of old house flies, the lifted sleeve which was too large, the lifted hand like a curled claw. The door opened so promptly that the boy knew the Negro must have been watching them all the time, an old man with neat grizzled hair, in a linen jacket, who stood barring the door with his body, saying, "Wipe yo foots, white man, fo you come in here. Major ain't home nohow."

"Get out of my way, nigger," his father said, without heat too, flinging the door back and the Negro also and entering, his hat still on his head. And now the boy saw the prints of the stiff foot on the doorjamb and saw them appear on the pale rug behind the machinelike deliberation of the foot which seemed to bear (or transmit) twice the weight which the body compassed. The Negro was shouting "Miss Lula! Miss Lula!" somewhere behind them, then the boy, deluged as though by a warm wave by a suave turn of carpeted stair and a pendant glitter of chandeliers and a mute gleam of gold frames, heard the swift feet and saw her too, a lady—perhaps he had never seen her like before either—in a gray, smooth gown with lace at the throat and an apron tied at the waist and the sleeves turned back, wiping cake or biscuit dough from her hands with a towel as she came up the hall, looking not at his father at all but at the tracks on the blond rug with an expression of incredulous amazement.

"I tried," the Negro cried. "I tole him to . . ."

"Will you please go away?" she said in a shaking voice. "Major de Spain is not at home. Will you please go away?"

His father had not spoken again. He did not speak again. He did not even look at her. He just stood stiff in the center of the rug, in his hat, the shaggy iron-gray brows twitching slightly above the pebble-colored eyes as he appeared to examine the house with brief deliberation. Then with the same deliberation he turned; the boy watched him pivot on the good leg and saw the stiff foot drag round the arc of the turning, leaving a final long and fading smear. His father never looked at it, he never once looked down at the rug. The Negro held the door. It closed behind them, upon the hysteric and indistinguishable woman-wail. His father stopped at the top of the steps and scraped his boot clean on the edge of it. At the gate he stopped again. He stood for a moment, planted stiffly on the stiff foot, looking back at the house. "Pretty and white, ain't it?" he said. "That's sweat. Nigger sweat. Maybe it ain't white enough yet to suit him. Maybe he wants to mix some white sweat with it."

Two hours later the boy was chopping wood behind the house within which his mother and aunt and the two sisters (the mother and aunt, not the two girls, he knew that; even at this distance and muffled by walls the flat loud voices of the two girls emanated an incorrigible idle inertia) were setting up the stove to prepare a meal, when he heard the hooves and saw the linen-clad man on a fine sorrel mare, whom he recognized even before he saw the rolled rug in front of the Negro youth following on a fat bay carriage horse—a suffused, angry face vanishing, still at full gallop, beyond the corner of the house where his father and brother were sitting in the two tilted chairs; and a moment later, almost before he could have put the axe down, he heard the hooves again and watched the sorrel mare go back out of the yard, already galloping again. Then his father began to shout one of the sisters' names, who presently emerged backward from the kitchen door dragging the rolled rug along the ground by one end while the other sister walked behind it.

"If you ain't going to tote, go on and set up the wash pot," the first said.

"You, Sarty!" the second shouted, "Set up the wash pot!" His father appeared at the door, framed against that shabbiness, as he had been against that other bland perfection, impervious to either, the mother's anxious face at his shoulder.

"Go on," the father said. "Pick it up." The two sisters stooped, broad, lethargic; stooping, they presented an incredible expanse of pale cloth and a flutter of tawdry ribbons.

"If I thought enough of a rug to have to git hit all the way from France I wouldn't keep hit where folks coming in would have to tromp on hit," the first said. They raised the rug.

"Abner," the mother said. "Let me do it."

"You go back and git dinner," his father said. "I'll tend to this."

From the woodpile through the rest of the afternoon the boy watched them, the rug spread flat in the dust beside the bubbling wash-pot, the two sisters stooping over it with that profound and lethargic reluctance, while the father stood over them in turn, implacable and grim, driving them though never raising his voice again. He could smell the harsh homemade lye they were using; he saw his mother come to the door once and look toward them with an expression not anxious now but very like despair; he saw his father turn, and he fell to with the axe and saw from the corner of his eye his father raise from the ground a flattish fragment of field stone and examine it and return to the pot, and this time his mother actually spoke: "Abner. Abner. Please don't. Please, Abner."

Then he was done too. It was dusk; the whippoorwills had already begun. He could smell coffee from the room where they would presently eat the cold food remaining from the mid-afternoon meal, though when he entered the house he realized they were having coffee again probably because there was a fire on the hearth, before which the rug now lay spread over the backs of the two chairs. The tracks of his father's foot were gone. Where they had been were now long, water-cloudy scoriations resembling the sporadic course of a lilliputian mowing machine.

It still hung there while they ate the cold food and then went to bed, scattered without order or claim up and down the two rooms, his mother in one bed, where his father would later lie, the older brother in the other, himself, the aunt, and the two sisters on pallets on the floor. But his father was not in bed yet. The last thing the boy remembered was the depthless, harsh silhouette of the hat and coat bending over the rug and it seemed to him that he had not even closed his eyes when the silhouette was standing over him, the fire almost dead behind it, the stiff foot prodding him awake. "Catch up the mule," his father said.

When he returned with the mule his father was standing in the black door, the rolled rug over his shoulder. "Ain't you going to ride?" he said.

"No. Give me your foot."

He bent his knee into his father's hand, the wiry, surprising power flowed smoothly, rising, he rising with it, on to the mule's bare back (they had owned a saddle once; the boy could remember it though not when or where) and with the same effortlessness his father swung the rug up in front of him. Now in the starlight they retraced the afternoon's path, up the dusty road rife with honeysuckle, through the gate and up the black tunnel of the drive to the lightless house, where he sat on the mule and felt the rough warp of the rug drag across his thighs and vanish.

"Don't you want me to help?" he whispered. His father did not answer and now he heard again that stiff foot striking the hollow portico with that wooden and clocklike deliberation, that outrageous overstatement of the weight it carried. The rug, hunched, not flung (the boy could tell that even in the darkness) from his father's shoulder struck the angle of wall and floor with a sound unbelievably loud, thunderous, then the foot again, unhurried and enormous; a light came on in the house and the boy sat, tense, breathing steadily and quietly and just a little fast, though the foot itself did not increase its beat at all, descending the steps now; now the boy could see him.

"Don't you want to ride now?" he whispered. "We kin both ride now," the light within the house altering now, flaring up and sinking. *He's coming down the stairs now,* he thought. He had already ridden the mule up beside the horse block; presently his father was up behind him and he doubled the reins over and slashed the mule across the neck, but before the animal could begin to trot the hard, thin arm came round him, the hard, knotted hand jerking the mule back to a walk.

In the first red rays of the sun they were in the lot, putting plow gear on the mules. This time the sorrel mare was in the lot before he heard it at all, the rider collarless and even bareheaded, trembling, speaking in a shaking voice as the woman in the house had done, his father merely looking up once before stooping again to the hame he was buckling, so that the man on the mare spoke to his stooping back:

"You must realize you have ruined that rug. Wasn't there anybody here, any of your women . . ." he ceased, shaking, the boy watching him, the older brother leaning now in the stable door, chewing, blinking slowly and steadily at nothing apparently. "It cost a hundred dollars. But you never had a hundred dollars. You never will. So I'm going to charge you twenty bushels of corn against your crop. I'll add it in your contract and when you come to the commissary you can sign it. That won't keep Mrs. de Spain quiet but maybe it will teach you to wipe your feet off before you enter her house again."

Then he was gone. The boy looked at his father, who still had not spoken or even looked up again, who was now adjusting the logger-head in the hame.

"Pap," he said. His father looked at him—the inscrutable face, the shaggy brows beneath which the gray eyes glinted coldly. Suddenly the boy went toward him, fast, stopping as suddenly. "You done the best you could!" he cried. "If he wanted hit done different why didn't he wait and tell you how? He won't git no twenty bushels! He won't git none! We'll gether hit and hide hit! I kin watch . . ."

"Did you put the cutter back in the straight stock like I told you?"

"No sir," he said.

"Then go do it."

That was Wednesday. During the rest of that week he worked steadily, at what was within his scope and some which was beyond it, with an industry that did not need to be driven nor even commanded twice; he had this from his mother, with the difference that some at least of what he did he liked to do, such as splitting wood with the half-size axe which his mother and aunt had earned, or saved money somehow, to present him with at Christmas. In company with the two older women (and on one afternoon, even one of the sisters), he built pens for the shoat and the cow which were a part of his father's contract with the landlord, and one afternoon, his father being absent, gone somewhere on one of the mules, he went to the field.

They were running a middle buster now, his brother holding the plow straight while he handled the reins, and walking beside the straining mule, the rich black soil shearing cool and damp against his bare ankles, he thought *Maybe this is the end of it. Maybe even that twenty bushels that seems hard to have to pay for just a rug will be a cheap price for him to stop forever and always from being what he used to be;* thinking, dreaming now, so that his brother had to speak sharply to him to mind the mule: *Maybe he even won't collect the twenty bushels. Maybe it will all add up and balance and vanish— corn, rug, fire; the terror and grief, the being pulled two ways like between two teams of horses—gone, done with for ever and ever.*

Then it was Saturday; he looked up from beneath the mule he was harnessing and saw his father in the black coat and hat. "Not that," his father said. "The wagon gear." And then, two hours later, sitting in the wagon bed behind his father and brother on the seat, the wagon accomplished a final curve, and he saw the weathered paintless store with its tattered tobacco and patent-medicine posters and the tethered wagons and saddle animals below the gallery. He mounted the gnawed steps behind his father and brother, and there again was the lane of quiet, watching faces for the three of them to walk through. He saw the man in spectacles sitting at the plank table and he did not need to be told this was a Justice of the Peace; he sent one glare of fierce, exultant, partisan defiance at the man in collar and cravat now, whom he had seen but twice before in his life, and that on a galloping horse, who now wore on his face an expression not of rage but of amazed unbelief which the boy could not have known was at the incredible circumstance of being sued by one of his own tenants, and came and stood against his father and cried at the Justice: "He ain't done it! He ain't burnt . . ."

"Go back to the wagon," his father said.

"Burnt?" the Justice said. "Do I understand this rug was burned too?"

"Does anybody here claim it was?" his father said. "Go back to the wagon." But he did not, he merely retreated to the rear of the room, crowded as that other had been, but not to sit down this time, instead, to stand pressing among the motionless bodies, listening to the voices:

"And you claim twenty bushels of corn is too high for the damage you did to the rug?"

"He brought the rug to me and said he wanted the tracks washed out of it. I washed the tracks out and took the rug back to him."

"But you didn't carry the rug back to him in the same condition it was in before you made the tracks on it."

His father did not answer, and now for perhaps half a minute there was no sound at all save that of breathing, the faint, steady suspiration of complete and intent listening.

"You decline to answer that, Mr. Snopes?" Again his father did not answer. "I'm going to find against you, Mr. Snopes. I'm going to find that you were responsible for the injury to Major de Spain's rug and hold you liable for it.

But twenty bushels of corn seems a little high for a man in your circumstances to have to pay. Major de Spain claims it cost a hundred dollars. October corn will be worth about fifty cents. I figure that if Major de Spain can stand a ninety-five dollar loss on something he paid cash for, you can stand a five-dollar loss you haven't earned yet. I hold you in damages to Major de Spain to the amount of ten bushels of corn over and above your contract with him, to be paid to him out of your crop at gathering time. Court adjourned."

It had taken no time hardly, the morning was but half begun. He thought they would return home and perhaps back to the field, since they were late, far behind all other farmers. But instead his father passed on behind the wagon, merely indicating with his hand for the older brother to follow with it, and he crossed the road toward the blacksmith shop opposite, pressing on after his father, overtaking him, speaking, whispering up at the harsh, calm face beneath the weathered hat: "He won't git no ten bushels neither. He won't git one. We'll . . ." until his father glanced for an instant down at him, the face absolutely calm, the grizzled eyebrows tangled above the cold eyes, the voice almost pleasant, almost gentle:

"You think so? Well, we'll wait till October anyway."

The matter of the wagon—the setting of a spoke or two and the tightening of the tires—did not take long either, the business of the tires accomplished by driving the wagon into the spring branch behind the shop and letting it stand there, the mules nuzzling into the water from time to time, and the boy on the seat with the idle reins, looking up the slope and through the sooty tunnel of the shed where the slow hammer rang and where his father sat on an upended cypress bolt, easily, either talking or listening, still sitting there when the boy brought the dripping wagon up out of the branch and halted it before the door.

"Take them on to the shade and hitch," his father said. He did so and returned. His father and the smith and a third man squatting on his heels inside the door were talking, about crops and animals; the boy, squatting too in the ammoniac dust and hoof-parings and scales of rust, heard his father tell a long and unhurried story out of the time before the birth of the older brother even when he had been a professional horsetrader. And then his father came up beside him where he stood before a tattered last year's circus poster on the other side of the store, gazing rapt and quiet at the scarlet horses, the incredible poisings and convolutions of tulle and tights and the painted leer of comedians, and said, "It's time to eat."

But not at home. Squatting beside his brother against the front wall, he watched his father emerge from the store and produce from a paper sack a segment of cheese and divide it carefully and deliberately into three with his pocket knife and produce crackers from the same sack. They all three squatted on the gallery and ate, slowly, without talking; then in the store again, they drank from a tin dipper tepid water smelling of the cedar bucket and of living beech trees. And still they did not go home. It was a horse lot this time, a tall rail fence upon and along which men stood and sat and out of which one by one horses were led, to be walked and trotted and then cantered back and forth along the road while the slow swapping and buying went on and the sun began to slant westward, they—the three of them—watching and listening, the older brother with his muddy eyes and his steady, inevitable tobacco, the father commenting now and then on certain of the animals, to no one in particular.

It was after sundown when they reached home. They ate supper by lamp-light, then, sitting on the doorstep, the boy watched the night fully accomplished, listening to the whippoorwills and the frogs, when he heard his mother's voice: "Abner! No! No! Oh, God. Oh, God. Abner!" and he rose, whirled, and saw the altered light through the door where a candle stub now burned in a bottle neck on the table and his father, still in the hat and coat, at once formal and burlesque as though dressed carefully for some shabby and ceremonial violence, emptying the reservoir of the lamp back into the five-gallon kerosene can from which it had been filled, while the mother tugged at his arm until he shifted the lamp to the other hand and flung her back, not savagely or viciously, just hard, into the wall, her hands flung out against the wall for balance, her mouth open and in her face the same quality of hopeless despair as had been in her voice. Then his father saw him standing in the door.

"Go to the barn and get that can of oil we were oiling the wagon with," he said. The boy did not move. Then he could speak.

"What . . ." he cried "What are you . . ."

"Go get that oil," his father said. "Go."

Then he was moving, running outside the house, toward the stable: this the old habit, the old blood which he had not been permitted to choose for himself, which had been bequeathed him willy nilly and which had run for so long (and who knew where, battening on what of outrage and savagery and lust) before it came to him. *I could keep on,* he thought. *I could run on and on and never look back, never need to see his face again. Only I can't. I can't,* the rusted can in his hand now, the liquid sploshing in it as he ran back to the house and into it, into the sound of his mother's weeping in the next room, and handed the can to his father.

"Ain't you going to even send a nigger?" he cried. "At least you sent a nigger before!"

This time his father didn't strike him. The hand came even faster than the blow had, the same hand which had set the can on the table with almost excruciating care flashing from the can toward him too quick for him to follow it, gripping him by the back of the shirt and on to tiptoe before he had seen it quit the can, the face stooping at him in breathless and frozen ferocity, the cold, dead voice speaking over him to the older brother who leaned against the table, chewing with that steady, curious, sidewise motion of cows:

"Empty the can into the big one and go on. I'll ketch up with you."

"Better tie him to the bedpost," the brother said.

"Do like I told you," the father said. Then the boy was moving, his bunched shirt and the hard, bony hand between his shoulder-blades, his toes just touching the floor, across the room and into the other one, past the sisters sitting with spread heavy thighs in the two chairs over the cold hearth, and to where his mother and aunt sat side by side on the bed, the aunt's arms about his mother's shoulders.

"Hold him," the father said. The aunt made a startled movement. "Not you," the father said. "Lennie. Take hold of him. I want to see you do it." His mother took him by the wrist. "You'll hold him better than that. If he gets loose don't you know what he is going to do? He will go up yonder." He jerked his head toward the road. "Maybe I'd better tie him."

"I'll hold him," his mother whispered.

"See you do then." Then his father was gone, the stiff foot heavy and measured upon the boards, ceasing at last.

Then he began to struggle. His mother caught him in both arms, he jerking and wrenching at them. He would be stronger in the end, he knew that. But he had no time to wait for it. "Lemme go!" he cried. "I don't want to have to hit you!"

"Let him go!" the aunt said. "If he don't go, before God, I am going up there myself!"

"Don't you see I can't?" his mother cried. "Sarty! Sarty! No! No! Help me, Lizzie!"

Then he was free. His aunt grasped at him but was too late. He whirled, running, his mother stumbled forward on to her knees behind him, crying to the nearer sister: "Catch him, Net! Catch him!" But that was too late too, the sister (the sisters were twins, born at the same time, yet either of them now gave the impression of being, encompassing as much living meat and volume and weight as any other two of the family) not yet having begun to rise from the chair, her head, face, alone merely turned, presenting to him in the flying instant an astonishing expanse of young female features untroubled by any surprise even, wearing only an expression of bovine interest. Then he was out of the room, out of the house, in the mild dust of the starlit road and the heavy rifeness of honeysuckle, the pale ribbon unspooling with terrific slowness under his running feet, reaching the gate at last and turning in, running, his heart and lungs drumming, on up the drive toward the lighted house, the lighted door. He did not knock, he burst in, sobbing for breath, incapable for the moment of speech; he saw the astonished face of the Negro in the linen jacket without knowing when the Negro had appeared.

"De Spain!" he cried, panted. "Where's . . ." then he saw the white man too emerging from a white door down the hall. "Barn!" he cried. "Barn!"

"What?" the white man said. "Barn?"

"Yes!" the boy cried. "Barn!"

"Catch him!" the white man shouted.

But it was too late this time too. The Negro grasped his shirt, but the entire sleeve, rotten with washing, carried away, and he was out that door too and in the drive again, and had actually never ceased to run even while he was screaming into the white man's face.

Behind him the white man was shouting, "My horse! Fetch my horse!" and he thought for an instant of cutting across the park and climbing the fence into the road, but he did not know the park nor how high the vine-massed fence might be and he dared not risk it. So he ran on down the drive, blood and breath roaring; presently he was in the road again though he could not see it. He could not hear either: the galloping mare was almost upon him before he heard her, and even then he held his course, as if the urgency of his wild grief and need must in a moment more find him wings, waiting until the ultimate instant to hurl himself aside and into the weed-choked roadside ditch as the horse thundered past and on, for an instant in furious silhouette against the stars, the tranquil early summer night sky which, even before the shape of the horse and rider vanished, strained abruptly and violently upward: a long, swirling roar incredible and soundless, blotting the stars, and he springing up and into the road again, running again, knowing it was too late yet still running even after he heard the shot and, an instant later, two shots, pausing now without knowing he had ceased to run, crying "Pap! Pap!", running again before he knew he had begun to run, stumbling, tripping over something and scrabbling up again without ceasing to run, looking backward over his shoulder at the glare as he got up, running on among the invisible trees, panting, sobbing, "Father! Father!"

At midnight he was sitting on the crest of a hill. He did not know it was midnight and he did not know how far he had came. But there was no glare behind him now and he sat now, his back toward what he had called home for four days anyhow, his face toward the dark woods which he would enter when breath was strong again, small, shaking steadily in the chill darkness, hugging himself into the remainder of his thin, rotten shirt, the grief and despair now no longer terror and fear but just grief and despair. *Father. My father,* he thought. "He was brave!" he cried suddenly, aloud but not loud, no more than a whisper: "He was! He was in the war! He was in Colonel Sartoris' cav'ry!" not knowing that his father had gone to that war a private in the fine old European sense, wearing no uniform, admitting the authority of and giving fidelity to no man or army or flag, going to war as Malbrouck[1] himself did: for booty—it meant nothing and less than nothing to him if it were enemy booty or his own.

The slow constellations wheeled on. It would be dawn and then sun-up after a while and he would be hungry. But that would be to-morrow and now he was only cold, and walking would cure that. His breathing was easier now and he decided to get up and go on, and then he found that he had been asleep because he knew it was almost dawn, the night almost over. He could tell that from the whippoorwills. They were everywhere now among the dark trees below him, constant and inflectioned and ceaseless, so that, as the instant for giving over to the day birds drew nearer and nearer, there was no interval at all between them. He got up. He was a little stiff, but walking would cure that too as it would the cold, and soon there would be the sun. He went on down the hill, toward the dark woods within which the liquid silver voices of the birds called unceasing—the rapid and urgent beating of the urgent and quiring heart of the late spring night. He did not look back.

[1] An allusion to an old French song, *Malbrouk s'en va-t-en guerre* (Marlborough is off to the wars).

OF
THIS TIME,
OF
THAT PLACE

LIONEL TRILLING
1 9 0 5 –

I<small>T WAS</small> a fine September day. By noon it would be summer again, but now it was
true autumn with a touch of chill in the air. As Joseph Howe stood on the porch
of the house in which he lodged, ready to leave for his first class of the year, he
thought with pleasure of the long indoor days that were coming. It was a moment when he could feel glad of his profession.

On the lawn the peach tree was still in fruit and young Hilda Aiken was
taking a picture of it. She held the camera tight against her chest. She wanted
the sun behind her, but she did not want her own long morning shadow in the
foreground. She raised the camera, but that did not help, and she lowered it,
but that made things worse. She twisted her body to the left, then to the right.
In the end she had to step out of the direct line of the sun. At last she snapped the
shutter and wound the film with intense care.

Howe, watching her from the porch, waited for her to finish and called
good morning. She turned, startled, and almost sullenly lowered her glance. In
the year Howe had lived at the Aikens', Hilda had accepted him as one of her
family, but since his absence of the summer she had grown shy. Then suddenly
she lifted her head and smiled at him, and the humorous smile confirmed his
pleasure in the day. She picked up her bookbag and set off for school.

The handsome houses on the streets to the college were not yet fully awake, but they looked very friendly. Howe went by the Bradby house where he would be a guest this evening at the first dinner party of the year. When he had gone the length of the picket fence, the whitest in town, he turned back. Along the path there was a fine row of asters and he went through the gate and picked one for his buttonhole. The Bradbys would be pleased if they happened to see him invading their lawn and the knowledge of this made him even more comfortable.

He reached the campus as the hour was striking. The students were hurrying to their classes. He himself was in no hurry. He stopped at his dim cubicle of an office and lit a cigarette. The prospect of facing his class had suddenly presented itself to him and his hands were cold; the lawful seizure of power he was about to make seemed momentous. Waiting did not help. He put out his cigarette, picked up a pad of theme paper, and went to his classroom.

As he entered, the rattle of voices ceased, and the twenty-odd freshmen settled themselves and looked at him appraisingly. Their faces seemed gross, his heart sank at their massed impassivity, but he spoke briskly.

'My name is Howe,' he said, and turned and wrote it on the blackboard. The carelessness of the scrawl confirmed his authority. He went on, 'My office is 412 Slemp Hall, and my office-hours are Monday, Wednesday and Friday from eleven-thirty to twelve-thirty.'

He wrote, 'M., W., F., 11:30–12:30.' He said, 'I'll be very glad to see any of you at that time. Or if you can't come then, you can arrange with me for some other time.'

He turned again to the blackboard and spoke over his shoulder. 'The text for the course is Jarman's *Modern Plays*, revised edition. The Co-op has it in stock.' He wrote the name, underlined 'revised edition' and waited for it to be taken down in the new notebooks.

When the bent heads were raised again he began his speech of prospectus. 'It is hard to explain—' he said, and paused as they composed themselves. 'It is hard to explain what a course like this is intended to do. We are going to try to learn something about modern literature and something about prose composition.'

As he spoke, his hands warmed and he was able to look directly at the class. Last year on the first day the faces had seemed just as cloddish, but as the term wore on they became gradually alive and quite likable. It did not seem possible that the same thing could happen again.

'I shall not lecture in this course,' he continued. 'Our work will be carried on by discussion and we will try to learn by an exchange of opinion. But you will soon recognize that my opinion is worth more than anyone else's here.'

He remained grave as he said it, but two boys understood and laughed. The rest took permission from them and laughed too. All Howe's private ironies protested the vulgarity of the joke, but the laughter made him feel benign and powerful.

When the little speech was finished, Howe picked up the pad of paper he had brought. He announced that they would write an extemporaneous theme. Its subject was traditional, 'Who I am and why I came to Dwight College.' By now the class was more at ease and it gave a ritualistic groan of protest. Then there was a stir as fountain pens were brought out and the writing-arms of the chairs were cleared, and the paper was passed about. At last, all the heads bent to work, and the room became still.

Howe sat idly at his desk. The sun shone through the tall clumsy windows. The cool of the morning was already passing. There was a scent of autumn and of varnish and the stillness of the room was deep and oddly touching. Now and then a student's head was raised and scratched in the old, elaborate students' pantomime that calls the teacher to witness honest intellectual effort.

Suddenly a tall boy stood within the frame of the open door. 'Is this,' he said, and thrust a large nose into a college catalogue, 'is this the meeting place of English 1A? The section instructed by Dr. Joseph Howe?'

He stood on the very sill of the door, as if refusing to enter until he was perfectly sure of all his rights. The class looked up from work, found him absurd and gave a low mocking cheer.

The teacher and the new student, with equal pointedness, ignored the disturbance. Howe nodded to the boy, who pushed his head forward and then jerked it back in a wide elaborate arc to clear his brow of a heavy lock of hair. He advanced into the room and halted before Howe, almost at attention. In a loud, clear voice he announced, 'I am Tertan, Ferdinand R., reporting at the direction of Head of Department Vincent.'

The heraldic formality of this statement brought forth another cheer. Howe looked at the class with a sternness he could not really feel, for there was indeed something ridiculous about this boy. Under his displeased regard the rows of heads dropped to work again. Then he touched Tertan's elbow, led him up to the desk and stood so as to shield their conversation from the class.

'We are writing an extemporaneous theme,' he said. 'The subject is, "Who I am and why I came to Dwight College." '

He stripped a few sheets from the pad and offered them to the boy. Tertan hesitated and then took the paper, but he held it only tentatively. As if with the effort of making something clear, he gulped, and a slow smile fixed itself on his face. It was at once knowing and shy.

'Professor,' he said, 'to be perfectly fair to my classmates'—he made a large gesture over the room—'and to you'—he inclined his head to Howe—'this would not be for me an extemporaneous subject.'

Howe tried to understand. 'You mean you've already thought about it— you've heard we always give the same subject? That doesn't matter.'

Again the boy ducked his head and gulped. It was the gesture of one who wishes to make a difficult explanation with perfect candor. 'Sir,' he said, and made the distinction with great care, 'the topic I did not expect, but I have given much ratiocination to the subject.'

Howe smiled and said, 'I don't think that's an unfair advantage. Just go ahead and write.'

Tertan narrowed his eyes and glanced sidewise at Howe. His strange mouth smiled. Then in quizzical acceptance, he ducked his head, threw back the heavy, dank lock, dropped into a seat with a great loose noise and began to write rapidly.

The room fell silent again and Howe resumed his idleness. When the bell rang, the students who had groaned when the task had been set now groaned again because they had not finished. Howe took up the papers, and held the class while he made the first assignment. When he dismissed it, Tertan bore down on him, his slack mouth held ready for speech.

'Some professors,' he said, 'are pedants. They are Dryasdusts.[1] However, some professors are free souls and creative spirits. Kant, Hegel and Nietzsche were

[1] Generic name used by Thomas Carlyle (1795–1881) in *Sartor Resartus* for a pedantic scholar; derived from the fictitious writer of prefaces to several of Scott's novels.

all professors.' With this pronouncement he paused. 'It is my opinion,' he continued, 'that you occupy the second category.'

Howe looked at the boy in surprise and said with good-natured irony, 'With Kant, Hegel and Nietzsche?'

Not only Tertan's hand and head but his whole awkward body waved away the stupidity. 'It is the kind and not the quantity of the kind,' he said sternly.

Rebuked, Howe said as simply and seriously as he could, 'It would be nice to think so.' He added, 'Of course I am not a professor.'

This was clearly a disappointment but Tertan met it. 'In the French sense,' he said with composure. 'Generically, a teacher.'

Suddenly he bowed. It was such a bow, Howe fancied, as a stage-director might teach an actor playing a medieval student who takes leave of Abelard[2]— stiff, solemn, with elbows close to the body and feet together. Then, quite as suddenly, he turned and left.

A queer fish, and as soon as Howe reached his office, he sifted through the batch of themes and drew out Tertan's. The boy had filled many sheets with his unformed headlong scrawl. 'Who am I?' he had begun. 'Here, in a mundane, not to say commercialized academe, is asked the question which from time long immemorably out of mind has accreted doubts and thoughts in the psyche of man to pester him as a nuisance. Whether in St. Augustine (or Austin as sometimes called) or Miss Bashkirtsieff or Frederic Amiel or Empedocles,[3] or in less lights of the intellect than these, this posed question has been ineluctable.'

Howe took out his pencil. He circled 'academe' and wrote 'vocab.' in the margin. He underlined 'time long immemorably out of mind' and wrote 'Diction!' But this seemed inadequate for what was wrong. He put down his pencil and read ahead to discover the principle of error in the theme. 'Today as ever, in spite of gloomy prophets of the dismal science (economics) the question is uninvalidated. Out of the starry depths of heaven hurtles this spear of query demanding to be caught on the shield of the mind ere it pierces the skull and the limbs be unstrung.'

Baffled but quite caught, Howe read on. 'Materialism, by which is meant the philosophic concept and not the moral idea, provides no aegis against the question which lies beyond the tangible (metaphysics). Existence without alloy is the question presented. Environment and heredity relegated aside, the rags and old clothes of practical life discarded, the name and the instrumentality of livelihood do not, as the prophets of the dismal science insist on in this connection, give solution to the interrogation which not from the professor merely but veritably from the cosmos is given. I think, therefore I am (cogito etc.)[4] but who am I? Tertan I am, but what is Tertan? Of this time, of that place, of some parentage, what does it matter?'

Existence without alloy: the phrase established itself. Howe put aside Tertan's paper and at random picked up another. 'I am Arthur J. Casebeer, Jr.,' he read. 'My father is Arthur J. Casebeer and my grandfather was Arthur J. Case-

[2] French scholastic philosopher and theologian (1079–1142) who was extremely popular as a teacher.

[3] St. Augustine (354–430), church father, author of *Confessions, City of God,* etc.; Maria Constantinowna Bashkirtsieff (1860–1884), Russian artist whose diaries were published in 1887; Henri Frédéric Amiel (1821–1881), Swiss scholar, poet, and philosopher; Empedocles (*ca.* 490–430 B.C.), Greek philosopher, poet, and statesman.

[4] *Cogito, ergo sum* (Latin, I think, therefore I am), a famous phrase of the philosopher René Descartes (1596–1650).

beer before him. My mother is Nina Wimble Casebeer. Both of them are college graduates and my father is in insurance. I was born in St. Louis eighteen years ago and we still make our residence there.'

Arthur J. Casebeer, who knew who he was, was less interesting than Tertan, but more coherent. Howe picked up Tertan's paper again. It was clear that none of the routine marginal comments, no 'sent. str.' or 'punct.' or 'vocab.' could cope with this torrential rhetoric. He read ahead, contenting himself with underscoring the errors against the time when he should have the necessary 'conference' with Tertan.

It was a busy and official day of cards and sheets, arrangements and small decisions, and it gave Howe pleasure. Even when it was time to attend the first of the weekly Convocations he felt the charm of the beginning of things when intention is still innocent and uncorrupted by effort. He sat among the young instructors on the platform, and joined in their humorous complaints at having to assist at the ceremony, but actually he got a clear satisfaction from the ritual of prayer, and prosy speech, and even from wearing his academic gown. And when the Convocation was over the pleasure continued as he crossed the campus, exchanging greetings with men he had not seen since the spring. They were people who did not yet, and perhaps never would, mean much to him, but in a year they had grown amiably to be part of his life. They were his fellow-townsmen.

The day had cooled again at sunset, and there was a bright chill in the September twilight. Howe carried his voluminous gown over his arm, he swung his doctoral hood by its purple neckpiece, and on his head he wore his mortarboard with its heavy gold tassel bobbing just over his eye. These were the weighty and absurd symbols of his new profession and they pleased him. At twenty-six Joseph Howe had discovered that he was neither so well off nor so bohemian as he had once thought. A small income, adequate when supplemented by a sizable cash legacy, was genteel poverty when the cash was all spent. And the literary life—the room at the Lafayette,[5] or the small apartment without a lease, the long summers on the Cape,[6] the long afternoons and the social evenings—began to weary him. His writing filled his mornings, and should perhaps have filled his life, yet it did not. To the amusement of his friends, and with a certain sense that he was betraying his own freedom, he had used the last of his legacy for a year at Harvard. The small but respectable reputation of his two volumes of verse had proved useful—he continued at Harvard on a fellowship and when he emerged as Doctor Howe he received an excellent appointment, with prospects, at Dwight.

He had his moments of fear when all that had ever been said of the dangers of the academic life had occurred to him. But after a year in which he had tested every possibility of corruption and seduction he was ready to rest easy. His third volume of verse, most of it written in his first years of teaching, was not only ampler but, he thought, better than its predecessors.

There was a clear hour before the Bradby dinner party, and Howe looked forward to it. But he was not to enjoy it, for lying with his mail on the hall table was a copy of this quarter's issue of *Life and Letters,* to which his landlord subscribed. Its severe cover announced that its editor, Frederic Woolley, had this

[5] Hotel that was well-known as a gathering place for intellectuals and bohemians in New York's Greenwich Village.
[6] Cape Cod.

month contributed an essay called 'Two Poets,' and Howe, picking it up, curious to see who the two poets might be, felt his own name start out at him with cabalistic power—Joseph Howe. As he continued to turn the pages his hand trembled.

Standing in the dark hall, holding the neat little magazine, Howe knew that his literary contempt for Frederic Woolley meant nothing, for he suddenly understood how he respected Woolley in the way of the world. He knew this by the trembling of his hand. And of the little world as well as the great, for although the literary groups of New York might dismiss Woolley, his name carried high authority in the academic world. At Dwight it was even a revered name, for it had been here at the college that Frederic Woolley had made the distinguished scholarly career from which he had gone on to literary journalism. In middle life he had been induced to take the editorship of *Life and Letters*, a literary monthly not widely read but heavily endowed, and in its pages he had carried on the defense of what he sometimes called the older values. He was not without wit, he had great knowledge and considerable taste, and even in the full movement of the 'new' literature he had won a certain respect for his refusal to accept it. In France, even in England, he would have been connected with a more robust tradition of conservatism, but America gave him an audience not much better than genteel. It was known in the college that to the subsidy of *Life and Letters* the Bradbys contributed a great part.

As Howe read, he saw that he was involved in nothing less than an event. When the Fifth Series of *Studies in Order and Value* came to be collected, this latest of Frederic Woolley's essays would not be merely another step in the old direction. Clearly and unmistakably, it was a turning point. All his literary life Woolley had been concerned with the relation of literature to morality, religion, and the private and delicate pieties, and he had been unalterably opposed to all that he had called 'inhuman humanitarianism.' But here, suddenly, dramatically late, he had made an about-face, turning to the public life and to the humanitarian politics he had so long despised. This was the kind of incident the histories of literature make much of. Frederic Woolley was opening for himself a new career and winning a kind of new youth. He contrasted the two poets, Thomas Wormser, who was admirable, Joseph Howe, who was almost dangerous. He spoke of the 'precious subjectivism of Howe's verse. 'In times like ours,' he wrote, 'with millions facing penury and want, one feels that the qualities of the *tour d'ivoire* are well-nigh inhuman, nearly insulting. The *tour d'ivoire* becomes the *tour d'ivresse*,[7] and it is not self-intoxicated poets that our people need.' The essay said more: 'The problem is one of meaning. I am not ignorant that the creed of the esoteric poets declares that a poem does not and should not *mean* anything, that it *is* something. But poetry is what the poet makes it, and if he is a true poet he makes what his society needs. And what is needed now is the tradition in which Mr. Wormser writes, the true tradition of poetry. The Howes do no harm, but they do no good when positive good is demanded of all responsible men. Or do the Howes indeed do no harm? Perhaps Plato would have said they do, that in some ways theirs is the Phrygian music that turns men's minds from the struggle. Certainly it is true that Thomas Wormser writes in the lucid Dorian mode[8] which sends men into battle with evil.'

[7] The ivory tower becomes the tower of intoxication, or madness.
[8] The Phrygian and Dorian modes were scales used in Greek and ecclesiastical music; the Phrygian was brisk and spirited and the Dorian, bold and grave.

It was easy to understand why Woolley had chosen to praise Thomas Wormser. The long, lilting lines of *Corn Under Willows* hymned, as Woolley put it, the struggle for wheat in the Iowa fields, and expressed the real lives of real people. But why out of the dozen more notable examples he had chosen Howe's little volume as the example of 'precious subjectivism' was hard to guess. In a way it was funny, this multiplication of himself into 'the Howes.' And yet this becoming the multiform political symbol by whose creation Frederic Woolley gave the sign of a sudden new life, this use of him as a sacrifice whose blood was necessary for the rites of rejuvenation, made him feel oddly unclean.

Nor could Howe get rid of a certain practical resentment. As a poet he had a special and respectable place in the college life. But it might be another thing to be marked as the poet of a willful and selfish obscurity.

As he walked to the Bradbys', Howe was a little tense and defensive. It seemed to him that all the world knew of the 'attack' and agreed with it. And, indeed, the Bradbys had read the essay but Professor Bradby, a kind and pretentious man, said, 'I see my old friend knocked you about a bit, my boy,' and his wife Eugenia looked at Howe with her child-like blue eyes and said, 'I shall *scold* Frederic for the untrue things he wrote about you. You aren't the least obscure.' They beamed at him. In their genial snobbery they seemed to feel that he had distinguished himself. He was the leader of Howeism. He enjoyed the dinner party as much as he had thought he would.

And in the following days, as he was more preoccupied with his duties, the incident was forgotten. His classes had ceased to be mere groups. Student after student detached himself from the mass and required or claimed a place in Howe's awareness. Of them all it was Tertan who first and most violently signaled his separate existence. A week after classes had begun Howe saw his silhouette on the frosted glass of his office door. It was motionless for a long time, perhaps stopped by the problem of whether or not to knock before entering. Howe called, 'Come in!' and Tertan entered with his shambling stride.

He stood beside the desk, silent and at attention. When Howe asked him to sit down, he responded with a gesture of head and hand, as if to say that such amenities were beside the point. Nevertheless, he did take the chair. He put his ragged, crammed briefcase between his legs. His face, which Howe now observed fully for the first time, was confusing, for it was made up of florid curves, the nose arched in the bone and voluted in the nostril, the mouth loose and soft and rather moist. Yet the face was so thin and narrow as to seem the very type of asceticism. Lashes of unusual length veiled the eyes and, indeed, it seemed as if there were a veil over the whole countenance. Before the words actually came, the face screwed itself into an attitude of preparation for them.

'You can confer with me now?' Tertan said.

'Yes, I'd be glad to. There are several things in your two themes I want to talk to you about.' Howe reached for the packet of themes on his desk and sought for Tertan's. But the boy was waving them away.

'These are done perforce,' he said. 'Under the pressure of your requirement. They are not significant; mere duties.' Again his great hand flapped vaguely to dismiss his themes. He leaned forward and gazed at his teacher.

'You are,' he said, 'a man of letters? You are a poet?' It was more declaration than question.

'I should like to think so,' Howe said.

At first Tertan accepted the answer with a show of appreciation, as though the understatement made a secret between himself and Howe. Then he chose to misunderstand. With his shrewd and disconcerting control of expression, he presented to Howe a puzzled grimace. 'What does that mean?' he said.

Howe retracted the irony. 'Yes. I am a poet.' It sounded strange to say.

'That,' Tertan said, 'is a wonder.' He corrected himself with his ducking head. 'I mean that is wonderful.'

Suddenly, he dived at the miserable briefcase between his legs, put it on his knees, and began to fumble with the catch, all intent on the difficulty it presented. Howe noted that his suit was worn thin, his shirt almost unclean. He became aware, even, of a vague and musty odor of garments worn too long in unaired rooms. Tertan conquered the lock and began to concentrate upon a search into the interior. At last he held in his hand what he was after, a torn and crumpled copy of *Life and Letters.*

'I learned it from here,' he said, holding it out.

Howe looked at him sharply, his hackles a little up. But the boy's face was not only perfectly innocent, it even shone with a conscious admiration. Apparently nothing of the import of the essay had touched him except the wonderful fact that his teacher was a 'man of letters.' Yet this seemed too stupid, and Howe, to test it, said, 'The man who wrote that doesn't think it's wonderful.'

Tertan made a moist hissing sound as he cleared his mouth of saliva. His head, oddly loose on his neck, wove a pattern of contempt in the air. 'A critic,' he said, 'who admits *prima facie* that he does not understand.' Then he said grandly, 'It is the inevitable fate.'

It was absurd, yet Howe was not only aware of the absurdity but of a tension suddenly and wonderfully relaxed. Now that the 'attack' was on the table between himself and this strange boy, and subject to the boy's funny and absolutely certain contempt, the hidden force of his feeling was revealed to him in the very moment that it vanished. All unsuspected, there had been a film over the world, a transparent but discoloring haze of danger. But he had no time to stop over the brightened aspect of things. Tertan was going on. 'I also am a man of letters. Putative.'

'You have written a good deal?' Howe meant to be no more than polite, and he was surprised at the tenderness he heard in his words.

Solemnly the boy nodded, threw back the dank lock, and sucked in a deep, anticipatory breath. 'First, a work of homiletics, which is a defense of the principles of religious optimism against the pessimism of Schopenhauer and the humanism of Nietzsche.'

'Humanism? Why do you call it humanism?'

'It is my nomenclature for making a deity of man,' Tertan replied negligently. 'Then three fictional works, novels. And numerous essays in science, combating materialism. Is it your duty to read these if I bring them to you?'

Howe answered simply, 'No, it isn't exactly my duty, but I shall be happy to read them.'

Tertan stood up and remained silent. He rested his bag on the chair. With a certain compunction—for it did not seem entirely proper that, of two men of letters, one should have the right to blue-pencil the other, to grade him or to question the quality of his 'sentence structure'—Howe reached for Tertan's papers. But before he could take them up, the boy suddenly made his bow-to-Abelard, the stiff inclination of the body with the hands seeming to emerge from the scholar's gown. Then he was gone.

But after his departure something was still left of him. The timbre of his curious sentences, the downright finality of so quaint a phrase as 'It is the inevitable fate' still rang in the air. Howe gave the warmth of his feeling to the new visitor who stood at the door announcing himself with a genteel clearing of the throat.

'Doctor Howe, I believe?' the student said. A large hand advanced into the room and grasped Howe's hand. 'Blackburn, sir, Theodore Blackburn, vice-president of the Student Council. A great pleasure, sir.'

Out of a pair of ruddy cheeks a pair of small eyes twinkled good-naturedly. The large face, the large body were not so much fat as beefy and suggested something 'typical'—monk, politician, or innkeeper.

Blackburn took the seat beside Howe's desk. 'I may have seemed to introduce myself in my public capacity, sir,' he said. 'But it is really as an individual that I came to see you. That is to say, as one of your students to be.'

He spoke with an English intonation and he went on, 'I was once an English major, sir.'

For a moment Howe was startled, for the roast-beef look of the boy and the manner of his speech gave a second's credibility to one sense of his statement. Then the collegiate meaning of the phrase asserted itself, but some perversity made Howe say what was not really in good taste even with so forward a student, 'Indeed? What regiment?'

Blackburn stared and then gave a little pouf-pouf of laughter. He waved the misapprehension away. '*Very* good, sir. It certainly is an ambiguous term.' He chuckled in appreciation of Howe's joke, then cleared his throat to put it aside. 'I look forward to taking your course in the romantic poets, sir,' he said earnestly. 'To me the romantic poets are the very crown of English literature.'

Howe made a dry sound, and the boy, catching some meaning in it, said, 'Little as I know them, of course. But even Shakespeare who is so dear to us of the Anglo-Saxon tradition is in a sense but the preparation for Shelley, Keats and Byron. And Wadsworth.'

Almost sorry for him, Howe dropped his eyes. With some embarrassment, for the boy was not actually his student, he said softly, 'Wordsworth.'

'Sir?'

'Wordsworth, not Wadsworth. You said Wadsworth.'

'Did I, sir?' Gravely he shook his head to rebuke himself for the error. 'Wordsworth, of course—slip of the tongue.' Then, quite in command again, he went on. 'I have a favor to ask of you, Doctor Howe. You see, I began my college course as an English major,'—he smiled—'as I said.'

'Yes?'

'But after my first year I shifted. I shifted to the social sciences. Sociology and government—I find them stimulating and very *real*.' He paused, out of respect for reality. 'But now I find that perhaps I have neglected the other side.'

'The other side?' Howe said.

'Imagination, fancy, culture. A well-rounded man.' He trailed off as if there were perfect understanding between them. 'And so, sir, I have decided to end my senior year with your course in the romantic poets.'

His voice was filled with an indulgence which Howe ignored as he said flatly and gravely, 'But that course isn't given until the spring term.'

'Yes, sir, and that is where the favor comes in. Would you let me take your romantic prose course? I can't take it for credit, sir, my program is full, but just for background it seems to me that I ought to take it. I do hope,' he concluded in a manly way, 'that you will consent.'

'Well, it's no great favor, Mr. Blackburn. You can come if you wish, though there's not much point in it if you don't do the reading.'

The bell rang for the hour and Howe got up.

'May I begin with this class, sir?' Blackburn's smile was candid and boyish.

Howe nodded carelessly and together, silently, they walked to the classroom down the hall. When they reached the door Howe stood back to let his student enter, but Blackburn moved adroitly behind him and grasped him by the arm to urge him over the threshold. They entered together with Blackburn's hand firmly on Howe's biceps, the student inducting the teacher into his own room. Howe felt a surge of temper rise in him and almost violently he disengaged his arm and walked to the desk, while Blackburn found a seat in the front row and smiled at him.

II

The question was, At whose door must the tragedy be laid?

All night the snow had fallen heavily and only now was abating in sparse little flurries. The windows were valanced high with white. It was very quiet; something of the quiet of the world had reached the class, and Howe found that everyone was glad to talk or listen. In the room there was a comfortable sense of pleasure in being human.

Casebeer believed that the blame for the tragedy rested with heredity. Picking up the book he read, 'The sins of the fathers are visited on their children.' This opinion was received with general favor. Nevertheless, Johnson ventured to say that the fault was all Pastor Manders'[9] because the Pastor had made Mrs. Alving go back to her husband and was always hiding the truth. To this Hibbard objected with logic enough, 'Well then, it was really all her husband's fault. He *did* all the bad things.' DeWitt, his face bright with an impatient idea, said that the fault was all society's. 'By society I don't mean upper-crust society,' he said. He looked around a little defiantly, taking in any members of the class who might be members of upper-crust society. 'Not in that sense. I mean the social unit.'

Howe nodded and said, 'Yes, of course.'

'If the society of the time had progressed far enough in science,' De Witt went on, 'then there would be no problem for Mr. Ibsen to write about. Captain Alving plays around a little, gives way to perfectly natural biological urges, and he gets a social disease, a venereal disease. If the disease is cured, no problem. Invent salvarsan and the disease is cured. The problem of heredity disappears and li'l Oswald just doesn't get paresis. No paresis, no problem—no problem, no play.'

[9] The play being discussed is *Ghosts* by Henrik Ibsen (1828–1906).

This was carrying the ark into battle, and the class looked at De Witt with respectful curiosity. It was his usual way and on the whole they were sympathetic with his struggle to prove to Howe that science was better than literature. Still, there was something in his reckless manner that alienated them a little.

'Or take birth-control, for instance,' De Witt went on. 'If Mrs. Alving had some knowledge of contraception, she wouldn't have had to have li'l Oswald at all. No li'l Oswald, no play.'

The class was suddenly quieter. In the back row Stettenhover swung his great football shoulders in a righteous sulking gesture, first to the right, then to the left. He puckered his mouth ostentatiously. Intellect was always ending up by talking dirty.

Tertan's hand went up, and Howe said, 'Mr. Tertan.' The boy shambled to his feet and began his long characteristic gulp. Howe made a motion with his fingers, as small as possible, and Tertan ducked his head and smiled in apology. He sat down. The class laughed. With more than half the term gone, Tertan had not been able to remember that one did not rise to speak. He seemed unable to carry on the life of the intellect without this mark of respect for it. To Howe the boy's habit of rising seemed to accord with the formal shabbiness of his dress. He never wore the casual sweaters and jackets of his classmates. Into the free and comfortable air of the college classroom he brought the stuffy sordid strictness of some crowded, metropolitan high school.

'Speaking from one sense,' Tertan began slowly, 'there is no blame ascribable. From the sense of determinism, who can say where the blame lies? The preordained is the preordained and it cannot be said without rebellion against the universe, a palpable absurdity.'

In the back row Stettenhover slumped suddenly in his seat, his heels held out before him, making a loud, dry, disgusted sound. His body sank until his neck rested on the back of his chair. He folded his hands across his belly and looked significantly out of the window, exasperated not only with Tertan, but with Howe, with the class, with the whole system designed to encourage this kind of thing. There was a certain insolence in the movement and Howe flushed. As Tertan continued to speak, Howe stalked casually toward the window and placed himself in the line of Stettenhover's vision. He stared at the great fellow, who pretended not to see him. There was so much power in the big body, so much contempt in the Greek-athlete face under the crisp Greek-athlete curls, that Howe felt almost physical fear. But at last Stettenhover admitted him to focus and under his disapproving gaze sat up with slow indifference. His eyebrows raised high in resignation, he began to examine his hands. Howe relaxed and turned his attention back to Tertan.

'Flux of existence,' Tertan was saying, 'produces all things, so that judgment wavers. Beyond the phenomena, what? But phenomena are adumbrated and to them we are limited.'

Howe saw it for a moment as perhaps it existed in the boy's mind—the world of shadows which are cast by a great light upon a hidden reality as in the old myth of the Cave.[10] But the little brush with Stettenhover had tired him, and he said irritably, 'But come to the point, Mr. Tertan.'

He said it so sharply that some of the class looked at him curiously. For three

10 Parable used by Plato (ca. 429–347 B.C.) in the *Republic*, Book VII.

months he had gently carried Tertan through his verbosities, to the vaguely respectful surprise of the other students, who seemed to conceive that there existed between this strange classmate and their teacher some special understanding from which they were content to be excluded. Tertan looked at him mildly, and at once came brilliantly to the point. 'This is the summation of the play,' he said and took up his book and read, '"Your poor father never found any outlet for the overmastering joy of life that was in him. And I brought no holiday into his home, either. Everything seemed to turn upon duty and I am afraid I made your poor father's home unbearable to him, Oswald." Spoken by Mrs. Alving.'

Yes that was surely the 'summation' of the play and Tertan had hit it, as he hit, deviously and eventually, the literary point of almost everything. But now, as always, he was wrapping it away from sight. 'For most mortals,' he said, 'there are only joys of biological urgings, gross and crass, such as the sensuous Captain Alving. For certain few there are the transmutations beyond these to a contemplation of the utter whole.'

Oh, the boy was mad. And suddenly the word, used in hyperbole, intended almost for the expression of exasperated admiration, became literal. Now that the word was used, it became simply apparent to Howe that Tertan was mad.

It was a monstrous word and stood like a bestial thing in the room. Yet it so completely comprehended everything that had puzzled Howe, it so arranged and explained what for three months had been perplexing him that almost at once its horror became domesticated. With this word Howe was able to understand why he had never been able to communicate to Tertan the value of a single criticism or correction of his wild, verbose themes. Their conferences had been frequent and long but had done nothing to reduce to order the splendid confusion of the boy's ideas. Yet, impossible though its expression was, Tertan's incandescent mind could always strike for a moment into some dark corner of thought.

And now it was suddenly apparent that it was not a faulty rhetoric that Howe had to contend with. With his new knowledge he looked at Tertan's face and wondered how he could have so long deceived himself. Tertan was still talking, and the class had lapsed into a kind of patient unconsciousness, a coma of respect for words which, for all that most of them knew, might be profound. Almost with a suffusion of shame, Howe believed that in some dim way the class had long ago had some intimation of Tertan's madness. He reached out as decisively as he could to seize the thread of Tertan's discourse before it should be entangled further.

'Mr. Tertan says that the blame must be put upon whoever kills the joy of living in another. We have been assuming that Captain Alving was a wholly bad man, but what if we assume that he became bad only because Mrs. Alving, when they were first married, acted toward him in the prudish way she says she did?'

It was a ticklish idea to advance to freshmen and perhaps not profitable. Not all of them were following.

'That would put the blame on Mrs. Alving herself, whom most of you admire. And she herself seems to think so.' He glanced at his watch. The hour was nearly over. 'What do you think, Mr. De Witt?'

De Witt rose to the idea; he wanted to know if society couldn't be blamed for educating Mrs. Alving's temperament in the wrong way. Casebeer was puzzled, Stettenhover continued to look at his hands until the bell rang.

Tertan, his brows louring in thought, was making as always for a private word. Howe gathered his books and papers to leave quickly. At this moment of his discovery and with the knowledge still raw, he could not engage himself with Tertan. Tertan sucked in his breath to prepare for speech and Howe made ready for the pain and confusion. But at that moment Casebeer detached himself from the group with which he had been conferring and which he seemed to represent. His constituency remained at a tactful distance. The mission involved the time of an assigned essay. Casebeer's presentation of the plea—it was based on the freshmen's heavy duties at the fraternities during Carnival Week—cut across Tertan's preparations for speech. 'And so some of us fellows thought,' Casebeer concluded with heavy solemnity, 'that we could do a better job, give our minds to it more, if we had more time.'

Tertan regarded Casebeer with mingled curiosity and revulsion. Howe not only said that he would postpone the assignment but went on to talk about the Carnival, and even drew the waiting constituency into the conversation. He was conscious of Tertan's stern and astonished stare, then of his sudden departure.

Now that the fact was clear, Howe knew that he must act on it. His course was simple enough. He must lay the case before the Dean. Yet he hesitated. His feeling for Tertan must now, certainly, be in some way invalidated. Yet could he, because of a word, hurry to assign to official and reasonable solicitude what had been, until this moment, so various and warm? He could at least delay and, by moving slowly, lend a poor grace to the necessary, ugly act of making his report.

It was with some notion of keeping the matter in his own hands that he went to the Dean's office to look up Tertan's records. In the outer office the Dean's secretary greeted him brightly, and at his request brought him the manila folder with the small identifying photograph pasted in the corner. She laughed. 'He was looking for the birdie in the wrong place,' she said.

Howe leaned over her shoulder to look at the picture. It was as bad as all the Dean's-office photographs were, but it differed from all that Howe had ever seen. Tertan, instead of looking into the camera, as no doubt he had been bidden, had, at the moment of exposure, turned his eyes upward. His mouth, as though conscious of the trick played on the photographer, had the sly superior look that Howe knew.

The secretary was fascinated by the picture. 'What a funny boy,' she said. 'He looks like Tartuffe!'[11]

And so he did, with the absurd piety of the eyes and the conscious slyness of the mouth and the whole face bloated by the bad lens.

'Is he *like* that?' the secretary said.

'Like Tartuffe? No.'

From the photograph there was little enough comfort to be had. The records themselves gave no clue to madness, though they suggested sadness enough. Howe read of a father, Stanislaus Tertan, born in Budapest and trained in engineering in Berlin, once employed by the Hercules Chemical Corporation—this was one of the factories that dominated the sound end of the town—but now without employment. He read of a mother Erminie (Youngfellow) Tertan, born in Manchester, educated at a Normal School at Leeds, now housewife by profession. The family lived on Greenbriar Street which Howe knew as a row of once elegant homes near what was now the factory district. The old mansion had long ago

[11] The sanctimonious hypocrite in Molière's comedy *Tartuffe,* first produced in 1667.

been divided into small and primitive apartments. Of Ferdinand himself there was little to learn. He lived with his parents, had attended a Detroit high school and had transferred to the local school in his last year. His rating for intelligence, as expressed in numbers, was high, his scholastic record was remarkable, he held a college scholarship for his tuition.

Howe laid the folder on the secretary's desk. 'Did you find what you wanted to know?' she asked.

The phrases from Tertan's momentous first theme came back to him. 'Tertan I am, but what is Tertan? Of this time, of that place, of some parentage, what does it matter?'

'No, I didn't find it,' he said.

Now that he had consulted the sad, half-meaningless record he knew all the more firmly that he must not give the matter out of his own hands. He must not release Tertan to authority. Not that he anticipated from the Dean anything but the greatest kindness for Tertan. The Dean would have the experience and skill which he himself could not have. One way or another the Dean could answer the question, 'What is Tertan?' Yet this was precisely what he feared. He alone could keep alive—not forever but for a somehow important time—the question, 'What is Tertan?' He alone could keep it still a question. Some sure instinct told him that he must not surrender the question to a clean official desk in a clear official light to be dealt with, settled and closed.

He heard himself saying, 'Is the Dean busy at the moment? I'd like to see him.'

His request came thus unbidden, even forbidden, and it was one of the surprising and startling incidents of his life. Later when he reviewed the events, so disconnected in themselves, or so merely odd, of the story that unfolded for him that year, it was over this moment, on its face the least notable, that he paused longest. It was frequently to be with fear and never without a certainty of its meaning in his own knowledge of himself that he would recall this simple, routine request, and the feeling of shame and freedom it gave him as he sent everything down the official chute. In the end, of course, no matter what he did to 'protect' Tertan, he would have had to make the same request and lay the matter on the Dean's clean desk. But it would always be a landmark of his life that, at the very moment when he was rejecting the official way, he had been, without will or intention, so gladly drawn to it.

After the storm's last delicate flurry, the sun had come out. Reflected by the new snow, it filled the office with a golden light which was almost musical in the way it made all the commonplace objects of efficiency shine with a sudden sad and noble significance. And the light, now that he noticed it, made the utterance of his perverse and unwanted request even more momentous.

The secretary consulted the engagement pad. 'He'll be free any minute. Don't you want to wait in the parlor?'

She threw open the door of the large and pleasant room in which the Dean held his Committee meetings, and in which his visitors waited. It was designed with a homely elegance on the masculine side of the eighteenth-century manner. There was a small coal fire in the grate and the handsome mahogany table was strewn with books and magazines. The large windows gave on the snowy lawn, and there was such a fine width of window that the white casements and walls seemed at this moment but a continuation of the snow, the snow but an extension of casement and walls. The outdoors seemed taken in and made safe, the indoors seemed luxuriously freshened and expanded.

Howe sat down by the fire and lighted a cigarette. The room had its intended effect upon him. He felt comfortable and relaxed, yet nicely organized, some young diplomatic agent of the eighteenth century, the newly fledged Swift carrying out Sir William Temple's business.[12] The rawness of Tertan's case quite vanished. He crossed his legs and reached for a magazine.

It was that famous issue of *Life and Letters* that his idle hand had found and his blood raced as he sifted through it, and the shape of his own name, Joseph Howe, sprang out at him, still cabalistic in its power. He tossed the magazine back on the table as the door of the Dean's office opened and the Dean ushered out Theodore Blackburn.

'Ah, Joseph!' the Dean said.

Blackburn said, 'Good morning, Doctor.' Howe winced at the title and caught the flicker of amusement over the Dean's face. The Dean stood with his hand high on the door-jamb and Blackburn, still in the doorway, remained standing almost under the long arm.

Howe nodded briefly to Blackburn, snubbing his eager deference. 'Can you give me a few minutes?' he said to the Dean.

'All the time you want. Come in.' Before the two men could enter the office, Blackburn claimed their attention with a long full 'er.' As they turned to him, Blackburn said, 'Can *you* give *me* a few minutes, Doctor Howe?' His eyes sparkled at the little audacity he had committed, the slightly impudent play with hierarchy. Of the three of them Blackburn kept himself the lowest, but he reminded Howe of his subaltern relation to the Dean.

'I mean, of course,' Blackburn went on easily, 'when you've finished with the Dean.'

'I'll be in my office shortly,' Howe said, turned his back on the ready 'Thank you, sir,' and followed the Dean into the inner room.

'Energetic boy,' said the Dean. 'A bit beyond himself but very energetic. Sit down.'

The Dean lighted a cigarette, leaned back in his chair, sat easy and silent for a moment, giving Howe no signal to go ahead with business. He was a young Dean, not much beyond forty, a tall handsome man with sad, ambitious eyes. He had been a Rhodes scholar. His friends looked for great things from him, and it was generally said that he had notions of education which he was not yet ready to try to put into practice.

His relaxed silence was meant as a compliment to Howe. He smiled and said, 'What's the business, Joseph?'

'Do you know Tertan—Ferdinand Tertan, a freshman?'

The Dean's cigarette was in his mouth and his hands were clasped behind his head. He did not seem to search his memory for the name. He said, 'What about him?'

Clearly the Dean knew something, and he was waiting for Howe to tell him more. Howe moved only tentatively. Now that he was doing what he had resolved

---

[12] Jonathan Swift (1667–1745), author of *Gulliver's Travels*, worked as secretary to Sir William Temple (1628–1699), English statesman and author, during the years 1689–1692 and 1696–1699.

not to do, he felt more guilty at having been so long deceived by Tertan and more need to be loyal to his error.

'He's a strange fellow,' he ventured. He said stubbornly, 'In a strange way he's very brilliant.' He concluded, 'But very strange.'

The springs of the Dean's swivel chair creaked as he came out of his sprawl and leaned forward to Howe. 'Do you mean he's so strange that it's something you could give a name to?'

Howe looked at him stupidly. 'What do you mean?' he said.

'What's his trouble?' the Dean said more neutrally.

'He's very brilliant, in a way. I looked him up and he has a top intelligence rating. But somehow, and it's hard to explain just how, what he says is always on the edge of sense and doesn't quite make it.'

The Dean looked at him and Howe flushed up. The Dean had surely read Woolley on the subject of 'the Howes' and the *tour d'ivresse*. Was that quick glance ironical?

The Dean picked up some papers from his desk, and Howe could see that they were in Tertan's impatient scrawl. Perhaps the little gleam in the Dean's glance had come only from putting facts together.

'He sent me this yesterday,' the Dean said. 'After an interview I had with him. I haven't been able to do more than glance at it. When you said what you did, I realized there was something wrong.'

Twisting his mouth, the Dean looked over the letter. 'You seem to be involved,' he said without looking up. 'By the way, what did you give him at midterm?'

Flushing, setting his shoulders, Howe said firmly, 'I gave him A-minus.'

The Dean chuckled. 'Might be a good idea if some of our nicer boys went crazy—just a little.' He said, 'Well,' to conclude the matter and handed the papers to Howe. 'See if this is the same thing you've been finding. Then we can go into the matter again.'

Before the fire in the parlor, in the chair that Howe had been occupying, sat Blackburn. He sprang to his feet as Howe entered.

'I said my office, Mr. Blackburn.' Howe's voice was sharp. Then he was almost sorry for the rebuke, so clearly and naively did Blackburn seem to relish his stay in the parlor, close to authority.

'I'm in a bit of a hurry, sir,' he said, 'and I did want to be sure to speak to you, sir.'

He was really absurd, yet fifteen years from now he would have grown up to himself, to the assurance and mature beefiness. In banks, in consular offices, in brokerage firms, on the bench, more seriously affable, a little sterner, he would make use of his ability to be administered by his job. It was almost reassuring. Now he was exercising his too-great skill on Howe. 'I owe you an apology, sir,' he said.

Howe knew that he did, but he showed surprise.

'I mean, Doctor, after your having been so kind about letting me attend your class, I stopped coming.' He smiled in deprecation. 'Extracurricular activities take up so much of my time. I'm afraid I undertook more than I could perform.'

Howe had noticed the absence and had been a little irritated by it after Blackburn's elaborate plea. It was an absence that might be interpreted as a comment on the teacher. But there was only one way for him to answer. 'You've no need to apologize,' he said. 'It's wholly your affair.'

Blackburn beamed. 'I'm so glad you feel that way about it, sir. I was worried you might think I had stayed away because I was influenced by—' he stopped and lowered his eyes.

Astonished, Howe said, 'Influenced by what?'

'Well, by—' Blackburn hesitated and for answer pointed to the table on which lay the copy of *Life and Letters*. Without looking at it, he knew where to direct his hand. 'By the unfavorable publicity, sir.' He hurried on. 'And that brings me to another point, sir. I am secretary of Quill and Scroll, sir, the student literary society, and I wonder if you would address us. You could read your own poetry, sir, and defend your own point of view. It would be very interesting.'

It was truly amazing. Howe looked long and cruelly into Blackburn's face, trying to catch the secret of the mind that could have conceived this way of manipulating him, this way so daring and inept—but not entirely inept—with its malice so without malignity. The face did not yield its secret. Howe smiled broadly and said, 'Of course I don't think you were influenced by the unfavorable publicity.'

'I'm still going to take—regularly, for credit—your romantic poets course next term,' Blackburn said.

'Don't worry, my dear fellow, don't worry about it.'

Howe started to leave and Blackburn stopped him with, 'But about Quill, sir?'

'Suppose we wait until next term? I'll be less busy then.'

And Blackburn said, 'Very good, sir, and thank you.'

In his office the little encounter seemed less funny to Howe, was even in some indeterminate way disturbing. He made an effort to put it from his mind by turning to what was sure to disturb him more, the Tertan letter read in the new interpretation. He found what he had always found, the same florid leaps beyond fact and meaning, the same headlong certainty. But as his eye passed over the familiar scrawl it caught his own name, and for the second time that hour he felt the race of his blood.

'The Paraclete,' Tertan had written to the Dean, 'from a Greek word meaning to stand in place of, but going beyond the primitive idea to mean traditionally the helper, the one who comforts and assists, cannot without fundamental loss be jettisoned. Even if taken no longer in the supernatural sense, the concept remains deeply in the human consciousness inevitably. Humanitarianism is no reply, for not every man stands in the place of every other man for this other comrade's comfort. But certain are chosen out of the human race to be the consoler of some other. Of these, for example, is Joseph Barker Howe, Ph.D. Of intellects not the first yet of true intellect and lambent instructions, given to that which is intuitive and irrational, not to what is logical in the strict word, what is judged by him is of the heart and not the head. Here is one chosen, in that he chooses himself to stand in the place of another for comfort and consolation. To him more than another I give my gratitude, with all respect to our Dean who reads this, a noble man, but merely dedicated, not consecrated. But not in the aspect of the Paraclete only is Dr. Joseph Barker Howe established, for he must be the Paraclete to another aspect of himself, that which is driven and persecuted by the lack of understanding in the world at large, so that he in himself embodies the full history of man's tribulations and, overflowing upon others, notably the present writer, is the ultimate end.'

This was love. There was no escape from it. Try as Howe might to remember that Tertan was mad and all his emotions invalidated, he could not destroy the effect upon him of his student's stern, affectionate regard. He had betrayed not only a power of mind but a power of love. And, however firmly he held before his attention the fact of Tertan's madness, he could do nothing to banish the physical sensation of gratitude he felt. He had never thought of himself as 'driven and persecuted' and he did not now. But still he could not make meaningless his sensation of gratitude. The pitiable Tertan sternly pitied him, and comfort came from Tertan's never-to-be-comforted mind.

III

In an academic community, even an efficient one, official matters move slowly. The term drew to a close with no action in the case of Tertan, and Joseph Howe had to confront a curious problem. How should he grade his strange student, Tertan?

Tertan's final examination had been no different from all his other writing, and what did one 'give' such a student? De Witt must have his A, that was clear. Johnson would get a B. With Casebeer it was a question of a B-minus or a C-plus, and Stettenhover, who had been crammed by the team tutor to fill half a blue-book with his thin feminine scrawl, would have his C-minus which he would accept with mingled indifference and resentment. But with Tertan it was not so easy.

The boy was still in the college process and his name could not be omitted from the grade sheet. Yet what should a mind under suspicion of madness be graded? Until the medical verdict was given, it was for Howe to continue as Tertan's teacher and to keep his judgment pedagogical. Impossible to give him an F: he had not failed. B was for Johnson's stolid mediocrity. He could not be put on the edge of passing with Stettenhover, for he exactly did not pass. In energy and richness of intellect he was perhaps even De Witt's superior, and Howe toyed grimly with the notion of giving him an A, but that would lower the value of the A De Witt had won with his beautiful and clear, if still arrogant, mind. There was a notation which the Registrar recognized—Inc., for Incomplete, and in the horrible comedy of the situation, Howe considered that. But really only a mark of M for Mad would serve.

In his perplexity, Howe sought the Dean, but the Dean was out of town. In the end, he decided to maintain the A-minus he had given Tertan at mid-term. After all, there had been no falling away from that quality. He entered it on the grade sheet with something like bravado.

Academic time moves quickly. A college year is not really a year, lacking as it does three months. And it is endlessly divided into units which, at their beginning, appear larger than they are—terms, half-terms, months, weeks. And the ultimate unit, the hour, is not really an hour, lacking as it does ten minutes. And so the new term advanced rapidly, and one day the fields about the town were all brown, cleared of even the few thin patches of snow which had lingered so long.

Howe, as he lectured on the romantic poets, became conscious of Blackburn emanating wrath. Blackburn did it well, did it with enormous dignity. He did not stir in his seat, he kept his eyes fixed on Howe in perfect attention, but he abstained from using his notebook, there was no mistaking what he proposed to himself as an attitude. His elbow on the writing-wing of the chair, his chin on the curled fingers of his hand, he was the embodiment of intellectual indignation. He was thinking his own thoughts, would give no public offense, yet would claim his due, was not to be intimidated. Howe knew that he would present himself at the end of the hour.

Blackburn entered the office without invitation. He did not smile; there was no cajolery about him. Without invitation he sat down beside Howe's desk. He did not speak until he had taken the blue-book from his pocket. He said, 'What does this mean, sir?'

It was a sound and conservative student tactic. Said in the usual way it meant, 'How could you have so misunderstood me?' or 'What does this mean for my future in the course?' But there were none of the humbler tones in Blackburn's way of saying it.

Howe made the established reply, 'I think that's for you to tell me.'

Blackburn continued icy. 'I'm sure I can't, sir.'

There was a silence between them. Both dropped their eyes to the blue-book on the desk. On its cover Howe had penciled: 'F. This is very poor work.'

Howe picked up the blue-book. There was always the possibility of injustice. The teacher may be bored by the mass of papers and not wholly attentive. A phrase, even the student's handwriting, may irritate him unreasonably. 'Well,' said Howe, 'Let's go through it.'

He opened the first page. 'Now here: you write, "In *The Ancient Mariner,* Coleridge lives in and transports us to a honey-sweet world where all is rich and strange, a world of charm to which we can escape from the humdrum existence of our daily lives, the world of romance. Here, in this warm and honey-sweet land of charming dreams we can relax and enjoy ourselves."'

Howe lowered the paper and waited with a neutral look for Blackburn to speak. Blackburn returned the look boldly, did not speak, sat stolid and lofty. At last Howe said, speaking gently, 'Did you mean that, or were you just at a loss for something to say?'

'You imply that I was just "bluffing"?' The quotation marks hung palpable in the air about the word.

'I'd like to know. I'd prefer believing that you were bluffing to believing that you really thought this.'

Blackburn's eyebrows went up. From the height of a great and firm-based idea he looked at his teacher. He clasped the crags for a moment and then pounced, craftily, suavely. 'Do you mean, Doctor Howe, that there aren't two opinions possible?'

It was superbly done in its air of putting all of Howe's intellectual life into the balance. Howe remained patient and simple. 'Yes, many opinions are possible, but not this one. Whatever anyone believes of *The Ancient Mariner,* no one can in reason believe that it represents a—a honey-sweet world in which we can relax.'

'But that is what I *feel*, sir.'

This was well-done, too. Howe said, 'Look, Mr. Blackburn. Do you really relax with hunger and thirst, the heat and the sea-serpents, the dead men with staring eyes, Life in Death and the skeletons? Come now, Mr. Blackburn.'

Blackburn made no answer, and Howe pressed forward. 'Now, you say of Wordsworth, "Of peasant stock himself, he turned from the effete life of the salons and found in the peasant the hope of a flaming revolution which would sweep away all the old ideas. This is the subject of his best poems."'

Beaming at his teacher with youthful eagerness, Blackburn said, 'Yes, sir, a rebel, a bringer of light to suffering mankind. I see him as a kind of Prothemeus.'

'A kind of what?'

'Prothemeus, sir.'

"Think, Mr. Blackburn. We were talking about him only today and I mentioned his name a dozen times. You don't mean Prothemeus. You mean—' Howe waited, but there was no response.

'You mean Prometheus.'

Blackburn gave no assent, and Howe took the reins. 'You've done a bad job here, Mr. Blackburn, about as bad as could be done.' He saw Blackburn stiffen and his genial face harden again. 'It shows either a lack of preparation or a complete lack of understanding.' He saw Blackburn's face begin to go to pieces and he stopped.

'Oh, sir,' Blackburn burst out, 'I've never had a mark like this before, never anything below a B, never. A thing like this has never happened to me before.'

It must be true, it was a statement too easily verified. Could it be that other instructors accepted such flaunting nonsense? Howe wanted to end the interview. 'I'll set it down to lack of preparation,' he said. 'I know you're busy. That's not an excuse, but it's an explanation. Now, suppose you really prepare, and then take another quiz in two weeks. We'll forget this one and count the other.'

Blackburn squirmed with pleasure and gratitude. "Thank you, sir. You're really very kind, very kind.'

Howe rose to conclude the visit. 'All right, then—in two weeks.'

It was that day that the Dean imparted to Howe the conclusion of the case of Tertan. It was simple and a little anti-climatic. A physician had been called in, and had said the word, given the name.

'A classic case, he called it,' the Dean said. 'Not a doubt in the world,' he said. His eyes were full of miserable pity, and he clutched at a word. 'A classic case, a classic case.' To his aid and to Howe's there came the Parthenon and the form of the Greek drama, the Aristotelian logic, Racine and the Well-Tempered Clavichord, the blueness of the Aegean and its clear sky.[13] Classic—that is to say, without a doubt, perfect in its way, a veritable model, and, as the Dean had been told, sure to take a perfectly predictable and inevitable course to a foreknown conclusion.

It was not only pity that stood in the Dean's eyes. For a moment there was fear too. 'Terrible,' he said, 'it is simply terrible.'

Then he went on briskly. 'Naturally, we've told the boy nothing. And,

[13] The Parthenon, the most celebrated example of Doric architecture, is a temple of Athena, built in the fifth century B.C.; Jean Baptiste Racine (1639–1699) was a famous French tragic poet; the *Well-Tempered Clavichord* is a series of piano exercises by Johann Sebastian Bach (1685–1750).

naturally, we won't. His tuition's paid by his scholarship, and we'll continue him on the rolls until the end of the year. That will be kindest. After that the matter will be out of our control. We'll see, of course, that he gets into the proper hands. I'm told there will be no change, he'll go on like this, be as good as this, for four to six months. And so we'll just go along as usual.'

So Tertan continued to sit in Section 5 of English 1A, to his classmates still a figure of curiously dignified fun, symbol to most of them of the respectable but absurd intellectual life. But to his teacher he was now very different. He had not changed—he was still the greyhound casting[14] for the scent of ideas, and Howe could see that he was still the same Tertan, but he could not feel it. What he felt as he looked at the boy sitting in his accustomed place was the hard blank of a fact. The fact itself was formidable and depressing. But what Howe was chiefly aware of was that he had permitted the metamorphosis of Tertan from person to fact.

As much as possible he avoided seeing Tertan's upraised hand and eager eye. But the fact did not know of its mere factuality, it continued its existence as if it were Tertan, hand up and eye questioning, and one day it appeared in Howe's office with a document.

'Even the spirit who lives egregiously, above the herd, must have its relations with the fellowman,' Tertan declared. He laid the document on Howe's desk. It was headed 'Quill and Scroll Society of Dwight College. Application for Membership.'

'In most ways these are crass minds,' Tertan said, touching the paper. 'Yet as a whole, bound together in their common love of letters, they transcend their intellectual lacks since it is not a paradox that the whole is greater than the sum of its parts.'

'When are the elections?' Howe asked.

'They take place tomorrow.'

'I certainly hope you will be successful.'

'Thank you. Would you wish to implement that hope?' A rather dirty finger pointed to the bottom of the sheet. 'A faculty recommender is necessary,' Tertan said stiffly, and waited.

'And you wish me to recommend you?'

'It would be an honor.'

'You may use my name.'

Tertan's finger pointed again. 'It must be a written sponsorship, signed by the sponsor.' There was a large blank space on the form under the heading, 'Opinion of Faculty Sponsor.'

This was almost another thing and Howe hesitated. Yet there was nothing else to do and he took out his fountain pen. He wrote, 'Mr. Ferdinand Tertan is marked by his intense devotion to letters and by his exceptional love of all things of the mind.' To this he signed his name, which looked bold and assertive on the white page. It disturbed him, the strange affirming power of a name. With a businesslike air, Tertan whipped up the paper, folding it with decision, and put it into his pocket. He bowed and took his departure, leaving Howe with the sense of having done something oddly momentous.

And so much now seemed odd and momentous to Howe that should not

14 Hunting term; searching for a scent or trail.

have seemed so. It was odd and momentous, he felt, when he sat with Blackburn's second quiz before him, and wrote in an excessively firm hand the grade of C-minus. The paper was a clear, an indisputable failure. He was carefully and consciously committing a cowardice. Blackburn had told the truth when he had pleaded his past record. Howe had consulted it in the Dean's office. It showed no grade lower than a B-minus. A canvass of some of Blackburn's previous instructors had brought vague attestations to the adequate powers of a student imperfectly remembered, and sometimes surprise that his abilities could be questioned at all.

As he wrote the grade, Howe told himself that his cowardice sprang from an unwillingness to have more dealings with a student he disliked. He knew it was simpler than that. He knew he feared Blackburn; that was the absurd truth. And cowardice did not solve the matter after all. Blackburn, flushed with a first success, attacked at once. The minimal passing grade had not assuaged his feelings and he sat at Howe's desk and again the blue-book lay between them. Blackburn said nothing. With an enormous impudence, he was waiting for Howe to speak and explain himself.

At last Howe said sharply and rudely, 'Well?' His throat was tense and the blood was hammering in his head. His mouth was tight with anger at himself for his disturbance.

Blackburn's glance was almost baleful. 'This is impossible, sir.'

'But there it is,' Howe answered.

'Sir?' Blackburn had not caught the meaning but his tone was still haughty.

Impatiently Howe said, 'There it is, plain as day. Are you here to complain again?'

'Indeed I am, sir.' There was surprise in Blackburn's voice that Howe should ask the question.

'I shouldn't complain if I were you. You did a thoroughly bad job on your first quiz. This one is a little, only a very little, better.' This was not true. If anything, it was worse.

'That might be a matter of opinion, sir.'

'It is a matter of opinion. Of my opinion.'

'Another opinion might be different, sir.'

'You really believe that?' Howe said.

'Yes.' The omission of the 'sir' was monumental.

'Whose, for example?'

'The Dean's, for example.' Then the fleshy jaw came forward a little. 'Or a certain literary critic's, for example.'

It was colossal and almost too much for Blackburn himself to handle. The solidity of his face almost crumpled under it. But he withstood his own audacity and went on. 'And the Dean's opinion might be guided by the knowledge that the person who gave me this mark is the man whom a famous critic, the most eminent judge of literature in this country, called a drunken man. The Dean might think twice about whether such a man is fit to teach Dwight students.'

Howe said in quiet admonition, 'Blackburn, you're mad,' meaning no more than to check the boy's extravagance.

But Blackburn paid no heed. He had another shot in the locker. 'And the Dean might be guided by the information, of which I have evidence, documentary evidence,'—he slapped his breast pocket twice—'that this same person personally recommended to the college literary society, the oldest in the country, that he personally recommended a student who is crazy, who threw the meeting into an uproar—a psychiatric case. The Dean might take that into account.'

Howe was never to learn the details of that 'uproar.' He had always to content himself with the dim but passionate picture which at that moment sprang into his mind, of Tertan standing on some abstract height and madly denouncing the multitude of Quill and Scroll who howled him down.

He sat quiet a moment and looked at Blackburn. The ferocity had entirely gone from the student's face. He sat regarding his teacher almost benevolently. He had played a good card and now, scarcely at all unfriendly, he was waiting to see the effect. Howe took up the blue-book and negligently sifted through it. He read a page, closed the book, struck out the C-minus and wrote an F.

'Now you may take the paper to the Dean,' he said. 'You may tell him that after reconsidering it, I lowered the grade.'

The gasp was audible. 'Oh, sir!' Blackburn cried. 'Please!' His face was agonized. 'It means my graduation, my livelihood, my future. Don't do this to me.'

'It's done already.'

Blackburn stood up. 'I spoke rashly, sir, hastily. I had no intention, no real intention, of seeing the Dean. It rests with you—entirely, entirely. I *hope* you will restore the first mark.'

'Take the matter to the Dean or not, just as you choose. The grade is what you deserve and it stands.'

Blackburn's head dropped. 'And will I be failed at mid-term, sir?'

'Of course.'

From deep out of Blackburn's great chest rose a cry of anguish. 'Oh, sir, if you want me to go down on my knees to you, I will, I will.'

Howe looked at him in amazement.

'I will, I will. On my knees, sir. This mustn't, mustn't happen.'

He spoke so literally, meaning so very truly that his knees and exactly his knees were involved and seeming to think that he was offering something of tangible value to his teacher, that Howe, whose head had become icy clear in the nonsensical drama, thought, 'The boy is mad,' and began to speculate fantastically whether something in himself attracted or developed aberration. He could see himself standing absurdly before the Dean and saying, 'I've found another. This time it's the vice-president of the Council, the manager of the debating team and secretary of Quill and Scroll.'

One more such discovery, he thought, and he himself would be discovered! And there, suddenly, Blackburn was on his knees with a thump, his huge thighs straining his trousers, his hand outstretched in a great gesture of supplication.

With a cry, Howe shoved back his swivel chair and it rolled away on its casters half across the little room. Blackburn knelt for a moment to nothing at all, then got to his feet.

Howe rose abruptly. He said, 'Blackburn, you will stop acting like an idiot. Dust your knees off, take your paper and get out. You've behaved like a fool and a malicious person. You have half a term to do a decent job. Keep your silly mouth shut and try to do it. Now get out.'

Blackburn's head was low. He raised it and there was a pious light in his eyes. 'Will you shake hands, sir?' he said. He thrust out his hand.

'I will not,' Howe said.

Head and hand sank together. Blackburn picked up his blue-book and walked to the door. He turned and said, 'Thank you, sir.' His back, as he departed, was heavy with tragedy and stateliness.

IV

After years of bad luck with the weather, the College had a perfect day for Commencement. It was wonderfully bright, the air so transparent, the wind so brisk that no one could resist talking about it.

As Howe set out for the campus he heard Hilda calling from the back yard. She called, 'Professor, professor,' and came running to him.

Howe said, 'What's this "professor" business?'

'Mother told me,' Hilda said. 'You've been promoted. And I want to take your picture.'

'Next year,' said Howe. 'I won't be a professor until next year. And you know better than to call anybody "professor."'

'It was just in fun,' Hilda said. She seemed disappointed.

'But you can take my picture if you want. I won't look much different next year.' Still, it was frightening. It might mean that he was to stay in this town all his life.

Hilda brightened. 'Can I take it in this?' she said, and touched the gown he carried over his arm.

Howe laughed. 'Yes, you can take it in this.'

'I'll get my things and meet you in front of Otis,' Hilda said. 'I have the background all picked out.'

On the campus the Commencement crowd was already large. It stood about in eager, nervous little family groups. As he crossed, Howe was greeted by a student, capped and gowned, glad of the chance to make an event for his parents by introducing one of his teachers. It was while Howe stood there chatting that he saw Tertan.

He had never seen anyone quite so alone, as though a circle had been woven about him to separate him from the gay crowd on the campus. Not that Tertan was not gay, he was the gayest of all. Three weeks had passed since Howe had last seen him, the weeks of examination, the lazy week before Commencement, and this was now a different Tertan. On his head he wore a panama hat, broad-brimmed and fine, of the shape associated with South American planters. He wore a suit of raw silk, luxurious, but yellowed with age and much too tight, and he sported a whangee cane.[15] He walked sedately, the hat tilted at a devastating angle, the stick coming up and down in time to his measured tread. He had, Howe guessed, outfitted himself to greet the day in the clothes of that ruined father whose existence was on record in the Dean's office. Gravely and arrogantly he surveyed the scene—in it, his whole bearing seemed to say, but not of it. With his haughty step, with his flashing eye, Tertan was coming nearer. Howe did not wish to be seen. He shifted his position slightly. When he looked again, Tertan was not in sight.

[15] Walking stick made from a plant similar to bamboo.

The chapel clock struck the quarter hour. Howe detached himself from his chat and hurried to Otis Hall at the far end of the campus. Hilda had not yet come. He went up into the high portico and, using the glass of the door for a mirror, put on his gown, adjusted the hood on his shoulders and set the mortarboard on his head. When he came down the steps, Hilda had arrived.

Nothing could have told him more forcibly that a year had passed than the development of Hilda's photographic possessions from the box camera of the previous fall. By a strap about her neck was hung a leather case, so thick and strong, so carefully stitched and so molded to its contents that it could only hold a costly camera. The appearance was deceptive, Howe knew, for he had been present at the Aikens' pre-Christmas conference about its purchase. It was only a fairly good domestic camera. Still, it looked very impressive. Hilda carried another leather case from which she drew a collapsible tripod. Decisively she extended each of its gleaming legs and set it up on the path. She removed the camera from its case and fixed it to the tripod. In its compact efficiency the camera almost had a life of its own, but Hilda treated it with easy familiarity, looked into its eye, glanced casually at its gauges. Then from a pocket she took still another leather case and drew from it a small instrument through which she looked first at Howe, who began to feel inanimate and lost, and then at the sky. She made some adjustment on the instrument, then some adjustment on the camera. She swept the scene with her eye, found a spot and pointed the camera in its direction. She walked to the spot, stood on it and beckoned to Howe. With each new leather case, with each new instrument, and with each new adjustment she had grown in ease and now she said, 'Joe, will you stand here?'

Obediently Howe stood where he was bidden. She had yet another instrument. She took out a tape-measure on a mechanical spool. Kneeling down before Howe, she put the little metal ring of the tape under the tip of his shoe. At her request, Howe pressed it with his toe. When she had measured her distance, she nodded to Howe who released the tape. At a touch, it sprang back into the spool. 'You have to be careful if you're going to get what you want,' Hilda said. 'I don't believe in all this snap-snap-snapping,' she remarked loftily. Howe nodded in agreement, although he was beginning to think Hilda's care excessive.

Now at last the moment had come. Hilda squinted into the camera, moved the tripod slightly. She stood to the side, holding the plunger of the shutter-cable. 'Ready,' she said. 'Will you relax, Joseph, please?' Howe realized that he was standing frozen. Hilda stood poised and precise as a setter, one hand holding the little cable, the other extended with curled dainty fingers like a dancer's, as if expressing to her subject the precarious delicacy of the moment. She pressed the plunger and there was the click. At once she stirred to action, got behind the camera, turned a new exposure. 'Thank you,' she said. 'Would you stand under that tree and let me do a character study with light and shade?'

The childish absurdity of the remark restored Howe's ease. He went to the little tree. The pattern the leaves made on his gown was what Hilda was after. He had just taken a satisfactory position when he heard in the unmistakable voice, 'Ah, Doctor! Having your picture taken?'

Howe gave up the pose and turned to Blackburn who stood on the walk, his hands behind his back, a little too large for his bachelor's gown. Annoyed that Blackburn should see him posing for a character study in light and shade, Howe said irritably, 'Yes, having my picture taken.'

Blackburn beamed at Hilda. 'And the little photographer?' he said. Hilda fixed her eyes on the ground and stood closer to her brilliant and aggressive camera. Blackburn, teetering on his heels, his hands behind his back, wholly prelatical and benignly patient, was not abashed at the silence. At last Howe said, 'If you'll excuse us, Mr. Blackburn, we'll go on with the picture.'

'Go right ahead, sir. I'm running along.' But he only came closer. 'Doctor Howe,' he said fervently, 'I want to tell you how glad I am that I was able to satisfy your standards at last.'

Howe was surprised at the hard, insulting brightness of his own voice, and even Hilda looked up curiously as he said, 'Nothing you have ever done has satisfied me, and nothing you could ever do would satisfy me, Blackburn.'

With a glance at Hilda, Blackburn made a gesture as if to hush Howe—as though all his former bold malice had taken for granted a kind of understanding between himself and his teacher, a secret which must not be betrayed to a third person. 'I only meant, sir,' he said, 'that I was able to pass your course after all.'

Howe said, 'You didn't pass my course. I passed you out of my course. I passed you without even reading your paper. I wanted to be sure the college would be rid of you. And when all the grades were in and I did read your paper, I saw I was right not to have read it first.'

Blackburn presented a stricken face. 'It was very bad, sir?'

But Howe had turned away. The paper had been fantastic. The paper had been, if he wished to see it so, mad. It was at this moment that the Dean came up behind Howe and caught his arm. 'Hello, Joseph,' he said. 'We'd better be getting along, it's almost late.'

He was not a familiar man, but when he saw Blackburn, who approached to greet him, he took Blackburn's arm, too. 'Hello, Theodore,' he said. Leaning forward on Howe's arm and on Blackburn's, he said, 'Hello, Hilda dear.' Hilda replied quietly, 'Hello, Uncle George.'

Still clinging to their arms, still linking Howe and Blackburn, the Dean said, 'Another year gone, Joe, and we've turned out another crop. After you've been here a few years, you'll find it reasonably upsetting—you wonder how there can be so many graduating classes while you stay the same. But of course, you don't stay the same.' Then he said, 'Well,' sharply, to dismiss the thought. He pulled Blackburn's arm and swung him around to Howe. 'Have you heard about Teddy Blackburn?' he asked. 'He has a job already, before graduation—the first man of his class to be placed.' Expectant of congratulations, Blackburn beamed at Howe. Howe remained silent.

'Isn't that good?' the Dean said. Still Howe did not answer and the Dean, puzzled and put out, turned to Hilda. 'That's a very fine-looking camera, Hilda.' She touched it with affectionate pride.

'Instruments of precision,' said a voice. 'Instruments of precision.' Of the three with joined arms, Howe was the nearest to Tertan, whose gaze took in all the scene except the smile and the nod which Howe gave him. The boy leaned on his cane. The broad-brimmed hat, canting jauntily over his eye, confused the image of his face that Howe had established, suppressed the rigid lines of the ascetic and brought out the baroque curves. It made an effect of perverse majesty.

'Instruments of precision,' said Tertan for the last time, addressing no one, making a casual comment to the universe. And it occurred to Howe that Tertan might not be referring to Hilda's equipment. The sense of the thrice-woven circle of the boy's loneliness smote him fiercely. Tertan stood in majestic jauntiness, superior to all the scene, but his isolation made Howe ache with a pity of which Tertan was more the cause than the object, so general and indiscriminate was it.

Whether in his sorrow he made some unintended movement toward Tertan which the Dean checked, or whether the suddenly tightened grip on his arm was the Dean's own sorrow and fear, he did not know. Tertan watched them in the incurious way people watch a photograph being taken, and suddenly the thought that, to the boy, it must seem that the three were posing for a picture together made Howe detach himself almost rudely from the Dean's grasp.

'I promised Hilda another picture,' he announced—needlessly, for Tertan was no longer there, he had vanished in the last sudden flux of visitors who, now that the band had struck up, were rushing nervously to find seats.

'You'd better hurry,' the Dean said. 'I'll go along, it's getting late for me.' He departed and Blackburn walked stately by his side.

Howe again took his position under the little tree which cast its shadow over his face and gown. 'Just hurry, Hilda, won't you?' he said. Hilda held the cable at arm's length, her other arm crooked and her fingers crisped. She rose on her toes and said 'Ready,' and pressed the release. 'Thank you,' she said gravely and began to dismantle her camera as he hurried off to join the procession.

COMMENTARY

It is not unheard of for an editor to include an example of his own work in an anthology he is making, but it is sufficiently unusual to call for a word of explanation. My thrusting upon the reader a story of my own will perhaps seem less immodest if I say that the idea of doing so originated not with me but with my publisher and that the argument he advanced for its propriety seemed to me to be cogent—he said that something was to be gained for the understanding of literature by a writer's setting down his thoughts about his own work, especially if he gave an account of the process by which a particular work had come into being.

One possibly instructive thing that such an account can do is to suggest the relation that exists between the actual facts of a writer's experience and the process of his imagination, particularly in the creation of character. Not all writers of fiction are concerned to create characters that seem to be "true to life." (In the present volume, for example, Hawthorne has no such concern.) But whenever the nature of the story does call for verisimilitude of character, it can usually be assumed—at least in modern literature—that the author's creation began with reference to an actual person.

An awareness of the relation between an actual person and a created character can have no part in our assessment of a work of fiction. Yet it is interesting in itself and it is useful in helping us understand the interplay between actuality and imagination. In the case of this story, I am conscious of how much I have relied on actuality in my representation of the two students. They were both in classes of mine in my early years of teaching at Columbia College, and I recall them as being very much as they appear in the story— so much so that if I were now to say what part my imagination played in the creation of the characters which derive from them, I should incline to claim for it nothing more than its having brought them together in the same story, for in actuality they had no connection with each other. But does this not do an injustice to my imagination, for surely it was at work in my acquaintance with the two actual students, in my observation of the details of their behavior, in the emotions and opinions I had about them?

The story had its origin, as may easily be supposed, in my feelings about the student who is represented under the name of Tertan. (I do not remember how I got this name for him, nor do I know if it is actually an Hungarian name or one that I made up, thinking it would pass for Hungarian. I have always pronounced it with the accent on the last syllable: Ter*tan*.) The moment at which the impulse came to me to write a story about him is not easily forgotten. Some time in the winter after he had been a member of one of my composition classes, I stood next to that unfortunate boy at the loan desk of the College Library; we were both waiting to charge out some books. I greeted him and he responded with a blank and haughty stare. I did not know whether I was being deliberately snubbed or whether his not recognizing me was the sign of some confusion of his mental processes. It seemed to me that both alternatives were possible. For some time I had known that he was suffering from a deep disturbance of the mind. How very deep it was and how much worse it had become since I had last seen him was made plain by his air of majestic self-reference. But also he had good reason to refuse to recognize me, for, by the end of the course he had taken with me, I had refused to recognize him—I had, that is, not consented to know him as he believed he deserved to be known, as he demanded to be known. Like his teacher in the story, I had at first been struck by his intellectual powers. But then, with the passage of time, it had become clear to me that no effort of instruction could possibly overcome the extravagant incoherence of his expression, both in speech and in writing, which I eventually had to understand as a symptom of an extreme mental pathology. He had discovered that I wrote for certain magazines he admired and this had led him to entertain an exaggerated respect for me. Very likely this flattered me into giving him a good deal of attention, which inevitably I diminished when I realized that he was beyond the help of teaching. He did not give me the affection that Tertan in the story gives Dr. Howe, and the respect he did show me was of a most abstract, impersonal kind, yet I had felt a bond with him. When I gave up my special efforts to improve his writing and when at last I communicated to the Dean of the College my opinion of his deranged condition, I felt, against all reason, that I had committed a great disloyalty.

Yet as I saw him standing at the loan desk I could not doubt that he was on the verge of actual insanity, that he was on the way to being beyond the reach of ordinary human feelings. The conflict between my knowledge of this fact and my unreasoning remorse at my "disloyalty" made an emotion which demanded a story. The story, as I at once conceived it, would present the sad irony of a passionate devotion to the intellectual life maintained by a person of deranged mind.

This was what the story was to present, but what was the story to *be*? I remember deciding that some other element was needed in addition to the student's plight and his teacher's emotions. To limit myself to these two elements would make a story that was merely static and linear—and merely pathetic. I did not want a pathetic story for Tertan. I thought he deserved something sterner than that. From the first, I conceived him to be an impressive figure, in some sense heroic, and he therefore made the demand on me that I come as close as I could to tragedy. For this a sense of emotional and physical space was needed, and the possibility of action and decision. I had no idea at all of how to go about getting what I wanted. Then, quite without my bidding, the image of the student who was the original of Blackburn popped up before me.

He had been in a class of mine two or three years earlier, and, as I say, his traits were quite precisely those that I have attributed to Blackburn. He had the same pompous busyness, the same impulse to manipulate his teachers, the same flaunting stupidity, the same sly malevolence together with the same readiness to collapse if strongly resisted or counterattacked. We got on very badly. He once really did threaten to use against me the influence he claimed to have with the Dean. The conference over his bad examination is more or less literally remembered, and in the course of that meeting he did, in a moment of intense supplication, offer to go down on his knees to me, although he did not actually do so. The thought occurred to me that this conduct was "insane," but the word presented itself more as a way of speaking than as a serious idea.

His sudden appearance in my mind to stand beside Tertan delighted me. It immediately helped me in several ways. Blackburn's malevolence rescued the teacher from being merely a sensitive, sympathetic, observing consciousness. By putting Howe in some danger, it made him that much more of a person; it made him someone with a fate and required that he should not only feel but act. And of course it gave added stature to Tertan by suggesting that, if Blackburn were to try to harm his teacher, Tertan must help or at least comfort him. Upon Howe I bestowed the insecurities I had felt as a new instructor, but I sought to give them greater point and justification by making Howe a poet, and a "difficult" and "controversial" poet at that. For the same reason I set the scene in a country college where the smallness and tightness of the community would make a newcomer more conscious of the judgments that were being passed on him.

But if the appearance of Blackburn delighted me, it also filled me with apprehension. There was, I thought, something beautifully appropriate in the juxtaposition of the two students—something all too appropriate! For it occurred to me that the juxtaposition might seem to express an idea which could be very easily formulated: that there are kinds of insanity that society does not accept and kinds of insanity that society does accept. This was an idea to which I could readily assent, and the story does of course lend support to its truth. But it was not what I wanted my story primarily to express. Not only would my feelings and the intention that arose from them be belied, but I felt that it would be an aesthetic misfortune if readers were able to make the formulation thus easily, for a story that can be "summed up" in such a way must prove lacking in power. If the reader can so readily make the point of a story explicit, he comes too quickly to terms with it and is able to put it out of his mind as a thing settled and done with.

But then it occurred to me that if my readers did understand the juxtaposition of the two students in this way, it would prove a great advantage. For the story would seem to them to say one thing when actually it was saying another.

I thought it likely that my readers would wish to reverse the judgment that society makes, that they would say that Blackburn's insanity (if that is what it is) should not be accepted by society, and that Tertan's insanity should be accepted. And it seemed to me that they might go one step further and conclude that Tertan, although apparently insane, was not really so. All the authority of certain moral ideas, quite generous ones, would urge them to this conclusion. For was not Tertan terribly alone, and in a socially disadvantaged position, and benevolent, and dedicated, and was he not by way of being a genius, and are not geniuses often said to be mad, although mistakenly?

I seem to have been right in my expectation. When the story was published, many readers wrote to me—and some telephoned—to say that they had been moved by it but disappointed because I had not made it sufficiently clear that Tertan was not really insane.

The truth is, I think, that they knew he was insane and did not want him to be. If the story has any power at all, it surely lies in its ability to generate resistance to the certitude that Tertan is deranged. The impulse to resist the undeniable fact comes, I suppose, from the common apprehension, conscious or unconscious, that the fabric of our reason is very delicate and always in danger. This impulse is reinforced by our modern anxiety at confronting a painful fate which cannot be accounted for in moral terms and which cannot be said to result from some fault of society.

And if I may speak further of the source of what power the story may have, I ought to mention the challenge it offers the reader to reconcile two dissimilar modes of judgment with each other. One is the judgment of morality, the other of science. Judged by morality, Tertan's behavior is sane and good, Blackburn's mad and bad. But no psychiatrist would adjudge Blackburn insane, and no psychiatrist would fail to say that Tertan must soon go to a mental hospital.

It perhaps does not need to be remarked that the story encourages the reader to take an adverse view of the judgment of science. In the classroom discussion of Ibsen's *Ghosts,* DeWitt's expressed belief that science can solve all moral problems is arrogant and shallow, forgivable only because DeWitt is so young. When I began the story with the little scene of Hilda and her camera, I did not have in mind the concluding scene in which Hilda prepares to take a picture with such scientific accuracy; but having begun the story with Hilda taking the picture, the use I might make of her and her camera was suggested to me by the little conversation about photographic distortion in the Dean's office: it gave me the opportunity to allow Tertan to resist the judgment that had been passed on him, to murmur his scornful phrase, "Instruments of precision." And in other details the story seems to take the traditional hostile attitude of literary humanism toward science. But this must not be accepted at its face value. Nothing, I fear, can reverse the diagnosis of Tertan's illness.

Perhaps I should mention that in writing the description of Tertan on Commencement Day, I had consciously in mind Coleridge's description of the daemonic poet at the end of "Kubla Khan" (page 488) and stole a few phrases from it.

THE
MAGIC
BARREL

B E R N A R D M A L A M U D

1 9 1 4 –

NOT LONG AGO there lived in uptown New York, in a small, almost meager room, though crowded with books, Leo Finkle, a rabbinical student in the Yeshivah University. Finkle, after six years of study, was to be ordained in June and had been advised by an acquaintance that he might find it easier to win himself a congregation if he were married. Since he had no present prospects of marriage, after two tormented days of turning it over in his mind, he called in Pinye Salzman, a marriage broker whose two-line advertisement he had read in the *Forward*.[1]

The matchmaker appeared one night out of the dark fourth-floor hallway of the graystone rooming house where Finkle lived, grasping a black, strapped portfolio that had been worn thin with use. Salzman, who had been long in the business, was of slight but dignified build, wearing an old hat, and an overcoat too short and tight for him. He smelled frankly of fish, which he loved to eat, and although he was missing a few teeth, his presence was not displeasing, because of an amiable manner curiously contrasted with mournful eyes. His voice, his lips, his wisp of beard, his bony fingers were animated, but give him a moment of repose and his mild blue eyes revealed a depth of sadness, a charac-

[1] The Jewish daily newspaper.

375

teristic that put Leo a little at ease although the situation, for him, was inherently tense.

He at once informed Salzman why he had asked him to come, explaining that his home was in Cleveland, and that but for his parents, who had married comparatively late in life, he was alone in the world. He had for six years devoted himself almost entirely to his studies, as a result of which, understandably, he had found himself without time for a social life and the company of young women. Therefore he thought it the better part of trial and error—of embarrassing fumbling—to call in an experienced person to advise him on these matters. He remarked in passing that the function of the marriage broker was ancient and honorable, highly approved in the Jewish community, because it made practical the necessary without hindering joy. Moreover, his own parents had been brought together by a matchmaker. They had made, if not a financially profitable marriage—since neither had possessed any worldly goods to speak of—at least a successful one in the sense of their everlasting devotion to each other. Salzman listened in embarrassed surprise, sensing a sort of apology. Later, however, he experienced a glow of pride in his work, an emotion that had left him years ago, and he heartily approved of Finkle.

The two went to their business. Leo had led Salzman to the only clear place in the room, a table near a window that overlooked the lamp-lit city. He seated himself at the matchmaker's side but facing him, attempting by an act of will to suppress the unpleasant tickle in his throat. Salzman eagerly unstrapped his portfolio and removed a loose rubber band from a thin packet of much-handled cards. As he flipped through them, a gesture and sound that physically hurt Leo, the student pretended not to see and gazed steadfastly out the window. Although it was still February, winter was on its last legs, signs of which he had for the first time in years begun to notice. He now observed the round white moon, moving high in the sky through a cloud menagerie, and watched with half-open mouth as it penetrated a huge hen, and dropped out of her like an egg laying itself. Salzman, though pretending through eyeglasses he had just slipped on, to be engaged in scanning the writing on the cards, stole occasional glances at the young man's distinguished face, noting with pleasure the long, severe scholar's nose, brown eyes heavy with learning, sensitive yet ascetic lips, and a certain, almost hollow quality of the dark cheeks. He gazed around at shelves upon shelves of books and let out a soft, contented sigh.

When Leo's eyes fell upon the cards, he counted six spread out in Salzman's hand.

"So few?" he asked in disappointment.

"You wouldn't believe me how much cards I got in my office," Salzman replied. "The drawers are already filled to the top, so I keep them now in a barrel, but is every girl good for a new rabbi?"

Leo blushed at this, regretting all he had revealed of himself in a curriculum vitae he had sent to Salzman. He had thought it best to acquaint him with his strict standards and specifications, but in having done so, felt he had told the marriage broker more than was absolutely necessary.

He hesitantly inquired, "Do you keep photographs of your clients on file?"

"First comes family, amount of dowry, also what kind promises," Salzman replied, unbuttoning his tight coat and settling himself in the chair. "After comes pictures, rabbi."

"Call me Mr. Finkle. I'm not yet a rabbi."

Salzman said he would, but instead called him doctor, which he changed to rabbi when Leo was not listening too attentively.

Salzman adjusted his horn-rimmed spectacles, gently cleared his throat and read in an eager voice the contents of the top card:

"Sophie P. Twenty-four years. Widow one year. No children. Educated high school and two years college. Father promises eight thousand dollars. Has wonderful wholesale business. Also real estate. On the mother's side comes teachers, also one actor. Well known on Second Avenue."

Leo gazed up in surprise. "Did you say a widow?"

"A widow don't mean spoiled, rabbi. She lived with her husband maybe four months. He was a sick boy she made a mistake to marry him."

"Marrying a widow has never entered my mind."

"This is because you have no experience. A widow, especially if she is young and healthy like this girl, is a wonderful person to marry. She will be thankful to you the rest of her life. Believe me, if I was looking now for a bride, I would marry a widow."

Leo reflected, then shook his head.

Salzman hunched his shoulders in an almost imperceptible gesture of disappointment. He placed the card down on the wooden table and began to read another:

"Lily H. High school teacher. Regular. Not a substitute. Has savings and new Dodge car. Lived in Paris one year. Father is successful dentist thirty-five years. Interested in professional man. Well Americanized family. Wonderful opportunity."

"I knew her personally," said Salzman. "I wish you could see this girl. She is a doll. Also very intelligent. All day you could talk to her about books and theyater and what not. She also knows current events."

"I don't believe you mentioned her age?"

"Her age?" Salzman said, raising his brows. "Her age is thirty-two years."

Leo said after a while, "I'm afraid that seems a little too old."

Salzman let out a laugh. "So how old are you, rabbi?"

"Twenty-seven."

"So what is the difference, tell me, between twenty-seven and thirty-two? My own wife is seven years older than me. So what did I suffer?—Nothing. If Rothschild's daughter wants to marry you, would you say on account her age, no?"

"Yes," Leo said dryly.

Salzman shook off the no in the yes. "Five years don't mean a thing. I give you my word that when you will live with her for one week you will forget her age. What does it mean five years—that she lived more and knows more than somebody who is younger? On this girl, God bless her, years are not wasted. Each one that it comes makes better the bargain."

"What subject does she teach in high school?"

"Languages. If you heard the way she speaks French, you will think it is music. I am in the business twenty-five years, and I recommend her with my whole heart. Believe me, I know what I'm talking, rabbi."

"What's on the next card?" Leo said abruptly.

Salzman reluctantly turned up the third card:

"Ruth K. Nineteen years. Honor student. Father offers thirteen thousand cash to the right bridegroom. He is a medical doctor. Stomach specialist with marvelous practice. Brother in law owns own garment business. Particular people."

Salzman looked as if he had read his trump card.

"Did you say nineteen?" Leo asked with interest.

"On the dot."

"Is she attractive?" He blushed. "Pretty?"

Salzman kissed his finger tips. "A little doll. On this I give you my word. Let me call the father tonight and you will see what means pretty."

But Leo was troubled. "You're sure she's that young?"

"This I am positive. The father will show you the birth certificate."

"Are you positive there isn't something wrong with her?" Leo insisted.

"Who says there is wrong?"

"I don't understand why an American girl her age should go to a marriage broker."

A smile spread over Salzman's face.

"So for the same reason you went, she comes."

Leo flushed. "I am pressed for time."

Salzman, realizing he had been tactless, quickly explained. "The father came, not her. He wants she should have the best, so he looks around himself. When we will locate the right boy he will introduce him and encourage. This makes a better marriage than if a young girl without experience takes for herself. I don't have to tell you this."

"But don't you think this young girl believes in love?" Leo spoke uneasily.

Salzman was about to guffaw but caught himself and said soberly, "Love comes with the right person, not before."

Leo parted dry lips but did not speak. Noticing that Salzman had snatched a glance at the next card, he cleverly asked, "How is her health?"

"Perfect," Salzman said, breathing with difficulty. "Of course, she is a little lame on her right foot from an auto accident that it happened to her when she was twelve years, but nobody notices on account she is so brilliant and also beautiful."

Leo got up heavily and went to the window. He felt curiously bitter and upbraided himself for having called in the marriage broker. Finally, he shook his head.

"Why not?" Salzman persisted, the pitch of his voice rising.

"Because I detest stomach specialists."

"So what do you care what is his business? After you marry her do you need him? Who says he must come every Friday night in your house?"

Ashamed of the way the talk was going, Leo dismissed Salzman, who went home with heavy, melancholy eyes.

Though he had felt only relief at the marriage broker's departure, Leo was in low spirits the next day. He explained it as arising from Salzman's failure to produce a suitable bride for him. He did not care for his type of clientele. But when Leo found himself hesitating whether to seek out another matchmaker, one more polished than Pinye, he wondered if it could be—his protestations to the contrary, and although he honored his father and mother—that he did not, in essence, care for the matchmaking institution? This thought he quickly put out of mind yet found himself still upset. All day he ran around in the woods—missed an important appointment, forgot to give out his laundry, walked out of a Broadway cafeteria without paying and had to run back with the ticket in his hand; had even not recognized his landlady in the street when she passed with a friend and courteously called out, "A good evening to you, Doctor Finkle." By nightfall, however, he had regained sufficient calm to sink his nose into a book and there found peace from his thoughts.

Almost at once there came a knock on the door. Before Leo could say enter, Salzman, commercial cupid, was standing in the room. His face was gray and meager, his expression hungry, and he looked as if he would expire on his feet. Yet the marriage broker managed, by some trick of the muscles, to display a broad smile.

"So good evening. I am invited?"

Leo nodded, disturbed to see him again, yet unwilling to ask the man to leave.

Beaming still, Salzman laid his portfolio on the table. "Rabbi, I got for you tonight good news."

"I've asked you not to call me rabbi. I'm still a student."

"Your worries are finished. I have for you a first-class bride."

"Leave me in peace concerning this subject." Leo pretended lack of interest.

"The world will dance at your wedding."

"Please, Mr. Salzman, no more."

"But first must come back my strength," Salzman said weakly. He fumbled with the portfolio straps and took out of the leather case an oily paper bag, from which he extracted a hard, seeded roll and a small, smoked white fish. With a quick motion of his hand he stripped the fish out of its skin and began ravenously to chew. "All day in a rush," he muttered.

Leo watched him eat.

"A sliced tomato you have maybe?" Salzman hesitantly inquired.

"No."

The marriage broker shut his eyes and ate. When he had finished he carefully cleaned up the crumbs and rolled up the remains of the fish, in the paper bag. His spectacled eyes roamed the room until he discovered, amid some piles of books, a one-burner gas stove. Lifting his hat he humbly asked, "A glass of tea you got, rabbi?"

Conscience-stricken, Leo rose and brewed the tea. He served it with a chunk of lemon and two cubes of lump sugar, delighting Salzman.

After he had drunk his tea, Salzman's strength and good spirits were restored.

"So tell me, rabbi," he said amiably, "you considered some more the three clients I mentioned yesterday?"

"There was no need to consider."

"Why not?"

"None of them suits me."

"What then suits you?"

Leo let it pass because he could give only a confused answer.

Without waiting for a reply, Salzman asked, "You remember this girl I talked to you—the high school teacher?"

"Age thirty-two?"

But, surprisingly, Salzman's face lit in a smile. "Age twenty-nine."

Leo shot him a look. "Reduced from thirty-two?"

"A mistake," Salzman avowed. "I talked today with the dentist. He took me to his safety deposit box and showed me the birth certificate. She was twenty-nine years last August. They made her a party in the mountains where she went for her vacation. When her father spoke to me the first time I forgot to write the age and I told you thirty-two, but now I remember this was a different client, a widow."

"The same one you told me about? I thought she was twenty-four?"

"A different. Am I responsible that the world is filled with widows?"

"No, but I'm not interested in them, nor for that matter, in school teachers."

Salzman pulled his clasped hand to his breast. Looking at the ceiling he devoutly exclaimed, "Yiddishe kinder, what can I say to somebody that he is not interested in high school teachers? So what then you are interested?"

Leo flushed but controlled himself.

"In what else will you be interested," Salzman went on, "if you not interested in this fine girl that she speaks four languages and has personally in the bank ten thousand dollars? Also her father guarantees further twelve thousand. Also she has a new car, wonderful clothes, talks on all subjects, and she will give you a first-class home and children. How near do we come in our life to paradise?"

"If she's so wonderful, why wasn't she married ten years ago?"

"Why?" said Salzman with a heavy laugh. "—Why? Because she is *partikiler*. This is why. She wants the *best*."

Leo was silent, amused at how he had entangled himself. But Salzman had aroused his interest in Lily H., and he began seriously to consider calling on her. When the marriage broker observed how intently Leo's mind was at work on the facts he had supplied, he felt certain they would soon come to an agreement.

Late Saturday afternoon, conscious of Salzman, Leo Finkle walked with Lily Hirschorn along Riverside Drive. He walked briskly and erectly, wearing with distinction the black fedora he had that morning taken with trepidation out of the dusty hat box on his closet shelf, and the heavy black Saturday coat he had thoroughly whisked clean. Leo also owned a walking stick, a present from a distant relative, but quickly put temptation aside and did not use it. Lily, petite and not unpretty, had on something signifying the approach of spring. She was au courant, animatedly, with all sorts of subjects, and he weighed her words and found her surprisingly sound—score another for Salzman, whom he uneasily sensed to be somewhere around, hiding perhaps high in a tree along the street, flashing the lady signals with a pocket mirror; or perhaps a cloven-hoofed Pan,[2] piping nuptial ditties as he danced his invisible way before them, strewing wild buds on the walk and purple grapes in their path, symbolizing fruit of a union, though there was of course still none.

Lily startled Leo by remarking, "I was thinking of Mr. Salzman, a curious figure, wouldn't you say?"

Not certain what to answer, he nodded.

[2] Greek god of pastures, forests, flocks, and herds; he is represented with the lower part of a goat and the upper part of a man.

She bravely went on, blushing, "I for one am grateful for his introducing us. Aren't you?"

He courteously replied, "I am."

"I mean," she said with a little laugh—and it was all in good taste, or at least gave the effect of being not in bad—"do you mind that we came together so?"

He was not displeased with her honesty, recognizing that she meant to set the relationship aright, and understanding that it took a certain amount of experience in life, and courage, to want to do it quite that way. One had to have some sort of past to make that kind of beginning.

He said that he did not mind. Salzman's function was traditional and honorable—valuable for what it might achieve, which, he pointed out, was frequently nothing.

Lily agreed with a sigh. They walked on for a while and she said after a long silence, again with a nervous laugh, "Would you mind if I asked you something a little bit personal? Frankly, I find the subject fascinating." Although Leo shrugged, she went on half embarrassedly, "How was it that you came to your calling? I mean was it a sudden passionate inspiration?"

Leo, after a time, slowly replied. "I was always interested in the Law."

"You saw revealed in it the presence of the Highest?"

He nodded and changed the subject. "I understand that you spent a little time in Paris, Miss Hirschorn?"

"Oh, did Mr. Salzman tell you, Rabbi Finkle?" Leo winced but she went on, "It was ages ago and almost forgotten. I remember I had to return for my sister's wedding."

And Lily would not be put off. "When," she asked in a trembly voice, "did you become enamored of God?"

He stared at her. Then it came to him that she was talking not about Leo Finkle, but of a total stranger, some mystical figure, perhaps even passionate prophet that Salzman had dreamed up for her—no relation to the living or dead. Leo trembled with rage and weakness. The trickster had obviously sold her a bill of goods, just as he had him, who'd expected to become acquainted with a young lady of twenty-nine, only to behold, the moment he laid eyes upon her strained and anxious face, a woman past thirty-five and aging rapidly. Only his self control had kept him this long in her presence.

"I am not," he said gravely, "a talented religious person," and in seeking words to go on, found himself possessed by shame and fear. "I think," he said in a strained manner, "that I came to God not because I loved Him, but because I did not."

This confession he spoke harshly because its unexpectedness shook him.

Lily wilted. Leo saw a profusion of loaves of bread go flying like ducks high over his head, not unlike the winged loaves by which he had counted himself to sleep last night. Mercifully, then, it snowed, which he would not put past Salzman's machinations.

He was infuriated with the marriage broker and swore he would throw him out of the room the minute he reappeared. But Salzman did not come that night, and when Leo's anger had subsided, an unaccountable despair grew in its place. At first he thought this was caused by his disappointment in Lily, but before long it became evident that he had involved himself with Salzman without a true knowledge of his own intent. He gradually realized—with an emptiness that seized him with six hands—that he had called in the broker to find him a bride because he was incapable of doing it himself. This terrifying insight he had derived as a result of his meeting and conversation with Lily Hirschorn. Her probing questions had somehow irritated him into revealing—to himself more than her—the true nature of his relationship to God, and from that it had come upon him, with shocking force, that apart from his parents, he had never loved anyone. Or perhaps it went the other way, that he did not love God so well as he might, because he had not loved man. It seemed to Leo that his whole life stood starkly revealed and he saw himself for the first time as he truly was—unloved and loveless. This bitter but somehow not fully unexpected revelation brought him to a point of panic, controlled only by extraordinary effort. He covered his face with his hands and cried.

The week that followed was the worst of his life. He did not eat and lost weight. His beard darkened and grew ragged. He stopped attending seminars and almost never opened a book. He seriously considered leaving the Yeshivah, although he was deeply troubled at the thought of the loss of all his years of study—saw them like pages torn from a book, strewn over the city—and at the devastating effect of this decision upon his parents. But he had lived without knowledge of himself, and never in the Five Books[3] and all the Commentaries—mea culpa[4]—had the truth been revealed to him. He did not know where to turn, and in all this desolating loneliness there was no *to whom*, although he often thought of Lily but not once could bring himself to go downstairs and make the call. He became touchy and irritable, especially with his landlady, who asked him all manner of personal questions; on the other hand, sensing his own disagreeableness, he waylaid her on the stairs and apologized abjectly, until mortified, she ran from him. Out of this, however, he drew the consolation that he was a Jew and that a Jew suffered. But gradually, as the long and terrible week drew to a close, he regained his composure and some idea of purpose in life: to go on as planned. Although he was imperfect, the ideal was not. As for his quest of a bride, the thought of continuing afflicted him with anxiety and heartburn, yet perhaps with this new knowledge of himself he would be more successful than in the past. Perhaps love would now come to him and a bride to that love. And for this sanctified seeking who needed a Salzman?

The marriage broker, a skeleton with haunted eyes, returned that very night. He looked, withal, the picture of frustrated expectancy—as if he had steadfastly waited the week at Miss Lily Hirschorn's side for a telephone call that never came.

Casually coughing, Salzman come immediately to the point: "So how did you like her?"

Leo's anger rose and he could not refrain from chiding the matchmaker: "Why did you lie to me, Salzman?"

Salzman's pale face went dead white, the world had snowed on him.

"Did you not state that she was twenty-nine?" Leo insisted.

"I give you my word—"

[3] The *Megilloth* (Song of Solomon, Ruth, Lamentations, Ecclesiastes, and Esther), used in the liturgy of the Jewish faith.
[4] (Latin) Through my fault.

"She was thirty-five, if a day. *At least* thirty-five."

"Of this don't be too sure. Her father told me—"

"Never mind. The worst of it was that you lied to her."

"How did I lie to her, tell me?"

"You told her things about me that weren't true. You made me out to be more, consequently less than I am. She had in mind a totally different person, a sort of semi-mystical Wonder Rabbi."

"All I said, you was a religious man."

"I can imagine."

Salzman sighed. "This is my weakness that I have," he confessed. "My wife says to me I shouldn't be a salesman, but when I have two fine people that they would be wonderful to be married, I am so happy that I talk too much." He smiled wanly. "This is why Salzman is a poor man."

Leo's anger left him. "Well, Salzman, I'm afraid that's all."

The marriage broker fastened hungry eyes on him.

"You don't want any more a bride?"

"I do," said Leo, "but I have decided to seek her in a different way. I am no longer interested in an arranged marriage. To be frank, I now admit the necessity of premarital love. That is, I want to be in love with the one I marry."

"Love?" said Salzman, astounded. After a moment he remarked, "For us, our love is our life, not for the ladies. In the ghetto they—"

"I know, I know," said Leo. "I've thought of it often. Love, I have said to myself, should be a by-product of living and worship rather than its own end. Yet for myself I find it necessary to establish the level of my need and fulfill it."

Salzman shrugged but answered, "Listen, rabbi, if you want love, this I can find for you also. I have such beautiful clients that you will love them the minute your eyes will see them."

Leo smiled unhappily. "I'm afraid you don't understand."

But Salzman hastily unstrapped his portfolio and withdrew a manila packet from it.

"Pictures," he said, quickly laying the envelope on the table.

Leo called after him to take the pictures away, but as if on the wings of the wind, Salzman had disappeared.

March came. Leo had returned to his regular routine. Although he felt not quite himself yet—lacked energy—he was making plans for a more active social life. Of course it would cost something, but he was an expert in cutting corners; and when there were no corners left he would make circles rounder. All the while Salzman's pictures had lain on the table, gathering dust. Occasionally as Leo sat studying, or enjoying a cup of tea, his eyes fell on the manila envelope, but he never opened it.

The days went by and no social life to speak of developed with a member of the opposite sex—it was difficult, given the circumstances of his situation. One morning Leo toiled up the stairs to his room and stared out the window at the city. Although the day was bright his view of it was dark. For some time he watched the people in the street below hurrying along and then turned with a heavy heart to his little room. On the table was the packet. With a sudden relentless gesture he tore it open. For a half-hour he stood by the table in a state of excitement, examining the photographs of the ladies Salzman had included.

Finally, with a deep sigh he put them down. There were six, of varying degrees of attractiveness, but look at them long enough and they all became Lily Hirschorn: all past their prime, all starved behind bright smiles, not a true personality in the lot. Life, despite their frantic yoohooings, had passed them by; they were pictures in a brief case that stank of fish. After a while, however, as Leo attempted to return the photographs into the envelope, he found in it another, a snapshot of the type taken by a machine for a quarter. He gazed at it a moment and let out a cry.

Her face deeply moved him. Why, he could at first not say. It gave him the impression of youth—spring flowers, yet age—a sense of having been used to the bone, wasted; this came from the eyes, which were hauntingly familiar, yet absolutely strange. He had a vivid impression that he had met her before, but try as he might he could not place her although he could almost recall her name, as if he had read it in her own handwriting. No, this couldn't be; he would have remembered her. It was not, he affirmed, that she had an extraordinary beauty—no, though her face was attractive enough; it was that *something* about her moved him. Feature for feature, even some of the ladies of the photographs could do better; but she leaped forth to his heart—had *lived,* or wanted to—more than just wanted, perhaps regretted how she had lived—had somehow deeply suffered: it could be seen in the depths of those reluctant eyes, and from the way the light enclosed and shone from her, and within her, opening realms of possibility: this was her own. Her he desired. His head ached and eyes narrowed with the intensity of his gazing, then as if an obscure fog had blown up in the mind, he experienced fear of her and was aware that he had received an impression, somehow, of evil. He shuddered, saying softly, it is thus with us all. Leo brewed some tea in a small pot and sat sipping it without sugar, to calm himself. But before he had finished drinking, again with excitement he examined the face and found it good: good for Leo Finkle. Only such a one could understand him and help him seek whatever he was seeking. She might, perhaps, love him. How she had happened to be among the discards in Salzman's barrel he could never guess, but he knew he must urgently go find her.

Leo rushed downstairs, grabbed up the Bronx telephone book, and searched for Salzman's home address. He was not listed, nor was his office. Neither was he in the Manhattan book. But Leo remembered having written down the address on a slip of paper after he had read Salzman's advertisement in the "personals" column of the *Forward.* He ran up to his room and tore through his papers, without luck. It was exasperating. Just when he needed the matchmaker he was nowhere to be found. Fortunately Leo remembered to look in his wallet. There on a card he found his name written and a Bronx address. No phone number was listed, the reason—Leo now recalled—he had originally communicated with Salzman by letter. He got on his coat, put a hat on over his skull cap and hurried to the subway station. All the way to the far end of the Bronx he sat on the edge of his seat. He was more than once tempted to take out the picture and see if the girl's face was as he remembered it, but he refrained, allowing the snapshot to remain in his inside coat pocket, content to have her so close. When the train pulled into the station he was waiting at the door and bolted out. He quickly located the street Salzman had advertised.

The building he sought was less than a block from the subway, but it was not an office building, nor even a loft, nor a store in which one could rent office space. It was a very old tenement house. Leo found Salzman's name in pencil on a soiled tag under the bell and climbed three dark flights to his apartment. When he knocked, the door was opened by a thin, asthmatic, gray-haired woman, in felt slippers.

"Yes?" she said, expecting nothing. She listened without listening. He could have sworn he had seen her, too, before but knew it was an illusion.

"Salzman—does he live here? Pinye Salzman," he said, "the matchmaker?"

She stared at him a long minute. "Of course."

He felt embarrassed. "Is he in?"

"No." Her mouth, though left open, offered nothing more.

"The matter is urgent. Can you tell me where his office is?"

"In the air." She pointed upward.

"You mean he has no office?" Leo asked.

"In his socks."

He peered into the apartment. It was sunless and dingy, one large room divided by a half-open curtain, beyond which he could see a sagging metal bed. The near side of a room was crowded with rickety chairs, old bureaus, a three-legged table, racks of cooking utensils, and all the apparatus of a kitchen. But there was no sign of Salzman or his magic barrel, probably also a figment of the imagination. An odor of frying fish made Leo weak to the knees.

"Where is he?" he insisted. "I've got to see your husband."

At length she answered, "So who knows where he is? Every time he thinks a new thought he runs to a different place. Go home, he will find you."

"Tell him Leo Finkle."

She gave no sign she had heard.

He walked downstairs, depressed.

But Salzman, breathless, stood waiting at his door.

Leo was astounded and overjoyed. "How did you get here before me?"

"I rushed."

"Come inside."

They entered. Leo fixed tea, and a sardine sandwich for Salzman. As they were drinking he reached behind him for the packet of pictures and handed them to the marriage broker.

Salzman put down his glass and said expectantly, "You found somebody you like?"

"Not among these."

The marriage broker turned away.

"Here is the one I want." Leo held forth the snapshot.

Salzman slipped on his glasses and took the picture into his trembling hand. He turned ghastly and let out a groan.

"What's the matter?" cried Leo.

"Excuse me. Was an accident this picture. She isn't for you."

Salzman frantically shoved the manila packet into his portfolio. He thrust the snapshot into his pocket and fled down the stairs.

Leo, after momentary paralysis, gave chase and cornered the marriage broker in the vestibule. The landlady made hysterical outcries but neither of them listened.

"Give me back the picture, Salzman."

"No." The pain in his eyes was terrible.

"Tell me who she is then."

"This I can't tell you. Excuse me."

He made to depart, but Leo, forgetting himself, seized the matchmaker by his tight coat and shook him frenziedly.

"Please," sighed Salzman. "*Please.*"

Leo ashamedly let him go. "Tell me who she is," he begged. "It's very important for me to know."

"She is not for you. She is a wild one—wild, without shame. This is not a bride for a rabbi."

"What do you mean wild?"

"Like an animal. Like a dog. For her to be poor was a sin. This is why to me she is dead now."

"In God's name, what do you mean?"

"Her I can't introduce to you," Salzman cried.

"Why are you so excited?"

"Why, he asks," Salzman said, bursting into tears. "This is my baby, my Stella, she should burn in hell."

Leo hurried up to bed and hid under the covers. Under the covers he thought his life through. Although he soon fell asleep he could not sleep her out of his mind. He woke, beating his breast. Though he prayed to be rid of her, his prayers went unanswered. Through days of torment he endlessly struggled not to love her; fearing success, he escaped it. He then concluded to convert her to goodness, himself to God. The idea alternately nauseated and exalted him.

He perhaps did not know that he had come to a final decision until he encountered Salzman in a Broadway cafeteria. He was sitting alone at a rear table, sucking the bony remains of a fish. The marriage broker appeared haggard, and transparent to the point of vanishing.

Salzman looked up at first without recognizing him. Leo had grown a pointed beard and his eyes were weighted with wisdom.

"Salzman," he said, "love has at last come to my heart."

"Who can love from a picture?" mocked the marriage broker.

"It is not impossible."

"If you can love her, then you can love anybody. Let me show you some new clients that they just sent me their photographs. One is a little doll."

"Just her I want," Leo murmured.

"Don't be a fool, doctor. Don't bother with her."

"Put me in touch with her, Salzman," Leo said humbly. "Perhaps I can be of service."

Salzman had stopped eating and Leo understood with emotion that it was now arranged.

Leaving the cafeteria, he was, however, afflicted by a tormenting suspicion that Salzman had planned it all to happen this way.

Leo was informed by letter that she would meet him on a certain corner, and she was there one spring night, waiting under a street lamp. He appeared carrying a small bouquet of violets and rosebuds. Stella stood by the lamp post, smoking. She wore white with red shoes, which fitted his expectations, although in a troubled moment he had imagined the dress red, and only the shoes white. She waited uneasily and shyly. From afar he saw that her eyes—clearly her father's—were filled with desperate innocence. He pictured, in her, his own redemption. Violins and lit candles revolved in the sky. Leo ran forward with flowers outthrust.

Around the corner, Salzman, leaning against a wall, chanted prayers for the dead.

PART

3

POETRY

ANONYMOUS

EDWARD

"Why dois your brand[1] sae[2] drap wi bluid,
    Edward, Edward?
Why dois your brand sae drap wi bluid,
  And why sae sad gang[3] yee O?"
"O I hae killed my hauke[4] sae guid,   5
    Mither, mither,
O I hae killed my hauke sae guid,
  And I had nae mair bot[5] hee O."

"Your haukis bluid was nevir sae reid,
    Edward, Edward,   10
Your haukis bluid was nevir sae reid,
  My deir son I tell thee O."
"O I hae killed my reid-roan steid,[6]
    Mither, mither,
O I hae killed my reid-roan steid,   15
  That erst[7] was sae fair and frie O."

"Your steid was auld, and ye hae gat mair,
    Edward, Edward,
Your steid was auld, and ye hae gat mair,
  Sum other dule[8] ye drie[9] O."   20
"O I hae killed my fadir[10] deir,
    Mither, mither,
O I hae killed my fadir deir,
  Alas, and wae is mee O!"

"And whatten penance wul ye drie for that,   25
    Edward, Edward?
And whatten penance wul ye drie, for that?
  My deir son, now tell me O."
"Ile set my feit in yonder boat,
    Mither, mither   30

---

[1] Sword. [2] So. [3] Go. [4] Hawk. [5] But. [6] Steed. [7] Once. [8] Grief. [9] Suffer.
[10] Father.

Ile set my feit in yonder boat,
        And Ile fare ovir the sea O."

"And what wul ye doe wi your towirs and your ha,[11]
        Edward, Edward?
And what wul ye doe wi your towirs and your ha,   35
    That were sae fair to see O?"
"Ile let thame stand tul they doun fa,
        Mither, mither,
Ile let thame stand tul they doun fa,
    For here nevir mair maun[12] I bee O."   40

"And what wul ye leive to your bairns[13] and your wife,
        Edward, Edward?
And what wul ye leive to your bairns and your wife,
    Whan ye gang ovir the sea O?"
"The warldis room, late them beg thrae[14] life,   45
        Mither, mither,
The warldis room, late them beg thrae life,
    For thame nevir mair wul I see O."

"And what wul ye leive to your ain mither deir,
        Edward, Edward?   50
And what wul ye leive to your ain mither deir?
    My deir son, now tell me O."
"The curse of hell frae me sall ye beir,
        Mither, mither,
The curse of hell frae me sall ye beir,   55
    Sic[15] counseils ye gave to me O."

COMMENTARY

It is obvious that the extraordinary force of this poem depends largely on
its element of surprise. There are two occasions of surprise, both intense, but
the one that comes midway in the poem is less shocking than the one
at the end because in some measure we have been led to anticipate it. We
know that we can expect the disclosure of an especially terrible deed when, to
the mother's question about the blood on his sword and the look on his face,
the son returns the first of his two prevaricating answers, saying that he has
killed his hawk. The substance of this lie is dismaying enough—in the days

11 Hall, house.   12 Must.   13 Children.   14 Through.   15 Such.

when hawking was a common sport of the nobility, there was felt to be a close communion between the falcon and the falconer. For a man to kill his horse, as Edward then says he did, perhaps goes even further against natural feeling. And if Edward had in fact killed neither the hawk nor the horse, if the blood on his sword and the look on his face are to be explained by some other killing, we expect it to be yet more horrifying, and of course it is—Edward has killed his father. Shocking as this revelation is, we have been at least a little prepared for it. But we are wholly unprepared for the second revelation, that he has killed his father at the behest of his mother.

In the face of the enormity it sets forth, "Edward" maintains an entire imperturbability. *We* are taken aback, but the poem is not even startled. The violence of its subject does not disorder the strict formality of its pattern; its composure is never ruffled. And this decorum transfers itself to the two characters: the mother's first question, which is asked in a tone that is not especially agitated, is answered in kind by the son, and once the question-and-answer mode of dialogue is established, it is sustained up to the end of the poem, when all the accumulated restraint releases itself in the explosion of the son's last terrible answer. The son is certainly not without emotion from the beginning—he is "sad," he speaks of his father as "deir" to him and bewails the murder, and his reply to his mother's question about his life in the future is bitter. Yet his emotions can scarcely be considered sufficient to his deed, and they do not become so until his last utterance. Up to that point he has submitted to his mother's questioning with a kind of grim courtesy; when at last the curse is torn from him, it is that much the more terrible because it has been so long held back. Yet even when he does utter the curse, which reveals his mother's part in the murder, his utterance is in the strict form the poem has established. What I have called the imperturbability of the poem creates the quiet out of which the terrible surprise leaps at us.

Of a piece with the poem's manner is its objectivity of view, which is uncompromising. Just as "Edward" refuses to make any emotional response to its subject, it refuses to make any moral comment on it—it is wholly detached from what it represents. By employing the dialogue form without a single narrative phrase, it refuses to assume even such involvement as is implied by *telling* what has happened; it undertakes to do nothing more than record what two persons said to each other. We are left free to judge the persons of the dialogue as we will, or must, while the poem itself is silent.

Nor does it say anything by way of explaining the dire happening that it reports. It does not consent to tell us the "whole story." This would consist of many episodes, of which the confrontation of the mother and the son would be only the last. If the events that took place before the dialogue have a claim upon our interest, it is a claim the poem does not recognize. We shall never know what sort of man the dead husband and father was, nor why his wife wanted him dead, nor by what means she induced her son to serve her purpose.

This frustration of our curiosity is strangely pleasurable. We do not find ourselves at a loss because the antecedent events of the poem have not been given us; we willingly consent to the high-handed way in which the poem denies the past. Its actually represented time is a brief moment of the immediate present. Of the five questions and seven answers that occupy this moment of the present, four questions and their answers have to do with the future. But to the past there is no reference at all until the last line, when the past is loosed in all its retributive ferocity. It has, of course, been lying in wait all through the poem. Doubtless the force of that last line is in large part achieved by its effect upon our moral sense: the intensity of our surprise does indeed relate to our horror at the mother's wickedness. Yet it is not only, and perhaps not even chiefly, the moral enormity that so satisfyingly disturbs us: it is rather the sudden, inexorable—we might almost say vengeful—return of the past, which the poem had seemed determined to exclude from its purview.

It has been said of "Edward" that it is "one of the best of all the ballads," and it may enhance our sense of the poem to be reminded that its characteristics are not unique but are shared by many poems in the same tradition.

Ballads divide, roughly, into two categories, literary and traditional, the latter sometimes called "popular" or "folk" ballads. In the eighteenth century there developed a considerable interest in the traditional ballads—the genre, in England and Scotland, took its rise in the fifteenth century—and many poets began to write in imitation of them or under their inspiration. But none of the traditional ballads can be assigned to any known author. This is not to say that they were not first composed by individual poets—no credence is now given to the theory, so attractive to many scholars in the nineteenth century, that the ballads were communal creations, that "the people" or "the folk" made them up by some process of composition the nature of which was never explained. The ballads are "popular" in the sense that they were made for and loved by the people, that is to say, by those members of a society who do not belong to the nobility: the literature of the people is distinguished from the literature of the court. But though each ballad was composed by an individual poet, his name was not attached to it and it did not long remain peculiarly his, nor did it necessarily circulate in its original form. For the ballads were not composed in writing nor were they meant to be read. They were intended to be sung and they had their existence in the memories of the people who sang them. The tune of a ballad was more likely to stay constant than its words, which might be altered by the whim of the singer, or by his failure to recall accurately what he had learned, or by his inability to understand one or another detail, such as a custom or an idiom no longer familiar to him. As a consequence, most of the traditional ballads exist in a number of versions.[1]

What may be thought of as the hallmark of the traditional ballads, the trait common to all examples of the genre, is their way of telling a story. Usually the story concerns an act of violence; it consists of a single situation which is presented at its point of climax, as near as possible to its conclusion. The method of presentation is dramatic rather than narrative, in the sense that it proceeds largely by dialogue; descriptions of scene and the use of what might be called stage-directions are kept to a minimum and are always very simple (in "Edward" there are none). Although the action is violent, the manner in which it is recounted is restrained. No effort is made to achieve originality of diction—the ballad-maker uses simple language and relies upon phrases that are traditional, or even clichés of the tradition. Explanation of motives and comment on morality are rigorously suppressed, and the attitude is one of detachment. It will readily be

[1] The taking down of the words of ballads from the lips of the singer began in the eighteenth century and still goes on.

seen that many of these characteristics derive from the fact that the ballads were sung.

In "Edward" two traditional devices of the ballad play a decisive part in the poem's dramatic effectiveness. One of these is called by scholars "incremental repetition," a parallelism of phrase and idea that is strictly maintained, often in the form of question and answer; in "Edward" the natural effectiveness of this device is pointed up by the reiteration of courteous vocatives: "Edward, Edward" and "Mither, mither." Incremental repetition often takes the form of the so-called "nuncupative testament"—*nuncupative* means oral, as distinguished from written, and the phrase refers to a series of questions and answers in which a person in an extreme and usually fatal situation is asked what, upon his death or exile, he will bequeath to each of his relatives. Characteristically the answers are bitter and ironic, and the answer to the last question is usually climactic in its fierceness.

Many of the traditional ballads came over to America and some of them are still sung in parts of the country. "Edward" is one of these, but the American version has none of the tragic import of the Scottish. The son explains the stain on his "shirt sleeve" first as the blood of his "little yellow dog," then as the blood of his "little yellow horse"; it is his brother, not his father, he has killed; the cause of the quarrel is fully explained; his mother is not implicated in the murder; he speaks of his departure not as exile but as escape, and he plans to take "Katie dear" with him "to bear [him] company."

THE THREE RAVENS

1. There were three ravens sat on a tree,
     Down a downe, hay downe, hay downe
   There were three ravens sat on a tree,
     With a downe
   There were three ravens sat on a tree,   5
   They were as blacke as they might be.
     With a downe derrie, derrie, derrie, downe, downe.

2. The one of them said to his mate,
   "Where shall we our breakfast take?"

3. "Downe in yonder greene field,   10
   There lies a knight slain under his shield.

4. "His hounds they lie down at his feete,
   So well they can their master keepe.

5. "His haukes they flie so eagerly,
   There's no fowle dare him come nie." 15

6. Downe there comes a fallow doe,
   As great with yong as she might goe.

7. She lift up his bloudy hed,
   And kist his wounds that were so red.

8. She got him up upon her backe,
   And carried him to earthen lake.[1] 20

9. She buried him before the prime,[2]
   She was dead herselfe ere even-song time.

10. God send every gentleman,
    Such haukes, such hounds, and such a leman.[3] 25

SIR PATRICK SPENS

The king sits in Dumferling toune,
    Drinking the blude-reid wine:
"O whar will I get a guid sailor,
    To sail this schip of mine?"

Up and spak an eldern knicht, 5
    Sat at the kings richt kne:
"Sir Patrick Spens is the best sailor
    That sails upon the se."

The king has written a braid[1] letter,
    And signd it wi his hand, 10
And sent it to Sir Patrick Spens,
    Was walking on the sand.

---

[1] Pit in the earth. [2] *Prime* is the old ecclesiastical name for the first hour of the day; *even-song* is the service of vespers, held in the evening. [3] Lover.

[1] Broad; that is, emphatic, explicit.

The first line that Sir Patrick red,
 A loud lauch lauched he;
The next line that Sir Patrick red,
 The teir blinded his ee.   15

"O wha is this has don this deid,
 This ill deid don to me,
To send me out this time o' the yeir,
 To sail upon the se!   20

"Mak hast, mak haste, my mirry men all,
 Our guid schip sails the morne."
"O say na sae,[2] my master deir,
 For I feir a deadlie storme.

"Late late yestreen[3] I saw the new moone,   25
 Wi the auld moone in hir arme,
And I feir, I feir, my deir master,
 That we will cum to harme."

O our Scots nobles were richt laith[4]
 To weet[5] their cork-heild schoone,[6]   30
Bot lang owre[7] a' the play wer playd,
 Thair hats they swam aboone.[8]

O lang, lang may their ladies sit,
 Wi thair fans into their hand,
Or eir they se Sir Patrick Spens   35
 Cum sailing to the land.

O lang, lang may the ladies stand,
 Wi thair gold kems in their hair,
Waiting for thair ain der lords,
 For they'll se thame na mair.   40

Haf owre, half owre to Aberdour,
 It's fiftie fadom deip,
And thair lies guid Sir Patrick Spens,
 Wi the Scots lords at his feit.

---

[2] Say not so. [3] Yesterday evening. [4] Right loath. [5] Wet. [6] Cork was not uncommonly used for the heels (and soles) of gentlemen's shoes in the sixteenth and seventeenth centuries. [7] Over; here, after. [8] Above; that is, on the water.

WESTRON WINDE, WHEN WILL THOU BLOW

Westron winde, when will thou blow,
The smalle raine downe can raine?
Christ, if my love were in my armes,
And I in my bed againe.

SIR THOMAS WYATT
1 5 0 3 – 1 5 4 2

THEY FLEE FROM ME

They flee from me that sometime did me seek,
With naked foot stalking in my chamber.
I have seen them gentle, tame, and meek,
That now are wild, and do not remember
That some time they put themselves in danger   5
To take bread at my hand; and now they range,
Busily seeking with a continual change.

Thanked be fortune, it hath been otherwise
Twenty times better; but once, in special,
In thin array, after a pleasant guise,[1]   10
When her loose gown from her shoulders did fall,
And she caught me in her arms long and small.[2]
Therewith all sweetly did me kiss,
And softly said, Dear heart, how like you this?

It was no dream; I lay broad waking.   15
But all is turned, thorough[3] my gentleness,
Into a strange fashion of forsaking;
And I have leave to go of her goodness,
And she also to use newfangleness.
But since that I so kindly am served,[4]   20
I fain[5] would know what she hath deserved.

---

[1] Looking pleasant.   [2] Thin.   [3] Through.   [4] Dealt with.   [5] Gladly with pleasure.

COMMENTARY

One of the things that are bound to strike us early in our acquaintance with this poem is the shift from the "they" of the first stanza to the "she" of the rest of the poem. In the first lines the poet seems to be recalling the high favor in which he stood with many women, or women in general. In the second stanza he recalls one erotic occasion "in special," with a woman who is strongly particularized. And the emotions that follow upon this encounter occupy his bitter and bewildered thought in the third stanza.

Some interpretations of the poem tell us that we must not take the "they" literally, that from the beginning the poet is really talking about "she." There is an advantage in this view—if we accept it, we can suppose that the happening the poet remembers "in special" is not the first love-encounter with one mistress out of many, but one peculiarly memorable encounter out of many with the same woman; of the two possibilities, the latter is the more interesting. But if "they" is really "she," it is by no means clear why the poet pluralized and generalized his mistress. In any case, the visual effect that "they" makes in the first stanza cannot be easily obliterated—one has the delighted impression that all the women the poet may ever have made love to are present at the same time in his chamber, all "stalking" together, a little multitude of glimpsed presences, rather like a flock or herd. The adjectives used of them evoke the image of delicate and charming animals: the "naked foot" evokes their lightness of step; their graceful stealth is suggested by their "stalking." This word has more than one meaning—it can refer to the action of a hunter trying to approach an animal without being seen, heard, or scented; or it can describe a way of walking, of humans or animals, with stiff, high, measured steps, like a long-legged bird— but Wyatt probably intended the now obsolete use of the word, which means the soft, cautious tread of an animal. No doubt he wished to create the image of a little herd of light-stepping deer which, in the park of some great manor house, become tame enough to take food from human hands.

But in the conclusion of the stanza three words occur which, for Wyatt's contemporary audience, would tend to modify, even to dispel, the enchanting picture of the preceding lines. Hunting was the chief sport of the gentlemen and ladies of the sixteenth century and they were conversant with its elaborate technical vocabulary. "Range," "seek," and "change" are hunting terms, all referring to the behavior of dogs. "Range" was the word used to describe the action of dogs who rove and stray in search of game. " 'Seek!' " (or " 'Seek out!' ") was the command to a dog to begin the search, and "a seek" was a series of notes upon the hunting horn calling the hounds to begin a chase. A "change" was an animal which the hounds meet by chance and then hunt instead of the quarry. These technical meanings are certainly not exclusive of others, and of course they contradict the idea that the pleasing animals, once "gentle, tame, and meek," have become "wild"—hunting dogs and hounds, even when fierce, are not wild. Yet it is probably not an accident that Wyatt uses three words associated with the hunt. The vocabulary of the field suggests that "they" who might once have been hunted have taken on the character of hunters.

"They" were perhaps never without their predatory aspect, and certainly "she" was not. The charm of the remembered erotic scene of the second stanza lies in the mistress's boldness in seduction, her overt display of her erotic power over her lover. Her ever-remembered utterance on the occasion makes this plain, and to Wyatt's audience her way of addressing her lover, "Dear heart," would have brought the idea of a deer, a hart, the pun being then a common one, the easier to make because there was no established difference in the spelling of the two words.

The "specialness" of the episode is superbly conveyed by the first line of the last stanza, "It was no dream; I lay broad waking," of which the very sound suggests the lover's incredulity over the delight of the event at the same time that he insists on its actuality.

Wyatt's poem makes a particular appeal to modern taste because of the directness and colloquial simplicity of its diction: it avoids, as modern poetry characteristically does, any reliance on "poetical" language. Another claim upon modern admiration is the way it handles its metre. The basic pattern of the verse is iambic pentameter, a line of five feet, the foot being typically of two syllables with the stress on the second; for example, the first line of the poem, "They flée from mé that sómetime díd me séek," conforms to this pattern. But many of the succeeding lines—"Busily seeking with a continual change"; "And she me caught in her arms long and small"; "It was no dream; I lay broad waking"—clearly violate this metrical scheme. The prevailing modern supposition is that Wyatt knew exactly what he was doing, that he broke the pattern to achieve the effects he desired. But according to older opinion, Wyatt wrote as he did out of ignorance or incompetence; he was thought to have a bad ear and no control over metrics.

This opinion was established, at least by implication, within a few years after Wyatt's death, in 1557, when Tottel's famous miscellany, *Songs and Sonnets,* was published. Although Wyatt would seem to have had a considerable reputation as a poet, his poems had never been printed in his lifetime, and the *Miscellany* was his first significant publication. To judge by the large space he gave to Wyatt's poems, the editor of the volume had a general admiration of the poet. But he took rather a dim view of Wyatt's skill as a metrist, revising the poems extensively to make them suit the taste of a period which esteemed verse that was "musical" in a mellifluous way. The text of the poem that I use in this book is that of Wyatt's manuscript, except that the spelling has been modernized. Here is the revised and "corrected" version as it appeared in the *Miscellany,* with the spelling modernized:

> They flee from me, that sometime did me seek
> With naked foot stalking within my chamber.
> Once have I seen them gentle, tame, and meek,
> That now are wild, and do not once remember
> That sometime they have put themselves in danger,
> To take bread at my hand; and now they range,
> Busily seeking in continual change.
> Thanked be fortune, it hath been otherwise
> Twenty times better; but once especial,
> In thin array, after a pleasant guise,
> When her loose gown did from her shoulders fall,
> And she me caught in her arms long and small,
> And therewithal so sweetly did me kiss,
> And softly said, "Dear heart, how like you this?"

It was no dream, for I lay broad awaking.
But all is turned now, through my gentleness,
Into a bitter fashion of forsaking;
And I have leave to go, of her goodness,
And she also to use newfangleness.
But since that I unkindly so am served,
How like you this? what hath she now deserved?

The emendations make a poem that is no doubt prettier than the original but, by that token, a poem less masculine and strong. They dispose of any questions about stress that the original version might present to us, but in doing this deprive the poem of a considerable part of its interest. When, for example, the two syllables are added to the line we have had occasion to notice and we read it as regular iambic pentameter, "It wás no dreám, for Í lay bróad awáking,"[1] it comes very smoothly off the tongue, but how much firmer, bolder, and more dramatic is the line as Wyatt actually wrote it. When we speak the original line aloud, our emphasis falls very decisively: once we are aware that it is not conforming to the pattern, we say, "It was nó dream," or perhaps, "It was no dréam," for either stress is possible and our freedom to choose between the two makes the phrase the more engaging. Then as we go on to the second half of the line, "I lay broad waking," our stress falls weightily on "broad" and we naturally tend to sustain the sound for a perceptible instant in order to accomplish the somewhat difficult transition to the stressed syllable that immediately follows, for in the line as Wyatt wrote it we naturally stress "waking" equally with "broad." The emended line, compared to the original, is light, easy, and relatively characterless, and the same judgment can be made on all the other editorial changes in the poem.

But aware as we may be of Wyatt's bold colloquialism and his roughness of metre, we must not leave out of account in our response to the poem the part played in it by formal strictness. The stanza that Wyatt uses is the so-called Rhyme Royal, which has a tradition going back to Chaucer and the Scottish poets; Shakespeare was later to use it for his *Rape of Lucrece*. The stanza moves with an energy that is at once vivacious and grave, and its inherent elegance makes a happy frame for the colloquial directness of the lines themselves.

There is one point at which we may regard the Tottel version with some degree of sympathy, in its revision of the last two lines of the poem. The editor's repetition of "How like you this?" would seem to express his sense that the stanza should be brought into a firmer relation with the rest of the poem, that it dissipates rather than discharges the energy that the first two stanzas have built up. Certainly the lover's plaint creates the effect of diffuseness, even of anticlimax. In fact, for many readers the meaning of these lines proves far too elusive, or, if discovered, inadequate to the earlier stanzas of the poem. It is not difficult to understand that the lover's "gentleness" should have been the cause of his mistress's indifference and infidelity. But why is the "fashion of forsaking" a "strange" one? (Although one would rather have it a "strange" than a "bitter" fashion, as in the revised version.) That the lover should have been given "leave to go" by the mistress's "goodness" is an irony which is either obscure or too

---

[1] The concluding extra syllable does not make it irregular. Even a strict adherence to rule does not require only a series of five iambics to a line.

simple, and it is certainly not clear why she has need of her own "goodness" to give her leave to "use newfangleness." Even if we have in mind the old meaning of "kindly"—that is, "naturally"—the irony of "But since that I so kindely am served" seems querulous (perhaps that is one reason why Tottel changes it to "unkindly") and the question about what the mistress "hath deserved" has the aspect of mere petulance.

Yet so great is the authority of what has gone before in the poem that many readers are not disposed to be severe upon the faults they find in the conclusion. Their love of the whole leads them to decide that the troubling part is not so much a failure as a puzzle.

WILLIAM SHAKESPEARE
1564–1616

SONNET 18

Shall I compare thee to a summer's day?
Thou art more lovely and more temperate:
Rough winds do shake the darling buds of May,
And summer's lease hath all too short a date:
Sometime too hot the eye of heaven shines,   5
And often is his gold complexion dimm'd;
And every fair from fair sometime declines,
By chance, or nature's changing course untrimm'd;
But thy eternal summer shall not fade,
Nor lose possession of that fair thou ow'st;[1]   10
Nor shall Death brag thou wander'st in his shade,
When in eternal lines to time thou grow'st.
    So long as men can breathe or eyes can see,
    So long lives this, and this gives life to thee.

SONNET 29

When in disgrace with fortune and men's eyes,
I all alone beweep my outcast state,

[1] Ownest.

And trouble deaf heaven with my bootless cries,
And look upon myself and curse my fate,
Wishing me like to one more rich in hope,
Featur'd like him, like him with friends possess'd,
Desiring this man's art, and that man's scope,
With what I most enjoy contented least,
Yet in these thoughts myself almost despising,
Haply I think on thee, and then my state,
Like to the lark at break of day arising,
From sullen earth sings hymns at heaven's gate,
    For thy sweet love rememb'red such wealth brings,
    That then I scorn to change my state with kings.

SONNET 30

When to the sessions of sweet silent thought,
I summon up remembrance of things past,
I sigh the lack of many a thing I sought,
And with old woes new[1] wail my dear time's waste:
Then can I drown an eye, unus'd to flow,
For precious friends hid in death's dateless night,
And week afresh love's long-since cancel'd woe,
And moan th' expense[2] of many a vanish'd sight.
Then can I grieve at grievances foregone,
And heavily from woe to woe tell o'er
The sad account of fore-bemoanèd moan,
Which I new pay as if not paid before.
    But if the while I think on thee, dear friend,
    All losses are restor'd, and sorrows end.

SONNET 33

Full many a glorious morning have I seen
Flatter the mountain-tops with sovereign[1] eye,
Kissing with golden face the meadows green;
Gilding pale streams with heavenly alchemy:
Anon permit the basest clouds to ride,
With ugly rack[2] on his celestial face,
And from the forlorn world his visage hide,

[1] Newly.   [2] Loss.

[1] Efficacious, healing.   [2] A group of storm clouds.

Stealing unseen to west with this disgrace:
Even so my sun one early morn did shine,
With all-triumphant splendor on my brow,
But out, alack, he was but one hour mine;
The region cloud[3] hath mask'd him from me now.
    Yet him for this, my love no whit disdaineth;
    Suns of the world may stain,[4] when heaven's sun staineth.

SONNET 55

Not marble, nor the gilded monuments
Of princes, shall outlive this powerful rhyme,
But you shall shine more bright in these contents
Than unswept stone,[1] besmear'd with sluttish time.
When wasteful war shall statues overturn,   5
And broils[2] root out the work of masonry,
Nor[3] Mars his sword,[4] nor war's quick fire shall burn
The living record of your memory.
'Gainst death and all-oblivious enmity
Shall you pace forth; your praise shall still find room,   10
Even in the eyes of all posterity
That wear this world out[5] to the ending doom.
    So till the judgment that yourself arise,
    You live in this, and dwell in lovers' eyes.

SONNET 73

That time of year thou mayst in me behold,
When yellow leaves, or none, or few, do hang
Upon those boughs which shake against the cold,
Bare ruin'd choirs,[1] where late the sweet birds sang.
In me thou see'st the twilight of such day,   5
As after sunset fadeth in the west,
Which by and by black night doth take away,
Death's second self, that seals up all in rest.

---

[3] Cloud of the upper air.   [4] Be darkened.

[1] Stone unswept by the wind and thus not eroded.   [2] Tumults. This line essentially
repeats the preceding one.   [3] Neither.   [4] The sword of Mars, the Roman god of war.
[5] Stay with.

[1] Choir lofts.

In me thou see'st the glowing of such fire,
That on the ashes of his[2] youth doth lie,   10
As the death-bed whereon it must expire,
Consum'd with that which it was nourish'd by.
    This thou perceiv'st, which makes thy love more strong,
    To love that well, which thou must leave ere long.

SONNET 107

Not mine own fears, nor the prophetic soul
Of the wide world, dreaming on things to come,
Can yet the lease of my true love control,
Suppos'd as forfeit to a confin'd doom.[1]
The mortal moon hath her eclipse endur'd,   5
And the sad augurs mock their own presage;[2]
Incertainties now crown themselves assur'd,
And peace proclaims olives[3] of endless age.
Now with the drops[4] of this most balmy time,
My love looks fresh, and Death to me subscribes,[5]   10
Since, spite of him, I'll live in this poor rhyme,
While he insults[6] o'er dull and speechless tribes.
    And thou in this shalt find thy monument,
    When tyrants' crests and tombs of brass are spent.[7]

SONNET 129

Th' expense of spirit in a waste of shame
Is lust in action; and till action, lust
Is perjur'd,[1] murd'rous, bloody, full of blame,
Savage, extreme, rude, cruel, not to trust,[2]
Enjoy'd no sooner but[3] despisèd straight,   5
Past reason hunted, and no sooner had
Past reason hated as a swallowed bait,
On purpose laid to make the taker mad:
Mad in pursuit, and in possession so,
Had,[4] having, and in quest to have, extreme,   10

    [2] Its (that is, the fire's).

    [1] Judgment.   [2] Prophesy.   [3] The olive, or olive branch, symbolizes peace.
[4] Dewdrops.   [5] Yields.   [6] Exalts insolently.   [7] Gone.

    [1] Made false to itself.   [2] Not to be trusted.   [3] Than.   [4] In the process of being
experienced.

A bliss in proof,—and prov'd, a very woe;
Before, a joy propos'd; behind, a dream.
    All this the world well knows; yet none knows well,
    To shun the heaven that leads men to this hell.

BEN JONSON
1572–1637

ON MY FIRST SON

Farewell, thou child of my right hand, and joy;
    My sin was too much hope of thee, lov'd boy.
Seven years thou wert lent to me, and I thee pay,[1]
    Exacted by thy fate, on the just day.
O, could I lose all father, now! For why   5
    Will man lament the state he should envy?
To have so soon 'scap'd world's and flesh's rage,
    And, if no other misery, yet age!
Rest in soft peace, and, ask'd, say, Here doth lie
    Ben Jonson his[2] best piece of poetry.   10
For whose sake, henceforth, all his vows be such,
    As what he loves may never like too much.

EPITAPH ON ELIZABETH, L.H.

Would'st thou hear what man can say
In a little? Reader, stay.
Underneath this stone doth lie
As much beauty as could die:
Which in life did harbour give   5
To more virtue than doth live.
If, at all, she had a fault,
Leave it buried in this vault.
One name was Elizabeth,
Th' other, let it sleep with death: 10

    [1] I pay (for thee) with thee.   [2] Ben Jonson's.

Fitter, where it died, to tell,
Than that it liv'd at all. Farewell.

SONG, TO CELIA

Drink to me only with thine eyes,
    And I will pledge with mine;
Or leave a kiss but in the cup,
    And I'll not look for wine.
The thirst that from the soul doth rise   5
    Doth ask a drink divine:
But might I of Jove's nectar sup,
    I would not change for thine.

I sent thee late a rosy wreath,
    Not so much honoring thee,   10
As giving it a hope that there
    It could not withered be.
But thou thereon didst only breathe,
    And sent'st it back to me:
Since when it grows, and smells, I swear,   15
    Not of itself, but thee.

JOHN DONNE
1572–1631

SONG

Go, and catch a falling star,
    Get with child a mandrake root,[1]
Tell me where all past years are,
    Or who cleft the Devil's foot,
Teach me to hear mermaids' singing,   5

[1] The forked root of the mandrake (mandragora) was thought to suggest the shape
of the human body.

Or to keep off envy's stinging,
   And find
   What wind
Serves to advance an honest mind.

If thou be'st born to[2] strange sights,   10
  Things invisible to see,
Ride ten thousand days and nights,
  Till age snow white hairs on thee,
Thou, when thou return'st, wilt tell me
All strange wonders that befell thee,   15
   And swear
   No where
Lives a woman true, and fair.

If thou find'st one, let me know,
  Such a pilgrimage were[3] sweet;   20
Yet do not, I would not go,
Though at next door we[4] might meet,
Though she were true, when you met her,
And last till you write your letter,
   Yet she   25
   Will be
False, ere I come, to two, or three.

THE INDIFFERENT

I can love both fair and brown,
Her whom abundance melts, and her whom want betrays,
Her who loves loneness best, and her who masks and plays,
Her whom the country form'd, and whom the town,
Her who believes, and her who tries,[1]   5
Her who still weeps with spongy eyes,
And her who is dry cork and never cries;
I can love her, and her, and you and you;
I can love any, so she be not true.

Will no other vice content you?   10
Will it not serve your turn to do as did your mothers?

  [2] Born for (seeing), prone to (see).   [3] Would be.   [4] The speaker and the
"woman true and fair."

  [1] Tests, examines.

Or have you all old vices spent,[2] and now would find out[3] others?
Or doth a fear that men are true torment you?
O, we are not, be not you so;
Let me, and do you, twenty know.   15
Rob me, but bind me not, and let me go.
Must I, who came to travail thorough[4] you,
Grow your fix'd subject because you are true?

Venus heard me sigh this song,
And by love's sweetest part,[5] variety, she swore   20
She heard not this till now, and that it should be so no more.
She went, examin'd, and return'd ere long,
And said, "Alas, some two or three
Poor heretics in love there be,
Which think to 'stablish dangerous constancy.   25
But I have told them, 'Since you be true,
You shall be true to them who are false to you.'"

THE GOOD-MORROW

I wonder, by my troth, what thou and I
Did till we lov'd? were we not wean'd till then?
But suck'd on country pleasures, childishly?
Or snorted we in the seven sleepers' den?[1]
'Twas so; but this,[2] all pleasures fancies be.   5
If ever any beauty I did see,
Which I desir'd, and got, 'twas but a dream of thee.

And now good-morrow to our waking souls,
Which watch not one another out of fear;
For love all love of other sights controls,   10
And makes one little room an everywhere.
Let sea-discoverers to new worlds have gone,[3]
Let maps to other, worlds on worlds have shown,
Let us possess one world, each hath one, and is one.

My face in thine eye, thine in mine appears,   15
And true plain hearts do in the faces rest;

[2] Exhausted.   [3] Discover.   [4] Through.   [5] Characteristic.

[1] The seven sleepers of Ephesus are seven Christian youths who, according to legend, hid in a cave to escape the persecution of the emperor Decius; they fell asleep and woke up two hundred years later.   [2] Except this love of ours.   [3] Go.

Where can we find two better hemispheres
Without sharp north, without declining west?
Whatever dies, was not mixed equally;
If our two loves be one, or thou and I   20
Love so alike that none do slacken,[4] none can die.

THE UNDERTAKING

I have done one braver thing
    Than all the Worthies did,
And yet a braver thence doth spring,
    Which is, to keep that hid.

It were but madness now t'impart   5
    The skill of specular[1] stone,
When he which can have learn'd the art
    To cut it, can find none.

So, if I now should utter this,
    Others (because no more   10
Such stuff to work upon there is)
    Would love but as before.

But he who loveliness within
    Hath found, all outward loathes,
For he who colour loves, and skin,   15
    Loves but their[2] oldest clothes.

If, as I have, you also do
    Virtue attir'd in woman see,
And dare love that, and say so too,
    And forget the he and she;   20

And if this love, though placèd so,
    From profane men you hide,
Which will no faith on this bestow,
    Or, if they do, deride:

[4] Neither slackens.

[1] Mirror-like. "Specular stone" is probably an allusion to the astrologer's crystal.
[2] Women's.

Then you have done a braver thing
    Than all the Worthies did;
And a braver thence will spring,
    Which is, to keep that hid.

HOLY SONNET VII

At the round earth's imagined corners,[1] blow
Your trumpets, angels, and arise, arise
From death, you numberless infinities
Of souls, and to your scattered bodies go;
All whom the flood did, and fire shall o'erthrow;   5
All whom war, dearth, age, agues, tyrannies,
Despair, law, chance, hath slain, and you whose eyes
Shall behold God, and never taste death's woe.
But let them sleep, Lord, and me mourn a space,
For, if above all these, my sins abound,   10
'Tis late to ask abundance of Thy grace,
When we are there; here on this lowly ground,[2]
Teach me how to repent; for that's as good
As if Thou hadst sealed my pardon, with Thy blood.

THE FUNERAL

Whoever comes to shroud me, do not harm
    Nor question much
That subtle wreath[1] of hair which crowns my arm;
The mystery, the sign you must not touch,
    For 'tis my outward soul,   5
Viceroy to that which, unto heaven being gone,
    Will leave this[2] to control,
And keep these limbs, her provinces, from dissolution.

For if the sinewy thread[3] my brain lets fall
    Through every part   10
Can tie those parts, and make me one of all,
Those hairs, which upward grew, and strength and art

[1] The "four corners" of the earth.   [2] The earth.

[1] Circlet.   [2] This soul (the circlet of hair).   [3] Spinal cord.

Have from a better brain,
Can better do it: except[4] she meant that I
    By this should know my pain,
As prisoners then[5] are manacled, when they're condemn'd to die.   15

Whate'er she meant by it, bury it with me,
    For since I am
Love's martyr, it might breed idolatry,
If into other hands these reliques came;   20
    As 'twas humility
To afford[6] to it all that a soul can do,
    So 'tis some bravery[7]
That since you would save none of me, I bury some of you.

A VALEDICTION
FORBIDDING MOURNING

As virtuous men pass mildly away,
    And whisper to their souls, to go
Whilst some of their sad friends do say,
    The breath goes now, and some say, no:

So let us melt, and make no noise,   5
    No tear-floods, nor sigh-tempests move,
'Twere profanation of our joys
    To tell the laity our love.

Moving of th' earth brings harms and fears,
    Men reckon what it did and meant,   10
But trepidation of the spheres,
    Though greater far, is innocent.[1]

Dull sublunary[2] lovers' love
    (Whose soul is sense[3]) cannot admit
Absence, because it does remove   15
    Those things which elemented[4] it.

---

[4] Unless.   [5] For that reason.   [6] Give.   [7] Boldness.

[1] "Trepidation," in Ptolemaic astronomy, referred to motion of the outermost of the nine transparent spheres that comprised the universe, which caused the "innocent" or harmless variation in the occurrence of the equinox.   [2] Terrestrial, and hence, inferior. [3] Sensuality.   [4] Constituted.

But we by a love, so much refin'd,
    That our selves know not what it is,
Inter-assurèd of the mind,
    Care less, eyes, lips, and hands to miss.   20

Our two souls therefore, which are one,
    Though I must go, endure not yet
A breach, but an expansion,
    Like gold to airy thinness beat.

If they be two, they are two so   25
    As stiff twin compasses[5] are two,
Thy soul the fix'd foot, makes no show
    To move, but doth, if th' other do.

And though it in the center sit,
    Yet when the other far doth roam,   30
It leans, and hearkens after it,
    And grows erect, as that comes home.

Such wilt thou be to me, who must
    Like th' other foot, obliquely run;
Thy firmness makes my circle just,[6]   35
    And makes me end, where I begun.

COMMENTARY

In 1912 the Oxford University Press published Professor H. J. C. Grierson's edition of the poems of John Donne, two handsomely printed volumes bound in the familiar Oxford dark-blue cloth. The first volume contained the poems, many of which had never before been printed; the second volume was devoted to notes which dealt with problems of the text and explicated the often obscure philosophical, scientific, and historical allusions. Perhaps no other work of English literary scholarship in our century is so famous or has had so much influence.

It would not be true to say that Donne had been unknown or unvalued in the nineteenth century and the first years of the twentieth. Edmund Gosse's biography in 1899 and three editions of the poetical works between 1872 and 1896 attest to a continuing awareness of the poet. But he was likely to be considered a minor figure, interesting chiefly for the vivacious idiosyncrasies

[5] One pair of dividers.   [6] Perfect.

of his style and for the discrepancy between the bold cynicism of his early poems and the passionate religious intensity of his later years when, after taking holy orders, he became one of the notable figures of the Church of England. Historians of literature were not disposed to study his work in any particularity and the criticism of the day scarcely took him into account. After Grierson's edition, however, Donne came to be seen as a pre-eminent figure not only of the seventeenth century but of the whole of English literature. The scholarly and critical studies of his work proliferated rapidly and are by now innumerable.

Yet Donne in his own time had been greatly admired; he had fallen into disesteem only in the eighteenth century. The reasons for the decline were formulated in Dr. Samuel Johnson's essay on Cowley in *The Lives of the English Poets*. In a passage that has become a *locus classicus* of English criticism, Johnson dealt with the group of seventeenth-century poets whom he called "metaphysical." He used the word, in the fashion of his time, with the intention of reproach, to characterize a kind of poetry that he considered so abstruse, fine-drawn, and far-fetched as to be quite out of accord with good sense and even nature itself. Johnson's name for the group established itself and is still in use, although without any of its former pejorative meaning.[1]

The first characteristic of the metaphysical poets remarked on by Johnson was their learning and their desire to exhibit it. They took pleasure in deriving the elements of their poems from esoteric knowledge of all kinds and, in what to Johnson seemed an extravagant desire to be original and striking, they brought together facts and ideas which he thought incongruous and therefore unnatural; they filled their poems, he said, with "enormous and disgusting hyperboles," their figures of speech were often "grossly absurd" and sometimes "indelicate." They gave precedence to ingenuity over emotion, with the result that "their courtship was void of fondness and their lamentations of sorrow. Their wish was only to say what they hoped had never been said before."

By their excessive concern with minute particularities they transgressed against a chief tenet of eighteenth-century poetic theory, which held that poetry's most impressive effects were to be gained through spacious generalizations. "Great thoughts," said Johnson, "are always general, and consist in positions not limited by exceptions, and in descriptions not descending to minuteness." Dryden, while belittling Donne as a poet, had conceded that he was to be praised for his wit, but Johnson, defining wit "as a kind of *discordia concors,* a combination of dissimilar images or discovery of occult resemblances in things apparently unlike," concluded that "of wit thus defined" Donne and his fellows "have more than enough." The versification of the metaphysical poets won as little approval from Johnson as their diction and imagery—he judged it to be wholly contrived and inept. He does not deny these poets a measure of respect, but the praise it yields is small indeed: "Yet great labor, directed by great abilities is never wholly lost: if they frequently threw away their wit upon false conceits, they likewise sometimes struck out unexpected truth; if their conceits were far-fetched, they were often worth the carriage. To write on their plan, it was at least necessary to read and think."

[1] Although Dryden had earlier said that "Donne affects the metaphysics," it was Johnson who gave currency to the adjective as a way of characterizing a mode of writing.

But early in the nineteenth century the pendulum of taste began its swing to a more favorable view of the metaphysical school, especially Donne. Coleridge anticipated modern opinion when he spoke of Donne's "force" and observed that his "most fantastic out of the way thoughts" were expressed in "the most pure and genuine mother English." Still, that a sense of Donne as odd and eccentric and not in the line of succession of the great English poets qualified Coleridge's admiration is made clear in his much-quoted lines describing Donne's poetical mode:

> With Donne, whose muse on dromedary trots,
> Wreathe iron pokers into true-love knots;
> Rhyme's sturdy cripple, fancy's maze and clue,
> Wit's forge and fire-blast, meaning's press and screw.

Later in the century, two other poets, Browning and Hopkins, both of them antagonistic to the prevailing belief that English verse was at its best when it was harmonious and "smooth," found an affinity with Donne and his dromedary-mounted muse and Rosetti and Swinburne held him in esteem especially for his love-poetry. But no poet of the nineteenth century could speak of him with Yeats's intensity of praise, an intensity that actually comes close to nonsense—writing to thank Professor Grierson for the gift of his edition, Yeats says of Donne that "he who is but a man like us all has seen God."

The new enthusiasm for Donne is explained, of course, by the confirmation he gave to an important tendency of modern poetry. A celebrated statement of what the new poets found in him was made by T. S. Eliot in his review of an anthology of the metaphysical poets that Grierson published in 1921. For Eliot the characteristic virtue of the seventeenth-century poets was their ability to "feel their thought," to experience it as if it were a sensation, "as immediately as the odor of a rose." At some point later in the century, Eliot goes on to say, there occurred a "dissociation of sensibility," and thought and feeling in poetry became separated from each other. Eliot does not refer explicitly to Johnson's objection that metaphysical poetry was excessively intellectual at the cost of feeling, but when he says of Donne that to him "a thought was an experience, it modified his sensibility," it is obviously Johnson's view which he has in mind and means to contradict. Yeats had said much the same thing in his letter to Grierson: "Your notes tell me exactly what I want to know. Poems that I could not understand or could but understand are now clear and I notice that the more precise and learned the thought the greater the beauty, the passion; the intricacies and subtleties of his imagination are the length and depths of the furrows made by his passion."

It was not only Donne's power of conjoining thought and emotion that seemed so important to the modern poets but also his taking it for granted that any of the seemingly disparate elements of experience might be brought together with interesting and significant effect. The conjunction of things and ideas not usually believed to consort with each other had seemed to Dr. Johnson to be a poetical vice, a departure from nature. The modern poets, and after them the modern critics, held it to be a poetical virtue, and exactly because it was natural, at least for poets. "When a poet's mind is perfectly equipped for its work," Eliot said, "it is constantly amalgamating disparate experience; the ordinary man's experience is chaotic, irregular, fragmentary. The latter falls in love or reads Spinoza, and these two experiences can have nothing to do with each other, or with the noise of the typewriter or the smell of cooking; in the mind of the poet these experiences are always forming wholes." This well-known passage exemplifies the tendency of modern writers to reject the belief that there are orders of experience, distinct in themselves and separate from each other, of which some are appropriate to art, others inappropriate.

Donne's versification was no less important to the new poets than the quality of his thought and feeling. What Dr. Johnson and most eighteenth-century readers heard as "rugged" verse and therefore unpleasing, what Coleridge heard as powerful but ungraceful, the trot of the dromedary, the limp of the sturdy cripple, was heard by the poets of the twentieth century as the authoritative accent of actuality. They understood—as had the readers of the seventeenth century—that Donne did not fail in an attempt to conform to the demands of a metrical system but that he wrote a kind of verse in which the rhythms of the natural speaking voice assert themselves against, and modify, the strict pattern of the metre. It is worth noting that Yeats received the gift of Grierson's edition at the point in his development when, under the influence of Ezra Pound, his verse was moving steadily away from the relatively soft and "poetic" mode of his early work to the harder, more downright and forceful versification (and diction) of his great period.

In reading "A Valediction: Forbidding Mourning" it is the voice of the poem that first engages our attention. The opening line is audacious in its avoidance of the metre that is to be established in the following lines of the stanza and maintained through the rest of the poem, although not in a strict or mechanical way; no matter how we read it, we cannot scan that opening line, and its bold freedom leads us to feel that it is saying something "actual" rather than "poetic." The succeeding lines, although controlled by metre, sustain this feeling; they sound in the ear as the utterance of a present speaker. It is in the ambience of the speaker's voice that the metaphysical elements of the poem are presented to us. The comparison between the significance of earthquakes and the "trepidation of the spheres" and the brief simile of the beaten gold, the elaborated simile of the pair of compasses, are the less likely to seem merely ingenious, or studied, or out of the way, because they are suffused with the tones of the voice that proposes them, its directness and masculine vigor, its gravity and its serious humor.

Dr. Johnson took particular notice of the compass simile, introducing his quotation of the three stanzas in which it is developed with this sentence: "To the following comparison of a man that travels and his wife that stays at home, with a pair of compasses, it may be doubted whether absurdity or ingenuity has a better claim." For Johnson the absurdity lay in the fact that compasses seemed to him to be incongruous with the emotional circumstances they were meant to represent. A pair of compasses suggests what is mechanical and unfeeling: it is metallic and stiff, and an instrument of precision employed in, and emblematic of, the sternly rational and abstract discipline of geometry; it therefore stands at the furthest remove from the emotion of love. The simile of the compasses substantiated Johnson's opinion that metaphysical poetry cannot express emotion and is "void of fondness."

Although we will perceive as readily as Dr. Johnson that there is some measure of unlikelihood in the comparison, this will not prevent our having pleasure in it. On the contrary, we will tend to be pleased exactly because we are taken aback. For us, the figure's suggestion of cold rationality and abstractness is modified by the humor with which it is developed, a humor which does not in the least diminish the direct sincerity of the utterance. Isaac Walton, in his brief life of his friend, tells us that Donne composed the poem in 1611 while he was on a diplomatic mission to France and that it was addressed to his wife Anne. The marriage was a famous one in its day, both because of the tempestuous courtship that preceded it and the unbroken tender devotion of the husband and wife. Walton mentions the circumstance in which the poem was written and the person to whom it was addressed out of his sense that the poem, for all the ingenuity of its "conceits," is a direct, personal, and fully felt communication, wholly appropriate to its occasion. With this judgment the modern reader would find it hard to disagree.

ROBERT HERRICK
1591–1674

DELIGHT IN DISORDER

A sweet disorder in the dress
Kindles in clothes a wantonness:[1]
A lawn[2] about the shoulders thrown
Into a fine distraction,[3]
An erring lace, which here and there   5
Enthralls the crimson stomacher,[4]
A cuff neglectful, and thereby
Ribbands to flow confusedly,
A winning wave, deserving note,
In the tempestuous petticoat,   10
A careless shoe-string, in whose tie
I see a wild civility,
Do more bewitch me, than when art
Is too precise in every part.

[1] Capriciousness.   [2] A scarf of fine linen.   [3] Confusion.   [4] Part of a dress that is near the stomach.

TO THE VIRGINS, TO MAKE
MUCH OF TIME

Gather ye rose-buds while ye may,
    Old Time is still a-flying:
And this same flower that smiles today,
    Tomorrow will be dying.

The glorious lamp of heaven, the Sun,   5
    The higher he's a-getting,
The sooner will his race be run,
    And nearer he's to setting.

That age is best, which is the first,
    When youth and blood are warmer,   10
But being spent, the worse, and worst
    Times, still succeed the former.

Then be not coy, but use your time;
    And while ye may, go marry:
For having lost but once your prime,   15
    You may for ever tarry.

UPON JULIA'S CLOTHES

Whenas[1] in silks my Julia goes,
Then, then (methinks) how sweetly flows
That liquefaction of her clothes.

Next, when I cast mine eyes and see
That brave[2] vibration each way free,   5
O how that glittering taketh me!

    [1] When.   [2] Handsome, splendid.

GEORGE HERBERT

1593–1633

THE QUIP

The merry World did on a day
With his train-bands[1] and mates agree
To meet together, where I lay,
And all in sport to jeer at me.

First, Beauty crept into a rose,   5
Which when I pluck'd not, Sir, said she,
Tell me, I pray, whose hands are those?[2]
But thou shalt answer, Lord, for me.

Then Money came, and chinking still,
What tune is this, poor man? said he: 10
I heard in music you had skill.
But thou shalt answer, Lord, for me.

Then came brave[3] Glory puffing by
In silks that whistled, who but he?
He scarce allow'd me half an eye.   15
But thou shalt answer, Lord, for me.

Then came quick Wit and Conversation,
And he would needs a comfort be,
And, to be short, make an oration.
But thou shalt answer, Lord, for me.   20

Yet when the hour of thy design
To answer these fine things shall come,
Speak not at large; say, I am thine;
And then they have their answer home.

[1] Citizen soldiers, here suggesting comrades.   [2] "What kind of hands would not
pluck the rose?"   [3] Handsomely dressed.

THE COLLAR

I struck the board;¹ and cried, "No more.
        I will abroad.
   What? shall I ever sigh and pine?
My lines² and life are free; free as the road,
    Loose as the wind, as large as store.³   5
        Shall I be still in suit?⁴
Have I no harvest but a thorn
To let me blood,⁵ and not restore
What I have lost with cordial⁶ fruit?
        Sure there was wine   10
Before my sighs did dry it: there was corn
    Before my tears did drown it.
   Is the year only lost to me?
     Have I no bays⁷ to crown it?
No flowers, no garlands gay? all blasted?   15
        All wasted?
Not so, my heart: but there is fruit,
     And thou hast hands.
   Recover all thy sigh-blown age
On double pleasures; leave thy cold dispute   20
Of what is fit and not. Forsake thy cage,
       Thy rope of sands,
Which petty thoughts have made, and made to thee
    Good cable, to enforce and draw,
        And be thy law,   25
While thou didst wink and wouldst not see.
      Away; take heed:
      I will abroad.
Call in thy death's-head there;⁸ tie up thy fears.
      He that forbears   30
   To suit⁹ and serve his need,
     Deserves his load."
But as I rav'd and grew more fierce and wild
     At every word,
Methought I heard one calling, *Child!*   35
    And I replied, *My Lord.*

¹ Table.   ² Appointed lot in life.   ³ As large as abundance.   ⁴ In attendance, in suit of (favor, reward).   ⁵ To bleed myself, with reference to the practice of bleeding to cure ills.   ⁶ Invigorating.   ⁷ Honorary garland of bay, or laurel.   ⁸ "Put aside thoughts of death."   ⁹ To seek after, woo.

THE PULLEY

When God at first made man,
Having a glass of blessings standing by,
Let us, said he, pour on him all we can:
Let the world's riches, which dispersèd lie,
    Contract into a span.[1]   5

So strength first made a way;
Then beauty flow'd, then wisdom, honour, pleasure.
When almost all was out, God made a stay,[2]
Perceiving that alone of all his treasure
    Rest in the bottom lay.   10

For if I should, said he,
Bestow this jewel also on my creature,
He would adore my gifts instead of me,
And rest in[3] nature, not the God of nature:
    So both[4] should losers be.   15

Yet let him keep the rest,
But keep them with repining restlessness:
Let him be rich and weary, that at least,
If goodness lead him not, yet weariness
    May toss him to my breast.   20

JOHN MILTON
1608–1674

ON SHAKESPEARE

What[1] needs my Shakespeare for his honor'd bones
The labor of an age in pilèd stones,

[1] A definitely limited space.   [2] A halt.   [3] Be content with.   [4] Both God and man.

[1] Why.

Or that his hallow'd relics should be hid
Under a star-ypointing[2] pyramid?
Dear son of memory, great heir of fame,   5
What need'st thou such weak witness of thy name?
Thou in our wonder and astonishment
Hast built thyself a livelong[3] monument.
For whilst to th' shame of slow-endeavoring art
Thy easy numbers[4] flow, and that each heart   10
Hath from the leaves of thy unvalu'd[5] book
Those Delphic[6] lines with deep impression took,
Then thou, our fancy of itself bereaving,
Dost make us marble with too much conceiving,[7]
And so sepúlcher'd in such pomp dost lie,   15
That kings for such a tomb would wish to die.

HOW SOON HATH TIME

How soon hath Time, the subtle thief of youth,
    Stol'n on his wing my three and twentieth year!
    My hasting days fly on with full career,[1]
    But my late spring no bud or blossom shew'th.
Perhaps my semblance might deceive the truth,   5
    That I to manhood am arriv'd so near,
    And inward ripeness doth much less appear,
    That[2] some more timely-happy spirits endu'th.[3]
Yet be it less or more, or soon or slow,
    It shall be still in strictest measure ev'n   10
    To that same lot, however mean or high,
Toward which Time leads me, and the will of Heav'n;
    All is, if I have grace to use it so,
    As ever in my great task-Master's eye.

WHEN I CONSIDER HOW
MY LIGHT IS SPENT

When I consider how my light is spent
    Ere half my days, in this dark world and wide,

---

[2] The prefix *y* survives from an Old English form of the word.   [3] Long-lasting.
[4] Verses, measures.   [5] Priceless, invaluable.   [6] Oracular or inspired, as the priestess was
who spoke for Apollo at Delphi.   [7] Imagining.

[1] Speed.   [2] Refers to *manhood*.   [3] Endows.

And that one talent[1] which is death to hide,
Lodg'd with me useless, though my soul more bent
To serve therewith my Maker, and present   5
My true account, lest he returning chide,
"Doth God exact day-labor, light denied?"
I fondly[2] ask. But Patience, to prevent
That murmur, soon replies, "God doth not need
Either man's work or his own gifts; who best   10
Bear his mild yoke,[3] they serve him best; his state
Is kingly: thousands at his bidding speed,
And post o'er land and ocean without rest:
They also serve who only stand and wait."

LYCIDAS[1]

*In this Monody the Author Bewails a Learned Friend, Unfortunately Drowned in
His Passage from Chester on the Irish Seas, 1637; and, by Occasion, Foretells the
Ruin of Our Corrupted Clergy, Then in Their Height.*

Yet once more, O ye laurels, and once more,
Ye myrtles brown,[2] with ivy never sere,
I come to pluck your berries harsh and crude,[3]
And with forced fingers rude
Shatter your leaves before the mellowing year.   5
Bitter constraint, and sad occasion dear[4]
Compels me to disturb your season due;
For Lycidas is dead, dead ere his prime,
Young Lycidas, and hath not left his peer.
Who would not sing for Lycidas? he knew   10
Himself to sing, and build the lofty rhyme.
He must not float upon his watery bier
Unwept, and welter to the parching wind,
Without the meed of some melodious tear.
    Begin, then, Sisters of the sacred well[5]   15
That from beneath the seat of Jove does spring;
Begin, and somewhat loudly sweep the string.
Hence with denial vain and coy excuse:
So may some gentle Muse[6]

---

[1] See the "Parable of the Talents," Matthew 25:14–30.   [2] Foolishly.   [3] The
yoke of servitude, bondage.

[1] Lycidas is the name of a shepherd in a poem by the Roman poet, Virgil. Milton's
"Lycidas" was Edward King (1612–1637), a college friend who drowned in the Irish Sea.
[2] Dark, dusky.   [3] Unripe. Laurel, myrtle, and ivy are symbols of immortality that poets
were crowned with in ancient Greece.   [4] Keenly felt.   [5] The Muses, Greek deities of
the arts and sciences to whom all creative inspiration was attributed.   [6] Here, poet, one
inspired by a Muse.

With lucky words favour my destined urn,   20
And as he passes turn,
And bid fair peace be to my sable[7] shroud!
For we[8] were nursed upon the self-same hill,
Fed the same flock, by fountain, shade, and rill.

     Together both, ere the high lawns appeared   25
Under the opening eyelids of the Morn,
We drove a-field, and both together heard
What time the gray-fly[9] winds[10] her sultry horn,
Battening[11] our flocks with the fresh dews of night,
Oft till the star that rose, at evening, bright   30
Toward heaven's descent had sloped his westering wheel.[12]
Meanwhile the rural ditties were not mute;
Tempered to[13] the oaten flute,
Rough Satyrs[14] danced, and Fauns[15] with cloven heel
From the glad sound would not be absent long;   35
And old Damaetas[16] loved to hear our song.

     But, oh! the heavy change, now thou art gone,
Now thou art gone and never must return!
Thee, Shepherd, thee the woods and desert caves,
With wild thyme and the gadding[17] vine o'ergrown,   40
And all their echoes, mourn.
The willows, and the hazel copses green,
Shall now no more be seen
Fanning their joyous leaves to thy soft lays.[18]
As killing as the canker[19] to the rose,   45
Or taint-worm to the weanling herds that graze,
Or frost to flowers, that their gay wardrobe wear,
When first the white-thorn blows;
Such, Lycidas, thy loss to shepherd's ear.

     Where were ye, Nymphs, when the remorseless deep   50
Closed o'er the head of your loved Lycidas?
For neither were ye playing on the steep
Where your old bards, the famous Druids,[20] lie,
Nor on the shaggy top of Mona[21] high,
Nor yet where Deva[22] spreads her wizard stream.   55
Ay me! I fondly dream
"Had ye been there"—for what could that have done?
What could the Muse herself that Orpheus bore,[23]
     The Muse herself, for her enchanting son,

---

[7] Black.   [8] Lycidas and the poet.   [9] Insect that flies with a loud humming noise.
[10] Blows.   [11] Fattening, feeding.   [12] Venus, the "evening star," appears in the western sky.   [13] In time with.   [14] In Greek mythology, goat-men who lived in the woodlands and spent much time in amorous pursuit of the nymphs.   [15] Satyr-like beings.
[16] Name for a herdsman that, like "Lycidas," comes from Virgil.   [17] Spreading aimlessly.   [18] Tunes, poems.   [19] Cankerworm.   [20] Priests and poets (bards), of ancient Britain.   [21] The isle of Anglesey, off the coast of Wales; it was a Druidic center.
[22] The river Dee, which runs through England and Wales.   [23] Calliope, Muse of epic poetry, was the mother of Orpheus, who was torn to pieces by drunken worshippers of Bacchus. His head floated down the Hebrus to the island of Lesbos.

Whom universal nature did lament, 60
When, by the rout that made the hideous roar,
His gory visage down the stream was sent,
Down the swift Hebrus to the Lesbian shore?

    Alas! what boots it[24] with uncessant care
To tend the homely, slighted, shepherd's trade, 65
And strictly meditate the thankless Muse?
Were it not better done, as others use,
To sport with Amaryllis in the shade,
Or with the tangles of Neaera's hair?[25]
Fame is the spur that the clear spirit doth raise 70
(That last infirmity of noble mind)
To scorn delights, and live laborious days;
But the fair guerdon[26] when we hope to find,
And think to burst out into sudden blaze,
Comes the blind Fury[27] with the abhorrèd shears, 75
And slits the thin-spun life. "But not the praise,"
Phoebus[28] replied, and touched my trembling ears:
"Fame is no plant that grows on mortal soil,
Nor in the glistering foil[29]
Set off to the world, nor in broad rumour lies, 80
But lives and spreads aloft by those pure eyes,
And perfect witness of all-judging Jove;
As he pronounces lastly on each deed,
Of such fame in heaven expect thy meed."

    O fountain Arethuse,[30] and thou honoured flood, 85
Smooth-sliding Mincius,[31] crowned with vocal reeds,
That strain I heard was of a higher mood.
But now my oat[32] proceeds,
And listens to the Herald of the Sea[33]
That came in Neptune's[34] plea. 90
He asked the waves, and asked the felon winds,
What hard mishap hath doomed this gentle swain?
And questioned every gust of rugged wings
That blows from off each beakèd promontory.
They knew not of his story; 95
And sage Hippotades[35] their answer brings;
That not a blast was from his dungeon strayed,
The air was calm, and on the level brine
Sleek Panope with all her sisters[36] played.

---

[24] Of what advantage is it?   [25] Amaryllis and Neaera are traditional names for nymphs.   [26] Reward.   [27] Probably Atropos, the Fate who cuts the thread of life. (Milton, perhaps intentionally, confuses the Fates and the Furies here.)   [28] Apollo, god of—among other things—poetic inspiration.   [29] A thin metal leaf used as a background for a precious stone to increase its brilliance.   [30] The traditional fountain of pastoral verse in Sicily. The nymph Arethusa, pursued by the river-god Alpheus (see line 132), was changed into a fountain by Diana.   [31] A river in Lombardy, Italy, that Virgil once lived near.   [32] Pastoral song (see "oaten flute," line 33 above).   [33] Triton, a merman, who here pleads the innocence of the sea in causing Lycidas' death.   [34] Neptune was the Roman god of the sea.   [35] Aeolus, god of the winds.   [36] Water nymphs.

It was that fatal and perfidious bark,
Built in the eclipse, and rigged with curses dark,
That sunk so low that sacred head of thine.
     Next, Camus,[37] reverend sire, went footing slow,
His mantle hairy, and his bonnet sedge,
Inwrought with figures dim, and on the edge
Like to that sanguine flower[38] inscribed with woe.
"Ah! who hath reft," quoth he, "my dearest pledge?"[39]
Last came, and last did go,
The Pilot of the Galilean Lake;[40]
Two massy keys he bore of metals twain
(The golden opes, the iron shuts amain).
He shook his mitred locks, and stern bespake:—
"How well could I have spared for thee, young swain,
Enow of such as, for their bellies' sake,
Creep, and intrude, and climb into the fold!
Of other care they little reckoning make
Than how to scramble at the shearers' feast,
And shove away the worthy bidden guest.
Blind mouths! that scarce themselves know how to hold
A sheep-hook, or have learnt aught else the least
That to the faithful herdman's art belongs!
What recks it them? What need they? They are sped;[41]
And, when they list,[42] their lean and flashy songs
Grate on their scrannel[43] pipes of wretched straw;
The hungry sheep look up, and are not fed,
But, swoln with wind and the rank mist they draw,
Rot inwardly, and foul contagion spread;
Besides what the grim wolf[44] with privy paw
Daily devours apace, and nothing said.
But that two-handed engine at the door
Stands ready to smite once, and smite no more."[45]
     Return, Alpheus;[46] the dread voice is past
That shrunk thy streams; return, Sicilian Muse,[47]
And call the vales, and bid them hither cast
Their bells and flowerets of a thousand hues.
Ye valleys low, where the mild whispers use
Of shades, and wanton winds, and gushing brooks,

100
105
110
115
120
125
130
135

---

[37] The river Cam, representing Cambridge University, where Milton and King first knew each other.   [38] The hyacinth, which is said to bear markings resembling the Greek word for "alas."   [39] "Who hath taken away my dearest child?"   [40] St. Peter, wearing a bishop's miter (he was the first bishop of Rome) and carrying the keys of heaven. Edward King is mourned as a poet, as a scholar, and now as a churchman.   [41] What does it matter to them? What do they need? They have fared well.   [42] Want, desire. [43] Feeble.   [44] Probably the Anglican Church.   [45] That is, the corrupt clergy will be punished finally and absolutely. What the "two-handed engine" is has been much debated. "Not less than 34 different explanations have been traced in print" (Le Comte, *A Milton Dictionary*). The likeliest explanation is that it refers to the two-handled sword of the Archangel Michael.   [46] The lover of Arethusa; they both symbolize pastoral poetry. He has fled from the "dread voice" of St. Peter.   [47] The muse of Theocritus, a poet of ancient Greece, and others who wrote pastorals.

On whose fresh lap the swart star[48] sparely looks,
Throw hither all your quaint enamelled eyes,
That on the green turf suck the honeyed showers,   140
And purple all the ground with vernal flowers.
Bring the rathe[49] primrose that forsaken dies,
The tufted crow-toe, and pale jessamine,
The white pink, and the pansy freaked[50] with jet,
The glowing violet,   145
The musk rose, and the well-attired woodbine,
With cowslips wan that hang the pensive head,
And every flower that sad embroidery wears;
Bid amaranthus all his beauty shed,
And daffadillies fill their cups with tears,   150
To strew the laureate hearse where Lycid lies.
For so, to interpose a little ease,
Let our frail thoughts dally with false surmise.
Ay me! whilst thee the shores and sounding seas
Wash far away, where'er thy bones are hurled;   155
Whether beyond the stormy Hebrides,
Where thou perhaps under the whelming tide
Visit'st the bottom of the monstrous[51] world;
Or whether thou, to our moist vows denied,
Sleep'st by the fable of Bellerus[52] old,   160
Where the great Vision of the guarded mount[53]
Looks toward Namancos and Bayona's hold.
Look homeward, Angel, now, and melt with ruth:
And, O ye dolphins, waft[54] the hapless youth.[55]
    Weep no more, woeful shepherds, weep no more,   165
For Lycidas, your sorrow, is not dead,
Sunk though he be beneath the watery floor.
So sinks the day-star[56] in the ocean bed,
And yet anon repairs his drooping head,
And tricks his beams, and with new-spangled ore   170
Flames in the forehead of the morning sky:
So Lycidas sunk low, but mounted high,
Through the dear might of Him that walked the waves,[57]
Where, other groves and other streams along,
With nectar pure his oozy locks he laves,   175
And hears the unexpressive[58] nuptial songs,
In the blest kingdoms meek of joy and love.
There entertain him all the Saints above,
In solemn troops, and sweet societies,

---

[48] Sirius, the Dog Star. It is called "swart" because it rises in the late summer when heat scorches and darkens vegetation.   [49] Early.   [50] Spotted.   [51] Full of sea monsters. [52] A mythical Cornish giant.   [53] Off Land's End in Cornwall, a large rock, traditionally guarded by the archangel Michael, points towards Namancos (Nemancos) and Bayona in Spain.   [54] Bear, carry (through water or air).   [55] Dolphins rescued Arion, a semi-mythical poet who was attacked at sea by sailors who intended to rob him.   [56] The sun. [57] Christ.   [58] Inexpressible.

That sing, and singing in their glory move,   180
And wipe the tears for ever from his eyes.
Now, Lycidas, the shepherds weep no more;
Henceforth thou art the Genius[59] of the shore,
In thy large recompense, and shalt be good
To all that wander in that perilous flood.   185
   Thus sang the uncouth swain to the oaks and rills,
While the still morn went out with sandals grey:
He touched the tender stops of various quills,[60]
With eager thought warbling his Doric[61] lay:
And now the sun had stretched out all the hills,   190
And now was dropt into the western bay;
At last he rose, and twitched his mantle blue:
To-morrow to fresh woods, and pastures new.

COMMENTARY

It is often said by critics and teachers of literature that "Lycidas" is the greatest
lyric poem in the English language, and very likely it is. But the word "greatest"
applied to a work of art is not always serviceable; the superlative judgment can
immobilize a reader's response to a work, or arouse his skeptical resistance. It
may be that we are given a more enlightening introduction to the poem by a
critic who held it in low esteem—so far from thinking that "Lycidas" was
superlatively great, Samuel Johnson thought it a very bad poem. Without
doubt Dr. Johnson was wrong in this judgment and the grounds on which he
bases it are quite mistaken. But his erroneous views, stated in his characteristically bold and unequivocal fashion, make plain how the poem ought to be
regarded.

   The sum of Dr. Johnson's objections is that "Lycidas" is insincere. It
purports to be a poem of mourning; the poet is expressing grief over the death
of a friend. But can we possibly believe in the truth of his emotion? Grief, Dr.
Johnson says in effect, inclines to be silent or at least to be simple in its utterance. It does not express itself so elaborately, with as much artifice as Milton
uses or with such a refinement of fancy and such a proliferation of reference
to ancient legend and lore. "Passion plucks no berries from myrtle or ivy," Dr.
Johnson said, "nor calls upon Arethuse and Mincius, nor tells of rough *satyrs*
or *fauns with cloven heels*. Where there is leisure for fiction, there is little grief."

   Of the poem's elaborateness of artifice, even of artificiality, there can be no
question. The poet does not speak in his own person but in the guise of a
"shepherd" or "swain." That is to say, he expresses his grief, such as it is,
through the literary convention known as the pastoral, so called because all the
persons represented in it are shepherds (the Latin word for shepherd is *pastor*).
This convention of poetry has a long history. It goes back to the Greek poet

---

[59] Protective spirit.   [60] Holes in different reeds, or pipes of Pan.   [61] Pastoral.

Theocritus (c. 310–250 B.C.), who, in certain of his poems, pretended that he and his poet-friends were shepherds of his native Sicily. Far removed from the sophistication and corruption of cities, the fancied shepherds of Theocritus devoted themselves to the care of their flocks and to two innocent pursuits—song and the cultivation of love and friendship. Their only ambition was to be accomplished in song; their only source of unhappiness was a lost love or the death of a friend, the latter being rather more grievous than the former and making the occasion for an *elegy,* a poem of lament. Virgil brought the pastoral convention into Roman literature with his *Eclogues,* and it was largely through his influence that it became enormously popular in the Renaissance. This popularity continued through the eighteenth century, but the mechanical way in which it came to be used in much of the verse of that period justifies Dr. Johnson in speaking of the pastoral mode as "easy, vulgar, and therefore disgusting." In the nineteenth century the convention lost its vogue, but even then it was used for two great elegies, Shelley's "Adonais" and Matthew Arnold's "Thyrsis." For the poets of our time it seems to have no interest.

The fictional nature of the pastoral was never in doubt. Nobody was supposed to believe and nobody did believe that the high-minded poetic herdsmen were real, in charge of actual flocks. Yet the fiction engaged men's imagination for so long a time because it fulfilled so real a desire of mankind—it speaks of simplicity and innocence, youth and beauty, love and art. And although the poets were far from claiming actuality for their pastoral fancies, they often used the convention to criticize actual conditions of life, either explicitly as Milton does in the passage on the English clergy (lines 108–131) or by implication.

The traditional and avowedly artificial nature of the pastoral was exactly suited to the occasion which produced "Lycidas." Milton could scarcely have felt at Edward King's death the "passion" that Dr. Johnson blames him for not expressing, for King, although a college mate, had not been a close friend. He composed "Lycidas" not on spontaneous impulse but at the invitation of a group of Cambridge men who were bringing out a volume of poems to commemorate King. For Milton to have pretended to an acute sense of personal loss would have been truly an insincerity. Yet he could not fail to respond to what we might call the general pathos of a former comrade's dying "ere his prime," and by means of the pastoral elegy he was able to do what was beautifully appropriate to the situation—he associated King's death with a long tradition in which the deaths of young men had been lamented. Ever since the dawn of literature the death of a young man has been felt to have an especial pathos— how often it is evoked in the *Iliad;* and few things in the Bible are more affecting than David's mourning for his young friend Jonathan and his young son Absolom. It is this traditional pathos that Milton evokes from the death of Edward King. Had he tried to achieve a more personal expression of feeling, we should have responded not more but less. What engages us is exactly the universality of the emotion.

The pastoral convention is also appropriate to King's commemoration in two other respects. One is the extent to which the pastoral elegy was known and cultivated by young men in the English universities of Milton's time, if only because in their study of the ancient languages they were assigned the task of composing verses in this genre. Milton's own earliest-known poems are such college exercises, and all the poets who are mentioned or referred to in "Lycidas"—Theocritus, Virgil, Ovid—were subjects of university study. And in Milton's age as in ours, the college days of a young man were thought to have something like a pastoral quality—from mature life men look back to that time as being more carefree, and to their relationships then as having been more generous, disinterested, and comradely than now: why else do college alumni return each spring to their old campuses? Our very word *alumnus* expresses what Milton means when he says that he and King were "nurs'd upon the self-same hill," for an *alumnus* is a foster child, a nursling of *alma mater,* the fostering mother.

Dr. Johnson did not make it an item in his charge of insincerity that Milton, mourning a young man dead, is so preoccupied with a young man alive —himself. But we cannot fail to see that this is the case. Milton begins his poem with an unabashed self-reference, to his feeling about himself as a young poet who has not yet reached the point of his development when he is ready to appear before the public. One reason he gives for overcoming his reluctance and undertaking the poem in memory of King is his hope that this will make it the more likely that someone will write to commemorate him when he dies. When he speaks about the poetic career and about poetic fame in relation to death, it is manifestly his own career and fame and his own death that he has in mind —the thought arouses him to a proud avowal of his sense of his high calling. And as the poem concludes, it is again to himself that he refers. Having discharged his duty of mourning, he turns from death and sorrow back to life and his own purposes:

> At last he rose, and twitch'd his mantle blue:
> To-morrow to fresh woods, and pastures new.

These passages have led many readers to conclude that "Lycidas" is not about Edward King at all but about John Milton. They are quite content that this should be so. They take the view that though the poem may fail in its avowed intention, it succeeds in an intention that it does not avow—they point to the fact that the most memorable and affecting parts of the poem are those in which Milton is his own subject. But in weighing this opinion we might ask whether it is ever possible to grieve for a person to whom we feel akin without grieving for ourselves, and, too, whether the intensity with which we are led to imagine our own inevitable death is not a measure of the kinship we feel with the person who has already died. Certainly nothing in "Lycidas" more strongly enforces upon us the pathos of untimely death than that it puts the poet in mind of his own death—for what he says of himself we are bound to feel of ourselves. And how better represent the sadness of death than to put it beside the poet's imagination of the fulness of life?

It must also be observed that Milton speaks of the death of Edward King and of his own imagined death and actual life in a context that does not permit our mere ordinary sense of the personal to prevail. He brings them into conjunction not only with the traditional pathos of young men dead ere their prime but also with the traditional evocations of the death of young gods, and their resurrection. No religious ceremonies of the ancient peoples were more fervently performed than those in which the death of a young male deity— Osiris, Adonis, Atys, Thammuz—was mourned and his resurrection rejoiced in. The myths of these gods and the celebration of their death and rebirth represented the cycles of the vital forces; the dying and reborn god symbolized the sun in its annual course, the processes of vegetation, the sexual and pro- creative energy, and sometimes, as in the case of Orpheus, poetic genius. Once we are aware of this, Milton's concern with himself takes on a larger significance. It is not himself-the-person that Milton is meditating upon but himself-the-poet: that is, he is thinking about himself in the service not of his own interests but of the interests of the "divine" power that he bears within him.

In this service Milton is properly associated with Edward King, who was also a poet—it does not matter that King was not distinguished in his art. But there was yet another aspect of the service of divine power in the fact that King was a clergyman, a priest of the Church of England, which licenses the inclusion in the elegy of St. Peter's explosion of wrath against the negligent and corrupt clergy of the time. This famous passage constitutes only a small part of the poem, but the importance that Milton gave it is made plain by his ex- tended reference to it in the "argument." Some readers will find a bitter con- demnation of clerical corruption inappropriate to an elegy, and will be jarred and dismayed by the sudden introduction of Christian personages and considerations into a poem that has been, up to this point, consistently pagan. That Milton is himself quite aware that the passage will seem incongruous to the pastoral form is indicated in the lines in which he invokes the "return" of the "Sicilian Muse," who has been scared away by St. Peter's "dread voice." But in Milton's thought ancient pagan literature and mythology and the Judaeo-Christian reli- gion were never really at odds with each other. It is a salient characteristic of his great and enormously learned mind that Milton gave allegiance to both, and used for Christian ideas the literary forms of paganism. In the pastoral convention he found a natural conjunction of the two: we can readily see that the poetic convention has affinity with the feelings attached to the pastoral life by Biblical Judaism and, more elaborately, by Christianity. The peaceable Abel was a shep- herd and so was Abraham. So was David, and a poet-shepherd at that, one of whose psalms begins, "The Lord is my Shepherd, I shall not want." It was shepherds who saw the Star of Bethlehem rise; Jesus is both the Lamb of God and the Good Shepherd. *Pastor* is the name for the priest of a parish, the con- gregation being his flock, and the form of a bishop's crozier is the shepherd's crook.[1]

---

[1] The affinity between the pagan and the Christian idealizations of the pastoral life was no doubt affirmed by the common belief that Virgil's fourth *Eclogue* was a prophecy of the birth of Christ. The Christian acceptance of the pagan convention imposed one small condition which it is amusing to note: Although I have referred throughout my comment to shepherds, the herdsmen of the Greek bucolic poets herded either sheep or goats, and, indeed, Milton took the name Lycidas from a character in a poem by Theocritus who was not a shepherd but a goatherd. But Christianity separates the sheep from the goats, regarding the latter with suspicion and even aversion—in fact, it assigns the physical attributes of the goat to the Devil himself—and does not permit their presence in pastoral poetry. When Spenser in *The Shepheardes Calender* mentions a "Goteheard," his anony- mous pedantic contemporary who annotated the poems explains: "By Gotes in scrypture he represented the wicked and reprobate, whose pastour also must needes be such."

As the poem moves toward its conclusion the mingling of pagan and Christian elements is taken wholly for granted. This conjunction of the two traditions exemplifies yet another characteristic of the poem, its inclusiveness. "Lycidas" gathers up all the world, things the most disparate in space and time and kind, and concentrates them in one place and moment, brings them to bear upon one event, the death of the poet-priest. The poem's action is, as it were, summarized in the lines about "the great Vision" of St. Michael the Angel who, from Land's End, the southernmost tip of England, looks afar to Spain but is abjured to "look homeward." So the poem looks afar to the ancient world and also turns its gaze upon contemporary England. From "the bottom of the monstrous world" it turns to heaven, and from all the waters of the world to all the flowers of all the seasons of the Earth, and from the isolation of Lycidas in death to the "sweet societies" of his resurrection and everlasting life through the agency of Christ. It plays literary games with the most solemn subjects, and juxtaposes the gravest ideas with the smallest blossoms, using their most delicate or homely names (culminating in the daffadillies, which sound like the very essence of irresponsible frivolity). And then, when it has brought all the world together, and life out of death and faith out of despair, it has its "uncouth swain," the shepherd-poet, with the jauntiness of a task fully discharged, announce that the mourning is now at an end. Life calls the poet to other work and he must answer the call.

SIR JOHN SUCKLING
1609–1642

WHY SO PALE AND WAN?

Why so pale and wan, fond lover?
    Prithee, why so pale?
Will, when looking well can't move her,
    Looking ill prevail?
    Prithee, why so pale?   5

Why so dull and mute, young sinner?
    Prithee, why so mute?
Will, when speaking well can't win her,
    Saying nothing do't?
    Prithee, why so mute?   10

Quit, quit for shame, this will not move:
    This cannot take her.
If of herself she will not love,
    Nothing can make her:
    The devil take her!   15

THE CONSTANT LOVER

Out upon it![1] I have lov'd
    Three whole days together;
And am like to love three more,
    If it prove fair weather.

Time shall moult away his wings,   5
    Ere he shall discover
In the whole wide world again
    Such a constant[2] lover.

[1] Phrase implying abhorrence.   [2] Faithful

But the spite on't is, no praise
　　Is due at all to me:
Love with me had made no stays,[3]
　　Had it any been but she.

Had it any been but she,
　　And that very face,
There had been at least ere this
　　A dozen dozen in her place.

ANDREW MARVELL
1 6 2 1 – 1 6 7 8

TO HIS COY MISTRESS

Had we but world enough, and time,
This coyness, Lady, were no crime.
We would sit down and think which way
To walk and pass our long love's day.
Thou by the Indian Ganges' side
Shouldst rubies find;[1] I by the tide
Of Humber[2] would complain.[3] I would
Love you ten years before the Flood,
And you should, if you please, refuse
Till the conversion of the Jews.
My vegetable love should grow
Vaster than empires, and more slow;
An hundred years should go to praise
Thine eyes and on thy forehead gaze;
Two hundred to adore each breast,
But thirty thousand to the rest;
An age at least to every part,
And the last age should show your heart.
For, Lady, you deserve this state,

[3] Standstill.

[1] Most rubies now come from Burma, but they might once have been mined from the Ganges Delta.　　[2] An estuary in England. Marvell's town, Hull, is on it.　　[3] Lament.

Nor would I love at lower rate. 20
     But at my back I always hear
Time's winged chariot[4] hurrying near;
And yonder all before us lie
Deserts of vast eternity.
Thy beauty shall no more be found, 25
Nor, in thy marble vault, shall sound
My echoing song; then worms shall try[5]
That long preserved virginity,
And your quaint honor turn to dust,
And into ashes all my lust: 30
The grave's a fine and private place,
But none, I think, do there embrace.
     Now therefore, while the youthful hue
Sits on thy skin like morning dew,
And while thy willing soul transpires 35
At every pore with instant fires,
Now let us sport us while we may,
And now, like amorous birds of prey,
Rather at once our time devour
Than languish in his slow-chapped[6] power. 40
Let us roll all our strength and all
Our sweetness up into one ball,
And tear our pleasures with rough strife
Through the iron gates of life:
Thus, though we cannot make our sun 45
Stand still, yet we will make him run.

THE GARDEN

How vainly men themselves amaze[1]
To win the palm, the oak, or bays;[2]
And their incessant labours see
Crown'd from some single herb or tree,
Whose short and narrow vergèd[3] shade 5
Does prudently their toils upbraid;
While all flow'rs and all trees do close[4]
To weave the garlands of repose.

---

[4] Probably an allusion to the chariot driven by Helios, the sun god of ancient Greece.
[5] Subject to a severe test.   [6] Slowly devouring (*chap*, "jaw").

[1] Perplex.   [2] Crowns made of these types of leaves were symbols, respectively, of fame in war, civil life, poetry.   [3] Bordered, limited.   [4] Combine, join together.

Fair Quiet, have I found thee here,
And Innocence, thy sister dear!
Mistaken long, I sought you then
In busy companies of men.
Your sacred plants, if here below,
Only among the plants will grow.
Society is all but rude,
To[5] this delicious solitude.

    10

    15

No white nor red[6] was ever seen
So am'rous as this lovely green.
Fond lovers, cruel as their flame,[7]
Cut in these trees their mistress' name.
Little, alas, they know, or heed,
How far these beauties hers exceed!
Fair trees, wheres'e'er your barks I wound,
No name shall but your own be found.

    20

When we have run our passion's heat,
Love hither makes his best retreat.
The gods, that mortal beauty chase,
Still in a tree did end their race:
Apollo hunted Daphne so,
Only that she might laurel grow;
And Pan did after Syrinx speed,
Not as a nymph, but for a reed.[8]

    25

    30

What wond'rous life is this I lead!
Ripe apples drop about my head;
The luscious clusters of the vine
Upon my mouth do crush their wine;
The nectarine, and curious peach,
Into my hands themselves do reach;
Stumbling on melons, as I pass,
Ensnar'd with flow'rs, I fall on grass.

    35

    40

Meanwhile the mind, from pleasure less,
Withdraws its happiness:
The mind, that ocean where each kind

[5] In comparison to.   [6] Of a woman's skin.   [7] Passion.   [8] Daphne and Syrinx, in Greek mythology, were nymphs who were pursued by Apollo (god of light and medicine) and Pan (god of forest and flocks), respectively. Both wanted to escape and both succeeded: Daphne was changed into a laurel and Syrinx into a reed.

Does straight[9] its own resemblance find;
Yet it creates, transcending these,
Far other worlds, and other seas;
Annihilating all that's made
To a green thought in a green shade.

Here at the fountain's sliding foot,
Or at some fruit-tree's mossy root,
Casting the body's vest aside,
My soul into the boughs does glide:
There, like a bird, it sits, and sings,
Then whets[10] and combs its silver wings,
And, till prepar'd for longer flight,
Waves in its plumes the various light.

Such was that happy garden-state,
While man there walk'd without a mate:
After a place so pure, and sweet,
What other help could yet be meet!
But 'twas beyond a mortal's share
To wander solitary there:
Two paradises 'twere in one
To live in paradise alone.

How well the skilful gardner drew
Of flow'rs and herbs this dial new;[11]
Where, from above, the milder sun
Does through a fragrant zodiac run;
And, as it works, th' industrious bee
Computes its time as well as we.
How could such sweet and wholesome hours
Be reckon'd but with herbs and flow'rs!

[9] Immediately.   [10] Preens.   [11] The garden is planted in the form of a sundial.

HENRY VAUGHAN

1622–1695

CHILDHOOD

I cannot reach it; and my striving eye
Dazzles at it, as at eternity.
    Were now that chronicle alive,
Those white designs which children drive,
And the thoughts of each harmless hour,   5
With their content, too, in my pow'r,
Quickly would I make my path even,
And by mere playing go to heaven.

    Why should men love
A wolf more than a lamb or dove?   10
Or choose hell-fire and brimstone streams
Before bright stars and God's own beams?
Who kisseth thorns will hurt his face,
But flowers do both refresh and grace,
And sweetly living (fie on men!)   15
Are, when dead, medicinal then.
If seeing much should make staid eyes,
And long experience should make wise,
Since all that age doth teach is ill,
Why should I not love childhood still?   20
Why, if I see a rock or shelf,
Shall I from thence cast down myself,
Or by complying with the world,
From the same precipice be hurl'd?
Those observations are but foul   25
Which make me[1] wise to lose my soul.

And yet the practice worldlings call
Business, and weighty action all,
Checking[2] the poor child for his play,
But gravely cast themselves away.   30

[1] Say I am.   [2] Reprimanding.

Dear, harmless age! the short, swift span
Where weeping virtue parts with man;
Where love without lust dwells, and bends
What way we please, without self-ends.[3]

An age of mysteries! which he   35
Must live twice that would God's face see;
Which angels guard, and with it play,
Angels! which foul men drive away.

How do I study now, and scan
Thee more than e'er I studied man,   40
And only see through a long night
Thy edges and thy bordering light!
O for thy center and mid-day!
For sure that is the Narrow Way![4]

THE WORLD

I saw eternity the other night
Like a great ring of pure and endless light,
    All calm as it was bright,
And round beneath it, time in hours, days, years,
    Driv'n by the spheres,[1]   5
Like a vast shadow mov'd, in which the world
    And all her train were hurl'd;
The doting lover in his quaintest strain[2]
    Did there complain;[3]
Near him, his lute, his fancy, and his flights,   10
    Wit's sour delights,
With gloves and knots,[4] the silly snares of pleasure,
    Yet his dear treasure
All scatter'd lay, while he his eyes did pour
    Upon a flow'r.   15

The darksome statesman,[5] hung with weights and woe,
Like a thick midnight-fog, mov'd there so slow

---

[3] Its own ends.   [4] "Straight is the gate, and narrow is the way, which leadeth unto life" (Matthew 7:14).

[1] According to ancient astronomy, which Vaughan uses for figurative purposes, the heavens were a series of concentric, crystalline spheres arranged around the earth.   [2] Most elaborate verse.   [3] Plead his cause.   [4] Love knots.   [5] Unscrupulous politician.

He did nor stay nor go;
Condemning thoughts, like sad eclipses, scowl
    Upon his soul, 20
And clouds of crying witnesses without
    Pursued him with one shout.
Yet digg'd the mole, and, lest his ways be found,
    Work'd under ground,
Where he did clutch his prey, but one[6] did see 25
    That policy:
Churches and altars fed him; perjuries
    Were gnats and flies;[7]
It rained about him blood and tears, but he
    Drank them as free.[8] 30

The fearful miser on a heap of rust
Sat pining all his life there, did scarce trust
    His own hands with the dust,
Yet would not place one piece[9] above, but lives
    In fear of thieves. 35
Thousands there were as frantic as himself,
    And hugg'd each one his pelf:
The downright epicure plac'd heav'n in sense[10]
    And scorn'd pretense
While others, slipp'd into a wide excess,[11] 40
    Said little less;
The weaker sort slight, trivial wares enslave,
    Who think them brave,[12]
And poor, despisèd Truth sat counting by[13]
    Their victory. 45

Yet some, who all this while did weep and sing,
And sing, and weep, soar'd up into the ring,[14]
    But most would use no wing.
"O fools!" said I, "thus to prefer dark night
    Before true light, 50
To live in grots, and caves, and hate the day
    Because it shows the way,
The way which from this dead and dark abode
    Leads up to God,
A way where you might tread the sun, and be 55
    More bright than he!"

---

[6] The speaker.   [7] Plentiful and of no importance.   [8] As freely as they ran; that is, he thrived on others' misfortunes.   [9] Invest one coin. See St. Matthew's admonition to invest in heavenly, rather than earthly, goods (Matthew 6:19–20).   [10] Sensual pleasures.   [11] Deviation from moderation.   [12] Splendid, handsome.   [13] Observing. [14] See line 2 above.

But as I did their madness so discuss
    One whisper'd thus:
"This ring the Bridegroom did for none provide
    But for His bride."[15]

ALEXANDER POPE
1688–1744

AN ESSAY
ON MAN Epistle I

ARGUMENT

Of the Nature and State of Man with respect to the UNIVERSE

Of *Man* in the abstract. I. That we can judge only with regard to our *own system,* being ignorant of the *relations* of systems and things. II. That Man is not to be deemed *imperfect,* but a Being suited to his *place* and *rank* in the creation, agreeable to the *general Order* of things, and conformable to *Ends* and *Relations* to him unknown. III. That it is partly upon his *ignorance* of *future* events, and partly upon the *hope* of a *future* state, that all his happiness in the present depends. IV. The *pride* of aiming at more knowledge, and pretending to more Perfection, the cause of Man's error and misery. The *impiety* of putting himself in the place of *God,* and judging of the fitness of unfitness, perfection or imperfection, justice or injustice of his dispensations. V. The *absurdity* of conceiting himself the *final cause* of the creation, or expecting that perfection in the *moral* world, which is not in the *natural.* VI. The *unreasonableness* of his complaints against *Providence,* while on the one hand he demands the Perfections of the Angels, and on the other the bodily qualifications of the Brutes; though, to possess any of the *sensitive faculties* in a higher degree, would render him miserable. VII. That throughout the whole visible world, an universal *order* and *gradation* in the sensual and mental faculties is observed, which causes a *subordination* of creature to creature, and of all creatures to Man. The gradations of *sense, instinct, thought, reflection, reason;* that Reason alone countervails all the other faculties. VIII. How much further this *order* and *subordination* of living creatures may extend, above and below us; were any part of which broken, not that part only, but the whole connected *creation* must be destroyed. IX. The *extravagance, madness,* and *pride* of such a desire. V. The consequence of all, the *absolute submission* due to Providence, both as to our *present* and *future* state.

15 In Revelation 21, the holy city of Jerusalem, the home of the twelve tribes of the children of Israel who are to be granted eternal life, is compared to a bride, and God to a bridegroom.

Awake, my St. John![1] leave all meaner things
To low ambition, and the pride of Kings.
Let us (since Life can little more supply
Than just to look about us and to die)
Expatiate free o'er all this scene of Man;   5
A mighty maze! but not without a plan;
A Wild, where weeds and flowers promiscuous shoot;
Or Garden, tempting with forbidden fruit.
Together let us beat this ample field,
Try what the open, what the covert yield;   10
The latent tracts, the giddy heights, explore
Of all who blindly creep, or sightless soar;
Eye Nature's walks, shoot Folly as it flies,
And catch the Manners living as they rise;
Laugh where we must, be candid where we can;   15
But vindicate the ways of God to Man.
    I. Say first, of God above, or Man below,
What can we reason, but from what we know?[2]
Of Man, what see we but his station here,
From which to reason, or to which refer?   20
Through worlds unnumbered though the God be known,
'Tis ours to trace him only in our own.
He, who through vast immensity can pierce,
See worlds on worlds compose one universe,
Observe how system into system runs,   25
What other planets circle other suns,
What varied Being peoples every star,
May tell why Heaven has made us as we are.
But of this frame the bearings, and the ties,
The strong connexions, nice dependencies,   30
Gradations just, has thy pervading soul
Looked through? or can a part contain the whole?
    Is the great chain,[3] that draws all to agree,
And drawn supports, upheld by God, or thee?
    II. Presumptuous Man! the reason wouldst thou find,   35
Why formed so weak, so little, and so blind?
First, if thou canst, the harder reason guess,
Why formed no weaker, blinder, and no less?
Ask of thy mother earth, why oaks are made
Taller or stronger than the weeds they shade?   40
Or ask of yonder argent fields[4] above,

---

[1] Henry St. John, Viscount Bolingbroke (1678–1751). His philosophical writings had some influence on Pope.   [2] That is, how can we reason (about God or man) except on the basis of what we already know?   [3] The "great chain of being," the conception of the structure of the universe put forth here, originated with the neoplatonist philosopher, Plotinus (third century), and was particularly influential in Europe in the seventeenth and early eighteenth centuries.   [4] The heavens. *Argent*, silvery white.

Why Jove's Satellites[5] are less than Jove?
    Of systems possible, if 'tis confest
That Wisdom infinite must form the best,
Where all must full or not coherent be,   45
And all that rises, rise in due degree;
Then, in the scale of reasoning life,[6] 'tis plain,
There must be, somewhere, such a rank as Man:
And all the question (wrangle e'er so long)
Is only this, if God has placed him wrong?   50
    Respecting Man, whatever wrong we call,
May, must be right, as relative to all.[7]
In human works, though laboured on with pain,
A thousand movements scarce one purpose gain;
In God's, one single can its end produce;   55
Yet serves to second too some other use.
So Man, who here seems principal alone,
Perhaps acts second to some sphere unknown,
Touches some wheel, or verges to some goal;
'Tis but a part we see, and not a whole.   60
    When the proud steed shall know why Man restrains
His fiery course, or drives him o'er the plains;
When the dull Ox, why now he breaks the clod,[8]
Is now a victim, and now Egypt's God:
Then shall Man's pride and dulness comprehend   65
His actions', passions', being's, use and end;
Why doing, suffering, checked, impelled; and why
This hour a slave, the next a deity.
    Then say not Man's imperfect, Heaven in fault;
Say rather, Man's as perfect as he ought: 70
His knowledge measured to his state and place;
His time a moment, and a point his space.
It to be perfect in a certain sphere,
What matter, soon or late, or here or there?
The blest to day is as completely so,   75
As who began a thousand years ago.
    III. Heaven from all creatures hides the book of Fate,
All but the page prescribed, their present state:
From brutes what men, from men what spirits know:
Or who could suffer Being here below?   80
The lamb thy riot[9] dooms to bleed today,
Had he thy Reason, would he skip and play?
Pleased to the last, he crops the flowery food,
And licks the hand just raised to shed his blood.
Oh blindness to the future! kindly given,   85

---

[5] The classical hierarchy of gods.   [6] Life having the ability to reason.   [7] The entire universe.   [8] That is, pulls a plow. The ox is a victim when it is used as meat, and Egypt's principal god, Osiris, was often represented as an ox.   [9] Extravagance.

That each may fill the circle marked by Heaven:
Who sees with equal eye, as God of all,
A hero perish, or a sparrow fall,
Atoms or systems into ruin hurled,
And now a bubble burst, and now a world.   90

      Hope humbly then; with trembling pinions soar;
Wait the great teacher Death; and God adore.
What future bliss, he gives not thee to know,
But gives that Hope to be thy blessing now.
Hope springs eternal in the human breast: 95
Man never Is, but always To be blest:
The soul, uneasy and confined from home,[10]
Rests and expatiates in a life to come.

      Lo, the poor Indian! whose untutored mind
Sees God in clouds, or hears him in the wind;   100
His soul, proud Science never taught to stray
Far as the solar walk, or milky way;
Yet simple Nature to his hope has given,
Behind the cloud-topped hill, an humbler heaven;
Some safer world in depth of woods embraced,   105
Some happier island in the watery waste,
Where slaves once more their native land behold,
No fiends torment, no Christians thirst for gold.
To Be, contents his natural desire,
He asks no Angel's wing, no Seraph's fire;[11]   110
But thinks, admitted to that equal sky,
His faithful dog shall bear him company.

      IV.   Go, wiser thou! and, in thy scale of sense,
Weigh thy Opinion against Providence;
Call imperfection what thou fanciest such,   115
Say, here he gives too little, there too much:
Destroy all creatures for thy sport or gust,[12]
Yet cry, If Man's unhappy, God's unjust;
If Man alone engross not Heaven's high care,
Alone made perfect here, immortal there: 120
Snatch from his hand the balance[13] and the rod,
Re-judge his justice, be the GOD of GOD.
In Pride, in reasoning Pride, our error lies;
All quit their sphere, and rush into the skies.
Pride still is aiming at the blest abodes,   125
Men would be Angels, Angels would be Gods.
Aspiring to be Gods, if Angels fell,
Aspiring to be Angels, Men rebel:
And who but[14] wishes to invert the laws

---

[10] Heaven, or eternity.   [11] The seraphim are the highest order of angels, especially distinguished by the ardor of their love.   [12] Inclination, taste.   [13] Scales.   [14] Merely, only.

Or Order, sins against th' Eternal Cause.   130
    V. Ask for what end the heavenly bodies shine,
Earth for whose use? Pride answers, " 'Tis for mine:
For me kind Nature wakes her genial[15] power,
Suckles each herb, and spreads out every flower;
Annual for me, the grape, the rose renew   135
The juice nectareous, and the balmy dew;
For me, the mine a thousand treasures brings;
For me, health gushes from a thousand springs;
Seas roll to waft me, suns to light me rise;
My footstool earth, my canopy the skies."   140
    But errs not Nature from this gracious end,
From burning suns when livid deaths[16] descend,
When earthquakes swallow, or when tempests sweep
Towns to one grave, whole nations to the deep?
"No" ('tis replied) "the first Almighty Cause   145
Acts not by partial, but by general laws;
Th' exceptions few; some change since all began:
And what created perfect?"—Why then Man?
If the great end be human Happiness,
The Nature deviates; and can Man do less?   150
As much that end a constant course requires
Of showers and sunshine, as of Man's desires;
As much eternal springs and cloudless skies,
As Men for ever temperate, calm, and wise.
If plagues or earthquakes break not Heaven's design,   155
Why then a Borgia,[17] or a Catiline?[18]
Who knows but he, whose hand the lightning forms,
Who heaves old Ocean, and who wings the storms;
Pours fierce Ambition in a Cæsar's mind,
Or turns young Ammon[19] loose to scourge mankind?   160
From pride, from pride, our very reasoning springs;
Account for moral, as for natural things:
Why charge we Heaven in those, in these acquit?
In both, to reason right is to submit.
    Better for Us, perhaps, it might appear   165
Were there all harmony, all virtue here;
That never air or ocean felt the wind;
That never passion discomposed the mind.
But ALL subsists by elemental strife;
And Passions are the elements of Life.   170
The general ORDER, since the whole began,
Is kept in Nature, and is kept in Man.

---

15 Generative.   16 Plagues.   17 The Borgias rose to prominence in Italy during the
Renaissance. Their name became a symbol of unbridled power, lust, and greed.   18 An
unscrupulous Roman who conspired to overthrow the government by force. He was exposed
by Cicero.   19 Alexander the Great, who was told by an oracle that he was the son of
Ammon, an Egyptian deity.

VI.   What would this Man? Now upward will he soar,
And little less than Angel, would be more;
Now looking downwards, just as grieved appears   175
To want the strength of bulls, the fur of bears.
Made for his use all creatures if he call,
Say what their use, had he the powers of all?
Nature to these, without profusion, kind,
The proper organs, proper powers assigned;   180
Each seeming want compensated of course,
Here with degrees of swiftness, there of force;[20]
All in exact proportion to the state;
Nothing to add, and nothing to abate.
Each beast, each insect, happy in its own: 185
Is Heaven unkind to Man, and Man alone?
Shall he alone, whom rational we call,
Be pleased with nothing, if not blessed with all?
      The bliss of Man (could Pride that blessing find)
Is not to act or think beyond mankind;   190
No powers of body or of soul to share,
But what his nature and his state can bear.
Why has not Man a microscopic eye?
For this plain reason, Man is not a Fly.
Say what the use, where finer optics given,   195
T' inspect a mite, not comprehend the heaven?
Or touch, if tremblingly alive all o'er,
To smart and agonize at every pore?
Or quick effluvia[21] darting through the brain,
Die of a rose in aromatic pain?   200
If nature thundered in his opening ears,
And stunned him with the music of the spheres,[22]
How would he wish that Heaven had left him still
The whispering Zephyr,[23] and the purling rill?
Who finds not Providence all good and wise,   205
Alike in what it gives, and what it denies?
VII.   Far as Creation's ample range extends,
The scale of sensual,[24] mental powers ascends:
Mark how it mounts, to Man's imperial race,
From the green myriads in the peopled grass: 210
What modes of sight betwixt each wide extreme,
The mole's dim curtain, and the lynx's beam:

[20] It is a certain axiom in the anatomy of creatures, that in proportion as they are formed for strength, their swiftness is lessened; or as they are formed for swiftness, their strength is abated (Pope's note). [21] Exhalations affecting the sense of smell. [22] Spheres of ancient astronomy, according to which nine spheres of transparent material holding the planets and stars surrounded the earth. Pythagoras thought the planets must make sounds that corresponded to their different rates of motion and that, as all things in nature are harmoniously made, the different sounds must harmonize. [23] Gentle breeze. [24] Sensory.

Of smell, the headlong lioness between,[25]
And hound sagacious on the tainted green;[26]
Of hearing, from the life that fills the flood,[27]   215
To that which warbles through the vernal wood:
The spider's touch, how exquisitely fine!
Feels at each thread, and lives along the line:
In the nice bee, what sense so subtly true
From poisonous herbs extracts the healing dew?   220
How Instinct varies in the groveling swine,
Compared, half-reasoning elephant, with thine!
Twixt that, and Reason, what a nice[28] barrier,
For ever separate, yet for ever near!
Remembrance and Reflection how allied;   225
What thin partitions Sense[29] from Thought divide:
And Middle natures, how they long to join,
Yet never pass th' insuperable line!
Without this just graduation, could they be
Subjected, these to those, or all to thee?   230
The powers of all subdued by thee alone,
Is not thy Reason all these powers in one?

    VIII. See, through this air, this ocean, and this earth,
All matter quick,[30] and bursting into birth.
Above, how high, progressive life may go!   235
Around, how wide! how deep extend below!
Vast chain of Being! which from God began,
Natures ethereal, human, angel, man,
Beast, bird, fish, insect, what no eye can see,
No glass can reach; from Infinite to thee,   240
From thee to Nothing.—On superior powers
Were we to press, inferior might on ours:
Or in the full creation leave a void,
Where, one step broken, the great scale's destroyed:
From Nature's chain whatever link you strike,   245
Tenth or ten thousandth, breaks the chain alike.

    And, if each system in gradation roll
Alike essential to th' amazing Whole,
The least confusion but in one, not all
That system only, but the Whole must fall.   250
Let Earth unbalanced from her orbit fly,
Planets and Suns run lawless through the sky;
Let ruling Angels from their spheres be hurled,

---

[25] The manner of the Lions hunting their prey in the deserts of Africa is this: At their first going out in the nighttime they set up a loud roar, and then listen to the noise made by the beasts in their flight, pursuing them by the ear, and not by the nostril. It is probable the story of the jackal's hunting for the lion was occasioned by observation of this defect of scent in that terrible animal (Pope's note). [26] Hunting grounds imbued with the scent of an animal. [27] Waterlife. [28] Fine, fragile. [29] Sensory perceptions. [30] Alive.

Being on Being wrecked, and world on world;
Heaven's whole foundations to their centre nod, 255
And Nature tremble to the throne of God.
All this dread ORDER break—for whom? for thee?
Vile worm!—Oh Madness! Pride! Impiety!
     IX.   What if the foot, ordained the dust to tread,
Or hand, to toil, aspired to be the head? 260
What if the head, the eye, or ear repined[31]
To serve mere engines to the ruling Mind?
Just as absurd for any part to claim
To be another, in this general frame:
Just as absurd, to mourn the tasks or pains, 265
The great directing MIND of ALL ordains.
     All are but parts of one stupendous whole,
Whose body Nature is, and God the soul;
That, changed through all, and yet in all the same;
Great in the earth, as in th' ethereal frame; 270
Warms in the sun, refreshes in the breeze,
Glows in the stars, and blossoms in the trees,
Lives through all life, extends through all extent,
Spreads undivided, operates unspent;
Breathes in our soul, informs our mortal part, 275
As full, as perfect, in a hair as heart;
As full, as perfect, in vile Man that mourns,
As the rapt Seraph that adores and burns:
To him no high, no low, no great, no small;
He fills, he bounds, connects, and equals all. 280
     X.   Cease then, nor ORDER Imperfection name:
Our proper bliss depends on what we blame.
Know thy own point: This kind, this due degree
Of blindness, weakness, Heaven bestows on thee.
Submit.—In this, or any other sphere, 285
Secure to be as blest as thou canst bear:
Safe in the hand of one disposing Power,
Or in the natal, or the mortal hour.
All Nature is but Art, unknown to thee;
All Chance, Direction, which thou canst not see; 290
All Discord, Harmony not understood;
All partial Evil, universal Good:
And, spite of Pride, in erring Reason's spite,
One truth is clear, WHATEVER IS, IS RIGHT.

    [31] Complained, was discontented.

COMMENTARY

Modern critics, even those who take the greatness of Pope for granted, are likely to use a tone of advocacy when they write about him. They are aware that the taste of most of their readers does not readily respond to the poet whose genius was universally acclaimed in his own time. Pope is the chief English poet of the eighteenth century and it is he who bore the brunt of the Romanticists' repudiation of the poetic standards of that age. To Wordsworth and Coleridge, he stood for everything in poetry that they contemned. They saw him as virtually an anti-poet, the corrupter of poetry's true essence. Only Byron among the Romanticists found it possible to admire him, and Byron's enthusiastic praise was thought by many to be a mere perversity. The nineteenth century's antagonism to Pope was brought to a climax and codified by Matthew Arnold in his famous essay, "The Study of Poetry." Speaking of the importance that poetry would have in the modern world and calling the roll of those English poets who were likely to be of the greatest spiritual value, Arnold explicitly excluded Pope and his great predecessor Dryden from the illustrious roster on the ground that they were really not poets at all. "Though they may write in verse," he said, "though they may in a certain sense be masters of the art of versification, Dryden and Pope are not classics of our poetry, they are classics of our prose."

In the early decades of the twentieth century the reputation of the two poets took a decided upward turn among serious students of literature: now no informed person would think it possible to say of either of them that he is not a classic of our poetry. The counter-revolution against nineteenth-century opinion as summed up by Arnold found its most notable agitator in T. S. Eliot, who, in his essays on Dryden, repelled "the reproach of the prosaic" that had so often been made and went on to question in a radical and telling way the whole nineteenth-century view of what was and what was not poetic.

Yet despite the thorough-going change in the estimate of Pope that has taken place among critics and scholars, it is still probably true that the great majority of readers who come to him for the first time and without critical indoctrination tend to resist him and to echo Arnold's judgment that he is not really a poet at all, that such virtues as are most salient in his work, those that Arnold identified as "regularity, uniformity, precision, and balance," are prose virtues; and perhaps they will go so far as to say that, of these virtues, not all pertain to the kind of prose that interests them most.

What probably makes the root of the difficulty is the verse form with which the genius of Pope is identified, the heroic couplet. It is likely to strike the unhabituated modern ear as limited, repetitive, and all too committed to syntax, justifying Keats's vehement charge that it was nothing but mechanical. The disaffected reader should know, however, that the better acquainted Keats became with the form, the more he admired it and admitted its influence upon his own verse.

Nothing could be simpler than the defining characteristics of the heroic couplet: two rhymed lines, each of five iambic feet, that is, feet of two syllables, the accent falling on the second. But as it came into wide use in the late seventeenth century and especially in the hands of Dryden, the simple form developed toward complexity and ever stricter demands were made upon it. It became the rule (which might, however, be broken now and then for the sake of variety) that each couplet be self-contained, its meaning complete. This tended to make for a sententious and even epigrammatic quality of utterance, which was much esteemed. Considerable attention was given to the caesura, a discernible pause in the progress of a line which is dictated not by the metre but by the natural rhythm of the language; variations in the placing of the caesura had the effect of helping the heroic couplet avoid its greatest danger, monotony. Rhetorical devices, such as parallelism and antithesis, were favored by the nature of the verse and came to be highly valued.

The chief advantage that Dryden ascribed to the heroic couplet will make it plain why the Romantic poets disliked the form and why many modern readers find it uncongenial. ". . . That benefit which I consider most in it," Dryden said, "is . . . that it bounds and circumscribes the fancy." And he goes on: "For imagination in a poet is a faculty so wild and lawless that, like an highranging spaniel, it must have clogs tied to it, lest it outrun the judgment. The great easiness of blank verse renders the poet too luxuriant; he is tempted to say many things which might better be omitted, or at least shut up in fewer words; but when the difficulty of artful rhyming is interposed, where the poet commonly confines his sense to his couplet, and must contrive that sense into such words that the rhyme shall naturally follow them, not they the rhyme; the fancy then gives leisure to the judgment to come in. . . . That which most regulates the fancy, and gives the judgment its busiest employment, is like to bring forth the richest and clearest thoughts."

Nothing could be further from the nineteenth-century sense of how the poet should go about his work, of what poetry should be and do. And although modern poetry has in some measure responded to the influence of Dryden and Pope, there are few contemporary practitioners or theorists of poetry who would give their approval to a conception of poetry that was directed chiefly to bringing forth *thoughts,* no matter how rich and clear.

By Pope's time the advantages of the heroic couplet no longer seemed to be in need of reasoned defense; it was the accepted form for most poetic undertakings of importance.[1] If Pope ever thought of the limitations of the form, it was only as a challenge to his virtuosity. To him it was beyond doubt that the couplet in skilled hands—in hands made skilful as much by study and practice as by native endowment—was an instrument capable of producing the widest and most delightful range of effects. In an often-quoted passage of "An Essay on Criticism" he brilliantly demonstrated how various the "music" of the couplet may be and how precisely it could be related to the meaning that is being expressed. This correspondence of sense and sound, he says, is something to which the poet must give close attention—

> 'Tis not enough no harshness gives offence,
> The sound must seem an Echo to the sense:

[1] But the taste of no period is monolithic and the dislike of the heroic couplet that was expressed by at least one considerable poet of the eighteenth century should be noted —Matthew Prior objected to it because it "produces too frequent an identity in the sound," moves too readily toward epigram, and is tiring to the reader.

He illustrates the precept by a couplet in which the sound of the verse is consonant with the "softness" of the action being referred to:

> Soft is the strain when Zephyr gently blows,
> And the smooth stream in smoother numbers flows.

There follows an example of a rough action expressed in a rough-sounding verse:

> But when loud surges lash the sounding shore,
> The hoarse, rough verse should like the torrent roar.

Then an example of laborious effort:

> When Ajax strives some rock's vast weight to throw,
> The line too labours, and the words move slow.

And, in contrast to this, lightness and speed:

> Not so when swift Camilla scours the plain,
> Flies o'er the unbending corn, and skims along the main.

This famous display of virtuosity will suggest how large a part in Pope's art was played by the poet's sense that he was a performer, that it was his purpose to give pleasure to an audience whose right to judge his performance depended only upon a proper training of its faculty of judgment, its taste. The characteristic relation of later poets to their audiences will be very different: the idea of performance will come to be abhorrent to them and they will conceive it to be their purpose to serve not the pleasure of the reader but only the truth of their own feelings, which the reader is probably not competent to judge.

The poetry of exposition and argument, to which the heroic couplet so happily lends itself, has virtually no place in the modern tradition. In the eighteenth century the word "didactic" was used in a neutral descriptive sense when applied to poetry; early in the nineteenth century its meaning became opprobrious and has remained so. It means nothing more dreadful than "teaching," but, although we believe that much is to be learned from poetry, we now believe that it must not intend to instruct. To the poets of Pope's age, however, our adverse opinion of didactic poetry would have seemed arbitrary and pointless; they thought it nothing but natural that poetry should engage itself directly with ideas.[2]

2 But, again, the broad cultural generalization must be modified—in 1746, Joseph Warton, an important critic, protested the fashion of didactic poetry. And it should be said that in his preface to "An Essay on Man" Pope raised the question, perhaps only in a formal way, of whether he should not have treated his subject in prose, and he apologizes, again perhaps only in a formal way, for not having treated parts of his discourse "more poetically." It would seem to have been the abstruseness of the subject that raised doubts that had not existed in connection with the earlier "Essay on Criticism," which was no less didactic but considerably easier.

But even if the modern reader should consent to give up his prejudice against didactic poetry in general, he is pretty sure to find that another barrier stands in the way of his coming to terms with "An Essay on Man." This is the poem's purpose of demonstrating that man has no justifiable complaint to make of the conditions of his life, that, if he truly comprehends the nature of the universe, he must see that his relation to it is wholly in accord with reason and be gratified that things are as they are and not otherwise.

Such a view can scarcely win assent in our day, when it has become virtually a commonplace of much of our influential literature that man's relation to the universe is so far out of accord with reason as to be absurd. Yet exactly the currency of this idea makes "An Essay on Man" of rather special interest to us, for the poem takes its impetus from the assumption that anyone who thinks about his relation to the universe will, as a first conclusion, judge it to be unreasonable to the point of absurdity. The Essay, of course, then undertakes to prove that the first conclusion is in error, but the arguments it advances in the demonstration are as desperate as they are ingenious. Where the ingenuity fails to convince us, the desperateness may yet succeed in moving us: there is something deeply affecting in the Essay's passionate defeated attempt to force the universe to be rational.

When it is said that man's relation to the universe is not in accord with reason, what is primarily meant is that there is no discernible answer to the question of why man suffers or why there is an overplus of pain as against pleasure in human existence. That the question should be asked at all implies the belief that the universe is controlled by principles that are analogous with those more or less rational principles that man has evolved for the control of his own behavior. It is expected, that is, that the answer will be given in terms of man's own reason in its various social aspects—the reason of the father in the family, of the judge in the court of law, of the king in the city or nation. And when the question about the reason of the universe is posed in the Judaeo-Christian tradition, it takes the form of asking why the perfect Father, Judge, and King, the God who is believed to be both omnipotent and wholly beneficent, should have ordained man's suffering. The terms of the question being what they are, the answer is not hard to make—it is possible to "justify the ways of God to man," as Milton expressed his intention in writing *Paradise Lost,* by telling the story of a man's fall from innocence through his disobedience to the divine command and of God's consequent anger. The pain of human life is explained as a punishment for sin, mitigated by the permitted hope of an eventual redemption. Such rationality as is thought to inhere in the human concept of morality and justice is proposed as the controlling principle of the universe.

This answer is in many ways satisfactory so long as the imagination is disposed to accept its terms and to sustain the belief in a God who is Father, Judge, and King, and who is susceptible to the emotions that are appropriate to each of his functions. But in the eighteenth century the imagination of educated men was not so disposed. "An Essay on Man" undertakes to "vindicate the ways of God to man," and the conscious echo of Milton's line informs us that Pope wanted to connect the purpose of his poem with that of *Paradise Lost.* Yet the elements out of which Pope constructed his argument were very different from those available to Milton. The God of the Essay is not personal except insofar as wisdom and beneficence may be attributed to him. Having once ordained his universe in perfection, he does not intervene in its processes. Where Milton, in the traditional way of religion, frames his explanation of man's destiny in terms of man's own thought and feeling, showing that God's ways are essentially in accord with man's ways taken at their best, Pope vindicates God's ways by demonstrating the difference—which does not, however, imply the discontinuity—between the divine and the human. The famous conclusion, "Whatever is, is right," asserts the rationality and perfection of the universe as God has created it, a rationality and perfection of which man's suffering—so runs the terrible line of reasoning!—is a necessary element.

At no point in "An Essay on Man" is the actuality of human suffering denied. Indeed, the poem is charged throughout with an awareness of pain, as well it might be, considering how much of it its author had endured. The opening lines are explicit about the unsatisfactoriness of life, which "can little more supply / Than just to look about us and to die." It is this acceptance of the fact of suffering that gives the poem its desperate tragic force, for the essence of its position is not merely that human suffering is inevitable but that without it the universe would be less rational and perfect than in fact it is. The argument is based on a conception of a universal order in which all created things stand on a scale of perfection from the lowest to the highest. On this scale there may be no gaps; the gradation from the lowest to the highest is continuous, constituting a "vast Chain of Being." From this premise of the order of Nature two conclusions follow. (1) Man has his place or "station" in this order of perfection, above the animals and below the angels, and if he did not occupy this place, there would be a link missing in the chain of being, a circumstance which, if it were thinkable, would be a diminution of the perfection of the universal order. (2) Situated where he is on the scale, or in the chain, man must be understood to have been endowed in a way that makes all his attributes appropriate to his station; both his power and his weakness are exactly right for that place. Which is to say that, in relation to the universal order, man himself is perfect.

More than once the point is made that nothing would be gained for man's well-being if his powers were greater than they are. It is said, in fact, that the contrary is so. If, for example, man were better able to foretell the future, he would have a greater apprehension of the calamities that are destined to befall him and he would therefore be the less able to bear his existence. But such considerations, adduced for what comfort they may give, are of no more than secondary importance to the argument; its primary intention is to demonstrate that the perfection of the universal order depends upon man's suffering.

It is generally said that Pope derived his general position and the particularities by which he expounded it from his friend Lord Bolingbroke, the St. John to whom all four epistles of the Essay are addressed, but an educated man of the time could scarcely have read any philosophy without gaining knowledge of a doctrine that was fashionable and received. Yet it was not everywhere received; Dr. Johnson, for one, would have none of it. Johnson had the highest admiration for Pope as a poet and he said of "An Essay on Man" that it "affords an egregious instance of the predominance of genius, the dazzling splendour of imagery, and the seductive powers of eloquence." But the praise he gives to the poet is the measure of his scorn of the philosopher. "Never," he goes on, "was penury of knowledge and vulgarity of sentiment so happily disguised," and he proceeds to show that the doctrine of the Essay may be reduced to a series of truisms and platitudes. "Surely," he says when the demolition is complete, "a man of no very comprehensive search may venture to say that he has heard all this before. . . ." And then, his antagonism to the philosopher having been given full vent, he is free to return to his praise of the poet: ". . . But it was never till now recommended by such a blaze of embellishments, or such sweetness of melody. The vigorous contraction of thoughts, the luxuriant amplification of others, the incidental illustrations, and sometimes the dignity, sometimes the softness of the verses, enchain philosophy, suspend criticism, and oppress judgment by overpowering pleasure." The double opinion recommends itself.

THOMAS GRAY
1716–1771

ELEGY WRITTEN IN A COUNTRY CHURCHYARD

The curfew tolls the knell of parting day,
    The lowing herd wind slowly o'er the lea,
The ploughman homeward plods his weary way,
    And leaves the world to darkness and to me.

Now fades the glimmering landscape on the sight,   5
    And all the air a solemn stillness holds,
Save where the beetle wheels his droning flight,
    And drowsy tinklings lull the distant folds;

Save that from yonder ivy-mantled tow'r
    The moping owl does to the moon complain   10
Of such, as wand'ring near her secret bow'r,
    Molest her ancient solitary reign.

Beneath those rugged elms, that yew-tree's shade,
    Where heaves the turf in many a mold'ring heap,

Each in his narrow cell forever laid,
    The rude[1] forefathers of the hamlet sleep. 15

The breezy call of incense-breathing morn,
    The swallow twitt'ring from the straw-built shed,
The cock's shrill clarion, or the echoing horn,
    No more shall rouse them from their lowly bed. 20

For them no more the blazing hearth shall burn,
    Or busy housewife ply her evening care;
No children run to lisp their sire's return,
    Or climb his knees the envied kiss to share.

Oft did the harvest to their sickle yield; 25
    Their furrow oft the stubborn glebe[2] has broke;
How jocund did they drive their team afield!
    How bow'd the woods beneath their sturdy stroke!

Let not Ambition mock their useful toil,
    Their homely joys, and destiny obscure; 30
Nor Grandeur hear with a disdainful smile
    The short and simple annals of the poor.

The boast of heraldry,[3] the pomp of pow'r,
    And all that beauty, all that wealth e'er gave,
Awaits alike th' inevitable hour: 35
    The paths of glory lead but to the grave.

Nor you, ye proud, impute to these the fault,
    If Mem'ry o'er their tomb no trophies raise,
Where through the long-drawn aisle and fretted vault
    The pealing anthem swells the note of praise. 40

Can storied urn,[4] or animated[5] bust,
    Back to its mansion call the fleeting breath?
Can Honour's voice provoke the silent dust,
    Or Flatt'ry soothe the dull cold ear of Death?

---

[1] Rustic.   [2] Soil.   [3] Recorded genealogies and their heraldic symbols; hence, noble birth.   [4] Funeral urn engraved with scenes from a story.   [5] Lifelike.

Perhaps in this neglected spot is laid   45
    Some heart once pregnant with celestial fire;
Hands that the rod of empire might have sway'd,
    Or wak'd to ecstasy the living lyre.

But Knowledge to their eyes her ample page,
    Rich with the spoils of time, did ne'er unroll;   50
Chill Penury repress'd their noble rage,
    And froze the genial current of the soul.

Full many a gem of purest ray serene,
    The dark unfathom'd caves of ocean bear;
Full many a flower is born to blush unseen,   55
    And waste its sweetness on the desert air.

Some village Hampden,[6] that with dauntless breast
    The little tyrant of his fields withstood;
Some mute inglorious Milton[7] here may rest,
    Some Cromwell,[8] guiltless of his country's blood.   60

Th' applause of list'ning senates to command,
    The threats of pain and ruin to despise,
To scatter plenty o'er a smiling land,
    And read their hist'ry in a nation's eyes,

Their lot forbade; nor circumscrib'd alone   65
    Their growing virtues, but their crimes confined;
Forbade to wade through slaughter to a throne,
    And shut the gates of mercy on mankind;

The struggling pangs of conscious truth to hide,
    To quench the blushes of ingenuous shame,   70
Or heap the shrine of Luxury and Pride
    With incense kindled at the Muse's flame.

[6] John Hampden (1594–1643), a Member of Parliament who resisted taxes levied by King Charles I because he thought them unjust. He was impeached but resisted arrest. [7] The poet John Milton (1608–1674). [8] Oliver Cromwell, a Puritan military leader during the English Civil War and Lord Protector of the Commonwealth (1653–1658).

Far from the madding[9] crowd's ignoble strife,
    Their sober wishes never learn'd to stray;
Along the cool sequester'd vale of life   75
    They kept the noiseless tenor of their way.

Yet ev'n these bones from insult to protect,
    Some frail memorial still erected nigh,
With uncouth rhymes and shapeless sculpture deck'd,
    Implores the passing tribute of a sigh.   80

Their name, their years, spelt by th' unletter'd Muse,
    The place of fame and elegy supply;
And many a holy text around she strews,
    That teach the rustic moralist to die.

For who, to dumb Forgetfulness a prey,   85
    This pleasing anxious being e'er resign'd,
Left the warm precincts of the cheerful day,
    Nor cast one longing ling'ring look behind?

On some fond breast the parting soul relies,
    Some pious drops the closing eye requires;   90
Ev'n from the tomb the voice of Nature cries,
    Ev'n in our ashes live their wonted[10] fires.

For thee, who mindful of th' unhonour'd dead
    Dost in these lines their artless tale relate;
If chance, by lonely contemplation led,   95
    Some kindred spirit shall inquire thy fate,

Haply some hoary-headed[11] swain may say,
    "Oft have we seen him at the peep of dawn
Brushing with hasty steps the dews away
    To meet the sun upon the upland lawn.   100

"There at the foot of yonder nodding beech
    That wreathes its old fantastic roots so high,
His listless length at noontide would he stretch,
    And pore upon the brook that babbles by.

[9] Wild, restless.   [10] Customary.   [11] Gray- or white-haired.

"Hard by yon wood, now smiling as in scorn,   105
    Mutt'ring his wayward fancies he would rove;
Now drooping, woeful-wan, like one forlorn,
    Or craz'd with care, or cross'd in hopeless love.

"One morn I miss'd him on the custom'd hill,
    Along the heath, and near his fav'rite tree;   110
Another came; nor yet beside the rill,
    Nor up the lawn, nor at the wood was he;

"The next, with dirges due, in sad array,
    Slow through the church-way path we saw him borne.
Approach and read (for thou canst read) the lay,   115
    Grav'd on the stone beneath yon agèd thorn."

THE EPITAPH

Here rests his head upon the lap of earth,
    A youth to Fortune and to Fame unknown;
Fair Science frown'd not on his humble birth,
    And Melancholy mark'd him for her own.   120

Large was his bounty, and his soul sincere;
    Heav'n did a recompense as largely send:
He gave to Mis'ry all he had, a tear;
    He gain'd from Heav'n ('twas all he wish'd) a friend.

No farther seek his merits to disclose,   125
    Or draw his frailties from their dread abode,
(There they alike in trembling hope repose)
    The bosom of his Father and his God.

WILLIAM BLAKE

1757–1827

THE ECCHOING GREEN[1]

The Sun does arise,
And make happy the skies.
The merry bells ring
To welcome the Spring.
The skylark and thrush,   5
The birds of the bush,
Sing louder around
To the bells' cheerful sound;
While our sports shall be seen
On the Ecchoing Green.   10

Old John, with white hair,
Does laugh away care,
Sitting under the oak,
Among the old folk.
They laugh at our play,   15
And soon they all say:
Such, such were the joys,
When we all, girls and boys,
In our youth time were seen,
On the Ecchoing Green.   20

Till the little ones, weary,
No more can be merry;
The sun does descend,
And our sports have an end:
Round the laps of their mothers   25
Many sisters and brothers,
Like birds in their nest,
Are ready for rest;
And sport no more seen,
On the darkening Green.   30

[1] The spelling of "Ecchoing" is Blake's.

THE LAMB

  Little Lamb, who made thee?
  Dost thou know who made thee?
Gave thee life and bid thee feed,
By the stream and o'er the mead;
Gave thee clothing of delight,   5
Softest clothing wooly bright;
Gave thee such a tender voice,
Making all the vales rejoice?
  Little Lamb, who made thee?
  Dost thou know who made thee?   10

  Little Lamb, I'll tell thee,
  Little Lamb, I'll tell thee:
He is callèd by thy name,
For He calls Himself a Lamb:
He is meek, and He is mild;   15
He became a little child:
I a child, and thou a lamb,
We are callèd by His name.
  Little Lamb, God bless thee.
  Little Lamb, God bless thee.   20

THE CLOD AND THE PEBBLE

"Love seeketh not Itself to please,
 Nor for itself hath any care,
 But for another gives its ease,
 And builds a Heaven in Hell's despair."

So sang a little Clod of Clay   5
Trodden with the cattle's feet,
But a Pebble of the brook
Warbled out these metres meet:

"Love seeketh only Self to please,
 To bind another to its delight,   10
 Joys in another's loss of ease,
 And builds a Hell in Heaven's despite."[1]

  [1] In spite of Heaven.

A POISON TREE

I was angry with my friend:
I told my wrath, my wrath did end.
I was angry with my foe:
I told it not, my wrath did grow.

And I water'd it in fears,   5
Night and morning with my tears;
And I sunnèd it with smiles,
And with soft deceitful wiles.

And it grew both day and night,
Till it bore an apple bright.   10
And my foe beheld it shine,
And he knew that it was mine,

And into my garden stole
When the night had veil'd the pole;[1]
In the morning glad I see   15
My foe outstretch'd beneath the tree.

AH, SUN-FLOWER!

Ah, Sun-flower! weary of time,
Who countest the steps of the Sun:
Seeking after that sweet golden clime
Where the traveller's journey is done;

Where the Youth pined away with desire,   5
And the pale Virgin shrouded in snow,
Arise from their graves and aspire,[1]
Where my Sun-flower wishes to go.

[1] Polestar or North Star.

[1] Ascend.

LONDON

I wander through each charter'd[1] street,
Near where the charter'd Thames does flow,
And mark in every face I meet
Marks of weakness, marks of woe.

In every cry of every man,   5
In every infant's cry of fear,
In every voice, in every ban
The mind-forg'd manacles I hear.

How the chimney-sweeper's cry
Every black'ning church appalls,   10
And the hapless soldier's sigh
Runs in blood down palace walls.

But most through midnight streets I hear
How the youthful harlot's curse
Blasts the new-born infant's tear   15
And blights with plagues the marriage hearse.

TYGER! TYGER!

Tyger! Tyger! burning bright
In the forests of the night,
What immortal hand or eye
Could frame thy fearful symmetry?

In what distant deeps or skies   5
Burnt the fire of thine eyes?
On what wings dare he aspire?
What the hand dare seize the fire?

[1] Privileged, licensed.

And what shoulder, & what art,
Could twist the sinews of thy heart?
And when thy heart began to beat,
What dread hand? & what dread feet?[1]

What the hammer? what the chain?
In what furnace was thy brain?
What the anvil? what dread grasp
Dare its deadly terrors clasp?

When the stars threw down their spears,
And water'd heaven with their tears,
Did he smile his work to see?
Did he who made the Lamb make thee?

Tyger! Tyger! burning bright
In the forests of the night,
What immortal hand or eye,
Dare frame thy fearful symmetry?

ROBERT BURNS
1759–1796

MARY MORISON

O Mary, at thy window be!
    It is the wish'd, the trysted hour.[1]
Those smiles and glances let me see,

---

[1] In revising the poem, Blake deleted a line that might seem necessary to the thought. He originally wrote:

What dread hand and what dread feet
Could fetch it from the furnace deep?

[1] The hour appointed for a tryst.

That make the miser's treasure poor.
  How blythely wad I bide the stoure,[2]   5
A weary slave frae sun to sun,
  Could I the rich reward secure—
The lovely Mary Morison!

Yestreen,[3] when to the trembling string
  The dance gaed[4] thro' the lighted ha',   10
To thee my fancy took its wing,
  I sat, but neither heard or saw:
  Tho' this was fair, and that was braw,[5]
And yon the toast of a' the town,
  I sigh'd and said amang them a':—   15
"Ye are na Mary Morison!"

O Mary, canst thou wreck his peace
  Wha[6] for thy sake wad gladly die?
Or canst thou break that heart of his
  Whase only faut is loving thee?   20
  If love for love thou wilt na gie,
At least be pity to me shown:
  A thought ungentle canna be
The thought o' Mary Morison.

ADDRESS TO THE UNCO GUID[1]

or The Rigidly Righteous

> My Son, these maxims make a rule,
>   An' lump them ay thegither:
> The Rigid Righteous is a fool,
>   The Rigid Wise anither;
> The cleanest corn that e'er was dight[2]
>   May hae some pyles o' caff[3] in;
> So ne'er a fellow-creature slight
>   For random fits o' daffin.[4]
>   SOLOMON (Eccles. vii. 16)

O ye, wha are sae guid yoursel,
  Sae pious and sae holy,

---

[2] Would I wait out the storm, or tumult.   [3] Yesterday evening.   [4] Went.   [5] Brave; that is, splendid, showy.   [6] Who.

[1] Uncommon good; that is, those who profess to be strict in matters of morals and religion.   [2] Winnowed.   [3] Chaff.   [4] Fooling, frolicking.

Ye've nought to do but mark and tell
    Your neebours' fauts and folly;
Whase life is like a weel-gaun⁵ mill,   5
    Supplied wi' store o' water;
The heapet happer's⁶ ebbing still,
    An' still the clap⁷ plays clatter!

Hear me, ye venerable core,
    As counsel for poor mortals   10
That frequent pass douce⁸ Wisdom's door
    For glaikit⁹ Folly's portals:
I for their thoughtless, careless sakes
    Would here propone¹⁰ defences—
Their donsie¹¹ tricks, their black mistakes,   15
    Their failings and mischances.

Ye see your state wi' theirs compared,
    And shudder at the niffer;¹²
But cast a moment's fair regard,
    What makes the mighty differ?¹³   20
Discount what scant occasion¹⁴ gave;
    That purity ye pride in;
And (what's aft mair than a' the lave¹⁵)
    Your better art o' hidin.

Think, when your castigated pulse   25
    Gies now and then a wallop,
What ragings must his veins convulse,
    That still eternal gallop!
Wi' wind and tide fair i' your tail,
    Right on ye scud¹⁶ your sea-way;   30
But in the teeth o' baith to sail,
    It makes an unco¹⁷ lee-way.

See Social-life and Glee sit down
    All joyous and unthinking,
Till, quite transmugrify'd,¹⁸ they're grown   35
    Debauchery and Drinking:
O, would they stay to calculate

---

⁵ Wheel-driven.   ⁶ Heaped hopper.   ⁷ Clapper (of the mill).   ⁸ Sober.   ⁹ Senseless, giddy.   ¹⁰ Propound, propose.   ¹¹ Unfortunate.   ¹² Exchange.   ¹³ Difference. ¹⁴ Chance, coincidence.   ¹⁵ What's often more than all the rest.   ¹⁶ Sail swiftly, before the wind.   ¹⁷ Strange, uncommon.   ¹⁸ Transmogrified; that is, transformed, metamorphosed (humorous).

Th' eternal consequences,
Or—your more dreaded hell to state—
Damnation of expenses! 40

Ye high, exalted, virtuous dames,
Tied up in godly laces,
Before ye gie poor Frailty names,
Suppose a change o'cases:
A dear-lov'd lad, convenience snug, 45
A treach'rous inclination—
But, let me whisper i' your lug,[19]
Ye're aiblins[20] nae temptation.

Then gently scan your brother man,
Still gentler sister woman; 50
Tho' they may gang a kennin[21] wrang,
To step aside is human:
One point must still be greatly dark,
The moving[22] *why* they do it;
And just as lamely can ye mark 55
How far perhaps they rue it.

Who made the heart, 't is He alone
Decidedly can try us:
He knows each chord, its various tone,
Each spring, its various bias: 60
Then at the balance[23] let's be mute,
We never can adjust it;
What's done we partly may compute,
But know not what's resisted.

A RED, RED ROSE

O, my luve is like a red, red rose,
That's newly sprung[1] in June.
O, my luve is like the melodie,
That's sweetly play'd in tune.

---

[19] Ear.   [20] Perhaps.   [21] Just enough to be perceived; a little.   [22] Reason.
[23] Scale (of justice).

[1] Burst forth; bloomed.

As fair art thou, my bonie[2] lass,
    So deep in luve am I,
And I will luve thee still, my dear,
    Till a' the seas gang dry.

Till a' the seas gang dry, my dear,
    And the rocks melt wi' the sun!
And I will luve thee still, my dear,
    While the sands o' life shall run.

And fare thee weel, my only luve,
    And fare thee weel a while!
And I will come again, my luve,
    Tho' it were ten thousand mile!

WILLIAM WORDSWORTH
1770–1850

SHE DWELT AMONG THE UNTRODDEN WAYS

She dwelt among the untrodden ways
    Beside the springs of Dove,
A Maid whom there were none to praise
    And very few to love:

A violet by a mossy stone
    Half hidden from the eye!
—Fair as a star, when only one
    Is shining in the sky.

She lived unknown, and few could know
    When Lucy ceased to be;
But she is in her grave, and, oh,
    The difference to me!

2 Bonny.

COMPOSED UPON WESTMINSTER BRIDGE

Earth has not anything to show more fair:
Dull would he be of soul who could pass by
A sight so touching in its majesty:
This city now doth, like a garment, wear
The beauty of the morning; silent, bare,   5
Ships, towers, domes, theatres, and temples lie
Open unto the fields, and to the sky;
All bright and glittering in the smokeless air.
Never did sun more beautifully steep
In his first splendour, valley, rock, or hill;   10
Ne'er saw I, never felt, a calm so deep!
The river glideth at his own sweet will:
Dear God! the very houses seem asleep;
And all that mighty heart is lying still!

THE WORLD IS TOO MUCH WITH US

The world is too much with us; late and soon,
Getting and spending, we lay waste our powers:
Little we see in Nature that is ours;
We have given our hearts away, a sordid boon!
This Sea that bares her bosom to the moon;   5
The winds that will be howling at all hours,
And are up-gathered now like sleeping flowers;
For this, for everything, we are out of tune;
It moves us not.—Great God! I'd rather be
A Pagan suckled in a creed outworn;   10
So might I, standing on this pleasant lea,
Have glimpses that would make me less forlorn;
Have sight of Proteus[1] rising from the sea;
Or hear old Triton blow his wreathèd horn.

SURPRISED BY JOY

Surprised by joy—impatient as the Wind
I turned to share the transport—Oh! with whom

[1] Proteus, like Triton (line 14), was a sea god. Both were sons of Poseidon (or Neptune), principal god of the sea. Proteus could change his shape at will; Triton controlled the waves by blowing on a conch shell.

But Thee,[1] deep buried in the silent tomb,
That spot which no vicissitude can find?
Love, faithful love, recalled thee to my mind—
But how could I forget thee? Through what power,
Even for the least division of an hour,
Have I been so beguiled as to be blind
To my most grievous loss!—That thought's return
Was the worst pang that sorrow ever bore,
Save one, one only, when I stood forlorn,
Knowing my heart's best treasure was no more;
That neither present time, nor years unborn
Could to my sight that heavenly face restore.

5

10

THE SOLITARY REAPER

Behold her, single in the field,
Yon solitary Highland Lass!
Reaping and singing by herself;
Stop here, or gently pass!
Alone she cuts and binds the grain,
And sings a melancholy strain;
O listen! for the Vale profound
Is overflowing with the sound.

5

No Nightingale did ever chaunt
More welcome notes to weary bands
Of travellers in some shady haunt,
Among Arabian sands:
A voice so thrilling ne'er was heard
In springtime from the Cuckoo-bird,
Breaking the silence of the seas
Among the farthest Hebrides.[1]

10

15

Will no one tell me what she sings?—
Perhaps the plaintive numbers flow
For old, unhappy, far-off things,
And battles long ago:
Or is it some more humble lay,
Familiar matter of to-day?
Some natural sorrow, loss, or pain,
That has been, and may be again?

20

1 Wordsworth's daughter Catherine.

1 Islands off the west coast of Scotland.

Whate'er the theme, the Maiden sang   25
As if her song could have no ending;
I saw her singing at her work,
And o'er the sickle bending:—
I listened, motionless and still;
And, as I mounted up the hill,   30
The music in my heart I bore,
Long after it was heard no more.

ODE: INTIMATIONS OF IMMORTALITY FROM RECOLLECTIONS OF EARLY CHILDHOOD

The Child is father of the Man;
And I could wish my days to be
Bound each to each by natural piety.[1]

I

There was a time when meadow, grove, and stream,
The earth, and every common sight,
        To me did seem
        Apparelled in celestial light,
The glory and the freshness of a dream.   5
It is not now as it hath been of yore;—
    Turn wheresoe'er I may,
        By night or day,
The things which I have seen I now can see no more.

II

    The Rainbow comes and goes,   10
    And lovely is the Rose;
    The Moon doth with delight
Look round her when the heavens are bare;
    Waters on a starry night
    Are beautiful and fair;   15

[1] As the epigraph to the Ode, Wordsworth uses the last three lines of a poem of his own:

My heart leaps up when I behold
        A rainbow in the sky:
So was it when my life began;
So is it now I am a man;
So be it when I shall grow old,
        Or let me die!
The child is father . . . [etc.]

The sunshine is a glorious birth;
But yet I know, where'er I go,
That there hath passed away a glory from the earth.

III

Now, while the birds thus sing a joyous song,
  And while the young lambs bound   20
   As to the tabor's sound,
To me alone there came a thought of grief:
A timely utterance gave that thought relief,
   And I again am strong:
The cataracts blow their trumpets from the steep;   25
No more shall grief of mine the season wrong;
I hear the Echoes through the mountains throng,
The Winds come to me from the fields of sleep,
   And all the earth is gay;
    Land and sea   30
   Give themselves up to jollity,
    And with the heart of May
   Doth every Beast keep holiday;—
    Thou Child of Joy,
Shout round me, let me hear thy shouts, thou happy Shepherd-boy! 35

IV

Ye blessèd Creatures, I have heard the call
Ye to each other make; I see
The heavens laugh with you in your jubilee;
My heart is at your festival,
   My head hath its coronal,   40
The fulness of your bliss, I feel—I feel it all.
   Oh, evil day! if I were sullen
   While Earth herself is adorning,
    This sweet May-morning,
   And the Children are culling   45
    On every side,
    In a thousand valleys far and wide,
    Fresh flowers; while the sun shines warm,
And the Babe leaps up on his Mother's arm:—
   I hear, I hear, with joy I hear!   50
   —But there's a Tree, of many, one,
A single Field which I have looked upon,
Both of them speak of something that is gone:
   The Pansy at my feet
   Doth the same tale repeat: 55
Whither is fled the visionary gleam?
Where is it now, the glory and the dream?

V

Our birth is but a sleep and a forgetting:
The Soul that rises with us, our life's Star,
    Hath had elsewhere its setting,   60
      And cometh from afar:
Not in entire forgetfulness,
And not in utter nakedness,
But trailing clouds of glory do we come
    From God, who is our home: 65
Heaven lies about us in our infancy!
Shades of the prison-house begin to close
    Upon the growing Boy,
But he beholds the light, and whence it flows
    He sees it in his joy;   70
The Youth, who daily farther from the east
    Must travel, still is Nature's Priest,
    And by the vision splendid
    Is on his way attended;
At length the Man perceives it die away,   75
And fade into the light of common day.

VI

Earth fills her lap with pleasures of her own;
Yearnings she hath in her own natural kind,
And, even with something of a Mother's mind,
    And no unworthy aim,   80
    The homely Nurse doth all she can
To make her Foster-child, her Inmate Man,
    Forget the glories he hath known,
And that imperial palace whence he came.

VII

Behold the Child among his new-born blisses,   85
A six years' Darling of a pigmy size!
See, where 'mid work of his own hand he lies,
Fretted by sallies of his mother's kisses,
With light upon him from his father's eyes!
See, at his feet, some little plan or chart,   90
Some fragment from his dream of human life,
Shaped by himself with newly-learnèd art;
    A wedding or a festival,
    A mourning or a funeral,
      And this hath now his heart,   95
      And unto this he frames his song:

Then will he fit his tongue
To dialogues of business, love, or strife;
         But it will not be long
         Ere this be thrown aside,
         And with new joy and pride
The little Actor cons another part;
Filling from time to time his "humorous stage"
With all the Persons, down to palsied Age,
That Life brings with her in her equipage;   105
         As if his whole vocation
         Were endless imitation.

                    VIII

Thou, whose exterior semblance doth belie
         Thy Soul's immensity;
Thou best Philosopher, who yet dost keep   110
Thy heritage, thou Eye among the blind,
That, deaf and silent, read'st the eternal deep,
Haunted for ever by the eternal mind,—
         Mighty Prophet! Seer blest!
         On whom those truths do rest,   115
Which we are toiling all our lives to find,
In darkness lost, the darkness of the grave;
Thou, over whom thy Immortality
Broods like the Day, a Master o'er a Slave,
A Presence which is not to be put by;   120
Thou little Child, yet glorious in the might
Of heaven-born freedom on thy being's height,
Why with such earnest pains dost thou provoke
The years to bring the inevitable yoke,
Thus blindly with thy blessedness at strife?   125
Full soon thy Soul shall have her earthly freight,
And custom lie upon thee with a weight,
Heavy as frost, and deep almost as life!

                    IX

         O joy! that in our embers
         Is something that doth live,   130
         That nature yet remembers
         What was so fugitive!
The thought of our past years in me doth breed
Perpetual benediction: not indeed
For that which is most worthy to be blest;   135
Delight and liberty, the simple creed
Of Childhood, whether busy or at rest,
With new-fledged hope still fluttering in his breast:—

Not for these I raise
The song of thanks and praise;
But for those obstinate questionings
Of sense and outward things,
Fallings from us, vanishings;
Blank misgivings of a Creature
Moving about in worlds not realised,
High instincts, before which our mortal Nature
Did tremble like a guilty Thing surprised:
But for those first affections,
Those shadowy recollections,
Which, be they what they may,
Are yet the fountain-light of all our day,
Are yet a master-light of all our seeing;
Uphold us, cherish, and have power to make
Our noisy years seem moments in the being
Of the eternal Silence: truths that wake,
To perish never;
Which neither listlessness, nor mad endeavour,
Nor Man nor Boy,
Nor all that is at enmity with joy,
Can utterly abolish or destroy!
Hence in a season of calm weather
Though inland far we be,
Our souls have sight of that immortal sea
Which brought us hither;
Can in a moment travel thither,—
And see the Children sport upon the shore,
And hear the mighty waters rolling evermore.

X

Then, sing, ye Birds, sing, sing a joyous song!
And let the young Lambs bound
As to the tabor's sound!
We, in thought, will join your throng,
Ye that pipe and ye that play,
Ye that through your hearts to-day
Feel the gladness of the May!
What though the radiance which was once so bright
Be now for ever taken from my sight,
Though nothing can bring back the hour
Of splendour in the grass, of glory in the flower;
We will grieve not, rather find
Strength in what remains behind;
In the primal sympathy
Which having been must ever be;
In the soothing thoughts that spring

Out of human suffering;
        In the faith that looks through death,   185
In years that bring the philosophic mind.

XI

And O, ye Fountains, Meadows, Hills, and Groves,
Forbode not any severing of our loves!
Yet in my heart of hearts I feel your might;
I only have relinquished one delight   190
To live beneath your more habitual sway.
I love the Brooks which down their channels fret,
Even more than when I tripped lightly as they;
The innocent brightness of a new-born Day
        Is lovely yet;   195
The Clouds that gather round the setting sun
Do take a sober colouring from an eye
That hath kept watch o'er man's mortality;
Another race hath been, and other palms are won.
Thanks to the human heart by which we live,   200
Thanks to its tenderness, its joys, and fears,
To me the meanest flower that blows can give
Thoughts that do often lie too deep for tears.

'RESOLUTION
AND INDEPENDENCE'

I

There was a roaring in the wind all night;
The rain came heavily and fell in floods;
But now the sun is rising calm and bright;
The birds are singing in the distant woods;
Over his own sweet voice the Stock-dove broods;   5
The Jay makes answer as the Magpie chatters;
And all the air is filled with pleasant noise of waters.

II

All things that love the sun are out of doors;
The sky rejoices in the morning's birth;
The grass is bright with rain-drops;—on the moors   10
The hare is running races in her mirth;
And with her feet she from the plashy earth
Raises a mist; that, glittering in the sun,
Runs with her all the way, wherever she doth run.

III

I was a Traveller then upon the moor;　　　　　　　　15
I saw the hare that raced about with joy;
I heard the woods and distant waters roar;
Or heard them not, as happy as a boy:
The pleasant season did my heart employ:
My old remembrances went from me wholly;　　　20
And all the ways of men, so vain and melancholy.

IV

But, as it sometimes chanceth, from the might
Of joy in minds that can no further go,
As high as we have mounted in delight
In our dejection do we sink as low;　　　　　　　25
To me that morning did it happen so;
And fears and fancies thick upon me came;
Dim sadness—and blind thoughts, I knew not, nor could name

V

I heard the sky-lark warbling in the sky;
And I bethought me of the playful hare:　　　　30
Even such a happy Child of earth am I;
Even as these blissful creatures do I fare;
Far from the world I walk, and from all care;
But there may come another day to me—
Solitude, pain of heart, distress, and poverty.　　35

VI

My whole life I have lived in pleasant thought,
As if life's business were a summer mood;
As if all needful things would come unsought
To genial faith, still rich in genial good;
But how can He expect that others should　　　40
Build for him, sow for him, and at his call
Love him, who for himself will take no heed at all?

VII

I thought of Chatterton,[1] the marvellous Boy,
The sleepless Soul that perished in his pride;
Of Him[2] who walked in glory and in joy　　　45

---

[1] Thomas Chatterton (1752–1770), a promising poet who committed suicide at the age of 17.　[2] Robert Burns (1759–1796), the Scottish poet, who had a difficult life and died early.

Following his plough, along the mountain-side:
By our own spirits are we deified:
We Poets in our youth begin in gladness;
But thereof come in the end despondency and madness.

VIII

Now, whether it were by peculiar grace,
A leading from above, a something given,
Yet it befell that, in this lonely place,
When I with these untoward thoughts had striven,
Beside a pool bare to the eye of heaven
I saw a Man before me unawares:
The oldest man he seemed that ever wore grey hairs.

50

55

IX

As a huge stone is sometimes seen to lie
Couched on the bald top of an eminence;
Wonder to all who do the same espy,
By what means it could thither come, and whence;
So that it seems a thing endued with sense:
Like a sea-beast crawled forth, that on a shelf
Of rock or sand reposeth, there to sun itself;

60

X

Such seemed this Man, not all alive nor dead,
Nor all asleep—in his extreme old age:
His body was bent double, feet and head
Coming together in life's pilgrimage;
As if some dire constraint of pain, or rage
Of sickness felt by him in times long past,
A more than human weight upon his frame had cast.

65

70

XI

Himself he propped, limbs, body, and pale face,
Upon a long grey staff of shaven wood:
And, still as I drew near with gentle pace,
Upon the margin of that moorish[3] flood
Motionless as a cloud the old Man stood,
That heareth not the loud winds when they call;
And moveth all together, if it move at all.

75

[3] On a moor.

XII

At length, himself unsettling, he the pond
Stirred with his staff, and fixedly did look
Upon the muddy water, which he conned,   80
As if he had been reading in a book:
And now a stranger's privilege I took;
And, drawing to his side, to him did say,
"This morning gives us promise of a glorious day."

XIII

A gentle answer did the old Man make,   85
In courteous speech which forth he slowly drew:
And him with further words I thus bespake,
"What occupation do you there pursue?
This is a lonesome place for one like you."
Ere he replied, a flash of mild surprise   90
Broke from the stable orbs of his yet-vivid eyes.

XIV

His words came feebly, from a feeble chest,
But each in solemn order followed each,
With something of a lofty utterance drest—
Choice word and measured phrase, above the reach   95
Of ordinary men; a stately speech;
Such as grave Livers do in Scotland use,
Religious men, who give to God and man their dues.

XV

He told, that to these waters he had come
To gather leeches,[4] being old and poor: 100
Employment hazardous and wearisome!
And he had many hardships to endure:
From pond to pond he roamed, from moor to moor;
Housing, with God's good help, by choice or chance;
And in this way he gained an honest maintenance.   105

XVI

The old Man still stood talking by my side;
But now his voice to me was like a stream

[4] Bloodsucking worms formerly used by physicians to reduce what was thought to be an excess of blood.

Scarce heard; nor word from word could I divide;
And the whole body of the Man did seem
Like one whom I had met with in a dream;
Or like a man from some far region sent,
To give me human strength, by apt admonishment.   110

XVII

My former thoughts returned: the fear that kills;
And hope that is unwilling to be fed;
Cold, pain, and labour, and all fleshy ills;
And mighty Poets in their misery dead.   115
—Perplexed, and longing to be comforted,
My question eagerly did I renew,
"How is it that you live, and what is it you do?"

XVIII

He with a smile did then his words repeat;   120
And said that, gathering leeches, far and wide
He travelled; stirring thus about his feet
The waters of the pools where they abide.
"Once I could meet with them on every side;
But they have dwindled long by slow decay;   125
Yet still I persevere, and find them where I may."

XIX

While he was talking thus, the lonely place,
The old Man's shape, and speech—all troubled me:
In my mind's eye I seemed to see him pace
About the weary moors continually,   130
Wandering about alone and silently.
While I these thoughts within myself pursued,
He, having made a pause, the same discourse renewed.

XX

And soon with this he other matter blended,
Cheerfully uttered, with demeanour kind,
But stately in the main; and, when he ended,   135
I could have laughed myself to scorn to find
In that decrepit Man so firm a mind.
"God," said I, "be my help and stay secure;
I'll think of the Leech-gatherer on the lonely moor!"   140

479   WILLIAM WORDSWORTH

Let us suppose that someone who had never read "Resolution and Independence" were to ask us what it is about and we were to comply with his request. Would there be much likelihood of his believing that this could make the material of one of the finest poems in the English language? I use the phrase "what it is about" in the simple and quite natural sense in which we employ it when we inquire about some story or play with which we have no acquaintance, expecting to be answered with a summary account of its chief happenings. We do not of course think we have been told much when we have been told only this, yet we do feel we have been supplied some ground for estimating the interest the story or play will have for us; we assume some relation between even a scant *résumé* and the real nature of a work. And in general we are right in this assumption. But not always, and not, surely, in the instance of "Resolution and Independence."

What is the poem about? It is about the poet's meeting with a very old man and the beneficent effect that this encounter has upon him. On a fine spring morning, the poet, who is a young or youngish man, is walking on the moors. He is in a happy frame of mind, but suddenly his spirits fall, and he is overcome by an intense anxiety about his future; he thinks about the disastrous fates that have befallen other poets and that might befall him. As he walks on in his painful state of depression and fear, he comes across a solitary decrepit figure standing in a shallow pool. To the poet's questions about his way of life, the old man replies with simple dignity. He makes a bare living by gathering leeches; the work grows ever more difficult for him; he is quite alone in the world. He is so old that it seems scarcely possible that he should go on living; and he has, as we say, nothing to live for; yet he utters no complaint and shows no self-pity. The poet is moved to shame for having been so much distressed by the mere imagination of misfortune; he resolves to make the old leech-gatherer his example of fortitude.

If this is a fair statement of what happens in "Resolution and Independence," it is certainly reasonable to conclude that the content of the poem is rather trivial and dull. What is more, it has the unpleasing quality of moral didacticism; it seems to have the intention of teaching a lesson in simple morality, or even something more boring than that, a lesson in mental hygiene: "Do not allow your imagination to bedevil you with thoughts of personal disaster. Confront the chances of life with a firm and equal mind." What, then, are the elements of the poem that make for its great quality?

The first of these is the idea of greatness itself. The chief characteristic of the old man is his dignity. The simile by which he is first described compares him to a "huge stone," a massive boulder such as we sometimes see "couched on the bald top of an eminence," which raises in our minds the question of how it came there. If we do not think rationally of the glacier or flood that transported the boulder to its present unlikely place but suppose that it had moved of its own volition, its imagined movement is wonderful and awesome, and no less so is the movement of the old man. He leans on a staff because he is feeble, but his posture is majestic; his staff is an attribute of his majesty. The difficulty with which he moves appears as a sign not of weakness but of firmness, of a nature that is not easily moved by circumstance.

> Motionless as a cloud the old Man stood,
> That heareth not the loud winds when they call;
> And moveth all together, if it move at all.

In all cultures the quality of majesty is associated with weightiness and a degree of immobility, or at least slowness of movement—a king in a hurry seems a contradiction in terms. The ceremonial robes of the king express the idea that he has no need to be active. And the impression of the old man's kingliness is borne out by his "stately" speech and the imperious "flash" of his "yet vivid eyes."

In addition to this majesty, the old man has for the poet something like a supernatural authority. He seems "like one whom I had met with in a dream"—

> Or like a man from some far region sent,
> To give me human strength, by apt admonishment.

The "far region" suggests a divine region; to the poet the Leech-gatherer is an agent or messenger of God, an angel in disguise. This idea is sustained as the poet speculates on how it came about that he met the old man at this particular moment, when the meeting is of such momentous significance to him. He wonders if the encounter takes place "by peculiar grace, / A leading from above, a something given." These are theological terms having reference to divine intervention in the lives of individual persons.

But if the old man, despite his actual feebleness, is a figure of majesty, so, in his way, is the poet, who speaks not merely in his own person but as the representative of all poets. For him the sorrow of poets in misfortune is the sorrow of kings in misfortune—he speaks of "mighty Poets in their misery dead." The characteristic attributes of poets are not only "joy" but "pride" and "glory." They are, indeed, even greater than kings, for their divine right is from themselves: "By our own spirits are we deified."

Yet it is by their own spirits that they are cast down—no sooner has the poet made his proud boast than he confronts the tragic fate that threatens the possessors of the poetic power. His words are shocking in their explicitness:

> We Poets in our youth begin in gladness;
> But thereof come in the end despondency and madness.

The life of poets, our poet is saying, follows the course of his own feelings of that very morning: his despondency had succeeded his high spirits as if caused by them. His joy and its evanescence have their visual counterpart in the hare he described in Stanza II:

> All things that love the sun are out of doors;
> The sky rejoices in the morning's birth;
> The grass is bright with rain-drops;—on the moors
> The hare is running races in her mirth;

> And with her feet she from the plashy earth
> Raises a mist; that, glittering in the sun,
> Runs with her all the way, wherever she doth run.

Wherever she doth run—but not for as long as she runs. For the earth will dry and the mist that enhaloes her will vanish. We know from other of his poems that Wordsworth feared the loss of his poetic gift, which he associated with his youth and which he often represented in terms of some effect of light.

The poem, we can say, is organized by an opposition between what is suggested, on the one hand, by the hare racing in its luminous mist, and, on the other hand, by the "huge stone" to which the Leech-gatherer is compared— on the one hand, movement, speed, brightness, but also evanescence; on the other hand, immobility and lack of sentience, but also endurance. The poetic temperament, which is characterized by its quick responsiveness, Wordsworth associates with the quick-moving hare. To this he opposes—what? What name are we to give to the other temperament?

We are tempted to call it religious because one of the salient facts about the old Leech-gatherer is that he belongs to a Scottish religious sect. And religion may indeed, and often does, play a part in what we seek to name. But it need not. And then, even apart from the fact that there have been many religious poets, religion and poetry have too much in common to permit us to set up any simple opposition between them. What stands here in contrast to the poetic temperament is the temperament that finds its fulfilment in strictness of control, in what we have come to call "character." The nature of the poet, at least in the modern view, is defined by sensitivity and free responsiveness. These traits no doubt have their connection with morality as well as creativity, yet a strict moral training will undertake to limit them in the interests of character. This is exemplified in a striking way by the statement of the famous physician Sir William Osler, who, in one of his lectures to medical students, spoke of the physician's need for the quality which he called "imperturbability." He also called it "immobility" and "impassiveness" and even went so far as to call it "callousness." He admitted that this quality might appear to patients and their friends as hardness of heart, an indifference to the suffering of others that verged upon the inhuman, but he went on to say how disconcerted the patient and his family would be if the physician lacked this quality, for upon his ability to shut off his sensitivity depend his "firmness and courage," his ability to make difficult decisions and carry them out.

The poem, then, may be said to ask this question: Must the poet, for the sake of his survival, take to himself some measure of imperturbability, of rock-like fortitude, even at the cost of surrendering some of the sensitivity and responsiveness which constitute the essence of his poetic power? The question has an intrinsic psychological interest. But what gives it its peculiar force in the poem is the circumstance in which it is posed, the aura of tragic destiny which attends this confrontation of two modes of human self-realization.

Considered from the point of view of prosodic technique, "Resolution and Independence" is a most remarkable achievement. We begin our understanding of how the poem "works" by taking note of the punctuation, the sheer amount and weight of it: in the first three stanzas almost every line has a strong stop at its end. This has the effect of making each line a decisive and dramatic statement. The energy of one line is not continuous with that of the next; each line initiates its own movement, of which we become the more conscious as it discharges its energy upon the semi-colon, colon, or period that stops it; the effect is like that of watching breaker after breaker rising up to hurl itself upon a cliff. After the first three stanzas, the punctuation becomes lighter, although it is still decisive, and now we become aware of the stanza rather than the line as the unit of energy. Each stanza is as discrete as, at the beginning of the poem, each line had been, for the lengthened last line of the stanza acts as a full stop. The poem is thus a series of initiations of energy and of resistances to it, an equal display of movement and solidity.

Many readers are disturbed, even distressed, by the concluding couplet. And with some reason, for there is no doubt that

> "God," said I, "be my help and stay secure;
> I'll think of the Leech-gatherer on the lonely moor!"

is in all ways an anticlimax. It is emotionally insufficient and its tone is downright jaunty, so that it almost seems to dismiss the great episode which it brings to an end. The casual appeal to God seems merely conventional and a negation of the powerful if vague reference to the divine "far region." To these objections an admirer of the poem can offer no defence, except to say that, although cogent, they do not much matter.

SAMUEL TAYLOR COLERIDGE
1772–1834

DEJECTION: AN ODE

> Late, late yestreen I saw the new Moon,
> With the old Moon in her arms;
> And I fear, I fear, my Master dear!
> We shall have a deadly storm.
>> *Ballad of Sir Patrick Spence.*[1]

I

Well! If the Bard was weather-wise, who made
    The grand old ballad of Sir Patrick Spence,
    This night, so tranquil now, will not go hence
Unroused by winds, that ply a busier trade

[1] See "Sir Patrick Spens," p. 396.

Than those which mould yon cloud in lazy flakes,   5
Or the dull sobbing draft, that moans and rakes
Upon the strings of this Æolian lute,[2]
          Which better far were mute.
     For lo! the New-moon winter-bright!
     And overspread with phantom light,   10
     (With swimming phantom light o'erspread
     But rimmed and circled by a silver thread)
I see the old Moon in her lap, foretelling
     The coming-on of rain and squally blast.
And oh! that even now the gust were swelling,   15
     And the slant night-shower driving loud and fast!
Those sounds which oft have raised me, whilst they awed,
          And sent my soul abroad,
Might now perhaps their wonted[3] impulse give,
Might startle this dull pain, and make it move and live!   20

II

A grief without a pang, void, dark, and drear,
     A stifled, drowsy, unimpassioned grief,
     Which finds no natural outlet, no relief,
          In word, or sigh, or tear—
O Lady! in this wan and heartless mood,   25
To other thoughts by yonder throstle[4] woo'd,
     All this long eve, so balmy and serene,
Have I been gazing on the western sky,
     And its peculiar tint of yellow green:
And still I gaze—and with how blank an eye!   30
And those thin clouds above, in flakes and bars,
That give away their motion to the stars;
Those stars, that glide behind them or between,
Now sparkling, now bedimmed, but always seen:
Yon crescent Moon, as fixed as if it grew   35
In its own cloudless, starless lake of blue;
I see them all so excellently fair,
I see, not feel, how beautiful they are!

III

          My genial spirits fail;
          And what can these avail   40
To lift the smothering weight from off my breast?

[2] In Greek mythology, Aeolus was god of the winds. An Aeolian lute is a stringed instrument that is hung so that the wind can blow over it, producing sounds of a rather melancholy kind.   [3] Customary, usual.   [4] Thrush.

It were a vain endeavour,
        Though I should gaze for ever
On that green light that lingers in the west:
I may not hope from outward forms to win   45
The passion and the life, whose fountains are within.

IV

O Lady! we receive but what we give,
And in our life alone does Nature live:
Ours is her wedding garment, ours her shroud!
        And would we aught behold, of higher worth,   50
Than that inanimate cold world allowed
To the poor loveless ever-anxious crowd,
        Ah! from the soul itself must issue forth
A light, a glory, a fair luminous cloud
                Enveloping the Earth—   55
And from the soul itself must there be sent
        A sweet and potent voice, of its own birth,
Of all sweet sounds the life and element!

V

O pure of heart! thou need'st not ask of me
What this strong music in the soul may be!   60
What, and wherein it doth exist,
This light, this glory, this fair luminous mist,
This beautiful and beauty-making power.
        Joy, virtuous Lady! Joy that ne'er was given,
Save to the pure, and in their purest hour,   65
Life, and Life's effluence, cloud at once and shower,
Joy, Lady! is the spirit and the power,
Which wedding Nature to us gives in dower
        A new Earth and new Heaven,
Undreamt of by the sensual and the proud—   70
Joy is the sweet voice, Joy the luminous cloud—
                We in ourselves rejoice!
And thence flows all that charms or ear or sight,
        All melodies the echoes of that voice,
All colours a suffusion from that light.   75

VI

There was a time when, though my path was rough,
        This joy within me dallied with distress,
And all misfortunes were but as the stuff
        Whence Fancy made me dreams of happiness:
For hope grew round me, like the twining vine,   80

And fruits, and foliage, not my own, seemed mine.
But now afflictions bow me down to earth:
Nor care I that they rob me of my mirth;
      But oh! each visitation
Suspends what nature gave me at my birth,   85
    My shaping spirit of Imagination.
For not to think of what I needs must feel,
    But to be still and patient, all I can;
And haply by abstruse research to steal
    From my own nature all the natural man—   90
    This was my sole resource, my only plan:
Till that which suits a part infects the whole,
And now is almost grown the habit of my soul.

VII

Hence, viper thoughts, that coil around my mind,
      Reality's dark dream!   95
I turn from you, and listen to the wind,
    Which long has raved unnoticed. What a scream
Of agony by torture lengthened out
That lute sent forth! Thou Wind, that rav'st without,
    Bare crag, or mountain-tairn, or blasted tree,   100
Or pine-grove whither woodman never clomb,
Or lonely house, long held the witches' home,
    Methinks were fitter instruments for thee,
Mad Lutanist! who in this month of showers,
Of dark-brown gardens, and of peeping flowers,   105
Mak'st Devils' yule, with worse than wintry song,
The blossoms, buds, and timorous leaves among.
    Thou Actor, perfect in all tragic sounds!
Thou mighty Poet, e'en to frenzy bold!
      What tell'st thou now about?   110
      'Tis of the rushing of an host in rout,
    With groans, of trampled men, with smarting wounds—
At once they groan with pain, and shudder with the cold!
But hush! there is a pause of deepest silence!
    And all that noise, as of a rushing crowd,   115
With groans, and tremulous shudderings—all is over—
    It tells another tale, with sounds less deep and loud!
      A tale of less affright,
      And tempered with delight,
As Otway's self[5] had framed the tender lay,—   120
      'Tis of a little child
      Upon a lonesome wild,
Not far from home, but she hath lost her way:

[5] Thomas Otway (1642–1685) wrote tragedies in blank verse.

And now moans low in bitter grief and fear,
And now screams loud, and hopes to make her mother hear. 125

VIII

'Tis midnight, but small thoughts have I of sleep:
Full seldom may my friends such vigils keep!
Visit her, gentle Sleep! with wings of healing,
    And may this storm be but a mountain-birth,
May all the stars hang bright above her dwelling, 130
       Silent as though they watched the sleeping Earth!
          With light heart may she rise,
          Gay fancy, cheerful eyes,
      Joy lift her spirit, joy attune her voice;
To her may all things live, from pole to pole, 135
Their life the eddying of her living soul!
    O simple spirit, guided from above,
Dear Lady! friend devoutest of my choice,
Thus mayest thou ever, evermore rejoice.

KUBLA KHAN
OR A VISION IN A DREAM
A Fragment

In Xanadu did Kubla Khan[1]
A stately pleasure-dome decree:
Where Alph, the sacred river, ran
  Through caverns measureless to man
    Down to a sunless sea. 5
So twice five miles of fertile ground
With walls and towers were girdled round:
And here were gardens bright with sinuous rills,
Where blossomed many an incense-bearing tree;
And here were forests ancient as the hills, 10
Enfolding sunny spots of greenery.

But oh! that deep romantic chasm which slanted
Down the green hill athwart[2] a cedarn cover!
A savage place! as holy and enchanted
As e'er beneath a waning moon was haunted 15
By woman wailing for her demon-lover!
And from this chasm, with ceaseless turmoil seething,

[1] Kubla Khan was founder of the Mongol dynasty in China. His court, in reality, was at Yenching, near Peking.　[2] Across.

As if this earth in fast thick pants were breathing,
A mighty fountain momently[3] was forced:
Amid whose swift half-intermitted burst   20
Huge fragments vaulted like rebounding hail,
Or chaffy grain beneath the thresher's flail:
And 'mid these dancing rocks at once and ever
It flung up momently the sacred river.
Five miles meandering with a mazy motion   25
Through wood and dale the sacred river ran,
Then reached the caverns measureless to man,
And sank in tumult to a lifeless ocean:
And 'mid this tumult Kubla heard from far
Ancestral voices prophesying war!   30
    The shadow of the dome of pleasure
    Floated midway on the waves;
    Where was heard the mingled measure
    From the fountain and the caves.
It was a miracle of rare device,   35
A sunny pleasure-dome with caves of ice!

    A damsel with a dulcimer
    In a vision once I saw:
    It was an Abyssinian maid,
    And on her dulcimer she played,   40
    Singing of Mount Abora.
    Could I revive within me,
    Her symphony and song,
    To such a deep delight 'twould win me,
That with music loud and long,   45
I would build that dome in air,
That sunny dome! those caves of ice!
And all who heard should see them there,
And all should cry, Beware! Beware!
His flashing eyes, his floating hair!   50
Weave a circle round him thrice,
And close your eyes with holy dread,
For he on honey-dew hath fed,
And drunk the milk of Paradise.

[3] Every moment, continuously.

GEORGE GORDON, LORD BYRON
1788-1824

SHE WALKS IN BEAUTY

She walks in beauty, like the night
    Of cloudless climes and starry skies;
And all that's best of dark and bright
    Meet in her aspect and her eyes:
Thus mellow'd to that tender light   5
    Which heaven to gaudy day denies.

One shade the more, one ray the less,
    Had half impair'd the nameless grace
Which waves in every raven tress,
    Or softly lightens o'er her face;   10
Where thoughts serenely sweet express
    How pure, how dear their dwelling-place.

And on that cheek, and o'er that brow,
    So soft, so calm, yet eloquent,
The smiles that win, the tints that glow,   15
    But tell of days in goodness spent,
A mind at peace with all below,
    A heart whose love is innocent!

WHEN WE TWO PARTED

When we two parted
    In silence and tears,
Half broken-hearted
    To sever for years,
Pale grew thy cheek and cold,   5
    Colder thy kiss;
Truly that hour foretold
    Sorrow to this.

The dew of the morning
 Sunk chill on my brow—   10
It felt like the warning
 Of what I feel now.
Thy vows are all broken,
 And light is thy fame:
I hear thy name spoken,   15
 And share in its shame.

They name thee before me,
 A knell to mine ear;
A shudder comes o'er me—
 Why wert thou so dear?   20
They know not I knew thee,
 Who knew thee too well:—
Long, long shall I rue thee,
 Too deeply to tell.

In secret we met—   25
 In silence I grieve,
That thy heart could forget,
 Thy spirit deceive.
If I should meet thee
 After long years,   30
How should I greet thee?—
 With silence and tears.

DON JUAN
An Episode from Canto II

Headnote

There are two things that the reader ought to know about Byron's Don Juan.
The first is that his name is not pronounced in the Spanish fashion (*hwan*), but as
if it were an English name spoken phonetically: Byron rimes it with "new one" and
"true one." The second is that he has only the faintest connection with the Don Juan
of legend. It is true that all his adventures involve love affairs of one kind or another,
but he is nothing like the universal seducer of Molière's play or Mozart's opera. Indeed, he is a rather modest and virtuous young man whose love affairs either happen
to him or are forced upon him by women. A native of Seville, he has been very
strictly brought up by his extravagantly prudish and intellectual mother. When he is
sixteen, his mother's friend, Donna Julia, "married, charming, chaste, and twenty-
three," falls in love with him and he with her. Their liaison is discovered by Donna
Julia's husband, a great scandal results, Donna Julia is packed off to a convent, and
Juan is hustled out of the country by his mother. He takes ship at Cadiz; before his
departure he has received from Julia a very touching letter of farewell and has been
greatly moved by it.

1

Oh ye! who teach the ingenuous youth of nations,
    Holland, France, England, Germany, or Spain,
I pray ye flog them upon all occasions,
    It mends their morals, never mind the pain:
The best of mothers and of educations   5
    In Juan's case were but employ'd in vain,
Since, in a way that's rather of the oddest, he
Became divested of his native modesty.

2

Had he but been placed at a public school,
    In the third form, or even in the fourth,[1]   10
His daily task had kept his fancy cool,
    At least, had he been nurtured in the north;
Spain may prove an exception to the rule,
    But then exceptions always prove its worth—
A lad of sixteen causing a divorce   15
Puzzled his tutors very much, of course.

3

I can't say that it puzzles me at all,
    If all things be consider'd; first, there was
His lady-mother, mathematical,
    A——never mind;—his tutor, an old ass;   20
A pretty woman—(that's quite natural,
    Or else the thing had hardly come to pass)
A husband rather old, not much in unity
With his young wife—a time, and opportunity.

4

Well—well; the world must turn upon its axis,   25
    And all mankind turn with it, heads or tails,
And live and die, make love and pay our taxes,
    And as the veering wind shifts, shift our sails;
The king commands us, and the doctor quacks us,
    The priest instructs, and so our life exhales,   30
A little breath, love, wine, ambition, fame,
Fighting, devotion, dust,—perhaps a name.

[1] Grade in a British secondary school. A "public school" in England is an endowed institution at which rather high fees are charged. It prepares for the public service or for the university.

5

I said, that Juan had been sent to Cadiz—
    A pretty town, I recollect it well—
'Tis there the mart of the colonial trade is,   35
    (Or was, before Peru learn'd to rebel,)
And such sweet girls—I mean, such graceful ladies,
    Their very walk would make your bosom swell;
I can't describe it, though so much it strike,
Nor liken it—I never saw the like: 40

6

An Arab horse, a stately stag, a barb[2]
    New-broke, a cameleopard,[3] a gazelle,
No—none of these will do—and then their garb,
    Their veil and petticoat—Alas! to dwell
Upon such things would very near absorb   45
    A canto—then their feet and ankles,—well,
Thank Heaven I've got no metaphor quite ready,
(And so, my sober Muse—come, let's be steady—

7

Chaste Muse!—well, if you must, you must)—the veil
    Thrown back a moment with the glancing hand,
While the o'erpowering eye, that turns you pale,   50
    Flashes into the heart:—All sunny land
Of love! when I forget you, may I fail
    To——say my prayers—but never was there plann'd
A dress through which the eyes give such a volley,   55
Excepting the Venetian Fazzioli.[4]

8

But to our tale: the Donna Inez sent
    Her son to Cadiz only to embark;
To stay there had not answer'd her intent,
    But why?—we leave the reader in the dark—   60
'Twas for a voyage the young man was meant,
    As if a Spanish ship were Noah's ark,
To wean him from the wickedness of earth,
And send him like a dove of promise forth.[5]

[2] A Barbary horse, one of a breed noted for speed and endurance.   [3] Giraffe.   [4] A dress worn in Venice in Byron's time.   [5] After the flood, Noah repeatedly sent out a dove from the ark. When the bird failed to return, Noah knew that the land was dry and that it was safe to leave the ark (Genesis 8:8–13).

9

Don Juan bade his valet pack his things   65
    According to direction, then received
A lecture and some money: for four springs
    He was to travel; and though Inez grieved
(As every kind of parting has its stings),
    She hoped he would improve—perhaps believed: 70
A letter, too, she gave (he never read it)
Of good advice—and two or three of credit.

10

In the mean time, to pass her hours away,
    Brave Inez now set up a Sunday school
For naughty children, who would rather play   75
    (Like truant rogues) the devil, or the fool;
Infants of three years old were taught that day,
    Dunces were whipt, or set upon a stool:
The great success of Juan's education
Spurr'd her to teach another generation.   80

11

Juan embark'd—the ship got under way,
    The wind was fair, the water passing rough;
A devil of a sea rolls in that bay,
    As I, who've cross'd it oft, know well enough;
And, standing upon deck, the dashing spray   85
    Flies in one's face, and makes it weather-tough:
And there he stood to take, and take again,
His first—perhaps his last—farewell of Spain.

12

I can't but say it is an awkward sight
    To see one's native land receding through   90
The growing waters; it unmans one quite,
    Especially when life is rather new:
I recollect Great Britain's coast looks white,
    But almost every other country's blue,
When gazing on them, mystified by distance,   95
We enter on our nautical existence.

13

So Juan stood, bewilder'd on the deck:
    The wind sung, cordage strain'd, and sailors swore,
And the ship creak'd, the town became a speck,
    From which away so fair and fast they bore.   100

The best of remedies is a beef-steak
    Against sea-sickness; try it, sir, before
You sneer, and I assure you this is true,
    For I have found it answer—so may you.

14

Don Juan stood, and, gazing from the stern,   105
    Beheld his native Spain receding far:
First partings form a lesson hard to learn,
    Even nations feel this when they go to war;
There is a sort of unexprest concern,
    A kind of shock that sets one's heart ajar: 110
At leaving even the most unpleasant people
And places, one keeps looking at the steeple.

15

But Juan had got many things to leave,
    His mother, and a mistress, and no wife,
So that he had much better cause to grieve   115
    Than many persons more advanced in life;
And if we now and then a sigh must heave
    At quitting even those we quit in strife,
No doubt we weep for those the heart endears—
That is, till deeper griefs congeal our tears.   120

16

So Juan wept, as wept the captive Jews
    By Babel's waters, still remembering Sion:[6]
I'd weep,—but mine is not a weeping Muse,
    And such light griefs are not a thing to die on;
Young men should travel, if but to amuse   125
    Themselves; and the next time their servants tie on
Behind their carriages their new portmanteau,
Perhaps it may be lined with this my canto.[7]

17

And Juan wept, and much he sigh'd and thought,
    While his salt tears dropp'd into the salt sea,   130
"Sweets to the sweet";[8] (I like so much to quote;
    You must excuse this extract,—'t is where she,
The Queen of Denmark, for Ophelia brought

[6] Zion, or Jerusalem; Babel, Babylon. [7] A division of a long poem. A canto, or song, was originally as much of a poem as a minstrel might recite without a break. [8] So says the queen, Gertrude, in *Hamlet* (Act V, Scene 1) as she scatters flowers over the grave of Ophelia, who, after the death of her father, Polonius, loses her sanity and then drowns.

Flowers to the grave;) and, sobbing often, he
Reflected on his present situation, 135
And seriously resolved on reformation.

18

"Farewell, my Spain! a long farewell!" he cried,
　　"Perhaps I may revisit thee no more,
But die, as many an exiled heart hath died,
　　Of its own thirst to see again thy shore: 140
Farewell, where Guadalquivir's waters glide!
　　Farwell, my mother! and, since all is o'er,
Farewell, too, dearest Julia!—(here he drew
Her letter out again, and read it through.)

19

"And oh! if e'er I should forget, I swear— 145
　　But that's impossible, and cannot be—
Sooner shall this blue ocean melt to air,
　　Sooner shall earth resolve itself to sea,
Than I resign thine image, oh, my fair!
　　Or think of anything, excepting thee; 150
A mind diseased no remedy can physic—
(Here the ship gave a lurch, and he grew sea-sick.)

20

"Sooner shall heaven kiss earth—(here he fell sicker)
　　Oh, Julia! what is every other woe?—
(For God's sake let me have a glass of liquor; 155
　　Pedro, Battista, help me down below.)
Julia, my love—(you rascal, Pedro, quicker)—
　　Oh, Julia!—(this curst vessel pitches so)—
Beloved Julia, hear me still beseeching!"
(Here he grew inarticulate with retching.) 160

21

He felt that chilling heaviness of heart,
　　Or rather stomach, which, alas! attends,
Beyond the best apothecary's art,
　　The loss of love, the treachery of friends,
Or death of those we dote on, when a part 165
　　Of us dies with them as each fond hope ends:
No doubt he would have been much more pathetic,
But the sea acted as a strong emetic.

22

Love's a capricious power: I've known it hold
    Out through a fever caused by its own heat,   170
But be much puzzled by a cough and cold,
    And find a quinsy[9] very hard to treat;
Against all noble maladies he's bold,
    But vulgar illnesses don't like to meet,
Nor that a sneeze should interrupt his sigh,   175
Nor inflammations redden his blind eye.

23

But worst of all is nausea, or a pain
    About the lower region of the bowels;
Love, who heroically breathes a vein,[10]
    Shrinks from the application of hot towels,   180
And purgatives are dangerous to his reign,
    Sea-sickness death: his love was perfect, how else
Could Juan's passion, while the billows roar,
Resist his stomach, ne'er at sea before?

COMMENTARY

Don Juan is one of the celebrated books of the nineteenth century, and the odds are that it is quite the gayest. It is a very long poem, consisting of sixteen cantos ranging in length from 60 to 160 stanzas. It breaks off in the middle of a lively erotic adventure which the hero has embarked upon, brought to an end not by the poet's intention but by his death, and that it should stop rather than conclude is entirely appropriate to its nature. The poem has been called formless, and in some sense this is true—at least it can be said that Byron intended it to have no more form than is supplied by a single hero whose adventures and sexual escapades the poet follows, having first contrived them. Byron said that he planned to have Juan die on the guillotine during the French Revolution. But before reaching this grim consummation, he could have carried Juan through as many adventures as it pleased him to write. He intended that the chief interest of the poem should not be in the hero's living his life and dying his death but in the poet's writing the poem. Yet it would be wrong to think of Juan as a "mere puppet"—he is too engaging a figure to be regarded so; we come to have too much affection for his innocence and sweetness and readiness; and this is not to mention Byron's affection for him, as being—although of course not literally—a representation of his own youth. Nevertheless, Juan is not meant to create the illusion of being an autonomous person, like many characters in literature. His dependent status is announced in the poem's opening stanza:

[9] Sore throat.   [10] Allows a vein to be lanced so as to let blood.

I want a hero: an uncommon want,
    When every year and month sends forth a new one,
Till, after cloying the gazettes with cant,
    The age discovers he is not the true one:
Of such as these I should not care to vaunt,
    I'll therefore take our ancient friend Don Juan—
We all have seen him in the pantomime.
Sent to the devil somewhat ere his time.[1]

Having announced his selection of a hero, Byron goes on to tell us what his literary methods are going to be. Most epic poets, he says, start in the middle of the story—he quotes the famous phrase from Horace's *Art of Poetry*—and then, by some device, give the reader an account of what has gone before:

Most epic poets plunge "in medias res"
    (Horace makes this the heroic turnpike road),
And then your hero tells, whene'er you please,
    What went before—by way of episode,
While seated after dinner at his ease,
    Beside his mistress in some soft abode,
Palace, or garden, paradise, or cavern,
Which serves the happy couple for a tavern.

"Most epic poets"—does *Don Juan*, then, presume to think of itself as an epic poem? It does fulfill one requirement of an epic: it is very long. But what epic poem ever spoke in a voice so colloquial and casual, so downright careless, so lacking in high seriousness? And what epic poem was ever at such pains to destroy all possibility of illusion, to make sure that the reader will not give the usual credence to the story he is being told? This epic poem—if that is what it is—mocks the very idea of epic poetry.

Don Juan is, in short, what we call a burlesque. The meaning of that word has been largely lost to a kind of theatrical entertainment which is devoted to rowdy humor, chiefly of a sexual kind, and to female nudity. But the modern burlesque show had its beginnings in actual burlesque—in, that is, the mockery of a serious play that was well known to the audience. Burlesque is a very old form of art—it was highly developed by the ancient Greeks—and many notable and even great works have been conceived in its spirit. Cervantes began *Don Quixote* as a burlesque of the elaborate prose romances of the sixteenth century. Fielding's *Joseph Andrews* is a burlesque of the moralism of Richardson's *Pamela*, and his *Tom Jones* teases the literary conventions of classical antiquity. Jane Austen's *Northanger Abbey* affectionately mocks the terror-novels of the day.

Burlesque is usually directed against a particular literary work or kind of work, with the intention of showing that it is false or foolish. But it may also be directed against the whole enterprise of literature, which it represents as an institution licensed to traduce reality. Parts of Flaubert's *Bouvard and Pécuchet* take this direction, as do parts of the great modern instance of burlesque, Joyce's *Ulysses*. And this is true also of *Don Juan*. The poet's ceaseless intrusion into

---

[1] As I remarked in the headnote, Byron's hero has in fact very little in common with the legendary Don Juan.

his story, his avowed manipulation of it, his "asides," which must surely occupy more space than the narrative, his open references to himself, all enforce the idea that he is much too sensible a man to be taken in by the conventions of poetry, that he knows literature for what it really is, an elaborate game. He is perfectly willing to play the game, being the best-natured of men, but he will not pretend, or ask the reader to believe, that it is reality.

But although the episode of Juan struggling to maintain his high-minded sorrow against the assaults of the rising nausea of his seasickness is a notable example of burlesque, it quite transcends its genre. It goes beyond the mockery of a literary tradition, that of the faithful grieving lover, to raise radically subversive questions about the dignity of human nature and the autonomy of the human mind.

In any culture we are pretty sure to find two opposing views of man's nature. According to one view, man is at least potentially a being of great dignity, a spiritual being in the sense that he is not wholly or finally conditioned by material considerations. His dignity, spirituality, and freedom derive from his power and courage. In simpler societies power and courage are thought to belong almost exclusively to socially dominant figures, to the king, the warrior, and the priest. All these personages express by their mode of dress and by their bearing and manner of speech the dignity they claim for themselves. (The comments on the "kingliness" of Wordsworth's old Leech-gatherer [page 480] are relevant here—one of the tendencies of the literature of the late eighteenth and early nineteenth centuries was to assert the dignity of people not of the dominant classes.) The other view concentrates upon man as an animal creature, who provokes not respect but laughter. Contrary to a common assumption, even quite primitive peoples do not take their animal functions wholly for granted; in every culture sexuality and defecation are thought to be funny— they are "accepted" as "natural" but they are thought to derogate from human dignity; they are always joked about. The same is true of the impulse to self-preservation: cowardice is thought to be "natural"—and funny.

Among the Greeks these two views of man's nature were expressed in two distinct literary forms. The view of man as a dignified, free, and spiritual being was represented by tragedy, with its persons of royal or noble birth, its grave and exalted language, its conscious suppression of all petty and sordid considerations. Comedy represented the view that man was bound by his animal nature; in the frankest possible way it took account of all the exigencies of animality, all the "low" conditions of human existence.

Aristotle said that tragedy showed men as better than they really are and that comedy showed men as worse than they really are. And of course he is right in suggesting that neither the bias of tragedy nor that of comedy tells the whole truth. But in defiance of Aristotle, as it were, comedy does claim truth for itself. If tragedy denies the comic view of man, it does so implicitly and silently; but comedy is quite often explicit in its opposition to tragedy— again and again it says straight out that the form and manner of tragedy are false and highfalutin. It claims reality for itself, insisting that reality is what is comprised by the "facts of life," by man's need and greed for food and drink, by his running away from danger, and by his copulation and defecation.

In general it can be said of the Greeks that they were able to hold the two views of man's nature in balance. They gave as much sanction to the subversive view of comedy as to the ideal view of tragedy. Yet at least one Greek, Plato, was distressed by man's double nature; his philosophy makes a strong commitment to the belief that man is most truly himself when he is free of the animal conditions of life. Christianity followed Plato in this—the essence of Christian morality lies in the wish to overcome the bondage of flesh. The way in which Christianity describes this bondage varies with the changes in the secular culture. The seventeenth century, for example, was a period of great intellectual achievement, and Christian thought at that time undertook to check intellectual pride by reminding man how conditioned by physical things his intellect was. It did this, we may say, in the manner of burlesque. The Christian poet John Donne took wry note of the fact that at a moment when his thoughts were fixed on God in prayer and meditation, a fly buzzing around his head could distract his attention from its great object and that no effort of will could restore his rapt concentration until the fly was silenced. And Pascal, one of the great mathematicians of all times as well as a profound psychologist of the religious emotions, based his whole sense of the religious life upon similar observations, upon the discrepancy between man's "greatness" and his "littleness," reminding us that, powerful as the human intellect is, a man is never in full control of the right exercise of his mind, which is always at the mercy of the most trivial material circumstances.

The early nineteenth century was an age that took pride not so much in intellectual as in emotional power; it looked upon love and passion as an indication of human freedom and dignity, and perhaps no one had done more to establish this idea than Byron himself. Whatever else Byron is burlesquing in *Don Juan* he is burlesquing his own early work, in which love and passion asserted themselves without regard to the facts of animal existence. He did indeed represent love and passion as meeting with opposition from the world and as ensuing often in pain and defeat, but this of course constitutes anything but a skeptical comment upon them—in literature the pain and defeat of a person who lives according to his belief in his spiritual nature are taken to be the affirmation of spirit itself. What Byron is now saying, however, is reductive enough; he is proposing that it is not by the great catastrophes that the life of spirit is brought into question but by the small ones. Man's sense of his autonomy and dignity is not limited by his tragic sufferings but by those that are traditionally thought to be comic—the cold in the head and the passing afflictions of the stomach.

PERCY BYSSHE SHELLEY

1792–1822

OZYMANDIAS[1]

I met a traveller from an antique land
Who said: Two vast and trunkless legs of stone
Stand in the desert. Near them, on the sand,
Half sunk, a shattered visage lies, whose frown,
And wrinkled lip, and sneer of cold command,   5
Tell that its sculptor well those passions read
Which yet survive, stamped on these lifeless things,
The hand that mocked them and the heart that fed;
And on the pedestal these words appear:
"My name is Ozymandias, king of kings: 10
Look on my works, ye Mighty, and despair!"
Nothing beside remains. Round the decay
Of that colossal wreck, boundless and bare
The lone and level sands stretch far away.

SONNET: ENGLAND IN 1819

An old, mad, blind, despised, and dying king,—
Princes, the dregs of their dull race, who flow
Through public scorn,—mud from a muddy spring;
Rulers who neither see, nor feel, nor know,
But leech-like to their fainting country cling,   5
Till they drop, blind in blood, without a blow;
A people starved and stabbed in the untilled field,—
An army, which liberticide[1] and prey
Makes a two-edged sword to all who wield,—
Golden and sanguine laws which tempt and slay,—   10
Religion Christless, Godless—a book sealed;
A Senate, Time's worst statute unrepealed,—
Are graves, from which a glorious Phantom may
Burst, to illumine our tempestuous day.

[1] Rameses II, Pharaoh of Egypt, whose statue stood at Thebes.

[1] Destruction of liberty.

TO NIGHT

Swiftly walk over the western Wave,
      Spirit of Night!
Out of the misty eastern cave
Where, all the long and lone daylight,
Thou wovest dreams of joy and fear,   5
Which make thee terrible and dear,—
      Swift be thy flight!

Wrap thy form in a mantle gray,
      Star-inwrought!
Blind with thine hair the eyes of Day,   10
Kiss her until she be wearied out,
Then wander o'er city, and sea, and land,
Touching all with thine opiate wand—
      Come, long-sought!

When I arose and saw the dawn,   15
      I sighed for thee;
When light rode high, and the dew was gone,
And noon lay heavy on flower and tree,
And the weary Day turned to his rest,
Lingering like an unloved guest,   20
      I sighed for thee.

Thy brother Death came, and cried,
      Wouldst thou me?
Thy sweet child Sleep, the filmy-eyed,
Murmured like a noon-tide bee,   25
Shall I nestle near thy side?
Wouldst thou me?—and I replied,
      No, . . . not thee!

Death will come when thou art dead,
      Soon, too soon—   30
Sleep will come when thou art fled;
Of neither would I ask the boon
I asked of thee, belovèd Night—
Swift be thine approaching flight,
      Come soon, soon!   35

TO ———

Music, when soft voices die,
Vibrates in the memory—
Odours, when sweet violets sicken,
Live within the sense they quicken.

Rose leaves, when the rose is dead,   5
Are heaped for the belovèd's bed;
And so thy thoughts, when thou art gone,
Love itself shall slumber on.

ODE TO THE WEST WIND

I

O wild West Wind, thou breath of Autumn's being,
Thou, from whose unseen presence the leaves dead
Are driven, like ghosts from an enchanter fleeing,

Yellow, and black, and pale, and hectic red,
Pestilence-stricken multitudes: O thou,   5
Who chariotest to their dark wintry bed

The wingèd seeds, where they lie cold and low,
Each like a corpse within its grave, until
Thine azure sister of the spring shall blow

Her clarion o'er the dreaming earth, and fill   10
(Driving sweet buds like flocks to feed in air)
With living hues and odors plain and hill:

Wild spirit, which art moving everywhere;
Destroyer and preserver;[1] hear, oh hear!

[1] The seemingly opposed powers of destruction and preservation were frequently
attributed to a single god in ancient times.

Thou on whose stream, 'mid the steep sky's commotion,   15
Loose clouds like earth's decaying leaves are shed,
Shook from the tangled boughs of Heaven and Ocean,

Angels of rain and lightning: there are spread
On the blue surface of thine airy surge,
Like the bright hair uplifted from the head   20

Of some fierce Maenad,[2] even from the dim verge
Of the horizon to the zenith's height
The locks of the approaching storm. Thou dirge

Of the dying year, to which this closing night
Will be the dome of a vast sepulchre,   25
Vaulted with all thy congregated might

Of vapours, from whose solid atmosphere
Black rain, and fire, and hail will burst: O, hear!

3

Thou who didst waken from his summer dreams
The blue Mediterranean, where he lay,   30
Lulled by the coil of his crystalline streams,

Beside a pumice[3] isle in Baiæ's bay,[4]
And saw in sleep old palaces and towers
Quivering within the wave's intenser day,

All overgrown with azure moss and flowers   35
So sweet, the sense faints picturing them! Thou
For whose path the Atlantic's level powers

2 In Greek mythology, mad or frenzied women who attended the god Dionysus, or
Bacchus.   3 Obsidian.   4 Bay of Naples. Baiae is a town on an inlet of the bay.

Cleave themselves into chasms, while far below
The sea-blooms and the oozy woods which wear
The sapless foliage of the ocean, know   40

Thy voice, and suddenly grow gray with fear,
And tremble and despoil themselves: O hear!

4

If I were a dead leaf thou mightest bear;
If I were a swift cloud to fly with thee;
A wave to pant beneath thy power, and share   45

The impulse of thy strength, only less free
Than thou, O, uncontrollable! If even
I were as in my boyhood, and could be

The comrade of thy wanderings over heaven,
As then, when to outstrip thy skiey speed   50
Scarce seemed a vision; I would ne'er have striven

As thus with thee in prayer in my sore need,
Oh! lift me as a wave, a leaf, a cloud!
I fall upon the thorns of life! I bleed!

A heavy weight of hours has chained and bowed   55
One too like thee: tameless, and swift, and proud.

5

Make me thy lyre, even as the forest is:
What if my leaves are falling like its own!
The tumult of thy mighty harmonies

Will take from both a deep, autumnal tone,   60
Sweet though in sadness. Be thou, Spirit fierce,
My spirit! Be thou me, impetuous one!

Drive my dead thoughts over the universe
Like withered leaves to quicken a new birth!
And, by the incantation of this verse,   65

Scatter, as from an unextinguished hearth
Ashes and sparks, my words among mankind!
Be through my lips to unawakened earth

The trumpet of a prophecy, O, Wind,
If Winter comes, can Spring be far behind? 70

JOHN KEATS
1795-1821

ON FIRST LOOKING INTO
CHAPMAN'S HOMER[1]

Much have I travell'd in the realms of gold,
    And many goodly states and kingdoms seen;
    Round many western islands have I been
Which bards in fealty to Apollo[2] hold.
Oft of one wide expanse had I been told 5
    That deep-brow'd Homer ruled as his demesne;
    Yet did I never breathe its pure serene
Till I heard Chapman speak out loud and bold:
Then felt I like some watcher of the skies
    When a new planet swims into his ken; 10
Or like stout Cortez[3] when with eagle eyes
    He star'd at the Pacific—and all his men
Look'd at each other with a wild surmise—
    Silent, upon a peak in Darien.[4]

WHEN I HAVE FEARS

When I have fears that I may cease to be
    Before my pen has glean'd my teeming brain,

[1] George Chapman, an Elizabethan poet, translated both the *Iliad* (1611) and the *Odyssey* (1614) of Homer. [2] God of light and medicine and probably the most widely revered god of ancient Greece. [3] A mistake for Balboa. [4] Former name for Panama.

Before high-pilèd books, in charact'ry,
    Hold like rich garners the full-ripen'd grain;
When I behold, upon the night's starr'd face,   5
    Huge cloudy symbols of a high romance,[1]
And think that I may never live to trace
    Their shadows, with the magic hand of chance;
And when I feel, fair creature of an hour!
    That I shall never look upon thee more,   10
Never have relish in the faery power
    Of unreflecting love!—then on the shore
Of the wide world I stand alone, and think
Till love and fame to nothingness do sink.

LA BELLE DAME SANS MERCI[1]

O what can ail thee, knight-at-arms,
    Alone and palely loitering?
The sedge has wither'd from the lake,
    And no birds sing.

O what can ail thee, knight at arms,   5
    So haggard and so woe-begone?
The squirrel's granary is full,
    And the harvest's done.

I see a lily on thy brow,
    With anguish moist and fever dew,   10
And on thy cheeks a fading rose
    Fast withereth too.

"I met a lady in the meads,
    Full beautiful—a faery's child;
Her hair was long, her foot was light,   15
    And her eyes were wild.

"I made a garland for her head,
    And bracelets too, and fragrant zone;[2]
She look'd at me as she did love,
    And made sweet moan.   20

---

[1] Here, romantic story.

[1] The title can be translated as "The Fair Lady without Pity." Keats revised this poem, but his first version, which is printed here, is generally regarded as superior.   [2] An encircling band, belt, girdle.

"I set her on my pacing steed,
　　And nothing else saw all day long,
For side-long would she bend, and sing
　　A faery's song.

"She found me roots of relish sweet,
　　And honey wild, and manna dew, ← _spiritual food_
And sure in language strange she said—
　　'I love thee true.'　　　　　　　　　　　　　　　25

"She took me to her elfin grot,[3] – _womblike_
　　And there she wept, and sigh'd full sore,
And there I shut her wild wild eyes
　　With kisses four.　　　　　　　　　　　　　　　30

"And there she lullèd me asleep,
　　And there I dream'd—Ah! woe betide!—
The latest dream I ever dream'd
　　On the cold hill side.　　　　　　　　　　　　　35

"I saw pale kings and princes too,
　　Pale warriors, death-pale were they all;
They cried—'La Belle Dame sans Merci
　　Hath thee in thrall!'　　　　　　　　　　　　　40

"I saw their starved lips in the gloom,
　　With horrid warning gapèd wide, —— _(warning dream)_
And I awoke, and found me here,
　　On the cold hill's side.

"And this is why I sojourn here,　　　　　　　　45
　　Alone and palely loitering,
Though the sedge is wither'd from the lake,
　　And no birds sing."

at this point Keats was actually ~~dreaming~~ dying of Tuberculosis.

ODE ON A GRECIAN URN

Thou still unravish'd bride of quietness,
　　Thou foster-child of silence and slow time,

[3] Fairy cave.

Sylvan historian, who canst thus express
　　A flowery tale more sweetly than our rhyme:
What leaf-fring'd legend haunts about thy shape　　　　5
　　Of dieties or mortals, or of both,
　　　　In Tempe[1] or the dales of Arcady?[2]
What men or gods are these? What maidens loth?
　　What mad pursuit? What struggle to escape?
　　　　What pipes and timbrels? What wild ecstasy?　　10

Heard melodies are sweet, but those unheard
　　Are sweeter; therefore, ye soft pipes, play on;
Not to the sensual ear, but, more endear'd,
　　Pipe to the spirit ditties of no tone:
Fair youth, beneath the trees, thou canst not leave　　15
　　Thy song, nor ever can those trees be bare;
　　　　Bold lover, never, never canst thou kiss,
Though winning near the goal—yet, do not grieve;
　　She cannot fade, though thou hast not thy bliss,
　　　　Forever wilt thou love, and she be fair!　　　　20

Ah, happy, happy boughs! that cannot shed
　　Your leaves, nor ever bid the Spring adieu;
And, happy melodist, unwearièd,
　　For ever piping songs for ever new;
More happy love! more happy, happy love!　　　　25
　　For ever warm and still to be enjoy'd,
　　　　For ever panting, and for ever young;
All breathing human passion far above,
　　That leaves a heart high-sorrowful and cloy'd,
　　　　A burning forehead, and a parching tongue.　　30

Who are these coming to the sacrifice?
　　To what green altar, O mysterious priest,
Lead'st thou that heifer lowing at the skies,
　　And all her silken flanks with garlands drest?
What little town by river or sea shore,　　　　35
　　Or mountain-built with peaceful citadel,
　　　　Is emptied of this folk, this pious morn?
And, little town, thy streets for evermore
　　Will silent be; and not a soul to tell
　　　　Why thou art desolate, can e'er return.　　　　40

[1] The name of a valley in Thessaly, in ancient Greece, that came to be a synonym for any beautiful rural spot.　　[2] Arcadia, a region in ancient Greece that is taken as the ideal region of rural felicity.

O Attic[3] shape! Fair attitude! with brede[4]
    Of marble men and maidens overwrought,
With forest branches and the trodden weed;
    Thou, silent form, dost tease us out of thought
As doth eternity: Cold Pastoral!   45
    When old age shall this generation waste,
        Thou shalt remain, in midst of other woe
Than ours, a friend to man, to whom thou say'st,
    Beauty is truth, truth beauty,—that is all
        Ye know on earth, and all ye need to know.   50

TO AUTUMN

Season of mists and mellow fruitfulness,
    Close bosom-friend of the maturing sun;
Conspiring with him how to load and bless
    With fruit the vines that round the thatch-eaves run;
To bend with apples the moss'd cottage-trees,   5
    And fill all fruit with ripeness to the core;
        To swell the gourd, and plump the hazel shells
    With a sweet kernel; to set budding more,
And still more, later flowers for the bees,
Until they think warm days will never cease,   10
        For summer has o'er-brimm'd their clammy cells.

Who hath not seen thee oft amid thy store?
    Sometimes whoever seeks abroad may find
Thee sitting careless on a granary floor,
    Thy hair soft-lifted by the winnowing wind;   15
Or on a half-reap'd furrow sound asleep,
    Drows'd with the fume of poppies, while thy hook
        Spares the next swath and all its twinèd flowers:
And sometimes like a gleaner thou dost keep
    Steady thy laden head across a brook;   20
    Or by a cider-press, with patient look,
        Thou watchest the last oozings hours by hours.

Where are the songs of Spring? Ay, where are they?
    Think not of them, thou hast thy music too,—

[3] Of Attica, the ancient region of which Athens was the capital. *Attic* has come to suggest simplicity, purity, and refinement.   [4] Embroidery, interweaving.

While barrèd clouds bloom the soft-dying day,
    And touch the stubble-plains with rosy hue;
Then in a wailful choir the small gnats mourn
    Among the river sallows,[1] borne aloft
        Or sinking as the light wind lives or dies;
And full-grown lambs loud bleat from hilly bourn,[2]   30
    Hedge-crickets sing; and now with treble soft
    The red-breast whistles from a garden-croft;
        And gathering swallows twitter in the skies.

ODE ON MELANCHOLY

No, no, go not to Lethe,[1] neither twist
    Wolf's-bane,[2] tight-rooted, for its poisonous wine;
Nor suffer thy pale forehead to be kiss'd
    By nightshade, ruby grape of Proserpine;[3]
Make not your rosary of yew-berries,   5
    Nor let the beetle, nor the death-moth[4] be
        Your mournful Psyche,[5] nor the downy owl[6]
A partner in your sorrow's mysteries;
    For shade to shade will come too drowsily,
        And drown the wakeful anguish of the soul.   10

But when the melancholy fit shall fall
    Sudden from heaven like a weeping cloud,
That fosters the droop-headed flowers all,
    And hides the green hill in an April shroud;
Then glut thy sorrow on a morning rose,   15
    Or on the rainbow of the salt sand-wave,
        Or on the wealth of globèd peonies;
Or if thy mistress some rich anger shows,
    Emprison her soft hand, and let her rave,
        And feed deep, deep upon her peerless eyes.   20

[1] Willows.   [2] Domain, land.

[1] In Greek mythology, a river in Hades whose water, if drunk, causes forgetfulness; hence, forgetfulness, oblivion.   [2] Wolf's-bane, nightshade, and Yew-berries are poisonous plants.   [3] Queen of Hades.   [4] Both the beetle and the death's-head moth have markings on the back of the thorax suggesting a human skull or death's-head.   [5] In Greek, the soul, which was recognized as the seat of the passions. It was pictorially represented as a beautiful maiden with the wings of a butterfly, and sometimes as a butterfly.   [6] The note of the owl is generally thought to be doleful.

She dwells with Beauty—Beauty that must die;
    And Joy, whose hand is ever at his lips
Bidding adieu; and aching Pleasure nigh,
    Turning to poison while the bee-mouth sips:
Ay, in the very temple of Delight   25
      Veil'd Melancholy has her sovran shrine,
          Though seen of none save him whose strenuous tongue
Can burst Joy's grape against his palate fine;
      His soul shall taste the sadness of her might,
          And be among her cloudy trophies hung.   30

ODE TO A NIGHTINGALE

My heart aches, and a drowsy numbness pains
    My sense, as though of hemlock[1] I had drunk,
Or emptied some dull opiate to the drains
    One minute past, and Lethe-wards[2] had sunk.
'Tis not through envy of thy happy lot,   5
    But being too happy in thine happiness—
      That thou, light wingèd Dryad[3] of the trees,
        In some melodious plot
Of beechen green, and shadows numberless,
      Singest of summer in full-throated ease.   10

O, for a draught of vintage! that hath been
    Cooled a long age in the deep-delvèd earth,
Tasting of Flora[4] and the country green,
    Dance, and Provençal song,[5] and sunburnt mirth!
O for a beaker full of the warm South,   15
    Full of the true, the blushful Hippocrene,[6]
      With beaded bubbles winking at the brim,
        And purple-stainèd mouth;
That I might drink, and leave the world unseen,
      And with thee fade away into the forest dim: 20

Fade far away, dissolve, and quite forget
    What thou among the leaves hast never known,

[1] A poisonous potion obtained from the hemlock.   [2] Lethe, in Greek mythology, was the river of oblivion from which all dead souls drank as they passed into Hades.   [3] Tree nymph.   [4] The Roman goddess of flowers and gardens.   [5] Song of Provence, a region in the south of France noted, during the Middle Ages, for its troubadours, or lyric poets. [6] Water of the Hippocrene, the fountain of the Muses in Greek mythology; hence, poetic inspiration.

The weariness, the fever, and the fret
    Here, where men sit and hear each other groan;
Where palsy shakes a few, sad, last gray hairs,
    Where youth grows pale, and specter-thin, and dies;   25
        Where but to think is to be full of sorrow
           And leaden-eyed despairs,
    Where Beauty cannot keep her lustrous eyes,
        Or new Love pine at them beyond tomorrow.   30

Away! away! for I will fly to thee,
    Not charioted by Bacchus and his pards,[7]
But on the viewless[8] wings of Poesy,
    Though the dull brain perplexes and retards:
Already with thee! tender is the night,   35
    And haply the Queen-Moon is on her throne,
        Clustered around by all her starry Fays;[9]
          But here there is no light,
Save what from heaven is with the breezes blown
    Through verdurous glooms and winding mossy ways.   40

I cannot see what flowers are at my feet,
    Nor what soft incense hangs upon the boughs,
But, in embalmèd[10] darkness, guess each sweet
    Wherewith the seasonable month endows
The grass, the thicket, and the fruit-tree wild;   45
    White hawthorn, and the pastoral eglantine;
        Fast fading violets covered up in leaves;
          And mid-May's eldest child.
The coming musk-rose, full of dewy wine,
    The murmurous haunt of flies on summer eves.   50

Darkling[11] I listen; and, for many a time,
    I have been half in love with easeful Death,
Called him soft names in many a musèd rime,
    To take into the air my quiet breath;
Now more than ever seems it rich to die,   55
    To cease upon the midnight with no pain,
        While thou art pouring forth thy soul abroad
          In such an ecstasy!
Still wouldst thou sing, and I have ears in vain—
    To thy high requiem become a sod.   60

[7] Leopards or panthers. Bacchus, or Dionysus, the god of wine, is frequently represented in a chariot drawn by tigers.   [8] Invisible.   [9] Fairies.   [10] Aromatic, balmy.   [11] In the dark.

Thou wast not born for death, immortal Bird!
　　No hungry generations tread thee down;
The voice I hear this passing night was heard
　　In ancient days by emperor and clown:
Perhaps the self-same song that found a path　　　　　65
　　Through the sad heart of Ruth, when, sick for home,
　　　　She stood in tears amid the alien corn;[12]
　　　　　　The same that oft-times hath
Charmed magic casements, opening on the foam
　　Of perilous seas, in faery lands forlorn.　　　　　70

Forlorn! the very word is like a bell
　　To toll me back from thee to my sole self,
Adieu! the fancy cannot cheat so well
　　As she is famed to do, deceiving elf.
Adieu! adieu! thy plaintive anthem fades　　　　　75
　　Past the near meadows, over the still stream,
　　　　Up the hillside; and now 'tis buried deep
　　　　　In the next valley glades:
　　Was it a vision, or a waking dream?
　　　　Fled is that music—Do I wake or sleep?　　　　　80

RALPH WALDO EMERSON
1 8 0 3 – 1 8 8 2

GIVE ALL TO LOVE

Give all to love;
Obey thy heart;
Friends, kindred, days,
Estate, good-fame,
Plans, credit and the Muse,—　　　　　5
Nothing refuse.

'Tis a brave master;
Let it have scope:

[12] See the Book of Ruth, Chapter 2.

Follow it utterly,
Hope beyond hope:
High and more high
It dives into noon,
With wing unspent,
Untold intent;
But it is a god,
Knows its own path
And the outlets of the sky.

It was never for the mean;
It requireth courage stout.
Souls above doubt,
Valor unbending,
It will reward,—
They shall return
More than they were,
And ever ascending.

Leave all for love;
Yet, hear me, yet,
One word more thy heart behoved,
One pulse more of firm endeavor,—
Keep thee today,
Tomorrow, forever,
Free as an Arab
Of thy beloved.

Cling with life to the maid;
But when the surprise,
First vague shadow of surmise
Flits across her bosom young,
Of a joy apart from thee,
Free be she, fancy-free;
Nor thou detain her vesture's hem,
Nor the palest rose she flung
From her summer diadem.

Though thou loved her as thyself,
As a self of purer clay,
Though her parting dims the day,
Stealing grace from all alive;
Heartily know,
When half-gods go,
The gods arrive.

BRAHMA[1]

If the red slayer thinks he slays,
    Or if the slain think he is slain,
They know not well the subtle ways
    I keep, and pass, and turn again.

Far or forgot to me is near;   5
    Shadow and sunlight are the same;
The vanished gods to me appear;
    And one to me are shame and fame.

They reckon ill who leave me out;
    When me they fly, I am the wings;   10
I am the doubter and the doubt,
    And I the hymn the Brahmin[2] sings.

The strong gods[3] pine for my abode,
    And pine in vain the sacred Seven;[4]
But thou, meek lover of the good!   15
    Find me, and turn thy back on heaven.

EDGAR ALLAN POE
1809–1849

TO HELEN

Helen, thy beauty is to me
    Like those Nicèan[1] barks of yore,
That gently, o'er a perfumed sea,

---

[1] The creator god of Hinduism. This poem was inspired by several passages of the *Bhagavat-Gita*. [2] Member of the priestly and meditative caste of Hinduism. [3] Indra, god of the sky and wielder of the thunderbolt; Agni, god of fire; and Yoma, god of death and judgment. These gods eventually will be absorbed into Brahma. [4] Maharshis or highest saints.

[1] Of Nicaea, an ancient city in Asia Minor.

The weary, way-worn wanderer bore
To his own native shore.   5

On desperate seas long wont to roam,
  Thy hyacinth hair, thy classic face,
Thy Naiad[2] airs have brought me home
  To the glory that was Greece
And the grandeur that was Rome.   10

Lo! in yon brilliant window-niche
  How statue-like I see thee stand,
  The agate lamp within thy hand!
Ah, Psyche,[3] from the regions which
  Are Holy Land!   15

ALFRED, LORD TENNYSON
1809–1892

ULYSSES

It little profits that an idle king,
By this still hearth, among these barren crags,
Match'd with an agèd wife, I mete and dole[1]
Unequal laws unto a savage race,
That hoard, and sleep, and feed, and know not me.   5
I cannot rest from travel; I will drink
Life to the lees; all times I have enjoy'd
Greatly, have suffer'd greatly, both with those
That loved me, and alone; on shore, and when
Through scudding drifts the rainy Hyades[2]   10
Vext the dim sea: I am become a name;
For always roaming with a hungry heart
Much have I seen and known;—cities of men

   [2] A water nymph.   [3] The reference is to the legend of Psyche, who, beloved of Cupid, lit a lamp to see him while asleep.

   [1] The speaker is Ulysses (Odysseus). The time is after his return to his kingdom of Ithaca from the travels described in Homer's *Odyssey*.   [2] A cluster of stars believed to cause rainy weather.

And manners, climates, councils, governments,
Myself not least, but honour'd of them all;—
And drunk delight of battle with my peers,
Far on the ringing plains of windy Troy.
I am a part of all that I have met;
Yet all experience is an arch wherethrough
Gleams that untravell'd world, whose margin fades
For ever and for ever when I move.
How dull it is to pause, to make an end,
To rust unburnish'd, not to shine in use!
As though to breathe were life! Life piled on life
Were all too little, and of one to me
Little remains; but every hour is saved
From that eternal silence, something more,
A bringer of new things; and vile it were
For some three suns to store and hoard myself,
And this grey spirit yearning in desire
To follow knowledge, like a sinking star,
Beyond the utmost bound of human thought.

     This is my son, mine own Telemachus,
To whom I leave the sceptre and the isle—
Well-loved of me, discerning to fulfil
This labour, by slow prudence to make mild
A rugged people, and through soft degrees
Subdue them to the useful and the good.
Most blameless is he, centred in the sphere
Of common duties, decent not to fail
In offices of tenderness, and pay
Meet adoration to my household gods,
When I am gone. He works his work, I mine.

     There lies the port; the vessel puffs her sail;
There gloom the dark, broad seas. My mariners,
Souls that have toil'd, and wrought, and thought with me—
That ever with a frolic welcome took
The thunder and the sunshine, and opposed
Free hearts, free foreheads—you and I are old;
Old age hath yet his honour and his toil;
Death closes all; but something ere the end,
Some work of noble note, may yet be done,
Not unbecoming men that strove with Gods.
The lights begin to twinkle from the rocks;
The long day wanes; the slow moon climbs; the deep
Moans round with many voices. Come, my friends,
'Tis not too late to seek a newer world.
Push off, and sitting well in order smite
The sounding furrows; for my purpose holds
To sail beyond the sunset, and the baths
Of all the western stars, until I die.
It may be that the gulfs will wash us down;

It may be we shall touch the Happy Isles,[3]
And see the great Achilles,[4] whom we knew.
Though much is taken, much abides; and though   65
We are not now that strength which in old days
Moved earth and heaven; that which we are, we are;—
One equal temper of heroic hearts,
Made weak by time and fate, but strong in will
To strive, to seek, to find, and not to yield.   70

THE LOTOS-EATERS[1]

"Courage!" he[2] said, and pointed toward the land,
"This mounting wave will roll us shoreward soon."
In the afternoon they came unto a land
In which it seemed always afternoon.
All round the coast the languid air did swoon,   5
Breathing like one that hath a weary dream.
Full-faced above the valley stood the moon;
And like a downward smoke, the slender stream
Along the cliff to fall and pause and fall did seem.

A land of streams; some, like a downward smoke,   10
Slow-dropping veils of thinnest lawn, did go;
And some through wavering lights and shadows broke,
Rolling a slumbrous sheet of foam below.
They saw the gleaming river seaward flow
From the inner land; far off, three mountain-tops,   15
Three silent pinnacles of aged snow,
Stood sunset-flush'd; and, dew'd with showery drops,
Up-clomb the shadowy pine above the woven copse.

The charmed sunset linger'd low adown
In the red West; through mountain clefts the dale   20
Was seen far inland, and the yellow down
Border'd with palm, and many a winding vale
And meadow, set with slender galingale;[3]
A land where all things always seemed the same!

[3] Elysium, the Greek paradise for heroes.   [4] Hero of the *Iliad*, as Ulysses is of the
Odyssey. Both epics deal with the Trojan war.

[1] In Homer's *Odyssey*, the Lotophagi, or lotos-eaters, ate fruit that caused a state of
dreamy forgetfulness and loss of all desire to return home.   [2] Odysseus, or Ulysses.   [3] A
kind of sedge.

And round about the keel with faces pale,
Dark faces pale against that rosy flame,
The mild-eyed melancholy Lotos-eaters came.

Branches they bore of that enchanted stem,
Laden with flower and fruit, whereof they gave
To each, but whoso did receive of them,
And taste, to him the gushing of the wave
Far far away did seem to mourn and rave
On alien shores; and if his fellow spake,
His voice was thin, as voices from the grave;
And deep-asleep he seem'd, yet all awake,
And music in his ears his beating heart did make.

They sat them down upon the yellow sand,
Between the sun and moon upon the shore;
And sweet it was to dream of Fatherland,
Of child, and wife, and slave; but evermore
Most weary seem'd the sea, weary the oar,
Weary the wandering fields of barren foam.
Then someone said, "We will return no more";
And all at once they sang, "Our island home
Is far beyond the wave; we will no longer roam."

CHORIC SONG

I

There is sweet music here that softer falls
Than petals from blown roses on the grass,
Or night-dews on still waters between walls
Of shadowy granite, in a gleaming pass;
Music that gentlier on the spirit lies,
Than tired eyelids upon tired eyes;
Music that brings sweet sleep down from the blissful skies.
Here are cool mosses deep,
And through the moss the ivies creep,
And in the stream the long-leaved flowers weep,
And from the craggy ledge the poppy hangs in sleep.

II

Why are we weigh'd upon with heaviness,
And utterly consumed with sharp distress,

While all things else have rest from weariness?
All things have rest: why should we toil alone,   60
We only toil, who are the first of things,
And make perpetual moan,
Still from one sorrow to another thrown:
Nor ever fold our wings,
And cease from wanderings,   65
Nor steep our brows in slumber's holy balm;
Nor hearken what the inner spirit sings,
"There is no joy but calm!"
Why should we only toil, the roof and crown of things?

III

Lo! in the middle of the wood,   70
The folded leaf is woo'd from out the bud
With winds upon the branch, and there
Grows green and broad, and takes no care,
Sun-steep'd at noon, and in the moon
Nightly dew-fed; and turning yellow   75
Falls, and floats adown the air.
Lo! sweeten'd with the summer light,
The full-juiced apple, waxing over-mellow,
Drops in a silent autumn night.
All its allotted length of days   80
The flower ripens in its place,
Ripens and fades, and falls, and hath no toil,
Fast-rooted in the fruitful soil.

IV

Hateful is the dark-blue sky,
Vaulted o'er the dark-blue sea.   85
Death is the end of life; ah, why
Should life all labour be?
Let us alone. Time driveth onward fast
And in a little while our lips are dumb.
Let us alone. What is it that will last?   90
All things are taken from us, and become
Portions and parcels of the dreadful Past.
Let us alone. What pleasure can we have
To war with evil? Is there any peace
In ever climbing up the climbing wave?   95
All things have rest, and ripen toward the grave
In silence—ripen, fall and cease:
Give us long rest or death, dark death, or dreamful ease.

V

How sweet it were, hearing the downward stream,
With half-shut eyes ever to seem   100
Falling asleep in a half-dream!
To dream and dream, like yonder amber light,
Which will not leave the myrrh-bush on the height;
To hear each other's whisper'd speech;
Eating the Lotos day by day,   105
To watch the crisping ripples on the beach,
And tender curving lines of creamy spray;
To lend our hearts and spirits wholly
To the influence of mild-minded melancholy;
To muse and brood and live again in memory,   110
With those old faces of our infancy
Heap'd over with a mound of grass,
Two handfuls of white dust, shut in an urn of brass!

VI

Dear is the memory of our wedded lives,
And dear the last embraces of our wives   115
And their warm tears; but all hath suffer'd change;
For surely now our household hearths are cold:
Our sons inherit us: our looks are strange:
And we should come like ghosts to trouble joy.
Or else the island princes over-bold   120
Have eat our substance, and the minstrel sings
Before them of the ten-years' war in Troy,
And our great deeds, as half-forgotten things.
Is there confusion in the little isle?
Let what is broken so remain.   125
The Gods are hard to reconcile:
'Tis hard to settle order once again.
There *is* confusion worse than death,
Trouble on trouble, pain on pain,
Long labour unto agèd breath,   130
Sore task to hearts worn out with many wars
And eyes grown dim with gazing on the pilot-stars.

VII

But, propt on beds of amaranth and moly,
How sweet (while warm airs lull us, blowing lowly)
With half-dropt eyelids still,   135
Beneath a heaven dark and holy,

To watch the long bright river drawing slowly
His waters from the purple hill—
To hear the dewy echoes calling
From cave to cave through the thick-twinèd vine—   140
To watch the emerald-colour'd water falling
Through many a wov'n acanthus-wreath divine!
Only to hear and see the far-off sparkling brine,
Only to hear were sweet, stretch'd out beneath the pine.

VIII

The Lotos blooms below the barren peak: 145
The Lotos blows by every winding creek:
All day the wind breathes low with mellower tone;
Through every hollow cave and alley lone
Round and round the spicy downs the yellow Lotos-dust is blown.
We have had enough of action, and of motion we,   150
Roll'd to starboard, roll'd to larboard, when the surge was seething free,
Where the wallowing monster spouted his foam-fountains in the sea.
Let us swear an oath, and keep it with an equal mind,
In the hollow Lotos-land to live and lie reclined
On the hills like Gods together, careless of mankind.   155
For they lie beside their nectar, and the bolts are hurl'd
Far below them in the valleys, and the clouds are lightly curl'd
Round their golden houses, girdled with the gleaming world:
Where they smile in secret, looking over wasted lands,
Blight and famine, plague and earthquake, roaring deeps and fiery
    sands,   160
Clanging fights, and flaming towns, and sinking ships, and praying
    hands.
But they smile, they find a music centred in a doleful song
Steaming up, a lamentation and an ancient tale of wrong,
Like a tale of little meaning though the words are strong;
Chanted from an ill-used race of men that cleave the soil,   165
Sow the seed, and reap the harvest with enduring toil,
Storing yearly little dues of wheat, and wine and oil;
Till they perish and they suffer—some, 'tis whisper'd—down in hell
Suffer endless anguish, others in Elysian valleys dwell,
Resting weary limbs at last on beds of asphodel.   170
Surely, surely, slumber is more sweet than toil, the shore
Than labour in the deep mid-ocean, wind and wave and oar;
Oh, rest ye, brother mariners, we will not wander more.

COME DOWN, O MAID

Come down, O maid, from yonder mountain height:
What pleasure lives in height (the shepherd sang)

In height and cold, the splendour of the hills?
But cease to move so near the Heavens, and cease
To glide a sunbeam by the blasted[1] Pine,   5
To sit a star upon the sparkling spire;
And come, for Love is of the valley, come,
For Love is of the valley, come thou down
And find him; by the happy threshold, he,
Or hand in hand with Plenty in the maize,   10
Or red with spirited purple of the vats,
Or foxlike in the vine; nor cares to walk
With Death and Morning on the silver horns,[2]
Nor wilt thou snare him in the white ravine,
Nor find him dropt upon the firths of ice,   15
That huddling slant in furrow-cloven falls
To roll the torrent out of dusky doors:
But follow; let the torrent dance thee down
To find him in the valley; let the wild
Lean-headed Eagles yelp alone, and leave   20
The monstrous ledges there to slope, and spill
Their thousand wreaths of dangling water-smoke,[3]
That like a broken purpose waste in air:
So waste not thou; but come; for all the vales
Await thee; azure pillars of the hearth   25
Arise to thee; the children call, and I
Thy shepherd pipe, and sweet is every sound.

ROBERT BROWNING
1812–1889

MY LAST DUCHESS

FERRARA

That's my last Duchess painted on the wall,
Looking as if she were alive. I call
That piece a wonder, now: Frà Pandolf's[1] hands
Worked busily a day, and there she stands.

[1] Blighted.   [2] The icy horns of mountains.   [3] Water vapor.

[1] An imaginary painter.

Will't please you sit and look at her? I said   5
"Frà Pandolf" by design, for never read
Strangers like you that pictured countenance,
The depth and passion of its earnest glance,
But to myself they turned (since none puts by
The curtain I have drawn for you, but I)   10
And seemed as they would ask me, if they durst,
How such a glance came there; so, not the first
Are you to turn and ask thus. Sir, 'twas not
Her husband's presence only, called that spot
Of joy into the Duchess' cheek: perhaps   15
Frà Pandolf chanced to say, "Her mantle laps
Over my lady's wrist too much," or "Paint
Must never hope to reproduce the faint
Half-flush that dies along her throat": such stuff
Was courtesy, she thought, and cause enough   20
For calling up that spot of joy. She had
A heart—how shall I say?—too soon made glad,
Too easily impressed: she liked whate'er
She looked on, and her looks went everywhere.
Sir, 'twas all one! My favor at her breast,   25
The dropping of the daylight in the West,
The bough of cherries some officious fool
Broke in the orchard for her, the white mule
She rode with round the terrace—all and each
Would draw from her alike the approving speech,   30
Or blush, at least. She thanked men,—good! but thanked
Somehow—I know not how—as if she ranked
My gift of a nine-hundred-years-old name
With anybody's gift. Who'd stoop to blame
This sort of trifling? Even had you skill   35
In speech—(which I have not)—to make your will
Quite clear to such an one, and say, "Just this
Or that in you disgusts me; here you miss,
Or there exceed the mark"—and if she let
Herself be lessoned so, nor plainly set   40
Her wits to yours, forsooth, and made excuse,
—E'en then would be some stooping; and I choose
Never to stoop. Oh sir, she smiled, no doubt,
Whene'er I passed her; but who passed without
Much the same smile? This grew; I gave commands;   45
Then all smiles stopped together. There she stands
As if alive. Will't please you rise? We'll meet
The company below, then. I repeat,
The Count your master's known munificence
Is ample warrant that no just pretence   50
Of mine for dowry will be disallowed;
Though his fair daughter's self, as I avowed
At starting, is my object. Nay, we'll go

Together down, sir. Notice Neptune, though,
Taming a sea-horse, thought a rarity,   55
Which Claus of Innsbruck cast in bronze for me!

SOLILOQUY OF THE SPANISH CLOISTER

Gr-r-r—there go, my heart's abhorrence!
    Water your damned flower-pots, do!
If hate killed men, Brother Lawrence,
    God's blood, would not mine kill you!
What? your myrtle-bush wants trimming?   5
    Oh, that rose has prior claims—
Needs its leaden vase filled brimming?
    Hell dry you up with its flames!

At the meal we sit together:
    Salve tibi![1] I must hear   10
Wise talk of the kind of weather,
    Sort of season, time of year:
Not a plenteous cork-crop: scarcely
    Dare we hope oak-galls, I doubt:
What's the Latin name for 'parsley'?   15
    What's the Greek name for Swine's Snout?

Whew! We'll have our platter burnished,
    Laid with care on our own shelf!
With a fire-new spoon we're furnished,
    And a goblet for ourself,   20
Rinsed like something sacrificial
    Ere 'tis fit to touch our chaps—
Marked with L for our initial!
    (He-he! There his lily snaps!)

Saint, forsooth! While brown Dolores   25
    Squats outside the Convent bank
With Sanchicha, telling stories,
    Steeping tresses in the tank,[2]
Blue-black, lustrous, thick like horsehairs,
    —Can't I see his dead eye glow,   30
Bright as 'twere a Barbary corsair's?
    (That is, if he'd let it show!)

---

[1] (Latin) Hail to thee.   [2] Of rain water.

When he finishes refection,
    Knife and fork he never lays
Cross-wise, to my recollection,   35
    As do I, in Jesu's praise.
I the Trinity illustrate,
    Drinking watered orange-pulp—
In three sips the Arian[3] frustrate;
    While he drains his at one gulp.   40

Oh, those melons? If he's able
    We're to have a feast! so nice!
One goes to the Abbot's table,
    All of use get each a slice.
How go on your flowers? None double?   45
    Not one fruit-sort can you spy?
Strange!—And I, too, at such trouble,
    Keep them close-nipped on the sly!

There's a great text in Galatians,[4]
    Once you trip on it, entails   50
Twenty-nine distinct damnations,
    One sure, if another fails:
If I trip him just a-dying,
    Sure of heaven as sure can be,
Spin him round and send him flying   55
    Off to hell, a Manichee?[5]

Or, my scrofulous French novel
    On grey paper with blunt type!
Simply glance at it, you grovel
    Hand and foot in Belial's[6] gripe: 60
If I double down its pages
    At the woeful sixteenth print,
When he gathers his greengages,
    Ope a sieve[7] and slip it in't?

Or, there's Satan—one might venture   65
    Pledge one's soul to him, yet leave

---

[3] The Arian heresy, which maintained that Father and Son were entirely separate beings and that Christ was a created being, inferior to the Father.   [4] Probably Galatians 3:10: For as many as are of the works of the law are under the curse: for it is written, Cursed is every one that continueth not in all things which are written in the book of the law to do them.   [5] A believer in the Manichean heresy, which holds that the world is composed of two irreducible opposing principles, light (or good) and darkness (or evil). [6] Satan's.   [7] Basket used chiefly for produce.

Such a flaw in the endenture
    As he'd miss till, past retrieve,
Blasted lay that rose-acacia
    We're so proud of! *Hy, Zy Hine* . . .   70
'St, there's Vespers! *Plena gratiâ*
    Ave, Virgo![8] Gr-r-r—you swine!

WALT WHITMAN
1819–1892

WHEN LILACS LAST IN THE DOORYARD BLOOM'D

1

When lilacs last in the dooryard bloom'd,
And the great star[1] early droop'd in the western sky in the night,
I mourn'd, and yet shall mourn with ever-returning spring.

Ever-returning spring, trinity sure to me you bring,
Lilac blooming perennial and drooping star in the west,   5
And thought of him I love.

2

O powerful western fallen star!
O shades of night—O moody, tearful night!
O great star disappear'd—O the black murk that hides the star!
O cruel hands that hold me powerless—O helpless soul of me!   10
O harsh surrounding cloud that will not free my soul.

3

In the dooryard fronting an old farm-house near the white-wash'd
    palings,

[8] Full of grace, Hail, Virgin (usually, *Ave Maria gratia plena*).

[1] The planet Venus, or the "evening star."

Stands the lilac-bush tall-growing with heart-shaped leaves of rich
 green,
With many a pointed blossom rising delicate, with the perfume strong
 I love,
With every leaf a miracle—and from this bush in the dooryard,   15
With delicate-color'd blossoms and heart-shaped leaves of rich green,
A sprig with its flower I break.

4

In the swamp in secluded recesses,
A shy and hidden bird is warbling a song.

Solitary the thrush,   20
The hermit withdrawn to himself, avoiding the settlements,
Sings by himself a song.

Song of the bleeding throat,
Death's outlet song of life, (for well dear brother I know,
If thou wast not granted to sing thou would'st surely die.)   25

5

Over the breast of the spring, the land, amid cities,
Amid lanes and through old woods, where lately the violets peep'd
 from the ground spotting the gray debris,
Amid the grass in the fields each side of the lanes, passing the endless
 grass,
Passing the yellow-spear'd wheat, every grain from its shroud in the
 dark-brown fields uprisen,
Passing the apple-tree blows of white and pink in the orchards,   30
Carrying a corpse to where it shall rest in the grave,
Night and day journeys a coffin.

6

Coffin that passes through lanes and streets,
Through day and night with the great cloud darkening the land,
With the pomp of the inloop'd flags with the cities draped in black,   35
With the show of the States themselves as of crape-veil'd women
 standing,
With processions long and winding and the flambeaus of the night,
With the countless torches lit, with the silent sea of faces and the
 unbared heads,
With the waiting depot, the arriving coffin, and the sombre faces,

With dirges through the night, with the thousand voices rising strong
    and solemn,   40
With all the mournful voices of the dirges pour'd around the coffin,
The dim-lit churches and the shuddering organs—where amid these
    you journey,
With the tolling tolling bells' perpetual clang,
Here, coffin that slowly passes,
I give you my sprig of lilac.   45

7

(Nor for you, for one alone,
Blossoms and branches green to coffins all I bring,
For fresh as the morning, thus would I chant a song for you O sane
    and sacred death.

All over bouquets of roses,
O death, I cover you over with roses and early lilies,   50
But mostly and now the lilac that blooms the first,
Copious I break, I break the sprigs from the bushes,
With loaded arms I come, pouring for you,
For you and the coffins all of you O death.)

8

O western orb sailing the heaven,   55
Now I know what you must have meant as a month since I walk'd,
As I walk'd in silence the transparent shadowy night,
As I saw you had something to tell as you bent to me night after night,
As you droop'd from the sky low down as if to my side, (while the
    other stars all look'd on,)
As we wander'd together the solemn night, (for something I know not
    what kept me from sleep,)   60
As the night advanced, and I saw on the rim of the west how full you
    were of woe,
As I stood on the rising ground in the breeze in the cool transparent
    night,
As I watch'd where you pass'd and was lost in the netherward black
    of the night,
As my soul in its trouble dissatisfied sank, as where you sad orb,
Concluded, dropt in the night, and was gone.   65

9

Sing on there in the swamp,
O singer bashful and tender, I hear your notes, I hear your call,
I hear, I come presently, I understand you,

But a moment I linger, for the lustrous star has detain'd me,
The star my departing comrade holds and detains me.

10

O how shall I warble myself for the dead one there I loved?
And how shall I deck my song for the large sweet soul that has gone?
And what shall my perfume be for the grave of him I love?

Sea-winds blown from east and west,
Blown from the Eastern sea and blown from the Western sea, till there
     on the prairies meeting,
These and with these and the breath of my chant,
I'll perfume the grave of him I love.

11

O what shall I hang on the chamber walls?
And what shall the pictures be that I hang on the walls,
To adorn the burial-house of him I love?

Pictures of growing spring and farms and homes,
With the Fourth-month eve at sundown, and the gray smoke lucid and
     bright,
With floods of the yellow gold of the gorgeous, indolent, sinking sun,
     burning, expanding the air,
With the fresh sweet herbage under foot, and the pale green leaves of
     the trees prolific,
In the distance the flowing glaze, the breast of the river, with a wind-
     dapple here and there,
With ranging hills on the banks, with many a line against the sky, and
     shadows,
And the city at hand with dwellings so dense, and stacks of chimneys,
And all the scenes of life and the workshops, and the workmen home-
     ward returning.

12

Lo, body and soul—this land,
My own Manhattan with spires, and the sparkling and hurrying tides,
     and the ships,
The varied and ample land, the South and the North in the light,
     Ohio's shores and flashing Missouri,
And ever the far-spreading prairies cover'd with grass and corn.

Lo, the most excellent sun so calm and haughty,
The violet and purple morn with just-felt breezes,
The gentle soft-born measureless light,   95
The miracle spreading bathing all, the fulfill'd noon,
The coming eve delicious, the welcome night and the stars,
Over my cities shining all, enveloping man and land.

13

Sing on, sing on you gray-brown bird,
Sing from the swamps, the recesses, pour your chant from the bushes,   100
Limitless out of the dusk, out of the cedars and pines.

Sing on dearest brother, warble your reedy song,
Loud human song, with voice of uttermost woe.

O liquid and free and tender!
O wild and loose to my soul—O wondrous singer!   105
You only I hear—yet the star holds me, (but will soon depart,)
Yet the lilac with mastering odor holds me.

14

Now while I sat in the day and look'd forth,
In the close of the day with its light and the fields of spring, and the
        farmers preparing their crops,
In the large unconscious scenery of my land with its lakes and forests,   110
In the heavenly aerial beauty, (after the perturb'd winds and the
        storms,)
Under the arching heavens of the afternoon swift passing, and the
        voices of children and women,
The many-moving sea-tides, and I saw the ships how they sail'd,
And the summer approaching with richness, and the fields all busy
        with labor,
And the infinite separate houses, how they all went on, each with its
        meals and minutia of daily usages,   115
And the streets how their throbbings throbb'd, and the cities pent—lo,
        then and there,
Falling upon them all and among them all, enveloping me with the rest,
Appear'd the cloud, appear'd the long black trail,
And I knew death, its thought, and the sacred knowledge of death.

Then with the knowledge of death as walking one side of me,   120
And the thought of death close-walking the other side of me,
And I in the middle as with companions, and as holding the hands of
        companions,

I fled forth to the hiding receiving night that talks not,
Down to the shores of the water, the path by the swamp in the
      dimness,
To the solemn shadowy cedars and ghostly pines so still.   125

And the singer so shy to the rest receiv'd me,
The gray-brown bird I know receiv'd us comrades three,
And he sang the carol of death, and a verse for him I love.

From deep secluded recesses,
From the fragrant cedars and the ghostly pines so still,   130
Came the carol of the bird.

And the charm of the carol rapt me,
As I held as if by their hands my comrades in the night,
And the voice of my spirit tallied the song of the bird.

Come lovely and soothing death,   135
Undulate round the world, serenely arriving, arriving,
In the day, in the night, to all, to each,
Sooner or later delicate death.

Prais'd be the fathomless universe,
For life and joy, and for objects and knowledge curious,   140
And for love, sweet love—but praise! praise! praise!
For the sure-enwinding arms of cool-enfolding death.

Dark mother always gliding near with soft feet,
Have none chanted for thee a chant of fullest welcome?
Then I chant it for thee, I glorify thee above all,   145
I bring thee a song that when thou must indeed come, come
*   unfalteringly.*

Approach strong deliveress,
When it is so, when thou hast taken them I joyously sing the dead,
Lost in the loving floating ocean of thee,
Laved in the flood of thy bliss O death.   150

From me to thee glad serenades,
Dances for thee I propose saluting thee, adornments and feastings for
*   thee,*

And the sights of the open landscape and the high-spread sky are
    fitting,
And life and the fields, and the huge and thoughtful night.

The night in silence under many a star,   155
The ocean shore and the husky whispering wave whose voice I know,
And the soul turning to thee O vast and well-veil'd death,
And the body gratefully nestling close to thee.

Over the tree-tops I float thee a song,
Over the rising and sinking waves, over the myriad fields and the
    prairies wide,   160
Over the dense-pack'd cities all and the teeming wharves and ways,
I float this carol with joy, with joy to thee O death.

    15
To the tally of my soul,
Loud and strong kept up the gray-brown bird,
With pure deliberate notes spreading filling the night.   165

Loud in the pines and cedars dim,
Clear in the freshness moist and the swamp-perfume,
And I with my comrades there in the night.

While my sight that was bound in my eyes unclosed,
As to long panoramas of visions.   170

And I saw askant the armies,
I saw as in noiseless dreams hundreds of battle-flags,
Borne through the smoke of the battles and pierc'd with missiles I saw
    them,
And carried hither and yon through the smoke, and torn and bloody,
And at last but a few shreds left on the staffs, (and all in silence,)   175
And the staffs all splinter'd and broken.

I saw battle-corpses, myriads of them,
And the white skeletons of young men, I saw them,
I saw the debris and debris of all the slain soldiers of the war,
But I saw they were not as was thought,   180
They themselves were fully at rest, they suffer'd not,
The living remain'd and suffer'd, mother suffer'd,
And the wife and the child and the musing comrade suffer'd,
And the armies that remain'd suffer'd.

16

Passing the visions, passing the night,   185
Passing, unloosing the hold of my comrades' hands,
Passing the song of the hermit bird and the tallying song of my soul,
Victorious song, death's outlet song, yet varying ever-altering song,
As low and wailing, yet clear the notes, rising and falling, flooding the
     night,
Sadly, sinking and fainting, as warning and warning, and yet again
     bursting with joy,   190
Covering the earth and filling the spread of the heaven,
As that powerful psalm in the night I heard from recesses,
Passing, I leave thee lilac with heart-shaped leaves,
I leave thee there in the door-yard, blooming, returning with spring.

I cease from my song for thee,   195
From my gaze on thee in the west, fronting the west, communing with
     thee,
O comrade lustrous with silver face in the night.

Yet each to keep and all, retrievements out of the night,
The song, the wondrous chant of the gray-brown bird,
And the tallying chant, the echo arous'd in my soul,   200
With the lustrous and drooping star with the countenance full of woe,
With the holders holding my hand nearing the call of the bird,
Comrades mine and I in the midst, and their memory ever to keep, for
     the dead I loved so well,
For the sweetest, wisest soul of all my days and lands—and this for his
     dear sake,
Lilac and star and bird twined with the chant of my soul,   205
There in the fragrant pines and the cedars dusk and dim.

OUT OF THE CRADLE
ENDLESSLY ROCKING

Out of the cradle endlessly rocking,
Out of the mocking-bird's throat, the musical shuttle,
Out of the Ninth-month midnight,
Over the sterile sands and the fields beyond, where the child leaving his bed
     wander'd alone, bareheaded, barefoot,
Down from the shower'd halo,   5
Up from the mystic play of shadows twining and twisting as if they were
     alive,
Out from the patches of briers and blackberries,
From the memories of the bird that chanted to me,

From your memories sad brother, from the fitful risings and fallings I
    heard, 10
From under that yellow half-moon late-risen and swollen as if with
    tears,
From those beginning notes of yearning and love there in the mist,
From the thousand responses of my heart never to cease,
From the myriad thence-arous'd words,
From the word stronger and more delicious than any, 15
From such as now they start the scene revisiting,
As a flock, twittering, rising, or overhead passing,
Borne hither, ere all eludes me, hurriedly,
A man, yet by these tears a little boy again,
Throwing myself on the sand, confronting the waves, 20
I, chanter of pains and joys, uniter of here and hereafter,
Taking all hints to use them, but swiftly leaping beyond them,
A reminiscence sing.

Once Paumanok,[1]
When the lilac-scent was in the air and Fifth-month grass was growing, 25
Up this seashore in some briers,
Two feather'd guests from Alabama, two together,
And their nest, and four light-green eggs spotted with brown,
And every day the he-bird to and fro near at hand,
And every day the she-bird crouch'd on her nest, silent, with bright
    eyes, 30
And every day I, a curious boy, never too close, never disturbing them,
Cautiously peering, absorbing, translating.

Shine! shine! shine!
Pour down your warmth, great sun!
While we bask, we two together. 35

Two together!
Winds blow south, or winds blow north,
Day come white, or night come black,
Home, or rivers and mountains from home,
Singing all time, minding no time, 40
While we two keep together.

Till of a sudden,
May-be kill'd, unknown to her mate,
One forenoon the she-bird crouch'd not on the nest,
Nor return'd that afternoon, nor the next, 45
Nor ever appear'd again.

[1] Indian name for Long Island.

And thenceforward all summer in the sound of the sea,
And at night under the full of the moon in calmer weather,
Over the hoarse surging of the sea,
Or flitting from brier to brier by day,
I saw, I heard at intervals the remaining one, the he-bird,   50
The solitary guest from Alabama.

Blow! blow blow!
Blow up sea-winds along Paumanok's shore;
I wait and I wait till you blow my mate to me.

Yes, when the stars glisten'd,   55
All night long on the prong of a moss-scallop'd stake,
Down almost amid the slapping waves,
Sat the lone singer wonderful causing tears.

He call'd on his mate,
He pour'd forth the meanings which I of all men know.   60

Yes my brother I know,
The rest might not, but I have treasur'd every note,
For more than once dimly down to the beach gliding,
Silent, avoiding the moonbeams, blending myself with the shadows,
Recalling now the obscure shapes, the echoes, the sounds and sights after their
        sorts,   65
The white arms out in the breakers tirelessly tossing,
I, with bare feet, a child, the wind wafting my hair,
Listen'd long and long.

Listen'd to keep, to sing, now translating the notes,
Following you my brother.   70

Soothe! soothe! soothe!
Close on its wave soothes the wave behind,
And again another behind, embracing and lapping, every one close,
But my love soothes not me, not me.

Low hangs the moon, it rose late,   75
It is lagging—O I think it is heavy with love, with love.

O madly the sea pushes upon the land,
With love, with love.

O night! do I not see my love fluttering out among the breakers?
What is that little black thing I see there in the white?   80

Loud! loud! loud!
Loud I call to you, my love!
High and clear I shoot my voice over the waves,
Surely you must know who is here, is here,
You must know who I am, my love.   85

Low-hanging moon!
What is that dusky spot in your brown yellow?
O it is the shape, the shape of my mate!
O moon do not keep her from me any longer.

Land! land! O land!   90
Whichever way I turn, O I think you could give me my mate back again if you
        only would,
For I am almost sure I see her dimly whichever way I look.

O rising stars!
Perhaps the one I want so much will rise, will rise with some of you.

O throat! O trembling throat!   95
Sound clearer through the atmosphere!
Pierce the woods, the earth,
Somewhere listening to catch you must be the one I want.

Shake out carols!
Solitary here, the night's carols!   100
Carols of lonesome love! death's carols!
Carols under the lagging, yellow, waning moon!
O under that moon where she droops almost down into the sea!
O reckless despairing carols.

But soft! sink low!   105
Soft! let me just murmur,
And do you wait a moment you husky-nois'd sea,
For somewhere I believe I heard my mate responding to me,
So faint, I must be still, be still to listen,
But not altogether still, for then she might not come immediately to me.   110

Hither my love!
Here I am! here!

With this just-sustain'd note I announce myself to you,
This gentle call is for you my love, for you.

Do not be decoy'd elsewhere,   115
That is the whistle of the wind, it is not my voice,
That is the fluttering, the fluttering of the spray,
Those are the shadows of leaves.

O darkness! O in vain!
O I am sick and sorrowful.   120

O brown halo in the sky near the moon, dropping upon the sea!
O troubled reflection in the sea!

O throat! O throbbing heart!
And I singing uselessly, uselessly all the night.   125

O past! O happy life! O songs of joy!
In the air, in the woods, over fields,
Loved! loved! loved! loved! loved!
But my mate no more, no more with me!
We two together no more.   130

The aria sinking,
All else continuing, the stars shining,
The winds blowing, the notes of the bird continuous echoing,
With angry moans the fierce old mother incessantly moaning,
On the sands of Paumanok's shore gray and rustling,   135
The yellow half-moon enlarged, sagging down, drooping, the face of the sea al-
        most touching,
The boy ecstatic, with his bare feet the waves, with his hair the atmosphere
        dallying,
The love in the heart long pent, now loose, now at last tumultuously bursting,
The aria's meaning, the ears, the soul, swiftly depositing,
The strange tears down the cheeks coursing,   140
The colloquy there, the trio, each uttering,
The undertone, the savage old mother incessantly crying,
To the boy's soul's questions sullenly timing, some drown'd secret hissing,
To the outsetting bard.

Demon or bard! (said the boy's soul,)   145
Is it indeed toward your mate you sing? or is it really to me?
For I, that was a child, my tongue's use sleeping, now I have heard you,

Now in a moment I know what I am for, I awake,
And already a thousand singers, a thousand songs, clearer, louder and more
     sorrowful than yours,   150
A thousand warbling echoes have started to life within me, never to die.

O you singer solitary, singing by yourself, projecting me,
O solitary me listening, never more shall I cease perpetuating you,
Never more shall I escape, never more the reverberations,
Never more the cries of unsatisfied love be absent from me,   155
Never again leave me to be the peaceful child I was before what there in the
     night,
By the sea under the yellow and sagging moon,
The messenger there arous'd, the fire, the sweet hell within,
The unknown want, the destiny of me.

O give me the clew! (it lurks in the night here somewhere,)   160
O if I am to have so much, let me have more!

A word then, (for I will conquer it,)
The word final, superior to all,
Subtle, sent up—what is it?—I listen;
Are you whispering it, and have all the time, you sea waves?   165
Is that it from your liquid rims and wet sands?

Whereto answering, the sea,
Delaying not, hurrying not,
Whisper'd me through the night, and very plainly before daybreak,
Lisp'd to me the low and delicious word death,
And again, death, death, death, death,   170
Hissing melodious, neither like the bird nor like my arous'd child's heart,
But edging near as privately for me rustling at my feet,
Creeping thence steadily up to my ears and laving me softly all over,
Death, death, death, death, death.   175

Which I do not forget,
But fuse the song of my dusky demon and brother,
That he sang to me in the moonlight on Paumanok's gray beach,
With the thousand responsive songs at random,
My own songs awaked from that hour,   180
And with them the key, the word up from the waves,
The word of the sweetest song and all songs,
That strong and delicious word which, creeping to my feet,
(Or like some old crone rocking the cradle, swathed in sweet garments, bending
     aside,)
The sea whisper'd me.   185

MATTHEW ARNOLD
1822–1888

SHAKESPEARE

Others abide[1] our question. Thou art free.
We ask and ask: Thou smilest and art still,
Out-topping knowledge. For the loftiest hill
That to the stars uncrowns his majesty,
Planting his steadfast footsteps in the sea,   5
Making the Heaven of Heavens his dwelling-place,
Spares but the cloudy border of his base
To the foil'd searching of mortality:
And thou, who didst the stars and sunbeams know,
Self-school'd, self-scann'd,[2] self-honour'd, self-secure,   10
Didst walk on Earth unguess'd at. Better so!
All pains the immortal spirit must endure,
All weakness that impairs, all griefs that bow,
Find their sole voice in that victorious brow.

TO MARGUERITE IN RETURNING A VOLUME OF THE LETTERS OF ORTIS

Yes: in the sea of life enisl'd,
With echoing straits between us thrown,
Dotting the shoreless watery wild,
We mortal millions live *alone*.
    The islands feel the enclasping flow,   5
And then their endless bounds they know.

But when the moon their hollow lights,
And they are swept by balms of spring,
And in their glens, on starry nights,
The nightingales divinely sing;   10
And lovely notes, from shore to shore,
Across the sounds and channels pour;

[1] Submit to, face.   [2] Self-examined (introspectively).

Oh then a longing like despair
Is to their farthest caverns sent;
For surely once, they feel, we were   15
Parts of a single continent.
Now round us spreads the watery plain—
Oh might our marges[1] meet again!

Who order'd, that their longing's fire
Should be, as soon as kindled, cool'd?   20
Who renders vain their deep desire?—
    A God, a God their severance rul'd;
And bade betwixt their shores to be
The unplumb'd, salt, estranging sea.

DOVER BEACH

The sea is calm to-night.
The tide is full, the moon lies fair
Upon the straits; on the French coast the light
Gleams and is gone;[1] the cliffs of England stand,
Glimmering and vast, out in the tranquil bay.   5
Come to the window, sweet is the night-air!
Only, from the long line of spray
Where the sea meets the moon-blanched land,
Listen! you hear the grating roar
Of pebbles which the waves draw back, and fling,   10
At their return, up the high strand,
Begin, and cease, and then again begin,
With tremulous cadence slow, and bring
The eternal note of sadness in.

Sophocles long ago   15
Heard it on the Ægæan, and it brought
Into his mind the turbid ebb and flow
Of human misery; we
Find also in the sound a thought,
Hearing it by this distant northern sea.   20

[1] Margins, boundaries.

[1] Lights on the French coast are visible from Dover, the closest point in England (about 20 miles) to the continent. The cliffs near Dover are white and quite high.

The Sea of Faith
Was once, too, at the full, and round earth's shore
Lay like the folds of a bright girdle furled.
But now I only hear
Its melancholy, long, withdrawing roar,   25
Retreating, to the breath
Of the night-wind, down the vast edges drear
And naked shingles[2] of the world.

Ah, love, let us be true
To one another! for the world, which seems   30
To lie before us like a land of dreams,
So various, so beautiful, so new,
Hath really neither joy, nor love, nor light,
Nor certitude, nor peace, nor help for pain;
And we are here as on a darkling plain   35
Swept with confused alarms of struggle and flight,
Where ignorant armies clash by night.

GEORGE MEREDITH
1828–1909

LUCIFER IN STARLIGHT

On a starred night Prince Lucifer uprose.
Tired of his dark dominion swung the fiend
Above the rolling ball in cloud part screened,
Where sinners hugged their spectre of repose.
Poor prey to his hot fit of pride were those.   5
And now upon his western wing he leaned,
Nor his huge bulk o'er Afric's sands careened,
Now the black planet shadowed Arctic snows.
Soaring through wider zones that pricked his scars
With memory of the old revolt from Awe,   10
He reached a middle height, and at the stars,
Which are the brain of heaven, he looked, and sank.

[2] Coarse beach gravel.

Around the ancient track marched, rank on rank,
The army of unalterable law.

EMILY DICKINSON
1830–1886

"GO TELL IT"—
WHAT A MESSAGE—

"Go tell it"—What a Message—
To whom—is specified—
Not murmur—not endearment—
But simply—we—obeyed—
Obeyed—a Lure—a Longing?   5
Oh Nature—none of this—
To Law—said sweet Thermopylae
I give my dying Kiss—

COMMENTARY

One of the tenets of modern literary criticism is that a poem is a self-contained entity, that it must be regarded as wholly independent of all considerations that are not proposed by its own elements. For example, any knowledge of the personal life of the poet, even of the circumstances that led to the writing of the poem, is considered irrelevant—it may be interesting in itself but it cannot tell us anything we need to know in order for the poem to have its right effect upon us. There are critics who go so far as to say that an interest in the personal existence of the poet interferes with our direct response to the poem.

This idea must be granted the merit of its intention. When we read "Resolution and Independence," it is not necessary to know that Wordsworth, shortly before he wrote the poem, actually did meet an old man such as he describes, or that he was soon to be married and might therefore be expected to feel anxiety over the future. For a precise response to "Ode to a Nightingale" we do not have to know that it was written not many weeks after Keats had witnessed the death of his younger brother. And if we felt it necessary to seek out such information, the poem could of course be thought by that much the less complete in itself, for in part it would then depend for its effect upon something outside itself.

But the truth is that extrinsic information, whether we wish it or not, and whether the critics in their strictness like it or not, often does impinge upon our awareness of a particular poem and become an element in our relation to it which we cannot ignore. When we read "Lycidas," we cannot dismiss from our minds the fact that the young poet who speaks so proudly of the profession of poetry and of his noble desire for fame is to become one of the world's great poets, as famous as ever he could have wished. How different our response to "Lycidas" would be if Milton had died not long after its composition! We should then not take the poem to be, among other things, the superb prelude to a triumphant career, but a vaunt which had been made pathetic and ironic by circumstance. In this instance, the mere awareness of Milton's reputation is an extraneous knowledge that inevitably plays some part in our reading of the poem, and it would be a strict critic indeed who would say that it should not.

Another kind of information which properly has its share in our response to a poem comes from our familiarity with other poems from the same pen. Anyone acquainted with the canon of Wordsworth's work knows that the poet conceived of his creative power as being dependent upon the emotions of his childhood and early youth and that he believed that the passing years would diminish it. Whoever has read even a few of Keats's poems is aware that the poet was preoccupied with the antithesis between what is eternal and "pure" and what is transient and mundane. Such awarenesses constitute some knowledge of the poets as persons, and this knowledge cannot fail to have its effect upon our way of responding to a single one of their poems, nor does there seem to be any good reason for supposing that this effect is anything but natural. It is a positive advantage in our reading of "Resolution and Independence" to know that Wordsworth's fear of losing his creative powers is not a momentary fancy but an emotion that conditioned his whole life. It can scarcely confuse our response to "Ode to a Nightingale" to know that Keats is *again* moved to a passionate consideration of the eternal and the transitory.

And in the case of Emily Dickinson's striking little poem, there is at least one personal fact about the author which it is essential we bring to our reading —that the poet is a woman. If we were not aware of this, we might well be made uncomfortable by the poem, for its tone and diction seem appropriate to a woman but not to a man, and we would surely be ill at ease if we thought a man had been the writer.

The poem is, as it were, based upon the femininity of the poet. The word femininity is never used in a neutral sense but always with the intention of praise; it connotes charm, delicacy, tenderness. These qualities are no doubt readily seen, or heard, in the poem, but they will be the more quickly perceived by the reader who has some previous acquaintance with Emily Dickinson's work and knows the extent to which the poet represents herself in the postures of femininity, as a young woman, or girl, of high sensitivity, delicate, fastidious, quick to be apprehensive yet courageous and even daring, standing in a daughterly relation to God, whom, on one occasion, with the licensed audacity of rebelliousness characteristic of her manner, she addresses as "Papa above" (page

546). The rules of the world are laid down by masculine beings and the point of many of her poems lies, as in the present one, in the opposition of the feminine creature to the masculine authority, which usually delights her even though she addresses it in irony or protest.

There are two speakers in the poem. They are of opposite sexes and they are half a world and some twenty-five centuries apart. When Emily Dickinson wrote, she could count on a prompt appreciation of what "message" it is that begins "Go tell it . . ." Most readers of the nineteenth century knew the story of the Spartans at Thermopylae—how the huge Persian army under the great king Xerxes moved to conquer Greece; how the small Greek army took its stand at Thermopylae, where, between the precipitous mountain on the one side and the sea on the other, there was a pass so narrow that only a few soldiers could enter it abreast; how, when the Greek position was betrayed, the greater part of the Greek forces withdrew, leaving only the Spartans under their king Leonidas to hold the pass; and how the Spartans, some three hundred in number, were exterminated. Upon the spot a monument was erected which bore this inscription: "Go, stranger, and tell Sparta that here, obeying her commands, we fell." What a message indeed!

The feminine voice—and perhaps we should say the modern feminine voice —questions the basis of the Spartans' act even though the message says unmistakably what that is: obedience. The feminine mind wishes to understand the heroism as an impulse, specifically as an impulse of love. The language used is that of erotic attraction—the poet speaks of the heroic deed as having been a response to "a Lure—a Longing"; she sees it as instinctual, rising out of Nature. And across the centuries the men of Thermopylae refuse her interpretation of their act. They address her by the name of the principle she has invoked, speaking to her as if she were Nature itself, and, brushing aside the idea of their having responded to a "Lure" or a "Longing," assert that it was not Love but Law that moved them.

Yet the feminine voice is not to be silenced. In the very act of reporting how it is refuted and rebuked, it asserts itself in the peculiarly feminine epithet by which it characterizes the great event—"sweet Thermopylae," it says. And the men of Thermopylae seem suddenly to assent to the feminine understanding of their sacrifice—the salute which they send to Law is a kiss. The striking inappropriateness of applying the adjective *sweet* to the grim heroic battle is matched by the inappropriateness—almost comic—of the men of Thermopylae sending a kiss to the Law of Sparta, the most rigorous the world has known. The imperturbable soldiers have been beguiled into taking the feminine view of their action, and Law and Love are made one.

The text of " 'Go tell it'—" that I have used is the one established by Professor Thomas H. Johnson; it reproduces exactly the punctuation of the manuscript. The numerous dashes are characteristic of the poet's practice; Professor Edith Stamm has advanced the theory (in *The Saturday Review,* March 30, 1963) that they are intended to guide the voice in reading.

PAPA ABOVE!

Papa above!
Regard a Mouse
O'erpowered by the Cat!
Reserve within thy kingdom
A "Mansion" for the Rat!   5

Snug in seraphic Cupboards
To nibble all the day,
While unsuspecting Cycles[1]
Wheel solemnly away!

THERE'S A CERTAIN SLANT OF LIGHT

There's a certain Slant of light,
Winter Afternoons—
That oppresses, like the Heft
Of Cathedral Tunes—

Heavenly Hurt, it gives us—   5
We can find no scar,
But internal difference,
Where the Meanings, are—

None may teach it—Any—
'Tis the Seal Despair—   10
An imperial affliction
Sent us of the Air—

When it comes, the Landscape listens—
Shadows—hold their breath—
When it goes, 'tis like the Distance   15
On the look of Death—

A CLOCK STOPPED—

A Clock stopped—
Not the Mantel's—

---

[1] Revolutions (of planets), ages; but there is an intentional pun on "bicycles" also.

Geneva's farthest skill
Cant put the puppet bowing—
That just now dangled still—   5

An awe come on the Trinket!
The Figures hunched, with pain—
Then quivered out of Decimals—
Into Degreeless Noon—

It will not stir for Doctor's—   10
This Pendulum of snow—
The Shopman importunes it—
While cool—concernless No—

Nods from the Gilded pointers—
Nods from the Seconds slim—   15
Decades of Arrogance between
The Dial life—
And Him—

I TASTE A LIQUOR NEVER BREWED

I taste a liquor never brewed—
From Tankards scooped in Pearl—
Not all the Frankfort Berries
Yield such an Alcohol!

Inebriate of Air—am I—   5
And Debauchee of Dew—
Reeling—thro endless summer days—
From inns of Molten Blue—

When "Landlords" turn the drunken Bee
Out of the Foxglove's door—   10
When Butterflies—renounce their "drams"—
I shall but drink the more!

Till Seraphs swing their snowy Hats—
And Saints—to windows run—
To see the little Tippler   15
From Manzanilla come!

BECAUSE I COULD NOT STOP
FOR DEATH

Because I could not stop for Death—
He kindly stopped for me—
The Carriage held but just Ourselves—
And Immortality.

We slowly drove—He knew no haste   5
And I had put away
My labor and my leisure too,
For His Civility—

We passed the School, where Children strove
At Recess—in the Ring—   10
We passed the Fields of Gazing Grain—
We passed the Setting Sun—

Or rather—He passed Us—
The Dews drew quivering and chill—
For only Gossamer, my Gown—   15
My Tippet[1]—only Tulle—

We paused before a House that seemed
A Swelling of the Ground—
The Roof was scarcely visible—
The Cornice—in the Ground—   20

Since then—'tis Centuries—and yet
Feels shorter than the Day
I first surmised the Horses Heads
Were toward Eternity—

I'VE SEEN A DYING EYE

I've seen a Dying Eye
Run round and round a Room—
In search of Something—as it seemed—
Then Cloudier become—
And then—obscure with Fog—   5

---

[1] Shoulder cape.

And then—be soldered down
Without disclosing what it be
'Twere blessed to have seen—

A NARROW FELLOW IN THE GRASS

A narrow Fellow in the Grass
Occasionally rides—
You may have met Him—did you not
His notice sudden is—

The Grass divides as with a Comb—   5
A spotted shaft is seen—
And then it closes at your feet
And opens further on—

He likes a Boggy Acre—
A Floor too cool for Corn—   10
But when a Boy and Barefoot—
I more than once at Noon
Have passed I thought a Whip Lash
Unbraiding in the Sun
When stooping to secure it   15
It wrinkled, and was gone—

Several of Nature's People
I know, and they know me—
I feel for them a transport
Of cordiality—   20

But never met this Fellow
Attended, or alone
Without a tighter breathing
And Zero at the Bone—

"HEAVENLY FATHER"—TAKE TO THEE

"Heavenly Father"—take to thee
The supreme iniquity

Fashioned by thy candid Hand
In a moment contraband—
Though to trust us—seem to us
More respectful—"We are Dust"—
We apologize to thee
For thine own Duplicity—

'TWAS LATER WHEN THE SUMMER WENT

'Twas later when the summer went
Than when the Cricket came—
And yet we knew that gentle Clock
Meant nought but Going Home—
'Twas sooner when the Cricket went
Than when the Winter came
Yet that pathetic Pendulum
Keeps esoteric Time.

ALGERNON CHARLES SWINBURNE
1837–1909

WHEN THE HOUNDS OF SPRING
Chorus from "Atlanta in Calydon"

When the hounds of spring are on winter's traces,
   The mother of months in meadow or plain
Fills the shadows and windy places
   With lisp of leaves and ripple of rain;
And the brown bright nightingale amorous
Is half assuaged for Itylus,

For the Thracian ships and the foreign faces,
    The tongueless vigil, and all the pain.[1]

Come with bows bent and with emptying of quivers,
    Maiden most perfect,[2] lady of light,   10
With a noise of winds and many rivers,
    With a clamour of waters, and with might;
Bind on thy sandals, O thou most fleet,
Over the splendour and speed of thy feet;
For the faint east quickens, the wan west shivers,   15
    Round the feet of the day and the feet of the night.

Where shall we find her, how shall we sing to her,
    Fold our hands round her knees, and cling?
O that man's heart were as fire and could spring to her,
    Fire, or the strength of the streams that spring!   20
For the stars and the winds are unto her
As raiment, as songs of the harp-player;
For the risen stars and the fallen cling to her,
    And the southwest-wind and the west-wind sing.

For winter's rains and ruins are over,   25
    And all the season of snows and sins;
The days dividing lover and lover,
    The light that loses, the night that wins;
And time remembered is grief forgotten,
And frosts are slain and flowers begotten,   30
And in green underwood and cover
    Blossom by blossom the spring begins.

The full streams feed on flower of rushes,
    Ripe grasses trammel a travelling foot,
The faint fresh flame of the young year flushes   35
    From leaf to flower and flower to fruit,
And fruit and leaf are as gold and fire,
And the oat[3] is heard above the lyre,

[1] The allusion is to the Greek legend that Procne, wife of Theseus, king of Thrace, killed her son, Itylus, to avenge herself on her husband, and subsequently became a nightingale. Theseus had married Procne's sister, telling her that Procne, whose tongue he had cut out, was dead. [2] Artemis, Greek goddess of hunting and childbirth. [3] Oaten pipe, a rustic musical instrument.

And the hoofèd heel of a satyr crushes
    The chestnut-husk at the chestnut-root.   40

And Pan by noon and Bacchus by night,[4]
    Fleeter of foot than the fleet-foot kid,
Follows with dancing and fills with delight
    The Maenad and the Bassarid;[5]
And soft as lips that laugh and hide   45
The laughing leaves of the trees divide,
And screen from seeing and leave in sight
    The god pursuing, the maiden hid.

The ivy falls with the Bacchanal's hair[6]
    Over her eyebrows hiding her eyes;   50
The wild vine slipping down leaves bare
    Her bright breast shortening into sighs;
The wild vine slips with the weight of its leaves,
But the berried ivy catches and cleaves
To the limbs that glitter, the feet that scare   55
    The wolf that follows, the fawn that flies.

THE GARDEN OF PROSERPINE[1]

Here, where the world is quiet;
    Here, where all trouble seems
Dead winds' and spent waves' riot
    In doubtful dreams of dreams;
I watch the green field growing   5
For reaping folk and sowing,
For harvest-time and mowing,
    A sleepy world of streams.

I am tired of tears and laughter,
    And men that laugh and weep,   10
Of what may come hereafter

---

[4] Pan and Bacchus were frolicsome gods of the forest and wine, respectively.   [5] The Maenads and Bassarids were women who were inspired to ecstatic frenzy by worship of Dionysus.   [6] The Bacchanals were similar to Maenads and Bassarids.

[1] Persephone, the goddess of Hades; Proserpine is her Latin name.

For men that sow to reap:
I am weary of days and hours,
Blown[2] buds of barren flowers,
Desires and dreams and powers   15
    And everything but sleep.

Here life has death for neighbour,
    And far from eye or ear
Wan waves and wet winds labour,
    Weak ships and spirits steer;   20
They drive adrift, and whither
They wot[3] not who make thither;
But no such winds blow hither,
    And no such things grow here.

No growth of moor or coppice,   25
    No heather-flower or vine,
But bloomless buds of poppies,
    Green grapes of Proserpine.
Pale beds of blowing rushes
Where no leaf blooms or blushes   30
Save this whereout she crushes
    For dead men deadly wine.

Pale, without name or number,
    In fruitless fields of corn,
They bow themselves and slumber   35
    All night till light is born;
And like a soul belated,
In hell and heaven unmated,
By cloud and mist abated
    Comes out of darkness morn.   40

Though one were strong as seven,
    He too with death shall dwell,
Nor wake with wings in heaven,
    Nor weep for pains in hell;
Though one were fair as roses,   45
His beauty clouds and closes;
And well though love reposes,
    In the end it is not well.

[2] Blossomed.   [3] Know.

Pale, beyond porch and portal,
    Crowned with calm leaves, she stands   50
Who gathers all things mortal
    With cold immortal hands;
Her languid lips are sweeter
Than love's who fears to greet her
To men that mix and meet her   55
    From many times and lands.

She waits for each and other,
    She waits for all men born;
Forgets the earth her mother,[4]
    The life of fruits and corn;   60
And spring and seed and swallow
Take wing for her and follow
Where summer song rings hollow
    And flowers are put to scorn.

There go the loves that wither,   65
    The old loves with wearier wings;
And all dead years draw thither,
    And all disastrous things;
Dead dreams of days forsaken,
Blind buds that snows have shaken,   70
Wild leaves that winds have taken,
    Red strays of ruined springs.

We are not sure of sorrow,
    And joy was never sure;
To-day will die to-morrow;   75
    Time stoops to no man's lure;
And love, grown faint and fretful,
With lips but half regretful
Sighs, and with eyes forgetful
    Weeps that no loves endure.   80

From too much love of living,
    From hope and fear set free,
We thank with brief thanksgiving
    Whatever gods may be
That no life lives for ever;   85
That dead men rise up never;

[4] Demeter, corn goddess, was the mother of Persephone; she governed all fruits of
the earth.

That even the weariest river
    Winds somewhere safe to sea.

Then star nor sun shall waken,
    Nor any change of light: 90
Nor sound of waters shaken,
    Nor any sound or sight:
Nor wintry leaves nor vernal,
Nor days nor things diurnal;
Only the sleep eternal   95
    In an eternal night.

THOMAS HARDY
1840–1928

THE SUBALTERNS

I

"Poor wanderer," said the leaden sky,
    "I fain would lighten thee,
But there are laws in force on high
    Which say it must not be."

II

—"I would not freeze thee, shorn one," cried   5
    The North, "knew I but how
To warm my breath, to slack my stride;
    But I am ruled as thou."

III

—"To-morrow I attack thee, wight,"
    Said Sickness. "Yet I swear   10
I bear thy little ark no spite,
    But am bid enter there."

IV

—"Come hither, Son," I heard Death say;
 "I did not will a grave
Should end thy pilgrimage to-day,   15
 But I, too, am a slave!"

V

We smiled upon each other then,
 And life to me had less
Of that fell look it wore ere when
 They owned their passiveness.   20

THE DARKLING[1] THRUSH

I leant upon a coppice gate
 When Frost was spectre-gray,
And Winter's dregs made desolate
 The weakening eye of day.
The tangled bine-stems[2] scored the sky   5
 Like strings of broken lyres,
And all mankind that haunted nigh[3]
 Had sought their household fires.

The land's sharp features seemed to be
 The Century's corpse ouleant,[4]   10
His crypt the cloudy canopy,
 The wind his death-lament.
The ancient pulse of germ and birth
 Was shrunken hard and dry,
And every spirit upon earth   15
 Seemed fervourless as I.

At once a voice arose among
 The bleak twigs overhead
In a full-hearted evensong
 Of joy illimited;[5]   20
An aged thrush, frail, gaunt, and small,
 In blast-beruffled[6] plume,
Had chosen thus to fling his soul
 Upon the growing gloom.

[1] In the dark. [2] Stems of woodbine. [3] Lived nearby. [4] Outlined. [5] Unlimited.
[6] Windblown.

So little cause for carolings
　　Of such ecstatic sound
Was written on terrestrial things
　　Afar or nigh around,
That I could think there trembled through
　　His happy good-night air
Some blessed Hope, whereof he knew
　　And I was unaware.

25

30

THE VOICE

Woman much missed, how you call to me, call to me,
Saying that now you are not as you were
When you had changed from the one who was all to me,
But as at first, when our day was fair.

Can it be you that I hear? Let me view you, then,
Standing as when I drew near to the town
Where you would wait for me: yes, as I knew you then,
Even to the original air-blue gown!

5

Or is it only the breeze, in its listlessness
Travelling across the wet mead to me here,
You being ever dissolved to wan wistlessness,[1]
Heard no more again far or near?

10

　　Thus I; faltering forward,
　　Leaves around me falling,
Wind oozing thin through the thorn from norward,[2]
　　And the woman calling.

15

"WHO'S IN THE NEXT ROOM?"

　　"Who's in the next room?—who?
　　　　I seemed to see
Somebody in the dawning passing through,
　　　　Unknown to me."
"Nay: you saw nought. He passed invisibly."

5

[1] Inattentiveness.　　[2] Northward.

"Who's in the next room—who?
        I seem to hear
Somebody muttering firm in a language new
        That chills the ear."
"No: you catch not his tongue who has entered there."   10

        "Who's in the next room?—who?
        I seem to feel
His breath like a clammy draught, as if it drew
        From the Polar Wheel."
"No: none who breathes at all does the door conceal."   15

        "Who's in the next room?—who?
        A figure wan
With a message to one in there of something due?
        Shall I know him anon?"
"Yea he; and he brought such; and you'll know him anon."   20

AFTERWARDS

When the Present has latched its postern behind my tremulous stay,
    And the May month flaps its glad green leaves like wings,
Delicate-filmed as new-spun silk, will the neighbours say,
    "He was a man who used to notice such things"?

If it be in the dusk when, like an eyelid's soundless blink,   5
    The dewfall-hawk comes crossing the shades to alight
Upon the wind-warped upland thorn, a gazer may think,
    "To him this must have been a familiar sight."

If I pass during some nocturnal blackness, mothy and warm,
    When the hedgehog travels furtively over the lawn,   10
One may say, "He strove that such innocent creatures should come to no harm,
    But he could do little for them; and now he is gone."

If, when hearing that I have been stilled at last, they stand at the door,
    Watching the full-starred heavens that winter sees,
Will this thought rise on those who will meet my face no more,   15
    "He was one who had an eye for such mysteries"?

And will any say when my bell of quittance is heard in the gloom,
    And a crossing breeze cuts a pause in its outrollings,
Till they rise again, as they were a new bell's boom,
    "He hears it not now, but used to notice such things?"   20

GERARD MANLEY HOPKINS
1844–1889

THE LEADEN ECHO
AND THE GOLDEN ECHO

(Maidens' song from
St. Winefred's Well[1])

THE LEADEN ECHO

How to kéep[2]—is there ány any, is there none such, nowhere known some, bow
    or brooch or braid or brace, láce, latch or catch or key to keep
Back beauty, keep it, beauty, beauty, beauty, . . . from vanishing away?
Ó is there no frowning of these wrinkles, rankèd wrinkles deep,
Dówn? no waving off of these most mournful messengers, still messengers, sad
    and stealing messengers of grey?
No there's none, there's none, O no there's none,   5
Nor can you long be, what you now are, called fair,
Do what you may do, what, do what you may,
And wisdom is early to despair:
Be beginning; since, no, nothing can be done
To keep at bay   10
Age and age's evils, hoar hair,
Ruck[3] and wrinkle, drooping, dying, death's worst, winding sheets, tombs and
    worms and tumbling to decay;
So be beginning, be beginning to despair.
O there's none; no no no there's none:
Be beginning to despair, to despair,   15
Despair, despair, despair, despair.

---

[1] St. Winefred was murdered by her would-be ravisher, the chieftain Caradoc. The water of her well, which gushed spontaneously out of the ground after her death, is believed to have curative powers.   [2] Hopkins made a practice of indicating with accent marks which syllables were to receive the strongest stress.   [3] Crease.

Spare!⁴

There ís one, yes I have one (Hush there!);

Only not within seeing of the sun,

Not within the singeing of the strong sun,   20

Tall sun's tingeing, or treacherous the tainting of the earth's air,

Somewhere elsewhere there is ah well where! one,

One. Yes I cán tell such a key, I dó know such a place,

Where whatever's prized and passes of us, everything that's fresh and fast flying

      of us, seems to us sweet of us and swiftly away with, done away with,

      undone,

Undone, done with, soon done with, and yet dearly and dangerously sweet   25

Of us, the wimpled⁵-water-dimpled, not-by-morning-matchèd face,

The flower of beauty, fleece of beauty, too too apt to, ah! to fleet,

Never fleets móre, fastened with the tenderest truth

To its own best being and its loveliness of youth: it is an everlastingness of, O

      it is an all youth!

Come then, your ways and airs and looks, locks, maiden gear, gallantry and

      gaiety and grace,   30

Winning ways, airs innocent, maiden manners, sweet looks, loose locks, long

      locks, lovelocks, gaygear, going gallant, girlgrace—

Resign them, sign them, seal them, send them, motion them with breath,

And with sighs soaring, soaring síghs deliver

Them; beauty-in-the-ghost,⁶ deliver it, early now, long before death

Give beauty back, beauty, beauty, beauty, back to God, beauty's self and beauty's

      giver.   35

See; not a hair is, not an eyelash, not the least lash lost; every hair

Is, hair of the head, numbered.

Nay, what we had lighthanded left in surly⁷ the mere mould⁸

Will have waked and have waxed and have walked with the wind what while

      we slept,

This side, that side hurling a heavyheaded hundredfold   40

What while we, while we slumbered.

O then, weary then why should we tread? O why are we so haggard at the

      heart, so care-coiled, care-killed, so fagged, so fashed,⁹ so cogged,¹⁰ so

      cumbered,

When the thing we freely fórfeit is kept with fonder a care,

Fonder a care kept than we could have kept it, kept

Far with fonder a care (and we, we should have lost it) finer, fonder   45

A care kept.—Where kept? Do but tell us where kept, where.—

Yonder.—What high as that! We follow, now we follow.—Yonder, yes yonder,

      yonder,

Yonder.

---

⁴ Forbear.   ⁵ Rippled.   ⁶ Spiritual beauty.   ⁷ Sullenly.   ⁸ Earth.   ⁹ Troubled.
¹⁰ Deceived.

COMMENTARY

The poems of Gerard Manley Hopkins were first published in 1918, nearly thirty years after the poet's death, and to their early readers they seemed difficult and odd. They now stand in very high repute, but even a half century of habituation has not made them exactly easy for us. As for their oddness, this the poet himself was ready enough to concede; on one occasion he described himself as being taken aback by it. In a letter to his friend and future editor, Robert Bridges, Hopkins said that the oddness of his poems "may make them repulsive at first" and told how shocked he was when he read one of them that a friend had borrowed and sent back to him. ". . . I opened and read some lines, as one commonly reads whether prose or verse, with the eyes, so to say, only, and it struck me aghast with a kind of raw nakedness and unmitigated violence I was unprepared for. . . ." It needed a perceptible moment for Hopkins to perceive the true nature of his own poem. ". . . But take breath," he went on, "and read it with your ears, as I always wish to be read, and my verse becomes all right."

To take breath and read with the ears is what we must learn to do with any poem of Hopkins. "Read Hopkins aloud," says his latest editor, W. H. Gardner, "and you will find that his obscurity is never entirely opaque. . . ."

Hopkins was born in 1844, of a gifted family of the comfortable middle class. An excellent student, he devoted himself at Oxford to the study of Greek and Latin, in which he distinguished himself. In his Oxford days he came under the influence of John Henry Newman, later Cardinal Newman, and converted to the Roman Catholic Church in 1866; two years later he entered the Society of Jesus. The duties of that exigent order were arduous and sometimes personally uncongenial to Hopkins, but he discharged them with exemplary assiduity and still found time to speculate profoundly upon the nature of prosody, to develop his theory of English verse, and to write the poems which were to establish his posthumous fame. If the poems seemed odd in 1918, when literary experiment in England began to be the order of the day, they would have seemed far odder in the poet's lifetime, yet Hopkins might have risked publication had not the Jesuit discipline prevented it.

Many elements contribute to the radical novelty of Hopkins' style, but his chief theoretical statement, his preface to the manuscript volume of his mature poems, deals with one subject only, that of rhythm. The preface is not polemical: it says nothing adverse about the practice of other poets. But the implication of Hopkins' theory is that English verse had curtailed its strength by submitting to the rule of metre, by conforming, even though not with mechanical exactitude, to fixed line-patterns. His conception of the course that English verse should take has a considerable affinity with Wyatt's practice (see page 400), although of the two poets Hopkins is much the more radical. Hopkins would have stood in opposition to the "correct" taste that had contrived the version of "They Flee from Me" which appeared in Tottel's *Miscellany* and that would have led Victorian readers to prefer this revised version to the original. He would have defended the rightness of Wyatt's departures from the pattern of the iambic pentameter line and of all the roughnesses and irregularities by which the poet exploited the actuality of the speaking voice. But in his preface Hopkins confined himself to explaining his own practice; he did not advance the idea which he obviously held, that the established system of English verse seemed to its practitioners to be the only possible one merely because of long habit. For his own prosody, he drew upon the verse systems of Welsh and Greek poetry and upon the tradition of English alliterative verse which had prevailed before the Renaissance.

He also drew upon music, of which he was an accomplished amateur, and for the better understanding of his rhythmic effects he devised a system of marks, analogous to the directive marks on a musical score, which he placed over syllables, words, and groups of words in order to show the reader how to read the poem with his ears. But on the manuscript of "The Leaden Echo and the Golden Echo" he wrote this note: "I have marked the stronger stresses, but with the degree of the stress so perpetually varying no marking is satisfactory. Do you think all had best be left to the reader?" He seems to have answered his own question affirmatively; and any reader who deals with the poem as a singer deals with a new song, "running through" it experimentally a few times to see how the voice should proceed, may reasonably feel that he is not betraying Hopkins' trust in him.

Although rhythm is Hopkins' chief aural concern, it is by no means the only one. He uses alliteration to an extent that no poet has ever ventured; and internal rhyme; and assonance; and subtle, planned progressions and modulations of vowel sounds. The following portion of the first line of "The Leaden Echo and the Golden Echo" illustrates all these effects: ". . . is there none such, nowhere known some, bow or brooch or braid or brace, láce, latch or catch or key to keep." The elaborate devices of Hopkins' prosody are especially in evidence throughout the poem because of its avowed vocal nature. It is not a "lyric" in the sense of being a poem to be set to music for singing and therefore kept simple and modest so that the music may have its way. It is a lyric in the sense of being the whole song itself, words and music together, the vocal line and the accompaniment, both of considerable complexity and virtuosity.

But no doubt because it is so much a song, two characteristics of Hopkins' verse are not strongly apparent in this particular poem. One is the intense visuality that Hopkins usually sought after, the rendering of the specificity of beauty that he called "inscape," though we do have an example of it in the lines descriptive of beautiful girlhood:

> Come then, your ways and airs and looks, locks, maiden gear,
>   gallantry and gaiety and grace,
> Winning ways, airs innocent, maiden manners, sweet looks,
>   loose locks, long locks, lovelocks, gaygear, going gallant,
>   girlgrace—

The other is Hopkins' idiosyncratic rhetoric, which often, but not here, makes for difficult or delayed comprehension. In the passage

> Not within the singeing of the strong sun,
> Tall sun's tingeing, or treacherous the tainting of the earth's
>   air . . .

the last phrase offers only a momentary resistance—we quickly see that "treacherous the tainting" is to be understood as "the treacherous tainting." Nor are we much puzzled by the charming rhetorical idiosyncrasy of "it is an everlasting of, O it is an all youth!"

In common with the rest of Hopkins' poems, "The Leaden Echo and the Golden Echo" is suffused with religious feeling, which, as in many of the poems, is aroused (and colored) by the perception of beauty, frequently human beauty, and, as in this case, by the recognition of its transience. The passing of youth is of course one of poetry's oldest-established and most frequently recurrent themes; sadness or despair are the emotions which generally accompany its statement, and Hopkins, taking these to be the natural first response to transience, proposes the comfort that will be given by the resignation of youthful beauty into God's keeping. The recommendation is perhaps less a serious religious idea than a tender religious conceit; as such, it has an appealing sweetness of intention and but little power to hold grievous feelings at bay. It does, however, serve as the occasion for a peculiarly fresh and poignant celebration of the passing physical beauty for which it seeks a spiritual permanence.

SPRING AND FALL

To a Young Child

Márgarét, are you gríeving
Over Goldengrove unleaving?
Leáves, líke the things of man, you
With your fresh thoughts care for, can you?
Áh! ás the heart grows older   5
It will come to such sights colder
By and by, nor spare a sigh
Though worlds of wanwood leafmeal[1] lie;
And yet you wíll weep and know why.
Now no matter, child, the name: 10
Sórrow's spríngs áre the same.
Nor mouth had, no nor mind, expressed
What heart heard of, ghost guessed:
It ís the blight man was born for,
It is Margaret you mourn for.   15

---

[1] Words Hopkins coined to suggest faded leaves fallen to the ground.

THE WINDHOVER[1]
To Christ Our Lord

I caught this morning morning's minion,[2] king-
    dom of daylight's dauphin,[3] dapple-dawn-drawn Falcon, in his riding
    Of the rolling level underneath him steady air, and striding
High there, how he rung[4] upon the rein of a wimpling[5] wing
In his ecstasy! then off, off forth on swing,   5
    As a skate's heel sweeps smooth on a bow-bend: the hurl and gliding
    Rebuffed the big wind. My heart in hiding
Stirred for a bird,—the achieve of, the mastery of the thing!

Brute beauty and valour and act, oh, air, pride, plume here
    Buckle! AND the fire that breaks from thee then, a billion   10
Times told lovelier, more dangerous, O my chevalier!

      No wonder of it: shéer plód makes plough down sillion[6]
Shine, and blue-bleak embers, ah my dear,
    Fall, gall themselves, and gash gold-vermilion.

PIED BEAUTY

Glory be to God for dappled things—
    For skies of couple-colour as a brinded cow;
      For rose-moles all in stipple upon trout that swim;
Fresh-firecoal chestnut-falls; finches' wings;
    Landscape plotted and pieced—fold,[1] fallow, and plough;   5
    And áll trádes, their gear and tackle and trim.

All things counter, original, spare, strange;
    Whatever is fickle, freckled (who knows how?)
      With swift, slow; sweet, sour; adazzle, dim;
He fathers-forth whose beauty is past change: 10
      Praise him.

[1] A small falcon that hovers in the air against the wind. The male is bluish gray.
[2] Darling, favorite.   [3] Prince.   [4] Coined word suggesting both *wrung* and *reined*.
[5] Rippling.   [6] A word coined from French *sillon,* furrow created by a plough.

[1] An undulation in the landscape.

CARRION COMFORT

Not, I'll not, carrion comfort, Despair, not feast on thee;
Not untwist—slack they may be—these last strands of man
In me ór, most weary, cry *I can no more*. I can;
Can something, hope, wish day come, not choose not to be.
But ah, but O thou terrible, why wouldst thou rude on me   5
Thy wring-world right foot rock? lay a lionlimb against me? scan
With darksome devouring eyes my bruisèd bones? and fan,
O in turns of tempest, me heaped there; me frantic to avoid thee and flee?

      Why? That my chaff might fly; my grain lie, sheer and clear.
Nay in all that toil, that coil, since (seems) I kissed the rod,[1]   10
Hand rather, my heart lo! lapped strength, stole joy, would laugh, chéer.
Cheer whom though? the hero whose heaven-handling flung me, fóot tród
Me? or me that fought him? O which one? is it each one? That night, that year
Of now done darkness I wretch lay wrestling with (my God!) my God.

A. E. HOUSMAN
1859–1936

LOVELIEST OF TREES

Loveliest of trees, the cherry now
Is hung with bloom along the bough,
And stands about the woodland ride
Wearing white for Eastertide.

Now, of my threescore years and ten,   5
Twenty will not come again,
And take from seventy springs a score,
It only leaves me fifty more.

[1] Willingly submitted to punishment or correction.

And since to look at things in bloom
Fifty springs are little room,
About the woodlands I will go
To see the cherry hung with snow.   10

BE STILL, MY SOUL, BE STILL

Be still, my soul, be still; the arms you bear are brittle,
    Earth and high heaven are fixt of old and founded strong.
Think rather,—call to thought, if now you grieve a little,
    The days when we had rest, O soul, for they were long.

Men loved unkindness then, but lightless in the quarry   5
    I slept and saw not; tears fell down, I did not mourn;
Sweat ran and blood sprang out and I was never sorry:
    Then it was well with me, in days ere I was born.

Now, and I muse for why and never find the reason,
    I pace the earth, and drink the air, and feel the sun.
Be still, be still, my soul; it is but for a season: 10
    Let us endure an hour and see injustice done.

Ay, look: high heaven and earth ail from the prime foundation;
    All thoughts to rive the heart are here, and all are vain:
Horror and scorn and hate and fear and indignation—   15
    Oh why did I awake? when shall I sleep again?

WILLIAM BUTLER YEATS
1865–1939

SAILING TO BYZANTIUM[1]

That is no country for old men. The young
In one another's arms, birds in the trees,
—Those dying generations—at their song,
The salmon-falls, the mackerel-crowded seas,
Fish, flesh, or fowl, commend all summer long   5
Whatever is begotten, born, and dies.
Caught in that sensual music all neglect
Monuments of unaging intellect.

An aged man is but a paltry thing,
A tattered coat upon a stick, unless   10
Soul clap its hands and sing, and louder sing
For every tatter in its mortal dress,
Nor is there singing school but studying
Monuments of its own magnificence;
And therefore I have sailed the seas and come   15
To the holy city of Byzantium.

O sages standing in God's holy fire
As in the gold mosaic of a wall,
Come from the holy fire, perne[2] in a gyre,
And be the singing-masters of my soul.   20
Consume my heart away, sick with desire
And fastened to a dying animal
It knows not what it is; and gather me
Into the artifice of eternity.

Once out of nature I shall never take   25
My bodily form from any natural thing.
But such a form as Grecian goldsmiths make
Of hammered gold and gold enamelling
To keep a drowsy Emperor awake;

[1] An ancient great city, the holy city of eastern Christendom.   [2] Turn, spin.

Or set upon a golden bough to sing
To lords and ladies of Byzantium
Of what is past, or passing, or to come.[3]

LEDA AND THE SWAN

A sudden blow: the great wings beating still
Above the staggering girl, her thighs caressed
By the dark webs, her nape caught in his bill,
He holds her helpless breast upon his breast.

How can those terrified vague fingers push   5
The feathered glory from her loosening thighs?
And how can body, laid in that white rush,
But feel the strange heart beating where it lies?

A shudder in the loins engenders there
The broken wall, the burning roof and tower   10
And Agamemnon dead.
                        Being so caught up,
So mastered by the brute blood of the air,
Did she put on his knowledge with his power
Before the indifferent beak could let her drop?

THE SECOND COMING

Turning and turning in the widening gyre
The falcon cannot hear the falconer;
Things fall apart; the centre cannot hold;
Mere anarchy is loosed upon the world,
The blood-dimmed tide is loosed, and everywhere   5
The ceremony of innocence is drowned;
The best lack all conviction, while the worst
Are full of passionate intensity.

Surely some revelation is at hand;
Surely the Second Coming is at hand.   10
The Second Coming! Hardly are those words out

    [3] I have read somewhere that in the Emperor's palace at Byzantium was a tree made
of gold and silver, and artificial birds that sang. (Yeats's note)

When a vast image out of *Spiritus Mundi*
Troubles my sight: somewhere in sands of the desert
A shape with lion body and the head of a man,
A gaze blank and pitiless as the sun,   15
Is moving its slow thighs, while all about it
Reel shadows of the indignant desert birds.
The darkness drops again; but now I know
That twenty centuries of stony sleep
Were vexed to nightmare by a rocking cradle,
And what rough beast, its hour come round at last,
Slouches towards Bethlehem to be born?

A PRAYER FOR MY DAUGHTER

Once more the storm is howling, and half hid
Under this cradle-hood and coverlid
My child sleeps on. There is no obstacle
But Gregory's wood and one bare hill
Whereby the haystack- and roof-levelling wind,   5
Bred on the Atlantic, can be stayed;
And for an hour I have walked and prayed
Because of the great gloom that is in my mind.

I have walked and prayed for this young child an hour
And heard the sea-wind scream upon the tower,   10
And under the arches of the bridge, and scream
In the elms above the flooded stream;
Imagining in excited reverie
That the future years had come,
Dancing to a frenzied drum,   15
Out of the murderous innocence of the sea.

May she be granted beauty and yet not
Beauty to make a stranger's eye distraught,
Or hers before a looking-glass, for such,
Being made beautiful overmuch,   20
Consider beauty a sufficient end,
Lose natural kindness and maybe
The heart-revealing intimacy
That chooses right, and never find a friend.

Helen being chosen found life flat and dull   25
And later had much trouble from a fool,
While that great Queen, that rose out of the spray,

Being fatherless could have her way
Yet chose a bandy-leggèd smith for man.
It's certain that fine women eat   30
A crazy salad with their meat
Whereby the Horn of Plenty is undone.

In courtesy I'd have her chiefly learned;
Hearts are not had as a gift but hearts are earned
By those that are not entirely beautiful;   35
Yet many, that have played the fool
For beauty's very self, has charm made wise,
And many a poor man that has roved,
Loved and thought himself beloved,
From a glad kindness cannot take his eyes.   40

May she become a flourishing hidden tree
That all her thoughts may like the linnet be,
And have no business but dispensing round
Their magnanimities of sound,
Nor but in merriment begin a chase,   45
Nor but in merriment a quarrel.
O may she live like some green laurel
Rooted in one dear perpetual place.

My mind, because the minds that I have loved,
The sort of beauty that I have approved,   50
Prosper but little, has dried up of late,
Yet knows that to be choked with hate
May well be of all evil chances chief.
If there's no hatred in a mind
Assault and battery of the wind   55
Can never tear the linnet from the leaf.

An intellectual hatred is the worst,
So let her think opinions are accursed.
Have I not seen the loveliest woman born
Out of the mouth of Plenty's horn,   60
Because of her opinionated mind
Barter that horn and every good
By quiet natures understood
For an old bellows full of angry wind?

Considering that, all hatred driven hence,   65
The soul recovers radical innocence
And learns at last that it is self-delighting,

Self-appeasing, self-affrighting,
And that its own sweet will is Heaven's will;
She can, though every face should scowl   70
And every windy quarter howl
Or every bellows burst, be happy still.

And may her bridegroom bring her to a house
Where all's accustomed, ceremonious;
For arrogance and hatred are the wares   75
Peddled in the thoroughfares.
How but in custom and in ceremony
Are innocence and beauty born?
Ceremony's name for the rich horn,
And custom for the spreading laurel tree.   80

EDWIN ARLINGTON ROBINSON
1869–1935

LUKE HAVERGAL

Go to the western gate, Luke Havergal,
There where the vines cling crimson on the wall,
And in the twilight wait for what will come.
The leaves will whisper there of her, and some,
Like flying words, will strike you as they fall;   5
But go, and if you listen she will call.
Go to the western gate, Luke Havergal—
Luke Havergal.

No, there is not a dawn in eastern skies
To rift the fiery night that's in your eyes;   10
But there, where western glooms are gathering,
The dark will end the dark, if anything:
God slays Himself with every leaf that flies,

And hell is more than half of paradise.
No, there is not a dawn in eastern skies—   15
In eastern skies.

Out of a grave I come to tell you this,
Out of a grave I come to quench the kiss
That flames upon your forehead with a glow
That blinds you to the way that you must go.   20
Yes, there is yet one way to where she is,
Bitter, but one that faith may never miss.
Out of a grave I come to tell you this—
To tell you this.

There is the western gate, Luke Havergal,   25
There are the crimson leaves upon the wall.
Go, for the winds are tearing them away—
Nor think to riddle the dead words they say,
Nor any more to feel them as they fall;
But go, and if you trust her she will call.   30
There is the western gate, Luke Havergal—
Luke Havergal.

MINIVER CHEEVY

Miniver Cheevy, child of scorn,
    Grew lean while he assailed the seasons;
He wept that he was ever born,
    And he had reasons.

Miniver loved the days of old   5
    When swords were bright and steeds were prancing.
The vision of a warrior bold
    Would set him dancing.

Miniver sighed for what was not,
    And dreamed, and rested from his labors;   10
He dreamed of Thebes and Camelot,
    And Priam's neighbors.

Miniver mourned the ripe renown
    That made so many a name so fragrant;
He mourned Romance, now on the town,
    And Art, a vagrant.

15

Miniver loved the Medici,
    Albeit he had never seen one;
He would have sinned incessantly
    Could he have been one.

20

Miniver cursed the commonplace
    And eyed a khaki suit with loathing;
He missed the mediæval grace
    Of iron clothing.

Miniver scorned the gold he sought,
    But sore annoyed was he without it;
Miniver thought, and thought, and thought,
    And thought about it.

25

Miniver Cheevy, born too late,
    Scratched his head and kept on thinking:
Miniver coughed, and called it fate,
    And kept on drinking.

30

MR. FLOOD'S PARTY

Old Eben Flood, climbing alone one night
Over the hill between the town below
And the forsaken upland hermitage
That held as much as he should ever know
On earth again of home, paused warily.
The road was his with not a native near;
And Eben, having leisure, said aloud,
For no man else in Tilbury Town to hear:

5

"Well, Mr. Flood, we have the harvest moon
Again, and we may not have many more;
The bird is on the wing, the poet says,

10

And you and I have said it here before.
Drink to the bird." He raised up to the light
The jug that he had gone so far to fill,
And answered huskily: "Well, Mr. Flood,   15
Since you propose it, I believe I will."

Alone, as if enduring to the end
A valiant armor of scarred hopes outworn,
He stood there in the middle of the road
Like Roland's ghost winding a silent horn.   20
Below him, in the town among the trees,
Where friends of other days had honored him,
A phantom salutation of the dead
Rang thinly till old Eben's eyes were dim.

Then, as a mother lays her sleeping child   25
Down tenderly, fearing it may awake,
He set the jug down slowly at his feet
With trembling care, knowing that most things break;
And only when assured that on firm earth
It stood, as the uncertain lives of men   30
Assuredly did not, he paced away,
And with his hand extended paused again:

"Well, Mr. Flood, we have not met like this
In a long time; and many a change has come
To both of us, I fear, since last it was   35
We had a drop together. Welcome home!"
Convivially returning with himself,
Again he raised the jug up to the light;
And with an acquiescent quaver said:
"Well, Mr. Flood, if you insist, I might.   40

"Only a very little, Mr. Flood—
For auld lang syne. No more, sir; that will do."
So, for the time, apparently it did,
And Eben evidently thought so too;
For soon amid the silver loneliness   45
Of night he lifted up his voice and sang,
Secure, with only two moons listening,
Until the whole harmonious landscape rang—
"For auld lang syne." The weary throat gave out,
The last word wavered; and the song being done,   50
He raised again the jug regretfully
And shook his head, and was again alone.

There was not much that was ahead of him,
And there was nothing in the town below—
Where strangers would have shut the many doors
That many friends had opened long ago.

55

WALTER DE LA MARE
1873-1956

THE LISTENERS

"Is there anybody there?" said the Traveller,
    Knocking on the moonlit door;
And his horse in the silence champed the grasses
    Of the forest's ferny floor:
And a bird flew up out of the turret,
    Above the Traveller's head:
And he smote upon the door again a second time;
    "Is there anybody there?" he said.
But no one descended to the Traveller;
    No head from the leaf-fringed sill
Leaned over and looked into his grey eyes,
    Where he stood perplexed and still.
But only a host of phantom listeners
    That dwelt in the lone house then
Stood listening in the quiet of the moonlight
    To that voice from the world of men:
Stood thronging the faint moonbeams on the dark stair,
    That goes down to the empty hall,
Hearkening in an air stirred and shaken
    By the lonely Traveller's call.
And he felt in his heart their strangeness,
    Their stillness answering his cry,
While his horse moved, cropping the dark turf,
    'Neath the starred and leafy sky;
For he suddenly smote on the door, even
    Louder, and lifted his head:—
"Tell them I came, and no one answered,
    That I kept my word," he said.
Never the least stir made the listeners,
    Though every word he spake

5

10

15

20

25

30

Fell echoing through the shadowiness of the still house
  From the one man left awake:
Ay, they heard his foot upon the stirrup,
  And the sound of iron on stone,
And how the silence surged softly backward,   35
  When the plunging hoofs were gone.

ROBERT FROST
1874–1963

STOPPING BY WOODS ON A SNOWY EVENING

Whose woods these are I think I know
His house is in the village though;
He will not see me stopping here
To watch his woods fill up with snow.

My little horse must think it queer   5
To stop without a farmhouse near
Between the woods and frozen lake
The darkest evening of the year.

He gives his harness bells a shake
To ask if there is some mistake.   10
The only other sound's the sweep
Of easy wind and downy flake.

The woods are lovely, dark and deep,
But I have promises to keep,
And miles to go before I sleep,   15
And miles to go before I sleep.

NEITHER OUT FAR
NOR IN DEEP

The people along the sand
All turn and look one way.
They turn their back on the land.
They look at the sea all day.

As long as it takes to pass   5
A ship keeps raising its hull;
The wetter ground like glass
Reflects a standing gull.

The land may vary more;
But wherever the truth may be—   10
The water comes ashore,
And the people look at the sea.

They cannot look out far.
They cannot look in deep.
But when was that ever a bar   15
To any watch they keep?

DESIGN

I found a dimpled spider, fat and white,
On a white heal-all, holding up a moth
Like a white piece of rigid satin cloth—
Assorted characters of death and blight
Mixed ready to begin the morning right,   5
Like the ingredients of a witches' broth—
A snow-drop spider, a flower like a froth,
And dead wings carried like a paper kite.

What had that flower to do with being white,   10
The wayside blue and innocent heal-all?
What brought that kindred spider to that height,
Then steered the white moth thither in the night?
What but design of darkness to appall?—
If design govern in a thing so small?   15

PROVIDE, PROVIDE

The witch that came (the withered hag)
To wash the steps with pail and rag,
Was once the beauty Abishag,

The picture pride of Hollywood.
Too many fall from great and good   5
For you to doubt the likelihood.

Die early and avoid the fate.
Or if predestined to die late,
Make up your mind to die in state.

Make the whole stock exchange your own!   10
If need be occupy a throne,
Where nobody can call *you* crone.

Some have relied on what they knew;
Others on being simply true.
What worked for them might work for you.   15

No memory of having starred
Atones for later disregard,
Or keeps the end from being hard.

Better to go down dignified
With boughten friendship at your side   20
Than none at all. Provide, provide!

DIRECTIVE

Back out of all this now too much for us,
Back in a time made simple by the loss
Of detail, burned, dissolved, and broken off
Like graveyard marble sculpture in the weather,
There is a house that is no more a house   5
Upon a farm that is no more a farm
And in a town that is no more a town.

The road there, if you'll let a guide direct you
Who only has at heart your getting lost,
May seem as if it should have been a quarry—   10
Great monolithic knees the former town
Long since gave up pretense of keeping covered.
And there's a story in a book about it:
Besides the wear of iron wagon wheels
The ledges show lines ruled southeast northwest,   15
The chisel work of an enormous Glacier
That braced his feet against the Arctic Pole.
You must not mind a certain coolness from him
Still said to haunt this side of Panther Mountain.
Nor need you mind the serial ordeal   20
Of being watched from forty cellar holes
As if by eye pairs out of forty firkins.
As for the woods' excitement over you
That sends light rustle rushes to their leaves,
Charge that to upstart inexperience.   25
Where were they all not twenty years ago?
They think too much of having shaded out
A few old pecker-fretted apple trees.
Make yourself up a cheering song of how
Someone's road home from work this once was,   30
Who may be just ahead of you on foot
Or creaking with a buggy load of grain.
The height of the adventure is the height
Of country where two village cultures faded
Into each other. Both of them are lost.   35
And if you're lost enough to find yourself
By now, pull in your ladder road behind you
And put a sign up CLOSED to all but me.
Then make yourself at home. The only field
Now left's no bigger than a harness gall.   40
First there's the children's house of make believe,
Some shattered dishes underneath a pine,
The playthings in the playhouse of the children.
Weep for what little things could make them glad.
Then for the house that is no more a house,   45
But only a belilaced cellar hole,
Now slowly closing like a dent in dough.
This was no playhouse but a house in earnest.
Your destination and your destiny's
A brook that was the water of the house,   50
Cold as a spring as yet so near its source,
Too lofty and original to rage.
(We know the valley streams that when aroused
Will leave their tatters hung on barb and thorn.)
I have kept hidden in the instep arch   55
Of an old cedar at the waterside

A broken drinking goblet like the Grail
Under a spell so the wrong ones can't find it,
So can't get saved, as Saint Mark says they mustn't.
(I stole the goblet from the children's playhouse.) 60
Here are your waters and your watering place.
Drink and be whole again beyond confusion.

WALLACE STEVENS

1879–1955

SUNDAY MORNING

1

Complacencies of the peignoir, and late
Coffee and oranges in a sunny chair,
And the green freedom of a cockatoo
Upon a rug mingle to dissipate
The holy hush of ancient sacrifice. 5
She dreams a little, and she feels the dark
Encroachment of that old catastrophe,
As a calm darkens among water-lights.
The pungent oranges and bright, green wings
Seem things in some procession of the dead, 10
Winding across wide water, without sound.
The day is like wide water, without sound,
Stilled for the passing of her dreaming feet
Over the seas, to silent Palestine,
Dominion of the blood and sepulchre. 15

2

Why should she give her bounty to the dead?
What is divinity if it can come
Only in silent shadows and in dreams?
Shall she not find in comforts of the sun,
In pungent fruit and bright, green wings, or else 20
In any balm or beauty of the earth,
Things to be cherished like the thought of heaven?
Divinity must live within herself:
Passions of rain, or moods in falling snow;

Grievings in loneliness, or unsubdued   25
Elations when the forest blooms; gusty
Emotions on wet roads on autumn nights;
All pleasures and all pains, remembering
The bough of summer and the winter branch.
These are the measures destined for her soul.   30

3

Jove in the clouds had his inhuman birth.
No mother suckled him, no sweet land gave
Large-mannered motions to his mythy mind.
He moved among us, as a muttering king,
Magnificent, would move among his hinds,   35
Until our blood, commingling, virginal,
With heaven, brought such requital to desire
The very hinds discerned it, in a star.
Shall our blood fail? Or shall it come to be
The blood of paradise? And shall the earth   40
Seem all of paradise that we shall know?
The sky will be much friendlier then than now,
A part of labor and a part of pain,
And next in glory to enduring love,
Not this dividing and indifferent blue.   45

4

She says, "I am content when wakened birds,
Before they fly, test the reality
Of misty fields, by their sweet questionings;
But when the birds are gone, and their warm fields
Return no more, where, then, is paradise?"   50
There is not any haunt of prophecy,
Nor any old chimera of the grave,
Neither the golden underground, nor isle
Melodious, where spirits gat them home,
Nor visionary south, nor cloudy palm   55
Remote on heaven's hill, that has endured
As April's green endures; or will endure
Like her remembrance of awakened birds,
Or her desire for June and evening, tipped
By the consummation of the swallow's wings.   60

5

She says, "But in contentment I still feel
The need of some imperishable bliss."
Death is the mother of beauty; hence from her,

Alone, shall come fulfilment to our dreams
And our desires. Although she strews the leaves   65
Of sure obliteration on our paths,
The path sick sorrow took, the many paths
Where triumph rang its brassy phrase, or love
Whispered a little out of tenderness,
She makes the willow shiver in the sun   70
For maidens who were wont to sit and gaze
Upon the grass, relinquished to their feet.
She causes boys to pile new plums and pears
On disregarded plate. The maidens taste
And stray impassioned in the littering leaves.   75

6

Is there no change of death in paradise?
Does ripe fruit never fall? Or do the boughs
Hang always heavy in that perfect sky,
Unchanging, yet so like our perishing earth,
With rivers like our own that seek for seas   80
They never find, the same receding shores
That never touch with inarticulate pang?
Why set the pear upon those river-banks
Or spice the shores with odors of the plum?
Alas, that they should wear our colors there,   85
The silken weavings of our afternoons,
And pick the strings of our insipid lutes!
Death is the mother of beauty, mystical,
Within whose burning bosom we devise
Our earthly mothers waiting, sleeplessly.   90

7

Supple and turbulent, a ring of men
Shall chant in orgy on a summer morn
Their boisterous devotion to the sun,
Not as a god, but as a god might be,
Naked among them, like a savage source.   95
Their chant shall be a chant of paradise,
Out of their blood, returning to the sky;
And in their chant shall enter, voice by voice,
The windy lake wherein their lord delights,
The trees, like serafin, and echoing hills,   100
That choir among themselves long afterward.
They shall know well the heavenly fellowship
Of men that perish and of summer morn.
And whence they came and whither they shall go
The dew upon their feet shall manifest.   105

8

She hears, upon that water without sound,
A voice that cries, "The tomb in Palestine
Is not the porch of spirits lingering.
It is the grave of Jesus, where he lay."
We live in an old chaos of the sun,   110
Or old dependency of day and night,
Or island solitude, unsponsored, free,
Of that wide water, inescapable.
Deer walk upon our mountains, and the quail
Whistle about us their spontaneous cries;   115
Sweet berries ripen in the wilderness;
And, in the isolation of the sky,
As evening, casual flocks of pigeons make
Ambiguous undulations as they sink,
Downward to darkness, on extended wings.   120

ANECDOTE OF THE JAR

I placed a jar in Tennessee,
And round it was, upon a hill.
It made the slovenly wilderness
Surround that hill.

The wilderness rose up to it,   5
And sprawled around, no longer wild.
The jar was round upon the ground
And tall and of a port in air.

It took dominion everywhere.
The jar was gray and bare.   10
It did not give of bird or bush,
Like nothing else in Tennessee.

PETER QUINCE AT THE CLAVIER

I

Just as my fingers on these keys
Make music, so the self-same sounds
On my spirit make a music too.

Music is feeling then, not sound;
And thus it is that what I feel,
Here in this room, desiring you,

Thinking of your blue-shadowed silk,
Is music. It is like the strain
Waked in the elders by Susanna:

Of a green evening, clear and warm,
She bathed in her still garden, while
The red-eyed elders, watching, felt

The basses of their being throb
In witching chords, and their thin blood
Pulse pizzicati of Hosanna.

2

In the green water, clear and warm,
Susanna lay.
She searched
The touch of springs,
And found
Concealed imaginings.
She sighed
For so much melody.

Upon the bank, she stood
In the cool
Of spent emotions.
She felt, among the leaves,
The dew
Of old devotions.

She walked upon the grass,
Still quavering.
The winds were like her maids,
On timid feet,
Fetching her woven scarves,
Yet wavering.

A breath upon her hand
Muted the night.
She turned—
A cymbal crashed,
And roaring horns.

3

Soon, with a noise like tambourines,
Came her attendant Byzantines.

They wondered why Susanna cried
Against the elders by her side:

And as they whispered, the refrain
Was like a willow swept by rain.

Anon their lamps' uplifted flame
Revealed Susanna and her shame.

And then the simpering Byzantines,
Fled, with a noise like tambourines.

4

Beauty is momentary in the mind—
The fitful tracing of a portal;
But in the flesh it is immortal.

The body dies; the body's beauty lives.
So evenings die, in their green going,
A wave, interminably flowing.
So gardens die, their meek breath scenting
The cowl of Winter, done repenting.
So maidens die, to the auroral
Celebration of a maiden's choral.

SOLDIER, THERE IS A WAR

Soldier, there is a war between the mind
And sky, between thought and day and night. It is
For that the poet is always in the sun,

Patches the moon together in his room
To his Virgilian cadences, up down,
Up down. It is a war that never ends.

Yet it depends on yours. The two are one.
They are a plural, a right and left, a pair,
Two parallels that meet if only in

The meeting of their shadows or that meet   10
In a book in a barrack, a letter from Malay.
But your war ends. And after it you return

With six meats and twelve wines or else without
To walk another room . . . Monsieur and comrade,
The soldier is poor without the poet's lines,   15

His petty syllabi, the sounds that stick,
Inevitably modulating, in the blood.
And war for war, each has its gallant kind.

How simply the fictive hero becomes the real;
How gladly with proper words the soldier dies,   20
If he must, or lives on the bread of faithful speech.

D. H. LAWRENCE
1885–1930

THE ELEPHANT IS SLOW TO MATE

The elephant, the huge old beast,
    is slow to mate;
he finds a female, they show no haste,
    they wait.

for the sympathy in their vast shy hearts
    slowly, slowly to rouse
as they loiter along the river-beds
    and drink and browse

and dash in panic through the brake
    of forest with the herd,   5
and sleep in massive silence, and wake
    together, without a word.

So slowly the great hot elephant hearts
    grow full of desire,
and the great beasts mate in secret at last,
    hiding their fire.

Oldest they are and the wisest of beasts
    so they know at last
how to wait for the loneliest of feasts,
    for the full repast.   10

They do not snatch, they do not tear;
    their massive blood
moves as the moon-tides, near, more near,
    till they touch in flood.

SNAKE

A snake came to my water-trough
On a hot, hot day, and I in pyjamas for the heat,
To drink there.

In the deep, strange-scented shade of the great dark carobtree
I came down the steps with my pitcher   5
And must wait, must stand and wait, for there he was at the trough
    before me.

He reached down from a fissure in the earth-wall in the gloom
And trailed his yellow-brown slackness soft-bellied down, over the
    edge of the stone trough
And rested his throat upon the stone bottom,
And where the water had dripped from the tap, in a small clearness,   10
He sipped with his straight mouth,
Softly drank through his straight gums, into his slack long body,
Silently.

Someone was before me at my water-trough,
And I, like a second comer, waiting.   15
He lifted his head from his drinking, as cattle do,
And looked at me vaguely, as drinking cattle do,

And flickered his two-forked tongue from his lips, and mused a
    moment,
And stooped and drank a little more,
Being earth-brown, earth-golden from the burning bowels of the earth   20
On the day of Sicilian July, with Etna smoking.

The voice of my education said to me
He must be killed,
For in Sicily the black, black snakes are innocent, the gold are
    venomous.

And voices in me said, If you were a man   25
You would take a stick and break him now, and finish him off.

But must I confess how I liked him,
How glad I was he had come like a guest in quiet, to drink at my
    water-trough
And depart peaceful, pacified, and thankless,
Into the burning bowels of this earth?   30

Was it cowardice, that I dared not kill him?
Was it perversity, that I longed to talk to him?
Was it humility, to feel so honoured?
I felt so honoured.

And yet those voices: 35
If you were not afraid, you would kill him!

And truly I was afraid, I was most afraid,
But even so, honoured still more
That he should seek my hospitality
From out the dark door of the secret earth.   40

He drank enough
And lifted his head, dreamily, as one who has drunken,
And flickered his tongue like a forked night on the air, so black,
Seeming to lick his lips,
And looked around like a god, unseeing, into the air,   45
And slowly turned his head,

And slowly, very slowly, as if thrice adream,
Proceeded to draw his slow length curving round
And climb again the broken bank of my wall-face.

And as he put his head into that dreadful hole, 50
And as he slowly drew up, snake-easing his shoulders, and entered
farther,
A sort of horror, a sort of protest against his withdrawing into that
horrid black hole,
Deliberately going into the blackness, and slowly drawing himself
after,
Overcame me now his back was turned.

I looked round, I put down my pitcher, 55
I picked up a clumsy log
And threw it at the water-trough with a clatter.

I think it did not hit him,
But suddenly that part of him that was left behind convulsed in
undignified haste,
Writhed like lightning, and was gone 60
Into the black hole, the earth-lipped fissure in the wall-front,
At which, in the intense still noon, I stared with fascination.

And immediately I regretted it.
I thought how paltry, how vulgar, what a mean act!
I despised myself and the voices of my accursed human education. 65

And I thought of the albatross,
And I wished he would come back, my snake.

For he seemed to me again like a king,
Like a king in exile, uncrowned in the underworld,
Now due to be crowned again. 70

And so, I missed my chance with one of the lords
Of life.

And I have something to expiate;
A pettiness.

EZRA POUND
1 8 8 5 –

A PACT

I make a pact with you, Walt Whitman—
I have detested you long enough.
I come to you as a grown child
Who has had a pig-headed father;
I am old enough now to make friends.   5
It was you that broke the new wood,
Now is a time for carving.
We have one sap and one root—
Let there be commerce between us.

ITE

Go, my songs, seek your praise from the young and from the intolerant,
    move among the lovers of perfection alone.
Seek ever to stand in the hard Sophoclean light
And take your wounds from it gladly.

LES MILLWIN

The little Millwins attend the Russian Ballet.
The mauve and greenish souls of the little Millwins
Were seen lying along the upper seats
Like so many unused boas.

The turbulent and undisciplined host of art students—   5
The rigorous deputation from "Slade"—
Was before them.

With arms exalted, with fore-arms
Crossed in great futuristic X's, the art students
Exulted, they beheld the splendours of *Cleopatra*.   10

And the little Millwins beheld these things;
With their large and anaemic eyes they looked out upon this configuration.

Let us therefore mention the fact,
For it seems to us worthy of record.

COME MY CANTILATIONS

Come my cantilations,
Let us dump our hatreds into one bunch and be done with them,
Hot sun, clear water, fresh wind,
Let me be free of pavements,
Let me be free of the printers.   5
Let come beautiful people
Wearing raw silk of good colour,
Let come the graceful speakers,
Let come the ready of wit,
Let come the gay of manner, the insolent and the exulting.   10
We speak of burnished lakes,
Of dry air, as clear as metal.

MARIANNE MOORE
1887–

POETRY

I, too, dislike it: there are things that are important beyond all this fiddle.
Reading it, however, with a perfect contempt for it, one discovers in
it after all, a place for the genuine.
    Hands that can grasp, eyes
      that can dilate, hair that can rise   5
        if it must, these things are important not because a

high-sounding interpretation can be put upon them but because they are
    useful. When they become so derivative as to become unintelligible,
    the same thing may be said for all of us, that we
        do not admire what   10
        we cannot understand: the bat
            holding on upside down or in quest of something to

eat, elephants pushing, a wild horse taking a roll, a tireless wolf under
    a tree, the immovable critic twitching his skin like a horse that
        feels a flea, the base-
    ball fan, the statistician—   15
        nor is it valid
            to discriminate "against business documents and

school-books"; all these phenomena are important. One must make a
        distinction
    however: when dragged into prominence by half poets, the result
        is not poetry,
    nor till the poets among us can be   20
        "literalists of
        the imagination"—above
            insolence and triviality and can present

for inspection, imaginary gardens with real toads in them, shall we have
    it. In the meantime, if you demand on the one hand,   25
    the raw material of poetry in
        all its rawness and
        that which is on the other hand
            genuine, then you are interested in poetry.

ELEPHANTS

Uplifted and waved until immobilized
wistaria-like, the opposing opposed
mouse-grey twined proboscises' trunk formed by two
trunks, fights itself to a spiraled inter-nosed

deadlock of dyke-enforced massiveness. It's a   5
knock-down drag-out fight that asks no quarter? Just
a pastime, as when the trunk rains on itself
the pool it siphoned up; or when—since each must

provide his forty-pound bough dinner—he broke
the leafy branches. These templars of the Tooth,
these matched intensities, take master care of
master tools. One, sleeping with the calm of youth, 10

at full length in the half dry sun-flecked stream-bed,
rests his hunting-horn-curled trunk on shallowed stone.
The sloping hollow of the sleeper's body 15
cradles the gently breathing eminence's prone

mahout, asleep like a lifeless six-foot
frog, so feather light the elephant's stiff
ear's unconscious of the crossed feet's weight. And the
defenceless human thing sleeps as sound as if 20

incised with hard wrinkles, embossed with wide ears,
invincibly tusked, made safe by magic hairs!
As if, as if, it is all ifs; we are at
much unease. But magic's masterpiece is theirs,—

Houdini's serenity quelling his fears. 25
Elephant ear-witnesses-to-be of hymns
and glorias, these ministrants all grey or
grey with white on legs or trunks, are a pilgrims'

pattern of revery not reverence,—a
religious procession without any priests, 30
the centuries-old carefullest unrehearsed
play. Blessed by Buddha's Tooth, the obedient beasts

themselves as toothed temples blessing the street, see
the white elephant carry the cushion that
carries the casket that carries the Tooth. 35
Amenable to what, matched with him, are gnat

trustees, he does not step on them as the white-
canopied blue-cushioned Tooth is augustly
and slowly returned to the shrine. Though white is
the colour of worship and of mourning, he 40

is not here to worship and he is too wise
to mourn,—a life prisoner but reconciled.

593 MARIANNE MOORE

With trunk tucked up compactly—the elephant's
sign of defeat—he resisted, but is the child

of reason now. His straight trunk seems to say: when   45
what we hoped for came to nothing, we revived.
As loss could not ever alter Socrates'
tranquillity, equanimity's contrived

by the elephant. With the Socrates of
animals as with Sophocles the Bee, on whose   50
tombstone a hive was incised, sweetness tinctures
his gravity. His held up fore-leg for use

as a stair, to be climbed or descended with
the aid of his ear, expounds the brotherhood
of creatures to man the encroacher, by the   55
small word with the dot, meaning know,—the verb bud.

These knowers 'arouse the feeling that they are
allied to man' and can change roles with their trustees.
Hardship makes the soldier; then teachableness
makes him the philosopher—as Socrates,   60

prudently testing the suspicious thing, knew
the wisest is he who's not sure that he knows.
Who rides on a tiger can never dismount;
asleep on an elephant, that is repose.

THOMAS STEARNS ELIOT
1888–1965

THE LOVE SONG
OF J. ALFRED PRUFROCK

S'io credesse che mia risposta fosse
A persona che mai tornasse al mondo,
Questa fiamma staria senza piu scosse.
Ma perciocche giammai di questo fondo
Non torno vivo alcun, s'i'odo il vero,
Senza tema d'infamia ti rispondo.

Let us go then, you and I,
When the evening is spread out against the sky
Like a patient etherised upon a table;
Let us go, through certain half-deserted streets,
The muttering retreats   5
Of restless nights in one-night cheap hotels
And sawdust restaurants with oyster-shells:
Streets that follow like a tedious argument
Of insidious intent
To lead you to an overwhelming question. . .   10
Oh, do not ask, "What is it?"
Let us go and make our visit.

In the room the women come and go
Talking of Michelangelo.

The yellow fog that rubs its back upon the window-panes,   15
The yellow smoke that rubs its muzzle on the window-panes
Licked its tongue into the corners of the evening,
Lingered upon the pools that stand in drains,
Let fall upon its back the soot that falls from chimneys,
Slipped by the terrace, made a sudden leap,   20
And seeing that it was a soft October night,
Curled once about the house, and fell asleep.

And indeed there will be time
For the yellow smoke that slides along the street,
Rubbing its back upon the window-panes;   25

There will be time, there will be time
To prepare a face to meet the faces that you meet;
There will be time to murder and create,
And time for all the works and days of hands
That lift and drop a question on your plate;   30
Time for you and time for me,
And time yet for a hundred indecisions,
And for a hundred visions and revisions,
Before the taking of a toast and tea.

        In the room the women come and go   35
Talking of Michelangelo.

        And indeed there will be time
To wonder, "Do I dare?" and, "Do I dare?"
Time to turn back and descend the stair,
With a bald spot in the middle of my hair—   40
[They will say: "How his hair is growing thin!"]
My morning coat, my collar mounting firmly to the chin,
My necktie rich and modest, but asserted by a simple pin—
[They will say: "But how his arms and legs are thin!"]
Do I dare   45
Disturb the universe?
In a minute there is time
For decisions and revisions which a minute will reverse.

        For I have known them all already, known them all:—
Have known the evenings, mornings, afternoons,   50
I have measured out my life with coffee spoons;
I know the voices dying with a dying fall
Beneath the music from a farther room.
        So how should I presume?

        And I have known the eyes already, known them all—   55
The eyes that fix you in a formulated phrase,
And when I am formulated, sprawling on a pin,
When I am pinned and wriggling on the wall,
Then how should I begin
To spit out all the butt-ends of my days and ways?   60
        And how should I presume?

        And I have known the arms already, known them all—
Arms that are braceleted and white and bare
[But in the lamplight, downed with light brown hair!]
Is it perfume from a dress   65

That makes me so digress?
Arms that lie along a table, or wrap about a shawl.
   And should I then presume?
   And how should I begin?

Shall I say, I have gone at dusk through narrow streets   70
And watched the smoke that rises from the pipes
Of lonely men in shirt-sleeves, leaning out of windows? . . .

   I should have been a pair of ragged claws
Scuttling across the floors of silent seas.

And the afternoon, the evening, sleeps so peacefully!   75
Smoothed by long fingers,
Asleep . . . tired . . . or it malingers,
Stretched on the floor, here beside you and me.
Should I, after tea and cakes and ices,
Have the strength to force the moment to its crisis?   80
But though I have wept and fasted, wept and prayed,
Though I have seen my head [grown slightly bald] brought in upon
    a platter,
I am no prophet—and here's no great matter;
I have seen the moment of my greatness flicker,
And I have seen the eternal Footman hold my coat, and snicker,   85
And in short, I was afraid.

   And would it have been worth it, after all,
After the cups, the marmalade, the tea,
Among the porcelain, among some talk of you and me,
Would it have been worth while,   90
To have bitten off the matter with a smile,
To have squeezed the universe into a ball
To roll it toward some overwhelming question,
To say: "I am Lazarus, come from the dead,
Come back to tell you all, I shall tell you all"—   95
If one, settling a pillow by her head,
   Should say: "That is not what I meant at all.
   That is not it, at all."

   And would it have been worth it, after all,
Would it have been worth while,   100
After the sunsets and the dooryards and the sprinkled streets,
After the novels, after the teacups, after the skirts that trail along the
    floor—
And this, and so much more?—

It is impossible to say just what I mean!
But as if a magic lantern threw the nerves in patterns on a screen: 105
Would it have been worth while
If one, settling a pillow or throwing off a shawl,
And turning toward the window, should say:
   "That is not it at all,
   That is not what I meant, at all."   110

No! I am not Prince Hamlet, nor was meant to be;
Am an attendant lord, one that will do
To swell a progress, start a scene or two,
Advise the prince; no doubt, an easy tool,
Deferential, glad to be of use,   115
Politic, cautious, and meticulous;
Full of high sentence, but a bit obtuse;
At times, indeed, almost ridiculous—
Almost, at times, the Fool.

   I grow old . . . I grow old . . .   120
I shall wear the bottoms of my trousers rolled.

   Shall I part my hair behind? Do I dare to eat a peach?
I shall wear white flannel trousers, and walk upon the beach.
I have heard the mermaids singing, each to each.

   I do not think that they will sing to me.   125

   I have seen them riding seaward on the waves
Combing the white hair of the waves blown back
When the wind blows the water white and black.

   We have lingered in the chambers of the sea
By sea-girls wreathed with seaweed red and brown   130
Till human voices wake us, and we drown.

LA FIGLIA CHE PIANGE

O quam te memorem virgo . . .

Stand on the highest pavement of the stair—
Lean on a garden urn—
Weave, weave the sunlight in your hair—
Clasp your flowers to you with a pained surprise—

Fling them to the ground and turn   5
With a fugitive resentment in your eyes:
But weave, weave the sunlight in your hair.

     So I would have had him leave,
So I would have had her stand and grieve,
So he would have left   10
As the soul leaves the body torn and bruised,
As the mind deserts the body it has used.
I should find
Some way incomparably light and deft,
Some way we both should understand,   15
Simple and faithless as a smile and shake of the hand.

     She turned away, but with the autumn weather
Compelled my imagination many days,
Many days and many hours:
Her hair over her arms and her arms full of flowers.   20
And I wonder how they should have been together!
I should have lost a gesture and a pose.
Sometimes these cogitations still amaze
The troubled midnight and the noon's repose.

THE HIPPOPOTAMUS

> *Similiter et omnes revereantur Diaconos, ut mandatum*
> *Jesu Christi; et Epīscopum, ut Jesum Christum, existen-*
> *tem filium Patris; Presbyteros autem, ut concilium Dei*
> *et conjunctionem Apostolorum. Sine his Ecclesia non*
> *vocatur; de quibus suadeo vos sic habeo.*
>
> S. IGNATII AD TRALLIANOS.

And When This Epistle Is Read among You, Cause That It be Read Also in the
Church of the Laodiceans.

The broad-backed hippopotamus
Rests on his belly in the mud;
Although he seems so firm to us
He is merely flesh and blood.

     Flesh and blood is weak and frail,   5
Susceptible to nervous shock;
While the True Church can never fail
For it is based upon a rock.

The hippo's feeble steps may err
In compassing material ends,
While the True Church need never stir
To gather in its dividends.

The 'potamus can never reach
The mango on the mango-tree;
But fruits of pomegranate and peach
Refresh the Church from over sea.

At mating time the hippo's voice
Betrays inflexions hoarse and odd,
But every week we hear rejoice
The Church, at being one with God.

The hippopotamus's day
Is passed in sleep: at night he hunts;
God works in a mysterious way—
The Church can sleep and feed at once.

I saw the 'potamus take wing
Ascending from the damp savannas,
And quiring angels round him sing
The praise of God, in loud hosannas.

Blood of the Lamb shall wash him clean
And him shall heavenly arms enfold,
Among the saints he shall be seen
Performing on a harp of gold.

He shall be washed as white as snow,
By all the martyr'd virgins kist,
While the True Church remains below
Wrapt in the old miasmal mist.

SWEENEY AMONG THE NIGHTINGALES

*Why Should I speak of the nightingale? The nightingale
sings of adulterous wrong.*

Apeneck Sweeney spreads his knees
Letting his arms hang down to laugh,

The zebra stripes along his jaw
Swelling to maculate giraffe.

The circles of the stormy moon
Slide westward to the River Plate,
Death and the Raven drift above
And Sweeney guards the hornèd gate.

Gloomy Orion and the Dog
Are veiled; and hushed the shrunken seas;
The person in the Spanish cape
Tries to sit on Sweeney's knees

Slips and pulls the table cloth
Overturns a coffee cup,
Reorganized upon the floor
She yawns and draws a stocking up;

The silent man in mocha brown
Sprawls at the window-sill and gapes;
The waiter brings in oranges,
Bananas, figs and hot-house grapes;

The silent vertebrate exhales,
Contracts and concentrates, withdraws;
Rachel *née* Rabinovitch
Tears at the grapes with murderous paws;

She and the lady in the cape
Are suspect, thought to be in league;
Therefore the man with heavy eyes
Declines the gambit, shows fatigue,

Leaves the room and reappears
Outside the window, leaning in,
Branches of wistaria
Circumscribe a golden grin;

The host with someone indistinct
Converses at the door apart,
The nightingales are singing near
The Convent of the Sacred Heart,

And sang within the bloody wood
When Agamemnon cried aloud,
And let their liquid siftings fall
To stain the stiff dishonoured shroud.   40

THE HOLLOW MEN

Mistah Kurtz—he dead.

A penny for the Old Guy

I
We are the hollow men
We are the stuffed men
Leaning together
Headpiece filled with straw. Alas!
Our dried voices, when   5
We whisper together
Are quiet and meaningless
As wind in dry grass
Or rats' feet over broken glass
In our dry cellar   10

Shape without form, shade without colour,
Paralysed force, gesture without motion;

Those who have crossed
With direct eyes, to death's other Kingdom
Remember us—if at all—not as lost   15
Violent souls, but only
As the hollow men
The stuffed men.

II
Eyes I dare not meet in dreams
In death's dream kingdom   20
These do not appear:
There, the eyes are
Sunlight on a broken column
There, is a tree swinging
And voices are   25
In the wind's singing

More distant and more solemn
Than a fading star.

    Let me be no nearer
In death's dream kingdom   30
Let me also wear
Such deliberate disguises
Rat's coat, crowskin, crossed staves
In a field
Behaving as the wind behaves   35
No nearer—

    Not that final meeting
In the twilight kingdom

    III
This is the dead land
This is cactus land   40
Here the stone images
Are raised, here they receive
The supplication of a dead man's hand
Under the twinkle of a fading star.

    Is it like this   45
In death's other kingdom
Waking alone
At the hour when we are
Trembling with tenderness
Lips that would kiss   50
Form prayers to broken stone.

    IV
The eyes are not here
There are no eyes here
In this valley of dying stars
In this hollow valley   55
This broken jaw of our lost kingdoms

    In this last of meeting places
We grope together
And avoid speech
Gathered on this beach of the tumid river   60

Sightless, unless
The eyes reappear
As the perpetual star
Multifoliate rose
Of death's twilight kingdom   65
The hope only
Of empty men.

         V
Here we go round the prickly pear
Prickly pear prickly pear
Here we go round the prickly pear   70
At five o'clock in the morning.

   Between the idea
And the reality
Between the motion
And the act   75
Falls the Shadow
                         For Thine is the Kingdom

   Between the conception
And the creation
Between the emotion
And the response   80
Falls the Shadow
                              Life is very long

   Between the desire
And the spasm
Between the potency
And the existence   85
Between the essence
And the descent
Falls the Shadow
                         For Thine is the Kingdom

   For Thine is
Life is
For Thine is the   90

   This is the way the world ends
This is the way the world ends
This is the way the world ends
Not with a bang but a whimper.   95

JOURNEY OF THE MAGI

"A cold coming we had of it,
Just the worst time of the year
For a journey, and such a long journey:
The ways deep and the weather sharp,
The very dead of winter."   5
And the camels galled, sore-footed, refractory,
Lying down in the melting snow.
There were times we regretted
The summer palaces on slopes, the terraces,
And the silken girls bringing sherbet.   10
Then the camel men cursing and grumbling
And running away, and wanting their liquor and women,
And the night-fires going out, and the lack of shelters,
And the cities hostile and the towns unfriendly
And the villages dirty and charging high prices: 15
A hard time we had of it.
At the end we preferred to travel all night,
Sleeping in snatches,
With the voices singing in our ears, saying
That this was all folly.   20

Then at dawn we came down to a temperate valley,
Wet, below the snow line, smelling of vegetation;
With a running stream and a water-mill beating the darkness,
And three trees on the low sky,
And an old white horse galloped away in the meadow.   25
Then we came to a tavern with vine-leaves over the lintel,
Six hands at an open door dicing for pieces of silver,
And feet kicking the empty wine-skins.
But there was no information, and so we continued
And arrived at evening, not a moment too soon   30
Finding the place; it was (you may say) satisfactory.

All this was a long time ago, I remember,
And I would do it again, but set down
This set down
This: were we led all that way for   35
Birth or Death? There was a Birth, certainly,
We had evidence and no doubt. I had seen birth and death,
But had thought they were different; this Birth was
Hard and bitter agony for us, like Death, our death.
We returned to our places, these Kingdoms,   40
But no longer at ease here, in the old dispensation,
With an alien people clutching their gods.
I should be glad of another death.

ANIMULA

"Issues from the hand of God, the simple soul"
To a flat world of changing lights and noise,
To light, dark, dry or damp, chilly or warm;
Moving between the legs of tables and of chairs,
Rising or falling, grasping at kisses and toys,   5
Advancing boldly, sudden to take alarm,
Retreating to the corner of arm and knee,
Eager to be reassured, taking pleasure
In the fragrant brilliance of the Christmas tree,
Pleasure in the wind, the sunlight and the sea;   10
Studies the sunlit pattern on the floor
And running stags around a silver tray;
Confounds the actual and the fanciful,
Content with playing-cards and kings and queens,
What the fairies do and what the servants say.   15
The heavy burden of the growing soul
Perplexes and offends more, day by day;
Week by week, offends and perplexes more
With the imperatives of "is and seems"
And may and may not, desire and control   20
The pain of living and the drug of dreams
Curl up the small soul in the window seat

Behind the *Encyclopædia Britannica*.
Issues from the hand of time the simple soul
Irresolute and selfish, misshapen, lame,   25
Unable to fare forward or retreat,
Fearing the warm reality, the offered good,
Denying the importunity of the blood,
Shadow of its own shadows, specter in its own gloom,
Leaving disordered papers in a dusty room;   30
Living first in the silence after the viaticum.

Pray for Guiterriez, avid of speed and power,
For Boudin, blown to pieces,
For this one who made a great fortune,
And that one who went his own way.   35
Pray for Floret, by the boarhound slain between the yew trees,
Pray for us now and at the hour of our birth.

JOHN CROWE RANSOM

1 8 8 8 –

HERE LIES A LADY

Here lies a lady of beauty and high degree.
Of chills and fever she died, of fever and chills,
The delight of her husband, her aunt, an infant of three,
And of medicos marveling sweetly on her ills.

For either she burned, and her confident eyes would blaze,   5
And her fingers fly in a manner to puzzle their heads—
What was she making? Why, nothing; she sat in a maze
Of old scraps of laces, snipped into curious shreds—

Or this would pass, and the light of her fire decline
Till she lay discouraged and cold, like a stalk white and blown,   10
And would not open her eyes, to kisses, to wine;
The sixth of these states was her last; the cold settled down.

Sweet ladies, long may ye bloom, and toughly I hope ye may thole,
But was she not lucky? In flowers and lace and mourning,
In love and great honor we bade God rest her soul   15
After six little spaces of chill, and six of burning.

BELLS FOR JOHN WHITESIDE'S DAUGHTER

There was such speed in her little body,
And such lightness in her footfall,
It is no wonder her brown study
Astonishes us all.

Her wars were bruited in our high window.   5
We looked among orchard trees and beyond,

607   JOHN CROWE RANSOM

Where she took arms against her shadow,
Or harried unto the pond

The lazy geese, like a snow cloud
Dripping their snow on the green grass,   10
Tricking and stopping, sleepy and proud,
Who cried in goose, Alas,

For the tireless heart within the little
Lady with rod that made them rise
From their noon apple-dreams, and scuttle   15
Goose-fashion under the skies!

But now go the bells, and we are ready;
In one house we are sternly stopped
To say we are vexed at her brown study,
Lying so primly propped.   20

BLUE GIRLS

Twirling your blue skirts, traveling the sward
Under the towers of your seminary,
Go listen to your teachers old and contrary
Without believing a word.

Tie the white fillets then about your lustrous hair   5
And think no more of what will come to pass
Than bluebirds that go walking on the grass
And chattering on the air.

Practice your beauty, blue girls, before it fail;
And I will cry with my loud lips and publish   10
Beauty which all our power shall never establish,
It is so frail.

For I could tell you a story which is true:
I know a lady with a terrible tongue,
Blear eyes fallen from blue,   15

All her perfections tarnished—and yet it is not long
Since she was lovelier than any of you.

ARCHIBALD MACLEISH
1 8 9 2 –

ARS POETICA

A poem should be palpable and mute
As a globed fruit

Dumb
As old medallions to the thumb

Silent as the sleeve-worn stone   5
Of casement ledges where the moss has grown—

A poem should be wordless
As the flight of birds

A poem should be motionless in time
As the moon climbs   10

Leaving, as the moon releases
Twig by twig the night-entangled trees,

Leaving, as the moon behind the winter leaves,
Memory by memory the mind—

A poem should be motionless in time   15
As the moon climbs

A poem should be equal to:
Not true

For all the history of grief
An empty doorway and a maple leaf   20

For love
The leaning grasses and two lights above the sea—

A poem should not mean
But be

THE END OF THE WORLD

Quite unexpectedly, as Vasserot
The armless ambidextrian was lighting
A match between his great and second toe,
And Ralph the lion was engaged in biting
The neck of Madame Sossman while the drum   5
Pointed, and Teeny was about to cough
In waltz-time swinging Jocko by the thumb—
Quite unexpectedly the top blew off:

And there, there overhead, there, there hung over
Those thousands of white faces, those dazed eyes,   10
There in the starless dark the poise, the hover,
There with vast wings across the cancelled skies,
There in the sudden blackness the black pall
Of nothing, nothing, nothing—nothing at all.

YOU, ANDREW MARVELL

And here face down beneath the sun,
And here upon earth's noonward height
To feel the always coming on,
The always rising of the night.

To feel creep up the curving east
The earthly chill of dusk and slow
Upon those under lands the vast
And ever-climbing shadow grow,

And strange at Ecbatan the trees
Take leaf by leaf the evening, strange,
The flooding dark about their knees,
The mountains over Persia change,

And now at Kermanshah the gate,
Dark, empty, and the withered grass,
And through the twilight now the late
Few travelers in the westward pass.

And Baghdad darken and the bridge
Across the silent river gone,
And through Arabia the edge
Of evening widen and steal on,

And deepen on Palmyra's street
The wheel rut in the ruined stone,
And Lebanon fade out and Crete
High through the clouds and overblown,

And over Sicily the air
Still flashing with the landward gulls,
And loom and slowly disappear
The sails above the shadowy hulls,

And Spain go under and the shore
Of Africa, the gilded sand,
And evening vanish and no more
The low pale light across that land,

Nor now the long light on the sea—
And here face downward in the sun
To feel how swift, how secretly,
The shadow of the night comes on. . . .

E. E. CUMMINGS
1894–1962

MY FATHER MOVED
THROUGH DOOMS OF LOVE

my father moved through dooms of love
through sames of am through haves of give,
singing each morning out of each night
my father moved through depths of height

this motionless forgetful where   5
turned at his glance to shining here;
that if (so timid air is firm)
under his eyes would stir and squirm

newly as from unburied which
floats the first who, his april touch   10
drove sleeping selves to swarm their fates
woke dreamers to their ghostly roots

and should some why completely weep
my father's fingers brought her sleep:
vainly no smallest voice might cry   15
for he could feel the mountains grow.

Lifting the valleys of the sea
my father moved through griefs of joy;
praising a forehead called the moon
singing desire into begin   20

joy was his song and joy so pure
a heart of star by him could steer
and pure so now and now so yes
the wrists of twilight would rejoice

keen as midsummer's keen beyond   25
conceiving mind of sun will stand,

so strictly (over utmost him
so hugely) stood my father's dream

his flesh was flesh his blood was blood:
no hungry man but wished him food;   30
No cripple wouldn't creep one mile
uphill to only see him smile.

Scorning the pomp of must and shall
my father moved through dooms of feel;
his anger was as right as rain   35
his pity was as green as grain

septembering arms of year extend
less humbly wealth to foe and friend
than he to foolish and to wise
offered immeasurable is   40

proudly and (by octobering flame
beckoned) as earth will downward climb,
so naked for immortal work
his shoulders marched against the dark

his sorrow was as true as bread: 45
no liar looked him in the head;
if every friend became his foe
he'd laugh and build a world with snow.

My father moved through theys of we,
singing each new leaf out of each tree   50
(and every child was sure that spring
danced when she heard my father sing)

then let men kill which cannot share,
let blood and flesh be mud and mire,
scheming imagine, passion willed,   55
freedom a drug that's bought and sold

giving to steal and cruel kind,
a heart to fear, to doubt a mind,
to differ a disease of same,
conform the pinnacle of am   60

though dull were all we taste as bright,
bitter all utterly things sweet,
maggoty minus and dumb death
all we inherit, all bequeath

and nothing quite so least as truth   65
—i say though hate were why men breathe—
because my father lived his soul
love is the whole and more than all

COMMENTARY

In our elementary schooling we are—or used to be—taught the "parts of speech" and how to distinguish one from another, only to discover that they all incline to be interchangeable, their nature being protean, and determined not by definition but by use. *Walk* is a verb until we take a walk, when it is a noun. *Clear* is an adjective until we clear the snow from the sidewalk, when it is a verb. *Further* is an adverb, but we further our sense of how English works when we confront the fact that nothing requires this word to be permanently adverbial. *Beyond* is a mere preposition, but we have no trouble in understanding that in The Great Beyond it arises to the substantive status of a noun.

The tendency to this kind of interchange among the parts of speech is very strong in English and seems to accelerate. But it does not make its way without resistance; we respond to some instances of it with more dubiety or surprise than we do to others. *Yonder* is an adjective—"Yonder peasant, who is he?"—or an adverb—"You can easily find out by walking yonder a way and asking him." And it can, under light duress, be made to serve as a noun; as in the Air Force song "The Wild Blue Yonder." But the phrase startles us a little; we recognize it as a more or less successful effort to manipulate the language in an interesting—a poetic—way, and as such we accept it, but it is not possible that any of us will make the same use of the word in ordinary speech. We are more startled, and likely to be pleased, when Gerard Manley Hopkins exclaims over a falcon in flight, "the achieve of, the mastery of the thing!" The phrase has much more energy and verve than if it had read "the achievement of, the mastery of the thing!" Yet there is but little chance that *achieve* will replace *achievement* in common usage.

A considerable part of the interest of E. E. Cummings' poem comes from our surprise over its use of parts of speech in ways that we are not accustomed to and are scarcely likely to adopt, although we can understand the mode of their use if we make the effort to do so. To say of the father that he moved "through sames of am" is to speak of the integrity of his being; he was always, as we say, himself. "Haves of give" recalls the statement of Jesus that "it is more blessed to give than to receive"; it says that for the father this was true in the most literal sense possible: for him to give was to have. His relationship to people is exemplified by the effect he has on three of them, a where, an if, and a why—the "motionless forgetful where" who turned at the father's glance "to shining here" is, we may suppose, a young man who, until touched into activity, had been lost in a passive self-absorption, not easily to be reached by actuality, not even his own, since that had not yet come into being. The "if (so timid . . .)" would seem to be another young man, distrustful of life and of his own powers, who under the father's vivifying influence undergoes metamorphosis and is transformed from a nonpersonal being, a "which," into an actual personal self, a "who," like a butterfly emerging from its chrysalis. The weeping "why" of the next stanza is manifestly a woman or a girl whose being, at the moment, is defined by her bewilderment or resentment at some pain inflicted upon her.

"Most poetry," a critic has said, "is on commonplace themes, and the freshness, what the poet supplies, is in the language." Cummings' theme may be said to be commonplace enough—how often have we heard the praise of integrity and sincerity, how often have we been asked to be aware of the beneficent power of sympathy and unselfishness! Often enough, surely, to make the virtuous qualities that are praised seem as dull, abstract, and imprecise as the words that are used to denote them. But when the old words are translated in ways that startle us and that require some little effort of energy on our part to perceive the equivalence, the virtues being praised shed their commonplaceness and shine with the freshness of invention.

Yet the novelty of Cummings' language cannot claim all the credit for the poem's engagingness, which in some part comes from the poet's conception of the best kind of goodness, that which is spontaneous, natural, and arises from and moves toward joy. The father is represented as being virtuous rather than moral or ethical, which suggest a state of being arrived at by intention and effort. His virtue is to be understood in the old sense of the word, which meant power—he has a natural power of goodness that makes its effect less through what he does than through what he is. And this power is represented as being analogous with the beneficent workings of Nature; the instances and images that Cummings finds appropriate to his father, who was a Unitarian clergyman, might serve as well for some pagan fertility god. The poet touches upon the existence of his father in each season of the cycle of the year, but he makes spring his characteristic time, his characteristic action being, in Lucretius' phrase, to bring living things into the borders of light.

MY GIRL'S TALL WITH HARD LONG EYES

my girl's tall with hard long eyes
as she stands, with her long hard hands keeping
silence on her dress, good for sleeping
is her long hard body filled with surprise
like a white shocking wire, when she smiles
a hard long smile it sometimes makes

5

gaily go clean through me tickling aches,
and the weak noise of her eyes easily files
my impatience to an edge—my girl's tall
and taut, with thin legs just like a vine   10
that's spent all of its life on a garden-wall,
and is going to die. When we grimly go to bed
with these legs she begins to heave and twine
about me, and to kiss my face and head.

ANYONE LIVED IN A
PRETTY HOW TOWN

anyone lived in a pretty how town
(and up so floating many bells down)
spring summer autumn winter
he sang his didn't he danced his did.

Women and men (both little and small)   5
cared for anyone not at all
they sowed their isn't they reaped their same
sun moon stars rain

children guessed (but only a few
and down they forgot as up they grew   10
autumn winter spring summer)
that noone loved him more by more

when by now and tree by leaf
she laughed his joy she cried his grief
bird by snow and stir by still   15
anyone's any was all to her

someones married their everyones
laughed their cryings and did their dance
(sleep wake hope and then) they
said their nevers they slept their dream   20

stars rain sun moon
(and only the snow can begin to explain
how children are apt to forget to remember
with up so floating many bells down)

one day anyone died i guess 25
(and noone stooped to kiss his face)
busy folk buried them side by side
little by little and was by was

all by all and deep by deep
and more by more they dream their sleep 30
noone and anyone earth by april
wish by spirit and if by yes.

Women and men (both dong and ding)
summer autumn winter spring
reaped their sowing and went their came 35
sun moon stars rain

ROBERT GRAVES
1895-

THE CLIMATE OF THOUGHT

The climate of thought has seldom been described.
It is no terror of Caucasian frost,
Nor yet that brooding Hindu heat
For which a loin-rag and a dish of rice
Suffice until the pestilent monsoon. 5
But, without winter, blood would run too thin;
Or, without summer, fires would burn too long.
In thought the seasons run concurrently.

Thought has a sea to gaze, not voyage on;
And hills, to rough the edge of the bland sky, 10
Not to be climbed in search of blander prospect;
Few birds, sufficient for such caterpillars
As are not fated to turn butterflies;
Few butterflies, sufficient for the flowers
That are the luxury of a full orchard; 15
Wind, sometimes, in the evening chimneys; rain

On the early morning roof, on sleepy sight;
Snow streaked upon the hilltop, feeding
The fond brook at the valley-head
That greens the valley and that parts the lips; 20
The sun, simple, like a country neighbour;
The moon, grand, not fanciful with clouds.

TO JUAN AT THE WINTER SOLSTICE

There is one story and one story only
That will prove worth your telling,
Whether as learned bard or gifted child;
To it all lines or lesser gauds belong
That startle with their shining 5
Such common stories as they stray into.

Is it of trees you tell, their months and virtues,
Or strange beasts that beset you,
Of birds that croak at you the Triple will?
Or of the Zodiac and how slow it turns 10
Below the Boreal Crown,
Prison of all true kings that ever reigned?

Water to water, ark again to ark,
From woman back to woman:
So each new victim treads unfalteringly 15
The never altered circuit of his fate,
Bringing twelve peers as witness
Both to his starry rise and starry fall.

Or is it of the Virgin's silver beauty,
All fish below the thighs? 20
She in her left hand bears a leafy quince;
When, with her right she crooks a finger smiling,
How may the King hold back?
Royally then he barters life for love.

Or of the undying snake from chaos hatched, 25
Whose coils contain the ocean,
Into whose chops with naked sword he springs,
Then in black water, tangled by the reeds,
Battles three days and nights,
To be spewed up beside her scalloped shore? 30

Much snow is falling, winds roar hollowly,
The owl hoots from the elder,
Fear in your heart cries to the loving-cup:
Sorrow to sorrow as the sparks fly upward.
The log groans and confesses   35
There is one story and one story only.

Dwell on her graciousness, dwell on her smiling,
Do not forget what flowers
The great boar trampled down in ivy time.
Her brow was creamy as the crested wave,   40
Her sea-blue eyes were wild
But nothing promised that is not performed.

ALLEN TATE
1 8 9 9 –

ODE TO THE CONFEDERATE DEAD

Row after row with strict impunity
The headstones yield their names to the element,
The wind whirrs without recollection;
In the riven troughs the splayed leaves
Pile up, of nature the casual sacrament   5
To the seasonal eternity of death,
Then driven by the fierce scrutiny
Of heaven to their business in the vast breath,
They sough the rumor of mortality.

Autumn is desolation in the plot   10
Of a thousand acres where these memories grow
From the inexhaustible bodies that are not
Dead, but feed the grass row after rich row:
Remember now the autumns that have gone—
Ambitious November with the humours of the year,   15
With a particular zeal for every slab,
Staining the uncomfortable angels that rot
On the slabs, a wing chipped here, an arm there:

The brute curiosity of an angel's stare
Turns you like them to stone,   20
Transforms the heaving air,
Till plunged to a heavier world below
You shift your sea-space blindly,
Heaving like the blind crab.

       Dazed by the wind, only the wind   25
       The leaves flying, plunge

You know who have waited by the wall
The twilit certainty of an animal;
Those midnight restitutions of the blood
You know—the immitigable pines, the smoky frieze   30
Of the sky, the sudden call; you know the rage—
The cold pool left by the mounting flood—
The rage of Zeno and Parmenides.
You who have waited for the angry resolution
Of those desires that should be yours tomorrow,
You know the unimportant shrift of death
And praise the vision
And praise the arrogant circumstance
Of those who fall
Rank upon rank, hurried beyond decision—   40
Here by the sagging gate, stopped by the wall.

       Seeing, seeing only the leaves
       Flying, plunge and expire

Turn your eyes to the immoderate past
Turn to the inscrutable infantry rising   45
Demons out of the earth—they will not last.
Stonewall, Stonewall, and the sunken fields of hemp,
Shiloh, Antietam, Malvern Hill, Bull Run.
Lost in that orient of the thick and fast
You will curse the setting sun.   50

       Cursing only the leaves crying
       Like an old man in a storm

You hear the shout—the crazy hemlocks point
With troubled fingers to the silence which
Smothers you, a mummy, in time.

The hound bitch   55

Toothless and dying, in a musty cellar
Hears the wind only.

Now that the salt of their blood

Stiffens the saltier oblivion of the sea,
Seals the malignant purity of the flood,
What shall we, who count our days and bow   60
Our heads with a commemorial woe,
In the ribboned coats of grim felicity,
What shall we say of the bones, unclean
—Their verdurous anonymity will grow—
The ragged arms, the ragged heads and eyes   65
Lost in these acres of the insane green?
The gray lean spiders come; they come and go;
In a tangle of willows without light
The singular screech-owl's bright
Invisible lyric seeds the mind   70
With the furious murmur of their chivalry.

We shall say only, the leaves

Flying, plunge and expire

We shall say only, the leaves whispering
In the improbable mist of nightfall   75
That flies on multiple wing:
Night is the beginning and the end,
And in between the ends of distraction
Waits mute speculation, the patient curse
That stones the eyes, or like the jaguar leaps   80
For his own image in a jungle pool, his victim.

What shall we say who have knowledge
Carried to the heart? Shall we take the act
To the grave? Shall we, more hopeful, set up the grave
In the house? The ravenous grave?

Leave now   85

The turnstile and the old stone wall:
The gentle serpent, green in the mulberry bush,
Riots with his tongue through the hush—
Sentinel of the grave who counts us all!

ROBERT PENN WARREN
1905–

BEARDED OAKS

The oaks, how subtle and marine,
Bearded, and all the layered light
Above them swims; and thus the scene,
Recessed, awaits the positive night.

So, waiting, we in the grass now lie   5
Beneath the langourous tread of light:
The grasses, kelp-like, satisfy
The nameless motions of the air.

Upon the floor of light, and time,
Unmurmuring, of polyp made,   10
We rest; we are, as light withdraws,
Twin atolls on a shelf of shade.

Ages to our construction went,
Dim architecture, hour by hour:
And violence, forgot now, lent   15
The present stillness all its power.

The storm of noon above us rolled,
Of light the fury, furious gold,
The long drag troubling us, the depth:
Dark is unrocking, unrippling, still.   20

Passion and slaughter, ruth, decay
Descend, minutely whispering down,
Silted down swaying streams, to lay
Foundation for our voicelessness.

All our debate is voiceless here,   25
As all our rage, the rage of stone;
If hope is hopeless, then fearless fear,
And history is thus undone.

Our feet once wrought the hollow street
With echo when the lamps were dead   30
At windows, once our headlight glare
Disturbed the doe that, leaping, fled.

I do not love you less that now
The caged heart makes iron stroke,
Or less that all that light once gave   35
The graduate dark should now revoke.

We live in time so little time
And we learn all so painfully,
That we may spare this hour's term
To practice for eternity.   40

STANLEY KUNITZ
1905–

FOREIGN AFFAIRS

We are two countries girded for the war,
Whisking our scouts across the pricked frontier
To ravage in each other's fields, cut lines
Along the lacework of strategic nerves,
Loot stores; while here and there,   5
In ambushes that trace a valley's curves,
Stark witness to the dangerous charge we bear,
A house ignites, a train's derailed, a bridge
Blows up sky-high, and water floods the mines.
Who first attacked? Who turned the other cheek?   10
Aggression perpetrated is as soon
Denied, and insult rubbed into the injury
By cunning agents trained in these affairs,
With whom it's touch-and-go, don't-tread-on-me,
I-dare-you-to, keep-off, and kiss-my-hand.   15
Tempers could sharpen knives, and do; we live
In states provocative
Where frowning headlines scare the coffee cream
And doomsday is the eighth day of the week.

Our exit through the slammed and final door 20
Is twenty times rehearsed, but when we face
The imminence of cataclysmic rupture,
A lesser pride goes down upon its knees.
Two countries separated by desire!—
Whose diplomats speed back and forth by plane, 25
Portmanteaus stuffed with fresh apologies
Outdated by events before they land.
Negotiations wear them out: they're driven mad
Between the protocols of tears and rapture.

Locked in our fated and contiguous selves, 30
These worlds that too much agitate each other,
Interdependencies from hip to head,
Twin principalities both slave and free,
We coexist, proclaiming Peace together.
Tell me no lies! We are divided nations 35
With malcontents by thousands in our streets,
These thousands torn by inbred revolutions.
A triumph is demanded, not moral victories
Deduced from small advances, small retreats.
Are the gods of our fathers not still daemonic? 40
On the steps of the Capitol
The outraged lion of our years roars panic,
And we suffer the guilty cowardice of the will,
Gathering its bankrupt slogans up for flight
Like gold from ruined treasuries. 45
And yet, and yet, although the murmur rises,
We are what we are, and only life surprises.

FOR THE WORD IS FLESH

O ruined father dead, long sweetly rotten
Under the dial, the time-dissolving urn,
Beware a second perishing, forgotten,
Heap fallen leaves of memory to burn
On the slippery rock, the black eroding heart, 5
Before the wedged frost splits it clean apart.

The nude hand drops no sacramental flower
Of blood among the tough upthrusting weeds.
Senior, in this commemorative hour,

What shall the quick commemorate, what deeds   10
Ephemeral, what dazzling words that flare
Like rockets from the mouth to burst in air?

Of hypochondriacs that gnawed their seasons
In search of proofs, Lessius found twenty-two
Fine arguments, Tolet gave sixty reasons   15
Why souls survive. And what are they to you?
And, father, what to me, who cannot blur
The mirrored brain with fantasies of Er,

Remembering such factual spikes as pierce
The supplicating palms, and by the sea   20
Remembering the eyes, I hear the fierce
Wild cry of Jesus on the holy tree,
Yet have of you no syllable to keep,
Only the deep rock crumbling in the deep.

Observe the wisdom of the Florentine   25
Who, feeling death upon him, scribbled fast
To make revision of a deathbed scene,
Gloating that he was accurate at last.
Let sons learn from their lipless fathers how
Man enters hell without a golden bough.   30

STANLEY BURNSHAW
1 9 0 6 –

HISTORICAL SONG OF THEN AND NOW

Earth early and huge,
No eye dared hope to travel
The palette of its rage

Till, late, they learned to wind
Shackles into its veins,   5
Shrank it to fit a cage.

So trust contracts to fear.
The tribes give up their feuds.
All wars are now one war.

And will you indict this breed   10
That strained against a code
Where safe-and-fed was good?

Fled from the mothering wood,
It found in its hand the thought
To light up endless day,   15

Revel with sleepless eye,
Make of itself a god,
And the veins a level sun—

Now it stumbles, dwarf in the maze
That the thinking hand had spun.   20
Blind in its blaze of stone,

Whom can this breed indict
That its sun is a blast of darkness,
That light is always night?

MODES OF BELIEF

Ever since I grew cold
In heart, I always hear
Most men that I behold
Cry like a creature caught
In tones of dying will,   5
Such as their eyelids bear
With cuneiforms of fail—

Where are the young and wild
Teeming in hope of power?
Though striving lifts the bud,   10
None can achieve the flower.
Where can the bud disperse

Within?   Must every man
Entomb a withered child?—

What early hearts can store   15
Of sweetness still endures
Fever of flood or drought,
Till groping up from within,
A self-bereaving curse
Masses in reefs of thought,   20
Burns and bites the blood—

W. H. AUDEN
1907–

MUSÉE DES BEAUX ARTS

About suffering they were never wrong,
The Old Masters: how well they understood
Its human position; how it takes place
While someone else is eating or opening a window or just walking
        dully along;
How, when the aged are reverently, passionately waiting   5
For the miraculous birth, there always must be
Children who did not specially want it to happen, skating
On a pond at the edge of the wood:
They never forgot
That even the dreadful martyrdom must run its course   10
Anyhow in a corner, some untidy spot
Where the dogs go on with their doggy life and the torturer's horse
Scratches its innocent behind on a tree.

In Brueghel's *Icarus,* for instance: how everything turns away
Quite leisurely from the disaster; the ploughman may   15
Have heard the splash, the forsaken cry,
But for him it was not an important failure; the sun shone
As it had to on the white legs disappearing into the green
Water; and the expensive delicate ship that must have seen
Something amazing, a boy falling out of the sky,   20
Had somewhere to get to and sailed calmly on.

IN MEMORY OF W. B. YEATS

1

He disappeared in the dead of winter:
The brooks were frozen, the airports almost deserted,
The snow disfigured the public statues;
The mercury sank in the mouth of the dying day.
O all the instruments agree   5
The day of his death was a dark cold day.

Far from his illness
The wolves ran on through the evergreen forests,
The peasant river was untempted by the fashionable quays;
By mourning tongues   10
The death of the poet was kept from his poems.

But for him it was his last afternoon as himself,
An afternoon of nurses and rumours;
The provinces of his body revolted,   15
The squares of his mind were empty,
Silence invaded the suburbs,
The current of his feeling failed: he became his admirers.

Now he is scattered among a hundred cities
And wholly given over to unfamiliar affections;
To find his happiness in another kind of wood   20
And be punished under a foreign code of conscience.
The words of a dead man
Are modified in the guts of the living.

But in the importance and noise of tomorrow
When the brokers are roaring like beasts on the floor of the Bourse,   25
And the poor have the sufferings to which they are fairly accustomed,
And each in the cell of himself is almost convinced of his freedom;
A few thousand will think of this day
As one thinks of a day when one did something slightly unusual.
O all the instruments agree   30
The day of his death was a dark cold day.

2

You were silly like us: your gift survived it all;
The parish of rich women, physical decay,
Yourself; mad Ireland hurt you into poetry.
Now Ireland has her madness and her weather still,   35
For poetry makes nothing happen: it survives
In the valley of its saying where executives
Would never want to tamper; it flows south

From ranches of isolation and the busy griefs,
Raw towns that we believe and die in; it survives,   40
A way of happening, a mouth.

3

Earth, receive an honoured guest;
William Yeats is laid to rest:
Let the Irish vessel lie
Emptied of its poetry.   45

Time that is intolerant
Of the brave and innocent,
And indifferent in a week
To a beautiful physique,

Worships language and forgives   50
Everyone by whom it lives;
Pardons cowardice, conceit,
Lays its honours at their feet.

Time that with this strange excuse
Pardoned Kipling and his views,   55
And will pardon Paul Claudel,
Pardons him for writing well.

In the nightmare of the dark
All the gods of Europe bark,
And the living nations wait,   60
Each sequestered in its hate;

Intellectual disgrace
Stares from every human face,
And the seas of pity lie
Locked and frozen in each eye.   65

Follow, poet, follow right
To the bottom of the night,
With your unconstraining voice
Still persuade us to rejoice;

With the farming of a verse   70
Make a vineyard of the curse,
Sing of human unsuccess
In a rapture of distress;

In the deserts of the heart
Let the healing fountain start,   75
In the prison of his days
Teach the free man how to praise.

629   W. H. AUDEN

In Memory of
SIGMUND FREUD[1]
(d. Sept. 1939)

(1940)

When there are so many we shall have to mourn,
When grief has been made so public, and exposed
   To the critique of a whole epoch
   The frailty of our conscience and anguish,

Of whom shall we speak? For every day they die   5
Among us, those who were doing us some good,
   And knew it was never enough but
   Hoped to improve a little by living.

Such was this doctor: still at eighty he wished
To think of our life, from whose unruliness   10
   So many plausible young futures
   With threats or flattery ask obedience.

But his wish was denied him; he closed his eyes
Upon that last picture common to us all,
   Of problems like relatives standing   15
   Puzzled and jealous about our dying.

For about him at the very end were still
Those he had studied, the nervous and the nights,
   And shades that still waited to enter
   The bright circle of his recognition   20

Turned elsewhere with their disappointment as he
Was taken away from his old interest
   To go back to the earth in London,
   An important Jew who died in exile.

Only Hate was happy, hoping to augment   25
His practice now, and his shabby clientèle

[1] Sigmund Freud (1856–1939) was the originator of psychoanalysis. As a Jew living in Austria, he was forced to flee the Nazis in 1938. He went to London, where he remained until he died.

Who think they can be cured by killing
And covering the gardens with ashes.

They are still alive but in a world he changed
Simply by looking back with no false regrets;   30
                    All that he did was to remember
                    Like the old and be honest like children.

He wasn't clever at all: he merely told
The unhappy Present to recite the Past
                    Like a poetry lesson till sooner   35
                    Or later it faltered at the line where

Long ago the accusations had begun,
And suddenly knew by whom it had been judged,
                    How rich life had been and how silly,
                    And was life-forgiven and most humble.   40

Able to approach the Future as a friend
Without a wardrobe of excuses, without
                    A set mask of rectitude or an
                    Embarrassing over-familiar gesture.

No wonder the ancient cultures of conceit   45
In his technique of unsettlement foresaw
                    The fall of princes, the collapse of
                    Their lucrative patterns of frustration.

If he succeeded, why, the Generalised Life
Would become impossible, the monolith   50
                    Of State be broken and prevented
                    The co-operation of avengers.

Of course they called on God: but he went his way,
Down among the Lost People like Dante, down
                    To the stinking fosse² where the injured   55
                    Lead the ugly life of the rejected.

    2 Ditch. There are several malodorous ditches full of lost souls in Dante's representation
of Hell, the *Inferno*.

And showed us what evil is: not as we thought
Deeds that must be punished, but our lack of faith,
        Our dishonest mood of denial,
        The concupiscence of the oppressor.   60

And if something of the autocratic pose,
The paternal strictness he distrusted, still
        Clung to his utterance and features,
        It was a protective imitation

For one who lived among enemies so long;   65
If often he was wrong and at times absurd,
        To us he is no more a person
        Now but a whole climate of opinion,

Under whom we conduct our differing lives:
Like weather he can only hinder or help,   70
        The proud can still be proud but find it
        A little harder, and the tyrant tries

To make him do but doesn't care for him much.
He quietly surrounds all our habits of growth;
        He extends, till the tired in even   75
        The remotest most miserable duchy

Have felt the change in their bones and are cheered,
And the child unlucky in his little State,
        Some hearth where freedom is excluded,
        A hive whose honey is fear and worry,   80

Feels calmer now and somehow assured of escape;
While as they lie in the grass of our neglect,
        So many long-forgotten objects
        Revealed by his undiscouraged shining

Are returned to us and made precious again;   85
Games we had thought we must drop as we grew up,
        Little noises we dared not laugh at,
        Faces we made when no one was looking.

But he wishes us more than this: to be free
Is often to be lonely; he would unite   90
        The unequal moieties fractured
        By our own well-meaning sense of justice.

Would restore to the larger the wit and will
The smaller possesses but can only use
        For arid disputes, would give back to   95
        The son the mother's richness of feeling.

But he would have us remember most of all
To be enthusiastic over the night
        Not only for the sense of wonder
        It alone has to offer, but also   100

Because it needs our love: for with sad eyes
Its delectable creatures look up and beg
        Us dumbly to ask them to follow;
        They are exiles who long for the future

That lies in our power. They too would rejoice   105
If allowed to serve enlightenment like him,
        Even to bear our cry of "Judas,"
        As he did and all must bear who serve it.

One rational voice is dumb: over a grave
The household of Impulse mourns one dearly loved.   110
        Sad is Eros, builder of cities,
        And weeping anarchic Aphrodite.[3]

COMMENTARY

Among the first acts of the Nazi party after it came to power in Germany in
1933 was the suppression of the teaching of psychoanalysis in the medical
schools and a ceremonial burning of the works of Sigmund Freud. This was in
part a response to the fact that the founder of psychoanalysis was a Jew, for

---

[3] Eros, the Greek god of love, was the son of Aphrodite, the goddess of beauty and
love. Both are symbols of libidinous energy, but Eros is perhaps more often constructive or
creative, whereas Aphrodite can be the cause of destruction.

one of the axioms of the Nazi ideology was that the Jews were the cause of all the misfortunes of the German people and the source of all that was bad in the Western world. It was also a response to the actual content of psychoanalysis, especially to its theory that many disorders of the personality have a sexual etiology and can be traced to the patient's experience of the family situation in early infancy.

Freud, living in Vienna, was naturally much distressed over the turn of events, but he persuaded himself that the hostility of the Nazis would not come closer home. He was, of course, mistaken—in 1938 Hitler sent his troops into Austria and united that nation with Germany under his rule. Freud was forbidden to carry on his work and he and his family lived under the threat of the concentration camp. Before the invasion actually took place, he had resisted all suggestions that he leave Vienna, and even now he was reluctant to think of leaving the city in which he had lived all but two of his eighty-two years. Eventually, however, the counsels of his friends and colleagues prevailed and he consented to emigrate, but it was only after prolonged negotiations with the Nazi officials and the payment by his friends abroad of a large sum of money in ransom that Freud was permitted to leave Austria and, with his family, was brought to England, a country which he had held in affectionate admiration since boyhood and which now received him with great honor. He settled in London, and, although much enfeebled by the illness which had made existence a torture for many years—cancer of the jaw, necessitating innumerable operations—he resumed his habits of arduous work, seeing patients and pupils and carrying forward the composition of a new book. He died a year later, three weeks after the beginning of the Second World War.

Freud had never concerned himself directly with politics but the therapeutic psychology of which he was the inventor had social and ultimately political implications of great moment. If these had ever been obscure, they became manifest upon the violent Nazi opposition to psychoanalysis and they constitute the informing theme of Auden's commemoration of Freud.

The theory of psychoanalysis is enormously complex, but at its heart is the quite simple idea that the individual human personality is formed, and in all too many instances malformed, by the interaction of the biological impulses or "drives" with the controlling authority of the family, which is continuous with the authority of society and the state. The individual in the course of his development incorporates this authority into his emotional system, in both its conscious and its unconscious parts. If the authority thus internalized is excessively strict—as it may be either because it mirrors the actual repressiveness of the parental control or because the individual for some reason imagines the external authority to be more exigent than it actually is—there will result a malfunction of the instinctual life, inhibiting the healthy development of the personality and causing great emotional pain. The malfunction begins in earliest childhood, though it may not manifest itself until a later time, and Freud's method of therapy is to lead the patient to bring into the light of consciousness the particular circumstances, actual or fancied, that may serve to explain where his emotional life went wrong, why the "internalized authority" is devoted to causing pain. As Auden's poem puts it, Freud

> . . . told
> The unhappy Present to recite the Past

> Like a poetry lesson till sooner
> Or later it faltered at the line where

> Long ago the accusations had begun,
> And suddenly knew by whom it had been judged . . .

"Accusations" and "judged" are the crucial words—neurotic suffering may be ascribed to the patient's having instituted in his unconscious mind a juridical process in which the prosecuting attorney accuses too fiercely, the judge condemns too readily and sentences too sternly, and the jailer carries out the imposed punishment too eagerly.

By the time the Nazis banned it in Germany and Austria, psychoanalysis had won a considerable degree of acceptance, but only against a stubborn and often bitter resistance. The physicians who criticized its theory seldom did so in a spirit of disinterested scientific objectivity; they were likely to share the moralizing fervor of the many laymen who denounced it as a threat to society. The therapeutic goal of psychoanalysis is scarcely subversive and nowadays it is even said by some to err in the direction of social conformity, for it undertakes to make it possible for the patient to live in reasonable accord not only with himself but with his society. Yet even from the little that has been said here about the basic theory of psychoanalysis, it will be plain that it is antagonistic to authoritarianism, though not to rational authority. What Auden's poem aptly speaks of as Freud's "technique of unsettlement" cannot really be said to have overtly and explicitly foreseen "the fall of princes," but it nevertheless did bring the very idea of arbitrary rule into question. It is therefore not surprising that it should have incurred the hatred of "the ancient cultures of conceit."

At the present time the judgment on psychoanalysis is divided. Many still regard it uneasily or hostilely, yet it has established itself as part of the substance of modern thought. Its influence is especially strong in the United States, where its premises and conclusions are taken for granted by many who have never read any of the works in which its theory is expounded. For many Freud is indeed

> . . . no more a person
> Now but a whole climate of opinion . . .

Writing not long after Freud's death, Auden naturally made the large public aspects of Freud's thought salient in his commemoration. With totalitarianism in the ascendant, the aspects of psychoanalysis that might well seem of first importance were those that bore upon politics, such as the opposition it offers to "the Generalised Life" and "the monolith / Of State." But the poem does not fail to take account of the effects that the technique of unsettlement may have upon the personal and private life, and not only in situations of extreme pathology, among "the Lost People," "the injured" who "Lead the ugly life of the rejected," but also among those who are not so grossly afflicted and who yet live less freely than they might, immobilizing themselves behind "a set mask of rectitude," having less courage, simplicity, and power of responsive emotion than it is within their capacity to have.

The last quatrain brilliantly expresses the paradoxical nature of Freud's thought. By ancient convention, rationality and impulse are believed to be at hopeless odds with each other. But Freud put his "rational voice" at the service of impulse, seeking its liberation. It may be questioned, however, whether the last two lines, fine as they are, represent Freud's thought with entire accuracy. It is certainly true that Freud was in avowed alliance with "Eros, builder of cities," the love that makes the family, society, and civilization. But nothing in his work affirms the beneficence of "anarchic Aphrodite," the irresistible, heedless love that we call passion.

The poem claims much for the intention of Freud's science, much for its achievement. Yet this large optimism is qualified by the tone in which it is asserted. One may hear a note of reserve in the large positive statements as though the recognition of Freud's purpose and achievement went along with the sense of how much is still to be accomplished for human happiness and with the awareness that any celebration of human advance must be of a muted kind when uttered at the beginning of a war that promises to be long and terrible. The restrained, slightly dry tone is in part an effect of the diction, which is determinedly plain. It is also, and perhaps to an even greater extent, an effect of the stanzaic form, which seems to have been consciously modelled on the so-called Alcaic strophe of Greek and Latin poetry. In this strophe the first two lines are of eleven syllables, the third of nine, the fourth of ten, and Auden conforms quite strictly to the pattern; there are only a very few quite minor departures. Unlike the Alcaic strophe, Auden's form has no set metrical pattern within the fixed number of syllables for each line, nor, indeed, any metrical pattern at all; but the rhythm of each line is controlled and made more or less homogeneous with that of its matching lines by the fixed number of syllables. One has the sense of prose that is always at the point of becoming metrical, or at least markedly cadenced, and always being prevented, falling back to its prose tone. And this effect of an energy continually checked, even if continually asserting itself, is supported by the interplay between the lengths of the lines of which the stanzas consist, the ranging first two lines with which each stanza begins, the sharply curtailed third, the fourth that a little recoups what its predecessor had lost.

THEODORE ROETHKE
1908–1963

FRAU BAUMAN, FRAU SCHMIDT, AND FRAU SCHWARTZE

Gone the three ancient ladies
Who creaked on the greenhouse ladders,
Reaching up white strings

To wind, to wind
The sweet-pea tendrils, the smilax,   5
Nasturtiums, the climbing
Roses, to straighten
Carnations, red
Chrysanthemums; the stiff
Stems, jointed like corn,   10
They tied and tucked,—
These nurses of nobody else.
Quicker than birds, they dipped
Up and sifted the dirt;
They sprinkled and shook;   15
They stood astride pipes,
Their skirts billowing out wide into tents,
Their hands twinkling with wet;
Like witches they flew along rows
Keeping creation at ease;   20
With a tendril for needle
They sewed up the air with a stem;
They teased out the seed that the cold kept asleep,—
All the coils, loops, and whorls.
They trellised the sun; they plotted for more than themselves.   25

I remember how they picked me up, a spindly kid,
Pinching and poking my thin ribs
Till I lay in their laps, laughing,
Weak as a whiffet;
Now, when I'm alone and cold in my bed,   30
They still hover over me,
These ancient leathery crones,
With their bandannas stiffened with sweat,
And their thorn-bitten wrists,
And their snuff-laden breath blowing lightly over me in my first sleep.   35

LIGHT LISTENED

O what could be more nice
Than her ways with a man?
She kissed me more than twice
Once we were left alone.
Who'd look when he could feel?   5
She'd more sides than a seal.

The close air faintly stirred.
Light deepened to a bell,

The love-beat of a bird.
She kept her body still   10
And watched the weather flow.
We live by what we do.

All's known, all, all around:
The shape of things to be;
A green thing loves the green   15
And loves the living ground.
The deep shade gathers night;
She changed with changing light.

We met to leave again
The time we broke from time;   20
A cold air brought its rain,
The singing of a stem.
She sang a final song;
Light listened when she sang.

DELMORE SCHWARTZ
1913–

IN THE NAKED BED, IN PLATO'S CAVE

In the naked bed, in Plato's cave,
Reflected headlights slowly slid the wall,
Carpenters hammered under the shaded window,
Wind troubled the window curtains all night long,
A fleet of trucks strained uphill, grinding,   5
Their freights covered, as usual.

The ceiling lightened again, the slanting diagram
Slid slowly forth.
                    Hearing the milkman's chop,
His striving up the stair, the bottle's chink,
I rose from bed, lit a cigarette,   10
And walked to the window. The stony street

Displayed the stillness in which buildings stand,
The street-lamp's vigil and the horse's patience.
The winter sky's pure capital
Turned me back to bed with exhausted eyes.   15

Strangeness grew in the motionless air. The loose
Film grayed. Shaking wagons, hooves' waterfalls,
Sounded far off, increasing, louder and nearer.
A car coughed, starting. Morning, softly
Melting the air, lifted the half-covered chair   20
From underseas, kindled the looking-glass,
Distinguished the dresser and the white wall.
The bird called tentatively, whistled, called,
Bubbled and whistled, so! Perplexed, still wet
With sleep, affectionate, hungry and cold. So, so,   25
O son of man, the ignorant night, the travail
Of early morning, the mystery of beginning
Again and again,
                    while History is unforgiven.

THE HEAVY BEAR
"the withness of the body" WHITEHEAD

The heavy bear who goes with me,
A manifold honey to smear his face,
Clumsy and lumbering here and there,
The central ton of every place,
The hungry beating brutish one   5
In love with candy, anger, and sleep,
Crazy factotum, dishevelling all,
Climbs the building, kicks the football,
Boxes his brother in the hate-ridden city.

Breathing at my side, that heavy animal,   10
That heavy bear who sleeps with me,
Howls in his sleep for a world of sugar,
A sweetness intimate as the water's clasp,
Howls in his sleep because the tight-rope
Trembles and shows the darkness beneath.   15
—The strutting show-off is terrified,
Dressed in his dress-suit, bulging his pants,
Trembles to think that his quivering meat
Must finally wince to nothing at all.

That inescapable animal walks with me,   20
Has followed me since the black womb held,
Moves where I move, distorting my gesture,
A caricature, a swollen shadow,
A stupid clown of the spirit's motive,
Perplexes and affronts with his own darkness,   25
The secret life of belly and bone,
Opaque, too near, my private, yet unknown,
Stretches to embrace the very dear
With whom I would walk without him near,
Touches her grossly, although a word   30
Would bare my heart and make me clear,
Stumbles, flounders, and strives to be fed
Dragging me with him in his mouthing care,
Amid the hundred million of his kind,
The scrimmage of appetite everywhere.   35

DYLAN THOMAS
1914-1953

THE FORCE THAT THROUGH THE
GREEN FUSE DRIVES THE FLOWER

The force that through the green fuse drives the flower
Drives my green age; that blasts the roots of trees
Is my destroyer.
And I am dumb to tell the crooked rose
My youth is bent by the same wintry fever.   5

The force that drives the water through the rocks
Drives my red blood; that dries the mouthing streams
Turns mine to wax.
And I am dumb to mouth unto my veins
How at the mountain spring that same mouth sucks.   10

The hand that whirls the water in the pool
Stirs the quicksand; that ropes the blowing wind

Hauls my shroud sail.
And I am dumb to tell the hanging man
How of my clay is made the hangman's lime.   15

The lips of time leech to the fountain head;
Love drips and gathers, but the fallen blood
Shall calm her sores.
And I am dumb to tell a weather's wind
How time has ticked a heaven round the stars.   20

And I am dumb to tell the lover's tomb
How at my sheet goes the same crooked worm.

FERN HILL

Now as I was young and easy under the apple boughs
About the lilting house and happy as the grass was green,
     The night above the dingle starry,
          Time let me hail and climb
     Golden in the heydays of his eyes,   5
And honoured among wagons I was prince of the apple towns
And once below a time I lordly had the trees and leaves
          Trail with daisies and barley
     Down the rivers of the windfall light.

And as I was green and carefree, famous among the barns   10
About the happy yard and singing as the farm was home,
     In the sun that is young once only,
          Time let me play and be
     Golden in the mercy of his means,
And green and golden I was huntsman and herdsman, the calves 15
Sang to my horn, the foxes on the hills barked clear and cold,
          And the sabbath rang slowly
     In the pebbles of the holy streams.

All the sun long it was running, it was lovely, the hay
Fields high as the house, the tunes from the chimneys, it was air 20
     And playing, lovely and watery
          And fire green as grass.
     And nightly under the simple stars

As I rode to sleep the owls were bearing the farm away,
All the moon long I heard, blessed among the stables, the nightjars   25
    Flying with the ricks, and the horses
        Flashing into the dark.

And then to awake, and the farm, like a wanderer white
With the dew, come back, the cock on his shoulder: it was all
    Shining, it was Adam and maiden,   30
        The sky gathered again
    And the sun grew round that very day.
So it must have been after the birth of the simple light
In the first, spinning place, the spellbound horses walking warm
    Out of the whinnying green stable   35
        On to the fields of praise.

And honoured among foxes and pheasants by the gay house
Under the new made clouds and happy as the heart was long,
    In the sun born over and over,
        I ran my heedless ways,   40
    My wishes raced through the house high hay
And nothing I cared, at my sky blue trades, that time allows
In all his tuneful turning so few and such morning songs
    Before the children green and golden
        Follow him out of grace,   45

Nothing I cared, in the lamb white days, that time would take me
Up to the swallow thronged loft by the shadow of my hand,
    In the moon that is always rising,
        Nor that riding to sleep
    I should hear him fly with the high fields   50
And wake to the farm forever fled from the childless land.
Oh as I was young and easy in the mercy of his means,
        Time held me green and dying
    Though I sang in my chains like the sea.

DO NOT GO GENTLE
INTO THAT GOOD NIGHT

Do not go gentle into that good night,
Old age should burn and rave at close of day;
Rage, rage against the dying of the light.

Though wise men at their end know dark is right,
Because their words had forked no lightning they   5
Do not go gentle into that good night.

Good men, the last wave by, crying how bright
Their frail deeds might have danced in a green bay,
Rage, rage against the dying of the light.

Wild men who caught and sang the sun in flight,   10
And learn, too late, they grieved it on its way,
Do not go gentle into that good night.

Grave men, near death, who see with blinding sight
Blind eyes could blaze like meteors and be gay,
Rage, rage against the dying of the light.   15

And you, my father, there on the sad height,
Curse, bless, me now with your fierce tears, I pray.
Do not go gentle into that good night.
Rage, rage against the dying of the light.

IN MY CRAFT OR SULLEN ART

In my craft or sullen art
Exercised in the still night
When only the moon rages
And the lovers lie abed
With all their griefs in their arms,   5
I labour by singing light
Not for ambition or bread
Or the strut and trade of charms
On the ivory stages
But for the common wages   10
Of their most secret heart.
Not for the proud man apart
From the raging moon I write
On these spindrift pages
Not for the towering dead   15
With their nightingales and psalms
But for the lovers, their arms

Round the griefs of the ages,
Who pay no praise or wages
Nor heed my craft or art.

JOHN BERRYMAN
1914–

CONVERSATION

Whether the moorings are invisible
Or gone, we said we could not tell.
But argument held one thing sure
That none of us that night could well endure:
The ship is locked with fog, no man aboard   5
Can see what he is moving toward,
There's little food, less love, no sleep,
The sea is dark and we are told it's deep.

Where is an officer who knows this coast?
If all such men long since have faced   10
Downward, one summon. Who knows how,
With what fidelity his voice heard now
Could shout directions from the ocean's floor?
Traditional characters no more
Their learnéd simple parts rehearse,   15
But bed them down at last from the time's curse.

A broken log fell out upon the hearth,
The flaming harbinger come forth
Of holocausts that night and day
Shrivel from the mind its sovereignty.   20
We watched the embers cool; those embers brought
To one man there the failing thought
Of cities stripped of knowledge, men,
Our continent a wilderness again.

These are conclusions of the night, we said;   25
And drank, and were not satisfied.
The fire died down, smoke in the air
Took the alarming postures of our fear;
The overhead horror, in the padded room
The man who cannot tell his name,   30
The guns and enemies that face
Into this delicate and dangerous place.

DREAM SONG: 14

Life, friends, is boring. We must not say so.
After all, the sky flashes, the great sea yearns,
we ourselves flash and yearn,
and moreover my mother told me as a boy
(repeatingly) 'Ever to confess you're bored   5
means you have no

Inner Resources.' I conclude now I have no
inner resources, because I am heavy bored.
Peoples bore me,
literature bores me, especially great literature,
Henry bores me, with his plights & gripes   10
as bad as achilles,

who loves people and valiant art, which bores me.
And the tranquil hills, & gin, look like a drag
and somehow a dog   15
has taken itself & its tail considerably away
into mountains or sea or sky, leaving
behind: me, wag.

DREAM SONG: 18
A Strut for Roethke

Westward, hit a low note, for a roarer lost
across the Sound but north from Bremerton,
hit a way down note.
And never cadenza again of flowers, or cost.

Him who could really do that cleared his throat
& staggered on.

The bluebells, pool-shallows, saluted his over-needs,
while the clouds growled, heh-heh, & snapped, & crashed.

No stunt he'll ever unflinch once more will fail
(O lucky fellow, eh Bones?)—drifted off upstairs,
downstairs, somewheres.
No more daily, trying to hit the head on the nail:
thirstless: without a think in his head:
back from wherever, with it said.

Hit a high long note, for a lover found
needing a lower into friendlier ground
to bug among worms no more
around um jungles where ah blurt 'What for?'
Weeds, too, he favoured as   most men don't favour men.
The Garden Master's gone.

ROBERT LOWELL
1917-

THE QUAKER GRAVEYARD
IN NANTUCKET
(*For Warren Winslow, Dead at Sea*)

*Let man have dominion over the fishes of the sea and the
fowls of the air and the beasts and the whole earth, and
every creeping creature that moveth upon the earth.*

I

A brackish reach of shoal off Madaket,—
The sea was still breaking violently and night
Had steamed into our North Atlantic Fleet,
When the drowned sailor clutched the drag-net. Light

Flashed from his matted head and marble feet,   5
He grappled at the net
With the coiled, hurdling muscles of his thighs:
The corpse was bloodless, a botch of reds and whites,
Its open, staring eyes
Were lustreless dead-lights   10
Or cabin-windows on a stranded hulk
Heavy with sand. We weight the body, close
Its eyes and heave it seaward whence it came,
Where the heel-headed dogfish barks its nose
On Ahab's void and forehead; and the name   15
Is blocked in yellow chalk.
Sailors, who pitch this portent at the sea
Where dreadnaughts shall confess
Its hell-bent deity,
When you are powerless   20
To sand-bag this Atlantic bulwark, faced
By the earth-shaker, green, unwearied, chaste
In his steel scales: ask for no Orphean lute
To pluck life back. The guns of the steeled fleet
Recoil and then repeat   25
The hoarse salute.

II

Whenever winds are moving and their breath
Heaves at the roped-in bulwarks of this pier,
The terns and sea-gulls tremble at your death
In these home waters. Sailor, can you hear   30
The Pequod's sea wings, beating landward, fall
Headlong and break on our Atlantic wall
Off 'Sconset, where the yawing S-boats splash
The bellbuoy, with ballooning spinnakers,
As the entangled, screeching mainsheet clears   35
The blocks: off Madaket, where lubbers lash
The heavy surf and throw their long lead squids
For blue-fish? Sea-gulls blink their heavy lids
Seaward. The winds' wings beat upon the stones,
Cousin, and scream for you and the caws rush   40
At the sea's throat and wring it in the slush
Of this old Quaker graveyard where the bones
Cry out in the long night for the hurt beast
Bobbing by Ahab's whaleboats in the East.

III

All you recovered from Poseidon died   45
With you, my cousin, and the harrowed brine

Is fruitless on the blue beard of the god,
Stretching beyond us to the castles in Spain,
Nantucket's westward haven. To Cape Cod
Guns, cradled on the tide,   50
Blast the eelgrass about a waterclock
Of bilge and backwash, roil the salt and sand
Lashing earth's scaffold, rock
Our warships in the hand
Of the great God, where time's contrition blues   55
Whatever it was these Quaker sailors lost
In the mad scramble of their lives. They died
When time was open-eyed,
Wooden and childish; only bones abide
There, in the nowhere, where their boats were tossed   60
Sky-high, where mariners had fabled news
Of IS, the whited monster. What it cost
Them is their secret. In the sperm-whale's slick
I see the Quakers drown and hear their cry:
"If God himself had not been on our side,   65
If God himself had not been on our side,
When the Atlantic rose against us, why,
Then it had swallowed us up quick."

IV

This is the end of the whaleroad and the whale
Who spewed Nantucket bones on the thrashed swell
And stirred the troubled waters to whirlpools   70
To send the Pequod packing off to hell:
This is the end of them, three-quarters fools,
Snatching at straws to sail
Seaward and seaward on the turntail whale,
Spouting out blood and water as it rolls,   75
Sick as a dog to these Atlantic shoals:
Clamavimus, O depths. Let the sea-gulls wail

For water, for the deep where the high tide
Mutters to its hurt self, mutters and ebbs.   80
Waves wallow in their wash, go out and out,
Leave only the death-rattle of the crabs,
The beach increasing, its enormous snout
Sucking the ocean's side.
This is the end of running on the waves;   85
We are poured out like water. Who will dance
The mast-lashed master of Leviathans
Up from this field of Quakers in their unstoned graves?

V

When the whale's viscera go and the roll
Of its corruption overruns this world   90
Beyond tree-swept Nantucket and Wood's Hole
And Martha's Vineyard, Sailor, will your sword
Whistle and fall and sink into the fat?
In the great ash-pit of Jehoshaphat
The bones cry for the blood of the white whale,   95
The fat flukes arch and whack about its ears,
The death-lance churns into the sanctuary, tears
The gun-blue swingle, heaving like a flail,
And hacks the coiling life out: it works and drags
And rips the sperm-whale's midriff into rags,   100
Gobbets of blubber spill to wind and weather,
Sailor, and gulls go round the stoven timbers
Where the morning stars sing out together
And thunder shakes the white surf and dismembers
The red flag hammered in the mast-head, Hide,   105
Our steel, Jonas Messias, in Thy side.

VI

OUR LADY OF WALSINGHAM

There once the penitents took off their shoes
And then walked barefoot the remaining mile;
And the small trees, a stream and hedgerows file
Slowly along the munching English lane,   110
Like cows to the old shrine, until you lose
Track of your dragging pain.
The stream flows down under the druid tree,
Shiloah's whirlpools gurgle and make glad
The castle of God. Sailor, you were glad   115
And whistled Sion by that stream. But see:

Our Lady, too small for her canopy,
Sits near the altar. There's no comeliness
At all or charm in that expressionless
Face with its heavy eyelids. As before,   120
This face, for centuries a memory,
Non est species, neque decor,
Expressionless, expresses God: it goes
Past castled Sion. She knows what God knows,
Not Calvary's Cross nor crib at Bethlehem   125
Now, and the world shall come to Walsingham.

VII

The empty winds are creaking and the oak
Splatters and splatters on the cenotaph,
The boughs are trembling and a gaff
Bobs on the untimely stroke   130
Of the greased wash exploding on a shoal-bell
In the old mouth of the Atlantic. It's well;
Atlantic, you are fouled with the blue sailors,
Sea-monsters, upward angel, downward fish:
Unmarried and corroding, spare of flesh   135
Mart once of supercilious, wing'd clippers,
Atlantic, where your bell-trap guts its spoil
You could cut the brackish winds with a knife
Here in Nantucket, and cast up the time
When the Lord God formed man from the sea's slime   140
And breathed into his face the breath of life,
And blue-lung'd combers lumbered to the kill.
The Lord survives the rainbow of His will.

MR. EDWARDS AND THE SPIDER

I saw the spiders marching through the air,
Swimming from tree to tree that mildewed day
    In latter August when the hay
      Came creaking to the barn. But where
        The wind is westerly,   5
Where gnarled November makes the spiders fly
Into the apparitions of the sky,
They purpose nothing but their ease and die
Urgently beating east to sunrise and the sea;

What are we in the hands of the great God?   10
It was in vain you set up thorn and briar
    In battle array against the fire
      And treason crackling in your blood;
        For the wild thorns grow tame
And will do nothing to oppose the flame;   15
Your lacerations tell the losing game
You play against a sickness past your cure.
How will the hands be strong? How will the heart endure?

A very little thing, a little worm,
Or hourglass-blazoned spider, it is said,   20

Can kill a tiger. Will the dead
Hold up his mirror and affirm
  To the four winds the smell
And flash of his authority? It's well
If God who holds you to the pit of hell,   25
Much as one holds a spider, will destroy,
Baffle and dissipate your soul. As a small boy

On Windsor Marsh, I saw the spider die
When thrown into the bowels of fierce fire:
  There's no long struggle, no desire   30
  To get up on its feet and fly—
    It stretches out its feet
And dies. This is the sinner's last retreat;
Yes, and no strength exerted on the heat
Then sinews the abolished will, when sick   35
And full of burning, it will whistle on a brick.

But who can plumb the sinking of that soul?
Josiah Hawley, picture yourself cast
  Into a brick-kiln where the blast
  Fans your quick vitals to a coal—   40
    If measured by a glass,
How long would it seem burning! Let there pass
A minute, ten, ten trillion; but the blaze
Is infinite, eternal: this is death,
To die and know it. This is the Black Widow, death. 45

THE FAT MAN IN THE MIRROR
(After Werfel)

What's filling up the mirror? O, it is not I;
Hair-belly like a beaver's house? An old dog's eye?
  The forenoon was blue
  In the mad King's zoo
Nurse was swinging me so high, so high!   5

The bullies wrestled on the royal bowling green;
Hammers and sickles on their hoods of black sateen . . .
  Sulking on my swing
  The tobacco King
Sliced apples with a pen-knife for the Queen.   10

This *I*, who used to mouse about the parafined preserves,
And jammed a finger in the coffee-grinder, serves
    Time before the mirror.
    But this pursey terror . . .
Nurse, it is a person. *It is nerves.*

Where's the Queen-Mother waltzing like a top to staunch
The blood of Lewis, King of Faerie? Hip and haunch
    Lard the royal grotto;
    Straddling Lewis' motto,
Time, the Turk, its sickle on its paunch.
                                   20

Nurse, Nurse, it rises on me . . . O, it starts to roll,
My apples, O, are ashes in the meerschaum bowl . . .
    If you'd only come,
    If you'd only come,
Darling, if . . . The apples that I stole,
                                   25

While Nurse and I were swinging in the Old One's eye . . .
Only a fat man with his beaver on his eye,
    Only a fat man,
    Only a fat man
Bursts the mirror. O, it is not I!
                                   30

FOR THE UNION DEAD

"Relinquunt Omnia Servare Rem Publicam."

The old South Boston Aquarium stands
in a Sahara of snow now. Its broken windows are boarded.
The bronze weathervane cod has lost half its scales.
The airy tanks are dry.

Once my nose crawled like a snail on the glass;
my hand tingled
to burst the bubbles
drifting from the noses of the cowed, compliant fish.

My hand draws back. I often sigh still
for the dark downward and vegetating kingdom
of the fish and reptile. One morning last March,
I pressed against the new barbed and galvanized

fence on the Boston Common. Behind their cage,
yellow dinosaur steamshovels were grunting
as they cropped up tons of mush and grass   15
to gouge their underworld garage.

Parking spaces luxuriate like civic
sandpiles in the heart of Boston.
A girdle of orange, Puritan-pumpkin colored girders
braces the tingling Statehouse,   20

shaking over the excavations, as it faces Colonel Shaw
and his bell-cheeked Negro infantry
on St. Gaudens' shaking Civil War relief,
propped by a plank splint against the garage's earthquake.

Two months after marching through Boston,   25
half the regiment was dead;
at the dedication,
William James could almost hear the bronze Negroes breathe.

Their monument sticks like a fishbone
in the city's throat.   30
Its Colonel is as lean
as a compass-needle.

He has an angry wrenlike vigilance,
a greyhound's gentle tautness;
he seems to wince at pleasure,   35
and suffocate for privacy.

He is out of bounds now. He rejoices in man's lovely,
peculiar power to choose life and die—
when he leads his black soldiers to death,
he cannot bend his back.   40

On a thousand small town New England greens,
the old white churches hold their air
of sparse, sincere rebellion; frayed flags
quilt the graveyards of the Grand Army of the Republic.

The stone statues of the abstract Union Soldier   45
grow slimmer and younger each year—

wasp-waisted, they doze over muskets
and muse through their sideburns . . .

Shaw's father wanted no monument
except the ditch,   50
where his son's body was thrown
and lost with his "niggers."

The ditch is nearer.
There are no statues for the last war here;
on Boylston Street, a commercial photograph   55
shows Hiroshima boiling

over a Mosler Safe, the "Rock of Ages"
that survived the blast. Space is nearer.
When I crouch to my television set,
the drained faces of Negro school-children rise like balloons.   60

Colonel Shaw
is riding on his bubble,
he waits
for the blessèd break.

The Aquarium is gone. Everywhere,   65
giant finned cars nose forward like fish;
a savage servility
slides by on grease.

JAMES DICKEY

1923 –

THE FIEND

He has only to pass by a tree   moodily walking   head down
A worried accountant   not with it   and he is swarming
He is gliding up the underside light of leaves   upfloating
In a seersucker suit   passing window after window of her building.

He finds her at last, chewing gum   talking on the telephone.   5
The wind sways him softly   comfortably sighing   she must bathe
Or sleep.   She gets up, and he follows her along the branch
Into another room.   She stands there for a moment   and the teddy
     bear
On the bed feels its guts spin as she takes it by the leg and tosses
It off.   She touches one button at her throat, and rigor mortis   10
Slithers into his pockets, making everything there—keys, pen
And secret love—stand up.   He brings from those depths the knife
And flicks it open   it glints on the moon one time   carries
Through the dead walls   making a wormy static on the TV screen.
He parts the swarm of gnats that live excitedly at this perilous level   15
Parts the rarefied light high windows give out into inhabited trees
Opens his lower body to the moon.   This night the apartments are
     sinking

To ground level   burying their sleepers in the soil   burying all floors
But the one where a sullen shopgirl gets ready to take a shower,
Her hair in rigid curlers, and the rest.   When she gives up   20
Her aqua terry-cloth robe the wind quits in mid-tree   the birds
Freeze to their perches round his head   a purely human light
Comes out of a one-man oak   around her an energy field   she
     stands
Rooted   not turning to anything else   then begins to move like a
     saint
Her stressed nipples rising like things about to crawl off her   as he
     gets   25
A hold on himself.   With that clasp she changes   senses   some-
     thing

Some breath through the fragile walls   some all-seeing eye
Of God   some touch that enfolds her body   some hand come up
     out of roots
That carries her as she moves   swaying   at this rare height. She
     wraps
The curtain around her and streams.   The room fades.   Then
     coming   30
Forth magnificently   the window blurred from within   she moves
     in a cloud
Chamber   the tree in the oak currents sailing   in clear air keep-
     ing pace
With her white breathless closet—he sees her mistily part her lips
As if singing to him   come up from river-fog   almost hears her
     as if
She sang alone in a cloud   its warmed light streaming into his
     branches   35
Out through the gauze glass of the window.   She takes off her bath-
     ing cap

The tree with him ascending   himself and the birds all moving
In darkness together   sleep crumbling the bark in their claws.
By this time he holds in his awkward, subtle limbs the limbs

Of a hundred understanding trees.   He has learned what a plant is
    like   40
When it moves near a human habitation   moving closer the later it
    is
Unfurling its leaves near bedrooms   still keeping its wilderness life
Twigs covering his body with only one way out   for his eyes into
    inner light
Of a chosen window   living with them night after night   watch-
    ing
Watching with them at times their favorite TV shows   learning—   45
Though now and then he hears a faint sound: gunshot, bombing,
Building-fall—how to read lips: the lips of laconic cowboys
Bank robbers   old and young doctors tense-faced   gesturing savagely
In wards and corridors   like reading the lips of the dead

The lips of men interrupting the program at the wrong time   50
To sell you a good used car on the Night Owl Show   men silently
    reporting
The news out the window.   But the living as well, three-dimensioned,
Silent as the small gray dead, must sleep at last   must save their lives
By taking off their clothes. It is his beholding that saves them:
God help the dweller in windowless basements   the one obsessed   55
With drawing curtains this night. At three o'clock in the morning
He descends   a medium-sized shadow   while that one sleeps and
    turns
In her high bed in loss   as he goes limb by limb   quietly down
The trunk with one lighted side. Ground upon which he could not
    explain
His presence he walks with toes uncurled from branches, his bird-
    movements   60
Dying hard. At the sidewalk he changes   gains weight   a solid
    citizen

Once more.   At apartments there is less danger from dogs, but he has
For those a super-quiet hand   a hand to calm sparrows and rivers,
And watchdogs in half-tended bushes lie with him watching their
    women
Undress   the dog's honest eyes and the man's the same pure beast's   65
Comprehending the same essentials. Not one of these beheld would
    ever give
Him a second look   but he gives them all a first look that goes

On and on   conferring immortality while it lasts   while the sub-
    urb's leaves
Hold still enough   while whatever dog he has with him holds its
    breath
Yet seems to thick-pant   impatient as he with the indifferent men   70
Drifting in and out of the rooms   or staying on, too tired to move
Reading the sports page   dozing   plainly unworthy   for what
    women want
Dwells in bushes and trees: what they want is to look outward,

To look with the light streaming into the April limbs   to stand
    straighter
While their husbands' lips dry out   feeling that something is there   75
That could dwell in no earthly house: that in poplar trees or beneath
The warped roundabout of the clothesline   in the sordid disorder
Of communal backyards   some being is there in the shrubs
Sitting comfortably on a child's striped rubber ball filled with rainwater
Muffling his glasses with a small studious hand against a sudden   80
Flash of houselight from within   or flash from himself   a needle's
    eye
Uncontrollable   blaze of uncompromised being. Ah, the lingerie
Hung in the bathroom! The domestic motions of single girls living to-
    gether
A plump girl girding her loins against her moon-summoned blood:
In that moon he stands   the only male lit by it, covered with leaf-
    shapes.   85
He coughs, and the smallest root responds   and in his lust he is set
By the wind in motion. That movement can restore the green eyes
Of middle age   looking   renewed   through the qualified light
Not quite reaching him where he stands again on the ususal branch
Of his oldest love   his tie not loosened   a plastic shield   90
In his breast pocket full of pencils and ballpoint pens given him by
    salesmen
His hat correctly placed to shade his eyes   a natural gambler's tilt
And in summer wears an eyeshade   a straw hat Caribbean style.
In some guise or other he is near them when they are weeping without
    sound
When the teen-age son has quit school   when the girl has broken
    up   95
With the basketball star   when the banker walks out on his wife.
He sees mothers counsel desperately with pulsing girls face down
On beds full of overstuffed beasts   sees men dress as women
In ante-bellum costumes with bonnets   sees doctors come, looking
    oddly
Like himself   though inside the houses   worming a medical arm   100
Up under the cringing covers   sees children put angrily to bed

Sees one told an invisible fairy story   with lips moving silently as
     his
Are also moving   the book's few pages bright. It will take years
But at last he will shed his leaves   burn his roots   give up
Invisibility   will step out   will make himself known to the one   105
He cannot see loosen her blouse   take off luxuriously   with lips
Compressed against her mouth-stain   her dress   her stockings
Her magic underwear.   To that one he will come   up frustrated
     pines
Down alleys   through window blinds   blind windows   kitchen
     doors
On summer evenings. It will be something small that sets him off: 110
Perhaps a pair of lace pants on a clothesline   gradually losing
Water to the sun   filling out in the warm light with a well-rounded
Feminine wind as he watches   having spent so many sleepless nights
Because of her   because of her hand on a shade always coming
     down
In his face   not leaving even a shadow stripped naked upon the
     brown paper   115
Waiting for her now in a green outdated car with a final declaration
Of love   pretending to read   and when she comes and takes down
Her pants, he will casually follow her in   like a door-to-door sales-
     man
The godlike movement of trees stiffening with him   the light
Of a hundred favored windows   gone wrong somewhere in his
     glasses   120
Where his knocked-off panama hat was   in his painfully vanishing
     hair.

ALLEN GINSBERG
1926–

A SUPERMARKET IN CALIFORNIA

    What thoughts I have of you tonight, Walt Whitman, for I walked down
the sidestreets under the trees with a headache self-conscious looking at the full
moon.

    In my hungry fatigue, and shopping for images, I went into the neon
fruit supermarket, dreaming of your enumerations!

What peaches and what penumbras! Whole families shopping at night! Aisles full of husbands! Wives in the avocados, babies in the tomatoes!—and you, Garcia Lorca, what were you doing down by the watermelons?

I saw you, Walt Whitman, childless, lonely old grubber, poking among the meats in the refrigerator and eyeing the grocery boys.
I heard you asking questions of each: Who killed the pork chops? What price bananas? Are you my Angel? 5
I wandered in and out of the brilliant stacks of cans following you, and followed in my imagination by the store detective.
We strode down the open corridors together in our solitary fancy tasting artichokes, possessing every frozen delicacy, and never passing the cashier.

Where are we going, Walt Whitman? The doors close in an hour. Which way does your beard point tonight?
(I touch your book and dream of our odyssey in the supermarket and feel absurd.)
Will we walk all night through solitary streets? The trees add shade to shade, lights out in the houses, we'll both be lonely. 10
Will we stroll dreaming of the lost America of love past blue automobiles in driveways, home to our silent cottage?
Ah, dear father, graybeard, lonely old courage-teacher, what America did you have when Charon quit poling his ferry and you got out on a smoking bank and stood watching the boat disappear on the black waters of Lethe?

TO AUNT ROSE

Aunt Rose—now—might I see you
with your thin face and buck tooth smile and pain
   of rheumatism—and a long black heavy shoe
   for your bony left leg
 limping down the long hall in Newark on the running carpet   5
   past the black grand piano
   in the day room
    where the parties were
  and I sang Spanish loyalist songs
   in a high squeaky voice   10
    (hysterical) the committee listening
   while you limped around the room
   collected the money—
 Aunt Honey, Uncle Sam, a stranger with a cloth arm
   in his pocket   15
    and huge young bald head
     of Abraham Lincoln Brigade

—your long sad face
                    your tears of sexual frustration
                        (what smothered sobs and bony hips   20
                            under the pillows of Osborne Terrace)
—the time I stood on the toilet seat naked
                    and you powdered my thighs with Calomine
                        against the poison ivy—my tender
                            and shamed first black curled hairs   25
what were you thinking in secret heart then
                    knowing me a man already—
and I an ignorant girl of family silence on the thin pedestal
                    of my legs in the bathroom—Museum of Newark.
                            Aunt Rose   30
Hitler is dead, Hitler is in Eternity; Hitler is with
                    Tamburlane and Emily Brontë

Though I see you walking still, a ghost on Osborne Terrace
                    down the long dark hall to the front door
                    limping a little with a pinched smile   35
                        in what must have been a silken
                        flower dress
            welcoming my father, the Poet, on his visit to Newark
                    —see you arriving in the living room
                        dancing on your crippled leg   40
                    and clapping hands his book
                        had been accepted by Liveright

Hitler is dead and Liveright's gone out of business
The Attic of the Past and *Everlasting Minute* are out of print
                        Uncle Harry sold his last silk stocking   45
                    Claire quit interpretive dancing school
                        Buba sits a wrinkled monument in Old
                            Ladies Home blinking at new babies
last time I saw you was the hospital
                    pale skull protruding under ashen skin   50
                    blue veined unconscious girl
                        in an oxygen tent
            the war in Spain has ended long ago
                    Aunt Rose

INDEX